Blackstone's

Magistrates' Cou
Handbook 2020

CW00540062

Blackstone's
Magistrates' Court
Handbook 2020

Anthony Edwards

OXFORD
UNIVERSITY PRESS

Great Clarendon Street, Oxford, OX2 6DP,
United Kingdom

Oxford University Press is a department of the University of Oxford.
It furthers the University's objective of excellence in research, scholarship,
and education by publishing worldwide. Oxford is a registered trade mark of
Oxford University Press in the UK and in certain other countries

© Anthony Edwards 2019

The moral rights of the author have been asserted

Fourth Edition published in 2016
Fifth Edition published in 2017
Sixth Edition published in 2018
Seventh Edition published in 2019

Impression: 1

Published in the United States of America by Oxford University Press
198 Madison Avenue, New York, NY 10016, United States of America

British Library Cataloguing in Publication Data
Data available

Library of Congress Cataloging in Publication Data
Data available

ISBN 978-0-19-884667-3

Printed and bound by
CPI Group (UK) Ltd, Croydon, CR0 4YY

Preface to the 2020 Edition

This book aims to provide ready access to the law relevant to busy criminal lawyers seeking immediate answers to the common issues that arise at court. The book became too long last year after major changes to incorporate material relevant to youths. I have tried heavily to reduce the length of the book without affecting the help the book can provide to lawyers working in the magistrates' courts. The format has also been changed to reduce the book's bulk so that it can be carried with a laptop. The index has been completely refreshed.

The pressures on space are always present. I have continued to concentrate on matters that arise without warning and to omit matters that more commonly arise on notice, or where there is time for preparation. I have removed the detail of many Practice Rules and much statutory material that is too complex to digest at short notice. Both are available online and the relevant references remain. I welcome comment on the changes made, particularly from legal advisers, and I welcome feedback generally. The intention is that it will continue to be the most easily accessed source of answers to questions that arise pre-trial at the magistrates' court level.

Sentencing

Where there is a reference merely to a fine, it is reference to an unlimited fine. The Sentencing Council has published general guidelines and expanded details of aggravating and mitigating factors. A summary appears at Appendix 7. Unless otherwise stated guidelines apply to those of 18 and over.

As the companion handbook for Youths in the criminal courts is not updated annually, a supplement is provided in Appendix 8.

I have attempted to state the law as at 31 July 2019.

Sections *in italics* relate to matters not yet in force at the time of going to print.

I wish to thank Alex Johnson of Oxford University Press for his help in the preparation of this edition of the *Handbook*. Any mistakes are my responsibility alone.

Anthony Edwards
London

Contents

Part A Procedure and Evidence

Contents

Icons List

The following icons are used throughout this book:

DO Dangerous Offender

EW Either Way

Sentence (icon) Sentence

SO Summary Only

SON Sexual Offence Notification: registration required under s 80 and Sch 3 Sexual Offences Act 2003. The periods for notification are set out at **D22**

(book icon) Cross-reference to Blackstone's Criminal Practice 2019

GC Grave Crimes

IO Indictable Only

Key points Key Points

Key points: General defence Key Points: General Defence

Key points: Sentencing Key Points: Sentencing

Key points on conviction Key Points on Conviction

Key points on acquittal Key Points on Acquital

Table of Cases

Table of Cases

Table of Cases

Table of Cases

Table of Cases

Table of Cases

Table of Cases

Table of Cases

Table of Cases

European Court of Human Rights

Table of Practice Directions

Table of Statutes

Table of Statutes

Table of Statutes

Table of Statutes

Table of Statutes

Table of Statutes

Table of Statutory Instruments

Table of Statutory Instruments

Table of Treaties and Conventions

Part A
Procedure and Evidence

A1 Abuse of Process

A1.1 Introduction

Abuse of process is something so unfair and wrong with the prosecution that the court should not allow a prosecutor to proceed with what is, in all other respects, a regular proceeding: *Hui-chi Ming v R* [1992] 1 AC 34.

A stay on these grounds falls into two main categories:

- where a fair trial of the particular defendant is impossible (eg due to loss of evidence);
- where there is a misuse of court process (where it offends the court's sense of justice and propriety to be asked to try the accused in the circumstances of the particular case). In relation to this category of case, the magistrates' court does not have jurisdiction to determine the issue and proceedings might be adjourned in order that the defence may seek a judicial review. It was confirmed in *Woolls v N Somerset Council* [2016] EWHC 1410 (Admin), applying *Nembhard v DPP* [2009] EWHC 194, that it is also proper for the magistrates to proceed to a conclusion and make findings of fact so that the abuse issue can be resolved by the court stating a case for the High Court. Cases involving human trafficking and not covered by s 45 Modern Slavery Act 2015 will be considered under this head (*L; HVN; THN; T v R* [2013] EWCA Crim 991).

A stay of proceedings based on an abuse of process will be rare and should be allowed only in exceptional circumstances (see *Attorney General's Reference No 1 of 1990* (1992) 95 Cr App R 296); and if the court process can compensate for any unfairness or wrongs, so as to allow for a fair trial, that is the way in which it should proceed.

On an application to stay for abuse of process, it is for the defendant to satisfy the court on a balance of probabilities that no fair trial is possible. The application should be decided on material adduced by the prosecution and defence, with both parties having the right (subject to usual judicial discretion) to call evidence (*R v Clerkenwell Magistrates' Court, exp Bell* [1991] Crim LR 468).

A1.2 Relevant grounds

A1.2.1 *Alternative remedy*

The exclusion of evidence under s 78 Police and Criminal Evidence Act 1984 (PACE) to secure a fair trial is to be preferred to using the abuse jurisdiction (see **A2.2.5**). In *R v DS and TS* [2015] EWCA Crim 662 the court held that whether the breach by the Crown is of a general or specific nature the consequences should be the same, and whether the failure related to evidence (*Boardman*, see **A2.2.5**) or disclosure (in this case), all such breaches affect the fairness of the trial and undermine public confidence in the criminal justice system. Whether a breach is dealt with by a stay or by exclusion of evidence under s 78 PACE the same considerations apply. They include:

- the gravity of the charges;
- the denial of justice to the complainants;
- the importance of disclosure in sexual offences;
- the necessity for proper attention to be paid to disclosure;
- the nature and materiality of the failures;
- any failures by the defence;
- the waste of court resources and the effect on the court;
- the availability of other sanctions.

A1.2.2 *Missing evidence or disclosure*

The issues identified in *R v Dobson* [2001] EWCA Crim 1606 are as follows:

- What was the duty of the police?
- Did the police fail in their duty by not obtaining or retaining the appropriate material?
- If so, was there serious prejudice which rendered a fair trial impossible in the light of such failure?
- Alternatively, did the police failure result from such bad behaviour, in the sense of bad faith or serious fault, as to render it unfair that the accused should be tried at all? The requirement for bad faith was doubted in *Clay v South Cambridgeshire JJ* [2014] EWHC 321 (Admin) which held that the issue was whether or not there could be a fair trial.

There is a duty on the police to contact identified witnesses (*Morris v DPP* [2014] EWHC 105 (Admin)). There is no *general* duty on the prosecution to retain CCTV evidence that might have given insight into whether a warning was given to a detainee during a breath test procedure (*Morris v Director of Public Prosecutions* [2008] EWHC 2788 (Admin)). This decision follows the leading case of *R v Feltham Magistrates' Court and another, ex p Ebrahim* [2001] EWHC Admin 130.

That case emphasizes that the early identification of the significance of the relevant material is a key factor to ensure that the prosecution are under a duty, not least under the code of practice made under the Criminal Procedure and Investigations Act 1996. The case confirms the possibility of using s 78 PACE to exclude some or all of the prosecution evidence if the failure to produce the material sought or to comply with disclosure obligations may render the trial unfair.

The duties of the prosecution are set out in the Attorney General's guidelines on the disclosure of unused material.

A1.2.3 *Failure to supply initial details of the prosecution case*

There is no jurisdiction to stay proceedings for failures in service of initial details of the prosecution case under Part 8 of the Criminal Procedure Rules; the appropriate remedy is to adjourn (*R v Leeds Youth Court, ex p P(A)* [2001] EWHC 215 (Admin)), although repeated failure to comply with the rules may provide for a stay in truly exceptional circumstances (*R v Willesden Magistrates' Court, ex p Clemmings* (1988) 152 JPN 46). A threat to stay a prosecution if there were further disclosure breaches did not give rise to any legitimate expectation on the part of the defendant so as to require the court to carry through its threat on the next occasion (*R v Leeds Youth Court, ex p AP and others* [2001] EWHC 215 (Admin)).

A1.2.4 *Improper motive*

The fact that there was a mixed motive for launching a private prosecution will justify a stay only if the conduct of the prosecutor is truly oppressive, as it was obvious that many private prosecutions would be brought with mixed motives (*Dacre v City of Westminster Magistrates' Court* [2009] 1 Cr App R 6).

In *Nembhard v Director of Public Prosecutions* [2009] EWHC 194 (Admin), the court ruled that a magistrates' court was correct to refuse to stay proceedings on the ground that a request to produce traffic documents was motivated by improper considerations—namely a desire to harass the defendant. In such cases the proper course of action would be either to stay the prosecution pending determination of the issue by the High Court, or to apply for judicial review of the decision to prosecute. This case is an important reminder that in instances where an abuse of state power is being alleged, a magistrates' court has no jurisdiction to stay proceedings (*R v Horseferry Road Magistrates' Court, ex p Paul James Bennett* [1994] 1 AC 42).

A1.2.5 *Misuse of executive power*

In *Warren* [2011] UKPC 10 it was emphasized that where officers of the state act unlawfully a balancing exercise must be carried out between the need to protect the integrity of the criminal justice process and the public interest in ensuring that those charged with grave crimes should be tried.

A1.2.6 *Delay*

In the absence of other compelling reasons, a lengthy delay, in itself, does not justify a stay of criminal proceedings (*Spiers v Ruddy* [2008] 1 AC 873, PC).

In *Ali v Crown Prosecution Service* [2007] EWCA Crim 691, proceedings brought seven years after the incident should have been stayed, as important documentary evidence, relevant to assessing the victim's credibility, had been lost. The court emphasized that:

> this is a rare case where prejudice following from the delay was not alleviated and probably could never have been cured during the course of the trial.

In *Halahan* [2014] EWCA Crim 2079, the court held that in a case where prejudice by delay, resulting in the loss of documents, was alleged, it is necessary to show more than speculation that the document would assist the defence. It was necessary that the missing evidence represented a significant and demonstrable chance of the disclosure of strongly supportive evidence emerging on a specific issue in the case.

However in *Brown v DPP* [2019] EWHC 798 (Admin) the court indicated that an undue delay in serving a requisition, issued within 6 months, for a summary only matter may give rise to the abuse jurisdiction.

A1.2.7 *Legitimate expectation*

The prosecution of a person who has received a promise, an undertaking, or a representation from the police that he will not be prosecuted is capable of being an abuse of process (*Croydon Justices, ex p Dean* [1993] QB 769). So too will be the prosecution of a person denied a caution by the failure of the police to make appropriate disclosure to enable legal advice to be given (*DPP v Ara* [2001] EWHC 493 (Admin)). *Abu Hamza* [2006] EWCA Crim 2918 suggests that there must be both an unequivocal representation and, as a result, an action by the defendant to their detriment. New facts coming to light may justify further proceedings. The administration of a caution may make it an abuse for there to be a later prosecution (*Jones v Whalley* [2007] 1 AC 63) but the Crown may in appropriate cases, where there is a proper basis, change its mind as to how to proceed. Much will turn on what was said to the suspect at the time the caution was imposed and what the complainant knew and said about the caution being imposed (*R (Lowden) v Gateshead MC* [2016] EWHC 3536 (Admin)).

The Crown is required, absent a change of circumstances, to proceed in a single prosecution with all the charges it proposes to bring arising out of the same incident (*Connelly v DPP* [1964] AC 1254; *R v Beedie* [1997] EWCA Crim 714). The abuse jurisdiction may be used to stay an appropriate case when the strict *autrefois doctrine* does not apply (*J* [2013] EWCA Crim 569).

A1.2.8 *Autrefois acquit*

This bar is confined to cases that are the same in fact and law. The rule will be construed narrowly and if this causes injustice amounting to oppression the remedy is to stay the proceedings. Although on an allegation of common assault the Crown offered no evidence, it could proceed with an allegation of occasioning ABH if the defendant had never been in peril of trial on the lesser offence (*R v JFJ* [2013] EWCA Crim 569). Where a case is dismissed for the failure of the prosecution to appear (s 15 Magistrates' Court Act (MCA) 1980) it is not an abuse to commence again as the defendant was not in jeopardy (*DPP v Jarman* [2013] EWHC 4391 (Admin)). Magistrates cannot dismiss a case without hearing evidence. *DPP v Bird* [2016] EWHC 4077 (Admin) confirms that the doctrine of *autrefois acquit* only applies if the defendant was put at risk of conviction and the case was heard on the merits; that is, the court could have convicted but did not do so.

A1.2.9 *Decisions to prosecute*

A decision to prosecute is susceptible to review, as an abuse of process, if it is one that no reasonable prosecutor would make, or which misapplies a policy, or is based on a policy which is unlawful (*Campaign against Anti-Semitism v DPP* [2019] EWHC 9 (Admin).

 See *Blackstone's Criminal Practice 2019* **D3**

A2 **Adjournments**

A2.1 **Criminal Practice Directions**

Detailed guidance is now given in CPD VI trial 24C.5–C24C.32.

A2.2 **Principles to be applied**

Part 3 of the Criminal Procedure Rules (Crim PR) (**Appendix 2**) requires active case management. This includes discouraging delay, and dealing with as many aspects of the case as possible on the same occasion and avoiding unnecessary hearings (r 3.2(2)(f)). At every hearing, if the case cannot be concluded there and then, the court must give directions so that it can be concluded at the next hearing or as soon as possible after that (r 3.9(1)). Unless this has been done already, the court must take the defendant's plea (r 3.9(2)(b)). This obligation does not depend on the extent of initial disclosure, service of evidence, disclosure of unused material, or the grant of legal aid. There are still many instances where an adjournment is required. In such instances advocates can expect those applications to be closely scrutinized (*R v Hereford Magistrates' Court, ex p Rowland* [1998] QB 110).

In *Crown Prosecution Service v Picton* [2006] EWHC 1108 (Admin), the court laid down the following general approach:

- A decision whether to adjourn is a decision within the discretion of the trial court. An appellate court will interfere only if very clear grounds for doing so are shown.
- Magistrates should pay great attention to the need for expedition in the prosecution of criminal proceedings; delays are scandalous; they bring the law into disrepute; summary justice should be speedy justice; an application for an adjournment should be rigorously scrutinized.
- Where an adjournment is sought by the prosecution, magistrates must consider both the interest of the defendant in getting the matter dealt with, and the interest of the public that criminal charges should be adjudicated upon: the guilty convicted as well as the innocent acquitted. With a more serious charge, the public interest that there be a trial will carry greater weight.
- Where an adjournment is sought by the accused, the magistrates must consider whether, if it is not granted, the accused will be able fully to present his defence and, if he will not be able to do so, the degree to which his ability to do so is compromised.
- In considering the competing interests of the parties, the magistrates should examine the likely consequences of the proposed adjournment, in particular, its likely length, and the need to decide the facts while recollections are fresh.
- The reason that the adjournment is required should be examined and, if it arises through the fault of the party asking for the adjournment, that is a factor against granting the adjournment, carrying weight in accordance

with the gravity of the fault. If that party was not at fault then that may favour an adjournment. Likewise, if the party opposing the adjournment has been at fault then that will favour an adjournment.
- The magistrates should take appropriate account of the history of the case, and whether there have been earlier adjournments and at whose request, and why.
- Lastly, of course, the factors to be considered cannot be comprehensively stated but depend upon the particular circumstances of each case, and they will often overlap. The court's duty is to do justice between the parties in the circumstances as they have arisen.

Because of the requirement for an explanation for the inability to proceed, an adjournment will not be granted when no explanation can be given (*R (Walden) and R (Stern) v Highbury Corner Magistrates' Court* [2003] EWHC 708 (Admin)).

In *Aravinthan Visvaratnam v Brent Magistrates' Court* [2009] EWHC 3017 (Admin), the court made these observations:

> The prosecution must not think that they are always allowed at least one application to adjourn the case. If that idea were to gain currency, no trial would ever start on the first date set for trial.

> So these are the competing considerations. I have no doubt that there is a high public interest in trials taking place on the date set for trial, and that trials should not be adjourned unless there is a good and compelling reason to do so. The sooner the prosecution understand this—that they cannot rely on their own serious failures properly to warn witnesses—the sooner the efficiency in the Magistrates' Court system improves. An improvement in timeliness and the achievement of a more effective and efficient system of criminal justice in the Magistrates' Court will bring about great benefits to victims and to witnesses and huge savings in time and money.

On an application for an adjournment by the defence, the court in *R (Anderson) v Guildford MC* [2015] EWHC 2454 (Admin) held that the issue was whether a fair trial could take place. Whilst speed was important an adjournment was granted where:

(1) The defence had voluntarily submitted a full and very detailed defence case statement even though initial disclosure had not yet been made.
(2) The defence had identified the need for two expert reports on the 'victim's' pathology (nature of the injury) and toxicology (drugs taken), and it was not for a court to prejudge whether these would be relevant or not.
(3) Other outstanding material identified a potential witness who might testify to the 'victim's' condition, and related to bad character.

This was notwithstanding that the not guilty plea had been entered on 16 April (by a duty solicitor), the trial was on 29 June, and the application to adjourn was made (by the defendant's own solicitor) on 1 June.

The power to adjourn was considered in *Bourne v Scarborough MC* [2017] EWHC 2828 (Admin). The power could be exercised by a legal adviser and the Crim PR allowing this were lawful. If the application was opposed, the adviser must be in possession of all the relevant facts and consider all the *Picton* criteria (including when the trial would be heard). If the defence seek an oral hearing that should normally be allowed, or at least written observations from the defence should be sought.

Where the court is misled into granting an adjournment, it may reverse that decision even though in *DPP v Woods* [2017] EWHC 1070 (Admin) it meant that the Crown had to offer no evidence as its witnesses had been de-warned.

A2.2.1 *Diversion from prosecution*

Although courts are discouraged from allowing adjournments for this reason and there is no right to such an adjournment (*R (F) v CPS and the Chief Constable of Merseyside* (2004) 168 JP 93), such adjournments are regularly granted whenever the Crown Prosecution Service (CPS) on review agree that such an outcome is appropriate. This happens particularly where the charging decision has been made by the police or when defendants are receiving informed legal advice for the first time. It also applies when there are issues of mental disorder. Whilst a plea of not guilty can be entered, the Crown will often be willing to consider informed representations to comply with their duties under the Code for Crown Prosecutors.

Paragraph 3.6 of the Code for Crown Prosecutors states that:

Code for Crown Prosecutors, para 3.6

3.6 Prosecutors review every case they receive from the police or other investigators. Review is a continuing process and prosecutors must take account of any change in circumstances that occurs as the case develops. This includes what becomes known of the defence case, any further reasonable lines of inquiry that should be pursued, and receipt of any unused material that may undermine the prosecution case or assist the defence case, to the extent that charges should be altered or discontinued or the prosecution should not proceed. If a case is to be stopped, care should be taken when choosing the method of termination, as this can affect the victim's position under the Victims' Right to Review scheme. Wherever possible, prosecutors should consult the investigator when considering changing the charges or stopping the case. Prosecutors and investigators work closely together, but the final responsibility for the decision whether or not a case should go ahead rests with the CPS.

In addition, paragraph 9 of the Director's Guidance on Adult Conditional Cautions states that:

9. Prosecutor's post-charge review—cases that should have been considered for a Conditional Caution

9.1 Where an offender is charged with an offence, but it appears upon review by a prosecutor that a Conditional Caution is more appropriate, the reviewing prosecutor should direct an authorised person to offer a Conditional Caution. This includes any case where authorised persons ordinarily make that decision. The current prosecution should be adjourned whilst this action is taken. The authorised person shall then offer a caution with conditions as specified by the prosecutor. If it proves then not to be possible to administer the caution an alternative out of court disposal may not be offered and the prosecution must continue.

Note that there are particular provisions in relation to foreign offender conditional cautions.

A2.2.2 *Legal aid*

A common issue that arises is in relation to adjournments for the purposes of legal aid being granted. Much will depend on the circumstances, and in particular, how much time the defendant has had, if any, to arrange appropriate representation. The court will also be mindful of payments that can be made to firms if legal aid is refused—thereby diluting the force of any argument that work would otherwise be unfunded. However, in *Stopya v District Court of Lublin Poland* [2012] EWHC 1787 (Admin) it was held that 'delays occasioned by means testing which are not occasioned by the fault of the requested person or his legal advisers cannot be held against the requested person'.

A2.2.3 *Absence of the defendant*

R (Drinkwater) v Solihull Magistrates' Court [2012] EWHC 765 (Admin) (applying *R v Jones* [2002] UKHL 5) suggested that a trial may take place in the absence of the defendant only in exceptional circumstances. However, the case did not take account of the amendments made to s 11 MCA 1980. The section requires that the trial proceed unless it is contrary to the interests of justice to do so. The defence should show acceptable reason for the failure to appear (s 11(2A)). A failure to make proper inquiry into a defendant's absence which, had it been carried out, would have led to the adjournment of the matter, will result in 'any resulting conviction following trial in absence being quashed' (*R (James) v Tower Bridge Magistrates' Court*, unreported, 9 June 2009, DC). (See also **A22.3**)

Where a defendant provides a medical note in relation to nonattendance, a court should give reasons for finding such medical excuses spurious, it being rarely, if ever, appropriate to reject a medical certificate (even if not meeting the normal requirements as to information required) without first giving the defendant an opportunity to respond (*Evans v East Lancashire Magistrates' Court* [2010] EWHC 2108 (Admin). See also

R v Bolton Magistrates' Court, exp Merna [1991] Crim LR 848).

The issues were re-examined and confirmed in *Killick v West London Magistrates' Court* [2012] EWHC 3864 (Admin):

> Section 11(1)(b) and (2A) of the Magistrates' Courts Act 1980 allow the court to proceed in the absence of a defendant unless it appears contrary to the interests of justice, but it should not do so if it considers that there is an acceptable reason for his failure to attend. The jurisdiction must be exercised with the utmost care and caution. The case should not proceed without the court satisfying itself that the claim for an adjournment may properly be rejected and that no unfairness will thereby be done.

> Where a defendant wished to resist a criminal charge and is shown by medical evidence to be unfit to attend court either as a result of involuntary illness or incapacity, it would be very rarely, if ever, right for the court to exercise its discretion in favour of proceeding. If the court suspects the grounds to be spurious or inadequate, it should express its doubts to give the defence a chance to resolve them. The court must distinguish genuine grounds from those that are spurious and designed to frustrate the process. If the court concludes the latter is the case, it may proceed as if there is a truly compelling reason for doing so, notwithstanding the justified non-attendance.

> If a court proceeds, it should set aside the order under section 142 of the Magistrates' Court Act 1980 if compelling medical evidence is then produced.

Criminal Practice Direction 5C contains specific provisions on the production of medical certificates.

A2.2.4 *Witnesses*

Where a party was unable, through no fault of his own, to call an important witness, an adjournment should be granted to give an opportunity for that witness to be traced and steps taken to secure attendance (*Khurshied v Peterborough Magistrates' Court* [2009] EWHC 1136 (Admin) and *Nadour v Chester Magistrates' Court* [2009] EWHC 1505 (Admin)). In *Essen v Director of Public Prosecutions* [2005] EWHC 1077 (Admin), the court was concerned with a failure of the CPS, due to administrative error, to warn its witnesses for trial. The court held that in the absence of some other counter-prevailing factor an adjournment ought not to be granted. The fact that a crime may go unpunished is not sufficient as:

> in that case no prosecutor, however dilatory, need attend to the requirement to be ready for trial on the set date... The prejudice to the defendant [of an adjournment in those circumstances] was manifest. The CPS had no ground for seeking clemency. It was the sole author of its own misfortune.

A prosecutor should always be given some time to make inquiries as to why a witness is not present (*R v Swansea Justices, exp Director of Public Prosecutions*, The Times, 30 March 1990).

A2.2.5 *Disclosure*

Section 7A(3) Criminal Procedure and Investigations Act 1996 requires that the Crown serve material as soon as reasonably practicable. The court must have regard to the overriding objective of the Criminal PR. The defence must identify the possible significance of missing disclosure. If the prosecution have failed to carry out their statutory duties in relation to disclosure under the Act, an adjournment may be granted, on the Crown's application (*Swash v Director of Public Prosecutions* [2009] EWHC 803 (Admin)). A wholesale failure on the part of the prosecution to comply with its disclosure obligations may require the prosecution to offer no evidence (*DPP v Graham Petrie* [2015] EWHC 48 (Admin)). The courts may exclude all prosecution evidence under s 78 Police and Criminal Evidence Act 1984 as it may then be unfair in the proceedings to admit that evidence alone at trial (*R (Ibrahim) v Feltham Magistrates' Court* 2001 EWHC 130 (Admin)). In *R v Boardman* [2015] EWCA Crim 175, all the key prosecution evidence was excluded under this provision. Where the material sought would amount to further disclosure, a defence case statement must be lodged and an application made under s 8 Criminal Procedure and Investigations Act 1996 (*R v Austin* [2013] EWCA Crim 1028). Adjournments in relation to unused material will not be granted if the defence do not follow the correct formal procedures (*DPP v Graham Petrie* 2015 EWHC 48 (Admin)).

The Magistrates' Court disclosure review in May 2014 considered the issues involved:

Magistrates' Court disclosure review

146. The question has been raised as to what should happen on the day of trial if the prosecution has not complied with its disclosure obligations.

147. The first point for consideration is whether the Crown has indeed failed to comply. In some cases it is reported that there are late section 8 CPIA applications and that the fault, if any, therefore lies with the defence. However, if the failure is clearly at the door of the prosecution, then it is the prosecution who must make the application for an adjournment to comply with its obligations.

148. If the application for an adjournment is refused, the consequence must be that the prosecution should offer no evidence, in line with the guidance set out in Chapter 1 of the CPS/ACPO Disclosure Manual. It would be against the professional code of conduct for prosecutors to proceed to trial having not complied with their statutory disclosure obligations. Generally an abuse of process argument is neither necessary nor appropriate.

149. A common and very unfortunate situation is that the prosecution serve, on the day of trial, disclosure or a notice stating that there is nothing to disclose. Here the Bench should proceed in the interests of justice, applying common sense. Although the defence would be entitled to make a section 8 application within 14 days, it will often be appropriate for the court to expect the defence to set out its full defence case in order to trigger the section 8 application.

150. In some situations, the section 8 application can be dealt with there and then. If, having heard such an application, the court decides that there is no obligation for further disclosure, then, unsatisfactory as late service may be, the interests of justice may require the case to proceed. Similarly, where disclosure is made on the day of the hearing, it will often be possible, without injustice, for there to be a short adjournment on the day of trial for the defence to assimilate the new information, but for the trial itself nevertheless to proceed.

151. There will be occasions when it is unreasonable to expect the defence to assimilate new information on the day of trial, or where the court orders section 8 disclosure on the day of trial, and the prosecution cannot comply. In those circumstances an adjournment may be appropriate.

152. The key point is that this position should never have been reached. It is not simply a failing of the prosecution. The defence has an obligation to draw this to the attention of the court in advance, and it is the responsibility of the court to ensure that proper disclosure has been made sufficiently in advance of the trial.

See also **A16**.

A2.2.6 *Ambush defence*

If a defendant raises matters for the first time in the proceedings (so-called ambush defences), the court is fully justified in adjourning the matter in order to allow the prosecution to deal with them properly (eg *R (Lawson) v Stratford Magistrates' Court* [2007] EWHC 2490 (Admin), where compliance with signage regulations in relation to a prosecution for speeding was raised for the first time in cross-examination). The general principles are established by the series of decisions in *R v Gleeson* [2003] EWCA Crim 3357, *R v Chorley Justices* [2006] EWHC 1795 (Admin), and *Malcolm v Director of Public Prosecutions* [2007] EWHC 363 (Admin).

In *R (Taylor) v Southampton Magistrates' Court* [2008] EWHC 3006 (Admin), it was held that, during a trial for failing to comply with a notice under s 172 Road Traffic Act 1988, a District Judge was right to adjourn the case in order for the prosecution to be able to gather evidence (if such evidence existed) to prove service of the notice. There was no question of bias, even though the court acted of its own motion. In this case there was no issue of 'ambush', the prosecution having not only been put to proof of all issues but the specific issue having been raised. That was not enough for the court in this instance, in the absence of a positive defence case that the notice had not in fact been served. The case should be contrasted with *R (Decani) v City of London Magistrates' Court* [2017] EWHC 3422 (Admin) where notice of the issue had been given and the Divisional Court held that the Crown should have been refused an adjournment.

 See *Blackstone's Criminal Practice 2019* **D4**

A3 Admissibility and Exclusion of Evidence

A3.1 Admissibility and exclusion

Given that magistrates deal with questions of both fact and law, the *voir dire* procedure adopted in the Crown Court is not always appropriate in summary proceedings when issues of admissibility arise. The timing of any challenge is a matter for the court, and whilst there is no right to have issues of admissibility determined as a preliminary issue (*R v Epping and Ongar Justices, ex p Manby* [1986] Crim LR 555s), s 8A Magistrates' Courts Act 1980 provides for pre-trial rulings on issues of admissibility. Previous rulings on admissibility can be reversed, but this should happen only exceptionally (see **A9** for relevant provisions and cases).

When a party is seeking to exclude evidence under s 76 Police and Criminal Evidence Act 1984 (PACE), a *voir dire* will be required as there is no discretion under s 76 (as opposed to s 78) and the prosecution carry the burden of disproving unfairness (*Vel v Owen* [1987] Crim LR 496).

When a party is inviting a court to exercise its discretion to exclude evidence under s 78 PACE, the court has a choice as to whether to deal with the issue when it arises or once all evidence has been heard. The *voir dire* procedure is appropriate to such applications, as an accused may otherwise be denied the opportunity to remain silent in relation to the substantive matter. *Halawa v Federation Against Copyright Theft* [1995] 1 Cr App R 496 established the relevant principles.

Police and Criminal Evidence Act 1984, s 78

78 (1) In any proceedings the court may refuse to allow evidence on which the prosecution proposes to rely to be given if it appears to the court that, having regard to all the circumstances, including the circumstances in which the evidence was obtained, the admission of the evidence would have such an adverse effect on the fairness of the proceedings that the court ought not to admit it.

It should be noted that s 78 may only be used to exclude prosecution evidence, not that led by a co-defendant.

A4 **Allocation and Plea before Venue**

A4.1 **Cases that must be sent to the Crown Court**

The court must send the case to the Crown Court if:

- there is an indictable-only offence;
- a notice has been served under s 51B (serious fraud) or s 51C (children) of the Crime and Disorder Act 1998; or
- the offence is related to an indictable/notice offence for which the defendant or another defendant is sent for trial (unless the defendant appears on a subsequent occasion when there is a discretion);
- the defendant is charged with an either-way offence or relevant (imprisonable or disqualifiable) summary offence, and is or has been sent to the Crown Court for a related offence;
- the defendant is jointly charged with another defendant who is or has been sent to the Crown Court for a related offence;
- the defendant is jointly charged or is charged with a related offence with a youth defendant who is or has been sent to the Crown Court for trial.

In each case where there is a co-defendant, the duty exists when the defendants appear on the same occasion, but becomes a discretion if this defendant appears on a subsequent occasion.

For the procedure on sending see **A26**.

A4.2 **Cases that may be sent to the Crown Court**

A plea before venue is conducted for all other either-way offences. The defendant is asked to indicate a plea. The plea must be indicated by the defendant personally and not by a lawyer on their behalf (s 17A Magistrates' Courts Act (MCA) 1980 and *Westminster City Council v Owadally* [2017] EWHC 1092 (Admin)), although under s 17B MCA 1980, an advocate can indicate a plea on an adult defendant's behalf to an either-way offence if that defendant's disorderly behaviour makes it impossible to conduct the proceedings in his presence, or (Sch 3 MCA 1980) the defendant is a company.

A4.3 **Where there is a guilty plea**

If the indication of plea is guilty, the court proceeds to sentence, and this may include a committal for sentence if Crown Court powers are required to deal with the defendant. It shall commit for sentence if the offence is a specified offence and the dangerous offender provisions apply on the facts of the particular case.

A4.4 **Not guilty or no indication of plea**

If the indication of plea is not guilty, the court proceeds to allocation. If there is no indication of plea, it is treated as a plea of not guilty.

The court receives representations from the Crown, which may include details of previous convictions of the defendant, and from the defence.

Allocation Procedure for Adults

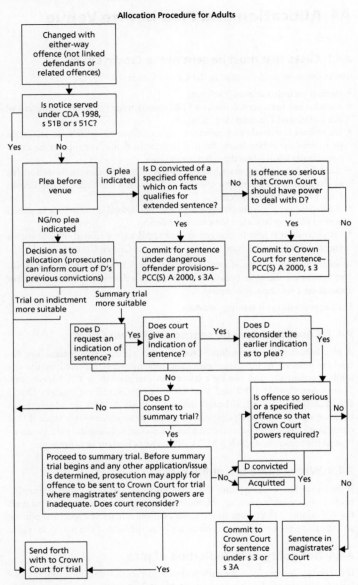

Figure 1 Allocation procedure for adults

The court determines, in accordance with s 19 MCA 1980 and the Allocation Guidelines, whether the case is more suitable for summary trial or trial on indictment.

A4.4.1 *Allocation procedure (s 19 MCA 1980)*

The court must hear representations from all parties before considering whether jurisdiction ought to be accepted or declined. The procedure where there is more than one charge or more than one defendant is set out in rule 9.2 of the Criminal Procedure Rules:

A4.4.2 *Allocation guideline*

The Sentencing Council has issued a definitive guideline in relation to the allocation of cases between the magistrates' court and Crown Court.

It is important to ensure that all cases are tried at the appropriate level.

1. In general, either way offences should be tried summarily unless:
   - the outcome would clearly be a sentence in excess of the court's powers for the offence(s) concerned after taking into account personal mitigation and any potential reduction for a guilty plea; or
   - for reasons of unusual legal, procedural or factual complexity, the case should be tried in the Crown Court. This exception may apply in cases where a very substantial fine is the likely sentence. Other circumstances where this exception will apply are likely to be rare and case specific; the court will rely on the submissions of the parties to identify relevant cases.
2. In cases with no factual or legal complications the court should bear in mind its power to commit for sentence after a trial and may retain jurisdiction notwithstanding that the likely sentence might exceed its powers.
3. Cases may be tried summarily even where the defendant is subject to a Crown Court Suspended Sentence Order or Community Order.
4. All parties should be asked by the court to make representations as to whether the case is suitable for summary trial. The court should refer to definitive guidelines (if any) to assess the likely sentence for the offence in the light of the facts alleged by the prosecution case, taking into account all aspects of the case including those advanced by the defence, including any personal mitigation to which the defence wish to refer.

Where the court decides that the case is suitable to be dealt with in the magistrates' court, it must warn the defendant that all sentencing options remain open and, if the defendant consents to summary trial and is convicted by the court or pleads guilty, the defendant may be committed to the Crown Court for sentence.

Committal for sentence

There is ordinarily no statutory restriction on committing an either-way case for sentence following conviction. The general power of the magistrates' court to commit to the Crown Court for sentence after a finding that a case is suitable for summary trial and/or conviction continues to be available where the court is of the opinion 'that the offence or the combination of the offence and one or more offences associated with it was so serious that the Crown Court should, in the court's opinion, have the power to deal with the offender in any way it could deal with him if he had been convicted on indictment'.

However, where the court proceeds to the summary trial of certain offences relating to criminal damage, upon conviction there is no power to commit to the Crown Court for sentence.

The court should refer to any definitive guideline to arrive at the appropriate sentence, taking into account all of the circumstances of the case including personal mitigation and the appropriate guilty plea reduction.

In borderline cases the court should consider obtaining a pre-sentence report before deciding whether to commit to the Crown Court for sentence.

Where the offending is so serious that the court is of the opinion that the Crown Court should have the power to deal with the offender, the case should be committed to the Crown Court for sentence even if a community order may be the appropriate sentence (this will allow the Crown Court to deal with any breach of a community order, if that is the sentence passed).

A4.5 Magistrates' court declines jurisdiction

If the court declines jurisdiction, it must send the case to the Crown Court. For the procedure on sending see **A26**.

A4.6 Magistrates' court accepts jurisdiction

If the court accepts jurisdiction, the defendant may request an indication whether the court is considering a custodial sentence. If the court is willing to give an indication, the defendant must be invited to reconsider his plea. If the indication was non-custodial and a plea of guilty is indicated, the court may neither impose a custodial sentence nor commit for sentence.

The defence must otherwise be asked if they consent to summary trial. This consent can, under s 23 MCA 1980, be given by the defendant's legal representative. If the defence elect trial on indictment, the case must be sent to the Crown Court. (See **A26**.)

If the defence consent to summary trial, the Crown may make further representations that the trial should be on indictment if new factors become relevant. However, there can be no change of venue once the trial has begun or an application in relation to the trial has been made.

If the case remains summary there is a trial, and in the event of a conviction the court may sentence within its own powers, unless:

- there is a specified offence and the requirements for an extended sentence are met by the facts of the particular case; or
- new factors have arisen during the trial, making the initial decision to accept jurisdiction inappropriate.

This follows the case law on 'expectation' preventing a court from changing its mind (*R v Nottingham Magistrates' Court, ex p Davidson* [2000] 1 Cr App R (S) 167). Under these procedures the court will have been fully advised about the defendant's previous convictions, and as the Crown will have had opportunities to emphasize particular seriousness, it will therefore be difficult for the court to say that the decision to accept summary jurisdiction did not give rise to a legitimate expectation of disposal within magistrates' court powers (*Sheffield Magistrates' Court, ex p Ojo* (2000) 164 JP 659). However, the allocation guideline emphasizes the powers to commit for sentence (see **A4.4.2**) and there may as a result now be no general expectation of a summary disposal. The power to commit for sentence certainly arises when there is an acceptance of jurisdiction that was so perverse as to be unlawful (*R (Nicholas) v Chester Magistrates' Court* [2009] EWHC 1504 (Admin)) or in total disregard of the relevant sentencing guideline (*Thornton v CPS* [2012] EWHC 346 (Admin)); or there have been new convictions since the allocation hearing; or the facts at trial were clearly more serious than originally described so that Crown Court sentencing powers are required.

A4.7 Either-way offences that must be tried summarily ss 22 and 22A MCA 1980

The court must determine venue for either-way offences but some either-way offences have venue dictated by value (criminal damage, save arson, aggravated vehicle-taking, and theft from a shop).

If the value of damage is less than £5,000, only summary trial will be offered. For multiple offences, the aggregate value must be considered (s 22(11) MCA 1980). A court has a discretion but not a duty to hear evidence in relation to value (*R v Canterbury Justices, exp Klisiak* [1981] 2 All ER 129). Value does not include consequential loss flowing from destruction (*R v Colchester Magistrates' Court, ex p Abbott* [2001] Crim LR 564). Where it is not clear whether or not the value exceeds £5,000, the defendant will be permitted, if he so wishes, to elect Crown Court trial but the maximum ten-year sentence is then available (*R v Alden* [2002] EWCA Crim 412).

Theft from a shop that does not exceed an aggregate value of £200 is a hybrid offence in that it can only be tried summarily (without a power to commit for sentence) unless the defendant elects to be tried on indictment: s 22A MCA 1980. If the defendant elects for trial on indictment full sentencing powers are available.

Section 22A MCA 1980 provides:

Magistrates' Courts Act 1980, s 22A

22A Low-value shoplifting to be a summary offence

(1) Low-value shoplifting is triable only summarily.
(2) But where a person accused of low-value shoplifting is aged 18 or over, and appears or is brought before the court before the summary trial of the offence begins, the court must give the person the opportunity of electing to be tried by the Crown Court for the offence and, if the person elects to be so tried—
　(a) subsection (1) does not apply, and
　(b) the court must proceed in relation to the offence in accordance with section 51(1) of the Crime and Disorder Act 1998.

The definition of low value shoplifting appears at **C15.21.3**.

Criminal Attempts Act 1981, s 1(5)

This section also applies to low-value shoplifting (which is defined in, and is triable only summarily by virtue of, s 22A of the Magistrates' Courts Act 1980).

See *Blackstone's Criminal Practice 2019* **D6**

A5 Amending Charge

A5.1 Amendment within the time limit

Prosecutors do not have an unfettered right to seek to amend charges that are not subject to any limitation of time (ie indictable and indictable-only charges). Amendments should be granted only where the application is judged to be proper and appropriate (*R v Redbridge Justices, ex p Whitehouse* (1992) 94 Cr App R 332).

A5.2 Amendment outside the time limit

An amendment outside the time limit, in order to allow the prosecution to proceed with a summary-only offence which would otherwise be time barred, may be permitted, provided that the new offence is based on the 'same misdoing', that it is in the interests of justice to allow the amendment (*R v Scunthorpe Justices, ex p McPhee and Gallagher* (1998) 162 JP 635, DC), and the matter to be amended was preferred *within* the relevant time limit (*Dougall v CPS* [2018] EWHC 1367(Admin).

The following principles emerge from *Scunthorpe Justices*:

- the purpose of the six-month time limit imposed by s 127 Magistrates' Courts Act (MCA) 1980 is to ensure that summary offences are charged and tried as soon as reasonably practicable after their alleged commission;
- where an information has been laid within the six-month period it can be amended after the expiry of that period;
- an information can be amended after the expiry of the six-month period, even to allege a different offence or different offences, provided that:
  - the different offence or offences allege the 'same misdoing' as the original offence; and
  - the amendment can be made in the interests of justice.

The phrase 'same misdoing' should not be construed too narrowly. It means that the new offence should arise out of the same (or substantially the same) facts as gave rise to the original offence.

In *Shaw v Director of Public Prosecutions* [2007] EWHC 207 (Admin), the court ruled that an amendment to charge an offence which was based on similar misdoing ought not to have been permitted, as the original offence carried only a financial penalty whereas the new offence carried imprisonment. The court ruled similarly in *R (Crown Prosecution Service) v Everest* [2005] EWHC 1124 (Admin), observing that the new offence carried a higher penalty, had a statutory defence that the defence had to establish, and that the defendant was not legally represented.

The amendment of a charge to substitute failing to provide a specimen of breath with failing to provide a specimen of urine was held to be proper in *Williams v Director of Public Prosecutions* [2009] EWHC 2354 (Admin), although the court did allow the appeal as the alteration had not been made in a timely fashion (applying *DPP v Hammerton* [2009] EWHC 921 (Admin)). By contrast in *Crann v CPS* [2013] EWHC 552 (Admin), a very late amendment was allowed as the offence was no more serious and had been anticipated.

When the prosecution seeks to change the name of a defendant out of time, a factual enquiry is necessary. The issue is whether there was a mistake as to identity, such as the wrong company in a group (when amendment is not permissible (see *Sainsbury's Supermarkets Ltd v HM Courts Service* [2006] EWHC 1749 (Admin)) or a misstatement of the name which could be amended, as in *Platinum Crown Investments Ltd v North East Essex MC* [2017] EWHC 2761 (Admin)).

A6 Appeals and Reopening

A6.1 Two routes of appeal under the Magistrates' Courts Act 1980; and judicial review availability

A6.1.1 *Appeals against conviction or sentence*

Under s 108 Magistrates' Courts Act (MCA) 1980, an appeal against conviction and/or sentence lies as of right to the Crown Court. A notice of appeal must be served within 21 days of final disposal of the case. Section 113 MCA 1980 creates an obligation on the magistrates' court to consider an application for bail pending appeal in every case where a notice of appeal has been lodged in accordance with the Criminal Procedure Rules (Crim PR) 34.3 and a properly constituted application for bail is made (*Thomas v CPS* [2015] EWHC 4079 (Admin)).

If a custodial sentence is imposed it is not the normal practice to grant bail pending an appeal, and there is no statutory right to bail. Where the appeal is against conviction and the defendant was convicted after trial, many courts will look more favourably on bail pending appeal, particularly when the custodial sentence is short. In *R v Imdad Shah* (1980) 144 JP 460, the court rejected an argument that bail should be granted where the sentence was a short one and there was a risk that the sentence would be served prior to the appeal being heard. The court ruled that in such cases an early listing should be sought. By way of contrast, in *R (G) v Inner London Crown Court* [2003] EWHC 2715 (Admin) the applicant successfully judicially reviewed a decision by a Crown Court to refuse bail in a 'short sentence' case.

A6.1.2 *Appeals by way of case stated*

Provision is made for appeals by way of case stated by s 111 MCA 1980 and Crim PR 35. The application, complying with Crim PR 35(2), must be made within 21 days of the decision sought to be appealed. This is a strict and non-extendable time limit (*Mishra v Colchester MC* [2017] EWHC 2869 (Admin)) and time runs from the giving of the decision and not from the giving of written reasons (*R v Ziegler* [2019] EWHC 19 (Admin)). The decision must be a final determination going to an issue of law or excess of jurisdiction (*R (Highbury Poultry Farm Produce Ltd) v Telford MC* [2018] EWHC 3122 (Admin)). The making of an application rules out any appeal on the facts under **A6.1.1**. A magistrates' court representation order covers the costs of seeking a case. The distinction between an appeal by way of case stated and an application for judicial review, and the circumstances in which they should be used, was considered in *Downes v RSPCA* [2017] EWHC 3622 (Admin). In *R (Parashar) v Sunderland MC* [2019] EWHC 514 (Admin) the court considered that judicial review may be an appropriate remedy where:

(a) it is properly arguable that the ability of the defendant to present his defence is so seriously compromised by the decision under challenge that an unfair trial is inevitable; and

(b) where an important point of principle is raised, likely to affect other cases; and

(c) where the case had some other exceptional feature which justifies the intervention of the High Court. The threshold for exceptionality is likely to be less high where the application is made pre-trial.

A6.2 **Reopening cases**

A6.2.1 *Jurisdiction*

Magistrates' Courts Act 1980, s 142

142 Power of magistrates' court to re-open cases to rectify mistakes etc

(1) A magistrates' court may vary or rescind a sentence or other order imposed or made by it when dealing with an offender if it appears to the court to be in the interests of justice to do so, and it is hereby declared that this power extends to replacing a sentence or order which for any reason appears to be invalid by another which the court has power to impose or make.

(1A) The power conferred on a magistrates' court by subsection (1) above shall not be exercisable in relation to any sentence or order imposed or made by it when dealing with an offender if—

    (a) the Crown Court has determined an appeal against—

        (i) that sentence or order;

        (ii) the conviction in respect of which that sentence or order was imposed or made; or

        (iii) any other sentence or order imposed or made by the magistrates' court when dealing with the offender in respect of that conviction (including a sentence or order replaced by that sentence or order); or

    (b) the High Court has determined a case stated for the opinion of that court on any question arising in any proceeding leading to or resulting from the imposition or making of the sentence or order.

(2) Where a person is convicted by a magistrates' court and it subsequently appears to the court that it would be in the interests of justice that the case should be heard again by different justices, the court may so direct.

(2A) The power conferred on a magistrates' court by subsection (2) above shall not be exercisable in relation to a conviction if—

    (a) the Crown Court has determined an appeal against—

        (i) the conviction; or

        (ii) any sentence or order imposed or made by the magistrates' court when dealing with the offender in respect of the conviction; or

    (b) the High Court has determined a case stated for the opinion of that court on any question arising in any proceeding leading to or resulting from the conviction ...

A6.2.2 *Principles*

Section 142 MCA 1980 relates to criminal proceedings and has no application to other areas of magistrates' court jurisdiction such as liability orders

(*Liverpool City Council v Plemora Distribution Ltd* [2002] EWHC 2467 (Admin)), and detention and forfeiture in relation to proceeds of crime. Further, the court enjoys no common law jurisdiction to reopen civil matters such as a civil injunction (*Samuda v Birmingham Justices* [2008] EWHC 205 (Admin)). A defendant who has been convicted in absence can properly attempt to reopen under this section. Culpability on the part of the offender is relevant to whether it is in the interests of justice to reopen, but it is not determinative. It will normally be in the interests of justice for a defendant to be able to defend himself, and unless the evidence indicates that his absence from trial is deliberate and voluntary, a rehearing would normally be the appropriate course (*R (Morsby) v Tower Bridge Magistrates' Court* [2007] EWHC 2766 (Admin)). See also *R (Manorgate Ltd) v Thames Magistrates' Court* [2013] EWHC 535 (Admin). Any inconvenience to the court in allowing a reopening can never outweigh the interests of justice (*R (Blick) v Doncaster Magistrates' Court* (2008) 172 JP 651). Section 142(2) MCA 1980 does not require a mistake in every case but merely that rectification be in the interests of justice. However, there must be new material before the court (*R (Nkromah) v Willesden MC* [2014] EWHC 4455(Admin)).

Persons made subject to a hospital order under s 37(3) Mental Health Act 1983 fall within the definition of 'offender', and a person can use s 142 MCA 1980 to reopen a hearing determining the issue under the Mental Health Act (*R (Bartram) v Southend Magistrates' Court* [2004] EWHC 2691 (Admin)). An order to commit an offender to prison for non-satisfaction of a confiscation order made under the Proceeds of Crime Act 2002 in the Crown Court is capable of being reopened.

The court has power to revisit the issue of a warrant following nonpayment of fines. A court does not have the power to rescind a costs order made in favour of a defendant who was not convicted as the section related only to orders post-conviction (*Coles v East Penwith Justices*, The Times, 27 July 1998).

A prosecutor cannot apply to reopen proceedings that have previously been withdrawn (*R (Green and Green Scaffolding Ltd) v Staines Magistrates' Court* (2008) 172 JP 353).

The nature of the remedy afforded under MCA 1980 is akin to a 'slip rule', allowing a court to rectify a clear mistake or injustice. An applicant who entered an unequivocal plea of guilty cannot apply to reopen a plea under this section (*R v Croydon Youth Court, ex p Director of Public Prosecutions* [1997] 2 Cr App R 411), unless the plea was inappropriate and so now equivocal; however, this exception did not apply where the allegation was of professional impropriety by the defendant's legal representative as this did not fall within the word 'mistake' (*Williamson v City of Westminster Magistrates' Court* [2012] EWHC 1444 (Admin)).

Section 142 should not be used to advance new arguments, neither should it be used as an 'appeal' mechanism (*Zykin v Crown Prosecution Service* [2009] EWHC 1469 (Admin); *R v Chajed* [2013] EWHC 188 (Admin)). Applications based on a change of law between conviction and application should not be entertained. The section may not be used to revisit an interlocutory ruling, but only after the conclusion of the case *(R (Poskitt) v Reading Magistrates' Court* [2018] EWHC 984 (Admin)).

A6.2.3 *Applications*

A procedure for an application under s 142 is provided by Crim PR 24.18.

There is no statutory time limit on reopening, but the former 28-day rule should act as a salutary guideline. Applications made much beyond this date might properly be refused on interests of justice grounds, as '[d]elay in matters of this sort is always harmful, memories fade, records may be lost and the essence of doing justice is that it should be done expeditiously' *(R v Ealing Magistrates' Court, ex p Sahota*, 1997 EWHC 993 (Admin)). It is not, however, a decisive factor. It is not enough for the magistrates simply to say that the length of time is such that it is no longer proper to open the case under s 142. More substantial reasoning than that has to be given, so that the applicant (and any court on appeal) can understand why it is no longer proper to deal with the matter.

It is possible for the section to apply when, in hindsight, the decision to proceed was made in error because all the facts that had a bearing on the exercise of judicial discretion were not known to the court. The power arises when the earlier decision would not have been reached had the full facts been known and the reason for that was not the defendant's fault *(R (Rathor) v Southampton MC* [2018] EWHC 3278 (Admin)).

Applications may be made by both defence and prosecution, but the exercise of such discretion in favour of a prosecutor will be rare, and can never extend to the overturning of an acquittal. A prosecutor could properly make an application to reopen where the court had erroneously failed to impose penalty points or some other appropriate order. Similarly, if the court had been unaware of factors relevant to sentence, it could be invited to reopen sentence, even if that meant a risk that it would be increased. However, if it is appropriate for the powers under s142 to be used to increase sentence then the power must be exercised very speedily *(R (Holme) v Liverpool Magistrates' Court* [2004] EWHC 3131 (Admin), where the court declined to allow the prosecution to exercise the power).

A6.2.4 *Interests of justice*

Justices are given wide discretion in determining what are relevant factors in relation to interests of justice, but decisions must be based on sound judicial reasoning. A defendant's late arrival at court was held not to be a proper ground, in itself, to refuse a rehearing *(R v Camberwell Green Magistrates' Court, exp Ibrahim* (1984) 148 JP 400). Factors a court ought to consider include:

- why the convicted person did not appear at the original trial (if that was the case);
- timeliness of the application;
- reason for any delay;

- importance of the decision being questioned—note that the importance to all parties, including defendant, prosecution, and other interested parties (such as victim), should be assessed;
- inconvenience and prejudice caused to opposing parties;
- whether a more appropriate appeal remedy is available. It will not normally be appropriate to allow a reopening where a defendant is denied a right of appeal due to an unequivocal guilty plea (*R v Croydon Youth Court, ex p Director of Public Prosecutions* [1997] 2 Cr App R 411).

In addition, the court must always consider rule 1 of the Crim PR and the overriding objective.

 See *Blackstone's Criminal Practice 2019* **D29**

A6.2.5 *Effect of reopening*

A conviction will be set aside, as will any sentence or ancillary orders flowing from it. The matter is treated as adjourned for trial. Justices who sat on the original hearing, or the hearing to reopen, cannot sit on the adjourned trial. The prosecution retain the right to offer no evidence and the court lacks power to insist that a prosecutor proceeds with the case (*R (Rhodes-Presley) v South Worcestershire Magistrates' Court* [2008] EWHC 2700 (Admin)).

If a sentence or order is reopened, the court may vary or rescind the original finding and substitute any other lawful sentence or order that would have been available to the court at the original hearing. The new orders take effect from the date of the old order unless the court directs otherwise. A court must be careful not to offend against any legitimate expectation given to the offender (*Jane v Broome*, The Times, 2 November 1988).

A6.3 Reopening of guilty plea

The procedure is set out in Crim PR 24.10 The following principles emerge from the authorities:

- the fact that the defendant was not legally represented when he entered his guilty plea is not on its own grounds for allowing a change of plea (*R v South Tameside Magistrates' Court, ex p Rowland* [1983] 3 All ER 689);
- a misunderstanding as to the nature of the charge being pleaded to may justify a change of plea (and may well be an equivocal plea in any event) (*P Foster Haulage Ltd v Roberts* [1978] 2 All ER 751);
- evidence of the previous guilty plea may be adduced at any later trial, although its probative value will generally be so low that a court ought to decline to admit it (*R v Rimmer* [1972] 1 WLR 268).

In *S (An Infant) v Recorder of Manchester* [1971] AC 481, the court held that:

- the power to reopen plea was a discretionary one;
- the power ought to be used sparingly;
- the power is available up until sentence has been passed;
- the question for the court is whether justice requires the change of plea to be permitted.

A7 Bad Character

A7.1 Introduction

The admissibility of bad character is regulated by ss 98–113 of the Criminal Justice Act 2003, but s 27(3) Theft Act 1968 remains available to the Crown in cases of handling. The common law rules are now subsidiary to the statutory regime. The Act is concerned with the admission of bad character in relation to:

- the defendant;
- any co-defendant;
- a person other than a defendant in the case.

The Criminal Procedure Rules (Crim PR Part 21) provide the regime for the admission of evidence of bad character. The court has the power to exclude otherwise admissible evidence of bad character on the grounds of non-compliance, if the effect would be to prejudice a party, for example by way of ambush defence (*R v Musone* [2007] EWCA Crim 1237). Provided that there is no prejudice, a court is free to admit evidence of bad character if to do so would satisfy the overriding objective of Crim PR 1. Attempts to argue that evidence ought to be admitted following procedural non-compliance only in exceptional cases have been rejected (*R (Robinson) v Sutton Coldfield Magistrates' Court* [2006] EWHC 307 (Admin)). In *Robinson*, the court did say, however, that:

> a court would ordinarily wish to know when the relevant enquiries had been initiated, and in broad terms why they have not been completed within the time allowed. Any application for an extension will be closely scrutinised by the court. A party seeking an extension cannot expect the indulgence of the court unless it clearly sets out the reasons why it is seeking that indulgence.

A7.2 What is bad character?

The Criminal Justice Act defines 'bad character' as the commission of an offence or other 'reprehensible behaviour'. It is important to note the effect of s 98 (see **A7.3**), which has the effect of excluding much bad character evidence from the statutory scheme, allowing for its admissibility subject only to the normal rules of probity and relevance.

In considering whether or not a party has committed an offence, regard can be had to:

- previous convictions;
- previous police cautions or youth cautions;
- offences for which the person has not been tried;
- offences for which the person has been acquitted (*R v Z* [2000] 2 AC 483) or found unfit to be tried (*R v Renda* [2005] EWCA Crim 2826).

Other examples include telling lies, taking illegal drugs (*R v AJC* [2006] EWCA Crim 284), being sexually promiscuous (*R v Ball* [2005] EWCA

Crim 2826), and collecting photographs of people being violently attacked (*R v Saleem* [2007] EWCA Crim 1923). In *R v M* [2014] EWCA Crim 1407, it was held that attempted suicide and probably self-harming do not amount to reprehensible behaviour but excessive drinking and illegal drug taking do fall within the meaning of the term. The Act also covers those with a disposition towards reprehensible conduct, for example an admission that a person is sexually attracted to children (*R v S* [2007] EWCA Crim 1387; but see also *R v Fox* [2009] EWCA Crim 653, where it was stated that such evidence ought not to be admitted).

It is important to note that a defendant is entitled to dispute that he is guilty of a matter that has resulted in conviction (or caution); the procedure for doing so is discussed in *R v C* [2010] EWCA Crim 2971.

There are some particular considerations at play when admitting police cautions as evidence of bad character. In *R v Olu and others* [2010] EWCA Crim 2975, the court held:

> We accept the submission that there is a very considerable difference not only between a caution and a conviction for the reasons given in the authorities to which we have referred, but there is also a very considerable difference between an admission contained in a caution without legal advice having been given and an admission made in a caution after legal advice or before a court by a plea. In such circumstances, the giving of legal advice or the formality of a court appearance will have made clear to the person the consequences of his admission. The processes that lead to a caution can differ widely between police area and police area; a court would be shutting its eyes to reality if it assumed that, where a person was not legally represented, the consequences of admitting an offence and accepting a caution were fully explained to a person in a manner that he understood the serious adverse consequences that would follow and what he was giving up by not exercising his right to legal advice— namely that what he was admitting would give him a criminal record, that the caution would be maintained on his PNC record for very many years and that it would be used against his interests in certain circumstances.

Penalty notices for disorder cannot, in themselves, be adduced as evidence of bad character and do not represent an admission (*R v Hamer* [2010] EWCA Crim 2053); *Hewson v CMP* [2018] EWHC 471 (Admin)) neither can unsubstantiated allegations contained in crime reports (*R v Braithwaite* [2010] EWCA Crim 1082).

A7.3 Bad character excluded from application

Section 98 provides:

Criminal Justice Act 2003, s 98

98 'Bad character'

References in this Chapter to evidence of a person's 'bad character' are to evidence of, or of a disposition towards, misconduct on his part, other than evidence which—

(a) has to do with the alleged facts of the offence with which the defendant is charged, or

---

(b) is evidence of misconduct in connection with the investigation or prosecution of that offence.

This means that the allegation itself (obviously of misconduct) does not need to be subject to an application to admit bad character. The section also covers:

- evidence of a previous conviction that might be a component of the offence alleged (eg a conviction for assault against a child in relation to a cruelty charge concerning that same child: *R v R* [2006] EWCA Crim 3196);
- preparatory acts (eg purchase of a murder weapon);
- background evidence (eg an act that provided motive for the offence: *R v Saleem* [2007] EWCA Crim 1923 and *R v McNeill* [2007] EWCA Crim 2927);
- a temporal connection is not essential for the evidence to be 'to do' with the offence if it goes to provide the motive, but it is otherwise if it is being used as evidence of propensity (*R v Sule* [2012] EWCA Crim 1130).

A7.4 **Non-defendant's bad character**

Section 100 provides:

Criminal Justice Act 2003, s 100

100 Non-defendant's bad character

(1) In criminal proceedings evidence of the bad character of a person other than the defendant is admissible if and only if—
    (a) it is important explanatory evidence,
    (b) it has substantial probative value in relation to a matter which—
        (i) is a matter in issue in the proceedings, and
        (ii) is of substantial importance in the context of the case as a whole, or
    (c) all parties to the proceedings agree to the evidence being admissible.
(2) For the purposes of subsection (1)(a) evidence is important explanatory evidence if—
    (a) without it, the court or jury would find it impossible or difficult properly to understand other evidence in the case, and
    (b) its value for understanding the case as a whole is substantial.
(3) In assessing the probative value of evidence for the purposes of subsection (1)(b) the court must have regard to the following factors (and to any others it considers relevant)—
    (a) the nature and number of the events, or other things, to which the evidence relates;
    (b) when those events or things are alleged to have happened or existed;
    (c) where—
        (i) the evidence is evidence of a person's misconduct, and
        (ii) it is suggested that the evidence has probative value by reason of similarity between that misconduct and other alleged misconduct,
    the nature and extent of the similarities and the dissimilarities between each of the alleged instances of misconduct;
    (d) where—
        (i) the evidence is evidence of a person's misconduct,
        (ii) it is suggested that that person is also responsible for the misconduct charged, and
        (iii) the identity of the person responsible for the misconduct charged is disputed,
    the extent to which the evidence shows or tends to show that the same person was responsible each time.

(4) Except where subsection (1)(c) applies, evidence of the bad character of a person other than the defendant must not be given without leave of the court.

A non-defendant includes a person who is not a witness in the case (*R v R Ahmed* [2017] EWCA Crim 1515).

A7.5 **Defendant's bad character**

Section 101 provides:

> ### Criminal Justice Act 2003, s 101
>
> #### 101 Defendant's bad character
>
> (1) In criminal proceedings evidence of the defendant's bad character is admissible if, but only if—
>   (a) all parties to the proceedings agree to the evidence being admissible,
>   (b) the evidence is adduced by the defendant himself or is given in answer to a question asked by him in cross-examination and intended to elicit it,
>   (c) it is important explanatory evidence,
>   (d) it is relevant to an important matter in issue between the defendant and the prosecution,
>   (e) it has substantial probative value in relation to an important matter in issue between the defendant and a co-defendant,
>   (f) it is evidence to correct a false impression given by the defendant, or
>   (g) the defendant has made an attack on another person's character.
> (2) Sections 102 to 106 contain provision supplementing subsection (1).
> (3) The court must not admit evidence under subsection (1)(d) or (g) if, on an application by the defendant to exclude it, it appears to the court that the admission of the evidence would have such an adverse effect on the fairness of the proceedings that the court ought not to admit it.
> (4) On an application to exclude evidence under subsection (3) the court must have regard, in particular, to the length of time between the matters to which that evidence relates and the matters which form the subject of the offence charged.

A7.6 **Important explanatory evidence**

Section 102 provides:

> ### Criminal Justice Act 2003, s 102
>
> #### 102 'Important explanatory evidence'
>
> For the purposes of section 101(1)(c) evidence is important explanatory evidence if—
>
> (a) without it, the court or jury would find it impossible or difficult properly to understand other evidence in the case, and
> (b) its value for understanding the case as a whole is substantial.

A case which is truly one of propensity cannot and must not be dressed up as a case of important explanatory evidence. To say the evidence fills out the picture is not the same as saying that the rest of the picture is either impossible or difficult to see without it (*R v Lee* [2012] EWCA Crim 316).

A7.7 Matter in issue between defendant and prosecution

Section 103 provides:

Criminal Justice Act 2003, s 103

103 Matter in issue between the defendant and the prosecution

(1) For the purposes of section 101(1)(d) the matters in issue between the defendant and the prosecution include—
- (a) the question whether the defendant has a propensity to commit offences of the kind with which he is charged, except where his having such a propensity makes it no more likely that he is guilty of the offence;
- (b) the question whether the defendant has a propensity to be untruthful, except where it is not suggested that the defendant's case is untruthful in any respect.

(2) Where subsection (1)(a) applies, a defendant's propensity to commit offences of the kind with which he is charged may (without prejudice to any other way of doing so) be established by evidence that he has been convicted of—
- (a) an offence of the same description as the one with which he is charged, or
- (b) an offence of the same category as the one with which he is charged.

(3) Subsection (2) does not apply in the case of a particular defendant if the court is satisfied, by reason of the length of time since the conviction or for any other reason, that it would be unjust for it to apply in his case.

(4) For the purposes of subsection (2)—
- (a) two offences are of the same description as each other if the statement of the offence in a written charge or indictment would, in each case, be in the same terms;
- (b) two offences are of the same category as each other if they belong to the same category of offences prescribed for the purposes of this section by an order made by the Secretary of State.

(5) A category prescribed by an order under subsection (4)(b) must consist of offences of the same type.

(6) Only prosecution evidence is admissible under section 101(1)(d).

Whilst the matter in issue includes propensity, the provision is more likely to be relevant to ruling out a defence such as innocent association (*R v Vo* [2013] EWCA Crim 2292); self-defence (*R v Cox* [2014] EWCA Crim 804); or identity (*R Richardson* [2014] EWCA Crim 1785). It may assist to establish the credibility of the complainant (*R v Blake* [2014] EWCA Crim 2341). It must not be used to bolster a weak case (see *R v H* [2014] EWCA Crim 420).

R v Mitchell [2016] UKSC 55 confirms that the issue for a court, asked to find bad character evidence from the propensity of a defendant to commit acts of the kind in question, was whether they were sure to the criminal standard that propensity existed. It was not necessary to prove the facts of each incident beyond reasonable doubt or that one incident should be considered separately from the others. However, propensity remains an incidental issue and could not alone establish guilt In that case the evidence was used to challenge a defence of self-defence when the defendant had made extensive use of knives in the past.

A7.8 Matter in issue between the defendant and a co-defendant

Section 104 provides:

Criminal Justice Act 2003, s 104

104 'Matter in issue between the defendant and a co-defendant'

(1) Evidence which is relevant to the question whether the defendant has a propensity to be untruthful is admissible on that basis under section 101(1) only if the nature or conduct of his defence is such as to undermine the co-defendant's defence.
(2) Only evidence—
(a) which is to be (or has been) adduced by the co-defendant, or
(b) which a witness is to be invited to give (or has given) in cross-examination by the co-defendant, is admissible under section 101(1)(e).

A7.9 Evidence to correct a false impression

Section 105 provides:

Criminal Justice Act 2003, s 105

105 'Evidence to correct a false impression'

(1) For the purposes of section 101(1)(f)—
(a) the defendant gives a false impression if he is responsible for the making of an express or implied assertion which is apt to give the court or jury a false or misleading impression about the defendant;
(b) evidence to correct such an impression is evidence which has probative value in correcting it.
(2) A defendant is treated as being responsible for the making of an assertion if—
(a) the assertion is made by the defendant in the proceedings (whether or not in evidence given by him),
(b) the assertion was made by the defendant—
(i) on being questioned under caution, before charge, about the offence with which he is charged, or
(ii) on being charged with the offence or officially informed that he might be prosecuted for it,
and evidence of the assertion is given in the proceedings,
(c) the assertion is made by a witness called by the defendant,
(d) the assertion is made by any witness in cross-examination in response to a question asked by the defendant that is intended to elicit it, or is likely to do so, or
(e) the assertion was made by any person out of court, and the defendant adduces evidence of it in the proceedings.
(3) A defendant who would otherwise be treated as responsible for the making of an assertion shall not be so treated if, or to the extent that, he withdraws it or disassociates himself from it.

> (4) Where it appears to the court that a defendant, by means of his conduct (other than the giving of evidence) in the proceedings, is seeking to give the court or jury an impression about himself that is false or misleading, the court may if it appears just to do so treat the defendant as being responsible for the making of an assertion which is apt to give that impression.
>
> (5) In subsection (4) 'conduct' includes appearance or dress.
>
> (6) Evidence is admissible under section 101(1)(f) only if it goes no further than is necessary to correct the false impression.
>
> (7) Only prosecution evidence is admissible under section 101(1)(f).

Material is only admissible (s 105(6)) if it goes no further than is necessary to correct the false impression (*R v Omotoso* [2018] EWCA Crim 1394).

A7.10 Attack on another person's character

Section 106 provides:

> ### Criminal Justice Act 2003, s 106
>
> #### 106 'Attack on another person's character'
>
> (1) For the purposes of section 101(1)(g) a defendant makes an attack on another person's character if—
>
>   (a) he adduces evidence attacking the other person's character,
>
>   (b) he (or any legal representative appointed under section 38(4) of the Youth Justice and Criminal Evidence Act 1999 (c. 23) to cross-examine a witness in his interests) asks questions in cross-examination that are intended to elicit such evidence, or are likely to do so, or
>
>   (c) evidence is given of an imputation about the other person made by the defendant—
>
>   (i) on being questioned under caution, before charge, about the offence with which he is charged, or
>
>   (ii) on being charged with the offence or officially informed that he might be prosecuted for it.
>
> (2) In subsection (1) 'evidence attacking the other person's character' means evidence to the effect that the other person—
>
>   (a) has committed an offence (whether a different offence from the one with which the defendant is charged or the same one), or
>
>   (b) has behaved, or is disposed to behave, in a reprehensible way; and 'imputation about the other person' means an assertion to that effect.
>
> (3) Only prosecution evidence is admissible under section 101(1)(g).

Only issues raised in evidence, and not during a procedural application, may be taken into account (*R v Omotoso* [2018] EWCA Crim1394).

 See *Blackstone's Criminal Practice 2019* **F13**

A7.11 Handling: special rules

Theft Act 1968, s 27

(3) Where a person is being proceeded against for handling stolen goods (but not for any offence other than handling stolen goods), then at any stage of the proceedings, if evidence has been given of his having or arranging to have in his possession the goods the subject of the charge, or of his undertaking or assisting in, or arranging to undertake or assist in, their retention, removal, disposal or realisation, the following evidence shall be admissible for the purpose of proving that he knew or believed the goods to be stolen goods:—

(a) evidence that he has had in his possession, or has undertaken or assisted in the retention, removal, disposal or realisation of, stolen goods from any theft taking place not earlier than twelve months before the offence charged; and

(b) (provided that seven days' notice in writing has been given to him of the intention to prove the conviction) evidence that he has within the five years preceding the date of the offence charged been convicted of theft or of handling stolen goods.

A7.11.1 Key points

Handling must be the only offence in issue. The provision goes only to proof of guilty knowledge, not dishonesty or possession (*Duffas* 1994 158 JP 245). Only the details admissible by reason of s 73(2) Police and Criminal Evidence Act 1984 should be admitted (*Hacker* 1994 1 All ER 45). *Hacker* also confirms that s 78 Police and Criminal Evidence Act 1984 can be used to exclude the evidence if it is unfair in the proceedings to admit it.

A8 **Bail**

A8.1 **Introduction**

The starting point is that there is a presumption in favour of bail being granted in criminal proceedings (see **A8.2** for the position in relation to defendants charged with murder appearing before a magistrates' court). The exceptions to that right under Sch 1 to the Bail Act 1976 are summarized in the following table:

Exception	Imprisonable— Pt I	Imprisonable— Pt IA triable only summarily	Non-imprisonable— Pt II
Fail to answer bail	Yes, but where there is a real likelihood of custody (para 2(1)(a))	Previously failed to answer bail in criminal proceedings and consequently court believes will fail to answer if bailed now, but only where real likelihood of custody (para 2)	Previously failed to answer bail in criminal proceedings and consequently court believes will fail to answer bail now (para 2)
Offend while on bail	Yes, but where real likelihood of custody (para 2(1)(b))	On bail at the date of the offence and consequently court believes would commit an offence on bail, but only if a real likelihood of custody (para 3)	NA
Interfere with witnesses or obstruct course of justice	Yes, but where real likelihood of custody (para 2(1)(c))	NA	NA
Substantial grounds for believing that if released on bail would commit an offence likely to cause physical or mental injury to an associated person, or cause an associated person to fear physical or mental injury	Yes (para 2ZA)	Yes (para 4)	NA
Arrested for breach of bail in same proceedings and substantial grounds to believe would fail to appear, commit offences, or interfere with witnesses or obstruct the course of justice	Yes, but must be a real likelihood of custody; if offence carries a life term the court may not grant bail unless satisfied there is no significant risk of failure to appear (para 6)	Yes, but must be real likelihood of custody (para 7)	Yes, including committing the offence by engaging in conduct likely to cause physical or mental injury to an associated person (paras 5 and 6)

Exception	Imprisonable— Pt I	Imprisonable— Pt IA triable only summarily	Non-imprisonable— Pt II
Indictable or either-way offence and defendant on bail at the time of the offence	Yes, but note that if the offence carries a life term the court may not grant bail unless it is satisfied that there is no significant risk of an offence on bail. Must be a real likelihood of custody (para 2A)	NA	NA
Own protection or welfare	Yes (para 3)	Yes (para 5)	Yes (para 3)
Serving sentence	Yes (para. 4)	Yes (para 6)	Yes (para 4)
Insufficient information	Yes (para 5)	Yes (para 8)	NA
Reports	Yes (para 7)	NA	NA
Drugs scheme	Yes (para 6A)	Yes (para 9)	NA
Homicide or rape	No bail unless exceptional circumstances justified if charged or convicted of a CJPOA 1994, s 25 offence and previous convictions for a s 25 offence	NA	NA
Murder	Not in the magistrates' court	NA	NA

A8.1.1 *General exceptions*

That presumption does not apply in the following cases:

- in extradition proceedings where the person is alleged to have been convicted of the offence;
- following committal to the Crown Court for sentence or for breach of a Crown Court order;
- after conviction, unless the proceedings are adjourned for inquiries to be made or a report to be prepared for sentence;
- on appeal against conviction or sentence.

Where a defendant aged 18 or over has tested positive for heroin, cocaine, or crack cocaine, and is unwilling to undergo an assessment of his drug misuse and/or any proposed follow-up treatment, different rules apply. The defendant cannot be granted bail unless the court is satisfied that there is no significant risk of an offence being committed while on bail.

Bail may be granted only in exceptional circumstances where a defendant is charged with or convicted of an offence of:

- murder, or
- attempted murder, or
- manslaughter, or
- rape, or
- attempted rape,

and the defendant has been previously convicted in the United Kingdom of any such offence or of culpable homicide. (If the previous conviction was manslaughter or culpable homicide, the provision applies only if the defendant received a sentence of imprisonment/long-term detention.) Convictions in EU member states can be taken into account.

Bail need not be granted to a person on bail at the time of committing an indictable offence (Sch 1, para 2A Bail Act 1976). Sections 14 and 15 of the Criminal Justice Act 2003 are partially in force and currently apply *only* to those charged with offences carrying life imprisonment.

Criminal Justice Act 2003, s 14

14 Offences committed on bail

(1) For paragraph 2A of Part 1 of Schedule 1 to the 1976 Act (defendant need not be granted bail where he was on bail on date of offence) there is substituted—

'2A(1) If the defendant falls within this paragraph he may not be granted bail unless the court is satisfied that there is no significant risk of his committing an offence while on bail (whether subject to conditions or not).
- The defendant falls within this paragraph if—
    (a) he is aged 18 or over, and
    (b) it appears to the court that he was on bail in criminal proceedings on the date of the offence.'

(2) After paragraph 9 of that Part there is inserted—

'9AA(1) This paragraph applies if—
    (a) the defendant is a child or young person, and
    (b) it appears to the court that he was on bail in criminal proceedings on the date of the offence.

(2) In deciding for the purposes of paragraph 2(1) of this Part of this Schedule whether it is satisfied that there are substantial grounds for believing that the defendant, if released on bail (whether subject to conditions or not), would commit an offence while on bail, the court shall give particular weight to the fact that the defendant was on bail in criminal proceedings on the date of the offence.'

Criminal Justice Act 2003, s 15(1) and (2)

15 Absconding by persons released on bail

(1) For paragraph 6 of Part 1 of Schedule 1 to the 1976 Act (defendant need not be granted bail if having been released on bail he has been arrested in pursuance of section 7) there is substituted—

'6(1) If the defendant falls within this paragraph, he may not be granted bail unless the court is satisfied that there is no significant risk that, if released on bail (whether subject to conditions or not), he would fail to surrender to custody.

(2) Subject to sub-paragraph (3) below, the defendant falls within this paragraph if—
   (a) he is aged 18 or over, and
   (b) it appears to the court that, having been released on bail in or in connection with the proceedings for the offence, he failed to surrender to custody.

(3) Where it appears to the court that the defendant had reasonable cause for his failure to surrender to custody, he does not fall within this paragraph unless it also appears to the court that he failed to surrender to custody at the appointed place as soon as reasonably practicable after the appointed time.

(4) For the purposes of sub-paragraph (3) above, a failure to give to the defendant a copy of the record of the decision to grant him bail shall not constitute a reasonable cause for his failure to surrender to custody.'

(2) After paragraph 9AA of that Part (inserted by section 14(2)) there is inserted—

'9AB (1) Subject to sub-paragraph (2) below, this paragraph applies if—
   (a) the defendant is a child or young person, and
   (b) it appears to the court that, having been released on bail in or in connection with the proceedings for the offence, he failed to surrender to custody

(2) Where it appears to the court that the defendant had reasonable cause for his failure to surrender to custody, this paragraph does not apply unless it also appears to the court that he failed to surrender to custody at the appointed place as soon as reasonably practicable after the appointed time.

(3) In deciding for the purposes of paragraph 2(1) of this Part of this Schedule whether it is satisfied that there are substantial grounds for believing that the defendant, if released on bail (whether subject to conditions or not), would fail to surrender to custody, the court shall give particular weight to—
   (a) where the defendant did not have reasonable cause for his failure to surrender to custody, the fact that he failed to surrender to custody, or
   (b) where he did have reasonable cause for his failure to surrender to custody, the fact that he failed to surrender to custody at the appointed place as soon as reasonably practicable after the appointed time.

(4) For the purposes of this paragraph, a failure to give to the defendant a copy of the record of the decision to grant him bail shall not constitute a reasonable cause for his failure to surrender to custody.'

A8.2 Right to apply for bail

An application for bail may be made at the first hearing of the case before a magistrates' court, save in respect of a defendant facing a charge of murder (or murder and any other charge(s)), in which case the issue of bail must be resolved before a Crown Court judge within 48 hours (excluding public holidays) beginning the day after the defendant's appearance in the magistrates' court (s 115 Coroners and Justice Act 2009). If bail is refused, an application may be made at the subsequent hearing, and may be based on the same grounds as the first. A refusal of bail on the grounds of insufficient information should not be counted as a decision to refuse bail, thereby exhausting one of the two attempts (*R v Calder Justices, ex p Kennedy* (1992) 156 JP 716). Similarly, a remand in absence should be discounted (*R v Dover and East Kent Justices, ex p Dean* (1991) 156 JP 357).

Note, however, that if a fully argued application is not made by the defendant at the first hearing, the effect is that one opportunity to argue for bail is lost, meaning that if bail is refused at the subsequent hearing, the two opportunities for bail have been spent. Similarly, if an argument is made at the first hearing but not at the second hearing, there is no right to a second application for bail at the third hearing. Advocates should always obtain certificates of full argument in order to support any further Crown Court bail application (s 5(6A) Bail Act 1976). This should appear on the bail form issued by the court.

Following two refusals to grant bail, further applications may be made if there are new arguments as to fact or law (Sch 1, Pt IIA Bail Act 1976). This includes but is not limited to a change in circumstances, for example:

- change in the case alleged against the defendant (*R v Reading Crown Court, ex p Malik* [1981] QB 451 and *R v Slough Justices, ex p Duncan* [1981] QB 451);
- increased surety (*R v Isleworth Crown Court, ex p Commissioners of Customs and Excise*, The Times, 27 July 1990);
- passage of time (*Neumeister v Austria (No 1)* (1979–80) 1 EHRR 91).

In *R (B) v Brent Youth Court* [2010] EWHC 1893 (Admin), the court held that a change of address presented for residence purposes amounted to a change of circumstances. It was not necessary that any new factor be exceptional in nature. The correct test is whether there are any new considerations which were not before the court when the accused was last remanded in custody. Similarly, an argument that the prosecution case against the defendant was significantly weaker than at first presented would qualify as a new argument. The court ended by saying that:

> even if the Bench had been entitled to form the view that each and every argument as to fact or law was an argument which it had heard previously, it manifestly failed to go on to consider whether, notwithstanding that, it should nonetheless consider substantively a bail application, given the provisions of Section 44 [Children and Young Persons Act 1933], having regard to the welfare of a child or young person.

A8.3 Grounds for refusing bail

The seriousness of the offence (and the likely penalty) cannot of itself justify a refusal of bail on the inference that the person is likely to abscond (*Lettelier v France* (1992) 14 EHRR 83), although a judge is perfectly entitled to regard that as a significant factor (*R (Thompson) v Central Criminal Court* [2005] EWHC 2345 (Admin)). Before bail can be refused on the grounds of interfering with witnesses or obstructing justice, the prosecution must point to an identifiable risk and provide supporting evidence (*Clooth v Belgium* (1991) 14 EHRR 717). The court should not take the prosecution case at its highest, but rather follow the statute and consider the strength overall of the prosecution evidence (*R (E) v Wood Green Crown Court* [2013] EWHC 1869 (Admin)).

In deciding whether to refuse bail the relevant considerations include (Sch 1, para 9 Bail Act 1976):

- the nature and seriousness of the offence or default (and the probable method of dealing with the defendant for it);
- the character, antecedents, associations, and community ties of the defendant;
- the defendant's record as respects the fulfilment of his obligations under previous grants of bail in criminal proceedings:
  - except in the case of a defendant whose case is adjourned for inquiries or a report, the strength of the evidence of his having committed the offence or having defaulted;
- the court is satisfied that there are substantial grounds for believing that the defendant, if released on bail (whether subject to conditions or not), would commit an offence while on bail, it is a relevant consideration that there is a risk that the defendant may do so by engaging in conduct that would, or would be likely to, cause physical or mental injury to any person other than the defendant;
- any other considerations that appear to be relevant.

A8.3.1 *Classifying the offence*

There are three categories of offences to consider:

- indictable imprisonable offences (Sch 1, Pt 1);
- summary-only imprisonable offences (which includes offences triable summarily only due to the value of the offence, eg criminal damage) (Sch 1, Pt 1A), although it is unclear whether the hybrid offence of low-value theft from a shop falls into this group because of the defendant's right to elect; and
- summary-only non-imprisonable offences (Sch 1, Pt II).

A8.4 **Indictable imprisonable offences**

Bail cannot be refused if there is no real prospect that the defendant will be sentenced to a custodial sentence in the proceedings.

A court may refuse bail on the grounds:

- that the defendant is already a serving prisoner (para 4 remand); or
- that there is insufficient information on which to base a decision (para 5 remand).

Refusal of bail can be for the defendant's own protection or, for a defendant under 18 years of age, his own welfare (para 3 remand).

Bail may be refused if there are substantial grounds for believing that, if released on bail, the defendant would:

- fail to surrender;
- commit further offences;

- commit an offence on bail by engaging in conduct that would or would be likely to cause physical or mental injury to an associated person, or that an associated person would fear physical or mental injury—under s 62 Family Law Act 1996, 'associated person' includes:
  - those who are or have been married to each other or in a civil partnership,
  - present or former cohabitants,
  - those who live or have lived in the same household other than as employees, tenants, or lodgers,
  - relatives,
  - those who are or have been engaged to marry or enter into a civil partnership,
  - those who have or have had intimate personal relationships of significant duration,
  - the parents of children and those with parental responsibility,
  - parties to the same family proceedings; or
- interfere with witnesses or otherwise obstruct the course of justice.

Bail may also be refused if the offender was:

- on bail at the time of the offence;
- arrested for breach of bail in the same proceedings and there are substantial grounds to believe he would fail to appear, commit offences, or interfere with witnesses or obstruct the course of justice.

A8.5 Summary-only imprisonable offences

Bail cannot be refused if there is no real prospect that the defendant will be sentenced to a custodial sentence in the proceedings.

Bail can be refused on one or more of the following grounds only:

- failure to surrender (if the defendant has previously failed to surrender);
- commission of further offences (if the instant offence was committed on bail);
- fear of commission of offences likely to cause an associated person to suffer or fear physical or mental injury;
- the defendant's own protection (for his own welfare if aged under 18);
- the defendant is serving custody;
- fear of failure to surrender, commission of offences, interference with witnesses, or obstruction of justice (if the defendant has been arrested for breach of bail in respect of the instant offence); and
- lack of sufficient information.

A8.6 Summary-only non-imprisonable offences (Sch 1, Pt II)

Bail can be denied only if there has been a previous failure to surrender in the proceedings and the court believes that if granted bail the defendant would fail to surrender again, or:

- for the defendant's own protection (for his own welfare if aged under 18);
- where the defendant is already in custody;

- where, following a breach of bail, or the defendant absconding, there are substantial grounds for believing that if released on bail the defendant would:
  - fail to surrender,
  - commit further offences, or
  - interfere with witnesses or otherwise obstruct the course of justice.

A8.7 Conditional bail

Conditional bail may be imposed if the court believes that it is necessary because there is a risk that:

- the defendant will fail to surrender; a surety should only be used for this reason (*R (Shea) v Winchester Crown Court* [2013] EWHC 1050 (Admin));
- the defendant will commit an offence while on bail;
- the defendant would interfere with witnesses or obstruct justice;
- the defendant would not cooperate with the making of presentence or other reports; or
- the defendant would not attend appointments with his legal adviser.

A person granted bail on a charge of murder must be required to undergo a psychiatric examination (s 3(6A) Bail Act 1976).

A8.8 Insufficient information

The accused need not be granted bail if the court is satisfied that, owing to lack of time since the commencement of the proceedings, it has not been practicable to obtain sufficient information for taking the bail decision. This may apply if the defence need to confirm an address, or immigration status, or the mental health of the defendant; or the police have enquiries outstanding which might make the allegation more serious. There is no restriction in the Bail Act which has the effect of limiting the number of times on which the provision can be used. While it should not allow the police to delay their enquiries, it has the benefit of not counting as a bail application.

A8.9 Pre-release conditions

Bail Act 1976, ss 3 and 8

3 General provisions

(1) A person granted bail in criminal proceedings shall be under a duty to surrender to custody, and that duty is enforceable in accordance with section 6 of this Act.
...

(4) He may be required, before release on bail, to provide a surety or sureties to secure his surrender to custody.
...

8 Bail with sureties

(1) This section applies where a person is granted bail in criminal proceedings on condition that he provides one or more surety or sureties for the purpose of securing that he surrenders to custody.

(2) In considering the suitability for that purpose of a proposed surety, regard may be had (amongst other things) to—
   (a) the surety's financial resources;
   (b) his character and any previous convictions of his; and
   (c) his proximity (whether in point of kinship, place of residence or otherwise) to the person for whom he is to be surety.

(3) Where a court grants a person bail in criminal proceedings on such a condition but is unable to release him because no surety or no suitable surety is available, the court shall fix the amount in which the surety is to be bound and subsections (4) and (5) below, or in a case where the proposed surety resides in Scotland subsection (6) below, shall apply for the purpose of enabling the recognizance of the surety to be entered into subsequently.

(4) Where this subsection applies the recognizance of the surety may be entered into before such of the following persons or descriptions of persons as the court may by order specify or, if it makes no such order, before any of the following persons, that is to say—
   (a) where the decision is taken by a magistrates' court, before a justice of the peace, a justices' clerk or a police officer who either is of the rank of inspector or above or is in charge of a police station or, if magistrates' courts rules so provide, by a person of such other description as is specified in the rules...

(5) Where a surety seeks to enter into his recognizance before any person in accordance with subsection (4) above but that person declines to take his recognizance because he is not satisfied of the surety's suitability, the surety may apply to—
   (a) the court which fixed the amount of the recognizance in which the surety was to be bound, or
   (b) a magistrates' court
   for that court to take his recognizance and that court shall, if satisfied of his suitability, take his recognizance.

(6) Where this subsection applies, the court, if satisfied of the suitability of the proposed surety, may direct that arrangements be made for the recognizance of the surety to be entered into in Scotland before any constable, within the meaning of the Police (Scotland) Act 1967, having charge at any police office or station in like manner as the recognizance would be entered into in England or Wales.

(7) Where, in pursuance of subsection (4) or (6) above, a recognizance is entered into otherwise than before the court that fixed the amount of the recognizance, the same consequences shall follow as if it had been entered into before that court. A surety may be taken by a police officer under these provisions unless the court otherwise orders.

Courts wish to see some evidence of a surety's means. A surety must understand the risks to them, including of imprisonment, if the defendant fails to appear and the recognizance cannot be found.

For the convenience of all parties sureties should normally be made continuous for each hearing at which the defendant is required to attend.

A surety may only be used to secure attendance and is not appropriate to prevent further offences (*R (Shea) v Winchester Crown Court* [2013] EWHC 1050 (Admin)).

A8.9.1 *Security*

This may be money or items of value. The Money Laundering Regulations require that those handling the money (including a court) are satisfied as to its source. There is no limitation on what may be provided as the security, though jointly owned property may not be accepted. The courts are ill equipped to hold substantial securities and solicitors will often give undertakings, backed by irrevocable authorities from the owner of the security, to account to the court should the defendant fail to appear.

A8.10 Electronic monitoring

Section 3AB Bail Act 1976 deals with electronic monitoring for adults; and s 3AC is applicable to all defendants. The court must be satisfied that without electronic monitoring bail would not be granted.

A8.11 Prosecution appeals against the grant of bail

The Bail (Amendment) Act 1993 allows a prosecutor to appeal the grant of bail in any case where the offence is imprisonable. The prosecution must have objected to bail, and following the grant of bail, must orally in court state their intention to appeal the decision. A written notice must be served on both the court and the defendant within two hours of the oral notice having been given. A delay of five minutes in giving an oral indication to the court (and after the defendant had been taken from the courtroom) was deemed to comply with the Act in *R v Isleworth Crown Court, ex p Clarke* [1998] 1 Cr App R 257. In *R (Cardin) v Birmingham Crown Court* [2017] EWHC 2101 (Admin) it was held that the two hours was to be liberally interpreted where there was no fault on the part of the Crown. This confirmed the decision in *R (Jeffrey) v Crown Court at Warwick* [2002] EWHC 2469, where it was held that s 1(7) of the Act should have read into it the following words:

unless such failure was caused by circumstances outside the control of the prosecution and not due to any fault on its part.

Service of the written notice on a jailer who hands the notice to a defendant suffices, and solicitors who accept such notices do so on the implicit understanding that they will be immediately communicated to the defendant.

A8.12 Breach of bail conditions

Offences in relation to bail are dealt with at **C3**.

Bail Act 1976, s 7

(4) a person arrested in pursuance of subsection (3) above—
  (a) shall, except where he was arrested within 24 hours of the time appointed for him to surrender to custody, be brought as soon as practicable and in any event within 24 hours after his arrest before a justice of the peace; and
  (b) in the said excepted case shall be brought before the court at which he was to have surrendered to custody.
(5) A justice of the peace before whom a person is brought under subsection (4) above may, subject to subsection (6) below, if of the opinion that that person—

(a) is not likely to surrender to custody, or
(b) has broken or is likely to break any condition of his bail, remand him in custody or commit him to custody, as the case may require, or alternatively, grant him bail subject to the same or to different conditions, but if not of that opinion shall grant him bail subject to the same conditions (if any) as were originally imposed.

Following an alleged breach of bail conditions, the defendant must be brought before a magistrates' court within 24 hours of arrest. This means that the hearing must commence at court within those 24 hours, and any delay must result in the defendant's automatic release from custody (*R v Governor of Glen Parva Young Offender Institution, ex p G (A Minor)* [1998] 2 Cr App R 349). A court can, however, bring a defendant into the dock and then adjourn the hearing until later in the court list (*R (Hussein) v Derby Magistrates' Court* [2001] 1 WLR 254). A magistrates' court has no power simply to commit an offender to the Crown Court in order for the breach to be decided (*R v Teeside Magistrates' Court, ex p Ellison* (2001) 165 JP 355).

Only one magistrate need deal with an alleged bail breach, and there is no requirement for formal evidence to be called by prosecution or defence. There is no defence of 'reasonable excuse' in relation to the breaking of bail conditions (*R (Vickers) v West London Magistrates' Court* [2004] Crim LR 63), although the reasons for breach would be relevant to the determination of whether or not to grant bail again.

In *R v Liverpool Justices, ex p Director of Public Prosecutions* (1992) 95 Cr App R 222, the court laid down the following guidance for a court to follow when considering bail breaches:

* strict rules of evidence did not apply and hearsay was admissible;
* the court must consider the type of evidence called and take account of the fact that there had been no cross-examination;
* the prosecution and defence can call witnesses if they so wish, and the other party has the right to cross-examine;
* the defendant has a right to give oral evidence.

In practice a statement will be made. No issue in relation to hearsay arises (*R (Thomas) v Greenwich Magistrates' Court* [2009] EWHC 1180 (Admin)).

If the breach is not proved, the defendant must be released on the same conditions as existed previously. If the breach is proved, that does not mean an automatic remand into custody; *R (DPP) v Havering Magistrates' Court* [2001] 1 WLR 805 confirms that it is simply a factor to be considered when the court decides whether or not it should re-bail the defendant and on what conditions. The statute does not require that they be more stringent.

A8.13 Criminal Procedure Rules applicable to the grant of bail

Part 14 of the Criminal Procedure Rules applies to bail.

A8.14 Provision of bail for youths

The rules relating to the provision of bail for youths are discussed in **B2**.

A8.15 Appeals in relation to bail

A8.15.1 *Appeal against conditional bail*

If a defendant is dissatisfied with the conditions of bail he may appeal to the Crown Court, provided that he has first applied to a magistrates' court to vary those conditions and has been unsuccessful. An appeal lies only in relation to the following conditions:

- residence (but not in relation to any bail hostel);
- surety or security;
- curfew;
- non-contact.

In other circumstances it may be necessary to apply for a judicial review.

A8.15.2 *Appeal against refusal of bail*

Following full argument in the magistrates' court (and a certificate of full argument having been issued; Crim PR 14 requires that the document confirming the refusal of bail contain such a certificate), an appeal lies as of right to the Crown Court.

There is no longer any appeal route to the High Court, save in an exceptional case by way of judicial review.

A8.15.3 *Bail pending appeal*

The procedure for making an application in the magistrates' court is at s 113 Magistrates' Courts Act 1980. *Thomas v CPS* [2015] EWHC 4079 (Admin) confirms that this provision creates an entitlement to apply for bail pending appeal in every case in which such a properly constituted application is made and places an obligation on the magistrates' court, whether by the sentencing tribunal or otherwise, to consider an application for bail pending appeal in every case where a properly constituted application for bail is made at the magistrates' court. It does not follow that in every case it would be necessary to hold an oral hearing on the application.

 See *Blackstone's Criminal Practice 2019* **D7**

A9 **Binding Rulings**

Section 8A Magistrates' Courts Act (MCA) 1980 deals with pre-trial rulings and s 8B allows a magistrates' court to make or vary binding rulings.

Sections 8A and 8B MCA 1980 provide:

Magistrates' Courts Act 1980, ss 8A and 8B

8A Power to make rulings at pre-trial hearing

(1) For the purposes of this section a hearing is a pre-trial hearing if—
    (a) it relates to an information—
        (i) which is to be tried summarily, and
        (ii) to which the accused has pleaded not guilty, and
    (b) it takes place before the start of the trial.

(2) ...

(3) At a pre-trial hearing, a magistrates' court may make a ruling as to any matter mentioned in subsection (4) if—
    (a) the condition in subsection (5) is met,
    (b) the court has given the parties an opportunity to be heard, and
    (c) it appears to the court that it is in the interests of justice to make the ruling.

(4) The matters are—
    (a) any question as to the admissibility of evidence;
    (b) any other question of law relating to the case.

(5) ...

(6) A ruling may be made under this section—
    (a) on an application by a party to the case, or
    (b) of the court's own motion.

(7) For the purposes of this section and section 8B, references to the prosecutor are to any person acting as prosecutor, whether an individual or body.

8B Effect of rulings at pre-trial hearing

(1) Subject to subsections (3) and (6), a ruling under section 8A has binding effect from the time it is made until the case against the accused or, if there is more than one, against each of them, is disposed of.

(2) The case against an accused is disposed of if—
    (a) he is acquitted or convicted,
    (b) the prosecutor decides not to proceed with the case against him, or
    (c) the information is dismissed.

(3) A magistrates' court may discharge or vary (or further vary) a ruling under section 8A if—
    (a) the condition in section 8A(5) is met,
    (b) the court has given the parties an opportunity to be heard, and
    (c) it appears to the court that it is in the interests of justice to do so.

(4) The court may act under subsection (3)—
    (a) on an application by a party to the case, or
    (b) of its own motion.

(5) No application may be made under subsection (4)(a) unless there has been a material change of circumstances since the ruling was made or, if a previous application has been made, since the application (or last application) was made.

(6) A ruling under section 8A is discharged in relation to an accused if—

(a) the magistrates' court commits or sends him to the Crown Court for trial for the offence charged in the information, or

(b) a count charging him with the offence is included in an indictment by virtue of section 40 of the Criminal Justice Act 1988.

Because of the binding nature of these rulings, it is not open to a later bench simply to reverse the ruling because it would have reached a different conclusion.

In *Brett v Director of Public Prosecutions* [2009] EWHC 440 (Admin), the court took a far less restrictive approach than that taken in previous cases in holding a judge to have erred in feeling that he was bound by a previous ruling under s 8A MCA 1980. However, a later court cannot simply annul a previous decision on the sole ground that it simply disagrees with it (*Crown Prosecution Service v Gloucester Justices and Loveridge* [2008] EWHC 1488 (Admin)). In *R (Jones) v South East Surrey Local Justice Area* [2010] EWHC 916 (Admin), the court, having previously disallowed a prosecution application to adjourn, later granted it due to the fact that the information presented on the renewed application was different and that it was in the interests of justice that the previous ruling be reversed.

Where the court acts of its own motion to vary a previous ruling, the grounds for discharge or variation are simply the interests of justice; and where an application is made by a party, there is an additional requirement for proof of material change of circumstances (*Crown Prosecution Service v Gloucester Justices and Alan Loveridge* [2008] EWHC 1488 (Admin)).

The decision of a magistrates' court to reverse its earlier decision was upheld when the court found the original application by the Crown to adjourn a trial was materially misleading (*DPP v Woods* [2017] EWHC 1070 (Admin)).

 See *Blackstone's Criminal Practice 2019* **D21**

A10 Case Management

A10.1 Overview

All parties are expected to manage cases proactively through the system. This applies as much in road traffic cases as in any criminal case (*R (Hassani) v West London Magistrates' Court* [2017] EWHC 1270 (Admin)). The most notable impact has been to limit the use of so-called ambush defences. However, a strong defendant, aware of the risks, is still able to put the Crown to proof.

For information on the completion of the preparation for effective trial form, see **Appendix 1**.

A10.2 Application of the rules to civil proceedings

The Criminal Procedure Rules (Crim PR) have no application in relation to civil proceedings in the magistrates' court, and the Civil Procedure Rules do not apply either. However, Rule 3A of the Magistrates' Courts Rules 1981 provides the court with case management powers identical to those enjoyed in relation to criminal cases.

A10.3 Alternative charges

When the Crown prefers an aggravated offence and in the alternative the underlying offence, the latter should be adjourned *sine die* if the court convicts on the more serious matter. If the defendant offers a plea to the lesser offence it should be noted but not taken (*Henderson v CPS* [2016] EWHC 464 (Admin)).

A10.4 The overriding objective and case management

Crim PR 1 and 3 deal with the overriding objective and case management powers. Extracts from these rules are reproduced in **Appendix 2**.

A10.5 Prosecution witnesses

Once the Crown has served witness statements as initial details of the prosecution case, it must, if the defence so request, call or at least tender as witnesses all those whose statements have been served, unless the statement is to be read or the witness is not capable of belief (*R v Russell Jones* [1995] 3 All ER 239). If the prosecution choose not to call a particular witness, and the court is satisfied that the interests of justice require that the witness be called, and that it would be unfair to the defence not to do so, the court may in appropriate cases call the witness itself (*R v Haringey Justices exp DPP* [1996] 1 All ER 828). These cases were not referred to in *Azzaz v DPP* [2015] EWHC 3016 when the case proceeded without the unwilling complainant, there being another witness to the events. Neither party made a hearsay application in relation to the statement of the missing witnesses nor sought to follow the procedure in *Haringey Justices*. The result of any cross-examination was speculative.

A10.6 Alibi notices

An alibi notice is required (in summary proceedings within 14 days of initial disclosure by the Crown) if the defendant believes that a witness may be able to assist his defence. Because it is based on belief, not actuality, it is *not* proper to wait until there is a signed proof from the witness in question (*In the matter of a wasted costs order against Joseph Hill & Company* [2013] EWCA Crim 775).

A10.7 Defence case statements

These are not obligatory in summary proceedings but if given should be served within 14 days of initial disclosure by the Crown. An application for further disclosure under s 8 Criminal Procedure and Investigations Act 1996 cannot be made unless a defence case statement has been served (see **A16**).

A10.8 Defence witnesses—notification of intention to call

Section 6C Criminal Procedure and Investigations Act 1996 imposes duties on a defendant intending to call defence witnesses at trial. Failure to comply is most likely to result in an adjournment and wasted costs, so solicitors should ensure that they have taken all reasonable steps to ensure that a defendant is made aware of his obligations to provide such information. Notice of the name, address, and date of birth, if available, should be given in summary proceedings within 14 days of initial disclosure. A form is prescribed at Criminal Procedure Rules forms 15.4. It is likely that the prosecution will supply such information to the police. There is a code of practice for arranging and conducting interviews of witnesses notified by the accused, and this governs police conduct.

A10.8.1 *Time limits*

The Criminal Procedure and Investigations Act 1996 (Defence Disclosure Time Limits) Regulations 2011, Reg 3 provides for time limits and extensions. The time for service begins with the day on which the prosecutor complies or purports to comply with s 3 Criminal Procedure and Investigations Act 1996 (initial duty of the prosecutor to disclose) and expires at the end of 14 days.

A10.9 Preparation for trial

Part 24.3 Crim PR requires that both prosecution and defence prepare their cases because, at the start of a trial,

(1) the prosecutor may summarize the prosecution case, concisely identifying the relevant law, outlining the facts, and indicating the matters likely to be in dispute;

(2) to help the members of the court to understand the case and resolve any issue in it, the court may invite the defendant concisely to identify what is in issue.

A10.10 Vulnerable persons

Criminal Practice Direction CPD General matters 1.3D: vulnerable people in the courts

3D.1 In respect of eligibility for special measures, 'vulnerable' and 'intimidated' witnesses are defined in sections 16 and 17 of the Youth Justice and Criminal Evidence Act 1999 (as amended by the Coroners and Justice Act 2009); 'vulnerable' includes those under 18 years of age and people with a mental disorder or learning disability; a physical disorder or disability; or who are likely to suffer fear or distress in giving evidence because of their own circumstances or those relating to the case.

3D.2 However, many other people giving evidence in a criminal case, whether as a witness or defendant, may require assistance: the court is required to take 'every reasonable step' to encourage and facilitate the attendance of witnesses and to facilitate the participation of any person, including the defendant (Rule 3.8(4)(a) and (b)). This includes enabling a witness or defendant to give their best evidence, and enabling a defendant to comprehend the proceedings and engage fully with his or her defence. The pre-trial and trial process should, so far as necessary, be adapted to meet those ends. Regard should be had to the welfare of a young defendant as required by section 44 of the Children and Young Persons Act 1933, and generally to Parts 1 and 3 of the Criminal Procedure Rules (the overriding objective and the court's powers of case management).

3D.3 Under Part 3 of the Rules, the court must identify the needs of witnesses at an early stage (Rule 3.2(2)(b)) and may require the parties to identify arrangements to facilitate the giving of evidence and participation in the trial (Crim PR 3.11(c)(iv) and (v)). There are various statutory special measures that the court may utilise to assist a witness in giving evidence. Crim PR Part 18 gives the procedures to be followed. Courts should note the 'primary rule' which requires the court to give a direction for a special measure to assist a child witness or qualifying witness and that in such cases an application to the court is not required (Crim PR 18.9).

CPD General matters 3E

[Provides for ground rules hearings to plan the questioning of a vulnerable witness or defendant.]

CPD General matters 3F

[Sets out detailed provisions for the use of intermediaries The process of appointment should begin with assessment by an intermediary and a report. The report will make recommendations to address the communication needs of the witness or defendant during trial. (See also **A27**.)]

CPD General matters 3G

[Sets out provisions for vulnerable defendants before the trial, sentencing, or appeal]

Note: there is a Judicial Protocol: Expedition of Cases Involving Witnesses Under 10 Years.

A10.11 Case law

The courts deprecate any attempts to take a tactical advantage.

In *Writtle v Director of Public Prosecutions* [2009] EWHC 236 (Admin), the court held:

> the present regime of case management should in general ensure that the issues in the case are identified well before a hearing. There will, of course, be cases where something occurs in the course of a trial which may properly give rise to a new issue, but this was not such a case. The days when the defence can assume that they will be able successfully to ambush the prosecution are over.

The court adopted the earlier ruling in *Malcolm v Director of Public Prosecutions* [2007] EWHC 363 (Admin), in which Burnton J stated that it is the duty of the defence to make clear to the prosecution and the court at an early stage both the defence and the issues it raises.

In *Director of Public Prosecutions v Bury Magistrates' Court* [2007] EWHC 3256 (Admin), the court deprecated the practice of the defence of failing to notify the court of prosecution failures when certifying a case ready for trial, in order to take a tactical advantage. Further, that defence breach of the rules may have an impact on the amount of any costs to be recovered (in this case wasted costs).

In *R (Lawson) v Stratford Magistrates' Court* [2007] EWHC 2490 (Admin), it was held that a court was correct to allow a prosecution adjournment in order to address issues raised for the first time by the defence during a closing speech. The issues related to signage and device calibration.

A10.12 Effects on the admissibility of evidence

There is no power under the Rules to make hearsay statements admissible other than by a proper application of the hearsay provisions of the Criminal Justice Act 2003. *T v R* [2012] EWCA Crim 2358 confirms that a failure to comply with procedural rules could not affect the law on the admissibility of evidence. This is confirmed in relation to expert evidence (form SFR1) by *Hunt v CPS* [2018] EWHC 3341 (Admin).

The court should have regard to s 114(2) Criminal Justice Act 2003.

For the answers given on a preparation for effective trial (PET) form to be admissible, a properly formulated application must be made to admit the hearsay evidence contained in that answer (*Valiati v DPP; KM v DPP* [2018] EWHC 2908 (Admin) and see **Appendix 1**). An unfair advantage must normally have been obtained from the way the form was completed.

Evidence cannot be admitted merely because no issue on it has been identified on the PET form. Being unhelpful was not a concession as to the truth of a statement (*Randell v DPP* [2018] EWHC 1048 (Admin)).

A failure to serve defence notices does not render the evidence inadmissible. The sanctions are adverse comment, cross-examination, and inference (*R (Tinnion) v Reading Crown Court* [2010] EWHC 2930 (Admin); *R v Ullah* [2011] EWCA Crim 3275).

A10.13 **Other consequences**

A failure by a defendant to serve a defence statement did not amount to a contempt of court on either the part of the advocate or defendant (*R v Rochford* [2010] EWCA Crim 1928 and *Joseph Hill & Co* [2013] EWCA Crim 775). In *SVS Solicitors* [2012] EWCA Crim 319, a wasted costs order was upheld in a case where the solicitors were said to be complicit in their client's disobedience of the Rules, failing to file a counter-notice to an application to admit hearsay evidence. The court stated (albeit *obiter*) that a solicitor instructed by a client to ignore the requirements of the Crim PR should withdraw from the case. It is wise to seek directions from the court in that eventuality.

 See *Blackstone's Criminal Practice 2019* **D4**

A11 Civil Orders

A full list of possible civil proceedings, and the relevant statutes, appears at **A19.1**. These proceedings are prescribed by reg 9 Criminal Legal Aid (General) Regulations 2013, so that criminal legal aid is available on forms CRM 14 and 15. Many orders may also be made on conviction and these appear in **Part D**. This section deals with civil orders that may be made on short notice.

A11.1 Closure orders

It should be noted that applications for closure orders will only be pre-scribed proceedings for the purposes of reg 9 Criminal Legal Aid (General) Regulations 2013 where a person has engaged in, or is likely to engage in, be-haviour that constitutes a criminal offence on the premises. This will include where the closure order relates to criminal behaviour and a combination of other grounds; but not closure orders that relate to nuisance or disorderly be-haviour only, unless they amount to a common law public nuisance.

> **Anti-social Behaviour Crime and Policing Act 2014, ss 76, 80, and 81**
>
> **76 Power to issue closure notices**
>
> (1) A police officer of at least the rank of inspector, or the local authority, may issue a closure notice if satisfied on reasonable grounds—
>   (a) that the use of particular premises has resulted, or (if the notice is not issued) is likely soon to result, in nuisance to members of the public, or
>   (b) that there has been, or (if the notice is not issued) is likely soon to be, disorder near those premises associated with the use of those premises,
>   and that the notice is necessary to prevent the nuisance or disorder from continuing, recurring or occurring.
>   ...
>
> **80 Power of court to make closure orders.**
>
> (1) Whenever a closure notice is issued an application must be made to a magistrates' court for a closure order (unless the notice has been cancelled under section 78).
> (2) An application for a closure order must be made—
>   (a) by a constable, if the closure notice was issued by a police officer;
>   (b) by the authority that issued the closure notice, if the notice was issued by a local authority.
> (3) The application must be heard by the magistrates' court not later than 48 hours after service of the closure notice.
> (4) In calculating when the period of 48 hours ends, Christmas Day is to be disregarded.
> (5) The court may make a closure order if it is satisfied—
>   (a) that a person has engaged, or (if the order is not made) is likely to engage, in disorderly, offensive or criminal behaviour on the premises, or
>   (b) that the use of the premises has resulted, or (if the order is not made) is likely to result, in serious nuisance to members of the public, or
>   (c) that there has been, or (if the order is not made) is likely to be, disorder near those premises associated with the use of those premises,

and that the order is necessary to prevent the behaviour, nuisance or disorder from continuing, recurring or occurring.

(6) A closure order is an order prohibiting access to the premises for a period specified in the order.
The period may not exceed 3 months.

(7) A closure order may prohibit access—
  (a) by all persons, or by all persons except those specified, or by all persons except those of a specified description;
  (b) at all times, or at all times except those specified;
  (c) in all circumstances, or in all circumstances except those specified.

(8) A closure order—
  (a) may be made in respect of the whole or any part of the premises;
  (b) may include provision about access to a part of the building or structure of which the premises form part.

(9) The court must notify the relevant licensing authority if it makes a closure order in relation to premises in respect of which a premises licence is in force.

81 Temporary orders.

(1) This section applies where an application has been made to a magistrates' court under section 80 for a closure order.

(2) If the court does not make a closure order it may nevertheless order that the closure notice continues in force for a specified further period of not more than 48 hours, if satisfied—
  (a) that the use of particular premises has resulted, or (if the notice is not continued) is likely soon to result, in nuisance to members of the public, or
  (b) that there has been, or (if the notice is not continued) is likely soon to be, disorder near those premises associated with the use of those premises,
  and that the continuation of the notice is necessary to prevent the nuisance or disorder from continuing, recurring or occurring.

(3) The court may adjourn the hearing of the application for a period of not more than 14 days to enable—
  (a) the occupier of the premises,
  (b) the person with control of or responsibility for the premises, or
  (c) any other person with an interest in the premises,
  to show why a closure order should not be made.

(4) If the court adjourns the hearing under subsection (3) it may order that the closure notice continues...

A11.2 Domestic violence protection orders

Crime and Security Act 2010, ss 27 and 28

27 Application for a domestic violence protection order

(1) If a DVPN (Domestic Violence protection notice) has been issued, a constable must apply for a domestic violence protection order ('a DVPO').

(2) The application must be made by complaint to a magistrates' court.

(3) The application must be heard by the magistrates' court not later than 48 hours after the DVPN was served pursuant to section 25(2).

(4) In calculating when the period of 48 hours mentioned in subsection (3) ends, Christmas Day, Good Friday, any Sunday and any day which is a bank holiday in

England and Wales under the Banking and Financial Dealings Act 1971 are to be disregarded.

(5) A notice of the hearing of the application must be given to (the respondent) P.

(6) The notice is deemed given if it has been left at the address given by P (when asked at the time of service of the DVPN).

(7) But if the notice has not been given because no address was given by P under section 25(3), the court may hear the application for the DVPO if the court is satisfied that the constable applying for the DVPO has made reasonable efforts to give P the notice.

(8) The magistrates' court may adjourn the hearing of the application.

(9) If the court adjourns the hearing, the DVPN continues in effect until the application has been determined.

(10) On the hearing of an application for a DVPO, section 97 of the Magistrates' Courts Act 1980 (summons to witness and warrant for his arrest) does not apply in relation to a person for whose protection the DVPO would be made, except where the person has given oral or written evidence at the hearing.

28 Conditions for and contents of a domestic violence protection order

(1) The court may make a DVPO if two conditions are met.

(2) The first condition is that the court is satisfied on the balance of probabilities that P has been violent towards, or has threatened violence towards, an associated person.

(3) The second condition is that the court thinks that making the DVPO is necessary to protect that person from violence or a threat of violence by P.

(4) Before making a DVPO, the court must, in particular, consider—
  (a) the welfare of any person under the age of 18 whose interests the court considers relevant to the making of the DVPO (whether or not that person is an associated person), and
  (b) any opinion of which the court is made aware—
    (i) of the person for whose protection the DVPO would be made, and
    (ii) in the case of provision included by virtue of subsection (8), of any other associated person who lives in the premises to which the provision would relate.

(5) But the court may make a DVPO in circumstances where the person for whose protection it is made does not consent to the making of the DVPO.

(6) A DVPO must contain provision to prohibit P from molesting the person for whose protection it is made.

(7) Provision required to be included by virtue of subsection (6) may be expressed so as to refer to molestation in general, to particular acts of molestation, or to both.

(8) If P lives in premises which are also lived in by a person for whose protection the DVPO is made, the DVPO may also contain provision—
  (a) to prohibit P from evicting or excluding from the premises the person for whose protection the DVPO is made,
  (b) to prohibit P from entering the premises,
  (c) to require P to leave the premises, or
  (d) to prohibit P from coming within such distance of the premises as may be specified in the DVPO.

(9) A DVPO must state that a constable may arrest P without warrant if the constable has reasonable grounds for believing that P is in breach of the DVPO.

(10) A DVPO may be in force for—
  (a) no fewer than 14 days beginning with the day on which it is made, and
  (b) no more than 28 days beginning with that day.

(11) A DVPO must state the period for which it is to be in force.

A11.2.1 Key points

1. These proceedings are civil in nature.
2. Whilst s 54 Magistrates' Courts Act (MCA) 1980 allowed for adjournments, this power to exceed the time limits in the legislation, this should only be used in the interests of justice and in circumstances sufficiently compelling to make them exceptional such as the loss of rights under the Human Rights Act 1998 (*MPC v Hooper* [2005] EWHC 340 (Admin); *R (Turner) v Highbury Corner Magistrates' Court* [2005] EWHC 2568 (Admin)).
3. Procedural safeguards were recommended in *R (Cleary) v Highbury Corner Magistrates' Court* [2006] EWHC 1869 (Admin) on the service of evidence, the use of hearsay evidence, and disclosure:

   As to the service of evidence fairness requires that the police must normally serve written versions of the evidence they propose to adduce in sufficient time before the hearing to enable the defendant fairly to deal with it.

   As to hearsay evidence, this is in principle admissible under section 1 of the Civil Evidence Act 1995. But, by section 2(1), a party proposing to adduce hearsay evidence in civil proceedings has to give the other party notice of that fact and, on request, such particulars of or relating to the evidence as is reasonable and practicable in the circumstances for the purpose of enabling him to deal with any matters arising from it being hearsay. Syntactically, the 'reasonable and practicable' requirement applies to the notice as well as the particulars.

   Section 3 provides that the rules may provide that another party to the proceedings may with the leave of the court call as a witness and cross-examine the maker of the hearsay statement. Thus to expect to adduce, as hearsay, evidence of a person who is not identified offends the spirit if not the letter of section 3, since a defendant cannot seek leave to call and cross-examine a witness whose identity is not revealed... an easy assumption that hearsay evidence is routine in these cases risks real injustice. The willingness of a civil court to admit hearsay evidence carries with it inherent dangers. It is much more difficult for a court to assess the truth of what they are being told if the original maker of the statement does not attend to be cross-examined. More attention should be paid by claimants to the need to state by convincing direct evidence why it is not reasonable and practicable to produce the original maker of the statement as a witness. Magistrates should have these matters well in mind. The use of the words 'if any' in section 4 of the 1995 Act shows that some hearsay evidence may be given no weight at all. Credible direct evidence of a defendant in an application for a closure order may well carry greater weight than uncross-examined hearsay from an anonymous witness or several anonymous witnesses [as to hearsay generally in civil proceedings see **A11.3**].

   The police should disclose documents which clearly and materially affect their case adversely or support the defendant's case.

4. Any breach of a domestic violence protection order is dealt with under s 63 Magistrates' Courts Act 1980 which provides for a penalty of up to £50 per day that the breach continues to a maximum of £5,000, or for committal to custody for a maximum of two months.

A11.3 Evidence

A11.3.1 *Hearsay*

Civil behaviour orders such as closure orders and domestic violence protection orders are now commonplace in criminal courts, and very often involve issues of hearsay. Hearsay evidence in these cases is not regulated by the Criminal Justice Act 2003 but, in so far as it relates to ancillary orders in criminal proceedings, by Part 31 of the Criminal Procedure Rules; and by the Civil Evidence Act 1995.

A11.3.2 *Procedure*

The procedure for a contested hearing is governed by s 55 MCA 1980 and rule 14 Magistrates' Court Rules 1981.

By s 2(1) Civil Evidence Act 1995 a party which proposes to adduce hearsay evidence must give notice of that intention to the other party or parties. A failure does not affect the admissibility of the evidence but may be taken into account in considering the exercise of its powers with respect to the course of proceedings and costs and as a matter adversely affecting the weight to be given to the evidence.

The Magistrates' Court (Hearsay Evidence in Civil Proceedings) Rules 1999 provide time limits:

- 21 days before the hearing date: notice of the intention to give hearsay evidence;
- within seven days: counter-notice with reasons why there should be cross-examination and a party must also give notice of any intention to attack the credibility of a hearsay witness.

A11.3.3 *Challenging the weight to be attached to hearsay evidence*

Regard should be had to s 4 Civil Evidence Act 1995, which provides:

Civil Evidence Act 1995, s 4

4 Considerations relevant to weighing of hearsay evidence

(1) In estimating the weight (if any) to be given to hearsay evidence in civil proceedings the court shall have regard to any circumstances from which any inference can reasonably be drawn as to the reliability or otherwise of the evidence.

(2) Regard may be had, in particular, to the following—

    (a) whether it would have been reasonable and practicable for the party by whom the evidence was adduced to have produced the maker of the original statement as a witness;

    (b) whether the original statement was made contemporaneously with the occurrence or existence of the matters stated;

    (c) whether the evidence involves multiple hearsay;

    (d) whether any person involved had any motive to conceal or misrepresent matters;

    (e) whether the original statement was an edited account, or was made in collaboration with another or for a particular purpose;

    (f) whether the circumstances in which the evidence is adduced as hearsay are such as to suggest an attempt to prevent proper evaluation of its weight.

A11.3.4 *Credibility and previous inconsistent statements*

Sections 5(2) and 6 Civil Evidence Act 1995 provide:

Civil Evidence Act 1995, ss 5(2) and 6

5 Competence and credibility

(2) Where in civil proceedings hearsay evidence is adduced and the maker of the original statement, or of any statement relied upon to prove another statement, is not called as a witness—

(a) evidence which if he had been so called would be admissible for the purpose of attacking or supporting his credibility as a witness is admissible for that purpose in the proceedings; and

(b) evidence tending to prove that, whether before or after he made the statement, he made any other statement inconsistent with it is admissible for the purpose of showing that he had contradicted himself. Provided that evidence may not be given of any matter of which, if he had been called as a witness and had denied that matter in cross-examination, evidence could not have been adduced by the cross-examining party.

6 Previous statements of witness

(1) Subject as follows, the provisions of this Act as to hearsay evidence in civil proceedings apply equally (but with any necessary modifications) in relation to a previous statement made by a person called as a witness in the proceedings.

(2) A party who has called or intends to call a person as a witness in civil proceedings may not in those proceedings adduce evidence of a previous statement made by that person, except—

(a) with the leave of the court, or

(b) for the purpose of rebutting a suggestion that his evidence has been fabricated.

This shall not be construed as preventing a witness statement (that is, a written statement of oral evidence which a party to the proceedings intends to lead) from being adopted by a witness in giving evidence or treated as his evidence.

(3) Where in the case of civil proceedings section 3, 4 or 5 of the Criminal Procedure Act 1865 applies, which make provision as to—

(a) how far a witness may be discredited by the party producing him,

(b) the proof of contradictory statements made by a witness, and

(c) cross-examination as to previous statements in writing,

this Act does not authorise the adducing of evidence of a previous inconsistent or contradictory statement otherwise than in accordance with those sections.

This is without prejudice to any provision made by rules of court under section 3 above (power to call witness for cross-examination on hearsay statement).

(4) Nothing in this Act affects any of the rules of law as to the circumstances in which, where a person called as a witness in civil proceedings is cross-examined on a document used by him to refresh his memory, that document may be made evidence in the proceedings.

(5) Nothing in this section shall be construed as preventing a statement of any description referred to above from being admissible by virtue of section 1 as evidence of the matters stated.

A12 Commencing Proceedings: Time Limits

A12.1 Time limits

A12.1.1 *Overview*

Generally speaking, under s 127 Magistrates' Courts Act 1980, summary only proceedings must be started within 6 months of the criminality complained of.

The following principles emerge from the case law:

- the date of the offence is excluded from the time calculation (*Radcliffe v Bartholomew* [1892] 1 QB 161);
- in relation to a continuing offence, it is the date of the last act that is relevant (*Director of Public Prosecutions v Baker* [2004] EWHC 2782 (Admin));
- month means calendar month;
- limitation ends at midnight on the last day;
- if there is doubt as to whether an information has been laid in time, it must be resolved in favour of the defendant (*Lloyd v Young* [1963] Crim LR 703)

A requisition is 'issued' once fully prepared in the CPS office. It will not be out of time if not sent to the court within 6 months of the offence (*Brown v DPP* [2019] EWHC 798 (Admin)).

The 6-month time limit does not apply to allegations of criminal damage of whatever value as they are either-way offences that, under £5000 in value, may only be tried summarily (*DPP v Bird* 2015 EWHC 4077 (Admin)). However the time limit does apply to low value theft from shops (**C 15.21.3**).

See **A5** for the rules relating to amendment of a charge to substitute an offence that would otherwise be time-barred.

A12.1.2 *Exceptions*

A large number of offences that can be tried only summarily are, in certain circumstances, exempt from the six-month time bar.

In relation to some offences, time runs only from when an offence is 'discovered' by the prosecutor, which means when there was a reasonable belief that an offence had been committed (*Tesco Stores Ltd v London Borough of Harrow* (2003) 167 JP 657, DC). Where the relevant statute provides for a certificate to be signed by a prosecutor as to when he first had knowledge of the relevant facts, and there is a defence challenge to such a certificate, the matter should be dealt with by an application to stay the case for abuse (*Lamont-Perkins v RSPCA* [2012] EWHC 1002 (Admin)). *Letherbarrow v Warwickshire County Council* [2015] EWHC 4820 (Admin) held that, where the time ran from the date on which evidence that a prosecutor considers sufficient to justify proceeding comes to his knowledge, the date referred to is that on which a decision-maker considered the evidence and not the date on which any employee became aware of the case. A prosecutor must be distinguished from an investigator. That decision is not merely whether there is a *prima facie* case but effectively the application of both parts of a prosecutor's duty (both evidential and public interest tests) to review a case before authorizing a prosecution. The matter as further considered in *CPS v Woodward* [2017] EWHC 1008 (Admin) which held that in cases where there is a time issue, it is for the prosecutor to show, to the relevant standard of proof, that there has been compliance. If there has been non-compliance, the prosecution is invalid. The prosecution may surmount the time bar hurdle by either of two means. The first is the issue of a certificate. The second is the adducing of evidence of fact showing who made the decision that a prosecution was justified and when. A certificate is not essential.

Where reliance is placed upon a certificate, then:

1. The certificate must strictly comply with the statutory requirements; and it must comply on its face, in the sense that deficiencies cannot be remedied by reference to extrinsic evidence.
2. A valid certificate is determinative of the matter unless the certificate is in-accurate on its face (ie plainly wrong on its face and patently misleading), or can be shown to be fraudulent. A certificate or further certificates may be issued or reissued at any time, at least until the close of the prosecution case.

In *Downes v RSPCA* [2017] EWHC 3622 (Admin) the court stated that:

> the circumstances in which it will be proper to try to go behind the certificate are likely to be few and far between, and I would encourage magistrates and District Judges to deal robustly with suggestions that certificates are wrong so as to be susceptible to challenge. Before the point can be argued, it seems to me that the defence must make clear that there is a *prima facie* case for undermining the certificate. Given that,... s 31(2)(a) provides the certificate is to be conclusive, I consider that it will seldom be proper to open up a lengthy evidential inquiry into the decision-making process leading to the laying of an information. If it were otherwise, then the presumptively conclusive nature of a s 31 certificate would be undermined.

 See *Blackstone's Criminal Practice 2019* **D2**

A13 **Costs**

Detailed provisions in relation to costs are contained in the Practice Direction (Costs in Criminal Proceedings) 2015 EWCA Crim 1568 (as amended) and in the Criminal Procedure Rules (Crim PR) Part 45.

A13.1 **Statutory basis for awarding defence costs (defence costs orders)**

Section 16(1) of the Prosecution of Offences Act 1985 provides:

> ### Prosecution of Offences Act 1985, s 16(1)
>
> #### 16 Defence costs
>
> (1) Where—
>   (a) an information laid before a justice of the peace for any area, charging any person with an offence, is not proceeded with;
>   (b) a magistrates' court dealing summarily with an offence dismisses the information;
> that court or, in a case falling within paragraph (a) above, a magistrates' court for that area, may make an order in favour of the accused for a payment to be made out of central funds in respect of his costs (a 'defendant's costs order').

Section 16(1) does not apply to proceedings in respect to breach of community penalty as the information does not charge a person with an offence. Similarly, the provision has no application in relation to civil proceedings (eg in relation to domestic violence protection orders).

Costs should generally be awarded to a defendant who can satisfy s 16(1). This includes:

- where the case is withdrawn so that a caution can be administered (*R (Stoddard) v Oxford Magistrates' Court* (2005) 169 JP 683);
- where there is a stay for abuse of process (*R (RE Williams & Sons (Wholesale) Ltd) v Hereford Magistrates' Court* [2008] EWHC 2585 (Admin));
- where a case is resolved by way of bind over (*Emohare v Thames Magistrates' Court* [2009] EWHC 689 (Admin)).

In *R (Spiteri) v Basildon Crown Court* [2009] EWHC 665 (Admin), the applicant successfully appealed a refusal to make a defendant's costs order on the grounds that he was acquitted on a 'technicality'. It was held that a costs order could not be refused on the sole ground that the applicant had brought the proceedings upon himself, as more was required, such as the defendant's having misled the prosecution as to the strength of the case against him. A similar point arose in *Dowler v MerseyRail* [2009] EWHC 558 (Admin), where the court ruled that, when refusing costs, courts should give reasons for the refusal contemporaneously with the ruling. In *R (Rees) v Snaresbrook Crown Court* [2012] EWHC 3879 (Admin), the court left open the possibility of refusing a defence costs order where the defendant had committed perjury or succeeded by ambushing the Crown.

A court should not limit the amount of costs recoverable from central funds to those of the final hearing, at which a bind over was accepted, where the Crown would not have discontinued the proceedings (*Newcombe v CPS* [2013] EWHC 2160 (Admin)).

A13.1.1 *Orders against a party to pay costs thrown away*

Such orders may benefit defendants who suffer financial prejudice as a result of CPS actions or failures to act.

Section 19 Prosecution of Offences Act 1985 provides:

Prosecution of Offences Act 1985, s 19

19 Provision for orders as to costs in other circumstances

(1) The Lord Chancellor may by regulations make provision empowering magistrates' courts ... in any case where the court is satisfied that one party to criminal proceedings has incurred costs as a result of an unnecessary or improper act or omission by, or on behalf of, another party to the proceedings, to make an order as to the payment of those costs.

The Regulations are the Costs in Criminal Cases (General) Regulations 1986.

Costs Practice Direction 4.1.1

Costs against a party to the proceedings

A Magistrates' Court ... may order the payment of any costs incurred as a result of any unnecessary or improper act or omission by or on behalf of any party to the proceedings as distinct from his legal representative: section 19 of the Act and regulation 3 of the General Regulations. In *R (Commissioners of Customs and Excise) v Leicester Crown Court* [2001] EWHC 33 (Admin) the court suggested a four-stage approach: (a) Has there been an unnecessary or improper, act or omission? (b) As a result have any costs been incurred by another party? (c) If the answers to (a) and (b) are 'yes', should the court exercise its discretion to order the party responsible to meet the whole or any part of the relevant costs, and if so what specific sum is involved? (d) What amount of costs should be paid?

In *DPP v Denning* (1991) 2 QB 532 an act was defined as unnecessary or improper if events would have occurred if the party had conducted itself properly. The word 'improper' does not necessarily connote some grave impropriety. In *R (Singh) v Ealing Magistrates' Court* [2014] EWHC 1443 (Admin) it was held that a mere mistake without repetition can be grounds for a costs order under s 19 if additional costs arise from someone on the prosecution side not conducting the case properly. It is not an answer to be unsure whether the CPS or police are responsible. The prosecution is indivisible. The section does, however, contain a discretion not a duty to make an order if there is a satisfactory explanation.

In considering an application under s 19 Prosecution of Offences Act 1985 the principles to be applied in respect of an application under that section and Regulation 3 were set out in *Evans* [2015] EWHC 263 (QB) and in *R v Cornish and Maidstone and Tunbridge Wells NHS Trust* [2016] EWHC 779 (QB).

It should be noted that these cases were concerned with an application for the total costs of a failed prosecution. More common will be applications in relation to unnecessary hearings or extra work caused by the failure of a party to comply in a timely fashion with an order of the court. It is suggested that failure to comply with a court order amounts to impropriety, as a party, however busy, can always apply for further time.

Prosecution of Offences Act 1985, s 19A

Costs against legal representatives etc

(1) In any criminal proceedings—

   ...

   (c) a magistrates' court,

   may disallow, or (as the case may be) order the legal or other representative concerned to meet, the whole of any wasted costs or such part of them as may be determined in accordance with regulations.

   ...

(3) In this section—

   'wasted costs' means any costs incurred by a party—

   (a) as a result of any improper, unreasonable, or negligent act or omission on the part of any representative or any employee of a representative; or

   (b) which, in the light of any such act or omission occurring after they were incurred, the court considers it is unreasonable to expect that party to pay.

The Practice Direction (Costs in Criminal Proceedings) 2015 EWCA Crim 1568 deals with wasted costs in paragraph 4.2:

Practice Direction (Costs in Criminal Proceedings) 2015 EWCA Crim 1568

Part 4.2.4

(iv) A three-stage test or approach is recommended when a wasted costs order is contemplated:

   (a) Has there been an improper, unreasonable or negligent act or omission?

   (b) As a result have any costs been incurred by a party?

   (c) If the answers to (a) & (b) are 'yes', should the court exercise its discretion to disallow or order the representative to meet the whole or any part of the relevant costs, and if so what specific sum is involved?

   ...

(vi) The judge must specify the sum to be allowed or ordered. Alternatively the relevant available procedure should be substituted should it be impossible to fix the sum.

Part 4.2.5

(i) The primary object is not to punish but to compensate, albeit as the order is sought against a non party, it can from that perspective be regarded as penal.

   ...

(iv) Because of the penal element a mere mistake is not sufficient to justify an order, there must be a more serious error.

   ...

(vi) The normal civil standard of proof applies but if the allegation is one of serious misconduct or crime clear evidence will be required to meet that standard.

In *Ridehalgh v Horsefield* [1994] Ch 205 the court stated:

Improper, unreasonable or negligent: ... In our view the meaning of these expressions is not open to serious doubt.

'Improper' means what it has been understood to mean in this context for at least half a century. The adjective covers, but is not confined to, conduct which would ordinarily be held to justify disbarment, striking off, suspension from practice or other serious professional penalty. It covers any significant breach of a substantial duty imposed by a relevant code of professional conduct. But it is not in our judgment limited to that. Conduct which would be regarded as improper according to the consensus of professional (including judicial) opinion can be fairly stigmatised as such whether or not it violates the letter of a professional code.

'Unreasonable' also means what it has been understood to mean in this context for at least half a century ... But conduct cannot be described as unreasonable simply because it leads in the event to an unsuccessful result or because other more cautious legal representatives would have acted differently. The acid test is whether the conduct permits of a reasonable explanation. If so, the course adopted may be regarded as optimistic and as reflecting on a practitioner's judgment, but it is not unreasonable.

... [W]e are clear that 'negligent' should be understood in an untechnical way to denote failure to act with the competence reasonably to be expected of ordinary members of the profession. In adopting an untechnical approach to the meaning of negligence in this context, we would however wish firmly to discountenance any suggestion that an applicant for a wasted costs order under this head need prove anything less than he would have to prove in an action for negligence: 'advice, acts or omissions in the course of their professional work which no member of the profession who was reasonably well-informed and competent would have given or done or omitted to do'; an error 'such as no reasonably well-informed and competent member of that profession could have made' ... We were invited to give the three adjectives (improper, unreasonable and negligent) specific, self-contained meanings, so as to avoid overlap between the three. We do not read these very familiar expressions in that way. Conduct which is unreasonable may also be improper, and conduct which is negligent will very frequently be (if it is not by definition) unreasonable. We do not think any sharp differentiation between these expressions is useful or necessary or intended.

Under the provisions of s 19B Prosecution of Offences Act 1985, to make a wasted costs order against a third party the court must find serious misconduct as required by s 19B Prosecution of Offenders Act 1986. There must therefore be a history of failure to address an underlying issue (*R v Allied Language Solutions* (2013) (QB)).

A13.2 Costs in relation to civil complaints

Section 64 Magistrates' Courts Act 1980 provides:

Magistrates' Courts Act 1980, s 64

64 Power to award costs and enforcement of costs

(1) On the hearing of a complaint, a magistrates' court shall have power in its discretion to make such order as to costs—
  (a) on making the order for which the complaint is made, to be paid by the defendant to the complainant;
  (b) on dismissing the complaint, to be paid by the complainant to the defendant, as it thinks just and reasonable; but if the complaint is for an order for the periodical payment of money, or for the revocation, revival or variation of such an order, or for the enforcement of such an order, the court may, whatever adjudication it makes, order either party to pay the whole or any part of the other's costs.

(2) The amount of any sum ordered to be paid under subsection (1) above shall be specified in the order, or order of dismissal, as the case may be.

The discretion here is narrower than under s 16 Prosecution of Offences Act 1985 (see **A13.1**), and can be invoked if the court makes an order or dismisses the complaint, or the proceedings are withdrawn (s 52 Courts Act 1971). Applicants may also rely upon *Baxendale-Walker v Law Society* [2007] 3 All ER 330 (and other similar cases) to avoid costs on the basis that they are public bodies acting in the wider public interest and should not be exposed to the risk of adverse costs orders:

- in relation to civil proceedings commenced under the Proceeds of Crime Act 2002 (*Perinpanathan v City of Westminster Magistrates' Court* [2010] EWCA Civ 40) in relation to cash seizure cases that have been successfully defended;
- in relation to proceedings under s 1 Crime and Disorder Act 1998 (ASBO application) (*Manchester City Council v Manchester Magistrates' Court* [2009] EWHC 1866 (Admin));
- in withdrawal cases—see *Chief Constable of Warwickshire v MT* 2015 EWHC 2303 (Admin).

A13.3 Costs in relation to witnesses

Costs in relation to character witnesses' attendance at court can be recovered only when the court has certified that the interests of justice required the witnesses' attendance (Costs in Criminal Cases (General) Regulations 1986 (SI 1986/1335), reg 15). Advocates should ensure that an application is made to the court either prior to or immediately after the witnesses' attendance.

 See *Blackstone's Criminal Practice 2019* **D33**

A14 Court-Appointed Legal Representatives

A14.1 Overview

In circumstances defined by s 34 Youth Justice and Criminal Evidence Act 1999 (complainants in proceedings for sexual offences); s 35 (child complainants and other child witnesses); and s 36 (more generally), a defendant is prohibited from cross-examining witnesses. In the event that the defendant has declined or is not eligible for legal funding, the court has power under s 38 to appoint a legal representative to carry out this function on behalf of the court.

A14.2 Key points

Fees for this work are authorized under s 19 Prosecution of Offences Act 1985 and are as agreed by the court or allowed following taxation at private client rates. Solicitors should not agree to fees that are less than those that would be allowed for in line with civil guideline costs rates. A duty solicitor can be required to conduct such cases but should ensure that they have sufficient time to undertake the work professionally.

In *Abbas v CPS* [2015] EWHC 579 (Admin), the court held that to allow for effective cross-examination there was a need for a pre-trial conference and also for presence at pre-trial applications such as over bad character or disclosure. Under the amended rule payment is possible until the conclusion of cross-examination. In *R Andrews* [2016] 4 Costs LR 705, the costs judge held that cross-examination of a witness continues until such time as any such witness might be recalled, noting that trials involving defendants in person tend to be chaotic.

Criminal Procedure Rule 23 applies. It identifies the information to which the representative is entitled.

A14.3 Statutory provisions

Youth Justice and Criminal Evidence Act 1999, ss 34, 35, 36, and 38

34 Complainants in proceedings for sexual offences

No person charged with a sexual offence may in any criminal proceedings cross-examine in person a witness who is the complainant, either—

(a) in connection with that offence, or
(b) in connection with any other offence (of whatever nature) with which that person is charged in the proceedings.

35 Child complainants and other child witnesses

(1) No person charged with an offence to which this section applies may in any criminal proceedings cross-examine in person a protected witness, either—

(a) in connection with that offence, or

(b) in connection with any other offence (of whatever nature) with which that person is charged in the proceedings.

(2) For the purposes of subsection (1) a 'protected witness' is a witness who—

    (a) either is the complainant or is alleged to have been a witness to the commission of the offence to which this section applies, and

    (b) either is a child or falls to be cross-examined after giving evidence in chief (whether wholly or in part)—

        (i) by means of a video recording made (for the purposes of section 27) at a time when the witness was a child, or

        (ii) in any other way at any such time.

(3) The offences to which this section applies are—

    (a) any offence under—

        (iva) any of sections 33 to 36 Sexual Offences Act 1956,

        (v) the Protection of Children Act 1978;

        (vi) part 1 of the Sexual Offences Act 2003 or any relevant superseded enactment; or

        (vii) sections 1 and 2 of the Modern Slavery Act 2015;

    (b) kidnapping, false imprisonment or an offence under section 1 or 2 of the Child Abduction Act 1984;

    (c) any offence under section 1 of the Children and Young Persons Act 1933;

    (d) any offence (not within any of the preceding paragraphs) which involves an assault on, or injury or a threat of injury to, any person.

(4) In this section 'child' means—

    (a) where the offence falls within subsection (3)(a), a person under the age of 17; or

    (b) where the offence falls within subsection (3)(b), (c) or (d), a person under the age of 14.

(5) For the purposes of this section 'witness' includes a witness who is charged with an offence in the proceedings.

36 Direction prohibiting accused from cross-examining particular witness

(1) This section applies where, in a case where neither of sections 34 and 35 operates to prevent an accused in any criminal proceedings from cross-examining a witness in person—

    (a) the prosecutor makes an application for the court to give a direction under this section in relation to the witness, or

    (b) the court of its own motion raises the issue whether such a direction should be given.

(2) If it appears to the court—

    (a) that the quality of evidence given by the witness on cross-examination—

        (i) is likely to be diminished if the cross-examination (or further cross-examination) is conducted by the accused in person, and

        (ii) would be likely to be improved if a direction were given under this section, and

    (b) that it would not be contrary to the interests of justice to give such a direction, the court may give a direction prohibiting the accused from cross-examining (or further cross-examining) the witness in person.

(3) In determining whether subsection (2)(a) applies in the case of a witness the court must have regard, in particular, to—

    (a) any views expressed by the witness as to whether or not the witness is content to be cross-examined by the accused in person;

(b) the nature of the questions likely to be asked, having regard to the issues in the proceedings and the defence case advanced so far (if any);

(c) any behaviour on the part of the accused at any stage of the proceedings, both generally and in relation to the witness;

(d) any relationship (of whatever nature) between the witness and the accused;

(e) whether any person (other than the accused) is or has at any time been charged in the proceedings with a sexual offence or an offence to which section 35 applies, and (if so) whether section 34 or 35 operates or would have operated to prevent that person from cross-examining the witness in person;

(f) any direction under section 19 which the court has given, or proposes to give, in relation to the witness.

(4) For the purposes of this section—

(a) 'witness', in relation to an accused, does not include any other person who is charged with an offence in the proceedings; and

(b) any reference to the quality of a witness's evidence shall be construed in accordance with section 16(5).....

38 Defence representation for purposes of cross-examination

(1) This section applies where an accused is prevented from cross-examining a witness in person by virtue of section 34, 35 or 36.

(2) Where it appears to the court that this section applies, it must—

(a) invite the accused to arrange for a legal representative to act for him for the purpose of cross-examining the witness; and

(b) require the accused to notify the court, by the end of such period as it may specify, whether a legal representative is to act for him for that purpose.

(3) If by the end of the period mentioned in subsection (2)(b) either—

(a) the accused has notified the court that no legal representative is to act for him for the purpose of cross-examining the witness, or

(b) no notification has been received by the court and it appears to the court that no legal representative is to so act,

the court must consider whether it is necessary in the interests of justice for the witness to be cross-examined by a legal representative appointed to represent the interests of the accused.

(4) If the court decides that it is necessary in the interests of justice for the witness to be so cross-examined, the court must appoint a qualified legal representative (chosen by the court) to cross-examine the witness in the interests of the accused.

(5) A person so appointed shall not be responsible to the accused.

 See *Blackstone's Criminal Practice 2019* **F7.2** and **F7.3**

A15 **Custody Time Limits**

A15.1 Overview

Category	Time limit
Cases sent to the Crown Court	An overall time limit of 182 days applies, which includes any time spent in custody at the magistrates' court.
Either-way offences	Maximum 56 days from first appearance to hearing evidence in a summary trial (unless case was originally destined for sending and court reverts to summary trial after 56 days have elapsed, in which case the limit is 70 days).
Summary-only offences	56 days to start of summary trial.
Youths	As above, save that indictable-only cases that are tried summarily in the youth court are subject to the same time limits as either-way cases (*R v Stratford Youth Court, exp S (A Minor)* [1998] 1 WLR 1758).

A15.2 Exceptions

Defendants who abscond from prison, or who have been released on bail following expiry of a custody time limit, but are then remanded following a breach of bail, do not enjoy the protections offered by custody time limits.

If a person is granted bail and is later remanded into custody, the earlier period on remand will count towards the custody time limit.

Custody time limits start at the end of the first day of remand and expire at midnight on the last day. A time limit expiring on one of the following days will be treated as having expired on the next preceding day which is not one of those days: a Saturday, a Sunday, Christmas Day, Good Friday, or a bank holiday.

A15.3 Extending custody time limits

In general, the following considerations are relevant:

• the prosecution should give two days' notice of an intention to apply, but lack of notice is not fatal to the application and the court retains a discretion to extend the time limits (*R v Governor of Canterbury Prison, ex p Craig* [1991] 2 QB 195);
• there is no power to extend once a time limit has lapsed (*R v Sheffield Justices, ex p Turner* [1991] 2 WLR 987);
• the court must be satisfied, on a balance of probabilities, that the need for the extension is due to the illness or absence of the accused, a necessary witness, a judge or magistrate; or a postponement which is occasioned by the ordering of separate trials, or some other good and sufficient cause; and that the prosecution have acted with all due diligence and expedition;
• the following have been held not to amount to good and sufficient cause, certainly in cases that are routine (*R (McAuley) v Coventry Crown Court*

[2012] EWHC 680 (Admin) and *R (Raeside) v Luton Crown Court* [2012]
EWHC 1064 (Admin)): lack of court time, listing difficulties attributable
to the nature of the case, lack of a suitably experienced judge (or lack of any
judge at all). Absent exceptional circumstances, resource difficulties do not
amount to a good and sufficient cause.

 See *Blackstone's Criminal Practice 2019* **D15.7–D15.38**

A16 **Disclosure**

A16.1 Overview

Disclosure comes in stages:

(1) Initial disclosure of the prosecution case.
(2) Common law disclosure.
(3) Disclosure in relation to unused material.
(4) Consideration also has to be given to third party disclosure.

A16.2 **Initial details of the prosecution case**

Part 8 of the Criminal Procedure Rules (Crim PR) requires that initial disclosure should be available no later than the start of the day of the first hearing.

Part 8 provides for disclosure of such information in relation to all cases in a magistrates' court. Criminal Practice Direction 2015 EWCA Crim 1567 directions 3A4 and 3A12 require that there is sufficient information to enable the defendant to make an informed decision on plea and for the court to decide whether the case is suitable for summary trial.

Frequent problems arise in relation to the service of video and other recorded evidence. If the Crown is not relying on the undisclosed video evidence then no issue in relation to initial disclosure arises. In any event, the prosecution are under a duty to serve only a summary of their case, not the case in its entirety. The defendant's remedy is to enter a not guilty plea and put the Crown to proof.

A16.3 **Extent of disclosure**

Part 8 of the Crim PR provides:

Criminal Procedure Rules, Pt 8

8.1 When this Part applies

This Part applies in a magistrates' court.

8.2

(1) The prosecutor must serve initial details of the prosecution case on the court officer—
  (a) as soon as practicable; and
  (b) in any event, no later than the beginning of the day of the first hearing.
(2) Where a defendant requests those details, the prosecutor must serve them on the defendant—
  (a) as soon as practicable; and
  (b) in any event, no later than the beginning of the day of the first hearing.
(3) Where a defendant does not request those details, the prosecutor must make them available to the defendant at, or before, the beginning of the day of the first hearing.

8.3 Content of initial details

Initial details of the prosecution case must include—

(a) where, immediately before the first hearing in the magistrates' court, the defendant was in police custody for the offence charged—
  (i) a summary of the circumstances of the offence, and
  (ii) the defendant's criminal record, if any;
(b) where paragraph (a) does not apply—
  (i) a summary of the circumstances of the offence,
  (ii) any account given by the defendant in interview, whether contained in that summary or in another document,
  (iii) any written witness statement or exhibit that the prosecutor then has available and considers material to plea, or to the allocation of the case for trial, or to sentence,
  (iv) the defendant's criminal record, if any, and
  (v) any available statement of the effect of the offence on a victim, a victim's family or others.

8.4

(1) This rule applies where—
  (a) the prosecutor wants to introduce information contained in a document listed in rule 8.3; and
  (b) the prosecutor has not—
    (i) served that document on the defendant, or
    (ii) made that information available to the defendant.
(2) The court must not allow the prosecutor to introduce that information unless the court first allows the defendant sufficient time to consider it.

 See *Blackstone's Criminal Practice 2019* **D5**

A16.4 **Common law disclosure**

There is a common law duty to disclose material which may assist the defence at bail hearings or in the early preparation of their case or in mitigation. Following the decision in *R v DPP, ex p Lee* [1999] 2 All ER 737, the prosecutor must always be alive to the need to make disclosure of material of which he is aware (either from his own consideration of the papers or because his attention has been drawn to it by the defence), and which he, as a responsible prosecutor, recognizes should be disclosed at an earlier stage. Examples include:

- previous convictions of a complainant or deceased if that information could reasonably be expected to assist the defence when applying for bail;
- material which will enable the defence to make preparations for trial which may be significantly less effective if disclosure is delayed (eg names of eyewitnesses who the prosecution do not intend to use);
- the withdrawal of support for the prosecution by a witness.

This material must be revealed to the prosecutor for service on the defence with the initial details of the prosecution case.

A16.5 **Disclosure of unused material**

Prosecution disclosure of unused material following a not guilty plea is regulated under s 3(1)(a) Criminal Procedure and Investigations Act (CPIA) 1996 and by the Judicial Protocol on disclosure of unused material:

> **Criminal Procedure and Investigations Act 1996, s 3(1)(a)**
>
> **3 Initial duty of prosecutor to disclose**
>
> (1) The prosecutor must—
>> (a) disclose to the accused any prosecution material which has not previously been disclosed to the accused and which might reasonably be considered capable of undermining the case for the prosecution against the accused or of assisting the case for the accused.....

In the magistrates' court there is no duty to serve a defence case statement but in the absence of one, a prosecutor may not be able to discover which information might be disclosable. Particular problems arise with CCTV. Courts are unlikely to adjourn for CCTV where its content is purely speculative. If an early request was made, forensic advantage could be taken of its absence (*DPP v Petrie* [2015] EWHC 48 (Admin)). However it is otherwise when the CCTV has been referred to in interview by the police, or has been viewed by the police who decided not to retain it because it did not assist their case, without performing their duty to consider whether it might assist the defendant's case. The court considered that the trial in the latter situation would not be fair (*Birmingham* [1992] Crim LR 117)).

A failure to disclose in accordance with the statutory scheme may lead to an adjournment (see **A2.2**). In the alternative, courts may exclude all or any prosecution evidence under s 78 Police and Criminal Evidence Act 1984 where there has been a failure in accordance with statutory time limits to provide initial or further disclosure, and this makes the trial unfair (*R (Ibrahim) v Feltham MC* [2001] EWHC 130 (Admin) and *R v Boardman* [2015] EWCA Crim 175). The need for a defence case statement cannot arise until initial disclosure had been served by the Crown.

A16.6 Section 8 disclosure applications

A party aggrieved in relation to prosecution disclosure can apply to the court under s 8 1996 Act, but *must* serve a defence case statement in order to do so.

> **Criminal Procedure and Investigations Act 1996, s 8**
>
> **8 Application by accused for disclosure**
>
> (1) This section applies where the accused has given a defence statement under section 5, 6 or 6B and the prosecutor has complied with section 7A(5) or purported to comply with it or has failed to comply with it.
> (2) If the accused has at any time reasonable cause to believe that there is prosecution material which is required by section 7A to be disclosed to him and has not been, he may apply to the court for an order requiring the prosecutor to disclose it to him.
> (3) For the purposes of this section prosecution material is material—
>> (a) which is in the prosecutor's possession and came into his possession in connection with the case for the prosecution against the accused,
>> (b) which, in pursuance of a code operative under Part II, he has inspected in connection with the case for the prosecution against the accused, or
>> (c) which falls within subsection (4).

(4) Material falls within this subsection if in pursuance of a code operative under Part II the prosecutor must, if he asks for the material, be given a copy of it or be allowed to inspect it in connection with the case for the prosecution against the accused.

(5) Material must not be disclosed under this section to the extent that the court, on an application by the prosecutor, concludes it is not in the public interest to disclose it and orders accordingly.

(6) Material must not be disclosed under this section to the extent that it is material the disclosure of which is prohibited by section 17 of the Regulation of Investigatory Powers Act 2000.

In road traffic cases, in the absence of some specific evidence which indicates that there is a problem with the Intoximeter EC/IR machine, extensive exploration of technicalities will normally be a waste of time (*R (Hassani) v West London MC* [2017] EWHC 1270 (Admin)). The issues were explored extensively in *R (DPP) v Manchester and Salford MC* [2017] EWHC 1708 (Admin) which held:

It is not enough to say that the defence case is that the amount drunk would not put the defendant over the limit or anywhere near it, and therefore the machine must be unreliable. What the evidence needed to do, in order to provide a basis for such a disclosure order was to address two critical features:

The first requirement is the basis for contending how the device might produce a printout which, on its face, demonstrated that it was operating in proper fashion, but which could generate a very significantly false positive reading, where, on the defence case, the true reading would have been well below the prosecution limit.

The second requirement is to identify how the material which was sought could assist to demonstrate how that might have happened.

A16.7 **Third party disclosure**

A16.7.1 *CPIA Code of Practice*

CPIA Code of Practice

3.5 In conducting an investigation, the investigator should pursue all reasonable lines of inquiry, whether these point towards or away from the suspect. What is reasonable in each case will depend on the particular circumstances...

3.6 If the officer in charge of an investigation believes that other persons may be in possession of material that may be relevant to the investigation, and if this has not been obtained under paragraph 3.5 above, he should ask the disclosure officer to inform them of the existence of the investigation and to invite them to retain the material in case they receive a request for its disclosure. The disclosure officer should inform the prosecutor that they may have such material. However, the officer in charge of an investigation is not required to make speculative enquiries of other persons; there must be some reason to believe that they may have relevant material. That reason may come from information provided to the police by the accused or from other inquiries made or from some other source.

...

4.3 Negative information is often relevant to an investigation. If it may be relevant it must be recorded. An example might be a number of people present in a particular place at a particular time who state that they saw nothing unusual.

A16.7.2 *Case law*

In *R v Alibhai* [2004] EWCA Crim 681, the Court of Appeal held that under the CPIA 1996 the prosecutor is only under a duty to disclose a third party's material if that material had come into the prosecutor's possession and the prosecutor was of the opinion that such material satisfied the disclosure test. Before taking steps to obtain third party material, the Court emphasized that it must be shown that there was a suspicion that the third party not only had relevant material and that the material was not merely neutral or damaging to the accused, but it also satisfied the disclosure test.

Furthermore, *R v Alibhai* states that even if there is the necessary suspicion, the prosecutor has a 'margin of consideration' as to what steps to take in any particular case and was not thus under an absolute obligation to obtain material that was suspected to satisfy the disclosure test.

There may be cases where the investigator, disclosure officer, or prosecutor believes that a third party (eg a local authority, a social services department, a hospital, a doctor, a school, a provider of forensic services) has material or information which might be relevant to the prosecution case. In such cases, investigators, disclosure officers, and prosecutors should take reasonable steps to identify, secure, and consider material held by any third party where it appears to the investigator, disclosure officer, or prosecutor that (a) such material exists, and (b) it may be relevant to an issue in the case.

A16.7.3 *Statutory procedure to obtain third party material*

If material evidence is in the hands of a third party a summons may be issued under s 97 Magistrates Courts Act 1980 (see **A32**). The statutory requirements in s 97 are more stringent than the disclosure test. Items sought under the summons procedure must be 'likely to be material evidence' (which the House of Lords in *R v Derby Magistrates' Court ex p B* [1995] 4 All ER 526 has construed to mean 'immediately admissible per se').

A16.8 **The judicial protocol on disclosure 2013**

The section on magistrates' courts confirms:

Judicial Protocol on the Disclosure of Unused Material in Criminal Cases, paras 30–37

30. The principles relating to disclosure apply equally in the magistrates' courts. It follows that whilst disclosure of unused material in compliance with the statutory test is undoubtedly essential in order to achieve justice, it is critical that summary trials are not delayed or made over-complicated by misconceived applications for, or inappropriate disclosure of, prosecution material.

31. Magistrates will rely on their legal advisers for guidance, and the latter should draw the attention of the parties and the court to the statutory provisions and the applicable case law. Cases raising disclosure issues of particular complexity should be referred to a District Judge (Magistrates' Courts), if available.

32. Although service of a defence statement is voluntary for summary trials (section 6 CPIA), the defendant cannot make an application for specific disclosure under section 8 CPIA, and the court cannot make any orders in this regard, unless a proper defence statement has been provided. It follows that although providing a defence statement is not mandatory, it remains a critical stage in the disclosure process. If disclosure issues are to be raised by the defence, a defence statement must be served well in advance of the trial date. Any section 8 application must be made in strict compliance with the Rules.

33. The case-management forms used in the magistrates' courts fulfil some of the functions of a defence statement, and the prosecution must take into account the information provided as to the defence case when conducting its ongoing review of unused material. As the Court of Appeal noted in R v Newell (supra), admissions can be made in the Trial Preparation Form and the defence is able to identify the matters that are not in issue. Admissions made in these circumstances may be admissible during the trial. However, other information on the form that does not come within the section relating to admissions should... not generally be introduced as part of the evidence at trial. However, the contents of the Trial Preparation Form do not replace the need to serve a defence statement if the defendant seeks to apply for disclosure under section 8 CPIA....

35. Although CCTV footage frequently causes difficulties, it is to be treated as any other category of unused material and it should only be disclosed if the material meets the appropriate test for disclosure under the CPIA. The defence should either be provided with copies of the sections of the CCTV or afforded an opportunity to view them. If the prosecution refuses to disclose CCTV material that the defence considers to be disclosable, the courts should not make standard or general directions requiring the prosecutor to disclose material of this kind in the absence of an application under section 8. When potentially relevant CCTV footage is not in the possession of the police, the guidance in relation to third party material will apply, although the police remain under a duty to pursue all reasonable lines of inquiry, including those leading away from a suspect, whether or not defence requests are made.

36. The previous convictions of witnesses and any disciplinary findings against officers in the case are frequently disclosable and care should be taken to disclose them as appropriate. Documents such as crime reports or records of emergency calls should not be provided on a routine basis, for instance as part of a bundle of disclosed documents, irrespective of whether the material satisfies the appropriate test for disclosure. Defence advocates should not request this material in standard or routine correspondence, and instead focussed consideration should be given to the circumstances of the particular case. Unjustified requests for disclosure of material of this kind are routinely made, frequently leading to unnecessary delays and adjournments. The prosecution should always consider whether the request is properly made out.

37. The supervisory role of the courts is critical in this context, and magistrates must guard against granting unnecessary adjournments and issuing unjustified directions.

See *Blackstone's Criminal Practice 2019* **D9**

A17 Hearsay

A17.1 Overview

Hearsay evidence in criminal proceedings is regulated by ss 114–126 Criminal Justice Act (CJA) 2003. The main legislative provisions are set out in **A17.3**.

A17.2 Criminal Procedure Rules

Part 20 of the Criminal Procedure Rules regulates the admission of hearsay evidence:

Criminal Procedure Rules, Pt 20

20.2 (1) This rule applies where a party wants to introduce hearsay evidence for admission under any of the following sections of the Criminal Justice Act 2003—
(a) section 114(1)(d) (evidence admissible in the interests of justice);
(b) section 116 (evidence where a witness is unavailable);
(c) section 117(1)(c) (evidence in a statement prepared for the purposes of criminal proceedings);
(d) section 121 (multiple hearsay).

A17.3 Legislative scheme

Sections 114–120 CJA 2003 are the main statutory provisions.

Criminal Justice Act 2003, s 114

114 Admissibility of hearsay evidence

(1) In criminal proceedings a statement not made in oral evidence in the proceedings is admissible as evidence of any matter stated if, but only if—
(a) any provision of this Chapter or any other statutory provision makes it admissible,
(b) any rule of law preserved by section 118 makes it admissible,
(c) all parties to the proceedings agree to it being admissible, or
(d) the court is satisfied that it is in the interests of justice for it to be admissible.
(2) In deciding whether a statement not made in oral evidence should be admitted under subsection (1)(d), the court must have regard to the following factors (and to any others it considers relevant)—
(a) how much probative value the statement has (assuming it to be true) in relation to a matter in issue in the proceedings, or how valuable it is for the understanding of other evidence in the case;
(b) what other evidence has been, or can be, given on the matter or evidence mentioned in paragraph (a);
(c) how important the matter or evidence mentioned in paragraph (a) is in the context of the case as a whole;
(d) the circumstances in which the statement was made;
(e) how reliable the maker of the statement appears to be;
(f) how reliable the evidence of the making of the statement appears to be;

> (g) whether oral evidence of the matter stated can be given and, if not, why it
>   cannot;
> (h) the amount of difficulty involved in challenging the statement;
> (i) the extent to which that difficulty would be likely to prejudice the party facing it.
> (3) Nothing in this Chapter affects the exclusion of evidence of a statement on
>   grounds other than the fact that it is a statement not made in oral evidence in the
>   proceedings.

It will rarely be appropriate to use s 114 in order to circumvent s 116 (cases where a witness is unavailable) (*R v Ibrahim* [2010] EWCA Crim 1176). This principle takes on a particular importance in the magistrates' court in relation to 'missing' or reluctant witnesses (eg in domestic abuse cases). While there would be occasions when, in domestic abuse proceedings, it would be necessary to admit hearsay evidence from the complainant the correct procedures must be followed. Section 114(1)(d) CJA 2003 (the interest of justice) could not be considered until all due enquiries and applications had been made and evidence heard under s 116 (*R v Jones (Kane)* [2015] EWCA Crim 1317). Section 114 should not be used simply to bypass other procedures available to the prosecution, for example the witness summons. In *R v Freeman* [2010] EWCA Crim 1997, the court quashed a conviction where s 114 was used in relation to a witness who had retracted his previous statement.

Regard must be had to all of the criteria in s 114(2), although not all factors need be decided in favour of admissibility.

Section 114(2)(e) requires the court to consider the reliability of the maker of the statement. The principles were considered further in *R v Riat and others* [2012] EWCA Crim 1509. The court must:

* be satisfied that there is proper statutory basis for admitting hearsay;
* identify if there is any material assisting in the test of credibility (s 124);
* consider as appropriate any interests of justice test;
* if there is no specific gateway, consider s 114(1)(d);
* consider any application to exclude under s 78 Police and Criminal Evidence Act 1984 or s 126 CJA 2003.

The criteria in s 114(2) are a useful aide-mémoire in identifying the relevant issues.

A focused decision must be made considering:

* the importance of the evidence in the case;
* the risks of unreliability;
* issues as to whether the reliability of the maker of the statement can be tested and assessed.

Of particular relevance are:

* the circumstances of the making of the hearsay statement,
* interest or disinterest of the maker,
* the existence of supporting evidence,
* information on the reliability of the maker,
* any means of testing reliability.

Criminal Justice Act 2003, ss 115 and 116

115 Statements and matters stated

(1) In this Chapter references to a statement or to a matter stated are to be read as follows.

(2) A statement is any representation of fact or opinion made by a person by whatever means; and it includes a representation made in a sketch, photofit or other pictorial form.

(3) A matter stated is one to which this Chapter applies if (and only if) the purpose, or one of the purposes, of the person making the statement appears to the court to have been—

    (a) to cause another person to believe the matter, or

    (b) to cause another person to act or a machine to operate on the basis that the matter is as stated.

The essential questions as to what is hearsay were identified in *R v Twist* [2011] EWCA Crim 1143:

(1) Identify the relevant fact/matter it is sought to prove.

(2) Is there a statement of that matter?

(3) If yes, was one of the purposes of the maker of the communication that the recipient or any other person should believe that matter or act upon it as true?

In *R v Midmore* [2017] EWCA Crim 533 a text was sent to a third party saying 'this one is the face melter', with a photograph of a chemical. In relation to the three elements, it was held:

(1) It established the defendant's shared intention to use the acid for a criminal as opposed to an innocent propose;

(2) It was an implied representation of intention, not just a comment from which intention could be inferred; *but*

(3) The third test was not met on the facts.

Similarly in *R v Noble and Johnson* [2016] EWCSA Crim 2219, a text message from a girlfriend of the defendant setting out an implication that the defendant was in a certain place and had a firearm was not hearsay as it was not intended that the defendant should believe it—he already knew—or act upon it.

A17.3.1 *Witnesses unable to attend*

116 Cases where a witness is unavailable

(1) In criminal proceedings a statement not made in oral evidence in the proceedings is admissible as evidence of any matter stated if—

    (a) oral evidence given in the proceedings by the person who made the statement would be admissible as evidence of that matter,

    (b) the person who made the statement (the relevant person) is identified to the court's satisfaction, and

    (c) any of the five conditions mentioned in subsection (2) is satisfied.

(2) The conditions are—
   (a) that the relevant person is dead;
   (b) that the relevant person is unfit to be a witness because of his bodily or mental condition;
   (c) that the relevant person is outside the United Kingdom and it is not reasonably practicable to secure his attendance;
   (d) that the relevant person cannot be found although such steps as it is reasonably practicable to take to find him have been taken;
   (e) that through fear the relevant person does not give (or does not continue to give) oral evidence in the proceedings, either at all or in connection with the subject matter of the statement, and the court gives leave for the statement to be given in evidence.

(3) For the purposes of subsection (2)(e) 'fear' is to be widely construed and (for example) includes fear of the death or injury of another person or of financial loss.

(4) Leave may be given under subsection (2)(e) only if the court considers that the statement ought to be admitted in the interests of justice, having regard—
   (a) to the statement's contents,
   (b) to any risk that its admission or exclusion will result in unfairness to any party to the proceedings (and in particular to how difficult it will be to challenge the statement if the relevant person does not give oral evidence),
   (c) in appropriate cases, to the fact that a direction under section 19 of the Youth Justice and Criminal Evidence Act 1999 (c. 23) (special measures for the giving of evidence by fearful witnesses etc) could be made in relation to the relevant person, and
   (d) to any other relevant circumstances.

(5) A condition set out in any paragraph of subsection (2) which is in fact satisfied is to be treated as not satisfied if it is shown that the circumstances described in that paragraph are caused—
   (a) by the person in support of whose case it is sought to give the state in evidence, or
   (b) by a person acting on his behalf, in order to prevent the relevant person giving oral evidence in the proceedings (whether at all or in connection with the subject matter of the statement).

In considering whether it is reasonably practicable to secure the attendance of a witness, the court must consider what steps have, and have not, been taken. The reasonableness will be judged in relation to many factors, including the resources available to the party (*R v Maloney* [1994] Crim LR 525).

Even where the attendance of a witness is not practicable (or some other factor in s 116 is present), the court should then go on to consider s 126 of the Act and s 78 Police and Criminal Evidence Act (PACE) 1984 in order to decide whether the evidence ought, in fairness, to be admitted. Section 126 CJA 2003, giving a discretion to exclude hearsay evidence, should also be used to exclude material that is barely relevant, which lacked significant probative value. The test was the same for the Crown and for the defence (unlike s 78 PACE) (*R v Drinkwater* [2016] EWCA Crim 16).

A17.3.2 *Business documents*

Criminal Justice Act 2003, ss 117 and 118

117 Business and other documents

(1) In criminal proceedings a statement contained in a document is admissible as evidence of any matter stated if—

    (a) oral evidence given in the proceedings would be admissible as evidence of that matter,

    (b) the requirements of subsection (2) are satisfied, and

    (c) the requirements of subsection (5) are satisfied, in a case where subsection (4) requires them to be.

(2) The requirements of this subsection are satisfied if—

    (a) the document or the part containing the statement was created or received by a person in the course of a trade, business, profession or other occupation, or as the holder of a paid or unpaid office,

    (b) the person who supplied the information contained in the statement (the relevant person) had or may reasonably be supposed to have had personal knowledge of the matters dealt with, and

    (c) each person (if any) through whom the information was supplied from the relevant person to the person mentioned in paragraph (a) received the information in the course of a trade, business, profession or other occupation, or as the holder of a paid or unpaid office.

(3) The persons mentioned in paragraphs (a) and (b) of subsection (2) may be the same person.

(4) The additional requirements of subsection (5) must be satisfied if the statement—

    (a) was prepared for the purposes of pending or contemplated criminal proceedings, or for a criminal investigation, but

    (b) was not obtained pursuant to—

        (i) a request under section 7 of the Crime (International Co-operation) Act 2003,

        (ii) an order under paragraph 6 of Schedule 13 to the Criminal Justice Act 1988, *(or)*

        (iii) an order under Part 2 of the Criminal Justice (European Investigation Order) Regulations 2017, *or*

        (iv) *an overseas production order under the Crime (Overseas Production Orders) Act 2019.*

    (all of which relate to overseas evidence)

(5) The requirements of this subsection are satisfied if—

    (a) any of the five conditions mentioned in section 116(2) is satisfied (absence of relevant person etc), or

    (b) the relevant person cannot reasonably be expected to have any recollection of the matters dealt with in the statement (having regard to the length of time since he supplied the information and all other circumstances).

(6) A statement is not admissible under this section if the court makes a direction to that effect under subsection (7).

(7) The court may make a direction under this subsection if satisfied that the statement's reliability as evidence for the purpose for which it is tendered is doubtful in view of—

    (a) its contents,

    (b) the source of the information contained in it,

(c) the way in which or the circumstances in which the information was supplied or received, or

(d) the way in which or the circumstances in which the document concerned was created or received.

If the Crown seeks to rely on a forensic match on central records, a statement confirming that match does not meet the requirements of s 117. There must also be evidence of the taking of that earlier forensic material from the defendant (*Chester-Nash v CPS* [2000] WL 571246).

A17.3.3 *Common law exceptions*

118 Preservation of certain common law categories of admissibility

(1) The following rules of law are preserved.

Public information etc

(1) Any rule of law under which in criminal proceedings—
   (a) published works dealing with matters of a public nature (such as histories, scientific works, dictionaries and maps) are admissible as evidence of facts of a public nature stated in them,
   (b) public documents (such as public registers, and returns made under public authority with respect to matters of public interest) are admissible as evidence of facts stated in them,
   (c) records (such as the records of certain courts, treaties, Crown grants, pardons and commissions) are admissible as evidence of facts stated in them, or
   (d) evidence relating to a person's age or date or place of birth may be given by a person without personal knowledge of the matter.

Reputation as to character

(2) Any rule of law under which in criminal proceedings evidence of a person's reputation is admissible for the purpose of proving his good or bad character.

[*Note*. The rule is preserved only so far as it allows the court to treat such evidence as proving the matter concerned.]

Reputation or family tradition

(3) Any rule of law under which in criminal proceedings evidence of reputation or family tradition is admissible for the purpose of proving or disproving—
   (a) pedigree or the existence of a marriage,
   (b) the existence of any public or general right, or
   (c) the identity of any person or thing.

[*Note*: The rule is preserved only so far as it allows the court to treat such evidence as proving or disproving the matter concerned.]

Res gestae

(4) Any rule of law under which in criminal proceedings a statement is admissible as evidence of any matter stated if—
   (a) the statement was made by a person so emotionally overpowered by an event that the possibility of concoction or distortion can be disregarded,
   (b) the statement accompanied an act which can be properly evaluated as evidence only if considered in conjunction with the statement, or
   (c) the statement relates to a physical sensation or a mental state (such as intention or emotion).

Confessions etc

(5) Any rule of law relating to the admissibility of confessions or mixed statements in criminal proceedings.

Admissions by agents etc

(6) Any rule of law under which in criminal proceedings—
   (a) an admission made by an agent of a defendant is admissible against the de-
       fendant as evidence of any matter stated, or
   (b) a statement made by a person to whom a defendant refers a person for informa-
       tion is admissible against the defendant as evidence of any matter stated.

Common enterprise

(7) Any rule of law under which in criminal proceedings a statement made by a party to a
common enterprise is admissible against another party to the enterprise as evidence of
any matter stated.

Expert evidence

(8) Any rule of law under which in criminal proceedings an expert witness may draw on
the body of expertise relevant to his field.

(9) With the exception of the rules preserved by this section, the common law rules
governing the admissibility of hearsay evidence in criminal proceedings are
abolished.

No notice was required to admit *res gestae* evidence under s 118(1)(4) CJA
2003. The law was described in *R v Andrews* [1987] AC 281 and the court
had considered whether the complainant was a person so emotionally overpowered that the court could rule out concoction or distortion. In *Barnaby v
DPP* [2015] EWHC 232 (Admin) the magistrates had been correct to admit
the content of three 999 calls and of the first statements by the victim to police
when they arrived six minutes after the calls. This decision was confirmed in
Ibrahim v CPS [2016] EWHC 1750 (Admin) when the district judge found
that the phone call had been made in the immediate aftermath of the assault.
The issue must be answered by considering the circumstances in which the
particular statement is made; because the *res gestae* principle deals with events
that are so unusual, startling, or dramatic as to dominate the thoughts of the
victim so that the utterance was an instinctive reaction to them, giving no real
opportunity for reasoned reflection. The time between the event and the statement is obviously a factor, but there may be special features quite apart from
the time factor that relate to the possibility of concoction or distortion. In
Morgan v DPP [2016] EWHC 3414 (Admin) hearsay evidence was admitted
when an allegation was made an hour after the incident in issue after considering the relevant issues which included:

- the demeanour of the complainant,
- the content of the 999 call,
- the body worn camera film,
- the way the complainant behaved during call and with police,
- the fact that she had remained outside the address for an hour for fear that
  the defendant was still there.

However, *res gestae* may not be used until the court has examined the reason that the witness does not attend the trial (*Wills & Anor v Crown Prosecution Service* [2016] EWHC 3779 (Admin)).

A17.3.4 *Prior statements*

Criminal Justice Act 2003, ss 119 and 120

119 Inconsistent statements

(1) If in criminal proceedings a person gives oral evidence and—
  (a) he admits making a previous inconsistent statement, or
  (b) a previous inconsistent statement made by him is proved by virtue of section 3, 4 or 5 of the Criminal Procedure Act 1865 (c. 18),
  the statement is admissible as evidence of any matter stated of which oral evidence by him would be admissible.
(2) If in criminal proceedings evidence of an inconsistent statement by any person is given under section 124(2)(c), the statement is admissible as evidence of any matter stated in it of which oral evidence by that person would be admissible.

In *Griffiths v CPS* [2018] EWHC 3062 (Admin)), a complainant was treated as a hostile witness and her earlier statements were put to her. In a questionable analysis they were admitted under s 119 CJA 2003. Her retraction statement did not say the earlier statements were untrue. The bench was entitled to have regard to them as representing the truth even though there was no chance for the defence to cross examine her on them. She had made in them admissions against herself which went to their credibility. It is difficult however to find a prior inconsistent statement.

120 Other previous statements of witnesses

(1) This section applies where a person (the witness) is called to give evidence in criminal proceedings.
(2) If a previous statement by the witness is admitted as evidence to rebut a suggestion that his oral evidence has been fabricated, that statement is admissible as evidence of any matter stated of which oral evidence by the witness would be admissible.
(3) A statement made by the witness in a document—
  (a) which is used by him to refresh his memory while giving evidence,
  (b) on which he is cross-examined, and
  (c) which as a consequence is received in evidence in the proceedings, is admissible as evidence of any matter stated of which oral evidence by him would be admissible.
(4) A previous statement by the witness is admissible as evidence of any matter stated of which oral evidence by him would be admissible, if—
  (a) any of the following three conditions is satisfied, and
  (b) while giving evidence the witness indicates that to the best of his belief he made the statement, and that to the best of his belief it states the truth.
(5) The first condition is that the statement identifies or describes a person, object or place.
(6) The second condition is that the statement was made by the witness when the matters stated were fresh in his memory but he does not remember them, and cannot reasonably be expected to remember them, well enough to give oral evidence of them in the proceedings.

(7) The third condition is that—

    (a) the witness claims to be a person against whom an offence has been committed,

    (b) the offence is one to which the proceedings relate,

    (c) the statement consists of a complaint made by the witness (whether to a person in authority or not) about conduct which would, if proved, constitute the offence or part of the offence,

    (d) [repealed]

    (e) the complaint was not made as a result of a threat or a promise, and

    (f) before the statement is adduced the witness gives oral evidence in connection with its subject matter.

(8) For the purposes of subsection (7) the fact that the complaint was elicited (for example, by a leading question) is irrelevant unless a threat or a promise was involved.

139 Use of documents to refresh memory

(1) A person giving oral evidence in criminal proceedings about any matter may, at any stage in the course of doing so, refresh his memory of it from a document made or verified by him at an earlier time if—

    (a) he states in his oral evidence that the document records his recollection of the matter at that earlier time, and

    (b) his recollection of the matter is likely to have been significantly better at that time than it is at the time of his oral evidence.

(2) Where—

    (a) a person giving oral evidence in criminal proceedings about any matter has previously given an oral account, of which a sound recording was made, and he states in that evidence that the account represented his recollection of the matter at that time,

    (b) his recollection of the matter is likely to have been significantly better at the time of the previous account than it is at the time of his oral evidence, and

    (c) a transcript has been made of the sound recording.

Where a person giving evidence seeks to refresh his memory in accordance with s 139 'from a document made or verified by him at an earlier time', verification involves a question of fact as to whether the witness has at an earlier time when the matter was fresh in his mind satisfied himself that the document that he wishes to use as a memory-refresher accurately recorded his recollection of the events in question. Evidence of verification may typically include the witness's signature on the document, but that is simply one form of evidence (*Cummings (Davina) v CPS* [2016] EWHC 3624 (Admin)). Provided there is compliance with s 139, copy documents may be used to refresh memory if the secondary document is likely to be an accurate reflection of the content of the original, provided that the witness verified either the original or the secondary document at a time when his or her recall was better than at the time of giving oral evidence. Whether or not the document becomes evidence in the case, the court will always consider and give appropriate weight to any discrepancy or risk of discrepancy between its content and an original or source document of which it is a copy or from which it is derived (*DPP v Sugden* [2018] EWHC 544 (Admin)).

See *Blackstone's Criminal Practice 2019* **A7.83–A7.86** and **F16**

A18 Identification Evidence

A18.1 *Turnbull* direction: visual identification

In *R v Turnbull* (1976) 63 Cr App R 132, the court laid down the following guidance:

First, whenever the case against an accused depends wholly or substantially on the correctness of one or more identifications of the accused which the defence alleges to be mistaken, the judge should warn the jury of the special need for caution before convicting the accused in reliance on the correctness of the identification or identifications. In addition he should instruct them as to the reason for the need for such a warning and should make some reference to the possibility that a mistaken witness can be a convincing one and that a number of such witnesses can all be mistaken. Provided this is done in clear terms the judge need not use any particular form of words.

Secondly, the judge should direct the jury to examine closely the circumstances in which the identification by each witness came to be made. How long did the witness have the accused under observation? At what distance? In what light? Was the observation impeded in any way, as for example, by passing traffic or a press of people? Had the witness ever seen the accused before? How often? If only occasionally, had he any special reason for remembering the accused? How long elapsed between the original observation and the subsequent identification to the police? Was there any material discrepancy between the description of the accused given to the police by the witness when first seen by them and his actual appearance? If in any case, whether it is being dealt with summarily or on indictment, the prosecution has reason to believe that there is such a material discrepancy it should supply the accused or his legal advisers with particulars of the description the police were first given. In all cases if the accused asks to be given particulars of such descriptions, the prosecution should supply them. Finally, he should remind the jury of any specific weaknesses which had appeared in the identification evidence.

Recognition may be more reliable than identification of a stranger; but even when the witness is purporting to recognise someone whom he knows, the jury should be reminded that mistakes in recognition of close relatives and friends are sometimes made.

All these matters go to the quality of the identification evidence. If the quality is good and remains good at the close of the accused's case, the danger of a mistaken identification is lessened; but the poorer the quality, the greater the danger.

In our judgment when the quality is good as for example when the identification is made after a long period of observation, or in satisfactory conditions by a relative, a neighbour, a close friend, a workmate and the like, the jury can safely be left to assess the value of the identifying evidence even though there is no other evidence to support it: provided always, however, that an adequate warning has been given about the special need for caution.

Were the Courts to adjudge otherwise, affronts to justice would frequently occur. A few examples, taken over the whole spectrum of criminal activity, will illustrate what the effects upon the maintenance of law and order would be if any law were enacted that no person could be convicted on evidence of visual identification alone.

A18.2 Audio identification

For the protections necessary when there is evidence of voice recognition, reference should be made to *Flynn and St John* [2008] EWCA Crim 970. But such evidence may be admitted, with appropriate warnings, when the quality of the recording is good and the length sufficient (*R v Kapikanya (Alick)* [2015] EWCA Crim 1507). In Facebook identification cases, reference should be made to *R v Alexander and McGill* [2012] EWCA Crim 2768.

 See *Blackstone's Criminal Practice 2019* **F19**

A19 Legal Aid

A19.1 Overview

Legal aid is available for criminal proceedings. These are defined by the Legal Aid, Sentencing and Punishment of Offenders Act 2012 as including the following:

> ### Legal Aid, Sentencing and Punishment of Offenders Act 2012, s 14
>
> **14 Criminal proceedings**
>
> In this Part 'criminal proceedings' means—
>
> (a) proceedings before a court for dealing with an individual accused of an offence,
> (b) proceedings before a court for dealing with an individual convicted of an offence, including proceedings in respect of a sentence or order,
> (c) proceedings for dealing with an individual under the Extradition Act 2003,
> (d) proceedings for binding an individual over to keep the peace or to be of good behaviour under section 115 of the Magistrates' Courts Act 1980 and for dealing with an individual who fails to comply with an order under that section,
> (e) proceedings on an appeal brought by an individual under section 44A of the Criminal Appeal Act 1968 (appeal in case of death of appellant),
> (f) proceedings on a reference under section 36 of the Criminal Justice Act 1972 on a point of law following the acquittal of an individual on indictment,
> (g) proceedings for contempt committed, or alleged to have been committed, by an individual in the face of a court, and
> (h) such other proceedings, before any court, tribunal or other person, as may be prescribed.

The proceedings referred to in s 14(h) are set out at reg 9 of the Criminal Legal Aid (General) Regulations 2013 (SI 2013/9):

> ### Criminal Legal Aid (General) Regulations 2013, reg 9
>
> **Criminal proceedings**
>
> 9. The following proceedings are criminal proceedings for the purposes of section 14(h) of the Act (criminal proceedings)—
>
> (a) civil proceedings in a magistrates' court arising from a failure to pay a sum due or to obey an order of that court where such failure carries the risk of imprisonment;
> (b) proceedings under sections 14B, 14D, 14G, 14H, 21B and 21D of the Football Spectators Act 1989 in relation to banning orders and references to a court;
> (c) proceedings under section 5A of the Protection from Harassment Act 1997 in relation to restraining orders on acquittal;
> ...
> (f) proceedings in relation to parenting orders made under section 8(1)(b) of the Crime and Disorder Act 1998(1) where an order under section 22 of the Antisocial Behaviour, Crime and Policing Act 2014 or a sexual harm prevention order under section 103A of the Sexual Offences Act 2003 is made;

(g) proceedings under section 8(1)(c) of the Crime and Disorder Act 1998 in relation to parenting orders made on the conviction of a child;

(h) proceedings under section 9(5) of the Crime and Disorder Act 1998 to discharge or vary a parenting order made as set out in sub-paragraph (f) or (g);

(i) proceedings under section 10 of the Crime and Disorder Act 1998 in relation to an appeal against a parenting order made as set out in sub-paragraph (f) or (g);

(j) proceedings under Part 1A of Schedule 1 to the Powers of Criminal Courts (Sentencing) Act 2000 in relation to parenting orders for failure to comply with orders under section 20 of that Act;

(ja) proceedings in a youth court (or on appeal from such a court) in relation to the breach or potential breach of a provision of an injunction under Part 1 of the Anti-social Behaviour, Crime and Policing Act 2014 where the person who is subject to the injunction is aged under 14;

(k) proceedings under sections 80, 82, 83 and 84 of the Anti-social Behaviour, Crime and Policing Act 2014 in relation to closure orders made under section 80(5)(a) of that Act where a person has engaged in, or is likely to engage in behaviour that constitutes a criminal offence on the premises;

(ka) proceedings under paragraph 3 of Schedule 2 to the Female Genital Mutilation Act 2003 in relation to female genital mutilation protection orders made other than on conviction and related appeals;

(kb) proceedings under paragraph 6 of Schedule 2 to the Female Genital Mutilation Act 2003 in relation to female genital mutilation protection orders made under paragraph 3 of that Schedule;

(l) proceedings under sections 20, 22, 26 and 28 of the Anti-social Behaviour Act 2003 in relation to parenting orders—
  (i) in cases of exclusion from school; or
  (ii) in respect of criminal conduct and anti-social behaviour;

(m) proceedings under sections 97, 100 and 101 of the Sexual Offences Act 2003 in relation to notification orders and interim notification orders;

(n) proceedings under sections 103A, 103E, 103F and 103H of the Sexual Offences Act 2003 in relation to sexual harm prevention orders;

...

(p) proceedings under sections 122A, 122D, 122E and 122G of the Sexual Offences Act 2003 in relation to sexual risk orders;

...

(r) proceedings under section 13 of the Tribunals, Courts and Enforcement Act 2007 on appeal against a decision of the Upper Tribunal in proceedings in respect of—
  (i) a decision of the Financial Conduct Authority
  (ia) a decision of the Prudential Regulation Authority;
  (ii) a decision of the Bank of England; or
  (iii) a decision of a person in relation to the assessment of any compensation or consideration under the Banking (Special Provisions) Act 2008 or the Banking Act 2009;

(s) proceedings before the Crown Court or the Court of Appeal in relation to serious crime prevention orders under sections 19, 20, 21 and 24 of the Serious Crime Act 2007;

(t) proceedings under sections 100, 101, 103, 104 and 106 of the Criminal Justice and Immigration Act 2008 in relation to violent offender orders and interim violent offender orders;

(u) proceedings under sections 26, 27 and 29 of the Crime and Security Act 2010 in relation to—

(i)   domestic violence protection notices; or

(ii) domestic violence protection orders;

(ua) proceedings under sections 14(1)(b) and (c), 15 and 20 to 22 of the Modern Slavery Act 2015 in relation to slavery and trafficking prevention orders;

(ub) proceedings under sections 23 and 27 to 29 of the Modern Slavery Act 2015 in relation to slavery and trafficking risk orders;

(uc) *proceedings under Part 2 of the Offensive Weapons Act 2019 in relation to a knife crime prevention order or an interim knife crime prevention order;*

and

(v) any other proceedings that involve the determination of a criminal charge for the purposes of Article 6(1) of the European Convention on Human Rights.

This provision (v) includes proceedings for contempt other than in the face of the court in the High Court. Legal aid is subject to a merits test, and means assessment in some cases. There is no means assessment:

- for those under 18 years;
- for those in receipt of income support;
- for those in receipt of income-based employment and support allowance (ESA);
- for those in receipt of income-based job-seeker's allowance (JSA);
- for those in receipt of guaranteed state pension credit; or
- for those in receipt of Universal Credit.

Legal aid extends automatically to the Crown Court if the case is committed for sentence (note that there is no additional contribution payable in respect of these Crown Court proceedings).

Legal aid automatically extends, without a merits test, to any case sent to the Crown Court, but proceedings in the Crown Court are subject to a means test. A contribution may then be required or legal aid be refused.

Appeals to the Crown Court require a fresh legal aid application to be lodged, and are subject to interests of justice and means criteria. A contribution may be payable in the Crown Court, dependent on means, or legal aid be refused.

A19.2 The interests of justice test

When assessing whether the grant of representation is in the interests of justice, regard should be had to the provisions of s 17(2) Legal Aid, Sentencing and Punishment of Offenders Act 2012 (the *Widgery* criteria). The defendant must be able to demonstrate one or more of the following:

- It is likely that I will lose my liberty.
- I have been given a sentence that is suspended or non-custodial. If I break this, the court may be able to deal with me for the original offence.
- It is likely that I will lose my livelihood.
- It is likely that I will suffer serious damage to my reputation.
- A substantial question of law may be involved.
- I may not be able to understand the court proceedings or present my own case.
- I may need witnesses to be traced or interviewed on my behalf.

- The proceedings may involve expert cross-examination of a prosecution witness.
- It is in the interests of another person that I am represented.
- Any other reasons.

Refusal on the basis of the interests of justice test can be appealed to justices or an officer of the Crown Court (Criminal Legal Aid (General) Regulations 2013 (SI 2013/9), regs 29 and 30), and regard should be had to the following:

- the likely penalty, not the theoretical maximum: *R v Highgate Justices, ex p Lewis* [1977] Crim LR 611. Where a defendant has received many prison sentences for identical offending it is irrational to refuse legal aid as it is likely that they will lose their livelihood (*R (David Sonn) v West London Magistrates' Court* [2000] CLW 40/13);
- in *R (Punatar) v Horseferry Road Magistrates' Court* [2002] EWHC 1196 (Admin), the solicitor attended court to defend an imprisonable matter and submitted an application for representation at the end of those proceedings. At that stage the imprisonable matter had been replaced by a non-imprisonable one and legal aid was refused. The court held that the refusal was wrong in law; the court should not apply hindsight but instead look at what had been in the mind of the solicitor when he made the decision to attend court;
- a 16-year-old would not have the skills to cross-examine a police officer effectively: *Scunthorpe Justices, ex p S*, The Times, 5 March 1998;
- in *R (GKR Law Solicitors) v Liverpool Magistrates' Court* [2008] EWHC 2974 (Admin), the court held that it was appropriate to grant representation to a defendant in relation to a special reasons hearing, where a witness in the case was the defendant's 12-year-old son. The child was a witness entitled to and requiring special measures, and consideration would need to be given to video-interviewing the young witness in order to ensure best evidence was given; such measures would be outside the competence and resources of the defendant;
- in *R v Chester Magistrates' Court, ex p Ball* (1999) 163 JP 757, it was said that any defendant of previous good character pleading not guilty to a charge equal to, or more significant than, s 5 Public Order Act 1986 in terms of nature and seriousness, should be granted legal aid regardless of his social or professional standing. This is very unlikely to include non-imprisonable road traffic or regulatory offences;
- in *R v Gravesend Magistrates' Court ex p Baker* [1977] 161 JP 765 the defendant was charged with driving with excess alcohol and put forward special reasons based on spiked drinks. The court held that the applicant should be granted legal aid because a scientific expert would be required and the assistance of a solicitor would be necessary to identify witnesses, to take proper proofs, and to extract the defence in the witness box.

A19.3 Transfer of representation

The law is contained in reg 14 Criminal Legal Aid (Determinations by a Court and Choice of Representative) Regulations 2013 (SI 2013/614):

Criminal Legal Aid (Determinations by a Court and Choice of Representative) Regulations 2013, reg 14

Change of provider

14 (1) Subject to paragraph (2), where an individual has selected a provider in criminal proceedings, the right conferred by section 27(4) of the Act does not include a right to select a provider in place of the original provider.

(1) The relevant court may determine that the individual can select a provider in place of the original provider in the circumstances set out in paragraphs (3) or (4).

(2) The circumstances are that the relevant court determines that—

    (a) there has been a breakdown in the relationship between the individual and the original provider such that effective representation can no longer be provided by the original provider; or

    (b) there is some other compelling reason why effective representation can no longer be provided by the original provider.

(3) The circumstances are that the relevant court determines that—

    (a) the original provider—

        (i) considers there to be a duty to withdraw from the case in accordance with the provider's professional rules of conduct; or

        (ii) is no longer able to represent the individual through circumstances outside the provider's control; and

    (b) the original provider has supplied the relevant court with details as to—

        (i) the nature of any such duty to withdraw from the case; or

        (ii) the particular circumstances that render the provider unable to represent the individual.

Solicitors seeking a transfer must exercise a proper and independent judgment when considering whether the supplicant's grounds were justified: *R (Sanjari) v Birmingham CC* 2015 EWHC 2037 (Admin).

Part 46 of the Criminal Procedure Rules provides the relevant procedure.

 See *Blackstone's Criminal Practice 2019* **D32**

A20 **Mental Disorder**

A20.1 **Fitness to plead**

In a strict legal sense the issue of fitness to plead does not arise in the magistrates' court as the relevant legislation does not provide for any summary procedures.

If the offence is an either-way offence the court may decline jurisdiction, but the defendant will not be able to consent to summary trial. However, if the accused is being tried for an imprisonable offence, and it is shown that the accused did the act or made the omission charged, *Lincoln (Kesteven) Justices, ex p O'Connor* [1983] 1 WLR 335 confirms that he can be made subject to a hospital order under s 37(3) Mental Health Act 1983.

Subject to having obtained two satisfactory reports, and the court can remand under s 35 Mental Health Act 1983 for that purpose, the court can then go on to make a hospital order under s 37(3). The stages are:

- raise issue of mental disorder;
- prove that the accused did the act or made the omission charged;
- obtain requisite medical assessment;
- make hospital order.

The prosecution will be required to prove only the *actus reus* of the offence (*R v Antoine* [2000] 2 All ER 208, HL). If the prosecution cannot prove the act or omission, the defendant must be discharged.

In the alternative, if the Crown will not follow that route, the defendant can plead not guilty and put the Crown to proof of the mental element.

The procedure under s 37(3) Mental Health Act 1983 is not available for indictable-only offences.

A20.2 **Fitness to stand trial**

If the defendant does not require a hospital/guardianship order under s 37(3) and suffers from mental disorder or some other significant impairment of intelligence, he may be able to participate in criminal proceedings if necessary with adaptations to the trial process tailored to suit his particular needs; see Criminal Practice Direction 3D–3F (**A10.10** and **A27**), including the use of an intermediary. However, if the defendant's illness or disability is so severe that he will be unable to participate in any way in his trial, then the Crown Prosecution Service (CPS) should be invited to consider discontinuing the proceedings, or the court could stay the proceedings on the grounds of an abuse of process, or of its own volition adjourn the case *sine die*.

A20.3 **Insanity**

Loake v CPS [2017] EWHC 2855 (Admin) confirms that insanity is available as a defence to all offences in the magistrates' court, because the M'Naghten Rules are not limited to *mens rea* but recognize the principle that criminal punishment should be imposed only upon those who are responsible for their actions (he does not know what he is doing is wrong, ie conduct being contrary to law). However the defendant does not have an absolute right to have the issue determined at trial if the court feels that a disposal under s 37(3) Mental Health Act 1983 might be more appropriate. There is no 'special verdict' of not guilty by reason of insanity; a finding of insanity prevents conviction (*R (Singh) v Stratford Magistrates' Court* [2007] EWHC 1582 (Admin)).

A20.4 Medical reports

In order to decide whether the person should be tried or made subject to the fitness to plead procedure, the court may need to consider the report of a medical practitioner, and a remand to hospital under s 11 Powers of Criminal Courts (Sentencing) Act 2000 may be ordered. The appropriate procedures and requirements are set out in the Criminal Procedure Rules (Crim PR) Rule 3.28. Procedures at the sentencing stage are set out at Crim PR 28.8. Solicitors may choose to commission their own expert to preserve client privilege.

Powers of Criminal Courts (Sentencing) Act 2000, s 11

11 Remand by magistrates' court for medical examination

(1) If, on the trial by a magistrates' court of an offence punishable on summary conviction with imprisonment, the court—
  (a) is satisfied that the accused did the act or made the omission charged, but
  (b) is of the opinion that an inquiry ought to be made into his physical or mental condition before the method of dealing with him is determined,
  the court shall adjourn the case to enable a medical examination and report to be made, and shall remand him.
(2) An adjournment under subsection (1) above shall not be for more than three weeks at a time where the court remands the accused in custody, nor for more than four weeks at a time where it remands him on bail.
(3) Where on an adjournment under subsection (1) above the accused is remanded on bail, the court shall impose conditions under paragraph (d) of section 3(6) of the Bail Act 1976 and the requirements imposed as conditions under that paragraph shall be or shall include requirements that the accused—
  (a) undergo medical examination by a registered medical practitioner or, where the inquiry is into his mental condition and the court so directs, two such practitioners; and
  (b) for that purpose attend such an institution or place, or on such practitioner, as the court directs and, where the inquiry is into his mental condition, comply with any other directions which may be given to him for that purpose by any person specified by the court or by a person of any class so specified.

A20.5 Legal aid

The Legal Aid Agency's (LAA) criminal legal aid manual confirms:

Criminal Legal Aid Manual, paras 3.5.6 and 3.5.7

3.5.6 Signing the form

For audit purposes and *with the exception of applicants with severe mental health problems,* the applicant must sign the application form in all cases.

3.5.7 Applicants with mental health problems

There are some applicants who, because of mental health problems, are unable to give instructions to their solicitor, to understand the declaration on the CRM14 & CRM15 and/or are unable to sign the application form. It is likely that these applicants will be detained under the Mental Health Act or will be being kept under medical supervision.

Where the applicant lacks capacity, within the meaning of the Mental Capacity Act 2005, to instruct a solicitor as their representative and to sign the declaration on the CRM14 and CRM15, the LAA's contract does allow the solicitor to get someone else to sign the application on the applicant's behalf.

The application form may be signed by

- The applicant's attorney or deputy appointed under the Mental Capacity Act 2005
- The applicant's nearest relative or guardian
- A person acting as a Litigation friend
- Any other person who is acting in the applicant's best interest and who has sufficient knowledge of the applicant's financial affairs to be able to sign the declaration on the applicant's behalf

The solicitor or any other member, employee or associate of the solicitor's firm cannot sign the form.

In addition to the signature, the third party must also be in a position to provide details of the applicant's finances or the application form will be rejected ... Solicitors should record in the 'Further Information' section of the application form where someone other than the applicant has signed the form, explaining why this was necessary. The person signing on the applicant's behalf must also print their name and state their relationship to the applicant.

In cases where the applicant does not have sufficient capacity to instruct a solicitor, is unwilling or physically unable to sign the declaration on the CRM14 and CRM15 forms themselves and there is no one available to sign on the applicant's behalf, then special circumstances may apply. We recognise the difficulties faced by the solicitor in obtaining information in these circumstances. A solicitor who wishes to act for the client in this situation should refer the application (as far as it can be completed) to the National Crime Team (NCT) for consideration. The NCT will work with you to build a picture of the applicant's circumstances and assess the level of risk the client presents.

Please note: Legal Advisers and Judges do not have the authority to accept unsigned forms for applicants in these circumstances,

A20.6 Force in mental health units

Under the Mental Health Units (Use of Force) Act 2018 a police officer who assists staff must wear and have operational body worn video. A failure goes to the admissibility of evidence.

A20.7 Diversion

The Code for Crown Prosecutors indicates that, in applying the public interest test, prosecutors should also have regard when considering culpability as to whether the suspect is, or was at the time of the offence, suffering from any significant mental or physical ill-health as in some circumstances this may mean that it is less likely that a prosecution is required. However, prosecutors will also need to consider how serious the offence was, whether it is likely to be repeated, and the need to safeguard the public or those providing care to such persons.

In legal guidance, presently under review, on mentally disordered offenders the following principle is set out:

The CPS uses the term 'mentally disordered offender' to describe a person who has a disability or disorder of the mind and has committed or is suspected of committing a criminal offence. This term covers a range of offences, disabilities, and disorders. A mental disorder may be relevant to:

- the decision to prosecute or divert;
- fitness to plead; and
- sentencing/disposal.

Each case must be considered on its merits, taking into account all available information about any mental health problem, and its relevance to the offence, in addition to the principles set out in the Code for Crown Prosecutors. The Code explains that there is a balance to be struck between the public interest in diverting a defendant with significant mental illness from the criminal justice system and other public interest factors in favour of prosecution including the need to safeguard the public.

If there is significant evidence to establish that a defendant or suspect has a significant mental illness, a prosecution may not be appropriate unless the offence is serious or there is a real possibility that it may be repeated.

If proceedings have been started or are being considered and the CPS is provided with a medical report which states that the strain of criminal proceedings may lead to a considerable worsening of the defendant's mental health, the implications of the report should be considered very carefully.

This is a difficult field because in some cases the defendant may have become disturbed and depressed by the mere fact that his or her conduct has been discovered, and any suggestions that continuing the criminal proceedings will significantly worsen the defendant's condition should be evaluated carefully. In serious cases where a prosecution is plainly needed unless there is clear evidence that continuing the case would be likely to result in a permanent deterioration in the defendant's condition, it may be appropriate to obtain an independent medical report. Where the prosecutor is satisfied that the probable effect on the defendant's health outweighs the public interest considerations in favour of a prosecution, the case should be discontinued and full reasons recorded on the file.

See *Blackstone's Criminal Practice 2019* **D20.72** and **E22**

A21 **Misbehaviour at Court**

A21.1 **Misbehaviour during allocation and summary trial**

Section 18(3) Magistrates' Courts Act 1980 provides:

Magistrates' Courts Act 1980, s 18(3)

18 Initial procedure on information against adult for offence triable either way

...

(3) The court may proceed in the absence of the accused in accordance with such of the provisions of sections 19 to 22 below as are applicable in the circumstances if the court considers that by reason of his disorderly conduct before the court it is not practicable for the proceedings to be conducted in his presence; and subsections (3) to (5) of section 23 below, so far as applicable, shall have effect in relation to proceedings conducted in the absence of the accused by virtue of this subsection (references in those subsections to the person representing the accused being for this purpose read as references to the person, if any, representing him).

...

A similar power exists in relation to youths by reason of s 24B(1) Magistrates' Courts Act 1980.

A21.2 **Contempt of Court Act 1981**

Section 12 Contempt of Court Act 1981 provides:

Contempt of Court Act 1981, s 12

12 Offences of contempt of magistrates' courts

(1) A magistrates' court has jurisdiction under this section to deal with any person who—
  (a) willfully insults the justice or justices, any witness before or officer of the court or any solicitor or counsel having business in the court, during his or their sitting or attendance in court or in going to or returning from the court; or
  (b) willfully interrupts the proceedings of the court or otherwise misbehaves in court.

(2) In any such case the court may order any officer of the court, or any constable, to take the offender into custody and detain him until the rising of the court; and the court may, if it thinks fit, commit the offender to custody for a specified period not exceeding one month or impose on him a fine not exceeding £2,500, or both.

(2A) A fine imposed under subsection (2) above shall be deemed, for the purposes of any enactment, to be a sum adjudged to be paid by a conviction.

(3) A magistrates' court may at any time revoke an order of committal made under subsection (2) and, if the offender is in custody, order his discharge.

(4) Section 135 of the Powers of Criminal Courts (Sentencing) Act 2000 (limit on fines in respect of young persons) and the following provisions of the Magistrates'

Courts Act 1980 apply in relation to an order under this section as they apply in relation to a sentence on conviction or finding of guilty of an offence; and those provisions of the Magistrates' Courts Act 1980 are section 36 (restriction on fines in respect of young persons); sections 75 to 91 (enforcement); section 108 (appeal to Crown Court); section 136 (overnight detention in default of payment); and section 142(1) (power to rectify mistakes).

It should be noted that there is no power to adjourn, and the matter must be dealt with before the end of the court day. There will be few cases that cannot be handled adequately by a suitable apology. See also Part 48 of the Criminal Procedure Rules.

Essential procedures, before any court considers a committal application, were set out in *Re L (a child); Re Oddin* [2016] EWCA Civ 173, including:

- there is complete clarity at the outset as to precisely what the foundation of the alleged contempt is;
- consideration is given to the question of whether the judge hearing the committal application should do so, or whether it should be heard by another judge;
- the accused has been given the opportunity to secure legal representation;
- that the standard of proof applied is the criminal standard; and
- any committal order sets out what the findings are that establish the contempt.

For procedures where the contempt is not in the face of the court see *R v Yaxley-Lennon* [2018] EWCA Crim 1356.

 See *Blackstone's Criminal Practice 2019* **B14.79–B14.128**

A22 Presence of Defendant in Court

A22.1 General principles

If a defendant has been bailed to attend court, his presence is mandatory unless and until it is excused by the court. Where a defendant on bail fails to appear, a warrant may be issued for his arrest. However, various exceptions apply.

Statutory provisions are contained in s 129 Magistrates' Court Act (MCA) 1980:

Magistrates' Court Act 1980, s 129

129 Further remand

(1) If a magistrates' court is satisfied that any person who has been remanded is unable by reason of illness or accident to appear or be brought before the court at the expiration of the period for which he was remanded, the court may, in his absence, remand him for a further time; and section 128(6) above shall not apply.

(2) Notwithstanding anything in section 128(1) above, the power of a court under subsection (1) above to remand a person on bail for a further time—

  (a) where he was granted bail in criminal proceedings, includes power to enlarge the recognizance of any surety for him to a later time;

(3) Where a person remanded on bail is bound to appear before a magistrates' court at any time and the court has no power to remand him under subsection (1) above, the court may in his absence—

  (a) where he was granted bail in criminal proceedings, appoint a later time as the time at which he is to appear and enlarge the recognizances of any sureties for him to that time;

  and the appointment of the time or the enlargement of his recognizance shall be deemed to be a further remand.

(4) Where a magistrates' court sends a person to the Crown Court for trial on bail and the recognizance of any surety for him has been conditioned in accordance with paragraph (a) of subsection (4) of section 128 above, the court may, in the absence of the surety, enlarge his recognizance so that he is bound to secure that the person so sent for trial appears also before the Crown Court.

On summons and certain other matters, the defendant may be represented by a legal representative.

Section 122 MCA 1980 provides:

Magistrates' Courts Act 1980, s 122

122 Appearance by counsel or solicitor

(1) A party to any proceedings before a magistrates' court may be represented by a legal representative.

(2) Subject to subsection (3) below, an absent party so represented shall be deemed not to be absent.

(3) Appearance of a party by legal representative shall not satisfy any provision of any enactment or any condition of a recognizance expressly requiring his presence.

Section 122(2) does not apply to a hearing at which a defendant is sent to the Crown Court. A personal attendance, but no contribution from the defendant, is required (*R (Lord Janner) v Westminster Magistrates' Court* [2015] EWHC 2578). For allocation hearings see **A4.2**. The defendant must personally enter the plea to an either-way offence.

A22.2 Defendants in custody

A further remand of a defendant in custody can be ordered if there is illness or accident in accordance with s 129 MCA 1980. There is no limit to the length of a remand under this provision.

However, further powers exist in s 128.

Magistrates Courts Act 1980, s 128

128(3A)

Subject to subsection (3B) below, where a person has been remanded in custody and the remand was not a remand under section 128A below for a period exceeding 8 clear days, the court may further remand him (otherwise than in the exercise of the power conferred by that section) on an adjournment under section 5, 10(1) 17C or 18(4) above without his being brought before it if it is satisfied—

(a) that he gave his consent, either in response to a question under subsection (1C) above or otherwise, to the hearing and determination in his absence of any application for his remand on an adjournment of the case under any of those provisions; and

(b) that he has not by virtue of this subsection been remanded without being brought before the court on more than two such applications immediately preceding the application which the court is hearing; and

...

(d) that he has not withdrawn his consent to their being so heard and determined.

(3B) The court may not exercise the power conferred by subsection (3A) above if it appears to the court, on an application for a further remand being made to it, that the person to whom the application relates has no legal representative acting for him in the case (whether present in court or not).

(3C) Where—

(a) a person has been remanded in custody on an adjournment of a case under section 5, 10(1) 17C or 18(4) above; and

(b) an application is subsequently made for his further remand on such an adjournment; and

(c) he is not brought before the court which hears and determines the application; and

(d) that court is not satisfied as mentioned in subsection (3A) above,

the court shall adjourn the case and remand him in custody for the period for which it stands adjourned.

(3D) An adjournment under subsection (3C) above shall be for the shortest period that appears to the court to make it possible for the accused to be brought before it.

(3E) Where—

(a) on an adjournment of a case under section 5, 10(1) 17C or 18(4) above a person has been remanded in custody without being brought before the court; and

(b) it subsequently appears—
    (i) to the court which remanded him in custody; or
    (ii) to an alternate magistrates' court to which he is remanded under section 130 below, that he ought not to have been remanded in custody in his absence, the court shall require him to be brought before it at the earliest time that appears to the court to be possible.

A22.3 Defendant's presence at trial

Section 11 MCA 1980 details the court's powers when a defendant does not appear for trial:

Magistrates' Courts Act 1980, s 11

11 Non-appearance of accused: general provisions

(1) Subject to the provisions of this Act, where at the time and place appointed for the trial or adjourned trial of an information the prosecutor appears but the accused does not—
    (a) if the accused is under 18 years of age, the court may proceed in his absence; and
    (b) if the accused has attained the age of 18 years, the court shall proceed in his absence unless it appears to the court to be contrary to the interests of justice to do so.
    This is subject to subsections (2), (2A), (3) and (4).

(2) Where a summons has been issued, the court shall not begin to try the information in the absence of the accused unless either it is proved to the satisfaction of the court, on oath or in such other manner as may be prescribed, that the summons was served on the accused within what appears to the court to be a reasonable time before the trial or adjourned trial or the accused has appeared on a previous occasion to answer to the information.

(2A) The court shall not proceed in the absence of the accused if it considers that there is an acceptable reason for his failure to appear.

(3) In proceedings to which this subsection applies, the court shall not in a person's absence sentence him to imprisonment or detention in a detention centre or make a detention and training order or an order under paragraph 8(2)(a) or (b) of Schedule 12 to the Criminal Justice Act 2003 that a suspended sentence passed on him shall take effect.

(3A) But where a sentence or order of a kind mentioned in subsection (3) is imposed or given in the absence of the offender, the offender must be brought before the court before being taken to a prison or other institution to begin serving his sentence (and the sentence or order is not to be regarded as taking effect until he is brought before the court).

(4) In proceedings to which this subsection applies, the court shall not in a person's absence impose any disqualification on him, except on resumption of the hearing after an adjournment under section 10(3) above; and where a trial is adjourned in pursuance of this subsection the notice required by section 10(2) above shall include notice of the reason for the adjournment ...

In deciding whether or not to proceed in the defendant's absence, the court has to have regard to the following principles (*R v Jones and others* [2002] UKHL 5; *Shirzadeh v Maidstone Magistrates' Court* [2003] EWHC 2216 (Admin)):

- the nature and circumstances of the defendant's behaviour in absenting himself from the trial or disrupting it, as the case may be, and in particular, whether his behaviour was deliberate, voluntary, and such as plainly waived his right to appear;
- (in the case of a defendant aged under 18 years) whether an adjournment might result in the defendant being caught or attending voluntarily and/or not disrupting the proceedings;
- (in the case of a defendant aged under 18 years) the likely length of such an adjournment;
- whether the defendant, though absent, is, or wishes to be, legally represented at the trial or has, by his conduct, waived his right to representation;
- whether an absent defendant's legal representatives are able to receive instructions from him during the trial and the extent to which they are able to present his defence (*Note*: it is a matter for the professional judgment of the advocate whether they should continue to represent the absent defendant (*R v Ulcay* [2007] EWCA Crim 2379));
- the extent of the disadvantage to the defendant in not being able to give his account of events, having regard to the nature of the evidence against him;
- the risk of the jury reaching an improper conclusion about the absence of the defendant;
- the seriousness of the offence, which affects defendant, victim, and public;
- the general public interest and the particular interest of victims and witnesses that a trial should take place within a reasonable time of the events to which it relates;
- the effect of delay on the memories of witnesses;
- where there is more than one defendant and not all have absconded, the undesirability of separate trials, and the prospects of a fair trial for the defendant(s) who are present.

The court in *Shirzadeh* identified four additional factors relevant to trial in the magistrates' court:

> [first] that there ought to be less risk from either a trained lay justice or a district judge in drawing an impermissible inference from a defendant's absence; secondly, in a magistrates' court the finder of fact may ask its own questions and test the evidence of prosecution witnesses; thirdly, a defendant in summary proceedings can apply to set aside any resulting conviction under section 142 of the Magistrates' Courts Act 1980; and fourthly, a defendant in summary proceedings has an automatic right of appeal to the Crown Court.

The decision to try a person in his absence must be exercised with great care and only in cases such as where the absence was a deliberate absconding (*R (Drinkwater) v Solihull Magistrates' Court* [2012] EWHC 765 (Admin)). (See also case law in **A2**.)

A22.4 Statutory declarations

Where a defendant is convicted in absence, having not known of the summons or proceedings, including within a single justice procedure, he may apply to the court for the conviction to be set aside. Section 14 MCA 1980 provides:

Magistrates' Courts Act 1980, s 14

14 Proceedings invalid where accused did not know of them

(1) Where a summons has been issued under section 1 above and a magistrates' court has begun to try the information to which the summons relates, then, if—

    (a) the accused, at any time during or after the trial, makes a statutory declaration that he did not know of the summons or the proceedings until a date specified in the declaration, being a date after the court has begun to try the information; and

    (b) within 21 days of that date the declaration is served on the designated officer for the court, without prejudice to the validity of the information,

the summons and all subsequent proceedings shall be void.

(2) For the purposes of subsection (1) above a statutory declaration shall be deemed to be duly served on the designated officer if it is delivered to him, or left at his office, or is sent in a registered letter or by the recorded delivery service addressed to him at his office.

(3) If on the application of the accused it appears to a magistrates' court (which for this purpose may be composed of a single justice) that it was not reasonable to expect the accused to serve such a statutory declaration as is mentioned in subsection (1) above within the period allowed by that subsection, the court may accept service of such a declaration by the accused after that period has expired; and a statutory declaration accepted under this subsection shall be deemed to have been served as required by that subsection.

(4) Where any proceedings have become void by virtue of subsection (1) above, the information shall not be tried again by any of the same justices.

The procedure is provided for by Criminal Procedure Rule 24.17.

See *Blackstone's Criminal Practice 2019* **D22**

A23 Pre-Charge Hearings

A23.1 Funding

Advocacy assistance, without a means test, is available for all the hearings in this section.

A23.2 Warrants of further detention and extended warrants of further detention

Police and Criminal Evidence Act 1984, ss 43 and 44

43

(1) Where, on an application on oath made by a constable and supported by an information, a magistrates' court is satisfied that there are reasonable grounds for believing that the further detention of the person to whom the application relates is justified, it may issue a warrant of further detention authorising the keeping of that person in police detention.

(2) A court may not hear an application for a warrant of further detention unless the person to whom the application relates—
   (a) has been furnished with a copy of the information; and
   (b) has been brought before the court for the hearing...
   ...

(4) A person's further detention is only justified for the purposes of this section or section 44 below if—
   (a) his detention without charge is necessary to secure or preserve evidence relating to an offence for which he is under arrest or to obtain such evidence by questioning him;
   (b) an offence for which he is under arrest is an indictable offence; and
   (c) the investigation is being conducted diligently and expeditiously.

(5) Subject to subsection (7) below, an application for a warrant of further detention may be made—
   (a) at any time before the expiry of 36 hours after the relevant time; or
   (b) in a case where—
      (i) it is not practicable for the magistrates' court to which the application will be made to sit at the expiry of 36 hours after the relevant time; but
      (ii) the court will sit during the 6 hours following the end of that period, at any time before the expiry of the said 6 hours...

(7) If—
   (a) an application for a warrant of further detention is made after the expiry of 36 hours after the relevant time; and
   (b) it appears to the magistrates' court that it would have been reasonable for the police to make it before the expiry of that period,
   the court shall dismiss the application.

(8) Where on an application such as is mentioned in subsection (1) above a magistrates' court is not satisfied that there are reasonable grounds for believing that the further detention of the person to whom the application relates is justified, it shall be its duty—

(a) to refuse the application; or

(b) to adjourn the hearing of it until a time not later than 36 hours after the relevant time.

(9) The person to whom the application relates may be kept in police detention during the adjournment.

(10) A warrant of further detention shall—

(a) state the time at which it is issued;

(b) authorise the keeping in police detention of the person to whom it relates for the period stated in it.

(11) Subject to subsection (12) below, the period stated in a warrant of further detention shall be such period as the magistrates' court thinks fit, having regard to the evidence before it.

(12) The period shall not be longer than 36 hours.

(13) If it is proposed to transfer a person in police detention to a police area other than that in which he is detained when the application for a warrant of further detention is made, the court hearing the application shall have regard to the distance and the time the journey would take.

(14) Any information submitted in support of an application under this section shall state—

(a) the nature of the offence for which the person to whom the application relates has been arrested;

(b) the general nature of the evidence on which that person was arrested;

(c) what inquiries relating to the offence have been made by the police and what further inquiries are proposed by them;

(d) the reasons for believing the continued detention of that person to be necessary for the purposes of such further inquiries.

(15) Where an application under this section is refused, the person to whom the application relates shall forthwith be charged or, subject to subsection (16) below, released, either on bail or without bail.

(16) A person need not be released under subsection (15) above—

(a) before the expiry of 24 hours after the relevant time; or

(b) before the expiry of any longer period for which his continued detention is or has been authorised under section 42 above.

(17) Where an application under this section is refused, no further application shall be made under this section in respect of the person to whom the refusal relates, unless supported by evidence which has come to light since the refusal.

44 Extension of warrants of further detention

(1) On an application on oath made by a constable and supported by an information a magistrates' court may extend a warrant of further detention issued under section 43 above if it is satisfied that there are reasonable grounds for believing that the further detention of the person to whom the application relates is justified.

(2) Subject to subsection (3) below, the period for which a warrant of further detention may be extended shall be such period as the court thinks fit, having regard to the evidence before it.

(3) The period shall not—

(a) be longer than 36 hours; or

(b) end later than 96 hours after the relevant time.

(4) Where a warrant of further detention has been extended under subsection (1) above, or further extended under this subsection, for a period ending before 96 hours after the relevant time, on an application such as is mentioned in that subsection a magistrates' court may further extend the warrant if it is satisfied as there mentioned; and subsections (2) and (3) above apply to such further extensions as they apply to extensions under subsection (1) above.

(5) A warrant of further detention shall, if extended or further extended under this section, be endorsed with a note of the period of the extension.

(6) Subsections (2), (3) and (14) of section 43 above shall apply to an application made under this section as they apply to an application made under that section.

(7) Where an application under this section is refused, the person to whom the application relates shall forthwith be charged or, subject to subsection (8) below, released, either on bail or without bail.

(8) A person need not be released under subsection (7) above before the expiry of any period for which a warrant of further detention issued in relation to him has been extended or further extended on an earlier application made under this section.

A23.3 Warrants of further detention and extensions in terrorist cases

Terrorism Act 2000, s 41

41 Arrest without warrant

(1) A constable may arrest without a warrant a person whom he reasonably suspects to be a terrorist.

(2) Where a person is arrested under this section the provisions of Schedule 8 (detention: treatment, review and extension) shall apply.

(3) Subject to subsections (4) to (7), a person detained under this section shall (unless detained under any other power) be released not later than the end of the period of 48 hours beginning—.

(a) with the time of his arrest under this section, or
(b) if he was being detained under Schedule 7 when he was arrested under this section, with the time when his examination under that Schedule began.

(4) If on a review of a person's detention under Part II of Schedule 8 the review officer does not authorise continued detention, the person shall (unless detained in accordance with subsection (5) or (6) or under any other power) be released.

(5) Where a police officer intends to make an application for a warrant under paragraph 29 of Schedule 8 extending a person's detention, the person may be detained pending the making of the application.

(6) Where an application has been made under paragraph 29 or 36 of Schedule 8 in respect of a person's detention, he may be detained pending the conclusion of proceedings on the application.

(7) Where an application under paragraph 29 or 36 of Schedule 8 is granted in respect of a person's detention, he may be detained, subject to paragraph 37 of that Schedule, during the period specified in the warrant.

(8) The refusal of an application in respect of a person's detention under paragraph 29 or 36 of Schedule 8 shall not prevent his continued detention in accordance with this section.

Schedule 8 Terrorism Act 2000, paras 29–36

29 (1) Each of the following—
(a) in England and Wales, a Crown Prosecutor,...
(d) in any part of the United Kingdom, a police officer of at least the rank of superintendent, may apply to a judicial authority for the issue of a warrant of further detention under this Part.

   (2) A warrant of further detention—
       (a) shall authorise the further detention under section 41 of a specified person for a specified period, and
       (b) shall state the time at which it is issued.
   (3) Subject to sub-paragraph (3A) and paragraph 36, the specified period in relation to a person shall be the period of seven days beginning—
       (a) with the time of his arrest under section 41, or
       (b) if he was being detained under Schedule 7 when he was arrested under section 41, with the time when his examination under that Schedule began.
 (3A) A judicial authority may issue a warrant of further detention in relation to a person which specifies a shorter period as the period for which that person's further detention is authorised if—
       (a) the application for the warrant is an application for a warrant specifying a shorter period; or
       (b) the judicial authority is satisfied that there are circumstances that would make it inappropriate for the specified period to be as long as the period of seven days mentioned in sub-paragraph (3)
   (4) In this Part 'judicial authority' means—
       (a) in England and Wales,... a District Judge (Magistrates' Courts) who is designated for the purpose of this Part by the Lord Chief Justice of England and Wales

Time limit

30 (1) An application for a warrant shall be made—
       (a) during the period mentioned in section 41(3), or
       (b) within six hours of the end of that period.
   (2) The judicial authority hearing an application made by virtue of sub-paragraph (1)(b) shall dismiss the application if he considers that it would have been reasonably practicable to make it during the period mentioned in section 41(3).
   (3) For the purposes of this Schedule, an application for a warrant is made when written or oral notice of an intention to make the application is given to a judicial authority.

Notice

   31 An application for a warrant may not be heard unless the person to whom it relates has been given a notice stating—
       (a) that the application has been made,
       (b) the time at which the application was made,
       (c) the time at which it is to be heard, and
       (d) the grounds upon which further detention is sought.

Grounds for extension

32 (1) A judicial authority may issue a warrant of further detention only if satisfied that—
       (a) there are reasonable grounds for believing that the further detention of the person to whom the application relates is necessary as mentioned in sub-paragraph (1A), and
       (b) the investigation in connection with which the person is detained is being conducted diligently and expeditiously.
 (1A) The further detention of a person is necessary as mentioned in this sub-paragraph if it is necessary—
       (a) to obtain relevant evidence whether by questioning him or otherwise;
       (b) to preserve relevant evidence; or

    (c) pending the result of an examination or analysis of any relevant evidence or of anything the examination or analysis of which is to be or is being carried out with a view to obtaining relevant evidence.

  (2) In this paragraph 'relevant evidence' means, in relation to the person to whom the application relates, evidence which—

    (a) relates to his commission of an offence under any of the provisions mentioned in section 40(1)(a), or

    (b) indicates that he is a person falling within section 40(1)(b)...

Representation

33 (3) A judicial authority may exclude any of the following persons from any part of the hearing—

    (a) the person to whom the application relates;

    (b) anyone representing him.

  (4) A judicial authority may, after giving an opportunity for representations to be made by or on behalf of the applicant and the person to whom the application relates, direct—

    (a) that the hearing of the application must be conducted, and

    (b) that all representations by or on behalf of a person for the purposes of the hearing must be made,

by such means (whether a live television link or other means) falling within sub-paragraph (5) as may be specified in the direction and not in the presence (apart from by those means) of the applicant, of the person to whom the application relates or of any legal representative of that person.

Information

34 (1) The person who has made an application for a warrant may apply to the judicial authority for an order that specified information upon which he intends to rely be withheld from—

    (a) the person to whom the application relates, and

    (b) anyone representing him.

  (2) Subject to sub-paragraph (3), a judicial authority may make an order under sub-paragraph (1) in relation to specified information only if satisfied that there are reasonable grounds for believing that if the information were disclosed—

    (a) evidence of an offence under any of the provisions mentioned in section 40(1)(a) would be interfered with or harmed,

    (b) the recovery of property obtained as a result of an offence under any of those provisions would be hindered,

    (c) the recovery of property in respect of which a forfeiture order could be made under section 23 or 23A would be hindered,

    (d) the apprehension, prosecution or conviction of a person who is suspected of falling within section 40(1)(a) or (b) would be made more difficult as a result of his being alerted,

    (e) the prevention of an act of terrorism would be made more difficult as a result of a person being alerted,

    (f) the gathering of information about the commission, preparation or instigation of an act of terrorism would be interfered with, or

    (g) a person would be interfered with or physically injured.

  (3) A judicial authority may also make an order under sub-paragraph (1) in relation to specified information if satisfied that there are reasonable grounds for believing that—

    (a) the detained person has benefited from his criminal conduct, and

    (b) the recovery of the value of the property constituting the benefit would be hindered if the information were disclosed.

(3A) For the purposes of sub-paragraph (3) the question whether a person has bene-fited from his criminal conduct is to be decided in accordance with Part 2 or 3 of the Proceeds of Crime Act 2002.

(4) The judicial authority shall direct that the following be excluded from the hearing of the application under this paragraph—
  (a) the person to whom the application for a warrant relates, and
  (b) anyone representing him.

Adjournments

35 (1) A judicial authority may adjourn the hearing of an application for a warrant only if the hearing is adjourned to a date before the expiry of the period mentioned in section 41(3).

  (2) This paragraph shall not apply to an adjournment under paragraph 33(2).

Extensions of warrants

36 (1) Each of the following—
  (a) in England and Wales, a Crown Prosecutor,...
  (d) in any part of the United Kingdom, a police officer of at least the rank of superintendent,
  may apply... for the extension or further extension of the period specified in a warrant of further detention.

(1A) The person to whom an application under sub-paragraph (1) may be made is—
  (a) a judicial authority;

(1B) An application for the extension or further extension of a period falls within this sub-paragraph if—
  (a) the grant of the application otherwise than in accordance with sub-paragraph (3AA)(b) would extend that period to a time that is no more than 14 days after the relevant time;

  (2) Where the period specified is extended, the warrant shall be endorsed with a note stating the new specified period.

  (3) Subject to sub-paragraph (3AA), the period by which the specified period is ex-tended or further extended shall be the period which—
  (a) begins with the time specified in sub-paragraph (3A); and
  (b) ends with whichever is the earlier of—
    (i) the end of the period of seven days beginning with that time; and
    (ii) the end of the period of 14 days beginning with the relevant time.

(3A) The time referred to in sub-paragraph (3)(a) is—
  (a) in the case of a warrant specifying a period which has not previously been extended under this paragraph, the end of the period specified in the warrant, and
  (b) in any other case, the end of the period for which the period specified in the warrant was last extended under this paragraph.

(3AA) A judicial authority... may extend or further extend the period specified in a war-rant by a shorter period than is required by sub-paragraph (3) if—
  (a) the application for the extension is an application for an extension by a period that is shorter than is so required; or
  (b) the judicial authority... is satisfied that there are circumstances that would make it inappropriate for the period of the extension to be as long as the period so required.

(3B) In this paragraph 'the relevant time', in relation to a person, means—
  (a) the time of his arrest under section 41, or
  (b) if he was being detained under Schedule 7 when he was arrested under section 41, the time when his examination under that Schedule began.

> (4) Paragraphs 30(3) and 31 to 34 shall apply to an application under this paragraph as they apply to an application for a warrant of further detention...
> (5) A judicial authority... may adjourn the hearing of an application under sub-paragraph (1) only if the hearing is adjourned to a date before the expiry of the period specified in the warrant.
> (6) Sub-paragraph (5) shall not apply to an adjournment under paragraph 33(2).

A23.4 Appeals against pre-charge bail decisions

A23.4.1 *Pre-charge bail conditions*

An application to the court, by way of appeal, from the decision to impose conditions on the grant of police bail, is provided for by s 47 Police and Criminal Evidence Act (PACE) 1984.

Police and Criminal Evidence Act 1984, s 47

> (1C) Subsections (1D) to (1F) below apply where a person released on bail under section 37, 37C(2)(b) or 37CA(2)(b) above is on bail subject to conditions.
> ...
> (1E) A magistrates' court may, on an application by or on behalf of the person, vary the conditions of bail; and in this subsection 'vary' has the same meaning as in the Bail Act 1976.
> (1F) Where a magistrates' court varies the conditions of bail under subsection (1E) above, that bail shall not lapse but shall continue subject to the conditions as so varied.

The procedure is provided for by rule 14.6 of the Criminal Procedure Rules (Crim PR):

A23.4.2 *Extension of pre-charge bail time limits*

The procedures are set out in ss 47ZC and 47ZF–J of PACE and Crim PR Parts 14.21 and 22.

For any extension to be granted the court must be satisfied that conditions B–D in s 47ZC and the provisions of s 47ZF(7) are met.

Police and Criminal Evidence Act 1984

47ZC

> ...
> (3) Condition B is that the decision-maker has reasonable grounds for believing—
> (a) in a case where the person in question is or is to be released on bail under section 37(7)(c) or 37CA(2)(b), that further time is needed for making a decision as to whether to charge the person with the relevant offence, or
> (b) otherwise, that further investigation is needed of any matter in connection with the relevant offence.
> (4) Condition C is that the decision-maker has reasonable grounds for believing—
> (a) in a case where the person in question is or is to be released on bail under section 37(7)(c) or 37CA(2)(b), that the decision as to whether to charge the person with the relevant offence is being made diligently and expeditiously, or
> (b) otherwise, that the investigation is being conducted diligently and expeditiously.

(5) Condition D is that the decision-maker has reasonable grounds for believing that the release on bail of the person in question is necessary and proportionate in all the circumstances (having regard, in particular, to any conditions of bail which are, or are to be, imposed).

47ZF(7)

(7) A case falls within this subsection if the nature of the decision or further investigations mentioned in condition B means that that decision is unlikely to be made or those investigations completed if the applicable bail period in relation to the person is not extended.

47ZF Applicable bail period: first extension of limit by court

(1) This section applies in relation to a person if—
   (a) the person's case is an SFO case,
   (b) a senior officer has authorised an extension of the applicable bail period in relation to the person under section 47ZD, (standard cases) or
   (c) an appropriate decision-maker has authorised an extension of the applicable bail period in relation to the person under section 47ZE (cases designated as exceptionally complex).
(2) Before the applicable bail period in relation to the person ends a qualifying applicant may apply to a magistrates' court for it to authorise an extension of the applicable bail period in relation to the person under this section....
(4) The (extension granted) is to end—
   (a) in a case falling within subsection (1)(a) or (b), at the end of the period of 6 months beginning with the person's bail start date;
   (b) in a case falling within subsection (1)(c), at the end of the period of 9 months beginning with the person's bail start date.
(5) [The court may] authorise the applicable bail period to be extended as specified in subsection (6).
(6) The applicable bail period is to end—
   (a) in a case falling within subsection (1)(a) or (b), at the end of the period of 9 months beginning with the person's bail start date;
   (b) in a case falling within subsection (1)(c), at the end of the period of 12 months beginning with the person's bail start date.

47ZG Applicable bail period: subsequent extensions of limit by court

(1) Subsections (2) to (6) apply where a court has authorised an extension of the applicable bail period in relation to a person under section 47ZF.
(2) Before the applicable bail period in relation to the person ends a qualifying applicant may apply to a magistrates' court for it to authorise an extension of the applicable bail period in relation to the person under this section.
(3) ... the court may authorise the applicable bail period to be extended as specified in subsection (4).
(4) The applicable bail period is to end at the end of the period of 3 months beginning with the end of the current applicable bail period in relation to the person....
(5) The applicable bail period is to end at the end of the period of 6 months beginning with the end of the current applicable bail period in relation to the person.
(6) Where a court has authorised an extension of the applicable bail period... a qualifying applicant may make further applications...

47ZH Sections 47ZF and 47ZG: withholding sensitive information

(1) This section applies where a qualifying applicant makes an application to a magistrates' court under section 47ZF or 47ZG in relation to a person.
(2) The qualifying applicant may apply to the court for it to authorise the specified information to be withheld from the person and any legal representative of the person.
(3) The court may grant an application under subsection (2) only if satisfied that there are reasonable grounds for believing that the specified information is sensitive information.
(4) For the purposes of this section information is sensitive information if its disclosure would have one or more of the following results—
  (a) evidence connected with an indictable offence would be interfered with or harmed;
  (b) a person would be interfered with or physically injured;
  (c) a person suspected of having committed an indictable offence but not yet arrested for the offence would be alerted;
  (d) the recovery of property obtained as a result of an indictable offence would be hindered.
(5) In this section "specified information" means the information specified in the application under subsection (2).

47ZI Sections 47ZF to 47ZH: proceedings in magistrates' court

(1) An application made to a magistrates' court under section 47ZF or 47ZG in relation to a person is to be determined by a single justice of the peace on written evidence unless subsection (2) or (3) applies.
(2) This subsection applies if—
  (a) the effect of the application would be to extend the applicable bail period in relation to the person so that it ends at or before the end of the period of 12 months beginning with the person's bail start date, and
  (b) a single justice of the peace considers that the interests of justice require an oral hearing.
(3) This subsection applies if—
  (a) the effect of the application would be to extend the applicable bail period in relation to the person so that it ends after the end of the period of 12 months beginning with the person's bail start date, and
  (b) the person, or the person who made the application, requests an oral hearing.
(4) If subsection (2) or (3) applies, the application is to be determined by two or more justices of the peace sitting otherwise than in open court.
(5) Where an application under section 47ZF or 47ZG in relation to a person is to be determined as mentioned in subsection (4), the justices may direct that the person and any legal representative of the person be excluded from any part of the hearing.
(6) The justices may give a direction under subsection (5) only if satisfied that there are reasonable grounds for believing that sensitive information would be disclosed at the part of the hearing in question.
(7) An application under section 47ZH is to be determined by a single justice of the peace on written evidence unless the justice determines that the interests of justice require an oral hearing.
(8) If the justice makes a determination under subsection (7)—
  (a) the application is to be determined by two or more justices of the peace sitting otherwise than in open court, and
  (b) the justices hearing the application must direct that the person to whom the application relates and any legal representative of the person be excluded from the hearing.
(9) In this section "sensitive information" has the meaning given in section 47ZH(4).

47ZJ Sections 47ZF and 47ZG: late applications to magistrates' court

(1) This section applies where—
  (a) an application under section 47ZF or 47ZG is made to a magistrates' court before the end of the applicable bail period in relation to a person, but
  (b) it is not practicable for the court to determine the application before the end of that period.
(2) The court must determine the application as soon as is practicable.
(3) The applicable bail period in relation to the person is to be treated as extended until the application is determined.
(4) If it appears to the court that it would have been reasonable for the application to have been made in time for it to have been determined by the court before the end of the applicable bail period in relation to the person, it may refuse the application.

A24 **Remand Periods**

A24.1 Continuing investigations

The power under s 128(7) and (8) Magistrates' Courts Act (MCA) 1980 to remand to police custody does not arise until the court has decided that bail cannot be granted and must relate to allegations that are not already before the court. The court should then consider whether the remand should be to custody or to a police station, depending on whether further evidence is likely to be obtained, and if to a police station how long is required, with 3 days being the maximum for an adult and 24 hours for a youth.

Under s 152 Criminal Justice Act 1988 the courts have power to commit a person facing certain drugs offences to police custody for up to 192 hours.

A24.2 **Prior to conviction**
A24.2.1 *In custody*

The courts may remand to custody for a maximum of 8 clear days on first remand.

A defendant may subsequently be remanded to custody for up to 28 clear days, provided the next stage in the proceedings will be dealt with. If it is known that the next stage cannot be dealt with in that period then 8-day remands will have to follow, until such time as completion of the next stage within 28 days is achievable.

However, the defendant can agree not to be produced for these hearings.

A further subsequent remand to custody for 28 clear days is allowed if the defendant is already in custody serving a sentence and will not be released before that date.

A24.2.2 *On bail*

The courts may remand on bail for 8 days, or longer if the defendant consents.

A24.3 Upon sending

After a case has been sent to the Crown Court, the magistrates have the power to adjourn for a period up to the date of trial. It is important to note that the expression 'remand' has a particular meaning within the MCA 1980, and the court is not remanding a person when it sends someone for trial—therefore, when a court sends a person for trial during his first appearance, it can do so in custody for a period in excess of 8 days.

For remands in absence see **A22**.

A24.4 **During trial**

No limit (s 10 MCA 1980).

A24.5 Post-conviction

Maximum 3 weeks if in custody; 4 weeks if on bail.

 See *Blackstone's Criminal Practice 2019* **D5.21–D5.37**

A25 **Reporting Restrictions**

A25.1 **Youths**

Section 39 Children and Young Persons Act 1933 has been disapplied from criminal proceedings. The law in relation to youth defendants in the adult court is set out in s 45 Youth Justice and Criminal Evidence Act 1999 (see **B7**).

A25.1.1 *Lifetime reporting restrictions in criminal proceedings for witnesses and victims under 18*

Section 45A Youth Justice and Criminal Evidence Act 1999 provides:

> ### Youth Justice and Criminal Evidence Act 1999, s 45A
>
> **Power to restrict reporting of criminal proceedings for lifetime of witnesses and victims under 18**
>
> (1) This section applies in relation to—
>   (a) any criminal proceedings in any court (other than a service court) in England and Wales, and
>   (b) any proceedings (whether in the United Kingdom or elsewhere) in any service court.
> (2) The court may make a direction ('a reporting direction') that no matter relating to a person mentioned in subsection (3) shall during that person's lifetime be included in any publication if it is likely to lead members of the public to identify that person as being concerned in the proceedings.
> (3) A reporting direction may be made only in respect of a person who is under the age of 18 when the proceedings commence and who is—
>   (a) a witness, other than an accused, in the proceedings;
>   (b) a person against whom the offence, which is the subject of the proceedings, is alleged to have been committed.
> (4) For the purposes of subsection (2), matters relating to a person in respect of whom the reporting direction is made include—
>   (a) the person's name,
>   (b) the person's address,
>   (c) the identity of any school or other educational establishment attended by the person,
>   (d) the identity of any place of work of the person, and
>   (e) any still or moving picture of the person.
> (5) The court may make a reporting direction in respect of a person only if it is satisfied that—
>   (a) the quality of any evidence given by the person, or
>   (b) the level of co-operation given by the person to any party to the proceedings in connection with that party's preparation of its case, is likely to be diminished by reason of fear or distress on the part of the person in connection with being identified by members of the public as a person concerned in the proceedings.
> (6) In determining whether subsection (5) is satisfied, the court must in particular take into account—
>   (a) the nature and alleged circumstances of the offence to which the proceedings relate;

(b) the age of the person;

(c) such of the following as appear to the court to be relevant—

  (i) the social and cultural background and ethnic origins of the person,

  (ii) the domestic, educational and employment circumstances of the person, and

  (iii) any religious beliefs or political opinions of the person;

(d) any behaviour towards the person on the part of—

  (i) an accused,

  (ii) members of the family or associates of an accused, or

  (iii) any other person who is likely to be an accused or a witness in the proceedings.

(7) In determining that question the court must in addition consider any views expressed—

  (a) by the person in respect of whom the reporting restriction may be made, and

  (b) where that person is under the age of 16, by an appropriate person other than an accused.

(8) In determining whether to make a reporting direction in respect of a person, the court must have regard to—

  (a) the welfare of that person,

  (b) whether it would be in the interests of justice to make the direction, and

  (c) the public interest in avoiding the imposition of a substantial and unreasonable restriction on the reporting of the proceedings.

(9) A reporting direction may be revoked by the court or an appellate court.

(10) The court or an appellate court may by direction ('an excepting direction') dispense, to any extent specified in the excepting direction, with the restrictions imposed by a reporting direction.

(11) The court or an appellate court may only make an excepting direction if—

  (a) it is satisfied that it is necessary in the interests of justice to do so, or

  (b) it is satisfied that—

    (i) the effect of the reporting direction is to impose a substantial and unreasonable restriction on the reporting of the proceedings, and

    (ii) it is in the public interest to remove or relax that restriction.

(12) No excepting direction shall be given under subsection (11)(b) by reason only of the fact that the proceedings have been determined in any way or have been abandoned.

(13) In determining whether to make an excepting direction in respect of a person, the court or the appellate court must have regard to the welfare of that person.

(14) An excepting direction—

  (a) may be given at the time the reporting direction is given or subsequently, and

  (b) may be varied or revoked by the court or an appellate court.

A25.2 Adults

A25.2.1 *Withholding names or other details*

Under s 11 Contempt of Court Act 1981, where a court exercises its powers to allow a name or any other matter to be withheld from the public in criminal proceedings, the court may make such directions as are necessary prohibiting the publication of that name or matter in connection with the proceedings.

In *Re Times Newspapers Ltd* [2008] EWCA Crim 2559 the court held that it is an important aspect of open justice that a defendant's name should be made public. However, the court may in appropriate circumstances order the identity of a defendant, or their address, to be protected from publicity. The power to do so is a common law power.

The Judicial College has published the following guidance:

> 4.4 ... Section 11 can only be invoked where the court allows a name or matter to be withheld from being mentioned in open court. It follows that there is no power to prohibit publication of any name or other matter which has been given in open court in the proceedings. For this reason, applications for an order under s. 11 may be heard in private provided there is good reason for doing so.
>
> Section 11 does not itself give the court power to withhold a name or other matter from the public. The power to do this must exist either at common law or from some other statutory provision.

Consistent with the requirement to protect the open justice principle and freedom of expression, courts should only make an order under s 11 where the nature or circumstances of the proceedings are such that hearing all evidence in open court would frustrate or render impractical the administration of justice. It follows that a defendant in a criminal trial must be named save in rare circumstances. It is not appropriate therefore to invoke the s 11 power to withhold matters for the benefit of a defendant's feelings or comfort or to prevent financial damage, or damage to reputation resulting from proceedings concerning a person's business. Nor can the power be invoked to prevent identification and embarrassment of the defendant's children, because of the defendant's public profile.

Where the ground for seeking a s 11 order is that the identification of a witness or a defendant will expose that person to a real and immediate risk to his life, engaging the state's duty to protect life under Article 2 of the European Convention on Human Rights (ECHR), the court will consider whether the fear is objectively well-founded. In practical terms, the applicant will have to provide clear and cogent evidence to show that publication of his name will create or materially increase a risk of death or serious injury.

In appropriate cases consideration should be given to s 46 Youth Justice and Criminal Evidence Act 1999 if the evidence of a witness may be affected by fear that the identity of her children may become known. *Re ITN News*, [2013] EWCA Crim 773 (Admin) confirms that this does not follow automatically from a special measures direction but requires a separate fact-finding exercise.

The court must balance the Article 10 rights of free expression and the Article 8 rights of the child. Particular weight is attached to the interests of the child if their interests were likely on the facts to be harmed, but there was a presumption that there should be open justice. In *R (A) v Lowestoft Magistrates' Court* [2013] EWHC 659 an elected councillor with a caution already was drunk in charge of the child. The child was under three years of age and would know nothing of the publicity. By contrast, in *Z v News Group Newspapers* [2013] EWHC 1150 (Fam), when a mother of eight children was involved in a benefit fraud, claiming by reference to disabilities and incapacities of those children, all of whom were innocent of any involvement, the balance was in favour of preventing the children (and so the mother) being named. The heavy burden to prevent publicity had been met, not least because the medical conditions of the children would be extensively examined and some of them were vulnerable. However, once the mother had been convicted the balance was in favour of naming her.

In rare circumstances, the right to private and family life under Article 8 ECHR may mean that normal media reporting has to be curtailed, but injunctions to cover these cases are dealt with by the High Court rather than the criminal courts. In *A v BBC* [2014] UKSC 325 the Supreme Court held that s 11 Contempt of Court Act 1981 could be used to protect a person's ECHR rights and not only to protect the public interest. It was not necessary for a restriction to have been in place for those who attended court. In this case the identification of the defendant would, on her deportation, have endangered her Article 3 rights and given her new grounds to seek asylum.

The court may in appropriate circumstances limit information to protect a person's safety or commercial interests, or to prevent disclosure of intimate personal details of a complainant. Each case turned on its own facts and involved a balancing exercise.

A25.2.2 *Postponement of reports*

Section 4(2) Contempt of Court Act 1981 provides:

Contempt of Court Act 1981, s 4(2)

4 Contemporary reports of proceedings

(2) In any such proceedings the court may, where it appears to be necessary for avoiding a substantial risk of prejudice to the administration of justice in those proceedings, or in any other proceedings pending or imminent, order that the publication of any report of the proceedings, or any part of the proceedings, be postponed for such period as the court thinks necessary for that purpose.

...

The provision was considered in *R. v Sarker; Re BBC* [2018] EWCA Crim 1341. The word 'substantial' does not mean 'weighty'. It means 'not insubstantial' or 'not minimal'. It is important to focus on what prejudice it is said would be occasioned by the reports sought to be postponed. Applications must be made in accordance with , rules 6.4 and 6.5 of the Criminal Procedure Rules.

The explanation for why the order is necessary needs to address, clearly (and ordinarily in writing):

(i) how contemporaneous, fair, and accurate reports of the trial will cause a substantial risk of prejudice, and

(ii) why a postponement order would avoid the identified risk of prejudice.

When dealing with applications for reporting restrictions, the default position is the general principle that all proceedings in courts and tribunals are conducted in public.

Even if an order would achieve the objective, he still has to consider whether the risk could satisfactorily be overcome by some less restrictive means. If so, it cannot be said to be 'necessary' to take the more drastic approach: If the judge is satisfied that there is no other way of eliminating the perceived risk of prejudice, it still does not necessarily follow that an order has to be made. The judge may still have to ask whether the degree of risk contemplated should be regarded as being 'the lesser of two evils'. It is at this stage that value judgments may have to be made as to the priority between the competing public interests, fair trial, and freedom of expression/open justice.

A26 **Sending and Transfer for Trial**

A26.1 **Overview**

In the following instances the court may decline or be deprived of jurisdiction to try a matter:

- indictable-only matters—sent to the Crown Court;
- either-way matters where jurisdiction is declined or the defendant has elected Crown Court trial—sent to the Crown Court; transfer cases—transferred to the Crown Court;
- voluntary bill of indictment (not covered in this book).

Method	Notes
Sending. Section 51 of the Crime and Disorder Act 1998	The court will send any indictable-only matter, along with any related either-way matters. This may involve sending one or more co-defendants, who shall be sent if appearing at the same time and may be sent if appearing on another occasion. Note: A sending is not a remand within the meaning of MCA 1980, ss 128, 128A, and therefore the initial 8-day limitation on a remand in custody does not apply.
	An either-way offence is related to an indictable offence if the charge for the either-way offence could be joined in the same indictment as the charge for the indictable offence.
	A summary offence is related to an indictable offence if it arises out of circumstances which are the same as or connected with those giving rise to the indictable offence. The court can send related summary offences if they are imprisonable or carry discretionary or obligatory disqualification from driving.
	In the case of a youth charged with an adult (not necessarily on the same occasion), the youth will be sent if it is in the interests of justice to try him with the adult. When sending cases a clear distinction must be made between either-way offences and summary-only cases (of which low-value shoplifting is one) (*R v Maxwell* [2017] EWCA Crim 1233).
Transfer cases. Note: See ss 51B and 51C of the Crime and Disorder Act 1998	Applicable to fraud cases and child cases.

The magistrates' court has no power (save in the special circumstances of s 52(7) Mental Health Act 1983) to conduct sending proceedings in the absence of the accused, but no contribution from the accused is required: *R (Lord Janner) v Westminster Magistrates' Court* [2015] EWHC 2578.

Where a person is arrested for an either-way offence and commits a summary-only assault while at the police station, there is no basis for dealing with the summary-only matter at the Crown Court; it did not arise out of the same facts, neither was it part of a series of offences, so s 40(1) Criminal Justice Act 1988 did not apply (*R v Walton* [2011] EWCA Crim 2832). An offence under s 6 Bail Act 1976 does not relate to the substantive offence for which bail was granted and so cannot be sent for trial to the Crown Court. (*R v Osman* [2017] EWCA Crim 2178).

A26.2 **Case management**

When sending a case to the Crown Court, the magistrates have certain management responsibilities, including to ask whether the defendant intends to plead guilty in the Crown Court (Criminal Procedure Rules, r 9.7) Because a discount for guilty plea can be reduced if a plea is not entered at the first hearing in the magistrates' court, even in indictable only matters, very careful consideration should be given to the completion of the case management form identifying, when possible, the issues in the case and which are in dispute (see **Appendix 2**).

A26.3 **Relevant legislation**

> The relevant legislation is set out in Crime and Disorder Act
> 1998, ss 50A–51D

 See *Blackstone's Criminal Practice 2019* **D10**

A27 Special Measures and Vulnerable Witnesses

A27.1 Special measures

Sections 16 and 17 Youth Justice and Criminal Evidence Act 1999 provide for special measures. Those aged under 18 may always benefit, as well as those meeting the requirements for incapacity (s 16). Witnesses who seek assistance may always benefit if the allegation is of the serious offences listed in the Youth Justice and Criminal Evidence Act 1999, Sch 1A, which will usually be tried in the Crown Court, as well as those who otherwise meet the criteria (s 17). Under Part 3 of the Criminal Procedure Rules, the courts are required to facilitate the participation of anyone taking part, both witnesses and defendant(s).

Youth Justice and Criminal Evidence Act 1999, ss 16 and 17

16 Witnesses eligible for assistance on grounds of age or incapacity

(1) For the purposes of this Chapter a witness in criminal proceedings (other than the accused) is eligible for assistance by virtue of this section—
   (a) if under the age of 18 at the time of the hearing; or
   (b) if the court considers that the quality of evidence given by the witness is likely to be diminished by reason of any circumstances falling within subsection (2).

(2) The circumstances falling within this subsection are—
   (a) that the witness—
      (i) suffers from mental disorder within the meaning of the Mental Health Act 1983, or
      (ii) otherwise has a significant impairment of intelligence and social functioning;
   (b) that the witness has a physical disability or is suffering from a physical disorder.

(3) In subsection (1)(a) 'the time of the hearing', in relation to a witness, means the time when it falls to the court to make a determination for the purposes of section 19(2) in relation to the witness.

(4) In determining whether a witness falls within subsection (1)(b) the court must consider any views expressed by the witness.

(5) In this Chapter references to the quality of a witness's evidence are to its quality in terms of completeness, coherence and accuracy; and for this purpose 'coherence' refers to a witness's ability in giving evidence to give answers which address the questions put to the witness and can be understood both individually and collectively.

17 Witnesses eligible for assistance on grounds of fear or distress about testifying

(1) For the purposes of this Chapter a witness in criminal proceedings (other than the accused) is eligible for assistance by virtue of this subsection if the court is satisfied that the quality of evidence given by the witness is likely to be diminished by reason of fear or distress on the part of the witness in connection with testifying in the proceedings.

(2) In determining whether a witness falls within subsection (1) the court must take into account, in particular—

(a) the nature and alleged circumstances of the offence to which the proceedings relate;
(b) the age of the witness;
(c) such of the following matters as appear to the court to be relevant, namely—
   (i) the social and cultural background and ethnic origins of the witness,
   (ii) the domestic and employment circumstances of the witness, and
   (iii) any religious beliefs or political opinions of the witness;
(d) any behaviour towards the witness on the part of—
   (i) the accused,
   (ii) members of the family or associates of the accused, or
   (iii) any other person who is likely to be an accused or a witness in the proceedings.
(3) In determining that question the court must in addition consider any views expressed by the witness.
(4) Where the complainant in respect of a sexual offence is a witness in proceedings relating to that offence (or to that offence and any other offences), the witness is eligible for assistance in relation to those proceedings by virtue of this subsection unless the witness has informed the court of the witness's wish not to be so eligible by virtue of this subsection.
(5) A witness in proceedings relating to a relevant offence (or to a relevant offence and any other offences) is eligible for assistance in relation to those proceedings by virtue of this subsection unless the witness has informed the court of the witness's wish not to be so eligible by virtue of this subsection.
(6) For the purposes of subsection (5) an offence is a relevant offence if it is an offence described in Schedule 1A.

The following special measures are available in the magistrates' court:

	Section 16 witnesses (children and vulnerable adults)	Section 17 witnesses (intimidated/fear or distress)
Section 23—screening witness from accused	Full availability	Full availability
Section 24—evidence via live link	Full availability	Full availability
Section 25—evidence given in private	Full availability	Full availability
Section 26—removal of wigs/gowns	Not applicable	Not applicable
Section 27—video-recorded evidence-in-chief	Full availability	Full availability
Section 28—video-recorded cross-examination and re-examination	Available in pilot Crown Courts	Not available
Section 29—examination through an intermediary	Full availability	Not applicable
Section 30—aids to communication	Full availability	Not applicable

A27.2 **Witness anonymity**

Sections 86–95 Coroners and Justice Act 2009 provide for the making and discharge of witness anonymity orders. These are to be regarded as a special measure of last practicable resort (*R v Mayers* [2008] EWCA Crim 2989).

 See *Blackstone's Criminal Practice 2019* **D14**

A28 **Submission of No Case**

A28.1 **Test for no case to answer**

In *R v Galbraith* (1981) 73 Cr App R 124, the court laid down the following test:

(1) If there is no evidence that the crime alleged has been committed by the defendant, there is no difficulty. The judge will of course stop the case.

(2) The difficulty arises where there is some evidence but it is of a tenuous character, for example because of inherent weakness, or vagueness, or because it is inconsistent with other evidence.

    (a) Where the judge comes to the conclusion that the prosecution evidence, taken at its highest, is such that a jury properly directed could not properly convict upon it, it is his duty, upon a submission being made, to stop the case.

    (b) Where, however, the prosecution evidence is such that its strength or weakness depends on the view to be taken of a witness's reliability, or other matters which are generally speaking within the province of the jury and where on one possible view of the facts there is evidence upon which a jury could properly come to the conclusion that the defendant is guilty, then the judge should allow the matter to be tried by the jury.

It follows that we think the second of the two schools of thought is to be preferred.

A28.2 **Dismissal of case**

A magistrates' court might only dismiss a charge in the following circumstances (*DPP v Bird* [2015] EWHC 4077 (Admin):

1   after hearing evidence;

2   where the prosecution had offered no evidence; or is not able to proceed and the case had not been adjourned; or

3   where the prosecution had not appeared at the time and place appointed for trial

 See *Blackstone's Criminal Practice 2019* **D16.54–D16.73**

A29 **Transfer/Remittal of Criminal Cases**

A29.1 **Transfer between courts**

Section 27A Magistrates' Courts Act 1980 provides for transfer between magistrates' courts:

Magistrates' Courts Act 1980, s 27A

27A Power to transfer criminal proceedings

(1) Where a person appears or is brought before a magistrates' court—
  (a) to be tried by the court for an offence, or
  (b) for the court to inquire into the offence as examining justices, the court may transfer the matter to another magistrates' court.
(2) The court may transfer the matter before or after beginning the trial or inquiry.
(3) But if the court transfers the matter after it has begun to hear the evidence and the parties, the court to which the matter is transferred must begin hearing the evidence and the parties again ...

A29.2 **Transfer of custodial remand hearings**

Magistrates Courts Act 1980, s 130

130 Transfer of remand hearings

(1) A magistrates' court adjourning a case under section 5, 10(1) or 18(4) above, and remanding the accused in custody, may, if he has attained the age of 17, order that he be brought up for any subsequent remands before an alternate magistrates' court nearer to the prison where he is to be confined while on remand.
(2) The order shall require the accused to be brought before the alternate court at the end of the period of remand or at such earlier time as the alternate court may require.
(3) While the order is in force, the alternate court shall, to the exclusion of the court which made the order, have all the powers in relation to further remand (whether in custody or on bail) and which that court would have had but for the order.
(4) The alternate court may, on remanding the accused in custody, require him to be brought before the court which made the order at the end of the period of remand or at such earlier time as that court may require; and, if the alternate court does so, or the accused is released on bail, the order under subsection (1) above shall cease to be in force....

A29.3 **Remittal of convicted defendants**

Provision is made for the remittal of convicted defendants by s 10 Powers of Criminal Courts (Sentencing) Act 2000:

Powers of Criminal Courts (Sentencing) Act 2000, s 10

10 Power of magistrates' court to remit case to another magistrates' court for sentence

(1) Where a person aged 18 or over ('the offender') has been convicted by a magistrates' court ('the convicting court') of an offence to which this section applies ('the instant offence') and—

    (a) it appears to the convicting court that some other magistrates' court ('the other court') has convicted him of another such offence in respect of which the other court has neither passed sentence on him nor committed him to the Crown Court for sentence nor dealt with him in any other way, and

    (b) the other court consents to his being remitted under this section to the other court,

the convicting court may remit him to the other court to be dealt with in respect of the instant offence by the other court instead of by the convicting court.

(2) This section applies to—

    (a) any offence punishable with imprisonment; and

    (b) any offence in respect of which the convicting court has a power or duty to order the offender to be disqualified under section 34, 35 or 36 of the Road Traffic Offenders Act 1988 (disqualification for certain motoring offences).

 See *Blackstone's Criminal Practice 2019* **D21.5**

A30 **Video/Live Links**

Sections 57A–57F Crime and Disorder Act 1998 provide for the use of live links in relation to preliminary hearings and sentence (see **A27** for special measure provisions). The Act creates a presumption that video links will be used.

At the first hearing in the magistrates' court, when the case is adjourned, magistrates will hear any representations from the defence about why subsequent hearings—a further bail application, plea before venue, mode of trial, the taking of a plea, or sentencing—should not take place over the video link.

Criminal Practice Direction 3N.1 deals with live link and telephone facilities:

Criminal Practice Direction 3N

3N.1 Where it is lawful and in the interests of justice to do so, courts should exercise their statutory and other powers to conduct hearings by live link or telephone.

...

3N.5 There may be circumstances in which the court should not require the use of live link or telephone facilities despite their being otherwise appropriate at a pre-trial hearing. In every case, in deciding whether any such circumstances apply the court will keep in mind that, for the purposes of what may be an essentially administrative hearing, it may be compatible with the overriding objective to proceed in the defendant's absence altogether, especially if he or she is represented, unless, exceptionally, a rule otherwise requires. The principle that the court always must consider proceeding in a defendant's absence is articulated in CrimPR 3.9(2)(a). Where at a pre-trial hearing bail may be under consideration, the provisions of CrimPR 14.2 will be relevant.

3N.6 Such circumstances will include any case in which the defendant's effective participation cannot be achieved by his or her attendance by such means, and CrimPR 3.2(4) and (5) except such cases from the scope of the obligation which that rule otherwise imposes on the court. That exception may apply where (this list is not exhaustive) the defendant has a disorder or disability, including a hearing, speech or sight impediment, or has communication needs to which the use of a live link or telephone is inimical (whether or not those needs are such as to require the appointment of an intermediary); or where the defendant requires interpretation and effective interpretation cannot be provided by live link or telephone, as the case may be.

3N.7 Finally, that exception sometimes may apply where the defendant's attendance in person at a pre-trial hearing will facilitate communication with his or her legal representatives. The court should not make such an exception merely to allow client and representatives to meet if that meeting can and should be held elsewhere. However, there will be cases in which defence representatives reasonably need to meet with a defendant, to take his or her instructions or to explain events to him or her, either shortly before or immediately after a pre-trial hearing and in circumstances in which that meeting cannot take place effectively by live link.

3N.8 Nothing prohibits the member or members of a court from conducting a pre-trial hearing by attending by live link or telephone from a location distant from all the other participants. Despite the conventional view that the venue for a court hearing is the court room in which that hearing has been arranged to take place, the Criminal Procedure Rules define ''court' as 'a tribunal with jurisdiction over criminal cases'.

A31 Witnesses, Issue of Summons, or Warrant

A31.1 Power to require attendance

Magistrates' Courts Act 1980, s 97

97 Summons to witness and warrant for his arrest

(1) Where a justice of the peace is satisfied that—

    (a) any person in England or Wales is likely to be able to give material evidence, or produce any document or thing likely to be material evidence, at the summary trial of an information or hearing of a complaint or of an application under the Adoption and Children Act 2002 (c. 38) by a magistrates' court, and

    (b) it is in the interests of justice to issue a summons under this subsection to secure the attendance of that person to give evidence or produce the document or thing,

    the justice shall issue a summons directed to that person requiring him to attend before the court at the time and place appointed in the summons to give evidence or to produce the document or thing.

(2) If a justice of the peace is satisfied by evidence on oath of the matters mentioned in subsection (1) above, and also that it is probable that a summons under that subsection would not procure the attendance of the person in question, the justice may instead of issuing a summons issue a warrant to arrest that person and bring him before such a court as aforesaid at a time and place specified in the warrant; but a warrant shall not be issued under this subsection where the attendance is required for the hearing of a complaint or of an application under the Adoption and Children Act 2002 (c. 38).

(2A) A summons may also be issued under subsection (1) above if the justice is satisfied that the person in question is outside the British Islands but no warrant shall be issued under subsection (2) above unless the justice is satisfied by evidence on oath that the person in question is in England or Wales.

(2B) A justice may refuse to issue a summons under subsection (1) above in relation to the summary trial of an information if he is not satisfied that an application for the summons was made by a party to the case as soon as reasonably practicable after the accused pleaded not guilty.

(2C) In relation to the summary trial of an information, subsection (2) above shall have effect as if the reference to the matters mentioned in subsection (1) above included a reference to the matter mentioned in subsection (2B) above.

(3) On the failure of any person to attend before a magistrates' court in answer to a summons under this section, if—

    (a) the court is satisfied by evidence on oath that he is likely to be able to give material evidence or produce any document or thing likely to be material evidence in the proceedings; and

    (b) it is proved on oath, or in such other manner as may be prescribed, that he has been duly served with the summons, and that a reasonable sum has been paid or tendered to him for costs and expenses; and

    (c) it appears to the court that there is no just excuse for the failure, the court may issue a warrant to arrest him and bring him before the court at a time and place specified in the warrant.

If any person attending or brought before a magistrates' court refuses without just excuse to be sworn or give evidence, or to produce any document or thing, the court may commit him to custody until the expiration of such period not exceeding one month as may be specified in the warrant or until he sooner gives evidence or produces the document or thing or impose on him a fine not exceeding £2,500 or both.

Conduct money should be served with any summons sufficient to enable the person to attend court.

The power to compel production of documents relates only to material evidence, and should not be used to compel the production of documents solely for the purpose of cross-examination (*R v Skegness Magistrates' Court, ex p Cardy* [1985] RTR 49). See also Part 17 of the Criminal Procedure Rules.

The alternative approach is to require the Crown to accept its responsibilities under paragraph 3.5 of the Code of Practice issued under the Criminal Procedure and Investigations Act 1996 to pursue all reasonable lines of enquiry, a duty recognized by paragraphs 46 to 48 of the Judicial Protocol on Disclosure of Unused Material (see **A16**).

 See *Blackstone's Criminal Practice 2019* **D21.27–D21.33**

Part B
Youths in the
Adult Court

B1 Age of Offender and the Position of Those Attaining 18

B1.1 Ascertainment of age

The age of the offender is important in relation to the court's power to impose different types of sentence. It is the duty of a court to determine their age when a young person is brought before the court. In most cases there is no dispute and a simple confirmation of the youth's date of birth will suffice. The court is, however, able to hear evidence on the issue. If there is a real doubt about the defendant's age, directions should be given for an age assessment to be carried out, usually through the Youth Offending Team (YOT) (*R (M) v Hammersmith MC* [2017] EWHC 1359 (Admin)). If the age is later found to be incorrect, this has no bearing on any orders made by the court (s 99 Children and Young Persons Act 1933).

B1.2 Youth becoming an adult during course of proceedings

B1.2.1 *Attaining 18 before first court appearance*

Notwithstanding the defendant's age at the date of allegation or charge, where a defendant is 18 years of age at the date of the first court appearance the hearing is in the adult magistrates' court. Section 24(1) Magistrates' Courts Act 1980 ('summary trial of information against child or young person for indictable offence') applies only to those who are under 18 years at the date of the first appearance in court. The youth court has no jurisdiction (*R v Amersham Juvenile Court, ex p Wilson* [1981] 2 All ER 315). This applies where the defendant does not appear and a warrant is issued prior to the defendant's 18th birthday. The charge must be laid again in the adult court (*R v Uxbridge Youth Court, ex p H* [1998] EWHC (Admin) 341).

B1.2.2 *Attaining 18 during court proceedings*

The relevant date is the date on which the plea is taken and/or the venue is determined. If the defendant attains 18 after the first appearance at court and the offence is indictable, and no plea has been taken/venue has not been determined, the adult sending and venue procedures apply. This includes the right to elect trial by jury (*Re Daley* [1983] 1 AC 327; *R v West London Justices, ex p Siley-Winditt* [2000] Crim LR 926).

Where the prosecution, during the course of the proceedings, seek to lay a new charge based on the same facts, the new charge must be laid in the adult court (*R v Chelsea Justices, ex p Director of Public Prosecutions* [1963] 3 All ER 657).

B1.3 Sentence

Sentencing Children and Young People: Definitive Guideline

SCG Guideline: Overarching Principles—Available Sentences, para 6

6. **Crossing a significant age threshold between commission of offence and sentence**

6.1 There will be occasions when an increase in the age of a child or young person will result in the maximum sentence on the date of the finding of guilt being greater than that available on the date on which the offence was committed (primarily turning 12, 15 or 18 years old).

6.2 In such situations the court should take as its starting point the sentence likely to have been imposed on the date at which the offence was committed. This includes young people who attain the age of 18 between the commission and the finding of guilt of the offence [footnote removed] but when this occurs the purpose of sentencing adult offenders [footnote removed] has to be taken into account, which is: the punishment of offenders; the reduction of crime (including its reduction by deterrence); the reform and rehabilitation of offenders; the protection of the public; and the making of reparation by offenders to persons affected by their offences.

6.3 When any significant age threshold is passed it will rarely be appropriate that a more severe sentence than the maximum that the court could have imposed at the time the offence was committed should be imposed. However, a sentence at or close to that maximum may be appropriate.

B1.3.1 *Sentencing principles*

For the purposes of sentence, the relevant age is the age of the defendant at the date of conviction or guilty plea (*R v Danga* [1992] QB 476), not the date of offence. As a matter of public policy, however, the courts have been willing to sentence having regard to the offence date, as opposed to conviction date. In *R v Ghafoor* [2002] EWCA Crim 1857, the court said:

> The starting point is the sentence that the defendant would have been likely to receive if he had been sentenced at the date of the commission of the offence. It has been described as a 'powerful factor'. That is for the obvious reason that ... the philosophy of restricting sentencing powers in relation to young persons reflects both (a) society's acceptance that young offenders are less responsible for their actions and therefore less culpable than adults, and (b) the recognition that, in consequence, sentencing them should place greater emphasis on rehabilitation and less on retribution and deterrence than in the case of adults. It should be noted that the 'starting point' is not the maximum sentence that could lawfully have been imposed, but the sentence that the offender would have been likely to receive.

In *R v Bowker* [2007] EWCA Crim 1608, the court said that *Ghafoor* was a powerful starting point but other factors (such as the need for deterrent sentencing, as to which see: Sentencing Children and Young People: Definitive Guideline) may justify departing from it.

B1.3.2 *Exceptions to general rule*

Where a court activates a conditional discharge, the relevant age for the purpose of resentencing is determined by the date on which the offender appears for resentence (s 136 Powers of Criminal Courts (Sentencing) Act 2000).

 See *Blackstone's Criminal Practice 2019* **E7.2**

B2 Bail

With the following exceptions, the bases on which the Crown may oppose bail, and on which an application for bail, whether unconditional or conditional, may be made for a youth appearing in the adult court, are the same as for an adult (see **A8**).

Under transitional arrangements, if the offence carries a sentence of life imprisonment and at the time of the offence the defendant was on bail, Sch 1, paras 9AA and 9AB to the Bail Act 1976 (as amended) provide:

Bail Act 1976, Sch 1, paras 9AA and 9AB

9AA (1) This paragraph applies if—
  (a) the defendant is a child or young person, and
  (b) it appears to the court that he was on bail in criminal proceedings on the date of the offence.

(2) In deciding for the purposes of paragraph 2(1) of this Part of this Schedule whether it is satisfied that there are substantial grounds for believing that the defendant, if released on bail (whether subject to conditions or not), would commit an offence while on bail, the court shall give particular weight to the fact that the defendant was on bail in criminal proceedings on the date of the offence.

9AB (1) Subject to sub-paragraph (2) below, this paragraph applies if—
  (a) the defendant is a child or young person, and
  (b) it appears to the court that, having been released on bail in or in connection with the proceedings for the offence, he failed to surrender to custody.

(2) Where it appears to the court that the defendant had reasonable cause for his failure to surrender to custody, this paragraph does not apply unless it also appears to the court that he failed to surrender to custody at the appointed place as soon as reasonably practicable after the appointed time.

(3) In deciding for the purposes of paragraph 2(1) of this Part of this Schedule whether it is satisfied that there are substantial grounds for believing that the defendant, if released on bail (whether subject to conditions or not), would fail to surrender to custody, the court shall give particular weight to—
  (a) where the defendant did not have reasonable cause for his failure to surrender to custody, the fact that he failed to surrender to custody, or
  (b) where he did have reasonable cause for his failure to surrender to custody, the fact that he failed to surrender to custody at the appointed place as soon as reasonably practicable after the appointed time.

(4) ...

If electronic monitoring is to be a condition of bail, the court must comply with s 3AA Bail Act 1976.

Bail Act 1976, ss 3AA(1)–(5)

3AA Conditions for the imposition of electronic monitoring requirements: children and young persons

(1) A court may not impose electronic monitoring requirements on a child or young person unless each of the following conditions is met.

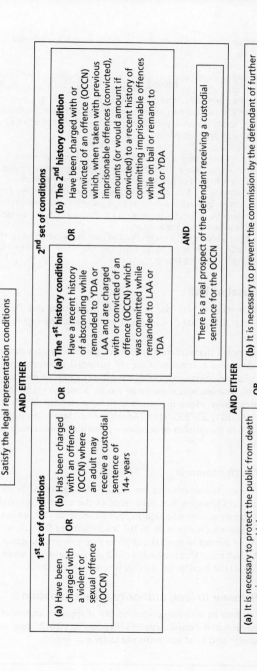

Figure 2 Remand to youth detention accommodation

The content of the figure reads:

Remand to Youth Detention Accommodation

Be aged between 12–17

AND

Satisfy the legal representation conditions

AND EITHER

1st set of conditions

(a) Have been charged with a violent or sexual offence (OCCN)

OR

(b) Has been charged with an offence (OCCN) where an adult may receive a custodial sentence of 14+ years

OR

2nd set of conditions

(a) The 1st history condition

Have a recent history of absconding while remanded to YDA or LAA and are charged with or convicted of an offence (OCCN) which was committed while remanded to LAA or YDA

OR

(b) The 2nd history condition

Have been charged with or convicted of an offence (OCCN) which, when taken with previous imprisonable offences (convicted), amounts (or would amount if convicted) to a recent history of committing imprisonable offences while on bail or remand to LAA or YDA

AND

There is a real prospect of the defendant receiving a custodial sentence for the OCCN

AND EITHER

(a) It is necessary to protect the public from death or serious personal injury

OR

(b) It is necessary to prevent the commission by the defendant of further imprisonable offences

OCCN = offence court currently considering

(2) The first condition is that the child or young person has attained the age of twelve years.
(3) The second condition is that—
  (a) the child or young person is charged with or has been convicted of a violent or sexual offence, or an offence punishable in the case of an adult with imprisonment for a term of fourteen years or more; or
  (b) he is charged with or has been convicted of one or more imprison-able offences which, together with any other imprisonable offences of which he has been convicted in any proceedings—
    (i) amount, or
    (ii) would, if he were convicted of the offences with which he is charged, amount, to a recent history of repeatedly committing imprisonable offences while remanded on bail or to local authority accommodation.
(4) The third condition is that the court is satisfied that the necessary provision for dealing with the person concerned can be made under arrangements for the electronic monitoring of persons released on bail that are currently available in each local justice area which is a relevant area.
(5) The fourth condition is that a youth offending team has informed the court that in its opinion the imposition of electronic monitoring requirements will be suitable in the case of the child or young person.

B2.1 Refusal of bail

If a youth is refused bail, the Legal Aid, Sentencing and Punishment of Offenders Act 2012, Part 3, Chapter 3 provides for the regime (see **B2.1.8** for ss 91–102).

It should be noted that remands both to local authority accommodation and to youth detention accommodation are custodial remands, and that time limits for such remands and custody time limits apply. In the case of a youth charged with murder, where the court has no power to grant bail, the court will still determine where the youth is to be remanded (*R (A) v Lewisham Youth Court* [2011] EWHC 1193 (Admin)) and there is no limit under the Bail Act 1976 to the number of occasions on which consideration can be given to this issue.

B2.1.1 *Youth remands*

Where a youth is not released on bail, s 91 Legal Aid, Sentencing and Punishment of Offenders Act 2012 requires the court to remand the child to local authority accommodation in accordance with s 92, unless one of the sets of conditions set out in ss 98 to 101 is fulfilled (see **B2.1.8**), in which case the court may instead remand the child to youth detention accommodation. Under s 92(2), a court that remands a child to local authority accommodation must designate the local authority that is to receive the child.

B2.1.2 *Remand to local authority accommodation*

The remand may be without conditions, but if appropriate, under s 93 Legal Aid, Sentencing and Punishment of Offenders Act 2012, after consultation with the designated local authority, the court may require:

- the child to comply with any conditions that could be imposed under section 3(6) of the Bail Act 1976;
- the child to comply with any conditions required for the purpose of securing compliance with electronic monitoring;
- the designated local authority to comply with any requirements to secure the child's compliance with a condition; and
- the designated local authority not to place the child with a named person.

An application may be made to the court in respect of a child who has been remanded to local authority accommodation to impose, vary, or revoke conditions.

B2.1.3 *Electronic monitoring as a condition of bail whilst remanded to local authority accommodation*

The court may not impose electronic monitoring of a child's compliance with a condition imposed under s 93 unless the conditions set out in s 94 (see **B2.1.8**) are satisfied.

B2.1.4 *Failure to surrender*

Where a child who is remanded on bail fails to surrender to court without reasonable cause, s 6 Bail Act 1976 will apply (see **C3**).

B2.1.5 *Breach of conditions of remand to local authority accommodation*

Under s 97 Legal Aid, Sentencing and Punishment of Offenders Act 2012, a constable may arrest a child without a warrant if the child has been remanded to local authority accommodation with conditions and the constable has reasonable grounds to suspect that the child has broken any of those conditions. The child must be brought before the court as soon as practicable and within 24 hours of the child's arrest. Where that 24-hour period includes the time appointed for the child's original court appearance then the child should appear before that same court.

If the court is of the opinion that a child has broken any of the conditions of a remand to local authority accommodation, the court may once again consider the conditions of bail and may attach new conditions to the remand to local authority accommodation or, if the conditions in ss 98–101 are met, remand the child to youth detention accommodation.

If the court is not of the opinion that the child has broken any of the conditions of his remand to local authority accommodation, it must remand the child subject to the original conditions imposed.

B2.1.6 *10- to 11-year-olds*

A child aged 10 to 11 years may only be remanded on bail or to local authority accommodation. If a child reaches the age of 12 during the course of a remand, it is possible that he may then be remanded to youth detention accommodation at the next court appearance should the relevant conditions (ss 98–101 Legal Aid, Sentencing and Punishment of Offenders Act 2012) be met.

B2.1.7 *Secure accommodation*

A child aged between 10 and 17 years who is remanded to local authority accommodation may be placed in secure local authority accommodation if the designated local authority obtains a court order permitting this under s 25 Children Act 1989 (as modified by the Children (Secure Accommodation) Regulations 1991 (SI 1991/1505)).

Section 25 Children Act 1989 provides:

Children Act 1989, s 25

25 Use of accommodation for restricting liberty

(1) Subject to the following provisions of this section, a child who is being looked after by a local authority or local authority in Wales may not be placed, and, if placed, may not be kept, in accommodation in England provided for the purpose of restricting liberty ('secure accommodation') unless it appears—
   (a) that—
      (i) he has a history of absconding and is likely to abscond from any other description of accommodation; and
      (ii) if he absconds, he is likely to suffer significant harm; or
   (b) that if he is kept in any other description of accommodation he is likely to injure himself or other persons.

(2) The Secretary of State may by regulations—
   (a) specify a maximum period—
      (i) beyond which a child may not be kept in secure accommodation in England without the authority of the court; and
      (ii) for which the court may authorise a child to be kept in secure accommodation in England;
   (b) empower the court from time to time to authorise a child to be kept in secure accommodation in England for such further period as the regulations may specify; and
   (c) provide that applications to the court under this section shall be made only by local authorities or local authorities in Wales.

(3) It shall be the duty of a court hearing an application under this section to determine whether any relevant criteria for keeping a child in secure accommodation are satisfied in his case.

(4) If a court determines that any such criteria are satisfied, it shall make an order authorising the child to be kept in secure accommodation and specifying the maximum period for which he may be so kept.

(5) On any adjournment of the hearing of an application under this section, a court may make an interim order permitting the child to be kept during the period of the adjournment in secure accommodation.

(6) No court shall exercise the powers conferred by this section in respect of a child who is not legally represented in that court unless, having been informed of his right to apply for the provision of representation under Part 1of LASPO 2012 and having had the opportunity to do so, he refused or failed to apply . . .

B2.1.8 *The statutory remand scheme*

Legal Aid, Sentencing and Punishment of Offenders Act 2012, ss 91–102

91 Remands of children otherwise than on bail

(1) This section applies where—
  (a) a court deals with a child charged with or convicted of one or more offences by remanding the child, and
  (b) the child is not released on bail.
(2) This section also applies where—
  (a) a court remands a child in connection with extradition proceedings, and
  (b) the child is not released on bail.
(3) Subject to subsection (4), the court must remand the child to local authority accommodation in accordance with section 92.
(4) The court may instead remand the child to youth detention accommodation in accordance with section 102 where—
  (a) in the case of a child remanded under subsection (1), the first or second set of conditions for such a remand (see sections 98 and 99) is met in relation to the child, or
  (b) in the case of a child remanded under subsection (2), the first or second set of conditions for such a remand in an extradition case (see sections 100 and 101) is met in relation to the child.
(5) This section is subject to section 128(7) of the Magistrates' Courts Act 1980 (remands to police detention for periods of not more than 3 days); but that provision has effect in relation to a child as if for the reference to 3 clear days there were substituted a reference to 24 hours.
(6) In this Chapter, 'child' means a person under the age of 18.
(7) References in this Chapter (other than in relation to extradition proceedings) to the remand of a child include a reference to—
  (a) the sending of a child for trial, and
  (b) the committal of a child for sentence, and related expressions are to be construed accordingly

...

93 Conditions etc on remands to local authority accommodation

(1) A court remanding a child to local authority accommodation may require the child to comply with any conditions that could be imposed under section 3(6) of the Bail Act 1976 if the child were then being granted bail.
(2) The court may also require the child to comply with any conditions imposed for the purpose of securing the electronic monitoring of the child's compliance with the conditions imposed under subsection (1) if—
  (a) in the case of a child remanded under section 91(1) (proceedings other than extradition proceedings), the requirements in section 94 are met, or
  (b) in the case of a child remanded under section 91(2) (extradition proceedings), the requirements in section 95 are met ...

94 Requirements for electronic monitoring

(1) The requirements referred to in section 93(2)(a) (requirements for imposing electronic monitoring condition: non-extradition cases) are those set out in subsections (2) to (6).

(2) The first requirement is that the child has reached the age of twelve.

(3) The second requirement is that the offence mentioned in section 91(1), or one or more of those offences, is an imprisonable offence.

(4) The third requirement is that—
   (a) the offence mentioned in section 91(1), or one or more of those offences, is a violent or sexual offence or an offence punishable in the case of an adult with imprisonment for a term of 14 years or more, or
   (b) the offence or offences mentioned in section 91(1), together with any other imprisonable offences of which the child has been convicted in any proceedings, amount or would, if the child were convicted of that offence or those offences, amount to a recent history of committing imprisonable offences while on bail or subject to a custodial remand.

(5) The fourth requirement is that the court is satisfied that the necessary provision for electronic monitoring can be made under arrangements currently available in each local justice area which is a relevant area.

(6) The fifth requirement is that a youth offending team has informed the court that, in its opinion, the imposition of an electronic monitoring condition will be suitable in the child's case …

98 First set of conditions for a remand to youth detention accommodation

(1) For the purposes of section 91(4)(a), the first set of conditions for a remand to youth detention accommodation is met in relation to a child if each of the following is met in relation to the child—
   (a) the age condition (see subsection (2)),
   (b) the offence condition (see subsection (3)),
   (c) the necessity condition (see subsection (4)), and
   (d) the first or second legal representation condition (see subsections (5) and (6)).

(2) The age condition is that the child has reached the age of twelve.

(3) The offence condition is that the offence mentioned in section 91(1), or one or more of those offences—
   (a) is a violent or sexual offence, or
   (b) is an offence punishable in the case of an adult with imprisonment for a term of 14 years or more.

(4) The necessity condition is that the court is of the opinion, after considering all the options for the remand of the child, that only remanding the child to youth detention accommodation would be adequate—
   (a) to protect the public from death or serious personal injury (whether physical or psychological) occasioned by further offences committed by the child, or
   (b) to prevent the commission by the child of imprisonable offences.

(5) The first legal representation condition is that the child is legally represented before the court.

(6) The second legal representation condition is that the child is not legally represented before the court and—
   (a) representation was provided to the child under Part 1 of this Act for the purposes of the proceedings, but was withdrawn—
      (i) because of the child's conduct, or
      (ii) because it appeared that the child's financial resources were such that the child was not eligible for such representation,
   (b) the child applied for such representation and the application was refused because it appeared that the child's financial resources were such that the child was not eligible for such representation, or

(c) having been informed of the right to apply for such representation and having had the opportunity to do so, the child refused or failed to apply.

99 Second set of conditions for a remand to youth detention accommodation

(1) For the purposes of section 91(4)(a), the second set of conditions for a remand to youth detention accommodation is met in relation to a child if each of the following is met in relation to the child—
  (a) the age condition (see subsection (2)),
  (b) the sentencing condition (see subsection (3)),
  (c) the offence condition (see subsection (4)),
  (d) the first or second history condition or both (see subsections (5) and (6)),
  (e) the necessity condition (see subsection (7)), and
  (f) the first or second legal representation condition (see subsections (8) and (9)).
(2) The age condition is that the child has reached the age of twelve.
(3) The sentencing condition is that it appears to the court that there is a real prospect that the child will be sentenced to a custodial sentence for the offence mentioned in section 91(1) or one or more of those offences.
(4) The offence condition is that the offence mentioned in section 91(1), or one or more of those offences, is an imprisonable offence.
(5) The first history condition is that—
  (a) the child has a recent history of absconding while subject to a custodial remand, and
  (b) the offence mentioned in section 91(1), or one or more of those offences, is alleged to be or has been found to have been committed while the child was remanded to local authority accommodation or youth detention accommodation.
(6) The second history condition is that the offence or offences mentioned in section 91(1), together with any other imprisonable offences of which the child has been convicted in any proceedings, amount or would, if the child were convicted of that offence or those offences, amount to a recent history of committing imprisonable offences while on bail or subject to a custodial remand.
(7) The necessity condition is that the court is of the opinion, after considering all the options for the remand of the child, that only remanding the child to youth detention accommodation would be adequate—
  (a) to protect the public from death or serious personal injury (whether physical or psychological) occasioned by further offences committed by the child, or
  (b) to prevent the commission by the child of imprisonable offences.
(8) The first legal representation condition is that the child is legally represented before the court.
(9) The second legal representation condition is that the child is not legally represented before the court and—
  (a) representation was provided to the child under Part 1 of this Act for the purposes of the proceedings, but was withdrawn—
    (i) because of the child's conduct, or
    (ii) because it appeared that the child's financial resources were such that the child was not eligible for such representation,
  (b) the child applied for such representation and the application was refused because it appeared that the child's financial resources were such that the child was not eligible for such representation, or
  (c) having been informed of the right to apply for such representation and having had the opportunity to do so, the child refused or failed to apply.

(10) In this Chapter 'custodial sentence' means a sentence or order mentioned in section 76(1) of the Powers of Criminal Courts (Sentencing) Act 2000.

(11) The reference in subsection (5)(b) to a child being remanded to local authority accommodation or youth detention accommodation includes—

(a) a child being remanded to local authority accommodation under section 23 of the Children and Young Persons Act 1969, and

(b) a child being remanded to prison under that section as modified by section 98 of the Crime and Disorder Act 1998 or under section 27 of the Criminal Justice Act 1948.

B3 Breach of Orders, and New Offences Committed during an Order

See Powers of Criminal Courts (Sentencing) Act 2000, Sch 1, Pt 1, paras 1–7 and Appendix 1 of Sentencing Children and Young People: Definitive Guideline.

B3.1 Referral orders

B3.1.1 *Which court will handle the case?*

> **Powers of Criminal Courts (Sentencing) Act 2000, Sch 1, Pt 1, para 1(2)**
>
> (2) the appropriate court is—
>
> (a) in the case of an offender aged under 18 at the time when (in pursuance of the referral back) he first appears before the court, a youth court acting in the local justice area in which it appears to the youth offender panel that the offender resides or will reside; and
>
> (b) otherwise, a magistrates' court (other than a youth court) acting in that area.

B3.1.2 *Powers of the court*

In dealing with the offender for such an offence, the appropriate court 'may deal with him in any way in which (assuming s 16 of this Act had not applied) he could have been dealt with for that offence by the court which made the order' (Sch 1, Pt 1, para 5(5)(a)). This provision disapplies the obligation to impose a referral order.

The court must be satisfied that the youth offender panel was entitled to make the finding of breach of the referral order, or that any discretion was exercised reasonably. Where a court is revoking and resentencing an offender, the court has the powers of the youth court, whatever the age of the defendant. As an alternative to revocation the court can impose a fine of up to £2,500 or the contract period may be increased up to a maximum of 12 months, and the court must have regard to the circumstances of the referral back and the extent of any compliance with it. The court may take no action.

B3.1.3 *Conviction while subject to a referral order*

See Powers of Criminal Courts (Sentencing) Act 2000, Sch 1, Pt 2, paras 11–14.

The court sentencing for the new offence may extend the compliance period of the referral order. The total period may not exceed 12 months. If sentencing for the new offence in any other way (other than by an absolute or conditional discharge), the referral order may be revoked, but it may also be allowed to continue. The court may, if it is in the interests of justice, deal with the offender in any manner in which the offender could have been dealt with by the original court. The extent of any compliance must be taken into account.

B3.2 Youth rehabilitation order—breach proceedings

B3.2.1 *Which court will handle the case?*

> **Criminal Justice and Immigration Act 2008, Sch 2, para 5(3)**
>
> (3) 'appropriate court' means—
>   (a) if the offender is aged under 18, a youth court acting in the relevant local justice area, and
>   (b) if the offender is aged 18 or over, a magistrates' court (other than a youth court) acting in that local justice area.

In a youth rehabilitation order (YRO) case, a warning is required if the supervising officer finds there is a failure to comply without reasonable excuse. If, following a further, second warning within the 12-month 'warned period', there is then a third failure to comply without reasonable excuse, the officer must refer the case to court for breach proceedings, although Youth Offending Teams will have additional discretion in exceptional circumstances following a third failure to comply. The officer also has the discretion to refer the case to court at an earlier warning stage.

B3.2.2 *Powers of the court*

When dealing with the breach of a YRO, the court has the following options:

* no action;
* a fine of up to £2,500;
* amend the YRO, but not with Intensive Supervision and Surveillance Requirement (ISSR) or Intensive Fostering, unless that already applies;
* revoke the YRO and resentence, within the powers of the original (sentencing) court.

Custody is an option for breach of a YRO only if the original offence is imprisonable or, in the case of a non-imprisonable offence, if, following 'wilful and persistent' non-compliance (Criminal Justice and Immigration Act 2008, Sch 2), a YRO with an ISSR or Intensive Fostering provision is made and that further YRO is then also subject to non-compliance. The court, if passing a custodial sentence, must state that a YRO with an ISSR or Intensive Fostering provision is not appropriate and the reasons why. This is in addition to meeting the existing criteria, that is, the court forming the opinion that the offence(s) is so serious that a community sentence cannot be justified.

Paragraph 6 provides:

> **Criminal Justice and Immigration Act 2008, Sch 2, para 6**
>
> 6   (1) This paragraph applies where—
>   (a) an offender appears or is brought before a youth court or other magistrates' court under paragraph 5, and
>   (b) it is proved to the satisfaction of the court that the offender has failed without reasonable excuse to comply with the youth rehabilitation order.

(1) The court may deal with the offender in respect of that failure in any one of the following ways—
   (a) by ordering the offender to pay a fine of an amount not exceeding £2,500;
   (b) by amending the terms of the youth rehabilitation order so as to impose any requirement which could have been included in the order when it was made—
      (i) in addition to, or
      (ii) substitution for any requirement or requirements already imposed by the order;
   (c) by dealing with the offender, for the offence in respect of which the order was made, in any way in which the court could have dealt with the offender for that offence (had the offender been before that court to be dealt with for it).
(2) Sub-paragraph (2)(b) is subject to sub-paragraphs (6) to (9).
(3) In dealing with the offender under sub-paragraph (2), the court must take into account the extent to which the offender has complied with the youth rehabilitation order.
(4) A fine imposed under sub-paragraph (2)(a) is to be treated, for the purposes of any enactment, as being a sum adjudged to be paid by a conviction.
(5) Any requirement imposed under sub-paragraph (2)(b) must be capable of being complied with before the date specified under paragraph 32(1) of Schedule 1.
(6) Where—
   (a) the court is dealing with the offender under sub-paragraph (2)(b), and
   (b) the youth rehabilitation order does not contain an unpaid work requirement, paragraph 10(2) of Schedule 1 applies in relation to the inclusion of such a requirement as if for '40' there were substituted '20'.
(7) The court may not under sub-paragraph (2)(b) impose—
   (a) an extended activity requirement, or
   (b) a fostering requirement, if the order does not already impose such a requirement.
(8) Where—
   (a) the order imposes a fostering requirement (the 'original requirement'), and
   (b) under sub-paragraph (2)(b) the court proposes to substitute a new fostering requirement ('the substitute requirement') for the original requirement, paragraph 18(2) of Schedule 1 applies in relation to the substitute requirement as if the reference to the period of 12 months beginning with the date on which the original requirement first had effect were a reference to the period of 18 months beginning with that date.
(9) Where—
   (a) the court deals with the offender under sub-paragraph (2)(b), and
   (b) it would not otherwise have the power to amend the youth rehabilitation order under paragraph 13 (amendment by reason of change of residence), that paragraph has effect as if references in it to the appropriate court were references to the court which is dealing with the offender.
(10) Where the court deals with the offender under sub-paragraph (2)(c), it must revoke the youth rehabilitation order if it is still in force.
(11) Sub-paragraphs (13) to (15) apply where—
   (a) the court is dealing with the offender under sub-paragraph (2)(c), and
   (b) the offender has wilfully and persistently failed to comply with a youth rehabilitation order.
(12) The court may impose a youth rehabilitation order with intensive supervision and surveillance notwithstanding anything in section 1(4) (a) or (b).
(13) If—
   (a) the order is a youth rehabilitation order with intensive supervision and surveillance, and
   (b) the offence mentioned in sub-paragraph (2)(c) was punishable with imprisonment,

the court may impose a custodial sentence notwithstanding anything in section 152(2) of the Criminal Justice Act 2003 (c. 44) (general restrictions on imposing discretionary custodial sentences).

(14) If—

(a) the order is a youth rehabilitation order with intensive supervision and surveillance which was imposed by virtue of sub-paragraph (13) or paragraph 8(12), and

(b) the offence mentioned in sub-paragraph (2)(c) was not punishable with imprisonment,

for the purposes of dealing with the offender under sub-paragraph (2)(c), the court is to be taken to have had power to deal with the offender for that offence by making a detention and training order for a term not exceeding 4 months.

(15) An offender may appeal to the Crown Court against a sentence imposed under sub-paragraph (2)(c).

B3.3 Youth rehabilitation orders made in the Crown Court

B3.3.1 *Powers of the court*

Criminal Justice and Immigration Act 2008, Sch 1, para 36

36 (1) Where the Crown Court makes a youth rehabilitation order, it may include in the order a direction that further proceedings relating to the order be in a youth court or other magistrates' court (subject to paragraph 7 of Schedule 2).

(2) In sub-paragraph (1), 'further proceedings', in relation to a youth rehabilitation order, means proceedings—

(a) for any failure to comply with the order within the meaning given by paragraph 1(2)(b) of Schedule 2, or

(b) on any application for amendment or revocation of the order under Part 3 or 4 of that Schedule.

Criminal Justice and Immigration Act 2008, Sch 2, para 7

7 (1) Sub-paragraph (2) applies if—

(a) the youth rehabilitation order was made by the Crown Court and contains a direction under paragraph 36 of Schedule 1, and

(b) a youth court or other magistrates' court would (apart from that sub-paragraph) be required, or has the power, to deal with the offender in one of the ways mentioned in paragraph 6(2).

(2) The court may instead—

(a) commit the offender in custody, or

(b) release the offender on bail,

until the offender can be brought or appear before the Crown Court.

(3) Where a court deals with the offender's case under sub-paragraph (2) it must send to the Crown Court—

(a) a certificate signed by a justice of the peace certifying that the offender has failed to comply with the youth rehabilitation order in the respect specified in the certificate, and

(b) such other particulars of the case as may be desirable;

and a certificate purporting to be so signed is admissible as evidence of the failure before the Crown Court.

B3.3.2 *Conviction while subject to a youth rehabilitation order*

If the defendant is convicted of a new offence while subject to a YRO, the court has power to revoke the sentence and resentence. If the sentence was imposed in the Crown Court, it must commit to the Crown Court for sentence, unless the Crown Court made an order allowing the magistrates' court to deal with any breach under Sch 1, para 36 Criminal Justice and Immigration Act 1998.

Paragraph 18 of Sch 2 to the Criminal Justice and Immigration Act 2008 provides:

Criminal Justice and Immigration Act 2008, Sch 2, para 18

18 (1) This paragraph applies where—
   (a) a youth rehabilitation order is in force in respect of an offender, and
   (b) the offender is convicted of an offence (the 'further offence') by a youth court or other magistrates' court ('the convicting court').
(2) Sub-paragraphs (3) and (4) apply where—
   (a) the youth rehabilitation order—
      (i) was made by a youth court or other magistrates' court, or
      (ii) was made by the Crown Court and contains a direction under paragraph 36 of Schedule 1, and
   (b) the convicting court is dealing with the offender for the further offence.
(3) The convicting court may revoke the order.
(4) Where the convicting court revokes the order under sub-paragraph (3), it may deal with the offender, for the offence in respect of which the order was made, in any way in which it could have dealt with the offender for that offence (had the offender been before that court to be dealt with for the offence).
(5) The convicting court may not exercise its powers under sub-paragraph (1) or (4) unless it considers that it would be in the interests of justice to do so, having regard to circumstances which have arisen since the youth rehabilitation order was made.
(6) In dealing with an offender under sub-paragraph (4), the sentencing court must take into account the extent to which the offender has complied with the order.
(7) A person sentenced under sub-paragraph (4) for an offence may appeal to the Crown Court against the sentence.
(8) Sub-paragraph (9) applies where—
   (a) the youth rehabilitation order was made by the Crown Court and contains a direction under paragraph 36 of Schedule 1, and
   (b) the convicting court would, but for that sub-paragraph, deal with the offender for the further offence.
(9) The convicting court may, instead of proceeding under sub-paragraph (3)—
   (a) commit the offender in custody, or
   (b) release the offender on bail,
      until the offender can be brought before the Crown Court.
(10) Sub-paragraph (11) applies if the youth rehabilitation order was made by the Crown Court and does not contain a direction under paragraph 36 of Schedule 1.
(11) The convicting court may—
   (a) commit the offender in custody, or
   (b) release the offender on bail,
      until the offender can be brought or appear before the Crown Court.

B3.4 Detention and training order: breach of the supervision requirements

B3.4.1 *Which court handles the case?*

Section 104(1) Powers of Criminal Courts (Sentencing) Act 2000 provides that such matters must be dealt with by the youth court, even if the defendant has reached the age of 18 years.

B3.4.2 *Detention and training order—new offences*

Powers of Criminal Courts (Sentencing) Act 2000, s 105(1)–(4)

105 Offences during currency of order

(1) This section applies to a person subject to a detention and training order if—
   (a) after his release and before the date on which the term of the order ends, he commits an offence punishable with imprisonment in the case of a person aged 21 or over ('the new offence'); and
   (b) whether before or after that date, he is convicted of the new offence.
(2) Subject to section 8(6) above (duty of adult magistrates' court to remit young offenders to youth court for sentence), the court by or before which a person to whom this section applies is convicted of the new offence may, whether or not it passes any other sentence on him, order him to be detained in such youth detention accommodation as the Secretary of State may determine for the whole or any part of the period which—
   (a) begins with the date of the court's order; and
   (b) is equal in length to the period between the date on which the new offence was committed and the date mentioned in subsection (1) above.
(3) The period for which a person to whom this section applies is ordered under subsection (2) above to be detained in youth detention accommodation—
   (a) shall, as the court may direct, either be served before and be followed by, or be served concurrently with, any sentence imposed for the new offence; and
   (b) in either case, shall be disregarded in determining the appropriate length of that sentence.
(4) Where the new offence is found to have been committed over a period of two or more days, or at some time during a period of two or more days, it shall be taken for the purposes of this section to have been committed on the last of those days.
   ...

 See *Blackstone's Criminal Practice 2019* **E7.15–E7.25**

B4 Jurisdiction of the Adult Magistrates' Court over Youths

B4.1 Youths in the adult court alone

A child or young person, who is not jointly charged with an adult and who is refused bail at the police station, may appear in an adult court when no youth court is sitting. The adult court may deal with the young person only for the purposes of making a decision with regard to a remand. It must then remit the young person to the next available youth court (s 46(2) Children and Young Persons Act 1933) (see further **B6**).

B4.2 Jointly charged with an adult

A child or young person *must* appear before the adult court if jointly charged with an adult.

A child or young person *may* appear before the adult court if:

- charged with aiding or abetting an adult;
- an adult is charged with aiding or abetting the child or young person;
- charged with an offence arising out of the same circumstances as those giving rise to proceedings against an adult

(s 46 Children and Young Persons Act 1933 and s 18 Children and Young Persons Act 1963).

B4.2.1 *What is a joint charge?*

It is not necessary for the charge to specify that the offence was committed 'jointly' or 'together with' the adult concerned (*R v Rowlands* [1972] 1 All ER 306).

Where there is a charge of taking a motor vehicle without consent or aggravated vehicle-taking, the driver and any passengers charged with allowing themselves to be carried are jointly charged (*R v Peterborough Justices, ex p Allgood* (1995) 159 JP 627, QBD).

B4.3 Severance of a youth from an adult

B4.3.1 *Sendings*

When the court sends the adult but is not obliged to send the youth, it shall, after following the plea before venue procedures (see **B5**), send the youth too if it considers it necessary in the interests of justice to do so (s 51(7) Crime and Disorder Act 1998).

Relevant issues have been identified by the Sentencing Council in two Guidelines which mirror each other: The Allocation Guideline and the Definitive Guideline on Sentencing Children and Young People, paragraphs 2.11–2.14.

Sentencing Children and Young People: Definitive Guideline, paras 2.11–2.14

2.11 The proper venue for the trial of any child or young person is normally the youth court. Subject to statutory restrictions, that remains the case where a child or young person is jointly charged with an adult. If the adult is sent for trial to the Crown Court, the court should conclude that the child or young person must be tried separately in the youth court unless it is in the interests of justice for the child or young person and the adult to be tried jointly.

2.12 Examples of factors that should be considered when deciding whether to send the child or young person to the Crown Court (rather than having a trial in the youth court) include:

whether separate trials will cause injustice to witnesses or to the case as a whole (consideration should be given to the provisions of ss 27 and 28 of the Youth Justice and Criminal Evidence Act 1999);

the age of the child or young person; the younger the child or young person, the greater the desirability that the child or young person be tried in the youth court;

the age gap between the child or young person and the adult; a substantial gap in age militates in favour of the child or young person being tried in the youth court;

the lack of maturity of the child or young person;

the relative culpability of the child or young person compared with the adult and whether the alleged role played by the child or young person was minor; and/or

the lack of previous findings of guilt on the part of the child or young person.

2.13 The court should bear in mind that the youth court now has a general power to commit for sentence (as discussed at paragraph 2.9); in appropriate cases this will permit a sentence to be imposed by the same court on adults and children and young people who have been tried separately.

2.14 The court should follow the plea before venue procedure (see flowcharts on page 217) prior to considering whether it is in the interests of justice for the child or young person and the adult to be tried jointly.

B4.4 Summary trials

If an adult and the youth plead not guilty to a joint charge, the trial must take place in the adult court (s 46(1)(a) Children and Young Persons Act 1933). It may do so if the allegation is of aiding and abetting, or arises out of the same circumstances (s 46(1)(b) Children and Young Persons Act 1933; s 18(a) and (b) Children and Young Persons Act 1963). (See **B4.2**.)

If the youth pleads guilty or is found guilty, the adult court may sentence under its limited powers or remit to the youth court (s 8(6) Powers of Criminal Courts (Sentencing) Act 2000).

If the adult pleads guilty and the youth not guilty, it is to be expected that the court will remit to the youth court for trial (s 29(2) Magistrates' Courts Act 1980) (see **B6**).

B4.5 Remittal

All cases not sent to the Crown Court, sentenced within the limited powers of the adult court (see **B8**) or listed for trial with an adult, will be remitted to the youth court (see **B6**).

B5 **Managing the Case**

In order to handle the case appropriately, the steps shown in Figure 3 must be followed where the youth is jointly charged with an adult. If the adult faces an indictable-only offence he must be sent to the Crown Court before dealing with this procedure. If the adult faces an either-way offence, this procedure should be followed but any plea should be taken first from the adult.

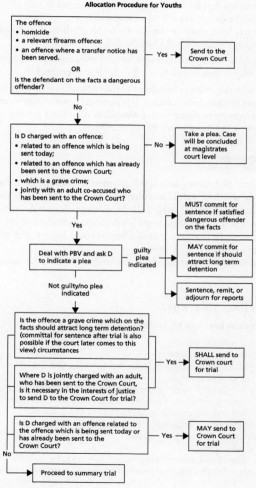

Allocation Procedure for Youths

The offence
• homicide
• a relevant firearm offence:
• an offence where a transfer notice has been served.

OR

Is the defendant on the facts a dangerous offender?

Yes → Send to the Crown Court

No

Is D charged with an offence:
• related to an offence which is being sent today;
• related to an offence which has already been sent to the Crown Court;
• which is a grave crime;
• jointly with an adult co-accused who has been sent to the Crown Court?

No → Take a plea. Case will be concluded at magistrates court level

Yes

Deal with PBV and ask D to indicate a plea

guilty plea indicated

MUST commit for sentence if satisfied dangerous offender on the facts

MAY commit for sentence if should attract long term detention

Sentence, remit, or adjourn for reports

Not guilty/no plea indicated

Is the offence a grave crime which on the facts should attract long term detention? (committal for sentence after trial is also possible if the court later comes to this view) circumstances

Where D is jointly charged with an adult, who has been sent to the Crown Court, is it necessary in the interests of justice to send D to the Crown Court for trial?

Yes → SHALL send to Crown court for trial

Is D charged with an offence related to the offence which is being sent today or has already been sent to the Crown Court?

Yes → MAY send to Crown Court for trial

No

Proceed to summary trial

Figure 3 Allocation procedure for youths

B5.1 Sendings to the Crown Court

The court *must* forthwith send the case to the Crown Court if the youth is charged with:

- homicide;
- an offence attracting a minimum sentence under s 51A Firearms Act 1968 or s 29(3) Violent Crime Reduction Act 2006, provided the youth was aged at least 16 at the date of the offence;
- a specified offence and on the facts of the case an extended sentence may be required (so that for youths, a minimum sentence of four years would be required) (the dangerous offender provisions); *or*
- if notice has been given by the Crown under s 51B (serious fraud) or s 51C (children) of the Crime and Disorder Act 1998 (see **B5.5**).

When a child or young person is sent for trial, the court may also send for trial any either-way or summary offence for which he is charged if:

- it appears to the court to be related to the indictable-only offence; *and*
- in the case of a summary offence, it is punishable with imprisonment or involves obligatory or discretionary disqualification from driving (s 51(6) and (11) Crime and Disorder Act 1998—see **B5.5**).

B5.1.1 Key points

- An offence of murder, attempted murder, manslaughter, causing or allowing the death of a child or vulnerable adult, or infanticide must be sent to the Crown Court for trial (s 24(1) Magistrates' Courts Act (MCA) 1980), along with any other offences with which the defendant is charged at the same time, if the charges for both offences could be joined in the same indictment (s 24(1A) MCA 1980).
- The relevant offences under the Firearms Act 1968 are set out in s 51A of that Act:

Firearms Act 1968, s 51A

51A Minimum sentence for certain offences under s 5

(1) This section applies where—
  (a) an individual is convicted of—
    (i) an offence under section 5(1)(a), (ab), (aba), (ac), (ad), (ae), (af) or of this Act,
    (ii) an offence under section 5(1A)(a) of this Act, or
    (iii) an offence under any of the provisions of this Act listed in subsection (1A) in respect of a firearm or ammunition specified in section 5(1)(a), (ab), (aba), (ac), (ad), (ae), (af) or (c) or section 5(1A)(a) of this Act, and
  (b) the offence was committed after the commencement of this section and at a time when he was aged 16 or over.
(1A) The provisions are—
  (a) section 16 (possession of firearm with intent to injure);
  (b) section 16A (possession of firearm with intent to cause fear of violence);

(c) section 17 (use of firearm to resist arrest);

(d) section 18 (carrying firearm with criminal intent);

(e) section 19 (carrying a firearm in a public place);

(f) section 20(1) (trespassing in a building with firearm).

(2) The court shall impose an appropriate custodial sentence (or order for detention) for a term of at least the required minimum term (with or without a fine) unless the court is of the opinion that there are exceptional circumstances relating to the offence or to the offender which justify its not doing so.

(3) Where an offence is found to have been committed over a period of two or more days, or at some time during a period of two or more days, it shall be taken for the purposes of this section to have been committed on the last of those days.

(4) In this section 'appropriate custodial sentence (or order for detention)' means—

(a) in relation to England and Wales—

(i) in the case of an offender who is aged 18 or over when convicted, a sentence of imprisonment, and

(ii) in the case of an offender who is aged under 18 at that time, a sentence of detention under section 91 of the Powers of Criminal Courts (Sentencing) Act 2000;

(b) ...

(5) In this section 'the required minimum term' means—

(a) in relation to England and Wales—

(i) in the case of an offender who was aged 18 or over when he committed the offence, five years, and

(ii) in the case of an offender who was under 18 at that time, three years...

(b) ...

B5.2 Other indictable and all summary matters

The court must proceed to plea before venue if the case could be sent; or take a plea if it is a summary-only offence. This applies even when appearing jointly with an adult, though if both plead not guilty the court will have to consider whether it is appropriate to join the cases.

Tottenham Youth Court, ex p Fawzy [1999] 1 WLR 1350 confirms that the adult court must make the decision on venue. There is no power to remit the youth to the youth court for that court to make the mode of trial decision.

B5.3 Guilty plea indications

If a guilty plea is indicated, the court should proceed to sentence if the court's powers are sufficient (see **B8**) or remit to the youth court (see **B6**) *unless*:

- the offence is a specified offence under the dangerous offender provisions and on the developing facts an extended sentence may be required (so that for a youth a minimum sentence of at least four years may be required), in which case it *must* commit to the Crown Court for sentence;

- the offence is related to an offence which is being sent that day, or related to a matter which has already been sent, in which case it *may* commit to the Crown Court for sentence;
- the offence is capable of being a grave crime, in which case it *may* commit for sentence if on the facts the offence might attract a sentence of long-term detention.

If the youth pleads guilty and the adult is committed for sentence under s 4 Powers of Criminal Courts (Sentencing) Act 2000, he must be remitted for sentence to the youth court, unless either he is committed to the Crown Court for seriousness or dangerousness, or the court imposes a discharge, referral order, financial penalty, or bind over under s 8 of the 2000 Act.

B5.3.1 Key points

- Offences are *grave crimes* if they comprise:
  - an offence punishable in the case of a person aged 21 or over with imprisonment for 14 years or more, not being an offence the sentence for which is fixed by law; or
  - an offence under s 3 Sexual Offences Act 2003 ('the 2003 Act') (sexual assault); or
  - an offence under s 13 2003 Act (child sex offences committed by children or young persons); or
  - an offence under s 25 2003 Act (sexual activity with a child family member); or
  - an offence under s 26 2003 Act (inciting a child family member to engage in sexual activity); or
  - an offence under subsection (1)(a), (ab), (aba), (ac), (ad), (ae), (af), or (c) of s 5 Firearms Act 1968 (prohibited weapons), or under subsection (1A)(a) of that section; or
  - an offence under s 51A(1A)(b), (e), or (f) Firearms Act 1968, which was committed in respect of a firearm or ammunition specified in s 5(1), (ab), (aba), (ac), (ad), (ae), (af), or (c), or s 5(1A)(a) of that Act; or
  - an offence under s 28 Violent Crime Reduction Act 2006 (using someone to mind a weapon).
- An offence requiring a sentence of 'long-term detention' because it should substantially exceed two years:
  - in determining whether a sentence of more than two years would be imposed, the court should ask itself what sentence was realistically possible, bearing in mind the sentencing range (*Crown Prosecution Service v Newcastle Upon Tyne Youth Court* [2010] EWHC 2773 (Admin));
  - the fact that a particular youth aged 12 to 14 years could not receive a detention and training order is not a ground for refusing jurisdiction when a sentence of more than two years' detention is not required; youths of this age should not be detained save in wholly exceptional circumstances (*R (B) v Norfolk Youth Court* and CPS [2013] EWHC 1459 (Admin));

- in *BH v Llandudno Youth Court* [2014] EWHC 1833 (Admin) the court considered all the relevant authorities and applied the guideline, emphasizing that the correct question is, bearing in mind the age and the previous good character of the child concerned (there an 11-year-old facing an allegation of inducing a boy under 13 to engage in a sexual act against s 8 Sexual Offences Act 2003), and any other mitigation that is known and uncontentious, and bearing in mind aggravating factors, is there a real prospect that the Crown Court would exercise its powers under s 91 PCC(S) Act 2000 to impose custody? (It concluded that there was not.);
- *R v H* [2014] EWCA Crim 2292 confirmed that while detention may have been appropriate for a 15-year-old in the same circumstances, a defendant who was 14 years old at the time of the offence had a youth rehabilitation order substituted. This was notwithstanding the seriousness of the burglary by 15 to 20 youths who entered a dwelling house and threatened violence, and his brandishing a carving knife to make his escape. He did not have 'a particularly bad record'—assaults on his mother; theft convictions; and various reprimands and warnings so as to be 'just' a persistent offender. The mitigation was a plea at the first opportunity; his being the only one arrested and being in the presence of much older boys who had serious criminal records and of whom he was in fear about attempting to separate himself;
- reference should be made to the definitive guideline at **B5.4**.

See *Blackstone's Criminal Practice 2019* **D24.27**

B5.4 Not guilty and no plea indications

If a youth is jointly charged with an adult who has been sent to the Crown Court, the court must first consider if the offence is a grave crime which on the facts should attract a sentence of long-term detention; and if it is, the court *must* send for trial. This is now subject to the provisions of the Definitive Guideline.

> ### Definitive Guideline on Sentencing Children and Young People, para 12.10
>
> 2.10 Before deciding whether to send the case to the Crown Court or retain jurisdiction in the youth court, the court should hear submissions from the prosecution and defence. As there is now a power to commit grave crimes for sentence [*footnote deleted*] the court should no longer take the prosecution case at its highest when deciding whether to retain jurisdiction.[*footnote deleted*] In most cases it is likely to be impossible to decide whether there is a real prospect that a sentence in excess of two years' detention will be imposed without knowing more about the facts of the case and the circumstances of the child or young person. In those circumstances the youth court should retain jurisdiction and commit for sentence if it is of the view, having heard more about the facts and the circumstances of the child or young person, that its powers of sentence are insufficient.
>
> Where the court decides that the case is suitable to be dealt with in the youth court it must warn the child or young person that all available sentencing options remain open

and, if found guilty, the child or young person may be committed to the Crown Court for sentence.

Children and young people should only be sent for trial or committed for sentence to the Crown Court when charged with or found guilty of an offence of such gravity that a custodial sentence substantially exceeding two years is a realistic possibility. For children aged 10 or 11, and children/young people aged 12–14 who are not persistent offenders, the court should take into account the normal prohibition on imposing custodial sentences

If the youth has not been sent for that reason but is jointly charged with an adult and it is necessary in the interests of justice (see **B4.3.1**) to send the youth to the Crown Court for trial, the court must then send the youth for that reason.

If the defendant is charged with an offence related to an offence which is sent that day, or has already been sent, the court *may* send to the Crown Court for trial.

In all other cases the court should proceed to summary trial or, if there is to be no effective trial of the adult, remit to the youth court (see **B6**).

B5.5 Statutory provisions

Refer to MCA 1980, ss 24A–24C and Crime and Disorder Act 1998, ss 51–51C

B6 Remittal to the Youth Court for Trial/Sentence

Under s 46 Children and Young Persons Act 1933 the magistrates' court shall remit to:

- a youth court acting for the same place as the remitting court; or
- a youth court acting for the place where the young offender habitually resides, except when:

  (a) a charge made jointly against a child or young person and a person who has attained the age of eighteen years shall be heard by a magistrates' court other than a youth court; and

  (b) where a child or young person is charged with an offence, the charge may be heard by a magistrates' court which is not a youth court if a person who has attained the age of eighteen years is charged at the same time with aiding, abetting, causing, procuring, allowing or permitting that offence; and

  (c) where, in the course of any proceedings before any magistrates' court other than a youth court, it appears that the person to whom the proceedings relate is a child or young person, nothing in this subsection shall be construed as preventing the court, if it thinks fit so to do, from proceeding with the hearing and determination of those proceedings.

It is generally good practice to remit for sentence to the young person's local court.

A power to remit to the youth court for trial is granted under s 29 Magistrates' Courts Act 1980 where there will be no effective trial of an adult in relation to a joint charge either because the adult(s) plead guilty or are sent to the Crown Court.

A duty to remit exists under s 8 Powers of Criminal Courts (Sentencing) Act 2000, for sentencing where the adult court's limited powers are not regarded as sufficient (see **B8**).

B7 **Reporting Restrictions**

In the adult court, unlike the youth court, discretionary provisions apply. The court must specifically apply the restrictions which relate to the identification of victims, other witnesses, and defendants by stating in open court that it is doing so. The conflicting demands of Articles 8 and 10 of the European Convention on Human Rights (ECHR) must be balanced (see **A25.2.1**). Section 39 Children and Young Persons Act 1933 has been disapplied from criminal proceedings, and the relevant provisions are now ss 45 and 45A Youth Justice and Criminal Evidence Act 1999. The latter is considered at **A25.1.1**.

Youth Justice and Criminal Evidence Act 1999, s 45

45 Power to restrict reporting of criminal proceedings involving persons under 18

(1) This section applies (subject to subsection (2)) in relation to—
   (a) any criminal proceedings in any court (other than a service court) in England and Wales
(2) This section does not apply in relation to any proceedings to which section 49 of the Children and Young Persons Act 1933 applies.
(3) The court may direct that no matter relating to any person concerned in the proceedings shall while he is under the age of 18 be included in any publication if it is likely to lead members of the public to identify him as a person concerned in the proceedings.
(4) The court or an appellate court may by direction ('an excepting direction') dispense, to any extent specified in the excepting direction, with the restrictions imposed by a direction under subsection (3) if it is satisfied that it is necessary in the interests of justice to do so.
(5) The court or an appellate court may also by direction ('an excepting direction') dispense, to any extent specified in the excepting direction, with the restrictions imposed by a direction under subsection (3) if it is satisfied—
   (a) that their effect is to impose a substantial and unreasonable restriction on the reporting of the proceedings, and
   (b) that it is in the public interest to remove or relax that restriction; but no excepting direction shall be given under this subsection by reason only of the fact that the proceedings have been determined in any way or have been abandoned.
(6) When deciding whether to make—
   (a) a direction under subsection (3) in relation to a person, or
   (b) an excepting direction under subsection (4) or (5) by virtue of which the restrictions imposed by a direction under subsection (3) would be dispensed with (to any extent) in relation to a person,
   the court or (as the case may be) the appellate court shall have regard to the welfare of that person.
(7) For the purposes of subsection (3) any reference to a person concerned in the proceedings is to a person—
   (a) against or in respect of whom the proceedings are taken, or
   (b) who is a witness in the proceedings.
(8) The matters relating to a person in relation to which the restrictions imposed by a direction under subsection (3) apply (if their inclusion in any publication is likely to have the result mentioned in that subsection) include in particular—

(a) his name,

(b) his address,

(c) the identity of any school or other educational establishment attended by him,

(d) the identity of any place of work, and

(e) any still or moving picture of him.

(9) A direction under subsection (3) may be revoked by the court or an appellate court.

(10) An excepting direction—

    (a) may be given at the time the direction under subsection (3) is given or subsequently; and

    (b) may be varied or revoked by the court or an appellate court.

Considering earlier statutory provisions, the following principles were set out in *R (Y) v Aylesbury Crown Court* [2012] EWHC 1140 (Admin):

- The defendant had to satisfy the court that there was a good reason for restriction.
- The good reason for a young person would in most cases be his welfare. Publicity would have significant effects on the young person's prospects and opportunities.
- The court must have regard to Article 10 ECHR. A restriction order must be necessary and proportionate, and for a pressing social need. There was a public interest in knowing the outcome of proceedings.
- There is a balance to be struck. Prior to conviction it was unlikely that there should be publicity. After conviction, the age of the defendant and seriousness of the crime would be particularly relevant.
- Partial publicity was possible.
- If there was an even balance there should be no publicity.

B8 Sentencing

B8.1 Overview of section 8 of the Powers of Criminal Courts (Sentencing) Act 2000

Only the following sentencing options are available in relation to young offenders appearing in the adult court. Any case requiring a greater sentence must be remitted to the youth court (see **B6**).

Age (last birthday)	10–13	14	15	16–17
Absolute discharge	Yes	Yes	Yes	Yes
Conditional discharge (note that a conditional discharge cannot be imposed if the offender has received a final warning/ youth caution in the previous 24 months unless exceptional circumstances are found). A conditional discharge in respect to a youth can be for a maximum period of 3 years.	Yes	Yes	Yes	Yes
Fine	Yes: maximum £250. Order must be made against parent/ guardian unless unreasonable in the circumstances	Yes: maximum £1,000. Order must be made against parent/ guardian unless unreasonable in the circumstances	Yes: maximum £1,000. Order must be made against parent/ guardian unless unreasonable in the circumstances	Yes: maximum £1,000
Referral order	Yes	Yes	Yes	Yes

B8.2 Victim surcharge

The court must add the relevant victim surcharge which for youths is as follows:

Offenders under 18 years at the time the offence was committed	Victim surcharge for offences:	
	before 28 June 2019	on or after 28 June 2019
A conditional discharge	£15	£16
A fine	£20	£21

Offenders under 18 years at the time the offence was committed	Victim surcharge for offences:	
	before 28 June 2019	on or after 28 June 2019
Youth rehabilitation order	£20	£21
Referral order	£20	£21

B8.3 Referral orders

The adult court may (but need not) make a referral order in circumstances where, in the youth court, such an order must be made. This obligation arises under s 17(1) Powers of Criminal Courts (Sentencing) Act 2000, where:

- the offence is punishable with imprisonment;
- the offender has pleaded guilty to the offence(s);
- the court is not imposing an absolute or conditional discharge, a hospital order, or a custodial sentence;
- the offender has never previously been convicted (in the United Kingdom) of an offence or bound over.

B8.4 Ancillary powers

In addition to exercising these powers, the court may make ancillary orders such as:

- an order (under s 150 Powers of Criminal Courts (Sentencing) Act 2000) binding over a parent or guardian to take proper care of the youth and exercise proper care over him, or a parenting order;
- ancillary orders such as disqualification from driving, endorsement of a driving licence, and to pay compensation and costs.

 See *Blackstone's Criminal Practice 2019* **D24.107** and **D24.108**

Part C
Offences

C1 **Animal Offences**

C1.1 **Animal cruelty**

Sections 4, 5, 6, 7, 8, and 9 Animal Welfare Act 2006 provide for offences in relation to unnecessary suffering, mutilation, docking of dogs' tails, administration of poisons, and fighting.

Animal Welfare Act 2006, ss 4(1)–(2), 5(1)–(2), (6), 6(1)–(12), 7, 8, and 9

4 Unnecessary suffering

(1) A person commits an offence if—
- (a) an act of his, or a failure of his to act, causes an animal to suffer,
- (b) he knew, or ought reasonably to have known, that the act, or failure to act, would have that effect or be likely to do so,
- (c) the animal is a protected animal, and
- (d) the suffering is unnecessary.

(2) A person commits an offence if—

- (a) he is responsible for an animal,
- (b) an act, or failure to act, of another person causes the animal to suffer,
- (c) he permitted that to happen or failed to take such steps (whether by way of supervising the other person or otherwise) as were reasonable in all the circumstances to prevent that happening, and
- (d) the suffering is unnecessary . . .

5 Mutilation

(1) A person commits an offence if—
- (a) he carries out a prohibited procedure on a protected animal;
- (b) he causes such a procedure to be carried out on such an animal.

(2) A person commits an offence if—
- (a) he is responsible for an animal,
- (b) another person carries out a prohibited procedure on the animal, and
- (c) he permitted that to happen or failed to take such steps (whether by way of supervising the other person or otherwise) as were reasonable in all the circumstances to prevent that happening.

...

(6) Nothing in this section applies to the removal of the whole or any part of a dog's tail.

6 Docking of dogs' tails

(1) A person commits an offence if—
- (a) he removes the whole or any part of a dog's tail, otherwise than for the purpose of its medical treatment;
- (b) he causes the whole or any part of a dog's tail to be removed by another person, otherwise than for the purpose of its medical treatment.

(2) A person commits an offence if—
- (a) he is responsible for a dog,
- (b) another person removes the whole or any part of the dog's tail, otherwise than for the purpose of its medical treatment, and

---

(c) he permitted that to happen or failed to take such steps (whether by way of supervising the other person or otherwise) as were reasonable in all the circumstances to prevent that happening.

(3) Subsections (1) and (2) do not apply if the dog is a certified working dog that is not more than 5 days old.

(4) For the purposes of subsection (3), a dog is a certified working dog if a veterinary surgeon has certified, in accordance with regulations made by the appropriate national authority, that the first and second conditions mentioned below are met.

(5) The first condition referred to in subsection (4) is that there has been produced to the veterinary surgeon such evidence as the appropriate national authority may by regulations require for the purpose of showing that the dog is likely to be used for work in connection with—
   (a) law enforcement,
   (b) activities of Her Majesty's armed forces,
   (c) emergency rescue,
   (d) lawful pest control, or
   (e) the lawful shooting of animals.

(6) The second condition referred to in subsection (4) is that the dog is of a type specified for the purposes of this subsection by regulations made by the appropriate national authority.

(7) It is a defence for a person accused of an offence under subsection (1) or to show that he reasonably believed that the dog was one in relation to which subsection (3) applies.

(8) A person commits an offence if—
   (a) he owns a subsection (3) dog, and
   (b) fails to take reasonable steps to secure that, before the dog is 3 months old, it is identified as a subsection (3) dog in accordance with regulations made by the appropriate national authority.

(9) A person commits an offence if—
   (a) he shows a dog at an event to which members of the public are admitted on payment of a fee,
   (b) the dog's tail has been wholly or partly removed (in England and Wales or elsewhere), and
   (c) removal took place on or after the commencement day.

(10) Where a dog is shown only for the purpose of demonstrating its working ability, subsection (9) does not apply if the dog is a subsection (3) dog.

(11) It is a defence for a person accused of an offence under subsection (9) to show that he reasonably believed—
   (a) that the event was not one to which members of the public were admitted on payment of an entrance fee,
   (b) that the removal took place before the commencement day, or
   (c) that the dog was one in relation to which subsection (10) applies.

(12) A person commits an offence if he knowingly gives false information to a veterinary surgeon in connection with the giving of a certificate for the purposes of this section.

7 Administration of poisons etc

(1) A person commits an offence if, without lawful authority or reasonable excuse, he—
   (a) administers any poisonous or injurious drug or substance to a protected animal, knowing it to be poisonous or injurious, or
   (b) causes any poisonous or injurious drug or substance to be taken by a protected animal, knowing it to be poisonous or injurious.

(2) A person commits an offence if—
   (a) he is responsible for an animal,

(b) without lawful authority or reasonable excuse, another person administers a poisonous or injurious drug or substance to the animal or causes the animal to take such a drug or substance, and

(c) he permitted that to happen or, knowing the drug or substance to be poisonous or injurious, he failed to take such steps (whether by way of supervising the other person or otherwise) as were reasonable in all the circumstances to prevent that happening.

(3) In this section, references to a poisonous or injurious drug or substance include a drug or substance which, by virtue of the quantity or manner in which it is administered or taken, has the effect of a poisonous or injurious drug or substance.

8 Fighting etc

(1) A person commits an offence if he—
   (a) causes an animal fight to take place, or attempts to do so;
   (b) knowingly receives money for admission to an animal fight;
   (c) knowingly publicises a proposed animal fight;
   (d) provides information about an animal fight to another with the intention of enabling or encouraging attendance at the fight;
   (e) makes or accepts a bet on the outcome of an animal fight or on the likelihood of anything occurring or not occurring in the course of an animal fight;
   (f) takes part in an animal fight;
   (g) has in his possession anything designed or adapted for use in connection with an animal fight with the intention of its being so used;
   (h) keeps or trains an animal for use for in connection with an animal fight;
   (i) keeps any premises for use for an animal fight.

(2) A person commits an offence if, without lawful authority or reasonable excuse, he is present at an animal fight.

(3) A person commits an offence if, without lawful authority or reasonable excuse, he—
   (a) knowingly supplies a video recording of an animal fight,
   (b) knowingly publishes a video recording of an animal fight,
   (c) knowingly shows a video recording of an animal fight to another, or
   (d) possesses a video recording of an animal fight, knowing it to be such a recording, with the intention of supplying it.

(4) Subsection (3) does not apply if the video recording is of an animal fight that took place—
   (a) outside Great Britain, or
   (b) before the commencement date.

(5) Subsection (3) does not apply—
   (a) in the case of paragraph (a), to the supply of a video recording for inclusion in a programme service;
   (b) in the case of paragraph (b) or (c), to the publication or showing of a video recording by means of its inclusion in a programme service;
   (c) in the case of paragraph (d), by virtue of intention to supply for inclusion in a programme service.

. . .

(7) In this section—
   'animal fight' means an occasion on which a protected animal is placed with an animal, or with a human, for the purpose of fighting, wrestling or baiting;

   . . .

   'programme service' has the same meaning as in the Communications Act 2003 (c. 21);

'video recording' means a recording, in any form, from which a moving image may by any means be reproduced and includes data stored on a computer disc or by other electronic means which is capable of conversion into a moving image.

(8) In this section—

    (a) references to supplying or publishing a video recording are to supplying or publishing a video recording in any manner, including, in relation to a video recording in the form of data stored electronically, by means of transmitting such data;

    (b) references to showing a video recording are to showing a moving image reproduced from a video recording by any means.

9 Duty of person responsible for animal to ensure welfare

(1) A person commits an offence if he does not take such steps as are reasonable in all the circumstances to ensure that the needs of an animal for which he is responsible are met to the extent required by good practice.

(2) For the purposes of this Act, an animal's needs shall be taken to include—

    (a) its need for a suitable environment,

    (b) its need for a suitable diet,

    (c) its need to be able to exhibit normal behaviour patterns,

    (d) any need it has to be housed with, or apart from, other animals, and

    (e) its need to be protected from pain, suffering, injury and disease.

(3) The circumstances to which it is relevant to have regard when applying subsection (1) include, in particular—

    (a) any lawful purpose for which the animal is kept, and

    (b) any lawful activity undertaken in relation to the animal.

(4) Nothing in this section applies to the destruction of an animal in an appropriate and humane manner.

SO But note that a magistrates' court may try an Information relating to an offence under this Act if the information is laid:

(a) before the end of the period of 3 years beginning with the date of the commission of the offence; and

(b) before the end of the period of 6 months beginning with the date on which evidence which the prosecutor thinks is sufficient to justify the proceedings comes to his knowledge.

Fine and/or 6 months' imprisonment (ss 4, 5, 6(1) and (2), 7, 8, and 9)

C1.1.1 *Sentencing*

Offences under Animal Welfare Act 2006, s 4 (unnecessary suffering), s 8 (fighting etc), s 9 (breach of duty of person responsible for animal to ensure welfare)

Triable only summarily:

Maximum: Unlimited fine and/or 6 months
Offence range: Band A fine—26 weeks' custody

STEP ONE: Determining the offence category

The court should determine **culpability** and **harm** cause with reference only to the following factors. **Where an offence does not fall squarely into a category,** individual factors may require a degree of weighting before making an overall assessment and determining the appropriate offence category.

CULPABILITY demonstrated by one or more of the following:		
Factors indicating high culpability	Factors indicating medium culpability	Factors indicating low culpability
1. Deliberate or gratuitous attempt to cause suffering 2. Prolonged or deliberate ill treatment or neglect 3. Ill treatment in a commercial context 4. A leading role in illegal activity	1. All cases not falling into high or low culpability	1. Well intentioned but incompetent care 2. Mental disorder or learning disability, where linked to the commission of the offence

HARM demonstrated by one or more of the following:	
Greater harm	Lesser harm
1. Death or serious injury/harm to animal 2. High level of suffering caused	1. All other cases

STEP TWO: Starting point and category range

Having determined the category at step one, the court should use the corresponding starting point to reach a sentence within the following category range. The starting point applies to all offenders irrespective of plea or previous convictions.

A case of particular gravity, reflected by multiple features of culpability in step one, could merit upward adjustment from the starting point before further adjustment for aggravating or mitigating features set out in the following table.

Harm	Culpability		
	High culpability	Medium culpability	Low culpability
Greater harm	**Starting point** 18 weeks' custody	**Starting point** Medium-level community order	**Starting point** Band C fine
	Category range 12–26 weeks' custody	**Category range** Low-level community order—high-level community order	**Category range** Band B fine—low-level community order
Lesser harm	**Starting point** High-level community order	**Starting point** Low-level community order	**Starting point** Band B fine
	Category range Low-level community order—12 weeks' custody	**Category range** Band C fine—medium-level community order	**Category range** Band A fine—Band C fine

The court should then consider further adjustment for any aggravating or mitigating factors. The following is a **non-exhaustive** list of additional factual elements providing the context of the offence and factors relating to the offender. Identify whether any combination of these, or other relevant factors, should result in an upward or downward adjustment from the sentence arrived at so far.

Factors increasing seriousness	
Statutory aggravating factors:	*Other aggravating factors:*
Previous convictions, having regard to (a) the **nature** of the offence to which the conviction relates and its **relevance** to the current offence; and (b) the **time** that has elapsed since the conviction	Distress caused to owner where not responsible for the offence Failure to comply with current court orders Offence committed on licence or post sentence supervision
Offence committed while on bail Offence motivated by or demonstrating hostility based on any of the following characteristics of the owner/keeper of the animal: religion, race, disability, sexual orientation, or transgender identity	Use of weapon Allowing person of insufficient experience or training to have care of animal(s) Use of technology to publicise or promote cruelty Ignores warning/professional advice/declines to obtain professional advice. Use of another animal to inflict death or injury Offender in position of responsibility Animal requires significant intervention to recover Animal being used in public service or as an assistance dog

Factors reducing seriousness or reflecting personal mitigation
No previous convictions **or** no relevant/recent convictions
Remorse
Good character and/or exemplary conduct
Serious medical condition requiring urgent, intensive, or long-term treatment
Age and/or lack of maturity where it affects the responsibility of the offender
Mental disorder or learning disability, where not linked to the commission of the offence
Sole or primary carer for dependent relatives
Offender has been given an inappropriate level of trust or responsibility
Voluntary surrender of animals to authorities
Cooperation with the investigation
Isolated incident

C1.1.2 *Deprivation order*

Section 33 Animal Welfare Act 2006 provides for a convicted person to be deprived of his animals:

Animal Welfare Act 2006, s 33

33 Deprivation

(1) If the person convicted of an offence under any of sections 4, 5, 6(1) and (2), 7, 8 and 9 is the owner of an animal in relation to which the offence was committed, the court by or before which he is convicted may, instead of or in addition to dealing with him in any other way, make an order depriving him of ownership of the animal and for its disposal.

(2) Where the owner of an animal is convicted of an offence under section 34(9) because ownership of the animal is in breach of a disqualification under section 34(2), the court by or before which he is convicted may, instead of or in addition to dealing with him in any other way, make an order depriving him of ownership of the animal and for its disposal.

(3) Where the animal in respect of which an order under subsection (1) or (2) is made has any dependent offspring, the order may include provision depriving the person to whom it relates of ownership of the offspring and for its disposal.

(4) Where a court makes an order under subsection (1) or (2), it may—

(a) appoint a person to carry out, or arrange for the carrying out of, the order;

(b) require any person who has possession of an animal to which the order applies to deliver it up to enable the order to be carried out;

(c) give directions with respect to the carrying out of the order;

(d) confer additional powers (including power to enter premises where an animal to which the order applies is being kept) for the purpose of, or in connection with, the carrying out of the order;

(e) order the offender to reimburse the expenses of carrying out the order.

(5) Directions under subsection (4)(c) may—

(a) specify the manner in which an animal is to be disposed of, or

(b) delegate the decision about the manner in which an animal is to be disposed of to a person appointed under subsection (4)(a).

(6) Where a court decides not to make an order under subsection (1) or (2) in relation to an offender, it shall—

(a) give its reasons for the decision in open court, and

(b) if it is a magistrates' court, cause them to be entered in the register of its proceedings.

(7) Subsection (6) does not apply where the court makes an order under section 34(1) in relation to the offender.

(8) In subsection (1), the reference to an animal in relation to which an offence was committed includes, in the case of an offence under section 8, an animal which took part in an animal fight in relation to which the offence was committed.

(9) In this section, references to disposing of an animal include destroying it.

C1.1.3 *Disqualification order*

Section 34 Animal Welfare Act 2006 provides for disqualification orders to be made against convicted persons, thereby making it an offence for them to be involved with owning, keeping, or otherwise in the control of animals:

Animal Welfare Act 2006, s 34

34 Disqualification

(1) If a person is convicted of an offence to which this section applies, the court by or before which he is convicted may, instead of or in addition to dealing with him in any other way, make an order disqualifying him under any one or more of subsections (2) to (4) for such period as it thinks fit.

(2) Disqualification under this subsection disqualifies a person—

(a) from owning animals,

(b) from keeping animals,

(c) from participating in the keeping of animals, and

(d) from being party to an arrangement under which he is entitled to control or influence the way in which animals are kept.

(3) Disqualification under this subsection disqualifies a person from dealing in animals.

(4) Disqualification under this subsection disqualifies a person—
   (a) from transporting animals, and
   (b) from arranging for the transport of animals.

(5) Disqualification under subsection (2), (3) or (4) may be imposed in relation to animals generally, or in relation to animals of one or more kinds.

(6) The court by which an order under subsection (1) is made may specify a period during which the offender may not make an application under section 43(1) for termination of the order.

...

(10) A person who breaches a disqualification imposed by an order under subsection (1) commits an offence [carrying a... fine and/or 6 months' imprisonment (s 32(2))].

(11) This section applies to an offence under any of sections 4, 5, 6(1) and (2), 7, 8, 9 and 13(6) and subsection (9).

The High Court, commenting that the Guideline did not assist on ancillary orders, gave the following guidance for s 9 cases in *Barker and another v RSPCA* [2018] EWHC 880:

(1) There can be an 'all animals' order, that is to say a prohibition against owning, keeping, etc of any animals. An example in an extreme case would be a case where there was no insight whatever into the need to protect the welfare of the animals in question and a culture of uncaring indifference towards them. An 'all animals' prohibition is not wrong in principle in a section 9 case. A person's treatment of a dog may shed light on his likely treatment of a cat or a parrot.

(2) There can be an order covering some kinds of animals but not others.

(3) There can an exclusory order, that is to say an order prohibiting the ownership, etc of all animals except those of certain kinds by reference to their genus of species although under section 34(5) it is not permissible to prohibit the ownership etc of individual animals.

The purpose of the disqualification was protection, not punishment. It was for the sentencing courts to select what they considered the appropriate period of disqualification, up to and including disqualification for life.

C1.1.3.1 *Sentencing for breach of s 34(10): see s 32(2)*

The Guideline states as follows.

STEP ONE: Determining the offence category

The court should determine the offence category with reference only to the factors listed in the following tables. In order to determine the category the court should assess **culpability** and **harm**.

The level of harm is determined by weighing up all the factors of the case to determine the harm that has been caused or was at risk of being caused.

In assessing any risk of harm posed by the breach, consideration should be given to the original offence(s) for which the order was imposed and the circumstances in which the breach arose.

Culpability	Harm
A: Serious and/or persistent breach B: All other cases	**Category 1** Breach causes or risks death or very serious harm or suffering to animal(s). Breach results in risk of or actual serious harm to individual(s) **Category 2** Cases falling between categories 1 and 3 **Category 3** Breach causes or risks little or no harm or suffering to animal(s) Breach results in very low risk of or little or no harm to individual(s)

Having determined the category at step one, the court should use the corresponding starting point to reach a sentence within the category range from the following appropriate sentence table. The starting point applies to all offenders irrespective of plea or previous convictions. The court should then consider further adjustment within the category range for aggravating or mitigating features.

Harm	Culpability	
	A	**B**
Category 1	**Starting point** 16 weeks' custody	**Starting point** 8 weeks' custody
	Category range 6 weeks'–26 weeks' custody	**Category range** Medium level community order—16 weeks' custody
Category 2	**Starting point** 8 weeks' custody	**Starting point** Medium-level community order
	Category range Medium-level community order—16 weeks' custody	**Category range** Band C Fine—High level community order
Category 3	**Starting point** Medium-level community order	**Starting point** Band A Fine
	Category range Band C Fine—High level community order	**Category range** Discharge—Band B Fine

The following table contains a **non-exhaustive** list of additional factual elements providing the context of the offence and factors relating to the offender. Identify whether any combination of these, or other relevant factors, should result in an upward or downward adjustment from the starting point. In some cases, having considered these factors, it may be appropriate to move outside the identified category range.

Factors increasing seriousness	
Statutory aggravating factors:	*Other aggravating factors:*
Previous convictions, having regard to (a) the nature of the offence to which the conviction relates and its relevance to the current offence; and (b) the time that has elapsed since the conviction Offence committed while on bail	Breach committed immediately or shortly after order made History of disobedience to court orders Breach conducted in commercial context Breach involves deceit regarding ownership of/ responsibility for animal Harm risked or caused to multiple animals (where not taken into account at step one) Offence committed on licence or while subject to post sentence supervision

Factors reducing seriousness or reflecting personal mitigation
Breach committed after long period of compliance
Genuine misunderstanding of terms of order
Prompt voluntary surrender/admission of breach or failure
Age and/or lack of maturity where it affects the responsibility of the offender
Mental disorder or learning disability where linked to the commission of the offence
Sole or primary carer for dependent relatives

C1.1.4 *Destruction orders*

Sections 37 and 38 Animal Welfare Act 2006 allow for destruction orders to be made in appropriate cases:

Animal Welfare Act 2006, ss 37 and 38

37 Destruction in the interests of the animal

(1) The court by or before which a person is convicted of an offence under any of sections 4, 5, 6(1) and (2), 7, 8(1) and (2) and 9 may order the destruction of an animal in relation to which the offence was committed if it is satisfied, on the basis of evidence given by a veterinary surgeon, that it is appropriate to do so in the interests of the animal.

(2) A court may not make an order under subsection (1) unless—
  (a) it has given the owner of the animal an opportunity to be heard, or
  (b) it is satisfied that it is not reasonably practicable to communicate with the owner.

(3) Where a court makes an order under subsection (1), it may—
  (a) appoint a person to carry out, or arrange for the carrying out of, the order;
  (b) require a person who has possession of the animal to deliver it up to enable the order to be carried out;
  (c) give directions with respect to the carrying out of the order (including directions about how the animal is to be dealt with until it is destroyed);
  (d) confer additional powers (including power to enter premises where the animal is being kept) for the purpose of, or in connection with, the carrying out of the order;
  (e) order the offender or another person to reimburse the expenses of carrying out the order.

(4) Where a court makes an order under subsection (1), each of the offender and, if different, the owner of the animal may—
  (a) in the case of an order made by a magistrates' court, appeal against the order to the Crown Court;
  (b) in the case of an order made by the Crown Court, appeal against the order to the Court of Appeal.
(5) Subsection (4) does not apply if the court by which the order is made directs that it is appropriate in the interests of the animal that the carrying out of the order should not be delayed.
(6) In subsection (1), the reference to an animal in relation to which an offence was committed includes, in the case of an offence under section 8(1) or (2), an animal which took part in an animal fight in relation to which the offence was committed.

38 Destruction of animals involved in fighting offences

(1) The court by or before which a person is convicted of an offence under section 8(1) or (2) may order the destruction of an animal in relation to which the offence was committed on grounds other than the interests of the animal.
(2) A court may not make an order under subsection (1) unless—
  (a) it has given the owner of the animal an opportunity to be heard, or
  (b) it is satisfied that it is not reasonably practicable to communicate with the owner.
(3) Where a court makes an order under subsection (1), it may—
  (a) appoint a person to carry out, or arrange for the carrying out of, the order;
  (b) require a person who has possession of the animal to deliver it up to enable the order to be carried out;
  (c) give directions with respect to the carrying out of the order (including directions about how the animal is to be dealt with until it is destroyed);
  (d) confer additional powers (including power to enter premises where the animal is being kept) for the purpose of, or in connection with, the carrying out of the order;
  (e) order the offender or another person to reimburse the expenses of carrying out the order.
(4) Where a court makes an order under subsection (1) in relation to an animal which is owned by a person other than the offender, that person may—
  (a) in the case of an order made by a magistrates' court, appeal against the order to the Crown Court;
  (b) in the case of an order made by the Crown Court, appeal against the order to the Court of Appeal.
(5) In subsection (1), the reference to an animal in relation to which the offence was committed includes an animal which took part in an animal fight in relation to which the offence was committed.

C1.1.5 Key points

- The 6-month limitation period for summary offences under this Act can be disapplied in certain circumstances (see s 31 of the 2006 Act, *RSPCA v Johnson* [2009] EWHC 2702 (Admin) and the cases at **A12.1.2**).
- References to a person responsible for an animal are to a person responsible for an animal, whether on a permanent or a temporary basis.
- References to being responsible for an animal include being in charge of it.
- A person who owns an animal shall always be regarded as being a person who is responsible for it.

- A person shall be treated as responsible for any animal for which a person under the age of 16 years of whom he has actual care and control is responsible.
- Protected animal refers to an animal commonly domesticated in the British Isles, under the control of man, or not living in a wild state.

Section 4 is to be interpreted so as to require the Crown to prove that the defendant knew or ought to have known that the suffering was unnecessary. *Riley v CPS* 2016 EWHC 2531 (Admin) confirms that an offence under s 4(1) has an element of *mens rea* (permitting unnecessary suffering) and so partners in a business could not be liable for events in their absence when there was no allegation of a systemic failure or a proper joint charge.

Section 8(1)(h) is to be interpreted to include those who have actual physical possession as well as those who retain control of the animal while it is elsewhere. The keeper of an animal may have it in their own home or retain it in the home or place of another. Equally a person may themselves train the animal to fight or arrange for another to carry out the training for them. There is no sensible basis to restrict the interpretation of s 8(1)(h) to the person who has actual physical possession or actually does the training themselves; to do so would unnecessarily restrict the offence and the policy of the legislation to criminalize those who are involved in training animals to fight (*Wright v Reading CC* [2017] EWHC 2643(Admin)).

In *RSPCA v McCormick* [2016] EWHC 928 (Admin) 'animal fight' in s 8(7) was held to mean an occasion on which a protected animal (an animal under control) is placed with an animal, or a human, for the purpose of fighting, wrestling, or baiting. The effect is that the other animal must also be under some degree of control and not wild. The case confirmed that, while s 8(7) is aimed at animal fights that are organized or controlled, the payment of money does not have to be involved.

A conviction should not be recorded under s 9, where the standard is objective, when there is a conviction under s 4 and the offending behaviour is no wider (*R (Gray and Gray) v Aylesbury County Court* [2013] EWHC 500 (Admin)).

The considerations to which it is relevant to have regard when determining for the purposes of this section whether suffering is unnecessary include:

- whether the suffering could reasonably have been avoided or reduced;
- whether the conduct which caused the suffering was in compliance with any relevant enactment or any relevant provisions of a licence or code of practice issued under an enactment;
- whether the conduct which caused the suffering was for a legitimate purpose, such as:
  - benefiting the animal, or
  - protecting a person, property, or another animal;
- whether the suffering was proportionate to the purpose of the conduct concerned;
- whether the conduct concerned was in all the circumstances that of a reasonably competent and humane person.

Nothing in this section applies to the destruction of an animal in an appropriate and humane manner.

When considering making a disqualification order under s 4 of the Act, regard can be had to any previous convictions (*Ward v RSPCA*, 2010 EWHC 347). To be in breach of a disqualification order (s 34(2) of the Animal Welfare Act 2006) by participating in the keeping of animals or being party to an arrangement under which the defendant is entitled to control or influence the way in which animals are kept, there must be something more than contact with, or mere influence on the keeping of, the animals. There must be evidence of an entitlement to control the animals (*Patterson v RSPCA* [2013] EWHC 4531(Admin)).

Expenses: Where there is a conviction under s 8, there is power to order the reimbursement of the expenses in keeping the animal (s 39 Animal Welfare Act 2006). Section 18 contains powers for the court to make orders for expenses where an animal is in distress. There are powers to make orders towards the expense of carrying out the court's orders in ss 33, 36, 37, 38, and 41. However, the cost of otherwise keeping an animal cannot be classified as prosecution costs (*R (Donovan) v Burnley CC* [2014] EWHC 742 (Admin)).

C1.1.6 *Animal welfare: s 9*

The welfare offence in this section extends to non-farmed animals; similar provisions are found in the Welfare of Farmed Animals (England) Regulations 2000 (SI 2000/1870) (made under Part 1 of the Agriculture (Miscellaneous Provisions) Act 1968), which ensure the welfare of livestock situated on agricultural land. A duty to ensure welfare will therefore apply to all animals for which someone is responsible, as defined in s 3. Where someone is responsible for an animal, he has a duty to take steps that are reasonable in all the circumstances to ensure its needs are met to the extent required by good practice (s 9(1)).

Section 9(3) specifies certain matters to which the courts should have regard when considering whether a person has committed an offence under this section. The provision recognizes that some otherwise lawful practices may prevent or hinder a person from ensuring that all of the welfare needs specified in s 9(2) can be met, and requires the courts to take this into account when considering what is reasonable in the circumstances of the case.

C1.2 Dangerous dogs

C1.2.1 *Dangerous Dogs Act 1991, s 1*

1 Dogs bred for fighting

(1) This section applies to—
   (a) any dog of the type known as the pit bull terrier;
   (b) any dog of the type known as the Japanese tosa; and
   (c) any dog of any type designated for the purposes of this section by an order of the Secretary of State, being a type appearing to him to be bred for fighting or to have the characteristics of a type bred for that purpose.
(2) No person shall—
   (a) breed, or breed from, a dog to which this section applies;
   (b) sell or exchange such a dog or offer, advertise or expose such a dog for sale or exchange;

(c) make or offer to make a gift of such a dog or advertise or expose such a dog as a gift;

(d) allow such a dog of which he is the owner or of which he is for the time being in charge to be in a public place without being muzzled and kept on a lead; or

(e) abandon such a dog of which he is the owner or, being the owner or for the time being in charge of such a dog, allow it to stray.

(3) After [30 November 1991] no person shall have any dog to which this section applies in his possession or custody except—

(a) in pursuance of the power of seizure conferred by the subsequent provisions of this Act; or

(b) in accordance with an order for its destruction made under those provisions;

(c) but the Secretary of State shall by order make a scheme for the payment to the owners of such dogs who arrange for them to be destroyed before that day of sums specified in or determined under the scheme in respect of those dogs and the cost of their destruction.

(4) Subsection (2)(b) and (c) above shall not make unlawful anything done with a view to the dog in question being removed from the United Kingdom before the day appointed under subsection (3) above.

(5) The Secretary of State may by order provide that the prohibition in subsection (3) above shall not apply in such cases and subject to compliance with such conditions as are specified in the order and any such provision may take the form of a scheme of exemption containing such arrangements (including provision for the payment of charges or fees) as he thinks appropriate.

(6) A scheme under subsection (3) or (5) above may provide for specified functions under the scheme to be discharged by such persons or bodies as the Secretary of State thinks.

(6A) A scheme under subsection (3) or (5) may in particular include provision requiring a court to consider whether a person is a fit and proper person to be in charge of a dog appropriate.

(7) Any person who contravenes this section is guilty of an offence and liable on summary conviction to imprisonment for a term not exceeding six months or a fine or both except that a person who publishes an advertisement in contravention of subsection (2)(b) or (c)—

(a) shall not on being convicted be liable to imprisonment if he shows that he published the advertisement to the order of someone else and did not himself devise it; and

(b) shall not be convicted if, in addition, he shows that he did not know and had no reasonable cause to suspect that it related to a dog to which this section applies.

SO 6 months' imprisonment and/or a fine

In relation to an offence under s 1(2)(b) or (c), see s 1(7) which limits liability and sentence in certain circumstances.

C1.2.2 *Sentencing guidelines*

Offences under s 1(7): STEP ONE: Determining the offence category

In order to determine the category the court should assess **culpability** and **harm**. The court should determine the offence category with reference only to the factors in the following tables. The level of culpability is determined by weighing up all the factors of the case. **Where there are characteristics present which fall under different levels of culpability, the court should balance these characteristics to reach a fair assessment of the offender's culpability.**

CULPABILITY demonstrated by one or more of the following:	
A—Factors indicating higher culpability:	B—Factors indicating lower culpability:
Possessing a dog known to be prohibited Breeding from a dog known to be prohibited Selling, exchanging, or advertising a dog known to be prohibited Offence committed for gain Dog used to threaten or intimidate. Permitting fighting. Training and/or possession of paraphernalia for dog fighting.	All other cases.

HARM	
The level of harm is assessed by weighing up all the factors of the case.	
Greater harm	Lesser harm
High risk to the public and/or animals	Low risk to the public and/or animals

STEP TWO: Starting point and category range

Having determined the category at step one, the court should use the corresponding starting point to reach a sentence within the following category range. The starting point applies to all offenders irrespective of plea or previous convictions.

Harm	Culpability	
	A	B
Greater harm	**Starting point** Medium-level community order	**Starting point** Band B fine
	Category range Band C fine—6 months' custody	**Category range** Band A fine—low-level community order
Lesser harm	**Starting point** Band C fine	**Starting point** Band A fine
	Category range Band B fine— medium-level community order	**Category range** Discharge—Band B fine

The court should then consider any adjustment for any aggravating or mitigating factors. A non-exhaustive list follows of additional factual elements providing the context of the offence and factors relating to the offender.

Identify whether any combination of these, or other relevant factors, should result in an upward or downward adjustment from the starting point.

Factors increasing seriousness	
Statutory aggravating factors:	*Other aggravating factors:*
Previous convictions, having regard to (a) the nature of the offence to which the conviction relates and its relevance to the current offence; and (b) the time that has elapsed since the conviction Offence committed while on bail	Presence of children or others who are vulnerable because of personal circumstances Ill-treatment or failure to ensure welfare needs of the dog (where connected to the offence and where not charged separately) Established evidence of community/wider impact Failure to comply with current court orders Offence committed on licence Offences taken into consideration

Factors reducing seriousness or reflecting personal mitigation
No previous convictions or no relevant/recent convictions
Unaware that dog was prohibited type despite reasonable efforts to identify type
Evidence of safety or control measures having been taken by owner
Prosecution results from owner notification
Evidence of responsible ownership
Remorse
Good character and/or exemplary conduct
Serious medical condition requiring urgent, intensive, or long-term treatment
Age and/or lack of maturity where it affects the responsibility of the offender
Mental disorder or learning disability
Sole or primary carer for dependent relatives
Determination and/or demonstration of steps having been taken to address offending behaviour
Lapse of time since the offence where this is not the fault of the offender ...

STEPS THREE to FIVE: (omitted: see D31)

Offences under section 1(7): STEP SIX

...

Other ancillary orders available include:

Disqualification from having a dog

The court **may** disqualify the offender from having custody of a dog for such period as it thinks fit. The test the court should consider is whether the offender is a fit and proper person to have custody of a dog.

Destruction order/contingent destruction order

In any case where the offender is not the owner of the dog, the owner must be given an opportunity to be present and make representations to the court. The court **shall** make a destruction order unless the court is satisfied that the dog would not constitute a danger to public safety. In reaching a decision, the court should consider the relevant circumstances, which must include:

- the temperament of the dog and its past behaviour;
- whether the owner of the dog, or the person for the time being in charge of it, is a fit and proper person to be in charge of the dog;

and **may** include:

• other relevant circumstances.

If the court is satisfied that the dog would not constitute a danger to public safety, it **shall** make a contingent destruction order requiring that the dog be exempted from the prohibition on possession or custody within the requisite period.

Where the court makes a destruction order, it **may** appoint a person to undertake destruction and order the offender to pay what it determines to be the reasonable expenses of destroying the dog and keeping it pending its destruction.

Fit and proper person

In determining whether a person is a fit and proper person to be in charge of a dog the following non-exhaustive factors may be relevant:

• any relevant previous convictions, cautions, or penalty notices;
• the nature and suitability of the premises that the dog is to be kept at by the person;
• where the police have released the dog pending the court's decision, whether the person has breached conditions imposed by the police; and
• any relevant previous breaches of court orders.

Note: the court must be satisfied that the person who is assessed by the court as a fit and proper person can demonstrate that they are the owner or the person ordinarily in charge of that dog at the time the court is considering whether the dog is a danger to public safety. Someone who has previously not been in charge of the dog should not be considered for this assessment, because it is an offence under the Dangerous Dogs Act 1991 to make a gift of a prohibited dog.

C1.2.3 *Dangerous Dogs Act 1991, section 3*

3 Keeping dogs under proper control

(1) If a dog is dangerously out of control in any place in England or Wales (whether or not a public place)—

  (a) the owner; and

  (b) if different, the person for the time being in charge of the dog, is guilty of an offence, or, if the dog while so out of control injures any person or assistance dog, an aggravated offence, under this subsection.

(1A) A person ('D') is not guilty of an offence under subsection (1) in a case which is a householder case.

(1B) For the purposes of subsection (1A) 'a householder case' is a case where—

  (a) the dog is dangerously out of control while in or partly in a building, or part of a building, that is a dwelling or is forces accommodation (or is both), and

  (b) at that time—

    (i) the person in relation to whom the dog is dangerously out of control ('V') is in, or is entering, the building or part as a trespasser, or

    (ii) D (if present at that time) believed V to be in, or entering, the building or part as a trespasser.

Section 76(8B) to (8F) of the Criminal Justice and Immigration Act 2008 (use of force at place of residence) apply for the purposes of this subsection as they apply for the purposes of subsection (8A) of that section (and for those purposes the reference in section 76(8D) to subsection (8A)(d) is to be read as if it were a reference to paragraph (b)(ii) of this subsection).

(2) In proceedings for an offence under subsection (1) above against a person who is the owner of a dog but was not at the material time in charge of it, it shall be a defence for the accused to prove that the dog was at the material time in the charge of a person whom he reasonably believed to be a fit and proper person to be in charge of it.

...

(4) A person guilty of an offence under subsection (1) above other than an aggravated offence is liable on summary conviction to imprisonment for a term not exceeding six months or a fine... or both; and a person guilty of an aggravated offence under that subsection is liable—

(a) on summary conviction, to imprisonment for a term not exceeding six months or a fine or both;

(b) on conviction on indictment, to imprisonment for a term not exceeding the relevant maximum specified in subsection (4A)

or a fine or both.

(4A) For the purposes of subsection (4)(b), the relevant maximum is—

(a) 14 years if a person dies as a result of being injured;

(b) 5 years in any other case where a person is injured;

(c) 3 years in any case where an assistance dog is injured (whether or not it dies).

(5) It is hereby declared for the avoidance of doubt that an order under section 2 of the Dogs Act 1871 (order on complaint that dog is dangerous and not kept under proper control)—

(a) may be made whether or not the dog is shown to have injured any person; and

(b) may specify the measures to be taken for keeping the dog under proper control, whether by muzzling, keeping on a lead, excluding it from specified places or otherwise.

(6) If it appears to a court on a complaint under section 2 of the said Act of 1871 that the dog to which the complaint relates is a male and would be less dangerous if neutered the court may under that section make an order requiring it to be neutered.

(7) The reference in section 1(3) of the Dangerous Dogs Act 1989 (penalties) to failing to comply with an order under section 2 of the said Act of 1871 to keep a dog under proper control shall include a reference to failing to comply with any other order made under that section; but no order shall be made under that section by virtue of subsection (6) above where the matters complained of arose before the coming into force of that subsection.

SO Non-aggravated offence

Fine and/or 6 months' imprisonment

EW Aggravated offence

Fine and/or on indictment terms of imprisonment, specified in s 4A

An offence is aggravated if the dog injures a person or assistance dog.

C1.2.4 *Sentencing guidelines*

The guidelines divide the offence under s 3(1) Dangerous Dogs Act 1991into four separate categories:

Category—Dangerous Dogs Act 1991 (section 3(1)):	Sentenced in:
Dog dangerously out of control in any place where death is caused	Normally, in the Crown Court
Dog dangerously out of control in any place where a person is injured	See **C1.2.4.1**
Dog dangerously out of control in any place where an assistance dog is injured or killed	See **C1.2.4.2**
Dog dangerously out of control in any place	See **C1.2.4.3**

C1.2.4.1 *Dog dangerously out of control, where a person is injured*

Owner or person in charge of a dog dangerously out of control in any place in England or Wales (whether or not a public place) where a person is injured: maximum five years' custody.

STEP ONE: Determining the offence category

In order to determine the category the court should assess **culpability** and **harm**. The court should determine the offence category with reference only to the factors in the following tables. The level of culpability is determined by weighing up all the factors of the case. **Where there are characteristics present which fall under different levels of culpability, the court should balance these characteristics to reach a fair assessment of the offender's culpability.**

CULPABILITY demonstrated by one or more of the following:		
A—Factors indicating high culpability	B—Factors indicating medium culpability	C—Factors indicating lesser culpability
Dog used as a weapon or to intimidate people Dog known to be prohibited Dog trained to be aggressive Failure to respond to official warnings or to comply with orders concerning the dog Offender disqualified from owning a dog.	All other cases where characteristics for categories A or C are not present, and in particular: • failure to respond to warnings or concerns expressed by others about the dog's behaviour • failure to act on previous knowledge of the dog's aggressive behaviour • lack of safety or control measures taken in situations where an incident could reasonably have been foreseen • failure to intervene in the incident (where it would have been reasonable to do so) • ill-treatment or failure to ensure welfare needs of the dog (where connected to the offence and where not charged separately)	Attempts made to regain control of the dog and/or intervene Provocation of the dog without fault of the offender Evidence of safety or control measures having been taken. Incident could not have reasonably been foreseen by the offender Momentary lapse of control/attention

HARM	
The level of harm is assessed by weighing up all the factors of the case	
Category 1	Serious injury (which includes disease transmission) Serious psychological harm
Category 2	Harm that falls between categories 1 and 3
Category 3	Minor injury and no significant psychological harm

STEP TWO: Starting point and category range

Having determined the category at step one, the court should use the corresponding starting point to reach a sentence within the following category range. The starting point applies to all offenders irrespective of plea or previous convictions.

Harm	Culpability		
	A	B	C
Category 1	**Starting point** 3 years' custody	**Starting point** 1 year 6 months' custody	**Starting point** High-level community order
	Category range 2 years 6 months'– 4 years' custody	**Category range** 6 months'–2 years 6 months' custody	**Category range** Medium-level community order– 6 months' custody
Category 2	**Starting point** 2 years 6 months'–4 years' custody	**Starting point** 6 months' custody	**Starting point** Band C fine
	Category range 1 year–3 years' custody	**Category range** Medium-level community order–1 year's custody	**Category range** Band B fine–high-level community order
Category 3	**Starting point** 6 months' custody	**Starting point** Low-level community order	**Starting point** Band B fine
	Category range High-level community order–1 year 6 months' custody	**Category range** Band C fine–6 months' custody	**Category range** Discharge–Band C fine

The table is for single offences. Concurrent sentences reflecting the overall criminality of offending will ordinarily be appropriate where offences arise out of the same incident or facts: please refer to the Offences Taken into Consideration and Totality guidelines.

The court should then consider any adjustment for any aggravating or mitigating factors. There follows a **non-exhaustive** list of additional factual elements providing the context of the offence and factors relating to the offender.

Identify whether any combination of these, or other relevant factors, should result in an upward or downward adjustment from the starting point.

Factors increasing seriousness	
Statutory aggravating factors:	*Other aggravating factors:*
Previous convictions, having regard to (a) the **nature** of the offence to which the conviction relates and its **relevance** to the current offence; and (b) the **time** that has elapsed since the conviction	Victim is a child or otherwise vulnerable because of personal circumstances
	Location of the offence
	Sustained or repeated attack
	Significant ongoing effect on witness(es) to the attack
Offence committed while on bail	Serious injury caused to others (where not charged separately)
Offence motivated by, or demonstrating hostility based on any of the following characteristics or presumed characteristics of the victim: religion, race, disability, sexual orientation, or transgender identity	Significant practical and financial effects of offence on relatives/carers
	Allowing person insufficiently experienced or trained, to be in charge of the dog
	Lack or loss of control of dog due to influence of alcohol or drugs
	Offence committed against those working in the public sector or providing a service to the public
	Injury to other animals
	Established evidence of community/wider impact
	Failure to comply with current court orders (except where taken into account in assessing culpability)
	Offence committed on licence
	Offences taken into consideration

Factors reducing seriousness or affecting personal mitigation
No previous convictions or no relevant/recent convictions
Isolated incident
No previous complaints against, or incidents involving, the dog
Evidence of responsible ownership
Remorse
Good character and/or exemplary conduct
Serious medical condition requiring urgent, intensive, or long-term treatment
Age and/or lack of maturity where it affects the responsibility of the offender
Mental disorder or learning disability
Sole or primary carer for dependent relatives
Determination and/or demonstration of steps having been taken to address offending behaviour

STEPS THREE to FIVE: (omitted: see D31)

STEP SIX

...

Other ancillary orders available include:

Disqualification from having a dog

The court **may** disqualify the offender from having custody of a dog. The test the court should consider is whether the offender is a fit and proper person to have custody of a dog.

Destruction order/contingent destruction order

In any case where the offender is not the owner of the dog, the owner must be given an opportunity to be present and make representations to the court.

If the dog is a **prohibited dog** refer to the guideline for possession of a prohibited dog in relation to destruction/contingent destruction orders.

The court **shall** make a destruction order unless the court is satisfied that the dog would not constitute a danger to public safety.

In reaching a decision, the court should consider the relevant circumstances which **must** include:

- the temperament of the dog and its past behaviour;
- whether the owner of the dog, or the person for the time being in charge of it is a fit and proper person to be in charge of the dog;

and **may** include:

- other relevant circumstances.

If the court is satisfied that the dog would not constitute a danger to public safety and the dog is not prohibited, it **may** make a contingent destruction order requiring the dog be kept under proper control. A contingent destruction order may specify the measures to be taken by the owner for keeping the dog under proper control, which include:

- muzzling;
- keeping on a lead;
- neutering in appropriate cases; and
- excluding it from a specified place.

Where the court makes a destruction order, it **may** appoint a person to undertake destruction and order the offender to pay what it determines to be the reasonable expenses of destroying the dog and keeping it pending its destruction.

Fit and proper person

In determining whether a person is a fit and proper person to be in charge of a dog the following non-exhaustive factors may be relevant:

- any relevant previous convictions, cautions or penalty notices;
- the nature and suitability of the premises that the dog is to be kept at by the person;
- where the police have released the dog pending the court's decision whether the person has breached conditions imposed by the police; and
- any relevant previous breaches of court orders.

C1.2.4.2 *Dog dangerously out of control, where an assistance dog is injured or killed*

Owner or person in charge of a dog dangerously out of control in any place in England or Wales (whether or not a public place) where an assistance dog is injured or killed: maximum three years' custody.

STEP ONE: Determining the offence category

In order to determine the category the court should assess **culpability** and **harm**. The court should determine the offence category with reference only to the factors in the following tables.

The level of culpability is determined by weighing up all the factors of the case. **Where there are characteristics present which fall under different levels of culpability, the court should balance these characteristics to reach a fair assessment of the offender's culpability.**

CULPABILITY demonstrated by one or more of the following:		
A—Factors indicating high culpability	B—Factors indicating medium culpability	C—Factors indicating lesser culpability
Dog used as a weapon or to intimidate people or dogs Dog known to be prohibited Dog trained to be aggressive Offender disqualified from owning a dog, or failed to respond to official warnings, or to comply with orders concerning the dog Offence motivated by, or demonstrating hostility to the victim (assisted person) based on the victim's disability (or presumed disability)	All other cases where characteristics for categories A or C are not present, and in particular: • failure to respond to warnings or concerns expressed by others about the dog's behaviour • failure to act on previous knowledge of the dog's aggressive behaviour • lack of safety or control measures taken in situations where an incident could reasonably have been foreseen • failure to intervene in the incident (where it would have been reasonable to do so) • ill treatment or failure to ensure welfare needs of the dog (where connected to the offence and where not charged separately)	Attempts made to regain control of the dog and/or intervene Provocation of the dog without fault of the offender Evidence of safety or control measures having been taken Incident could not have reasonably been foreseen by the offender Momentary lapse of control/attention

HARM	
The level of harm is assessed by weighing up all the factors of the case.	
Category 1	Fatality or serious injury to an assistance dog and/or serious impact on the assisted person (whether psychological or other harm caused by the offence)
Category 2	Harm that falls between categories 1 and 3
Category 3	Minor injury to assistance dog and impact of the offence on the assisted person is limited

STEP TWO: Starting point and category range

Having determined the category at step one, the court should use the corresponding starting point to reach a sentence within the following category range. The starting point applies to all offenders irrespective of plea or previous convictions.

C1 Animal Offences

Harm	Culpability		
	A	**B**	**C**
Category 1	**Starting point** 2 years' custody	**Starting point** 9 months' custody	**Starting point** Medium-level community order
	Category range 1 year–2 years 6 months' custody	**Category range** Medium-level community order–1 year's custody	**Category range** Low-level community order–high level community order
Category 2	**Starting point** 1 year's custody	**Starting point** High-level community order	**Starting point** Band B fine
	Category range 6 months'–1 year 6 months' custody	**Category range** Low-level community order–6 months' custody	**Category range** Band A fine–low-level community order
Category 3	**Starting point** High-level community order	**Starting point** Band C fine	**Starting point** Band A fine
	Category range Medium-level community order–6 months' custody	**Category range** Band B fine–high-level community order	**Category range** Discharge–Band B fine

The court should then consider any adjustment for any aggravating or mitigating factors. Following is a **non-exhaustive** list of additional factual elements providing the context of the offence and factors relating to the offender.

Identify whether any combination of these, or other relevant factors, should result in an upward or downward adjustment from the starting point.

Factors increasing seriousness	
Statutory aggravating factors:	*Other aggravating factors:*
Previous convictions, having regard to (a) the **nature** of the offence to which the conviction relates and its **relevance** to the current offence; and (b) the **time** that has elapsed since the conviction	Location of the offence
	Sustained or repeated attack
	Significant ongoing effect on witness(es) to the attack
	Allowing person insufficiently experienced or trained, to be in charge of the dog
	Lack or loss of control of dog owing to influence of alcohol or drugs
Offence committed while on bail	Offence committed against those working in the public sector or providing a service to the public
Offence motivated by, or demonstrating hostility based on any of the following characteristics or presumed characteristics of the victim: religion, race, disability, sexual orientation, or transgender identity	Injury to other animals
	Cost of retraining an assistance dog
	Established evidence of community/wider impact
	Failure to comply with current court orders (except where taken into account in assessing culpability)
	Offence committed on licence
	Offences taken into consideration

Factors reducing seriousness or reflecting personal mitigation
No previous convictions **or** no relevant/recent convictions
Isolated incident
No previous complaints against, or incidents involving the dog
Evidence of responsible ownership
Remorse
Good character and/or exemplary conduct
Serious medical condition requiring urgent, intensive, or long-term treatment
Age and/or lack of maturity where it affects the responsibility of the offender
Mental disorder or learning disability
Sole or primary carer for dependent relatives
Determination and/or demonstration of steps having been taken to address offending behaviour

STEPS THREE to FIVE: (omitted: see D31)

STEP SIX:

...

Other ancillary orders available include
Disqualification from having a dog

The court **may** disqualify the offender from having custody of a dog. The test the court should consider is whether the offender is a fit and proper person to have custody of a dog.

Destruction order/contingent destruction order

In any case where the offender is not the owner of the dog, the owner must be given an opportunity to be present and make representations to the court.

If the dog is a **prohibited dog** refer to the guideline for possession of a prohibited dog in relation to destruction/contingent destruction orders.

The court **shall** make a destruction order unless the court is satisfied that the dog would not constitute a danger to public safety.

In reaching a decision, the court should consider the relevant circumstances which **must** include:

- the temperament of the dog and its past behaviour;
- whether the owner of the dog, or the person for the time being in charge of it is a fit and proper person to be in charge of the dog;

and **may** include:

- other relevant circumstances.

If the court is satisfied that the dog would not constitute a danger to public safety and the dog is not prohibited, it **may** make a contingent destruction order requiring the dog be kept under proper control. A contingent destruction order may specify the measures to be taken by the owner for keeping the dog under proper control, which include:

- muzzling;

- keeping on a lead;
- neutering in appropriate cases; and
- excluding it from a specified place.

Where the court makes a destruction order, it **may** appoint a person to undertake destruction and order the offender to pay what it determines to be the reasonable expenses of destroying the dog and keeping it pending its destruction.

Fit and proper person

In determining whether a person is a fit and proper person to be in charge of a dog the following non-exhaustive factors may be relevant:

- any relevant previous convictions, cautions or penalty notices;
- the nature and suitability of the premises that the dog is to be kept at by the person;
- where the police have released the dog pending the court's decision whether the person has breached conditions imposed by the police; and
- any relevant previous breaches of court orders.

C1.2.4.3 *Dog dangerously out of control in any place*

Owner or person in charge of a dog dangerously out of control in any place in England or Wales (whether or not a public place): maximum 6 months' custody.

STEP ONE: Determining the offence category

In order to determine the category the court should assess **culpability** and **harm**. The court should determine the offence category with reference only to the factors in the following tables.

The level of culpability is determined by weighing up all the factors of the case. **Where there are characteristics present which fall under different levels of culpability, the court should balance these characteristics to reach a fair assessment of the offender's culpability.**

CULPABILITY demonstrated by one or more of the following:	
A—Factors indicating high culpability	B—Factors indicating lower culpability
Dog used as a weapon or to intimidate people	Attempts made to regain control of the dog and/or intervene
Dog known to be prohibited	Provocation of dog without fault of the offender
Dog trained to be aggressive	Evidence of safety or control measures having been taken
Offender disqualified from owning a dog, or failed to respond to official warnings, or to comply with orders concerning the dog	Incident could not have reasonably been foreseen by the offender
	Momentary lapse of control/attention

HARM	
The level of harm is assessed by weighing up all the factors of the case.	
Greater harm	Presence of children or others who are vulnerable because of personal circumstances. Injury to other animals
Lesser harm	Low risk to the public

STEP TWO: Starting point and category range

Having determined the category at step one, the court should use the corresponding starting point to reach a sentence within the following category range. The starting point applies to all offenders irrespective of plea or previous convictions.

Harm	Culpability	
	A	**B**
Greater Harm	**Starting point** Medium-level community order	**Starting point** Band B fine
	Category range Band C fine–6 months' custody	**Category range** Band A fine–Band C fine
Lesser harm	**Starting point** Band C fine	**Starting point** Band A fine
	Category range Band B fine–low-level community order	**Category range** Discharge–Band B fine

The court should then consider any adjustment for any aggravating or mitigating factors. Following is a **non-exhaustive** list of additional factual elements providing the context of the offence and factors relating to the offender.

Identify whether any combination of these, or other relevant factors, should result in an upward or downward adjustment from the starting point.

Factors increasing seriousness	
Statutory aggravating factors:	*Other aggravating factors:*
Previous convictions, having regard to (a) the **nature** of the offence to which the conviction relates and its **relevance** to the current offence; and (b) the **time** that has elapsed since the conviction	Location of the offence
	Significant ongoing effect on the victim and/or others
	Failing to take adequate precautions to prevent the dog from escaping
	Allowing person insufficiently experienced or trained, to be in charge of the dog
Offence committed while on bail	Ill treatment or failure to ensure welfare needs of the dog (where connected to the offence and where not charged separately)
Offence motivated by, or demonstrating hostility based on any of the following characteristics or presumed characteristics of the victim: religion, race, disability, sexual orientation or transgender identity	Lack or loss of control of dog owing to influence of alcohol or drugs
	Offence committed against those working in the public sector or providing a service to the public
	Established evidence of community/wider impact
	Failure to comply with current court orders (unless this has already been taken into account in assessing culpability)
	Offence committed on licence.
	Offences taken into consideration

Factors reducing seriousness or reflecting personal mitigation
No previous convictions **or** no relevant/recent convictions
Isolated incident
No previous complaints against, or incidents involving the dog
Evidence of responsible ownership
Remorse
Good character and/or exemplary conduct
Serious medical condition requiring urgent, intensive, or long-term treatment
Age and/or lack of maturity where it affects the responsibility of the offender
Mental disorder or learning disability
Sole or primary carer for dependent relatives
Determination and/or demonstration of steps having been taken to address offending behaviour

STEPS THREE to FIVE: (omitted: see D31)

STEP SIX

...

Other ancillary orders available include:
Disqualification from having a dog

The court **may** disqualify the offender from having custody of a dog. The test the court should consider is whether the offender is a fit and proper person to have custody of a dog.

Destruction order/contingent destruction order

In any case where the offender is not the owner of the dog, the owner must be given an opportunity to be present and make representations to the court.

If the dog is a **prohibited dog** refer to the guideline for possession of a prohibited dog in relation to destruction/contingent destruction orders.

If the dog is not prohibited and the court is satisfied that the dog would constitute a danger to public safety the court **may** make a destruction order.

In reaching a decision, the court should consider the relevant circumstances which **must** include:

- the temperament of the dog and its past behaviour;
- whether the owner of the dog, or the person for the time being in charge of it is a fit and proper person to be in charge of the dog;

and **may** include:

- other relevant circumstances.

If the court is satisfied that the dog would not constitute a danger to public safety and the dog is not prohibited, it **may** make a contingent destruction order requiring the dog be kept under proper control. A contingent destruction order may specify the measures to be taken by the owner for keeping the dog under proper control, which include:

- muzzling;
- keeping on a lead;
- neutering in appropriate cases; and
- excluding it from a specified place.

Where the court makes a destruction order, it **may** appoint a person to undertake destruction and order the offender to pay what it determines to be the reasonable expenses of destroying the dog and keeping it pending its destruction.

Fit and proper person

In determining whether a person is a fit and proper person to be in charge of a dog the following non-exhaustive factors may be relevant:

- any relevant previous convictions, cautions, or penalty notices;
- the nature and suitability of the premises that the dog is to be kept at by the person;
- where the police have released the dog pending the court's decision whether the person has breached conditions imposed by the police; **and**
- any relevant previous breaches of court orders.

C1.2.5 *Dangerous Dogs Act 1991, sections 4(1)–(3) and 4A*

4 Destruction and disqualification orders

(1) Where a person is convicted of an offence under section 1 or 3(1) above or of an offence under an order made under section 2 above the court—
  (a) may order the destruction of any dog in respect of which the offence was committed and, subject to subsection (1A) below, shall do so in the case of an offence under section 1 or an aggravated offence under section 3(1) above; and
  (b) may order the offender to be disqualified, for such period as the court thinks fit, for having custody of a dog.
(1A) Nothing in subsection (1)(a) above shall require the court to order the destruction of a dog if the court is satisfied—
  (a) that the dog would not constitute a danger to public safety; and
  (b) where the dog was born before 30th November 1991 and is subject to the prohibition in section 1(3) above, that there is a good reason why the dog has not been exempted from that prohibition.
(1B) For the purposes of subsection (1A)(a), when deciding whether a dog would constitute a danger to public safety, the court—
  (a) must consider—
    (i) the temperament of the dog and its past behaviour, and
    (ii) whether the owner of the dog, or the person for the time being in charge of it, is a fit and proper person to be in charge of the dog, and
  (b) may consider any other relevant circumstances.
(2) Where a court makes an order under subsection (1)(a) above for the destruction of a dog owned by a person other than the offender, the owner may appeal to the Crown Court against the order.
(3) A dog shall not be destroyed pursuant to an order under subsection (1)
  (a) above—

(a) until the end of the period for giving notice of appeal against the conviction or, against the order; and
(b) if notice of appeal is given within that period, until the appeal is determined or withdrawn, unless the offender and, in a case to which subsection (2) above applies, the owner of the dog give notice to the court that made the order that there is to be no appeal

...

4A Contingent destruction orders

(1) Where—
   (a) a person is convicted of an offence under section 1 above or an aggravated offence under section 3(1) above;
   (b) the court does not order the destruction of the dog under section 4(1)(a) above; and
   (c) in the case of an offence under section 1 above, the dog is subject to the prohibition in section 1(3) above,
   (d) the court shall order that, unless the dog is exempted from that prohibition within the requisite period, the dog shall be destroyed.
(2) Where an order is made under subsection (1) above in respect of a dog, and the dog is not exempted from the prohibition in section 1(3) above within the requisite period, the court may extend that period.
(3) Subject to subsection (2) above, the requisite period for the purposes of such an order is the period of two months beginning with the date of the order.
(4) Where a person is convicted of an offence under section 3(1) above, the court may order that, unless the owner of the dog keeps it under proper control, the dog shall be destroyed.
(5) An order under subsection (4) above—
   (a) may specify the measures to be taken for keeping the dog under proper control, whether by muzzling, keeping on a lead, excluding it from specified places or otherwise; and
   (b) if it appears to the court that the dog is a male and would be less dangerous if neutered, may require it to be neutered.
(6) Subsections (2) to (4) of section 4 above shall apply in relation to an order under subsection (1) or (4) above as they apply in relation to an order under subsection (1)(a) of that section.

C1.2.6 Key points

- In relation to destruction orders, see the guidance issued by the Court of Appeal in *R v Flack* [2008] EWCA Crim 204 and *R v Davies* [2010] EWCA Crim1923, reviewed in *Kelleher v DPP* [2012] EWHC 2978 (Admin) and *R (Killeen) v Birmingham Crown Court and others* [2018] EWHC 174 (Admin).
- Essentially the court must consider whether the dog constitutes a danger to the public. If it does not then no order is made. If it does, the court must consider whether a contingent destruction order would remove that danger. In the case of an aggravated offence, the burden of proof to show that the dog does not represent a danger is on the defence. The normal burden of proof applies in non-aggravated cases.
- For 'type' see *Crown Court at Knightsbridge, ex p Dune* [1993] 4 All ER 491.
- 'Dangerously out of control' is defined under s 10(3) of the Act:

Dangerous Dogs Act 1991, s 10(3)

(3) For the purposes of this Act a dog shall be regarded as dangerously out of control on any occasion on which there are grounds for reasonable apprehension that it will injure any person or assistance dog, whether or not it actually does so, but references to a dog injuring a person or assistance dog or there being grounds for reasonable apprehension that it will do so do not include references to any case in which the dog is being used for a lawful purpose by a constable or a person in the service of the Crown.

- Regard must be had to the behaviour of the dog and the degree of control exercised by its handler. The fact that the dog has not displayed any previous bad traits was of relevance but not conclusive (*R v Gedminintaite* [2008] EWCA Crim 814).
- It is sufficient that the danger is only to other dogs (*Briscoe v Shattock* (1998) 163 JP 201), but hunting and killing rabbits and other small animals is part of a dog's nature and does not make it dangerous (*Sansom v Chief Constable of Kent* [1981] Crim LR 617).
- The owner of the dog has a defence under s 3(2) if another fit and proper person was in charge of the dog at the material time. Whether a person is a fit and proper person will depend on all of the circumstances. The dog must have been left with an identifiable person; it was not sufficient merely to say that different members of a family looked after the dog at different times (*R v Huddart* [1999] Crim LR 568).
- Although s 3 creates an offence of strict liability, there must still be some causal connection between having charge of the dog and the occurrence of the serious injury (*R v Robinson-Pierre* [2013] EWCA Crim 2396).
- It is irrelevant that the owner did not anticipate the behaviour of the dog (*R v Bezzina* (1994) 158 JP 671).
- A person who relinquishes physical control of a dog by passing the lead to another may remain in joint control of the dog (*L v Crown Prosecution Service*, unreported, 10 February 2010). Plain evidence is required to demonstrate that control has been passed to another (*R v Huddart* [1999] Crim LR 568).
- 'Public place' includes the inside of a vehicle which is itself in a public place (*Bates v DPP* (1993) 157 JP 1004).
- There are no defences in relation to s 1 (see *DPP v Kellett* (1994) 158 JP 1138 (intoxication) and *Cichon v DPP* [1994] Crim LR (welfare of the animal—unmuzzling to allow the dog to be sick)).

 See *Blackstone's Criminal Practice 2019* **B20**

C2 Breach Offences

C2.1 Criminal behaviour order

Anti-social Behaviour Crime and Policing Act 2014, s 30

30 Breach of order

(1) A person who without reasonable excuse—
   (a) does anything he or she is prohibited from doing by a criminal behaviour order, or
   (b) fails to do anything he or she is required to do by a criminal behaviour order, commits an offence.

(2) A person guilty of an offence under this section is liable—
   (a) on summary conviction, to imprisonment for a period not exceeding 6 months or to a fine, or to both;
   (b) on conviction on indictment, to imprisonment for a period not exceeding 5 years or to a fine, or to both.

(3) If a person is convicted of an offence under this section, it is not open to the court by or before which the person is convicted to make an order under subsection (1)(b) of section 12 of the Powers of Criminal Courts (Sentencing) Act 2000 (conditional discharge).

 Fine and/or 6 months'/5 years' imprisonment.

C2.1.1 *Sentencing*

STEP ONE: Determining the offence category

The court should determine the offence category with reference only to the factors listed in the following tables. In order to determine the category the court should assess **culpability** and **harm**.

Culpability
A—High culpability
Very serious or persistent breach
B—Medium culpability
Deliberate breach falling between A and C
C—Low culpability
Minor breach
Breach just short of reasonable excuse

The level of **harm** is determined by weighing up all the factors of the case to determine the harm that has been caused or was at risk of being caused.

In assessing any risk of harm posed by the breach, consideration should be given to the original offence(s) or activity for which the order was imposed and the circumstances in which the breach arose.

Harm
Category 1
Breach causes very serious harm or distress
Breach demonstrates a continuing risk of serious criminal and/or anti-social behaviour
Category 2
Cases falling between categories 1 and 3
Category 3
Breach causes little or no harm or distress
Breach demonstrates a continuing risk of minor criminal and/or anti-social behaviour

STEP TWO: Starting point and category range

Having determined the category at step one, the court should use the corresponding starting point to reach a sentence within the category range from the following appropriate sentence table. The starting point applies to all offenders irrespective of plea or previous convictions.

Harm	Culpability		
	A	**B**	**C**
Category 1	**Starting point** 2 years' custody	**Starting point** 1 year's custody	**Starting point** 12 weeks' custody
	Category range 1–4 years' custody	**Category range** High-level community order–2 years' custody	**Category range** Medium-level community order–1 year's custody
Category 2	**Starting point** 1 year's custody	**Starting point** 12 weeks' custody	**Starting point** High-level community order
	Category range High-level community order–2 years' custody	**Category range** Medium level community order–1 year's custody	**Category range** Low-level community order–26 weeks' custody
Category 3	**Starting point** 12 weeks' custody	**Starting point** High-level community order	**Starting point** Medium-level community order
	Category range Medium-level community order–1 year's custody	**Category range** Low-level community order–26 weeks' custody	**Category range** Band B fine–High level community order

NOTE: A Conditional Discharge MAY NOT be imposed for breach of a criminal behaviour order.

The following table contains a **non-exhaustive** list of additional factual elements providing the context of the offence and factors relating to the offender. Identify whether any combination of these, or other relevant factors, should result in an upward or downward adjustment from the starting point. In some cases, having considered these factors, it may be appropriate to move outside the identified category range.

Factors increasing seriousness	
Statutory aggravating factors:	*Other aggravating factors:*
Previous convictions, having regard to (a) the nature of the offence to which the conviction relates and its relevance to the current offence; and (b) the time that has elapsed since the conviction Offence committed while on bail	Offence is a further breach, following earlier breach proceedings Breach committed shortly after order made History of disobedience of court orders or orders imposed by local authorities Breach constitutes a further offence (where not separately prosecuted) Targeting of a person the order was made to protect or a witness in the original proceedings Victim or protected subject of order breached is particularly vulnerable due to age, disability, culture, religion, language, or other factors Offence committed on licence or while subject to post-sentence supervision

Factors reducing seriousness or reflecting personal mitigation
Genuine misunderstanding of terms of order
Breach committed after long period of compliance
Prompt voluntary surrender/admission of breach or failure
Age and/or lack of maturity where it affects the responsibility of the offender
Mental disorder or learning disability
Sole or primary carer for dependent relatives
Offence committed on licence or while subject to post-sentence supervision

C2.1.2 Key points

- The prosecution must be in a position to prove that the person before the court is the person in respect of whom the order was made (*Barber v Crown Prosecution Service* [2004] EWHC 2605 (Admin)).
- In *R v Nicholson* [2006] EWCA Crim 1518, it was held that forgetfulness, misunderstanding, or ignorance could amount in law to a reasonable excuse.
- The fact that a person is appealing against the imposition of an order does not give rise to a reasonable excuse (*West Midlands Probation Board v Daly* [2008] EWHC 15 (Admin)).
- A belief that the order has come to an end is capable of amounting to a reasonable excuse (*Barber v Crown Prosecution Service* [2004] EWHC 2605 (Admin)).
- Where conduct forming the breach would also be a criminal offence in its own right, a court was not bound by the maximum sentence available for that offence, but should have regard to proportionality. It would be wrong for a prosecutor to proceed with a breach of an order simply because it was thought that the penalty for the substantive offence was too lenient (*R v Stevens* [2006] EWCA Crim 255).
- The burden of negativing reasonable excuse, once raised by evidence by the defence, falls on the prosecution (*R v Charles* [2009] EWCA Crim 1570).
- A defendant's state of mind is relevant to the issue of reasonable excuse (*JB v Crown Prosecution Service* [2012] EWHC 72 (Admin)).

 See *Blackstone's Criminal Practice 2019* **D25**

C2.2 Breach of protective orders

• Restraining order

Protection from Harassment Act 1997, s 5(5);

(5) If without reasonable excuse the defendant does anything which he is prohibited from doing by an order under this section [or s 5A], he is guilty of an offence.

• Non-molestation orders

Family Law Act 1996, s 42A

(1) A person who without reasonable excuse does anything that he is prohibited from doing by a non-molestation order is guilty of an offence.

(2) In the case of a non-molestation order made by virtue of section 45(1) [ex parte orders], a person can be guilty of an offence under this section only in respect of conduct engaged in at a time when he was aware of the existence of the order.

 Fine and/or 6 months'/5 years' imprisonment

C2.2.1 *Sentencing*

STEP ONE: Determining the offence category

The court should determine the offence category with reference only to the factors listed in the following tables. In order to determine the category the court should assess **culpability** and **harm**.

In assessing culpability, the court should consider the **intention** and **motivation** of the offender in committing any breach. The level of harm is determined by weighing up all the factors of the case to determine the harm that has been caused or was intended to be caused.

Culpability	Harm
A—High culpability	**Category 1**
Very serious and/or persistent breach	Breach causes very serious harm or distress
B—Medium culpability	**Category 2**
Deliberate breach falling between A and C	Cases falling between categories 1 and 3
C—Low culpability	**Category 3**
Minor breach	Breach causes little or no harm or distress*
Breach just short of reasonable excuse	

* Where a breach is committed in the context of a background of domestic abuse, the sentence should take care not to underestimate the harm which may be present in a breach.

C2 Breach Offences

STEP TWO: Starting point and category range

Having determined the category at step one, the court should use the corresponding starting point to reach a sentence within the category range from the following appropriate sentence table. The starting point applies to all offenders irrespective of plea or previous convictions.

Harm	Culpability		
	A	**B**	
Category 1	**Starting point** 2 years' custody	**Starting point** 1 year's custody	**Starting point** 12 weeks' custody
	Category range 1–4 years' custody	**Category range** High-level community order–2 years' custody	**Category range** Medium-level community order–1 year's custody
Category 2	**Starting point** 1 year's custody	**Starting point** 12 weeks' custody	**Starting point** High-level community order
	Category range High-level community order–2 years' custody	**Category range** Medium-level community order–1 year's custody	**Category range** Low-level community order–26 weeks' custody
Category 3	**Starting point** 12 weeks' custody	**Starting point** High-level community order	**Starting point** Low-level community order
	Category range Medium-level community order–1 year's custody	**Category range** Low-level community order–26 weeks' custody	**Category range** Band B fine–High-level community order

The preceding table refers to single offences. Where there are multiple offences consecutive sentences may be appropriate—please refer to the Offences Taken Into Consideration and Totality guideline.

The following table contains a **non-exhaustive** list of additional factual elements providing the context of the offence and factors relating to the offender. Identify whether any combination of these, or other relevant factors, should result in an upward or downward adjustment from the starting point. In some cases, having considered these factors, it may be appropriate to move outside the identified category range.

Factors increasing seriousness	
Statutory aggravating factors:	*Other aggravating factors:*
Previous convictions, having regard to (a) the **nature** of the offence to which the conviction relates and its **relevance** to the current offence; and (b) the **time** that has elapsed since the conviction Offence committed while on bail	Breach committed shortly after order made History of disobedience to court orders (where not already taken into account as a previous conviction) Breach involves a further offence (where not separately prosecuted) Using contact arrangements with a child/children to instigate offence and/or proven history of violence or threats by offender Breach results in victim or protected person being forced to leave their home Impact upon children or family members Victim or protected subject of order breached is particularly vulnerable Offender takes steps to prevent victim or subject harmed by breach from reporting an incident or seeking assistance Offence committed on licence or while subject to post-sentence supervision

Factors reducing seriousness or reflecting personal mitigation
Breach committed after long period of compliance
Prompt voluntary surrender/admission of breach or failure
Age and/or lack of maturity where it affects the responsibility of the offender
Mental disorder or learning disability where linked to the commission of the offence
Sole or primary carer for dependent relatives
Contact not initiated by offender—a careful examination of all the circumstances is required before weight is given to this factor

C2.2.2 Key points

- A delusional schizophrenic's belief that his neighbour was committing crime could not be regarded as a reasonable excuse for such a breach, and the test of whether his conduct breached an order was objective. The belief was relevant to sentence, however (*R v Grazanfer* [2015] EWCA Crim 642).
- When considering a breach of a restraining order the word 'harass' in an order is to be read, as it would be under the Protection from Harassment Act 1997, so that a defendant would not be in breach of the order if he could make good the defence under s 1(3)(c) of that Act that, in the particular circumstances, the pursuit of the course of conduct had been reasonable (*R v O'Neill* [2016] EWCA Crim 92).
- Note that there is also an either-way offence carrying five years on indictment, under s 3 Protection from Harassment Act 1997, where there is a breach without reasonable excuse of a civil injunction obtained by an individual under ASBPCA.

 See *Blackstone's Criminal Practice 2019* **B14.134**

C2.3 Breach of sexual harm prevention order (SHPO)

Offence: breach of SHPO or interim SHPO, etc

(1) A person who, without reasonable excuse, does anything that the person is prohibited from doing by—
   (a) a sexual harm prevention order,
   (b) an interim sexual harm prevention order,
   (c) a sexual offences prevention order,
   (d) an interim sexual offences prevention order, or
   (e) a foreign travel order,
     commits an offence.

EW

 6 months' imprisonment and/or a fine/5 years' imprisonment
A conditional discharge may not be imposed.

C2.3.1 *Sentencing*

STEP ONE: Determining the offence category

The court should determine the offence category with reference only to the factors listed in the following tables. In order to determine the category the court should assess **culpability** and **harm**.

In assessing culpability, the court should consider the **intention** and **motivation** of the offender in committing any breach.

Culpability	
A	Very serious or persistent breach
B	Deliberate breach falling between A and C
C	Minor breach
	Breach just short of reasonable excuse

The level of **harm** is determined by weighing up all the factors of the case to determine the harm that has been caused or was at risk of being caused.

In assessing any risk of harm posed by the breach, consideration should be given to the original offence(s) for which the order was imposed and the circumstances in which the breach arose.

Harm	
Category 1	Breach causes or risks very serious harm or distress
Category 2	Cases falling between categories 1 and 3
Category 3	Breach causes or risks little or no harm or distress

STEP TWO: Starting point and category range

Having determined the category at step one, the court should use the corresponding starting point to reach a sentence within the category range from the following appropriate sentence table. The starting point applies to all offenders irrespective of plea or previous convictions.

Harm	Culpability		
	A	**B**	**C**
Category 1	**Starting point** 3 years' custody	**Starting point** 2 years' custody	**Starting point** 1 year's custody
	Category range 2–4 years 6 months' custody	**Category range** 36 weeks–3 years' custody	**Category range** High-level community order–2 years' custody
Category 2	**Starting point** 2 years' custody	**Starting point** 1 year's custody	**Starting point** High-level community order

Harm	Culpability		
	A	**B**	**C**
	Category range 36 weeks–3 years' custody	**Category range** High-level community order –2 years' custody	**Category range** Medium-level community order–26 weeks' custody
Category 3	**Starting point** 1 year's custody	**Starting point** 26 weeks' custody	**Starting point** Medium-level community order
	Category range High-level community order–2 years' custody	**Category range** Medium-level community order–36 weeks' custody	**Category range** Band B fine–High-level community order

The following table contains a **non-exhaustive** list of additional factual elements providing the context of the offence and factors relating to the offender. Identify whether any combination of these, or other relevant factors, should result in an upward or downward adjustment from the starting point. In some cases, having considered these factors, it may be appropriate to move outside the identified category range.

Factors increasing seriousness	
Statutory aggravating factors:	*Other aggravating factors:*
Previous convictions, having regard to (a) the nature of the offence to which the conviction relates and its relevance to the current offence; and (b) the time that has elapsed since the conviction Offence committed while on bail	Breach committed immediately or shortly after order made History of disobedience of court orders (where not already taken into account as a previous conviction) Breach involves a further offence (where not separately prosecuted) Targeting of particular individual the order was made to protect Victim or protected subject of order is particularly vulnerable Offender takes steps to prevent victim or subject harmed by breach from reporting an incident or seeking assistance Offence committed on licence or while subject to post sentence supervision

Factors reducing seriousness or reflecting personal mitigation
Breach committed after long period of compliance
Prompt voluntary surrender/admission of breach
Age and/or lack of maturity where it affects the responsibility of the offender
Mental disorder or learning disability where linked to the commission of the offence
Sole or primary carer for dependent relatives

C2.4 Breach of Sexual Offences Act 2003 notification requirements

See **C14.23**.

C2.5 Breach of a Modern Slavery Act protection order

Modern Slavery Act 2015, s 30

(1) A person who, without reasonable excuse, does anything that the person is prohibited from doing ... commits an offence.

EW

6 months' imprisonment and/or a fine/5 years' imprisonment

C2.6 Breach of a female genital mutilation protection order

Female Genital Mutilation Act 2003, s 5A and Sch 2, para 4(1)

4(1) A person who without reasonable excuse does anything that the person is prohibited from doing by an FGM protection order is guilty of an offence.

EW

6 months' imprisonment and/or a fine/5 years' imprisonment

C2.7 Breach of a forced marriage protection order

Family Law Act 1996, s 63CA

(1) A person who without reasonable excuse does anything that the person is prohibited from doing by a forced marriage protection order is guilty of an offence.
(2) In the case of a forced marriage protection order made [ex parte] a person can be guilty of an offence under this section only in respect of conduct engaged in at a time when the person was aware of the existence of the order.

EW

6 months' imprisonment and/or a fine/5 years' imprisonment

C2.8 Serious crime prevention order

Serious Crime Act 2007, s 25

(1) A person who, without reasonable excuse, fails to comply with a serious crime prevention order commits an offence.

6 months' imprisonment and/or a fine/5 years' imprisonment

C2.9 Breach of a football banning order

Football Spectators Act 1989, s 14J

(1) A person subject to a banning order who fails to comply with—
   (a) any requirement imposed by the order, or
   (b) any requirement imposed under section 19(2B) or (2C) below, is guilty of an offence.

SO In its definitive guideline on breach offences, the Sentencing Council has suggested that reference should be made to the penalties for breach of a criminal behaviour order and the penalty adjusted to take account of the maximum available sentences.

6 months and/or a fine

C2.10 Breach of bail

See **C3.1**.

C2.11 Breach of dispersal order

Anti-social Behaviour Crime and Policing Act 2014

34 Authorisations to use powers under section 35

(1) A police officer of at least the rank of inspector may authorise the use in a specified locality, during a specified period of not more than 48 hours, of the powers given by section 35.
   'Specified' means specified in the authorisation.
(2) An officer may give such an authorisation only if satisfied on reasonable grounds that the use of those powers in the locality during that period may be necessary for the purpose of removing or reducing the likelihood of—
   (a) members of the public in the locality being harassed, alarmed or distressed, or
   (b) the occurrence in the locality of crime or disorder.
(3) In deciding whether to give such an authorisation an officer must have particular regard to the rights of freedom of expression and freedom of assembly set out in Articles 10 and 11 of the Convention.
   'Convention' has the meaning given by section 21(1) of the Human Rights Act 1998.
(4) An authorisation under this section—

   (a) must be in writing,
   (b) must be signed by the officer giving it, and
   (c) must specify the grounds on which it is given.

35 Directions excluding a person from an area

(1) If the conditions in subsections (2) and (3) are met and an authorisation is in force under section 34, a constable in uniform may direct a person who is in a public place in the locality specified in the authorisation—

(a) to leave the locality (or part of the locality), and

(b) not to return to the locality (or part of the locality) for the period specified in the direction ('the exclusion period').

(2) The first condition is that the constable has reasonable grounds to suspect that the behaviour of the person in the locality has contributed or is likely to contribute to—

(a) members of the public in the locality being harassed, alarmed or distressed, or

(b) the occurrence in the locality of crime or disorder.

(3) The second condition is that the constable considers that giving a direction to the person is necessary for the purpose of removing or reducing the likelihood of the events mentioned in subsection (2)(a) or (b).

(4) The exclusion period may not exceed 48 hours.

The period may expire after (as long as it begins during) the period specified in the authorisation under section 34.

(5) A direction under this section—

(a) must be given in writing, unless that is not reasonably practicable;

(b) must specify the area to which it relates;

(c) may impose requirements as to the time by which the person must leave the area and the manner in which the person must do so (including the route).

(6) The constable must (unless it is not reasonably practicable) tell the person to whom the direction is given that failing without reasonable excuse to comply with the direction is an offence.

(7) If the constable reasonably believes that the person to whom the direction is given is under the age of 16, the constable may remove the person to a place where the person lives or a place of safety.

(8) Any constable may withdraw or vary a direction under this section; but a variation must not extend the duration of a direction beyond 48 hours from when it was first given.

(9) Notice of a withdrawal or variation of a direction—

(a) must be given to the person to whom the direction was given, unless that is not reasonably practicable, and

(b) if given, must be given in writing unless that is not reasonably practicable.

(10) In this section 'public place' means a place to which at the material time the public or a section of the public has access, on payment or otherwise, as of right or by virtue of express or implied permission.

(11) In this Part "exclusion period" has the meaning given by subsection (1)(b).

36 Restrictions

(1) A constable may not give a direction under section 35 to a person who appears to the constable to be under the age of 10.

(2) A constable may not give a direction under section 35 that prevents the person to whom it is given having access to a place where the person lives.

(3) A constable may not give a direction under section 35 that prevents the person to whom it is given attending at a place which the person is—

(a) required to attend for the purposes of the person's employment, or a contract of services to which the person is a party,

(b) required to attend by an obligation imposed by or under an enactment or by the order of a court or tribunal, or

(c) expected to attend for the purposes of education or training or for the purposes of receiving medical treatment,

at a time when the person is required or expected (as the case may be) to attend there.

(4) A constable may not give a direction to a person under section 35 if the person is one of a group of persons who are—

(a) engaged in conduct that is lawful under section 220 of the Trade Union and Labour Relations (Consolidation) Act 1992 (peaceful picketing), or

(b) taking part in a public procession of the kind mentioned in subsection (1) of section 11 of the Public Order Act 1986 in respect of which—

(i) written notice has been given in accordance with that section, or

(ii) written notice is not required to be given as provided by subsections (1) and (2) of that section.

(5) In deciding whether to give a direction under section 35 a constable must have particular regard to the rights of freedom of expression and freedom of assembly set out in Articles 10 and 11 of the Convention.

'Convention' has the meaning given by section 21(1) of the Human Rights Act 1998.

37 Surrender of property

...

38 Record-keeping

...

39 Offences

(1) A person given a direction under section 35 who fails without reasonable excuse to comply with it commits an offence.

(3) A person given a direction under section 37 who fails without reasonable excuse to comply with it commits an offence.

SO

s 39(1) level 4 fine/3 months' imprisonment

s 39(3) level 2 fine

C2.11.1 *Sentencing*

The Guideline for breach offences states in relation to this offence

A court is ... entitled to use, and may be assisted by, a guideline for an analogous offence subject to differences in the elements of the offences and the statutory maxima.

In sentencing this breach offence the court should refer to the sentencing approach in step one of the guideline for breach of a criminal behaviour order to determine culpability and harm, and determine an appropriate sentence bearing in mind the maximum penalty for the offence.

C2.11.2 Key points

- The power to issue dispersal notices has also been given to police community support officers (s 40).
- To prove an offence under s 39 it must be established that the officer issuing the dispersal notice was acting lawfully. This means that the prosecution

must prove the validity of the authorization (*Carter v DPP* [2009] EWHC 2197 (Admin)) and the reasonableness of the grounds for issuing the notice to the particular defendant (*Buckley v DPP* [2006] EWHC 1888 (Admin)).
- Unless there were exceptional circumstances, reasonable [grounds] under s 34 had normally to depend, in part at least, on some behaviour of the group which indicates in some way or other that harassment, alarm, or intimidation had or was likely to occur (*Buckley v DPP*).

 Blackstone's Criminal Practice 2018 **B11.117–B11.121**

C2.12 Breach of a stalking protection order and notification requirements

Stalking Protection Act 2019, s 8
(1) A person who, without reasonable excuse, breaches a stalking protection order or an interim stalking protection order commits an offence.

EW

 6 months' imprisonment and/or a fine/5 years' imprisonment

Stalking Protection Act 2019, s 11

11 Offences relating to notification
(1) A person commits an offence if the person—
  (a) fails, without reasonable excuse, to comply with [notification requirements] or with [requirement to give fingerprints or photographs], or
  (b) notifies to the police, in purported compliance with [notification requirements] any information which the person knows to be false.

EW

 6 months' imprisonment and/or a fine/5 years

C2.13 Breach of a knife crime prevention order

Offensive Weapons Act 2019, s 29
(1) *A person commits an offence if, without reasonable excuse, the person breaches a knife crime prevention order or an interim knife crime prevention order.*

EW

 6 months and/or a fine/2 years' imprisonment

Offensive Weapons Act 2019, s 25

Offences relating to notification

(1) *A person commits an offence if the person—*
  (a) *fails, without reasonable excuse, to comply with [notification requirements], or*
  (b) *notifies to the police, in purported compliance with [notification requirements] (2)(5) any information which the person knows to be false.*

 6 months and/or a fine/2 years' imprisonment

C2.14 Other breach offences

C2.14.1

Breach of disqualification from acting as a director

Company Directors Disqualification Act 1986 (s13)

A full guideline appears in the Guideline for breach offences

C2.14.2 *Other offences*

The Sentencing Council guideline on breach has the following additional comments:

> Where an offence is not covered by a sentencing guideline a court is also entitled to use, and may be assisted by, a guideline for an analogous offence subject to differences in the elements of the offences and the statutory maxima.

In sentencing the following breach offences, the court should refer to the sentencing approach in step one of the guideline for breach of a criminal behaviour order to determine culpability and harm, and determine an appropriate sentence bearing in mind the maximum penalty for the offence.

Community protection notice Part 4, Chapter 1 Anti-social Behaviour, Crime and Policing Act 2014 (stops a person, business or organisation committing ASB which spoils the community's quality of life.)	Triable summarily only	A person guilty of an offence under this section is liable on summary conviction—to a fine not exceeding level 4 on the standard scale, in the case of an individual; to a fine of up to £20,000, in the case of a body. (If dealt with by way of fixed penalty, a fixed penalty notice of up to £100.)
Breach of public spaces protection order Part 4, Chapter 2 Anti-social Behaviour, Crime and Policing Act 2014 (stops people committing ASB in a particular public place.)	Triable summarily only	A person guilty of an offence under this section is liable on summary conviction to a fine not exceeding level 3 on the standard scale. (If dealt with by way of fixed penalty, a fixed penalty notice of up to £100.)

C2 Breach Offences

Closure power	Triable summarily only	A person guilty of obstructing a person acting under s 79 or 85(1) is liable on summary conviction—(a) to imprisonment for a period not exceeding 3 months, or (b) to a fine.
Part 4, Chapter 3 Anti-social Behaviour, Crime and Policing Act 2014 (allows the police or local council to close premises where ASB is being committed, or is likely to be committed.)		A person who is guilty of remaining on or entering premises in contravention of a closure order is liable on summary conviction—(a) to imprisonment for a period not exceeding 6 months, or (b) to a fine, or to both.

C3 Administration of Justice

C3.1 Bail: failure to surrender

> ### Bail Act 1976, s 6(1) and (2)
>
> #### 6 Offence of absconding by person released on bail
>
> (1) If a person who has been released on bail in criminal proceedings fails without reasonable cause to surrender to custody he shall be guilty of an offence.
> (2) If a person who—
>   (a) has been released on bail in criminal proceedings, and
>   (b) having reasonable cause therefor, has failed to surrender to custody, fails to surrender to custody at the appointed place as soon after the appointed time as is reasonably practicable he shall be guilty of an offence.

SO But with power to commit to the Crown Court. However a Bail Act offence is not 'related to' the substantive matter in which bail was granted and must be tried in the court that granted bail (*R v Osman* [2017] EWCA Crim 2178)

▦ Fine and/or 3 months'/12 months' imprisonment

C3.1.1 *Sentencing*

STEP ONE: Determining the offence category

The court should determine the offence category with reference only to the factors listed in the following tables. In order to determine the category the court should assess culpability and harm.

Culpability	Harm
A Failure to surrender represents deliberate attempt to evade or delay justice **B** Cases falling between categories A and C **C** Reason for failure to surrender just short of reasonable cause	The level of harm is determined by weighing up all the factors of the case to determine the harm that has been caused or was intended to be caused. **Category 1** Failure to attend Crown Court hearing results in substantial delay and/or interference with the administration of justice **Category 2** Failure to attend magistrates' court hearing results in substantial delay and/or interference with the administration of justice* **Category 3** Cases in either the magistrates' court or Crown Court not in categories 1 and 2

* In particularly serious cases where the failure to attend is in the magistrates' court and the consequences of the delay have a severe impact on victim(s) and /or witness(es) warranting a sentence outside of the powers of the magistrates' court, the case should be committed to the Crown Court pursuant to section 6(6)(a) of the Bail Act 1976 and the Crown Court should sentence the case according to the range in Category A1.

STEP TWO: Starting point and category range

Having determined the category at step one, the court should use the corresponding starting point to reach a sentence within the category range from the following appropriate sentence table. The starting point applies to all offenders irrespective of plea or previous convictions.

Where a custodial sentence is available within the category range and the substantive offence attracts a custodial sentence, a consecutive custodial sentence should normally be imposed for the failure to surrender offence.

	Culpability		
	A	**B**	**C**
Category 1	**Starting point** 6 weeks' custody	**Starting point** 21 days' custody	**Starting point** Medium-level community order*
	Category range 28 days'–26 weeks' custody1	**Category range** High-level community order*–13 weeks' custody	**Category range** Low level community order*–6 weeks' custody
Category 2	**Starting point** 21 days' custody	**Starting point** Medium-level community order*	**Starting point** Band B fine
	Category range High-level community order* – 13 weeks' custody	**Category range** Band B fine–6 weeks' custody	**Category range** Band A fine–Low level community order*
Category 3	**Starting point** 14 days' custody	**Starting point** Band C fine	**Starting point** Band A fine
	Category range Low-level community order*–6 weeks' custody	**Category range** Band A fine–Medium-level community order*	**Category range** Discharge–Band B fine
Maximum sentence in magistrates' court–3 months' imprisonment Maximum sentence in Crown Court–12 months' imprisonment			

* To include a curfew and/or unpaid work requirement only

1 In A1 cases which are particularly serious and where the consequences of the delay have a severe impact on victim(s) and /or witness(es), a sentence in excess of the specified range may be appropriate

The following table contains a non-exhaustive list of additional factual elements providing the context of the offence and factors relating to the offender. Identify whether any combination of these, or other relevant factors, should result in an upward or downward adjustment from the starting point.

In some cases, having considered these factors, it may be appropriate to move outside the identified category range.

Factors increasing seriousness	
Statutory aggravating factor:	*Other aggravating factors:*
Previous convictions, having regard to (a) the nature of the offence to which the conviction relates and its relevance to the current offence; and (b) the time that has elapsed since the conviction	History of breach of court orders or police bail
	Distress to victim(s) and /or witness(es)
	Offence committed on licence or while subject to post sentence supervision
	Factors reducing seriousness or reflecting personal mitigation
	Genuine misunderstanding of bail or requirements
	Prompt voluntary surrender
	Sole or primary carer for dependent relatives

C3.1.2 Key points

- Guidance by Justices' Clerks' Society in September 2014 advises that all courts should arrange for the surrender to bail to occur on appearance in the court room and not before on signing in with a court official. The effect is that those who arrive late, but whose cases are not called, will not be committing an offence. This reconciles *DPP v Richards* [1988] 3 All ER 406 (magistrates' courts) *with R v Scott Evans* [2011] 1WLR 1192 (Crown Courts) as appears below.
- In *R v Scott* [2007] EWCA Crim 2757, the court rejected an argument that surrendering to bail 30 minutes late was *de minimis* so as to make proceeding with a Bail Act charge *Wednesbury* unreasonable. The court held:

  We are prepared for the sake of argument to accept the possibility that there could be circumstances where a defendant's late arrival at court was so truly marginal that it would be Wednesbury unreasonable to pursue it but it would be a rare case. Even if a delay is small it can still cause inconvenience and waste of time. If a culture of lateness is tolerated the results can be cumulative and bad for the administration of justice.

- In *R v Gateshead Justices, ex p Usher* [1981] Crim LR 491, DC, a period of seven minutes was held to be *de minimis*; however, in *Scott* the court said that no gloss should be placed on the clear wording in the Bail Act and *Usher* established no clear principle of law.
- Proof of *bail* terms: s 6 Bail Act 1976 provides:

Bail Act 1976, s 6(8) and (9)

6 Offence of absconding by person released on bail

(8) In any proceedings for an offence under subsection (1) or (2) above a document purporting to be a copy of the part of the prescribed record which relates to the time and place appointed for the person specified in the record to surrender to custody and to be duly certified to be a true copy of that part of the record shall be evidence of the time and place appointed for that person to surrender to custody.

(9) For the purposes of subsection (8) above—
   (a) 'the prescribed record' means the record of the decision of the court, officer or constable made in pursuance of section 5(1) of this Act;
   (b) the copy of the prescribed record is duly certified if it is certified by the appropriate officer of the court or, as the case may be, by the constable who took the decision or a constable designated for the purpose by the officer in charge of the police station from which the person to whom the record relates was released.

- In *R v Liverpool Justices, ex p Santos*, The Times, 23 January 1997, the court held that reliance on mistaken information provided by a solicitor may be found a reasonable excuse for failing to surrender. The court went on to say that all relevant factors would need to be considered, and a mistake on the part of a solicitor in calculating the bail date did not automatically excuse the defendant's non-attendance.
- A failure to give the defendant a written bail notice does not amount to a reasonable excuse.
- A genuine, albeit mistaken, belief that bail was to another date would not amount to a reasonable excuse (*Laidlaw v Atkinson*, The Times, 2 August 1986).
- A reasonable excuse need be proved only to the civil standard (*R v Carr-Bryant* (1944) 29 Cr App R 76).
- A person who had overtly subjected himself to the court's direction (see *R v Central Criminal Court, ex p Guney* [1995] 2 All ER 577), or reported to court officials as directed, had surrendered to custody (see *Director of Public Prosecutions v Richards* [1988] QB 701 in relation to the magistrates' court). If the defendant later left court, no offence would be committed (although the court could issue a warrant for arrest). It is not essential that there be a formal surrender to an official (*R v Rumble* [2003] EWCA Crim 770), but simply arriving at the court at the proper time may not be enough (*R v Render* (1987) 84 Cr App R 294). In *Evans* [2011] EWCA Crim 2842, the court made clear that in the Crown Court a defendant who advises the usher and his own lawyer of his presence but then leaves, does not surrender to bail. He must be identified before the judge, or surrender to the dock officer.
- If a person is acquitted of the offence for which he was on bail, that does not mitigate the penalty for failing to surrender (*R v Maguire* [1993] RTR 306).
- Under s 68 Policing and Crime Act 2017 it is an offence carrying 12 months' imprisonment on indictment, if a person is on bail in respect of an offence mentioned in s41(1) or (2) Counter-Terrorism Act 2008, and their release on bail is subject to a travel restriction condition and they fail to comply with that condition.

 See *Blackstone's Criminal Practice 2019* **D7.97**

C3.2 Contempt of court

C3.2.1 *Magistrates' Court Act 1980, s 97*

(4) If any person attending or brought before a magistrates' court refuses without just excuse to be sworn or give evidence, or to produce any document or thing, the court may commit him to custody until the expiration of such period not exceeding one month as may be specified in the warrant or until he sooner gives evidence or produces the document or thing or impose on him a fine not exceeding £2,500 or both.

C3.2.2 *Contempt of Court Act 1981, s 12*

(1) A magistrates' court has jurisdiction under this section to deal with any person who—
  (a) wilfully insults the justice or justices, any witness before or officer of the court or any solicitor or counsel having business in the court, during his or their sitting or attendance in court or in going to or returning from the court; or
  (b) wilfully interrupts the proceedings of the court or otherwise misbehaves in court.
(2) In any such case the court may order any officer of the court, or any constable, to take the offender into custody and detain him until the rising of the court; and the court may, if it thinks fit, commit the offender to custody for a specified period not exceeding one month or impose on him a fine not exceeding £2,500, or both.

See *Blackstone's Criminal Practice 2019* **B 14.80–B14.128**

C3.3 **Escape from lawful custody**

At common law it is an offence to escape from legal custody.

 Life

C3.3.1 Key points

- The prosecution must prove that the defendant was in custody, that he knew (or was reckless as to whether he was or not); that the custody was lawful; and that he intentionally escaped from it (*R v Dhillon* [2005] EWCA Crim 2996).
- The escape may be from police custody following arrest (*R v Timmis* [1976] Crim LR 129).
- A prisoner is deemed to be in legal custody while he is confined in, or is being taken to or from, any prison or young offender institution (s 13 Prison Act 1952).
- Whether a person can be said to be in custody at any particular time is a question of fact to be decided by reference to the circumstances of each individual case. For a person to be in custody, his liberty must be subject to such restraint or restriction that he can be said to be confined by another in the sense that that person's immediate freedom of movement is under the direct control of another (*E v DPP* [2002] EWHC 433 (Admin)).
- A youth refused bail and remanded to local authority accommodation with a security requirement (now a remand to youth detention accommodation under s 91(5) Legal Aid, Punishment and Sentencing of Offenders Act 2012) but not placed in such accommodation as no placement was available was in lawful custody when he absented himself from court (*E v DPP*).

- A youth refused bail and remanded to local authority accommodation who had been collected from the cells by a Youth Offending Team worker and told to wait while she arranged a placement was held to be in lawful custody (*H v DPP* [2003] EWHC 878 (Admin)).

C3.4 Perverting the course of justice

It is an offence at common law to do an act tending and intended to pervert the course of public justice.

GC

 Life

IO

C3.4.1 Key points

- Acts which could amount to perverting the course of justice include destroying or concealing evidence, interfering with jurors or witnesses, and confessing to another's crime.
- Making false allegations against another person, intending that he be prosecuted or knowing that he might be, would constitute an offence (*R v Rowell* [1978] 1 WLR 132).
- Where it is alleged that a false allegation has been made, the prosecution must show that the defendant intended that the police take it seriously. It is not necessary to prove that the defendant intended anyone to be arrested (*R v Cotter* [2002] EWCA Crim 1033).
- False complaints which do not risk the arrest of an innocent person might in certain circumstances be more appropriately charged as wasting police time (see **C3.4** *R v Cotter*).
- When dealing with a suspected false sexual allegation reference should be made to the detailed CPS Legal Guidance *Perverting the Course of Justice: Charging in Cases Involving Rape and/or Domestic Violence Allegations.*

📖 See *Blackstone's Criminal Practice 2018* **B 14.29–B14.44**

C3.5 Wasting police time

> **Criminal Law Act 1967, s 5**
>
> (3) Where a person causes any wasteful employment of the police by knowingly making to any person a false report tending to show that an offence has been committed, or to give rise to apprehension for the safety of any persons or property, or tending to show that he has information material to any police inquiry, he shall be liable . . .

SO

▦ 6 month/level 4 fine

C3.5.1 Key points

- No proceedings shall be instituted for an offence under this section except by or with the consent of the DPP (s 5(3)).

📖 See *Blackstone's Criminal Practice 2018* **B14.78**

C3.6 Witness intimidation

Criminal Justice and Public Order Act 1994, s 51(1)–(5)

51 Intimidation, etc of witnesses, jurors and others

(1) A person commits an offence if—

  (a) he does an act which intimidates, and is intended to intimidate, another person ('the victim'),

  (b) he does the act knowing or believing that the victim is assisting in the investigation of an offence or is a witness or potential witness or a juror or potential juror in proceedings for an offence, and

  (c) he does it intending thereby to cause the investigation or the course of justice to be obstructed, perverted or interfered with.

(2) A person commits an offence if—

  (a) he does an act which harms, and is intended to harm, another person or, intending to cause another person to fear harm, he threatens to do an act which would harm that other person,

  (b) he does or threatens to do the act knowing or believing that the person harmed or threatened to be harmed ('the victim'), or some other person, has assisted in an investigation into an offence or has given evidence or particular evidence in proceedings for an offence, or has acted as a juror or concurred in a particular verdict in proceedings for an offence, and

  (c) he does or threatens to do it because of that knowledge or belief.

(3) For the purposes of subsections (1) and (2) it is immaterial that the act is or would be done, or that the threat is made—

  (a) otherwise than in the presence of the victim, or

  (b) to a person other than the victim.

(4) The harm that may be done or threatened may be financial as well as physical (whether to the person or a person's property) and similarly as respects an intimidatory act which consists of threats.

(5) The intention required by subsection (1)(c) and the motive required by subsection (2)(c) above need not be the only or the predominating intention or motive with which the act is done or, in the case of subsection (2), threatened.

6 months and/or fine/5 years

C3.6.1 *Sentencing*

Offence seriousness (culpability and harm)		
A. Identify the appropriate starting point		
Starting points based on first-time offender pleading not guilty		
Examples of nature of activity	**Starting point**	**Range**
Sudden outburst in chance encounter	6 weeks' custody	Medium-level community order–18 weeks' custody
Conduct amounting to a threat; staring at, approaching, or following witnesses; talking about the case; trying to alter or stop evidence	18 weeks' custody	12 weeks' custody–Crown Court
Threats of violence to witnesses and/or their families; deliberately seeking out witnesses	Crown Court	Crown Court

Offence seriousness (culpability and harm)
A. Identify the appropriate starting point
Starting points based on first-time offender pleading not guilty
Factors indicating higher culpability
1. Breach of bail conditions
2. Offender involves others
Factors indicating greater degree of harm
1. Detrimental impact on administration of justice
2. Contact made at or in vicinity of victim's home

C3.6.2 Key points

For there to be an offence under s 51(1) Criminal Justice and Public Order Act 1994 the witness, etc must be proved to have been intimidated. Intent alone is not enough. It might, however, be possible to establish an attempt (*R v ZN* [2013] EWCA Crim 989).

See *Blackstone's Criminal Practice 2019* **B14.46**

C4 Communication Network Offences

C4.1 Improper use of public electronic communications network

Communications Act 2003, s 127(1) and (2)

127 Improper use of public electronic communications network

(1) A person is guilty of an offence if he—
   (a) sends by means of a public electronic communications network a message or other matter that is grossly offensive or of an indecent, obscene or menacing character; or
   (b) causes any such message or matter to be so sent.
(2) A person is guilty of an offence if, for the purpose of causing annoyance, inconvenience or needless anxiety to another, he—

   (a) sends by means of a public electronic communications network, a message that he knows to be false,
   (b) causes such a message to be sent; or
   (c) persistently makes use of a public electronic communications network

SON

 Fine/6 months' imprisonment

C4.1.1 *Sentencing*

Communications Act 2003, s 127(1) and 127(2)

Triable only summarily:

Maximum: Unlimited fine and/or 6 months

Offence range: Band A fine–15 weeks' custody

STEP ONE: Determining the offence category

The court should determine the offence category using the following table.

Category 1	Higher culpability **and** greater harm
Category 2	Higher culpability **and** lesser harm **or** lower culpability **and** greater harm
Category 3	Lower culpability **and** lesser harm

The court should determine the offender's culpability and the harm caused with reference **only** to the following factors. Where an offence does not fall squarely into a category, individual factors may require a degree of weighting before making an overall assessment and determining the appropriate offence category.

CULPABILITY demonstrated by one or more of the following:	
High culpability	**Low culpability**
Targeting of a vulnerable victim	All other cases
Targeting offending (in terms of timing or location) to maximise effect	
Use of threats (including blackmail)	
Threat to disclose intimate material or sexually explicit images	
Campaign demonstrated by multiple calls and/or wide distribution	
False calls to emergency services	
Offence motivated by, or demonstrating, hostility based on any of the following characteristics or presumed characteristics of the victim(s): religion, race, disability, sexual orientation, or transgender identity	

HARM demonstrated by one or more of the following:	
Greater harm	**Lesser harm**
Substantial distress or fear to victim(s) **or** moderate impact on several victims	All other cases
Major disruption	

STEP TWO: Starting point and category range

Having determined the category at step one, the court should use the corresponding starting point to reach a sentence within the category range in the following table. The starting point applies to all offenders irrespective of plea or previous convictions.

Harm	Culpability	
	High culpability	**Low culpability**
Greater harm	**Category 1**	**Category 2**
	Starting point	Starting point
	9 weeks' custody	Medium-level community order
	Category range	Category range
	High-level community order–15 weeks' custody	Low-level community order–high-level community order
Lesser harm	**Category 2**	**Category 3**
	Starting point	Starting point
	Medium-level community order	Band B fine
	Category range	Category range
	Low-level community order–high-level community order	Band A fine–Band C fine

The court should then consider adjustment for any aggravating or mitigating factors. The following is a **non-exhaustive** list of additional factual elements providing the context of the offence and factors relating to the offender.

Identify whether any combination of these, or other relevant factors, should result in an upward or downward adjustment from the sentence arrived at so far.

Factors increasing seriousness	
Statutory aggravating factors:	*Other aggravating factors:*
Previous convictions, having regard to (a) the **nature** of the offence to which the conviction relates and its **relevance** to the current offence; and (b) the **time** that has elapsed since the conviction Offence committed while on bail	Failure to comply with current court orders including restraining order Offence committed on licence or post sentence supervision Offence committed while subject to sex offender notification requirements Offence linked to domestic abuse Abuse of trust Targeting emergency services (where not taken into account at step one)

Factors reducing seriousness or reflecting personal mitigation
No previous convictions **or** no relevant/recent convictions
Remorse
Good character and/or exemplary conduct
Isolated incident
Age and/or lack of maturity where it affects the responsibility of the offender
Mental disorder or learning disability
Sole or primary carer for dependent relatives
Limited awareness or understanding of the offence

C4.1.2 *Time limits (see also A12.1.2)*

Communications Act 2003, s 127

(5) An information or complaint relating to an offence under this section may be tried by a magistrates' court in England and Wales or Northern Ireland if it is laid or made—

  (a) before the end of the period of 3 years beginning with the day on which the offence was committed, and

  (b) before the end of the period of 6 months beginning with the day on which evidence comes to the knowledge of the prosecutor which the prosecutor considers sufficient to justify proceedings...

(7) A certificate of a prosecutor as to the date on which evidence described in subsection (5)(b) or (6)(b) came to his or her knowledge is conclusive evidence of that fact.

C4.1.3 Key points

- In *Director of Public Prosecutions v Collins* [2006] UKHL 40, the court held that to be guilty of an offence under s 127:
  - the defendant must have intended his words to be offensive to those to whom they related; or
  - must be aware that they might be taken to be so.
- It does not matter if the material sent was not received. The question of whether something is in fact offensive is to be determined by reference to whether or not reasonable persons would find the message grossly offensive, judged by the standards of an open and just multiracial society.

In *DPP v Smith (Kingsley Anthony)* [2017] EWHC 359 (Admin) the court emphasized that in deciding whether a particular message is grossly offensive, a court needs to be careful not to criminalize speech that, however contemptible, is no more than offensive.

It has to be asked whether taking account of the context and all the relevant circumstances, and applying the standards of a reasonable person in an open and just multi-racial and multi-faith society, it is proved that a particular message was grossly offensive to those to whom it related or was of a menacing character, and whether it would have created a sense of apprehension or fear in a person of reasonable fortitude who received or read it:

- Parliament cannot have intended to criminalize the conduct of a person using language which is, for reasons unknown to him, grossly offensive to those to whom it relates, or which may even be thought, however wrongly, to represent a polite or acceptable usage. On the other hand, a culpable state of mind will ordinarily be found where a message is couched in terms showing an intention to insult those to whom the message relates, or giving rise to the inference that a risk of doing so must have been recognized by the sender. The same will be true where facts known to the sender of a message about an intended recipient render the message peculiarly offensive to that recipient, or likely to be so, whether or not the message in fact reaches the recipient.
- While it is an offence to send by public electronic communication network a message of a menacing character (Communications Act 2003, s 127(1)(a)), the mental element requires the sender either to have intended that the message be of a menacing character, or to have been aware or to have recognized the risk that it might create fear or apprehension in any reasonable member of the public who reads or sees it.
- If the message was intended as a joke, however poor, the offence will rarely be made out (*Chambers v DPP* [2012] EWHC 2157 (QB)).
- For a call to be menacing within s 127(1)(a) Communications Act 2003 it must be more than offensive or nasty and anti-Semitic (*Karsten v Wood Green Crown Court* [2014] EWHC 2900 (Admin)).
- European Convention (ECHR) rights to freedom of expression will rarely provide a defence (see *Connolly v Director of Public Prosecutions* [2007] EWHC 237 (Admin), a case concerned with a different statute).

 See *Blackstone's Criminal Practice 2019* **B18.30**

C4.2 Sending indecent material through the post

Postal Services Act 2000, s 85

85 Prohibition on sending certain articles by post

(1) A person commits an offence if he sends by post a postal packet which encloses any creature, article or thing of any kind which is likely to injure other postal packets in course of their transmission by post or any person engaged in the business of a postal operator.

(2) Subsection (1) does not apply to postal packets which enclose anything permitted (whether generally or specifically) by the postal operator concerned.

(3) A person commits an offence if he sends by post a postal packet which encloses—
  (a) any indecent or obscene print, painting, photograph, lithograph, engraving, cinematograph film or other record of a picture or pictures, book, card or written communication, or
  (b) any other indecent or obscene article (whether or not of a similar kind to those mentioned in paragraph (a)).

(4) A person commits an offence if he sends by post a postal packet which has on the packet, or on the cover of the packet, any words, marks or designs which are of an indecent or obscene character.

(5) A person who commits an offence under this section shall be liable—
  (a) on summary conviction, to a fine not exceeding the statutory maximum,
  (b) on conviction on indictment, to a fine or to imprisonment for a term not exceeding twelve months or to both. '

EW

Summary trial—fine; on indictment—12 months' imprisonment and/or a fine

C4.2.1 Key points

Whether something is obscene is to be judged objectively.

The section is compatible with Article 10 ECHR (*R v Kirk* [2006] EWCA Crim 725).

See *Blackstone's Criminal Practice 2019* **B18.25**

C4.3 Indecent or offensive or threatening letters, etc

Malicious Communications Act 1988, s 1

1 Offence of sending letters etc with intent to cause distress or anxiety

(1) Any person who sends to another person—
  (a) a letter, electronic communication or article of any description which conveys—
    (i) a message which is indecent or grossly offensive;
    (ii) a threat; or
    (iii) information which is false and known or believed to be false by the sender; or
  (b) any article or electronic communication which is, in whole or part, of an indecent or grossly offensive nature,

is guilty of an offence if his purpose, or one of his purposes, in sending it is that it should, so far as falling within paragraph (a) or (b) above, cause distress or anxiety to the recipient or to any other person to whom he intends that it or its contents or nature should be communicated.

(2) A person is not guilty of an offence by virtue of subsection (1)(a)(ii) above if he shows—
  (a) that the threat was used to reinforce a demand made by him on reasonable grounds; and
  (b) that he believed, and had reasonable grounds for believing, that the use of the threat was a proper means of reinforcing the demand.
(2A) In this section 'electronic communication' includes—
  (a) any oral or other communication by means of an electronic communications network; and
  (b) any communication (however sent) that is in electronic form.
(3) In this section references to sending include references to delivering or transmitting and to causing to be sent, delivered or transmitted and 'sender' shall be construed accordingly.

 6 months' and/or fine/2 years' imprisonment

C4.3.1 Key points

See *Connolly v Director of Public Prosecutions* [2008] 1 WLR 276 for Articles 9 (religion) and 10 (free speech) considerations. Articles 9(2) and 10(2) allow for restrictions on the relevant rights.

 See *Blackstone's Criminal Practice 2019* **B18.30**

C4.4 Offences involving intent to cause distress, etc

Criminal Justice and Courts Act 2015, s 33

33 Disclosing private sexual photographs and films with intent to cause distress

(1) It is an offence for a person to disclose a private sexual photograph or film if the disclosure is made—
  (a) without the consent of an individual who appears in the photograph or film, and
  (b) with the intention of causing that individual distress.
(2) But it is not an offence under this section for the person to disclose the photograph or film to the individual mentioned in subsection (1)(a) and (b).
(3) It is a defence for a person charged with an offence under this section to prove that he or she reasonably believed that the disclosure was necessary for the purposes of preventing, detecting or investigating crime.
(4) It is a defence for a person charged with an offence under this section to show that—
  (a) the disclosure was made in the course of, or with a view to, the publication of journalistic material, and
  (b) he or she reasonably believed that, in the particular circumstances, the publication of the journalistic material was, or would be, in the public interest.

(5) It is a defence for a person charged with an offence under this section to show that—
  (a) he or she reasonably believed that the photograph or film had previously been disclosed for reward, whether by the individual mentioned in subsection (1)(a) and (b) or another person, and
  (b) he or she had no reason to believe that the previous disclosure for reward was made without the consent of the individual mentioned in subsection (1)(a) and (b).
(6) A person is taken to have shown the matters mentioned in subsection or (5) if—
  (a) sufficient evidence of the matters is adduced to raise an issue with respect to it, and
  (b) the contrary is not proved beyond reasonable doubt.
(7) For the purposes of subsections (1) to (5)—
  (a) 'consent' to a disclosure includes general consent covering the disclosure, as well as consent to the particular disclosure, and
  (b) 'publication' of journalistic material means disclosure to the public at large or to a section of the public.
(8) A person charged with an offence under this section is not to be taken to have disclosed a photograph or film with the intention of causing distress merely because that was a natural and probable consequence of the disclosure.

EW 6 months' imprisonment and/or fine/2 years' imprisonment.

C4.4.1 *Interpretation*

Criminal Justice and Courts Act 2015, ss 34–35 define the meaning of 'disclose' and 'photograph or film' and of 'private' and 'sexual'.

C4.4.2 *Sentencing*

Where offence committed in a domestic context, also refer to the Overarching principles: Domestic abuse guideline in **Appendix 5.**

STEP ONE: Determining the offence category

The court should determine the offence category with reference only to the factors in the following tables. In order to determine the category the court should assess **culpability** and **harm**.

The level of culpability is determined by weighing up all the factors of the case. Where there are characteristics present which fall under different levels of culpability, the court should balance these characteristics to reach a fair assessment of the offender's culpability.

Culpability demonstrated by one or more of the following:
AHigher culpability • Conduct intended to maximise distress and/or humiliation • Images circulated widely/publicly • Significant planning and/or sophisticated offence • Repeated efforts to keep images available for viewing

Culpability demonstrated by one or more of the following:
B—Medium culpability • Some planning • Scope and duration that falls between categories A and C • All other cases that fall between categories A and C
C—Lesser culpability • Offender's responsibility substantially reduced by mental disorder or learning disability • Little or no planning • Conduct intended to cause limited distress and/or humiliation • Offence was limited in scope and duration

Harm	
Category 1	The level of harm is assessed by weighing up all the factors of the case: • Very serious distress caused to the victim • Significant psychological harm caused to the victim • Offence has a considerable practical impact on the victim
Category 2	Harm that falls between categories 1 and 3, and in particular: • Some distress caused to the victim • Some psychological harm caused to the victim • Offence has some practical impact on the victim
Category 3	• Limited distress or harm caused to the victim

STEP TWO: Starting point and category range

Having determined the category at step one, the court should use the corresponding starting point to reach a sentence within the following category range. The starting point applies to all offenders irrespective of plea or previous convictions.

Harm	Culpability		
	A	**B**	**C**
Category 1	**Starting point** 1 year's custody	**Starting point** 26 weeks' custody	**Starting point** 12 weeks' custody
	Category range 26 weeks–1 year 6 months' custody	**Category range** 12 weeks'–1 year's custody	**Category range** High-level community order–26 weeks' custody
Category 2	**Starting point** 26 weeks' custody	**Starting point** 12 weeks' custody	**Starting point** High-level community order
	Category range 12 weeks'–1 year's custody	**Category range** High-level community order–26 weeks' custody	**Category range** Low-level community order– 12 weeks' custody
Category 3	**Starting point** 12 weeks' custody	**Starting point** High-level community order	**Starting point** Low-level community order
	Category range High-level community order–26 weeks' custody	**Category range** Low-level community order–12 weeks' custody	**Category range** Discharge–High-level community order

Where offence committed in a domestic context, also refer to the Overarching principles:

Domestic abuse guideline

The court should then consider any adjustment for any aggravating or mitigating factors. The following is a non-exhaustive list of additional factual elements providing the context of the offence and factors relating to the offender.

Identify whether any combination of these, or other relevant factors, should result in an upward or downward adjustment from the starting point.

Factors increasing seriousness	
Statutory aggravating factors:	*Other aggravating factors:*
Previous convictions, having regard to (a) the nature of the offence to which the conviction relates and its relevance to the current offence; and (b) the time that has elapsed since the conviction	Impact of offence on others, particularly children
	Victim is particularly vulnerable (not all vulnerabilities are immediately apparent)
Offence committed while on bail	Failure to comply with current court orders
Offence motivated by, or demonstrating hostility based on any of the following characteristics or presumed characteristics of the victim: religion, race, disability, sexual orientation, or transgender identity	Offence committed on licence or post sentence supervision
	Offences taken into consideration

Factors reducing seriousness or reflecting personal mitigation
No previous convictions or no relevant/recent convictions
Offender took steps to limit circulation of images
Remorse
Good character and/or exemplary conduct
Serious medical condition requiring urgent, intensive or long-term treatment
Age and/or lack of maturity
Mental disorder or learning disability (where not taken into account at step one)
Sole or primary carer for dependent relatives
Determination and/or demonstration of steps having been taken to address offending behaviour

C5 Computer Misuse

C5.1 Unauthorized access to computer material

Computer Misuse Act 1990, s 1

(1) A person is guilty of an offence if—
   (a) he causes a computer to perform any function with intent to secure access to any program or data held in any computer;
   (b) the access he intends to secure is unauthorised; and
   (c) he knows at the time when he causes the computer to perform the function that that is the case.
(2) The intent a person has to have to commit an offence under this section need not be directed at—

   (a) any particular program or data;
   (b) a program or data of any particular kind; or
   (c) a program or data held in any particular computer.

EW

 6 months/2 years and/or a fine

C5.1.1 Key points

- For the offence to be made out there must be an interaction with the computer's programs but the interaction need not be successful.
- s 1 was designed to combat all forms of unauthorized access to the actual data involved (*Bow Street Stipendiary Magistrate ex p United States* 2000 2 AC 216).
- Definitions are provided in s 17 Computer Misuse Act 1990.

C5.2 Unauthorized access with intent to commit or facilitate commission of further offences

Computer Misuse Act 1990, s 2

(1) A person is guilty of an offence under this section if he commits an offence under section 1 above ('the unauthorised access offence') with intent—
   (a) to commit an offence to which this section applies; or
   (b) to facilitate the commission of such an offence (whether by himself or by any other person);
   and the offence he intends to commit or facilitate is referred to below in this section as the further offence.

(2) This section applies to offences—
  (a) for which the sentence is fixed by law; or
  (b) for which a person who has attained the age of twenty-one years and has no previous convictions may be sentenced to imprisonment for a term of five years but for the restrictions imposed by section 33 of the Magistrates' Courts Act 1980).

(3) It is immaterial for the purposes of this section whether the further offence is to be committed on the same occasion as the unauthorised access offence or on any future occasion.

(4) A person may be guilty of an offence under this section even though the facts are such that the commission of the further offence is impossible.

 6 months/5 years and/or a fine

C5.3 Unauthorized acts with intent to impair, or with recklessness as to impairing, operation of computer, etc

Computer Misuse Act 1990, s 3

3 (1) A person is guilty of an offence if—
  (a) he does any unauthorised act in relation to a computer;
  (b) at the time when he does the act he knows that it is unauthorised; and
  (c) either subsection (2) or subsection (3) below applies.

(2) This subsection applies if the person intends by doing the act—
  (a) to impair the operation of any computer;
  (b) to prevent or hinder access to any program or data held in any computer;
  (c) to impair the operation of any such program or the reliability of any such data.

(3) This subsection applies if the person is reckless as to whether the act will do any of the things mentioned in paragraphs (a) to (c) of subsection (2) above.

(4) The intention referred to in subsection (2) above, or the recklessness referred to in subsection (3) above, need not relate to—
  (a) any particular computer;
  (b) any particular program or data; or
  (c) a program or data of any particular kind.

(5) In this section—
  (a) a reference to doing an act includes a reference to causing an act to be done;
  (b) 'act' includes a series of acts;
  (c) a reference to impairing, preventing or hindering something includes a reference to doing so temporarily.

 6 months/10 years and/or a fine

C5 Computer Misuse

C5.3.1 Key points

The offence is made out if a bogus email is placed on another person's computer (*Zezev and Yarimaka v Governor of HMP Brixton* 202 EWHC 589 (Admin)).

C5.4 Making, supplying, or obtaining articles for use in offence under section 1, 3, or 3ZA Computer Misuse Act 1990

Computer Misuse Act 1990, s 3A

(1) A person is guilty of an offence if he makes, adapts, supplies or offers to supply any article intending it to be used to commit, or to assist in the commission of, an offence under section 1, 3 or 3ZA.
(2) A person is guilty of an offence if he supplies or offers to supply any article believing that it is likely to be used to commit, or to assist in the commission of, an offence under section 1, 3 or 3ZA.
(3) A person is guilty of an offence if he obtains any article—
    (a) intending to use it to commit, or to assist in the commission of, an offence under section 1, 3 or 3ZA, or
    (b) with a view to its being supplied for use to commit, or to assist in the commission of, an offence under section 1, 3 or 3ZA.
(4) In this section 'article' includes any program or data held in electronic form.

EW

6 months/2 years and/or a fine

See *Blackstone's Criminal Practice 2019* **B17.14**

236

C6 Criminal Damage

C6.1 Destroying or damaging property

Criminal Damage Act 1971, s 1

1 Destroying or damaging property

(1) A person who without lawful excuse destroys or damages any property belonging to another intending to destroy or damage any such property or being reckless as to whether any such property would be destroyed or damaged shall be guilty of an offence.

(2) A person who without lawful excuse destroys or damages any property, whether belonging to himself or another—

(a) intending to destroy or damage any property or being reckless as to whether any property would be destroyed or damaged; and

(b) intending by the destruction or damage to endanger the life of another or being reckless as to whether the life of another would be thereby endangered;

shall be guilty of an offence.

(3) An offence committed under this section by destroying or damaging property by fire shall be charged as arson.

EW (If racially aggravated (see **C6.1.4**) but otherwise venue dictated by value and charge)

SO If value does not exceed £5,000 and offence is under s 1(1) and does not involve arson; the offence remains an indictable offence for all other purposes (*Fennell* [2000] EWCA Crim 3544) such as for time limits (*DPP v Bird* [2015] EWHC 4077 (Admin)) and costs. An offence under s 1(2) is indictable only

IO s 1(2) or s 1(3)

▥ If SO: 3 months' imprisonment and/or fine level 4 (if value > £5,000, 6 months/10 years); but if on indictment s 1(2) or s 1(3), Life

DO s 1(2) offence

C6.1.1 *Sentencing:*

There are now five sentencing guidelines relevant to these provisions. In C6.1.1 appear the guidelines for arson, criminal damage not exceeding £5000, and exceeding £5000. The guideline for criminal damage by endangering life is at 6.1.3. The guideline for threats to cause criminal damage appears at 6.2.

1 Arson (criminal damage by fire)
2 Criminal damage (other than by fire) value exceeding £5,000/ Racially or religiously aggravated criminal damage
3 Criminal damage (other than by fire) value exceeding £5,000/ Racially or religiously aggravated criminal damage

Arson (criminal damage by fire)

Courts should consider requesting a report from: liaison and diversion services, a medical practitioner, or where it is necessary, ordering a psychiatric report, to ascertain both whether the offence is linked to a mental disorder or learning disability (to assist in the assessment of culpability) and whether any mental health disposal should be considered.

STEP ONE: Determining the offence category

The court should determine the offence category with reference only to the factors in the following tables. In order to determine the category the court should assess **culpability** and **harm**.

The level of culpability is determined by weighing up all the factors of the case. Where there are characteristics present which fall under different levels of culpability, the court should balance these characteristics to reach a fair assessment of the offender's culpability.

Culpability demonstrated by one or more of the following
A—High culpability
• High degree of planning or premeditation • Revenge attack • Use of accelerant • Intention to cause very serious damage to property • Intention to create a high risk of injury to persons
B—Medium culpability
• Some planning • Recklessness as to whether very serious damage caused to property • Recklessness as to whether serious injury caused to persons • Other cases that fall between categories A and C because: • Factors are present in A and C which balance each other out and/or • The offender's culpability falls between the factors described in A and C
C—Lesser culpability
• Little or no planning; offence committed on impulse • Recklessness as to whether some damage to property caused • Offender's responsibility substantially reduced by mental disorder or learning disability • Involved through coercion, intimidation, or exploitation

Culpability demonstrated by one or more of the following
Harm
The level of harm is assessed by weighing up all the factors of the case.
Category 1
• Serious physical and/or psychological harm caused • Serious consequential economic or social impact of offence • High value of damage caused
Category 2
• Harm that falls between categories 1 and 3
Category 3
• No or minimal physical and/or psychological harm caused • Low value of damage caused

STEP TWO: Starting point and category range

Having determined the category at step one, the court should use the corresponding starting point to reach a sentence within the following category range. The starting point applies to all offenders irrespective of plea or previous convictions.

Where the offender is dependent on or has a propensity to misuse drugs or alcohol, which **is linked to the offending**, a community order with a drug rehabilitation requirement under se 209, or an alcohol treatment requirement under s 212 Criminal Justice Act 2003 may be a proper alternative to a short or moderate custodial sentence.

Where the offender suffers from a medical condition that is susceptible to treatment but does not warrant detention under a hospital order, a community order with a mental health treatment requirement under s 207 Criminal Justice Act 2003 may be a proper alternative to a short or moderate custodial sentence.

In exceptional cases within category 1A, sentences of above 8 years may be appropriate.

Harm		Culpability	
	A	**B**	**C**
Category 1	**Starting point** 4 years' custody	**Starting point** 1 year 6 months' custody	**Starting point** 9 months' custody
	Category range 2–8 years' custody	**Category range** 9 months–3 years' custody	**Category range** 6 months–1 year 6 months' custody

Harm		Culpability	
Category 2	**Starting point** 2 years' custody	**Starting point** 9 months' custody	**Starting point** High-level community order
	Category range 1–4 years' custody	**Category range** 6 months–1 year 6 months' custody	**Category range** Medium-level community order–9 months' custody
Category 3	**Starting point** 1 year's custody	**Starting point** High-level community order	**Starting point** Low-level community order
	Category range 6 months–2 years' custody	**Category range** Medium-level community order– 9 months' custody	**Category range** Discharge–High-level community order

The court should then consider any adjustment for any aggravating or mitigating factors. The following is a **non-exhaustive** list of additional factual elements providing the context of the offence and factors relating to the offender.

Identify whether any combination of these, or other relevant factors, should result in an upward or downward adjustment from the starting point.

Factors increasing seriousness
Statutory aggravating factors
<ul><li>Previous convictions, having regard to (a) the nature of the offence to which the conviction relates and its relevance to the current offence; and (b) the time that has elapsed since the conviction</li><li>Offence committed while on bail</li><li>Offence motivated by, or demonstrating hostility based on any of the following characteristics or presumed characteristics of the victim: religion, race, disability, sexual orientation, or transgender identity</li></ul>
Other aggravating factors
<ul><li>Commission of offence while under the influence of alcohol or drugs</li><li>Offence committed for financial gain</li><li>Offence committed to conceal other offences</li></ul>
Victim is particularly vulnerable
<ul><li>Offence committed within a domestic context</li><li>Fire set in or near a public amenity</li><li>Damage caused to heritage and/or cultural assets</li><li>Significant impact on emergency services or resources</li><li>Established evidence of community/wider impact</li><li>Failure to comply with current court orders</li><li>Offence committed on licence or post sentence supervision</li></ul>

Factors increasing seriousness
Offences taken into consideration

Factors reducing seriousness or reflecting personal mitigation
• No previous convictions **or** no relevant/recent convictions • Steps taken to minimise the effect of the fire or summon assistance • Remorse • Good character and/or exemplary conduct • Serious medical condition requiring urgent, intensive, or long-term treatment • Age and/or lack of maturity • Mental disorder or learning disability (where not taken into account at step one) • Sole or primary carer for dependent relatives • Determination and/or demonstration of steps having been taken to address   addiction or offending behaviour

Criminal damage (other than by fire) value exceeding £5,000/ Racially or religiously aggravated criminal damage

STEP TWO: Determining the offence category

The court should determine the offence category with reference only to the factors in the following tables. In order to determine the category the court should assess **culpability** and **harm.**

The level of **culpability** is determined by weighing up all the factors of the case. Where there are characteristics present which fall under different levels of culpability, the court should balance these characteristics to reach a fair assessment of the offender's culpability.

Culpability demonstrated by one or more of the following
A–High culpability
• High degree of planning or premeditation • Revenge attack • Intention to cause very serious damage to property • Intention to create a high risk of injury to persons
B–Medium culpability

• Some planning
• Recklessness as to whether very serious damage caused to property
• Recklessness as to whether serious injury caused to persons
• Other cases that fall between categories A and C because:
  o Factors are present in A and C which balance each other out and/or
  o The offender's culpability falls between the factors described in A and C

C–Lesser culpability
• Little or no planning; offence committed on impulse • Recklessness as to whether some damage to property caused • Offender's responsibility substantially reduced by mental disorder or learning disability • Involved through coercion, intimidation or exploitation

C6 Criminal Damage

Culpability demonstrated by one or more of the following
Harm
The level of harm is assessed by weighing up all the factors of the case
Category 1
• Serious distress caused • Serious consequential economic or social impact of offence • High value of damage
Category 2
• Harm that falls between categories 1 and 3
Category 3
• No or minimal distress caused • Low value damage

STEP TWO: Starting point and category range

Having determined the category at step one, the court should use the corresponding starting point to reach a sentence within the following category range. The starting point applies to all offenders irrespective of plea or previous convictions.

Where the offender is dependent on or has a propensity to misuse drugs or alcohol, which **is linked to the offending**, a community order with a drug rehabilitation requirement under s 209, or an alcohol treatment requirement under s 212 Criminal Justice Act 2003 may be a proper alternative to a short or moderate custodial sentence.

Where the offender suffers from a medical condition that is susceptible to treatment but does not warrant detention under a hospital order, a community order with a mental health treatment requirement under s 207 Criminal Justice Act 2003 may be a proper alternative to a short or moderate custodial sentence.

Maximum: 10 years' custody (basic offence)

Harm		Culpability	
	A	**B**	**C**
Category 1	**Starting point** 1 year 6 months' custody	**Starting point** 6 months' custody	**Starting point** High level community order
	Category range 6 months–4 years' custody	**Category range** High-level community order– 1 year 6 months' custody	**Category range** Medium-level community order–9 months' custody
Category 2	**Starting point** 6 months' custody	**Starting point** High-level community order	**Starting point** Low-level community order
	Category range High-level community order–1 year 6 months' custody	**Category range** Medium-level community order–9 months' custody	**Category range** Band C fine–High-level community order

Harm		Culpability	
Category 3	**Starting point** High-level community order	**Starting point** Low-level community order	**Starting point** Band B fine
	Category range Medium-level community order–9 months' custody	**Category range** Band C fine–High-level community order	**Category range** Discharge–Low-level community order

The court should then consider any adjustment for any aggravating or mitigating factors. The following is a **non-exhaustive** list of additional factual elements providing the context of the offence and factors relating to the offender.

Identify whether any combination of these, or other relevant factors, should result in an upward or downward adjustment from the starting point.

Factors increasing seriousness
Statutory aggravating factors
• Previous convictions, having regard to (a) the nature of the offence to which the conviction relates and its relevance to the current offence; and (b) the time that has elapsed since the conviction • Offence committed while on bail • Offence motivated by, or demonstrating hostility based on any of the following characteristics or presumed characteristics of the victim: disability, sexual orientation, or transgender identity
Other aggravating factors
• Damaged items of great value to the victim (whether economic, commercial, sentimental, or personal value) • Commission of offence while under the influence of alcohol or drugs
Victim is particularly vulnerable
• Offence committed in a domestic context • Damage caused to heritage and/or cultural assets • Significant impact on emergency services or resources • Established evidence of community/wider impact • Failure to comply with current court orders • Offence committed on licence or post sentence supervision
Offences taken into consideration
Factors reducing seriousness or reflecting personal mitigation
• No previous convictions **or** no relevant/recent convictions
• Remorse • Good character and/or exemplary conduct • Serious medical condition requiring urgent, intensive, or long-term treatment • Age and/or lack of maturity • Mental disorder or learning disability (where not taken into account at step one) • Sole or primary carer for dependent relatives • Determination and/or demonstration of steps having been taken to address addiction or offending behaviour

Racially or religiously aggravated criminal damage offences only

Having determined the category of the basic offence to identify the sentence of a non-aggravated offence, the court should now consider the level of racial or religious aggravation involved and apply an appropriate uplift to the sentence in accordance with the following guidance. The following is a list of factors which the court should consider to determine the level of aggravation. Where there are characteristics present which fall under different levels of aggravation, the court should balance these to reach a fair assessment of the level of aggravation present in the offence.

Maximum sentence for the aggravated offence on indictment is 14 years' custody (maximum for the basic offence is 10 years' custody).

Care should be taken to avoid double counting factors already taken into account in assessing the level of harm at step one.

High level of racial or religious aggravation	Sentence uplift
Racial or religious aggravation was the predominant motivation for the offence. Offender was a member of, or was associated with, a group promoting hostility based on race or religion. Aggravated nature of the offence caused severe distress to the victim or the victim's family **(over and above the distress already considered at step one).** Aggravated nature of the offence caused serious fear and distress throughout local community or more widely.	Increase the length of custodial sentence if already considered for the basic offence or consider a custodial sentence, if not already considered for the basic offence.
Medium level of racial or religious aggravation	**Sentence uplift**
Racial or religious aggravation formed a significant proportion of the offence as a whole. Aggravated nature of the offence caused some distress to the victim or the victim's family **(over and above the distress already considered at step one).** Aggravated nature of the offence caused some fear and distress throughout local community or more widely.	Consider a significantly more onerous penalty of the same type or consider a more severe type of sentence than for the basic offence.
Low level of racial or religious aggravation	**Sentence uplift**
Aggravated element formed a minimal part of the offence as a whole. Aggravated nature of the offence caused minimal or no distress to the victim or the victim's family **(over and above the distress already considered at step one).**	Consider a more onerous penalty of the same type identified for the basic offence.

Magistrates may find that, although the appropriate sentence for the basic offence would be within their powers, the appropriate increase for the aggravated offence would result in a sentence in excess of their powers. If so, they must commit for sentence to the Crown Court.

Criminal damage (other than by fire) value not exceeding £5,000/ Racially or religiously aggravated criminal damage

Note:

Where an offence of criminal damage is added to the indictment at the Crown Court the statutory maximum sentence is 10 years' custody regardless of the value of the damage. In such cases where the value does not exceed £5,000, the exceeding £5,000 guideline should be used but regard should also be had to this guideline.

STEP ONE: Determining the offence category

The court should determine the offence category with reference only to the factors in the following tables. In order to determine the category the court should assess **culpability** and **harm.**

The level of **culpability** is determined by weighing up all the factors of the case. Where there are characteristics present which fall under different levels of culpability, the court should balance these characteristics to reach a fair assessment of the offender's culpability.

Culpability demonstrated by one or more of the following:
• A–High culpability
• High degree of planning or premeditation • Revenge attack • Intention to cause very serious damage to property • Intention to create a high risk of injury to persons
B–Medium culpability
• Some planning • Recklessness as to whether very serious damage caused to property • Recklessness as to whether serious injury caused to persons • Other cases that fall between categories A and C because: • Factors are present in A and C which balance each other out and/or • The offender's culpability falls between the factors described in A and C
C–Lesser culpability
• Little or no planning; offence committed on impulse • Recklessness as to whether some damage to property caused • Offender's responsibility substantially reduced by mental disorder or learning disability • Involved through coercion, intimidation or exploitation
Harm
The level of harm is assessed by weighing up all the factors of the case.
Category 1
• Serious distress caused • Serious consequential economic or social impact of offence • High value of damage
Category 2
• All other cases

STEP TWO: Starting point and category range

Having determined the category at step one, the court should use the corresponding starting point to reach a sentence within the following category range. The starting point applies to all offenders irrespective of plea or previous convictions.

Where the offender is dependent on or has a propensity to misuse drugs or alcohol, which **is linked to the offending**, a community order with a drug rehabilitation requirement under s 209, or an alcohol treatment requirement under s 212 Criminal Justice Act 2003 may be a proper alternative to a short or moderate custodial sentence.

Where the offender suffers from a medical condition that is susceptible to treatment but does not warrant detention under a hospital order, a community order with a mental health treatment requirement under s 207 Criminal Justice Act 2003 may be a proper alternative to a short or moderate custodial sentence.

Maximum Level 4 fine and/or 3 months custody (basic offence)

Harm		Culpability	
	A	B	C
Category 1	**Starting point** High-level community order	**Starting point** Low-level community order	**Starting point** Band B fine
	Category range Medium-level community order–3 months' custody	**Category range** Band C fine–High-level community order	**Category range** Discharge–Low-level community order
Category 2	**Starting point** Low-level community order	**Starting point** Band B fine	**Starting point** Band A fine
	Category range Band C fine–High-level community order	**Category range** Discharge–Low-level community order	**Category range** Discharge–Band B fine

The court should then consider any adjustment for any aggravating or mitigating factors. The following is a **non-exhaustive** list of additional factual elements providing the context of the offence and factors relating to the offender.

Identify whether any combination of these, or other relevant factors, should result in an upward or downward adjustment from the starting point.

Factors increasing seriousness
Statutory aggravating factors
• Previous convictions, having regard to (a) the nature of the offence to which the conviction relates and its relevance to the current offence; and (b) the time that has elapsed since the conviction • Offence committed while on bail • Offence motivated by, or demonstrating hostility based on any of the following characteristics or presumed characteristics of the victim: disability, sexual orientation, or transgender identity

Factors increasing seriousness
Other aggravating factors
• Damaged items of great value to the victim (whether economic, commercial, sentimental, or personal value) • Commission of offence while under the influence of alcohol or drugs
Victim is particularly vulnerable
• Offence committed within a domestic context • Damage caused to heritage and/or cultural assets • Significant impact on emergency services or resources • Established evidence of community/wider impact • Failure to comply with current court orders • Offence committed on licence or post sentence supervision
Offences taken into consideration
Factors reducing seriousness or reflecting personal mitigation
• No previous convictions **or** no relevant/recent convictions • Remorse • Good character and/or exemplary conduct • Serious medical condition requiring urgent, intensive, or long-term treatment • Age and/or lack of maturity • Mental Disorder or learning disability (where not taken into account at step one) • Sole or primary carer for dependent relative • Determination and/or demonstration of steps having been taken to address addiction or offending behaviour

Racially or religiously aggravated criminal damage offences only

Having determined the category of the basic offence to identify the sentence of a non-aggravated offence, the court should now consider the level of racial or religious aggravation involved and apply an appropriate uplift to the sentence in accordance with the following guidance. The following is a list of factors which the court should consider to determine the level of aggravation. Where there are characteristics present which fall under different levels of aggravation, the court should balance these to reach a fair assessment of the level of aggravation present in the offence.

Maximum sentence for the aggravated offence on indictment is 14 years' custody (maximum for the basic offence is 10 years' custody)

Care should be taken to avoid double counting factors already taken into account in assessing the level of harm at step one

High level of racial or religious aggravation	Sentence uplift
Racial or religious aggravation was the predominant motivation for the offence. Offender was a member of, or was associated with, a group promoting hostility based on race or religion. Aggravated nature of the offence caused severe distress to the victim or the victim's family **(over and above the distress already considered at step one)**. Aggravated nature of the offence caused serious fear and distress throughout local community or more widely.	Increase the length of custodial sentence if already considered for the basic offence or consider a custodial sentence, if not already considered for the basic offence.

High level of racial or religious aggravation	Sentence uplift
Medium level of racial or religious aggravation	**Sentence uplift**
Racial or religious aggravation formed a significant proportion of the offence as a whole. Aggravated nature of the offence caused some distress to the victim or the victim's family **(over and above the distress already considered at step one)**. Aggravated nature of the offence caused some fear and distress throughout local community or more widely.	Consider a significantly more onerous penalty of the same type **or consider** a more severe type of sentence than for the basic offence.
Low level of racial or religious aggravation	**Sentence uplift**
Aggravated element formed a minimal part of the offence as a whole. Aggravated nature of the offence caused minimal or no distress to the victim or the victim's family **(over and above the distress already considered at step one)**.	Consider a more onerous penalty of the same type identified for the basic offence.

Magistrates may find that, although the appropriate sentence for the basic offence would be within their powers, the appropriate increase for the aggravated offence would result in a sentence in excess of their powers. If so, they must commit for sentence to the Crown Court.

C6.1.2 Key points

- There is no bar on charging attempted criminal damage where, due to value, the matter can be tried summarily only (*R v Bristol Justices, ex p E* [1999] 1 WLR 390).
- Lawful excuse is defined in s 5:

Criminal Damage Act 1971, s 5(2)–(5)

5 'Without lawful excuse'

(2) A person charged with an offence to which this section applies, shall, whether or not he would be treated for the purposes of this Act as having a lawful excuse apart from this subsection, be treated for those purposes as having a lawful excuse—

   (a) if at the time of the act or acts alleged to constitute the offence he believed that the person or persons whom he believed to be entitled to consent to the destruction of or damage to the property in question had so consented, or would have so consented to it if he or they had known of the destruction or damage and its circumstances; or

   (b) if he destroyed or damaged or threatened to destroy or damage the property in question or, in the case of a charge of an offence under section 3 above, intended to use or cause or permit the use of something to destroy or damage it, in order to protect property belonging to himself or another or a right or interest in property which was or which he believed to be vested in himself or another, and at the time of the act or acts alleged to constitute the offence he believed—

      (i) that the property, right or interest was in immediate need of protection; and

      (ii) that the means of protection adopted or proposed to be adopted were or would be reasonable having regard to all the circumstances.

---

(3) For the purposes of this section it is immaterial whether a belief is justified or not if it is honestly held.

(4) For the purposes of subsection (2) above a right or interest in property includes any right or privilege in or over land, whether created by grant, licence or otherwise.

(5) This section shall not be construed as casting doubt on any defence recognised by law as a defence to criminal charges.

- A person can avail himself of the defence of lawful excuse, notwithstanding the fact that he was intoxicated (*Jaggard v Dickinson* (1981) 72 Cr App R 33). The test is subjective, that is, whether the belief is held honestly, not whether it is justified or reasonable. Conduct due to mental illness resulting from alcohol psychosis or hallucinosis may not be reckless if the defendant was thereby not aware of the risk (*R v Coley* [2013] EWCA Crim 223). However, whether a person is acting to protect property has an objective element (*R v Hunt* (1977) 66 Cr App R 105).

- It is clear that s 5(5) is intended to cover the situation whereby damage is caused to protect life or prevent injury (*R v Baker*, The Times, 26 November 1996).

- Damage does not need to be destruction and encompasses harm that is not permanent, such as graffiti. If expense or inconvenience is involved in putting right the matter then damage will have been caused (eg stamping on a policeman's helmet so that it had to be pushed back into shape). Damaging something that can be restored (eg deleting a computer program) constitutes damage (*Cox v Riley* (1986) 83 Cr App R 54). Spitting on a police officer's uniform is unlikely to cause damage (*A v R* [1978] Crim LR 689). The soaking of a blanket and the flooding of the floor of a police cell were held to amount to damage in *R v Fiak* [2005] EWCA Crim 2381, and the daubing of water-soluble paint on a pavement was equally found to amount to damage in *Hardman v Chief Constable of Avon and Somerset* [1986] Crim LR 330.

- Determining whether something has been damaged is a matter of fact and degree to be determined by the magistrates or the jury (*Roe v Kingerlee* [1986] Crim LR 735).

- It is an offence to damage jointly owned property. Section 10 provides:

Criminal Damage Act 1971, s 10

10 Interpretation

(1) In this Act 'property' means of a tangible nature, whether real or personal, including money and—

(a) including wild creatures which have been tamed or are ordinarily kept in captivity, and any other wild creatures or their carcasses if, but only if, they have been reduced into possession which has not been lost or abandoned or are in the course of being reduced into possession; but

(b) not including mushrooms growing wild on any land or flowers, fruit or foliage of a plant growing wild on any land.

For the purposes of this subsection 'mushroom' includes any fungus and 'plant' includes any shrub or tree.

> (2) Property shall be treated for the purposes of this Act as belonging to any person—
>   (a) having the custody or control of it;
>   (b) having in it any proprietary right or interest (not being an equitable interest arising only from an agreement to transfer or grant an interest); or
>   (c) having a charge on it.
> (3) Where property is subject to a trust, the persons to whom it belongs shall be so treated as including any person having a right to enforce the trust.
> (4) Property of a corporation sole shall be so treated as belonging to the corporation notwithstanding a vacancy in the corporation.

- The prosecution will have proved that the defendant was reckless if, having regard to all the available evidence, the court is sure:
  - that he was aware of a risk that property would be destroyed/damaged; and
  - that in the circumstances which were known to him it was unreasonable for him to take that risk.
- This test allows for some of the personal characteristics of a defendant to be taken into account (see *R v G* [2003] UKHL 50).

C6.1.3 *Criminal damage (by endangering life): Criminal Damage Act 1971, section 1(2)*

 An offence under s 1(2) is triable only on indictment: Life

IO See **C6.1**.

C6.1.3.1 Sentencing

Criminal damage/arson with intent to endanger life or reckless as to whether life endangered

Courts should consider requesting a report from: liaison and diversion services, a medical practitioner, or where it is necessary, ordering a psychiatric report, to ascertain both whether the offence is linked to a mental disorder or learning disability (to assist in the assessment of culpability) and whether any mental health disposal should be considered.

STEP ONE: Determining the offence category

The court should determine the offence category with reference only to the factors in the following tables. In order to determine the category the court should assess **culpability** and **harm.**

Within this guideline culpability is fixed: culpability A is for intent, culpability B is for recklessness.

Culpability A
• Offender intended to endanger life
Culpability B
• Offender was reckless as to whether life was endangered

Harm
The level of harm is assessed by weighing up all the factors of the case.
Category 1
• Very serious physical and/or psychological harm caused • High risk of very serious physical and/or psychological harm • Serious consequential economic or social impact of offence caused • Very high value of damage caused
Category 2
• Significant physical and/or psychological harm caused • Significant risk of serious physical and/or psychological harm • Significant value of damage caused • All other harm that falls between categories 1 and 3
Category 3
• No or minimal physical and/or psychological harm caused • Low risk of serious physical and/or psychological harm • Low value of damage caused

Step two: Starting point and category range

Having determined the category at step one, the court should use the corresponding starting point to reach a sentence within the following category range. The starting point applies to all offenders irrespective of plea or previous convictions.

Where the offender is dependent on or has a propensity to misuse drugs or alcohol, which **is linked to the offending**, a community order with a drug rehabilitation requirement under s 209, or an alcohol treatment requirement under s 212 Criminal Justice Act 2003 may be a proper alternative to a short or moderate custodial sentence.

Where the offender suffers from a medical condition that is susceptible to treatment but does not warrant detention under a hospital order, a community order with a mental health treatment requirement under s 207 Criminal Justice Act 2003 may be a proper alternative to a short or moderate custodial sentence.

In exceptional cases within category 1A, sentences of above 12 years may be appropriate

Harm	Culpability	
	A	**B**
Category 1	**Starting point** 8 years' custody	**Starting point** 6 years' custody
	Category range 5 years–12 years' custody	**Category range** 4 years–10 years' custody
Category 2	**Starting point** 6 years' custody	**Starting point** 4 years' custody
	Category range 4–8 years' custody	**Category range** 2–6 years' custody

Harm	Culpability	
Category 3	**Starting point** 2 years' custody	**Starting point** 1 year's custody
	Category range 6 months–4 years' custody	**Category range** High level community order–2 years 6 months' custody

The seriousness of the offence should be the **initial** factor in determining which requirements to include in a community order. Offence-specific guidelines refer to three sentencing levels within the community order band based on offence seriousness (low, medium and high). See the following for **non-exhaustive** examples of requirements that might be appropriate in each.

At least one requirement **MUST** be imposed for the purpose of punishment and/or a fine imposed in addition to the community order unless there are exceptional circumstances which relate to the offence or the offender that would make it unjust in all the circumstances to do so. For further information see Imposition of community and custodial sentences.

A suspended sentence **MUST NOT** be imposed as a more severe form of community order. A suspended sentence is a custodial sentence.

Low	Medium	High
Offences only just cross community order threshold, where the seriousness of the offence or the nature of the offender's record means that a discharge or fine is inappropriate In general, only one requirement will be appropriate and the length may be curtailed if additional requirements are necessary	Offences that obviously fall within the community order band	Offences only just fall below the custody threshold or the custody threshold is crossed but a community order is more appropriate in the circumstances More intensive sentences which combine two or more requirements may be appropriate
Suitable requirements might include: • Any appropriate rehabilitative requirement(s) • 40–80 hours of unpaid work • Curfew requirement within the lowest range (for example up to 16 hours per day for a few weeks) • Exclusion requirement, for a few months • Prohibited activity requirement • Attendance centre requirement (where available)	Suitable requirements might include: • Any appropriate rehabilitative requirement(s) • Greater number of hours of unpaid work (for example 80–150 hours) • Curfew requirement within the middle range (for example up to 16 hours for 2–3 months) • Exclusion requirement lasting in the region of 6 months • Prohibited activity requirement	Suitable requirements might include: • Any appropriate rehabilitative requirement(s) • 150–300 hours of unpaid work • Curfew requirement for example up to 16 hours per day for 4–12 months • Exclusion requirement lasting in the region of 12 months
* If order does not contain a punitive requirement, suggested fine levels are indicated below:		
BAND A FINE	**BAND B FINE**	**BAND C FINE**

Care should be taken to avoid double counting factors already taken into account in assessing the level of harm at step one.

Factors increasing seriousness
Statutory aggravating factors
• Previous convictions, having regard to a) the nature of the offence to which the conviction relates and its relevance to the current offence; and b) the time that has elapsed since the conviction • Offence committed while on bail • Offence motivated by, or demonstrating hostility based on any of the following characteristics or presumed characteristics of the victim: religion, race, disability, sexual orientation, or transgender identity
Other aggravating factors
• Commission of offence while under the influence of alcohol or drugs • Revenge attack • Significant degree of planning or premeditation • Use of accelerant • Fire set in or near a public amenity
Victim is particularly vulnerable
• Offence committed within a domestic context • Damage caused to heritage and/or cultural assets • Multiple people endangered • Significant impact on emergency services or resources • Established evidence of community/wider impact • Failure to comply with current court orders • Offence committed on licence or post sentence supervision
Offences taken into consideration
Factors reducing seriousness or reflecting personal mitigation
• No previous convictions or no relevant/recent convictions • Offender's responsibility substantially reduced by mental disorder or learning disability • Lack of premeditation • Involved through coercion, intimidation or exploitation • Remorse • Good character and/or exemplary conduct • Serious medical condition requiring urgent, intensive, or long-term treatment • Age and/or lack of maturity • Sole or primary carer for dependent relatives • Determination and/or demonstration of steps having been taken to address addiction or offending behaviour

C6.1.4 *Racially or religiously aggravated criminal damage: Crime and Disorder Act 1998, section 30*

EW

 6 months' imprisonment and/or fine/14 years' imprisonment

C6.2 **Threats to destroy or damage property**

> ### Criminal Damage Act 1971, s 2
>
> #### 2 Threats to destroy or damage property
>
> A person who without lawful excuse makes to another a threat, intending that that other would fear it would be carried out—
>
> (a) to destroy or damage any property belonging to that other or a third person; or
> (b) to destroy or damage his own property in a way which he knows is likely to endanger the life of that other or third person;
>
> shall be guilty of an offence.

 Fine and/or 6 months'/10 years' imprisonment

C6.2.1 *Sentencing*

In cases of threats to cause damage by fire, courts should consider requesting a report from: liaison and diversion services, a medical practitioner, or where it is necessary, ordering a psychiatric report, to ascertain both whether the offence is linked to a mental disorder or learning disability (to assist in the assessment of culpability) and whether any mental health disposal should be considered.

STEP ONE–Determining the offence category

The court should determine the offence category with reference only to the factors in the following tables. In order to determine the category the court should assess **culpability** and **harm.**

The level of **culpability** is determined by weighing up all the factors of the case. Where there are characteristics present which fall under different levels of culpability, the court should balance these characteristics to reach a fair assessment of the offender's culpability.

Culpability demonstrated by one or more of the following
A– High culpability
Significant planning or premeditation
Offence motivated by revenge
• Offence committed to intimidate, coerce, or control • Threat to burn or bomb property
B–Medium culpability
Cases that fall between categories A and C because:
• Factors are present in A and C which balance each other out and/or • The offender's culpability falls between the factors described in A and C

Culpability demonstrated by one or more of the following
C–Lesser culpability
• Little or no planning; offence committed on impulse • Offender's responsibility substantially reduced by mental disorder or learning disability • Involved through coercion, intimidation or exploitation
Harm
The level of harm is assessed by weighing up all the factors of the case
Category 1
• Serious distress caused to the victim • Serious disruption/inconvenience caused to others • High level of consequential financial harm and inconvenience caused to the victim
Category 2
• Harm that falls between categories 1 and 3
Category 3
• No or minimal distress caused to the victim

Where the offender is dependent on or has a propensity to misuse drugs or alcohol, which **is linked to the offending**, a community order with a drug rehabilitation requirement under s 209, or an alcohol treatment requirement under s 212 Criminal Justice Act 2003 may be a proper alternative to a short or moderate custodial sentence

Where the offender suffers from a medical condition that is susceptible to treatment but does not warrant detention under a hospital order, a community order with a mental health treatment requirement under s 207 Criminal Justice Act 2003 may be a proper alternative to a short or moderate custodial sentence.

STEP TWO: Starting point and category range

Having determined the category at step one, the court should use the corresponding starting point to reach a sentence within the following category range. The starting point applies to all offenders irrespective of plea or previous convictions.

Harm		Culpability	
	A	**B**	**C**
Category 1	**Starting point** 1 year 6 months' custody	**Starting point** 6 months' custody	**Starting point** High-level community order
	Category range 6 months–4 years' custody	**Category range** High-level community order–1 year 6 months' custody	**Category range** Medium-level community order–9 months' custody

C6 Criminal Damage

Harm		Culpability	
Category 2	**Starting point** 6 months' custody	**Starting point** High-level community order	**Starting point** Low-level community order
	Category range High-level community order–1 year 6 months' custody	**Category range** Medium-level community order–9 months' custody	**Category range** Band C fine–High-level community order
Category 3	Starting point High-level community order	Starting point Low-level community order	Starting point Band B fine
	Category range Medium-level community order–9 months' custody	**Category range** Band C fine–High-level community order	**Category range** Discharge–Low-level community order

The court should then consider any adjustment for any aggravating or mitigating factors. The following is a **non-exhaustive** list of additional factual elements providing the context of the offence and factors relating to the offender.

Identify whether any combination of these, or other relevant factors, should result in an upward or downward adjustment from the starting point.

Factors increasing seriousness

Statutory aggravating factors

- Previous convictions, having regard to (a) the nature of the offence to which the conviction relates and its relevance to the current offence; and (b) the time that has elapsed since the conviction
- Offence committed while on bail
- Offence motivated by, or demonstrating hostility based on any of the following characteristics or presumed characteristics of the victim: religion, race, disability, sexual orientation, or transgender identity

Other aggravating factors

- Commission of offence while under the influence of alcohol or drugs

Victim is particularly vulnerable

- Offence committed in a domestic context
- Threats made in the presence of children
- Considerable damage threatened
- Damage threatened to heritage and/or cultural assets
- Established evidence of community/wider impact
- Failure to comply with current court orders
- Offence committed on licence or post sentence supervision

Offences taken into consideration

Factors reducing seriousness or reflecting personal mitigation

- No previous convictions **or** no relevant/recent convictions
- Remorse
- Good character and/or exemplary conduct
- Serious medical condition requiring urgent, intensive, or long-term treatment
- Age and/or lack of maturity
- Mental disorder or learning disability (where not taken into account at step one)
- Sole or primary carer for dependent relatives
- Determination and/or demonstration of steps having been taken to address addiction or offending behaviour

C6.2.2 `Key points`

- Whether a threat has been made under s 2(a) is to be assessed objectively with reference to the words and actions of the defendant (*R v Cakmak* [2002] EWCA Crim 500).
- The term 'without lawful excuse' is defined in s 5 of the Act:

> ### Criminal Damage Act 1971, s 5
>
> **5 'Without lawful excuse'**
>
> (1) This section applies to any offence under section 1(1) above and any offence under section 2 or 3 above other than one involving a threat by the person charged to destroy or damage property in a way which he knows is likely to endanger the life of another or involving an intent by the person charged to use or cause or permit the use of something in his custody or under his control so to destroy or damage property.

C6.3 Possessing anything with intent to destroy or damage property

> ### Criminal Damage Act 1971, s 3
>
> **3 Possessing anything with intent to destroy or damage property**
>
> A person who has anything in his custody or under his control intending without lawful excuse to use it or cause or permit another to use it—
>
> (a) to destroy or damage any property belonging to some other person; or
> (b) to destroy or damage his own or the user's property in a way which he knows is likely to endanger the life of some other person;
>
> shall be guilty of an offence.

`EW`

 Fine and/or 6 months'/10 years' imprisonment

C6.3.1 `Key points`

A conditional intent will suffice (*R v Buckingham* (1976) 63 Cr App R 159).

 See *Blackstone's Criminal Practice* 2019 **B8**

C7 **Drugs**

- A statutory defence is provided by s 28 Misuse of Drugs Act 1971:

Misuse of Drugs Act 1971, s 28

28 Proof of lack of knowledge etc to be a defence in proceedings for certain offences

(1) This section applies to offences under any of the following provisions of this Act, that is to say section 4(2) and (3), section 5(2) and (3), section 6(2) and section 9.

(2) Subject to subsection (3) below, in any proceedings for an offence to which this section applies it shall be a defence for the accused to prove that he neither knew of nor suspected nor had reason to suspect the existence of some fact alleged by the prosecution which it is necessary for the prosecution to prove if he is to be convicted of the offence charged.

(3) Where in any proceedings for an offence to which this section applies it is necessary, if the accused is to be convicted of the offence charged, for the prosecution to prove that some substance or product involved in the alleged offence was the controlled drug which the prosecution alleges it to have been, and it is proved that the substance or product in question was that controlled drug, the accused—

    (a) shall not be acquitted of the offence charged by reason only of proving that he neither knew nor suspected nor had reason to suspect that the substance or product in question was the particular controlled drug alleged; but

    (b) shall be acquitted thereof—

        (i) if he proves that he neither believed nor suspected nor had reason to suspect that the substance or product in question was a controlled drug; or

        (ii) if he proves that he believed the substance or product in question to be a controlled drug, or a controlled drug of a description, such that, if it had in fact been that controlled drug or a controlled drug of that description, he would not at the material time have been committing any offence to which this section applies.

(4) Nothing in this section shall prejudice any defence which it is open to a person charged with an offence to which this section applies to raise apart from this section.

- In considering a defence under s 28(3)(b), self-induced intoxication should not be considered (*R v Young* [1984] 2 All ER 164).

C7.2 Key points: Sentencing

- A minimum sentence of seven years must, unless not justified in all the circumstances, be imposed where an adult is convicted of a Class A drug trafficking offence (which excludes possession alone) if the offender has been convicted of two other drug trafficking offences in the circumstances set out in **D20**. Such offences may be tried on indictment only (s 91(5) Powers of Criminal Courts (Sentencing) Act 2000).
- Sentences are prescribed by Sch 4 to the Misuse of Drugs Act 1971 in the table in the next section. Sentencing Guidance for drugs not referred to in that schedule appears at **C7.10.1**.

C7.3 Drugs—Class A: fail to attend/remain for initial or follow-up assessment (Sentencing Guideline at p 323)

Drugs Act 2005, s 12(1)–(3)

12 Attendance at initial assessment

This section applies if a person is required to attend an initial assessment and remain for its duration by virtue of section 9(2).

(3) A person is guilty of an offence if without good cause—

    (a) he fails to attend an initial assessment at the specified time and place, or

    (b) he attends the assessment at the specified time and place but fails to remain for its duration.

...

SO

6 months' imprisonment and/or level 4 fine

MISUSE OF DRUGS ACT 1971, Sch 4

Schedule 4

Prosecution and Punishment of Offences

Section Creation offence	General Nature of Offence	Mode of Prosecution	Punishment			
			Class A drug involved	Class B drug involved	Class C drug involved	General
Section 4(2)	Production, or being concerned in the production, of a controlled drug.	(a) Summary	6 months or fine, or both	6 months or fine, or both	3 months or £2,500 or both	
		(b) On indictment	Life	14 years	14 years	
Section 4(3)	Supplying or offering to supply a controlled drug or being concerned in the doing of either activity by another	(a) Summary	6 months or fine, or both	6 months or fine, or both	3 months or £2,500, or both	
		(b) On indictment	Life	14 years	14 years	
Section 5(2)	Having possession of a controlled drug.	(a) Summary	6 months or fine, or both	3 months or £2,500, or both	3 months or £1,000, or both	
		(b) On indictment	7 years	5 years	2 years	
Section 5(3)	Having possession of a controlled drug with intent to supply it to another.	(a) Summary	6 months or fine, or both	6 months or fine, or both	3 months or £2,500, or both	
		(b) On indictment	Life	14 years	14 years	
Section 6(2)	Cultivation of cannabis plant.	(a) Summary				6 months or fine, or both
		(b) On indictment				14 years
Section 8	Being the occupier, or concerned in the management, of premises and permitting or suffering certain activities to take place there.	(a) Summary	6 months or fine, or both	6 months or fine, or both	3 months or £2,500, or both	
		(b) On indictment	14 years	14 years	14 years	
...						

Drugs Act 2005, s 14(1) and (3)

14 Attendance at follow-up assessment

(1) This section applies if a person is required to attend a follow-up assessment and remain for its duration by virtue of section 10(2).

...

(3) A person is guilty of an offence if without good cause—
   (a) he fails to attend a follow-up assessment at the specified time and place, or
   (b) he attends the assessment at the specified time and place but fails to remain for its duration.

...

SO

6 months and/or level 4 fine

C7.3.1 *Sentencing*

Note that this guideline refers to s 12 offences only. **Drugs—Class A—fail to attend/remain for initial assessment (revised 2017)**

Drugs Act 2005, s 12

Triable only summarily:

Maximum: Level 4 fine and/or 3 months

Offence range: Band A fine–high-level community order

STEP ONE: Determining the offence category

The court should determine the offence category using the following table.

Category 1	Higher culpability **and** greater harm
Category 2	Higher culpability **and** lesser harm **or** lower culpability **and** greater harm
Category 3	Lower culpability **and** lesser harm

The court should determine the offender's culpability and the harm caused with reference **only** to the following factors. Where an offence does not fall squarely into a category, individual factors may require a degree of weighting before making an overall assessment and determining the appropriate offence category.

CULPABILITY demonstrated by one or more of the following:	
Factor indicating higher culpability	**Factor indicating lower culpability**
Deliberate failure to attend/remain	All other cases

HARM demonstrated by one or more of the following:	
Factor indicating greater harm	**Factor indicating lesser harm**
Aggressive, abusive or disruptive behaviour	All other cases

STEP TWO: Starting point and category range

Having determined the category at step one, the court should use the corresponding starting point to reach a sentence within the category range in the following table. The starting point applies to all offenders irrespective of plea or previous convictions.

| Harm | Culpability | |
	High culpability	**Low culpability**
Greater harm	**Category 1**	**Category 2**
	Starting point	Starting point
	Medium-level community order	Band C fine
	Category range	Category range
	Low-level community order–high-level community order	Band B fine–low-level community order
Lesser harm	**Category 2**	**Category 3**
	Starting point	Starting point
	Band C fine	Band B fine
	Category range	Category range
	Band B fine–low-level community order	Band A fine–Band C fine

The court should then consider further adjustment for any aggravating or mitigating factors. The following is a **non-exhaustive** list of additional factual elements providing the context of the offence and factors relating to the offender. Identify whether any combination of these, or other relevant factors, should result in an upward or downward adjustment from the sentence arrived at so far.

Factors increasing seriousness	
Statutory aggravating factors:	*Other aggravating factors:*
Previous convictions, having regard to (a) the **nature** of the offence to which the conviction relates and its **relevance** to the current offence; and (b) the **time** that has elapsed since the conviction	Failure to comply with current court orders Offence committed on licence or post-sentence supervision Offender's actions result in a waste of resources
Offence committed while on bail Offence motivated by, or demonstrating hostility based on any of the following characteristics or presumed characteristics of the owner/keeper of the animal: religion, race, disability, sexual orientation, or transgender identity	

Factors reducing seriousness or reflecting personal mitigation
No previous convictions **or** no relevant/recent convictions
Remorse
Good character and/or exemplary conduct
Serious medical condition requiring urgent, intensive, or long-term treatment
Age and/or lack of maturity where it affects the responsibility of the offender
Mental disorder or learning disability
Sole or primary carer for dependent relatives
Determination and/or demonstration of steps having been taken to address addiction or offending behaviour
Attempts made to rearrange appointments

C7.4 Drugs—Class A: fail/refuse to provide a sample

There are a considerable number of condition precedents that need to be satisfied before a lawful request for a sample can be made.

Police and Criminal Evidence Act 1984, s 63B

63B Testing for presence of Class A drugs

(1) A sample of urine or a non-intimate sample may be taken from a person in police detention for the purpose of ascertaining whether he has any specified Class A drug in his body if—

    (a) either the arrest condition or the charge condition is met;

    (b) both the age condition and the request condition are met; and

    (c) the notification condition is met in relation to the arrest condition, the charge condition or the age condition (as the case may be).

(1A) The arrest condition is that the person concerned has been arrested for an offence but has not been charged with that offence and either—

    (a) the offence is a trigger offence; or

    (b) a police officer of at least the rank of inspector has reasonable grounds for suspecting that the misuse by that person of a specified Class A drug caused or contributed to the offence and has authorised the sample to be taken.

(2) The charge condition is either—

    (a) that the person concerned has been charged with a trigger offence; or

    (b) that the person concerned has been charged with an offence and a police officer of at least the rank of inspector, who has reasonable grounds for suspecting that the misuse by that person of any specified Class A drug caused or contributed to the offence and has authorised the sample to be taken.

(3) The age condition is—

    (a) if the arrest condition is met, that the person concerned has attained the age of 18;

    (b) if the charge condition is met, that he has attained the age of 14.

(4) The request condition is that a police officer has requested the person concerned to give the sample.

(4A) ...

(4B) ...

(5) Before requesting the person concerned to give a sample, an officer must—

    (a) warn him that if, when so requested, he fails without good cause to do so he may be liable to prosecution, and

    (b) in a case within subsection (1A)(b) or (2)(b) above, inform him of the giving of the authorisation and of the grounds in question.

(5A) ...

(5B) ...

(5C) Despite subsection (1)(a) above, a sample may be taken from a person under this section if—

    (c) he was arrested for an offence (the first offence),

    (d) the arrest condition is met but the charge condition is not met,

    (e) before a sample is taken by virtue of subsection (1) above he would (but for his arrest as mentioned in paragraph (d) below) be required to be released from police detention,

    (f) he continues to be in police detention by virtue of his having been arrested for an offence not falling within subsection (1A) above, and

    (g) the sample is taken before the end of the period of 24 hours starting with the time when his detention by virtue of his arrest for the first offence began.

(5D) A sample must not be taken from a person under this section if he is detained in a police station unless he has been brought before the custody officer.

(6) A sample may be taken under this section only by a person prescribed by regulations made by the Secretary of State by statutory instrument.

(6A) ...

(6B) ...

(7) A person who fails without good cause to give any sample which may be taken from him under this section shall be guilty of an offence.

 3 months and/or level 4 fine

C7.4.1 *Sentencing*

Police and Criminal Evidence Act 1984, s 63B

Triable only summarily:

Maximum: Level 4 fine and/or 3 months

Offence range: Band A fine–high-level community order

STEP ONE: Determining the offence category

The court should determine the offence category using the following table.

Category 1	Higher culpability **and** greater harm
Category 2	Higher culpability **and** lesser harm **or** lower culpability **and** greater harm
Category 3	Lower culpability **and** lesser harm

The court should determine the offender's culpability and the harm caused with reference **only** to the following factors. Where an offence does not fall squarely into a category, individual factors may require a degree of weighting before making an overall assessment and determining the appropriate offence category.

CULPABILITY demonstrated by one or more of the following:	
Factors indicating higher culpability	**Factors indicating lower culpability**
Deliberate refusal	All other cases

HARM demonstrated by one or more of the following:	
Factors indicating greater harm	**Factors indicating lesser harm**
Aggressive, abusive or disruptive behaviour	All other cases

STEP TWO: Starting point and category range

Having determined the category at step one, the court should use the starting point to reach a sentence within the appropriate category range in the following table. The starting point applies to all offenders irrespective of plea or previous convictions.

Offence category	Starting point	Range
Category 1	Medium-level community order	Medium-level community order–high-level community order
Category 2	Band C fine	Band B fine–low-level community order
Category 3	Band B fine	Band A fine–Band C fine

The court should then consider adjustment for any aggravating or mitigating factors. The following is a **non-exhaustive** list of additional factual elements providing the context of the offence and factors relating to the offender. Identify whether any combination of these, or other relevant factors, should result in an upward or downward adjustment from the sentence arrived at so far.

Factors increasing seriousness	
Statutory aggravating factors:	*Other aggravating factors:*
Previous convictions, having regard to (a) the **nature** of the offence to which the conviction relates and its **relevance** to the current offence; and (b) the **time** that has elapsed since the conviction Offence committed while on bail Offence motivated by, or demonstrating hostility based on any of the following characteristics or presumed characteristics of the victim: religion, race, disability, sexual orientation, or transgender identity	Failure to comply with current court orders Offence committed on licence or post-sentence supervision Offender's actions result in a waste of resources

Factors reducing seriousness or reflecting personal mitigation
No previous convictions **or** no relevant/recent convictions
Remorse
Good character and/or exemplary conduct
Serious medical condition requiring urgent, intensive, or long-term treatment
Age and/or lack of maturity where it affects the responsibility of the offender
Mental disorder or learning disability
Sole or primary carer for dependent relatives
Determination and/or demonstration of steps having been taken to address addiction or offending behaviour

C7.5 Drugs—Fraudulent evasion of a prohibition by bringing into or taking out of the United Kingdom a controlled drug

Misuse of Drugs Act 1971, s 3

3 Restriction of importation and exportation of controlled drugs

(1) Subject to subsection (2) below—
  a. the importation of a controlled drug; and
  b. the exportation of a controlled drug, are hereby prohibited.
(2) Subsection (1) above does not apply—
  a. to the importation or exportation of a controlled drug which is for the time being excepted from paragraph (a) or, as the case may be, paragraph (b) of subsection (1) above by regulations under section 7 of this Act or by provision made in a temporary class drug order by virtue of section 7A; or
  b. to the importation or exportation of a controlled drug under and in accordance with the terms of a licence issued by the Secretary of State and in compliance with any conditions attached thereto.

Customs and Excise Management Act 1979, s 170(2)

170 Penalty for fraudulent evasion of duty, etc

(2) Without prejudice to any other provision of the Customs and Excise Acts 1979, if any person is, in relation to any goods, in any way knowingly concerned in any fraudulent evasion or attempt at evasion—
  (a) of any duty chargeable on the goods;
  (b) of any prohibition or restriction for the time being in force with respect to the goods under or by virtue of any enactment; or
  (c) of any provision of the Customs and Excise Acts 1979 applicable to the goods, he shall be guilty of an offence under this section and may be detained.

6 months' imprisonment and/or £20,000 or three times the value of the drugs if greater/life (class A); 6 months' imprisonment and/or £20,000 or three times the value of the drugs if greater/14 years' imprisonment (classes B); 3 months imprisonment and/or three times the value of the drugs or £500 if greater/5 years (Class C)

GC (if Class A or B)

C7.5.1 *Sentencing*

STEP ONE: Determining the offence category

Culpability demonstrated by offender's role. One or more of these characteristics may demonstrate the offender's role. The list is not exhaustive.	Category of harm. Indicative output or potential output (upon which the starting point is based):
LEADING role: • directing or organizing production on a commercial scale; • substantial links to, and influence on, others in a chain; • expectation of substantial financial gain; • uses business as cover; • abuses a position of trust or responsibility.	**Category 1** • heroin, cocaine—5kg; • ecstasy—10,000 tablets; • LSD—250,000 tablets; • amphetamine—20kg; • cannabis—200kg; • ketamine—5kg.
SIGNIFICANT role: • operational or management function within a chain; • involves others in the operation whether by pressure, influence, intimidation, or reward; • motivated by financial or other advantage, whether or not operating alone; • some awareness and understanding of scale of operation. **LESSER role:** • performs a limited function under direction; • engaged by pressure, coercion, intimidation; • involvement through naivety/exploitation; • no influence on those above in a chain; • very little, if any, awareness or understanding of the scale of operation; • if own operation, solely for own use (considering reasonableness of account in all the circumstances).	**Category 2** • heroin, cocaine—1kg; • ecstasy—2,000 tablets; • LSD—25,000 squares; • amphetamine—4kg; • cannabis—40kg; • ketamine—1kg. Category 3 • heroin, cocaine—150g; • ecstasy—300 tablets; • LSD—2,500 squares; • amphetamine—750g; • cannabis—6kg; • ketamine—150g. Category 4 • heroin, cocaine—5g; • ecstasy—20 tablets; • LSD—170 squares; • amphetamine—20g; • cannabis—100g; • ketamine—5g.

STEP TWO: Starting point and category range

CLASS A	Leading role	Significant role	Lesser role
Category 1	**Starting point** 14 years' custody **Category range** 12–16 years' custody	**Starting point** 10 years' custody **Category range** 9–12 years' custody	**Starting point** 8 years' custody **Category range** 6–9 years' custody
Category 2	**Starting point** 11 years' custody **Category range** 9–13 years' custody	**Starting point** 8 years' custody **Category range** 6 years 6 months–10 years' custody	**Starting point** 6 years' custody **Category range** 5–7 years' custody
Category 3	**Starting point** 8 years 6 months' custody **Category range** 6 years 6 months'–10 years' custody	**Starting point** 6 years' custody **Category range** 5–7 years' custody	**Starting point** 4 years 6 months' **custody** Category range 3 years 6 months–5 years' custody

Category 4

Where the quantity falls below the indicative amount set out for category 4 on the previous page, first identify the role for the importation offence, then refer to the starting point and ranges for possession or supply offences, depending on intent.

Where the quantity is significantly larger than the indicative amounts for category 4 but below category 3 amounts, refer to the category 3 ranges above.

CLASS B	Leading role	Significant role	Lesser role
Category 1	**Starting point** 8 years' custody **Category range** 7–10 years' custody	**Starting point** 5 years 6 months' custody **Category range** 5–7 years' custody	**Starting point** 4 years' custody **Category range** 2 years 6 months–5 years' custody
Category 2	**Starting point** 6 years' custody **Category range** 4 years 6 months–8 years' custody	**Starting point** 4 years' custody **Category range** 2 years 6 months–5 years' custody	**Starting point** 2 years' custody **Category range** 18 months–3 years' custody
Category 3	**Starting point** 4 years' custody **Category range** 2 years 6 months–5 years' custody	**Starting point** 2 years' custody **Category range** 18 months–3 years' custody	1 year's custody **Range** 12 weeks–18 months' custody
	*	*	*

*Category 4

Where the quantity falls below the indicative amount set out for category 4 on the previous page, first identify the role for the importation offence, then refer to the starting point and ranges for possession or supply offences, depending on intent.

Where the quantity is significantly larger than the indicative amounts for category 4 but below category 3 amounts, refer to the category 3 ranges above.

CLASS C	Leading role	Significant role	Lesser role
Category 1	**Starting point** 5 years' custody **Category range** 4–8 years' custody	**Starting point** 3 years' custody **Category range** 2–5 years' custody	**Starting point** 18 months' custody **Category range** 1–3 years' custody
Category 2	**Starting point** 3 years 6 months' custody **Category range** 2–5 years' custody	**Starting point** 18 months' custody **Category range** 1–3 years' custody	**Starting point** 26 weeks' custody **Range** 12 weeks–18 months' custody
Category 3	**Starting point** 18 months' custody **Category range** 1–3 years' custody	**Starting point** 26 weeks' custody **Range** 12 weeks–18 months' custody	**Starting point** High-level community order **Range** Medium-level community order–12 weeks
Category 4	*	*	*

* Where the quantity falls below the indicative amount set out in the guideline for category 4, first identify the role for the importation offence, then refer to the starting point and ranges for possession or supply offences, depending on intent. Where the quantity is significantly larger than the indicative amounts for category 4 but below category 3 amounts, refer to the category 3 ranges.

Factors increasing seriousness	Factors reducing seriousness or reflecting personal mitigation
Statutory aggravating factors: Previous convictions, having regardto (a) nature of the offence to which conviction relates and relevance to current offence; and (b) time elapsed since offender used or permitted a person under 18 to deliver a controlled drug to a third person Offence committed on bail **Other aggravating factors include:** Sophisticated nature of concealment and/or attempts to avoid detection Attempts to conceal or dispose of evidence, where not charged separately Exposure of others to more than usual danger, for example drugs cut with harmful substances	Lack of sophistication as to nature of concealment. Involvement due to pressure, intimidation, or coercion falling short of duress, except where already taken into account at step 1 Mistaken belief of the offender regarding the type of drug, taking into account the reasonableness of such belief in all the circumstances Isolated incident Low purity No previous convictions or no relevant or recent convictions Offender's vulnerability was exploited. Remorse Good character and/or exemplary conduct

Factors increasing seriousness	Factors reducing seriousness or reflecting personal mitigation
Presence of weapon, where not charged separately High purity Failure to comply with current court orders. Offence committed on licence	Determination and/or demonstration of steps having been taken to address addiction or offending behaviour Serious medical conditions requiring urgent, intensive, or long-term treatment Age and/or lack of maturity where it affects the responsibility of the offender Mental disorder or learning disability. Sole or primary carer for dependent relatives.

C7.5.1.1 Additional steps

Consider any factors which indicate a reduction, such as assistance to the prosecution; reduction for guilty plea; dangerousness; totality principle; compensation and ancillary orders; reasons; consideration for remand time.

C7.6 Drugs—Supplying or offering to supply a controlled drug; possession of a controlled drug with intent to supply it to another; being concerned in supply

Misuse of Drugs Act 1971, ss 4(3) and 5(3)

4 Restriction of production and supply of controlled drugs

(3) Subject to section 28 of this Act, it is an offence for a person—

  (a) to supply or offer to supply a controlled drug to another in contravention of subsection (1) above; or

  (b) to be concerned in the supplying of such a drug to another in contravention of that subsection; or

  (c) to be concerned in the making to another in contravention of that subsection of an offer to supply such a drug.

  ...

5 Restriction of possession of controlled drugs

(4) Subject to section 28 of this Act, it is an offence for a person to have a controlled drug in his possession, whether lawfully or not, with intent to supply it to another in contravention of section 4(1) of this Act.

EW

GC (if class A or B)

 See p 262 (see table at **C7.3**)

C7.6.1 *Sentencing*

STEP ONE: Determining the offence category

Culpability demonstrated by offender's role. One or more of these characteristics may demonstrate the offender's role. The list is not exhaustive	Category of harm. Indicative output or potential output (upon which the starting point is based)
LEADING role: • directing or organizing production on a commercial scale; • substantial links to, and influence on, others in a chain; • expectation of substantial financial gain; • uses business as cover; • abuses a position of trust or responsibility. **SIGNIFICANT role:** • operational or management function within a chain; • involves others in the operation whether by pressure, influence, intimidation, or reward; • motivated by financial or other advantage, whether or not operating alone; • some awareness and understanding of scale of operation. • supply, other than by a person in a position of responsibility, to a prisoner for gain without coercion. **LESSER role:** • performs a limited function under direction; • engaged by pressure, coercion, intimidation; • involvement through naivety/exploitation; • no influence on those above in a chain; • very little, if any, awareness or understanding of the scale of operation; • if own operation, solely for own use (considering reasonableness of amount in all the circumstances).	**Category 1** • heroin, cocaine—5kg; • ecstasy—10,000 tablets; • LSD—250,000 tablets; • amphetamine—20kg; • cannabis—200kg; • ketamine—5kg. **Category 2** • heroin, cocaine—1kg; • ecstasy—2,000 tablets; • LSD—25,000 squares; • amphetamine—4kg; • cannabis—40kg; • ketamine—1kg. **Category 3** Where the offence is selling directly to users* ('street dealing'), the starting point is not based on quantity, OR Where the offence is suppy of drugs in prison by a prison employee, the starting point is not based on quantity. • heroin, cocaine—150g; • ecstasy—300 tablets; • LSD—2,500 squares; • amphetamine—750g; • cannabis—6kg; • ketamine—150g. **Category 4** • heroin, cocaine—5g; • ecstasy—20 tablets; • LSD—170 squares; • amphetamine—20g; • cannabis—100g; • ketamine—5g. OR Where the offence is selling directly to users* ('street dealing') the starting point is not based on quantity—go to category 3.

* Including test purchase officers.

STEP TWO: Starting point and category range

CLASS A	Leading role	Significant role	Lesser role
Category 1	14 years' custody Range: 12–16 years' custody	10 years' custody Range: 9–12 years' custody	7 years' custody Range: 6–9 years' custody
Category 2	11 years' custody Range: 9–13 years' custody	8 years' custody Range 6 years 6 months–10 years' custody	5 years' custody Range: 3 years 6 months–7 years' custody
Category 3	8 years 6 months' custody Range: 6 years 6 months–10 years' custody	4 years 6 months' custody Range: 3 years 6 months–7 years' custody	3 years' custody Range: 2–4 years 6 months' custody
Category 4	5 years 6 months' custody Range: 4 years 6 months–7 years 6 months' custody	3 years 6 months' custody Range: 2–5 years' custody	18 months' custody Range: High-level community order–3 years' custody

CLASS B	Leading role	Significant role	Lesser role
Category 1	8 years' custody Range: 7–10 years' custody	5 years 6 months' custody Range: 5–7 years' custody	3 years' custody Range: 2 years 6 months–5 years' custody
Category 2	6 years' custody Range: 4 years 6 months–8 years' custody	4 years' custody Range: 2 years 6 months–5 years' custody	1 year's custody Range: 26 weeks–3 years' custody
Category 3	4 years' custody Range: 2 years 6 months–5 years' custody	1 year's custody Range: 26 weeks–3 years' custody	High-level community order Range: Low-level community order–26 weeks' custody
Category 4	18 months' custody Range: 26 weeks–3 years' custody	High-level community order Range: Medium-level community order–26 weeks' custody	Low-level community order Range: Band B fine–medium-level community order

CLASS C	Leading role	Significant role	Lesser role
Category 1	5 years' custody Range: 4–8 years' custody	3 years' custody Range: 2–5 years' custody	18 months' custody Range: 1–3 years' custody
Category 2	3 years 6 months' custody Range: 2–5 years' custody	18 months' custody Range: 1–3 years' custody	26 weeks' custody Range: 12 weeks–18 months' custody
Category 3	18 months' custody Range: 1–3 years' custody	26 weeks' custody Range: 12 weeks' to 18 months' custody	High-level community order Range: Low-level community order–12 weeks' custody

CLASS C	Leading role	Significant role	Lesser role
Category 4	26 weeks' custody Range: High-level community order– 18 months' custody	High-level community order Range: Low-level community order–12 weeks' custody	Low-level community order Range: Band A fine–medium-level community order

Factors increasing seriousness	Factors reducing seriousness or reflecting personal mitigation
Statutory aggravating factors:	Involvement due to pressure,
Previous convictions, having regard to	intimidation, or coercion falling short
(a) nature of the offence to which conviction relates and relevance to current offence; and	of duress, except where already taken into account at step 1
(b) time elapsed since conviction	Supply only of drug to which offender addicted
Offender used or permitted a person under 18	Mistaken belief of the offender regarding
to deliver a controlled drug to a third person	the type of drug, taking into account the
Offender 18 or over supplies or offers to supply a drug on, or in the vicinity of, school premises either when school in use as such or at a time between one hour before and one hour after they are to be used	reasonableness of such belief in all the circumstances
	Isolated incident
Offence committed on bail	Low purity
Other aggravating factors include:	No previous convictions or no relevant or recent convictions
Targeting of any premises intended to locate vulnerable individuals or supply to such	Offender's vulnerability was exploited
individuals and/or supply to those under 18	Remorse
Exposure of others to more than usual danger, for example drugs cut with harmful substances	Good character and/or exemplary conduct Determination and/or demonstration
Attempts to conceal or dispose of evidence, where not charged separately	of steps having been taken to address addiction or offending behaviour
Presence of others, especially children and/or non-users	Serious medical conditions requiring urgent, intensive, or long-term treatment
Presence of weapon, where not charged separately	Age and/or lack of maturity where it affects
Charged as importation of a very small amount.	the responsibility of the offender
High purity	Mental disorder or learning disability
Failure to comply with current court orders	Sole or primary carer for dependent relatives
Offence committed on licence	
Established evidence of community impact	

C7.6.2 Key points

- Purchasing drugs on behalf of a third party, and passing those drugs to that party, even for no profit, amounts to supply.
- So-called social supply should be charged as simple possession. In *R v Denslow* [1998] Crim LR 566 the court observed:

We wonder why it was thought necessary to charge supply in the circumstances of this case. How could it possibly serve the interests of the public that there should be either a trial or if not a trial as conventionally understood a hearing to determine this matter of law? It was inevitable that the appellant would be dealt with at worst as though he were in possession of the drugs and, as turned out in this case, as though he were without any criminal responsibility for that particular part of the transaction. We are told that a plea had been offered to a charge of possession. It ought to have been accepted. We hope that those words will be borne in mind by prosecuting authorities in the future.

- A person who places drugs in the hands of a third party merely for safe keeping does not supply drugs (*R v Maginnis* [1987] AC 303).
- An offer to supply can be made by words or conduct, and once made cannot be withdrawn.
- To be concerned in the supply of drugs under s 4(3)(b) Misuse of Drugs Act 1971 does not require proof of an actual supply but rather involvement in the process of supply. It is not limited to actual or past supply (*R v Martin (Dwain Ashley)* [2014] EWCA Crim 1940 and *R v Abi-Khalil* [2017] EWCA Crim 17).

C7.7 Drugs—Production of a controlled drug and cultivation of cannabis

C7.7.1 *Sentencing*

Misuse of Drugs Act 1971, ss 4(2)(a), (b) and 6

4 Restriction of production and supply of controlled drugs

(2) Subject to section 28 of this Act, it is an offence for a person—
  (a) to produce a controlled drug in contravention of subsection (1) above; or
  (b) to be concerned in the production of such a drug in contravention of that subsection by another.

6 Restriction of cultivation of cannabis plant

(1) Subject to any regulations under section 7 of this Act for the time being in force, it shall not be lawful for a person to cultivate any plant of the genus Cannabis.
(2) Subject to section 28 of this Act, it is an offence to cultivate any such plant in contravention of subsection (1) above.

EW

GC

 See p 262

STEP ONE: Determining the offence category

Culpability demonstrated by offender's role. One or more of these characteristics may demonstrate the offender's role. The list is not exhaustive.	Category of harm. Indicative output or potential output (upon which the starting point is based):
LEADING role: • directing or organizing production on a commercial scale; • substantial links to, and influence on, others in a chain; • expectation of substantial financial gain; • uses business as cover; • abuses a position of trust or responsibility.	**Category 1** • heroin, cocaine—5kg; • ecstasy—10,000 tablets; • LSD—250,000 tablets; • amphetamine—20kg; • cannabis—operation capable of producing industrial quantities for commercial use; • ketamine—5kg.
SIGNIFICANT role: • operational or management function within a chain; • involves others in the operation whether by pressure, influence, intimidation, or reward; • motivated by financial or other advantage, whether or not operating alone; • some awareness and understanding of scale of operation. **LESSER role:** • performs a limited function under direction; • engaged by pressure, coercion, intimidation; • involvement through naivety/exploitation; • no influence on those above in a chain; • very little, if any, awareness or understanding of the scale of operation; • if own operation, solely for own use (considering reasonableness of account in all the circumstances).	**Category 2** • heroin, cocaine—1kg; • ecstasy—2,000 tablets; • LSD—25,000 squares; • amphetamine—4kg; • cannabis—operation capable of producing significant quantities for commercial use; • ketamine—1kg. **Category 3** • heroin, cocaine—150g; • ecstasy—300 tablets; • LSD—2,500 squares; • amphetamine—750g; • cannabis—28 plants;* • ketamine—150g. **Category 4** • heroin, cocaine—5g; • ecstasy—20 tablets; • LSD—170 squares; • amphetamine—20g; • cannabis—9 plants (domestic operation);* • ketamine—5g. *with an assumed yield of 40g per plant.

STEP TWO: Starting point and category range

CLASS A	Leading role	Significant role	Lesser role
Category 1	14 years' custody Range: 12–16 years' custody	10 years' custody Range: 9–12 years' custody	7 years' custody Range: 6–9 years' custody
Category 2	11 years' custody Range: 9–13 years' custody	8 years' custody Range: 6 years 6 months–10 years' custody	5 years' custody Range: 3 years 6 months–7 years' custody
Category 3	8 years 6 months' custody Range: 6 years 6 months–10 years' custody	5 years' custody Range: 3 years 6 months–7 years' custody	3 years 6 months' custody Range: 2–5 years' custody

CLASS A	Leading role	Significant role	Lesser role
Category 4	5 years 6 months' custody Range: 4 years 6 months– 7 years 6 months' custody	3 years 6 months' custody Range: 2–5 years' custody	Starting point 18 months' custody Range: High-level community order– 3 years' custody

CLASS B	Leading role	Significant role	Lesser role
Category 1	8 years' custody Range: 7–10 years' custody	5 years 6 months' custody Range: 5–7 years' custody	3 years' custody Range: 2 years 6 months–5 years' custody
Category 2	6 years' custody Range: 4 years 6 months– 8 years' custody	4 years' custody Range: 2 years 6 months– 5 years' custody	1 year's custody Range: 26 weeks– 3 years' custody
Category 3	4 years' custody Range: 2 years 6 months– 5 years' custody	1 year's custody Range: 26 weeks–3 years' custody	High-level community order Range: Low- level community order–26 weeks' custody
Category 4	1 year's custody Range: High-level community order–3 years' custody	High-level community order Range: Medium-level community order–26 weeks' custody	Band C fine Range: Discharge– medium-level community penalty

CLASS C	Leading role	Significant role	Lesser role
Category 1	5 years' custody Range: 4–8 years' custody	3 years' custody Range: 2–5 years' custody	18 months' custody Range: 1–3 years' custody
Category 2	3 years 6 months' custody Range: 2–5 years' custody	18 months' custody Range: 1–3 years' custody	26 weeks' custody Range: High-level community order– 18 months' custody
Category 3	18 months' custody Range: 1–3 years' custody	26 weeks' custody Range: High-level community order to 18 months' custody	High-level community order Range: Low- level community order–12 weeks' custody
Category 4	26 weeks' custody Range: High-level community order–18 months' custody	High-level community order Range: Low-level community order–12 weeks' custody	Band C fine Range: Discharge– medium-level community penalty

Factors increasing seriousness	Factors reducing seriousness or reflecting personal mitigation
Statutory aggravating factors: Previous convictions, having regard to (a) nature of the offence to which conviction relates and relevance to current offence; and (b) time elapsed since conviction Offence committed on bail **Other aggravating factors include:** Nature of any likely supply Level of any profit element Use of premises accompanied by unlawful access to electricity/other utility supply of others Ongoing/large-scale operation as evidenced by presence and nature of specialist equipment Exposure of others to more than usual danger, for example drugs cut with harmful substances	Involvement due to pressure, intimidation, or coercion falling short of duress, except where already taken into account at step 1 Isolated incident Low purity No previous convictions or no relevant or recent convictions Offender's vulnerability was exploited Remorse Good character and/or exemplary conduct Determination and/or demonstration of steps having been taken to address addiction or offending behaviour
Attempts to conceal or dispose of evidence, where not charged separately Presence of others, especially children and/or non-users Presence of weapon, where not charged separately High purity or high potential yield Failure to comply with current court orders Offence committed on licence Established evidence of community impact	Serious medical conditions requiring urgent, intensive, or long-term treatment Age and/or lack of maturity where it affects the responsibility of the offender Mental disorder or learning disability Sole or primary carer for dependent relatives

C7.7.2 Key points

- In sentencing cases involving the cultivation of cannabis it is the capacity to produce that is central rather than the quantity (*R v Wiseman* [2013] EWCA Crim 2499).
- It is the plant that must be cultivated, not the cannabis produced from the plant.
- The accused does not need to know that the plant was in fact cannabis (*R v Champ* (1981) 73 Cr App R 267).
- The defence of necessity (commonly pleaded by sufferers of certain illnesses) is not a defence available in law for this charge (*R v Quayle and others* [2006] 1 All ER 988).

C7.8 Drugs—Permitting premises to be used

Misuse of Drugs Act 1971, s 8

8 Occupiers etc of premises to be punishable for permitting certain activities to take place there

A person commits an offence if, being the occupier or concerned in the management of any premises, he knowingly permits or suffers any of the following activities to take place on those premises, that is to say—

C7 Drugs

(a) producing or attempting to produce a controlled drug in contravention of section 4(1) of this Act;
(b) supplying or attempting to supply a controlled drug to another in contravention of section 4(1) of this Act, or offering to supply a controlled drug to another in contravention of section 4(1);
(c) preparing opium for smoking;
(d) smoking cannabis, cannabis resin or prepared opium.

 See p 262

C7.8.1 *Sentencing*

STEP ONE: Determining the offence category

Category 1	Higher culpability and greater harm
Category 2	Lower culpability and greater harm; or higher culpability and lesser harm
Category 3	Lower culpability and lesser harm

Factors indicating culpability (non-exhaustive)	Factors indicating harm (non-exhaustive)
Higher culpability: Permits premises to be used primarily for drug activity, for example crack house Permits use in expectation of substantial financial gain Uses legitimate business premises to aid and/or conceal illegal activity, for example public house or club Lower culpability: Permits use for limited or no financial gain No active role in any supply taking place Involvement through naivety	**Greater harm:** Regular drug-related activity Higher quantity of drugs, for example: heroin, cocaine—more than 5g; cannabis—more than 50g. Lesser harm: Infrequent drug-related activity Lower quantity of drugs, for example: heroin, cocaine—up to 5g; cannabis—up to 50g.

STEP TWO: Starting point and category range

Class A:

Offence category	Starting point	Category range
Category 1	2 years 6 months custody	18 months–4 years
Category 2	36 weeks' custody	High-level community order–18 months' custody
Category 3	Medium-level community order	Low-level community order to high-level community order

Class B:

Offence category	Starting point	Category range
Category 1	1 year's custody	26 weeks' to 18 months' custody
Category 2	High-level community order	Low-level community order to 26 weeks' custody
Category 3	Band C fine	Band A fine to low-level community order

Class C:

Offence category	Starting point	Category range
Category 1	12 weeks' custody	High-level community order–26 weeks' custody (max 12 weeks when tried summarily)
Category 2	Low-level community order	Band C fine–high-level community order
Category 3	Band A fine	Discharge to Band C fine

Factors increasing seriousness	Factors reducing seriousness or reflecting personal mitigation
Statutory aggravating factors: Previous convictions, having regard to (a) nature of the offence to which conviction relates and relevance to current offence; and (b) time elapsed since conviction Offence committed on bail Other aggravating factors include: Length of time over which premises used for drug activity Volume of drug activity permitted Premises adapted to facilitate drug activity Location of premises, for example proximity to school Attempts to conceal or dispose of evidence, where not charged separately Presence of others, especially children and/or non-users High purity Presence of weapons, where not charged separately Failure to comply with current court orders Offence committed on licence Established evidence of community impact	Involvement due to pressure, intimidation, or coercion falling short of duress Isolated incident Low purity No previous convictions or no relevant or recent convictions Offender's vulnerability was exploited Remorse Good character and/or exemplary conduct Determination and/or demonstration of steps having been taken to address addiction or offending behaviour Serious medical conditions requiring urgent, intensive or long-term treatment Age and/or lack of maturity where it affects the responsibility of the offender Mental disorder or learning disability Sole or primary carer for dependent relatives

C7.8.2 Key points

Where the allegation is permitting premises to be used for the supply of drugs, in order to establish the offence the Crown must prove not only that the defendant knowingly permitted the supply of the drugs, but also that a supply of the drugs had actually taken place on the premises (*R v McGee* [2012]

EWCA Crim 613 (Class A); *R v Auguiste* [2003] EWCA Crim 3329 (Class B). The prohibited activity may include offering to supply drugs, which on the facts might be inferred, and supply included the whole process of supply (*R v McNaught* [2018] EWCA Crim 1588).

C7.9 Drugs—Possession of a controlled drug

Misuse of Drugs Act 1971, s 5(2) and (4)

5 Restriction of possession of controlled drugs

(2) Subject to section 28 of this Act [see C6.1] and to subsection (4) below, it is an offence for a person to have a controlled drug in his possession in contravention of subsection (1) above.

...

(4) In any proceedings for an offence under subsection (2) above in which it is proved that the accused had a controlled drug in his possession, it shall be a defence for him to prove—

    (a) that, knowing or suspecting it to be a controlled drug, he took possession of it for the purpose of preventing another from committing or continuing to commit an offence in connection with that drug and that as soon as possible after taking possession of it he took all such steps as were reasonably open to him to destroy the drug or to deliver it into the custody of a person lawfully entitled to take custody of it; or

    (b) that, knowing or suspecting it to be a controlled drug, he took possession of it for the purpose of delivering it into the custody of a person lawfully entitled to take custody of it and that as soon as possible after taking possession of it he took all such steps as were reasonably open to him to deliver it into the custody of such a person.

 See p 262. See table at **C7.3**

C7.9.1 *Sentencing*

STEP ONE: Determine the offence category

Category 1	Class A drug
Category 2	Class B drug
Category 3	Class C drug

STEP TWO: Starting point and range

Offence category	Starting point	Category range
Category 1 (Class A)	Band C fine	Band A fine–51 weeks' custody
Category 2 (Class B)	Band B fine	Discharge–26 weeks' custody
Category 3 (Class C)	Band A fine	Discharge–medium-level community order

Factors increasing seriousness	Factors reducing seriousness or reflecting personal mitigation
Statutory aggravating factors: Previous convictions, having regard to	No previous convictions or no relevant or recent convictions
(a) nature of the offence to which conviction relates and relevance to current offence; and	Remorse
(b) time elapsed since conviction	Good character and/or exemplary conduct
Offence committed on bail	Offender is using cannabis to help with a diagnosed medical condition
Other aggravating factors include:	Determination and/or demonstration of steps having been taken to address addiction or offending behaviour
Possession of drug in prison	
Presence of others, especially children and/or non-users	Serious medical conditions requiring urgent, intensive, or long-term treatment
Possession of drug in school or licensed premises	Isolated incident
	Age and/or lack of maturity where it affects the responsibility of the offender
Failure to comply with current court orders	
Offence committed on licence	Mental disorder or learning disability
Attempts to conceal or dispose of evidence, where not charged separately	Sole or primary carer for dependent relatives
Charged as importation of a very small amount	
Established evidence of community impact	

C7.9.2 Key points

A person must know that he is in possession of the drug; therefore a person holding drugs believing that they were something else would not be guilty (assuming the court believed the defendant). Note, however, that suspicion would be sufficient (see s 28 Misuse of Drugs Act 1971); and see later on containers.

- A person who 'forgot' that he had drugs would still be in possession of those drugs, but a person who had no knowledge at all would not (*R v Martindale* [1986] 3 All ER 25).
- A person need not be in physical possession of a drug, provided he is in control (sole or joint): see s 37(3) Misuse of Drugs Act 1971. It is not sufficient that the defendant might have knowledge of a confederate's possession of drugs; the test is whether the drugs were part of a common pool from which all could draw (*R v Searle* [1971] Crim LR 592).
- The fact that the quantity of drug was so minuscule as to be incapable of being used does not amount to a defence (*R v Boyesen* [1982] AC 768); it is merely an indication that the defendant may not have had knowledge of its presence.
- If a person is in possession of a container and he knows there is something inside, he will be in possession of the contents, even if he does not know their characteristics (*R v Lambert* [2002] 2 AC 545). If, however, the defendant had no right to open the container, he may not be in possession of its contents (*Warner v Metropolitan Police Commissioner* [1969] 2 AC 256), nor if he believed the contents to be different from what in fact they were (*R v McNamara* (1988) 87 Cr App R 246) and see s 28 Misuse of Drugs Act 1971 at **C7.1**.
- Possession of drugs for religious purposes is not afforded any special protection under the European Convention (*R v Taylor* [2002] 1 Cr App R 519).

C7 Drugs

 See *Blackstone's Criminal Practice* 2019 **B19**

C7.9.3 *Obstruction under the Misuse of Drugs Act 1971*

Section 23(4) Misuse of Drugs Act 1971 provides:

Misuse of Drugs Act 1971, s 23(4)

23 Powers to search and obtain evidence

(4) A person commits an offence if he—
  (a) intentionally obstructs a person in the exercise of his powers under this section; or
  (b) conceals from a person acting in the exercise of his powers under subsection (1) above any such books, documents, stocks or drugs as are mentioned in that subsection; or
  (c) without reasonable excuse (proof of which shall lie on him) fails to produce any such books or documents as are so mentioned where their production is demanded by a person in the exercise of his power under that subsection.

EW

 6 months' imprisonment and/or fine/2 years' imprisonment

For there to be obstruction, the officer must be acting in the execution of his office. The officer must comply strictly with the requirements of the Police and Criminal Evidence Act 1984 in relation to a stop and search (*R v Bristol* [2007] EWHC 3214 (Admin); *B v DPP* [2008] EWHC 1655 (Admin); *R (Michaels) v Highbury Corner Magistrates' Court* [2009] EWHC 2928 (Admin)).

C7.10 **Drugs—Psychoactive substances**

Psychoactive Substances Act 2016, ss 1, 4–9,

Overview

(1) This Act contains provision about psychoactive substances.
(2) Section 2 defines what is meant by a 'psychoactive substance'.
(3) Sections 4 to 10 contain provision about offences relating to psychoactive substances.
(4) Section 11 provides for exceptions to those offences.
(5) Sections 12 to 35 contain powers for dealing with prohibited activities in respect of psychoactive substances, in particular powers to give prohibition notices and make prohibition orders.
(6) Sections 36 to 54 contain enforcement powers.

...

Offences

4 *Producing a psychoactive substance*

(1) A person commits an offence if—
  (a) the person intentionally produces a psychoactive substance,
  (b) the person knows or suspects that the substance is a psychoactive substance, and
  (c) the person—
    (i) intends to consume the psychoactive substance for its psychoactive effects, or
    (ii) knows, or is reckless as to whether, the psychoactive substance is likely to be consumed by some other person for its psychoactive effects.
(2) This section is subject to section 11 (exceptions to offences).

5 Supplying, or offering to supply, a psychoactive substance

(1) A person commits an offence if—
  (a) the person intentionally supplies a substance to another person,
  (b) the substance is a psychoactive substance,
  (c) the person knows or suspects, or ought to know or suspect, that the substance is a psychoactive substance, and
  (d) the person knows, or is reckless as to whether, the psychoactive substance is likely to be consumed by the person to whom it is supplied, or by some other person, for its psychoactive effects.
(2) A person ('P') commits an offence if—
  (a) P offers to supply a psychoactive substance to another person ('R'), and
  (b) P knows or is reckless as to whether R, or some other person, would, if P supplied a substance to R in accordance with the offer, be likely to consume the substance for its psychoactive effects.
(3) For the purposes of subsection (2)(b), the reference to a substance's psychoactive effects includes a reference to the psychoactive effects which the substance would have if it were the substance which P had offered to supply to R.
(4) This section is subject to section 11 (exceptions to offences).

6 Aggravation of offence under section 5

(1) This section applies if—
  (a) a court is considering the seriousness of an offence under section 5, and
  (b) at the time the offence was committed the offender was aged 18 or over.
(2) If condition A, B or C is met the court—
  (a) must treat the fact that the condition is met as an aggravating factor (that is to say, a factor that increases the seriousness of the offence), and
  (b) must state in open court that the offence is so aggravated.
(3) Condition A is that the offence was committed on or in the vicinity of school premises at a relevant time.
(4) For the purposes of subsection (3) a 'relevant time' is—
  (a) any time when the school premises are in use by persons under the age of 18;
  (b) one hour before the start and one hour after the end of any such time.
(5) In this section—
  'school premises' means land used for the purposes of a school, other than any land occupied solely as a dwelling by a person employed at the school;
  'school' has the same meaning—
  (a) in England and Wales, as in section 4 of the Education Act 1996;...
(6) Condition B is that in connection with the commission of the offence the offender used a courier who, at the time the offence was committed, was under the age of 18.

(7) For the purposes of subsection (6) a person ('P') uses a courier in connection with an offence under section 5 if P causes or permits another person (the courier)—

    (a) to deliver a substance to a third person, or

    (b) to deliver a drug-related consideration to P or a third person.

(8) A drug-related consideration is a consideration of any description which—

    (a) is obtained in connection with the supply of a psychoactive substance, or

    (b) is intended to be used in connection with obtaining a psychoactive substance.

(9) Condition C is that the offence was committed in a custodial institution.

(10) In this section—

    'custodial institution' means any of the following—

    (a) a prison;

    (b) a young offender institution, secure training centre, secure college, young offenders institution, young offenders centre, juvenile justice centre or remand centre;

    (c) a removal centre, a short-term holding facility or pre-departure accommodation;

    (d) service custody premises;

    'removal centre', 'short-term holding facility' and 'pre-departure accommodation' have the meaning given by section 147 of the Immigration and Asylum Act 1999; 'service custody premises' has the meaning given by section 300(7) of the Armed Forces Act 2006.

7 Possession of psychoactive substance with intent to supply

(1) A person commits an offence if—

    (a) the person is in possession of a psychoactive substance,

    (b) the person knows or suspects that the substance is a psychoactive substance, and

    (c) the person intends to supply the psychoactive substance to another person for its consumption, whether by any person to whom it is supplied or by some other person, for its psychoactive effects.

(2) This section is subject to section 11 (exceptions to offences).

8 Importing or exporting a psychoactive substance

(1) A person commits an offence if—

    (a) the person intentionally imports a substance,

    (b) the substance is a psychoactive substance,

    (c) the person knows or suspects, or ought to know or suspect, that the substance is a psychoactive substance, and

    (d) the person—

        (i) intends to consume the psychoactive substance for its psychoactive effects, or

        (ii) knows, or is reckless as to whether, the psychoactive substance is likely to be consumed by some other person for its psychoactive effects.

(2) A person commits an offence if—

    (a) the person intentionally exports a substance,

    (b) the substance is a psychoactive substance,

    (c) the person knows or suspects, or ought to know or suspect, that the substance is a psychoactive substance, and

    (d) the person—

        (i) intends to consume the psychoactive substance for its psychoactive effects, or

        (ii) knows, or is reckless as to whether, the psychoactive substance is likely to be consumed by some other person for its psychoactive effects.

(3) In a case where a person imports or exports a controlled drug suspecting it to be a psychoactive substance, the person is to be treated for the purposes of this section as if the person had imported or exported a psychoactive substance suspecting it to be such a substance.

.In this subsection 'controlled drug' has the same meaning as in the Misuse of Drugs Act 1971.

(4) Section 5 of the Customs and Excise Management Act 1979 (time of importation, exportation, etc) applies for the purposes of this section as it applies for the purposes of that Act.

(5) This section is subject to section 11 (exceptions to offences).

9 Possession of a psychoactive substance in a custodial institution

(1) A person commits an offence if—
   (a) the person is in possession of a psychoactive substance in a custodial institution,
   (b) the person knows or suspects that the substance is a psychoactive substance, and
   (c) the person intends to consume the psychoactive substance for its psychoactive effects.

(2) In this section 'custodial institution' has the same meaning as in section 6.

(3) This section is subject to section 11 (exceptions to offences)....

EW ss 4–8

6 months and/or fine/7 years' imprisonment

EW s 9

6 months and/or fine/2 years' imprisonment

C7.10.1 *Sentencing— Council Guidance on sentencing drug offences involving newer and less common drugs*

By virtue of s 125 (1) (b) Coroners and Justice Act 2009, sentencers may also refer to [The Drug Offences] Guideline when sentencing other relevant offences, for example, offences under the Psychoactive Substances Act 2016.

Drug offences—assessing harm

For most offences, the Drug Offences guideline uses class and quantity of the drug as the key element of assessing the harm caused by the offence, with higher quantities indicating higher harm. The Council intended, and case law has clearly shown, that where the drug in question is not listed in the guideline, the assessment of harm will be based on the equivalent level of harm caused by the relevant quantity of that drug.

Newer drugs—assessing harm

C7 Drugs

There has been an increase in the number of cases before the courts involving newer drugs, such as synthetic opioids, which may have much higher potency and potential to cause harm than more common drugs. Where these newer drugs are covered by the guideline but not specifically listed in the section on assessment of harm, the approach to assessing harm in these cases should be as with all cases of controlled drugs not explicitly mentioned in the guidelines. Sentencers should expect to be provided with expert evidence to assist in determining the potency of the particular drug and in equating the quantity in the case with the quantities set out in the guidelines in terms of the harm caused.

In *R v Waka* [2018] EWCA Crim 125, the psychoactive substances offence was closest to street dealing of cannabis. In the case of M-Kat (mephedrone), reference should be made for comparative weights to amphetamine and not cannabis (*R v Pitts* [2014] EWCA Crim 1615).

C7.10.2 Key points

Psychoactive Substances Act 2016, ss 2, 3, and 11

2 Meaning of 'psychoactive substance' etc

(1) In this Act 'psychoactive substance' means any substance which—
    (a) is capable of producing a psychoactive effect in a person who consumes it, and
    (b) is not an exempted substance (see section 3).
(2) For the purposes of this Act a substance produces a psychoactive effect in a person if, by stimulating or depressing the person's central nervous system, it affects the person's mental functioning or emotional state; and references to a substance's psychoactive effects are to be read accordingly.
(3) For the purposes of this Act a person consumes a substance if the person causes or allows the substance, or fumes given off by the substance, to enter the person's body in any way.

A psychoactive substance may produce its effect by directly or indirectly stimulating or depressing the central nervous system (*R v Rochester* [2018] EWCA Crim 1936).

3 Exempted substances

(1) In this Act 'exempted substance' means a substance listed in Schedule 1.

...

[SCHEDULE 1 Section 3—summary

EXEMPTED SUBSTANCES

Controlled drugs

Medicinal products

Alcohol

Nicotine and tobacco products

Caffeine

Food

Including drink;]

...

Nitrous oxide is not necessarily a medicinal product under the Human Medicines Regulations 2012 and so is not automatically excluded from the effect of the Psychoactive Substances Act 2016. The substance must, to be an offence, be intended to be consumed its psychoactive effects and not for one of its lawful uses. The Crown must prove the unlawful intention (*R v Chapman and others* [2017] EWCA Crim 1743).

11 Exceptions to offences

(1) It is not an offence under this Act for a person to carry on any activity listed in sub-section (3) if, in the circumstances in which it is carried on by that person, the activity is an exempted activity.

(2) In this section 'exempted activity' means an activity listed in Schedule 2.

(3) The activities referred to in subsection (1) are—

(a) producing a psychoactive substance;
(b) supplying such a substance;
(c) offering to supply such a substance;
(d) possessing such a substance with intent to supply it;
(e) importing or exporting such a substance;
(f) possessing such a substance in a custodial institution (within the meaning of section 9) ...

[Schedule 2 EXEMPTED ACTIVITIES—summary

Healthcare-related activities

Research]

C8 **Harassment Offences**

C8.1 **Harassment (without violence)**

Protection from Harassment Act 1997, ss 1 and 2(1)

1 Prohibition of harassment

(1) A person must not pursue a course of conduct—
   (a) which amounts to harassment of another, and
   (b) which he knows or ought to know amounts to harassment of the other.
(2) For the purposes of this section, the person whose course of conduct is in question ought to know that it amounts to harassment of another if a reasonable person in possession of the same information would think the course of conduct amounted to harassment of the other.
(3) Subsection (1) does not apply to a course of conduct if the person who pursued it shows—
   (a) that it was pursued for the purpose of preventing or detecting crime,
   (b) that it was pursued under any enactment or rule of law or to comply with any condition or requirement imposed by any person under any enactment, or
   (c) that in the particular circumstances the pursuit of the course of conduct was reasonable.

2 Offence of harassment

(1) A person who pursues a course of conduct in breach of section 1 is guilty of an offence.

SO (Either way if racially or religiously aggravated)

IIII 6 months' imprisonment and/or fine (2 years if racially or religiously aggravated)

C8.1.1 *Sentencing*

Where offence committed in a domestic context, also refer to the Overarching principles: Domestic abuse guideline. See **Appendix 5**.

STEP ONE: Determining the offence category

The court should determine the offence category with reference only to the factors in the following tables. In order to determine the category the court should assess culpability and harm.

The level of culpability is determined by weighing up all the factors of the case. Where there are characteristics present which fall under different levels of culpability, the court should balance these characteristics to reach a fair assessment of the offender's culpability.

Culpability demonstrated by one or more of the following:
A—High culpability:
Conduct intended to maximise fear or distress
High degree of planning and/or sophisticated offence
Persistent action over a prolonged period
Threat of serious violence
Offence motivated by, or demonstrating hostility based on any of the following characteristics or presumed characteristics of the victim: age, sex, disability, sexual orientation, or transgender identity
B—Medium culpability:
Cases that fall between categories A and C, in particular:
Conduct intended to cause some fear or distress
Some planning
Threat of some violence
Scope and duration of offence that falls between categories A and C
C—Lesser culpability:
Offender's responsibility substantially reduced by mental disorder or learning disability
Little or no planning
Offence was limited in scope and duration

HARM	
The level of harm is assessed by weighing up all the factors of the case.	
Category 1	• Very serious distress caused to the victim • Significant psychological harm caused to the victim • Victim caused to make considerable changes to lifestyle to avoid contact
Category 2	Harm that falls between categories 1 and 3, and in particular: • Some distress caused to the victim • Some psychological harm caused to the victim • Victim caused to make some changes to lifestyle to avoid contact
Category 3	• Limited distress or harm caused to the victim

STEP TWO: Starting point and category range

Having determined the category at step one, the court should use the corresponding starting point to reach a sentence within the following category range. The starting point applies to all offenders irrespective of plea or previous convictions.

Harm	Culpability		
	A	**B**	
Category 1	**Starting point** 12 weeks' custody	**Starting point** High-level community order	**Starting point** Medium-level community order
	Category range High- level community order–26 weeks' custody	**Category range** Medium-level community order–16 weeks' custody	**Category range** Low-level community order–12 weeks' custody

C8 Harassment Offences

Harm	Culpability		
	A	**B**	
Category 2	**Starting point** High-level community order	**Starting point** Medium-level community order	**Starting point** Low-level community order
	Category range Medium-level community order–16 weeks' custody	**Category range** Low-level community order–12 weeks' custody	**Category range** Band B fine–Medium-level community order
Category 3	**Starting point** Medium-level community order	**Starting point** Low-level community order	**Starting point** Band B fine
	Category range Low-level community order–12 weeks' custody	**Category range** Band B fine–Medium-level community order	**Category range** Discharge–Low-level community order

The court should then consider any adjustment for any aggravating or mitigating factors. The following is a non-exhaustive list of additional factual elements providing the context of the offence and factors relating to the offender.

Identify whether any combination of these, or other relevant factors, should result in an upwards or downwards adjustment from the starting point.

Factors increasing seriousness	Factors reducing seriousness or reflecting personal mitigation
Statutory aggravating factors: Previous convictions, having regard to (a) the nature of the offence to which the conviction relates and its relevance to the current offence; and (b) the time that has elapsed since the conviction Offence committed while on bail	No previous convictions or no relevant/recent convictions Remorse Good character and/or exemplary conduct Serious medical condition requiring urgent, intensive, or long-term treatment Age and/or lack of maturity
Other aggravating factors: Using a position of trust to facilitate the offence Victim is particularly vulnerable (not all vulnerabilities are immediately apparent) Grossly violent or offensive material sent Impact of offence on others, particularly children Exploiting contact arrangements with a child to commit the offence Offence committed against those working in the public sector or providing a service to the public Failure to comply with current court orders Offence committed on licence or post sentence Supervision Offences taken into consideration	Mental disorder or learning disability (where not taken into account at step one) Sole or primary carer for dependent relatives Determination and/or demonstration of steps having been taken to address offending behaviour

Racially Or Religiously Aggravated Harassment/Stalking Offences Only

Having determined the category of the basic offence to identify the sentence of a non-aggravated offence, the court should now consider the level of racial or religious aggravation involved and apply an appropriate uplift to the sentence in accordance with the following guidance. The following is a list of factors which the court should consider to determine the level of aggravation. Where there are characteristics present which fall under different levels of aggravation, the court should balance these to reach a fair assessment of the level of aggravation present in the offence.

Maximum sentence for the aggravated offence on indictment is 2 years' custody (maximum for the basic offence is 6 months' custody).

HIGH LEVEL OF RACIAL OR RELIGIOUS AGGRAVATION	SENTENCE UPLIFT
Racial or religious aggravation was the predominant motivation for the offence Offender was a member of, or was associated with, a group promoting hostility based on race or religion (where linked to the commission of the offence) Aggravated nature of the offence caused severe distress to the victim or the victim's family (over and above the distress already considered at step one) Aggravated nature of the offence caused serious fear and distress throughout local community or more widely	Increase the length of custodial sentence if already considered for the basic offence or consider a custodial sentence, if not already considered for the basic offence

MEDIUM LEVEL OF RACIAL OR RELIGIOUS AGGRAVATION	SENTENCE UPLIFT
• Racial or religious aggravation formed a significant proportion of the offence as a whole • Aggravated nature of the offence caused some distress to the victim or the victim's family (over and above the distress already considered at step one) • Aggravated nature of the offence caused some fear and distress throughout local community or more widely	Consider a significantly more onerous penalty of the same type or consider a more severe type of sentence than for the basic offence

LOW LEVEL OF RACIAL OR RELIGIOUS AGGRAVATION	SENTENCE UPLIFT
Aggravated element formed a minimal part of the offence as a whole • Aggravated nature of the offence caused minimal or no distress to the victim or the victim's family (over and above the distress already considered at step one)	Consider a more onerous penalty of the same type identified for the basic offence

Magistrates may find that, although the appropriate sentence for the basic offence would be within their powers, the appropriate increase for the aggravated offence would result in a sentence in excess of their powers. If so, they must commit for sentence to the Crown Court.

C8.1.2 Key points

The question of what constitutes a course of conduct has been considered in a number of cases, and the answer will always be fact-sensitive. In *R v Curtis* [2010] EWCA Crim 123, the court allowed a defence appeal where the defendant, in the context of there being a volatile relationship, had been responsible for six incidents over a period of nine months. The court held that the conduct must be unacceptable to a degree which would sustain criminal liability and also must be oppressive, and went on to say:

> Courts are well able to separate the wheat from the chaff at an early stage of the proceedings. They should be astute to do so. In most cases courts should have little difficulty in applying the 'close connection' test. Where the claim meets that requirement, and the quality of the conduct said to constitute harassment is being examined, courts will have in mind that irritations, annoyances, even a measure of upset, arise at times in everybody's day-to-day dealings with other people. Courts are well able to recognise the boundary between conduct which is unattractive, even unreasonable, and conduct which is oppressive and unacceptable. To cross the boundary from the regrettable to the unacceptable the gravity of the misconduct must be of an order which would sustained [sic] criminal liability under section 2.

- References to harassing a person include alarming the person or causing the person distress (s 7). The person whose course of conduct is in question ought to know that it will cause another to fear that violence will be used against him on any occasion, if a reasonable person in possession of the same information would think the course of conduct would cause the other so to fear on that occasion.
- *R v O'Neill* [2016] EWCA Crim 92 confirmed that the definition in s 7 is inclusive and not exhaustive. 'Harassment' is generally understood to involve improper, oppressive, and unreasonable conduct that is targeted at an individual and calculated to produce the consequences described in s 7. Harassment cannot simply be equated with 'causing alarm or distress'. The danger of doing this is that not all conduct, even if unattractive, unreasonable, and causing alarm or distress, will be of an order justifying the sanction of the criminal law. By s 1(3) Act '... reasonable and/or lawful courses of conduct may be excluded'. But the Crown does not need to prove that a defendant's conduct is unreasonable.
- In *R v Haque* [2011] EWCA Crim 1871, the following requirements were identified for there to be proof of harassment:
  - the conduct must be targeted at an individual;
  - conduct must be calculated to produce the consequences in s 7 (alarm or distress);
  - conduct must have been oppressive and unreasonable;
  - provocation may possibly be relevant to causation and reasonableness;
  - there must also be proof that the defendant knew or ought to have known that conduct would cause the complainant to fear violence.
- In *R v Widdows* [2011] EWCA Crim 1500, the court held that the concept of harassment is at the core of the 1997 Act—though the word is not used in s 4—and considered the explanation of 'harassment' in *Majrowski v Guy's and St Thomas' NHS Trust* [2007] 1 AC 224 ('stalkers, racial abusers,

disruptive neighbours, bullying at work and so forth') and in *Thomas v News Group Newspapers Ltd* [2001] EWCA Civ 1233 (where the practice of stalking was said to be a prime example). The section is not normally appropriate for use as a means of criminalizing conduct, not charged as violence, during incidents in a long and predominantly affectionate relationship in which both parties persisted and wanted to continue.

• The defence of M'Naghten Rules insanity was considered in *Loake v CPS* [2017] EWHC 2855 (Admin). The defence is available to a defendant charged with an offence of harassment under s 2 but the 'course' of conduct may make it very difficult to meet the requirements for insanity in relation to each separate event (see also **A20**).

• The naming of two complainants in one charge is not duplicitous, but unlike the charge under s 4, there need only be conduct against at least two people on at least one occasion each (*Director of Public Prosecutions v Dunn* (2008) 165 JP 130).

 See *Blackstone's Criminal Practice 2019* **B2.174–B2.187**

C8.2 Harassment—putting people in fear of violence

Protection from Harassment Act 1997, s 4

4 Putting people in fear of violence

(1) A person whose course of conduct causes another to fear, on at least two occasions, that violence will be used against him is guilty of an offence if he knows or ought to know that his course of conduct will cause the other so to fear on each of those occasions …

(2) For the purposes of this section, the person whose course of conduct is in question ought to know that it will cause another to fear that violence will be used against him on any occasion if a reasonable person in possession of the same information would think the course of conduct would cause the other so to fear on that occasion.

(3) It is a defence for a person charged with an offence under this section to show that—

    (a) his course of conduct was pursued for the purpose of preventing or detecting crime,

    (b) his course of conduct was pursued under any enactment or rule of law or to comply with any condition or requirement imposed by any person under any enactment, or

    (c) the pursuit of his course of conduct was reasonable for the protection of himself or another or for the protection of his or another's property.

EW

6 months' imprisonment and/or fine/10 years' imprisonment (14 years if racially or religiously aggravated)

DO

C8.2.1 *Sentencing*

Where offence committed in a domestic context, also refer to the Overarching principles: Domestic abuse guideline, see **Appendix 5**.

STEP ONE: Determining the offence category

The court should determine the offence category with reference only to the factors in the following tables. In order to determine the category the court should assess culpability and harm.

The level of culpability is determined by weighing up all the factors of the case. Where there are characteristics present which fall under different levels of culpability, the court should balance these characteristics to reach a fair assessment of the offender's culpability.

Culpability demonstrated by one or more of the following:
A—Very high culpability
the extreme nature of one or more culpability B factors or the extreme culpability indicated by a combination of culpability B factors may elevate to category A
B—High culpability
Conduct intended to maximise fear or distress
High degree of planning and/or sophisticated offence
Persistent action over a prolonged period
Offence motivated by, or demonstrating, hostility based on any of the following characteristics or presumed characteristics of the victim: age, sex, disability, sexual orientation, or transgender identity
C—Medium culpability
Cases that fall between categories B and D, and in particular:
Conduct intended to cause some fear or distress
Some planning
Scope and duration of offence that falls between categories B and D
D—Lesser culpability
Offender's responsibility substantially reduced by mental disorder or learning disability
Conduct unlikely to cause significant fear or distress
Little or no planning
Offence was limited in scope and duration

HARM	
The level of harm is assessed by weighing up all the factors of the case.	
Category 1	Very serious distress caused to the victim
	Significant psychological harm caused to the victim
	Victim caused to make considerable changes to lifestyle to avoid contact
Category 2	Harm that falls between categories 1 and 3, and in particular:
	Some distress caused to the victim
	Some psychological harm caused to the victim
	Victim caused to make some changes to lifestyle to avoid contact
Category 3	Limited distress or harm caused to the victim

STEP TWO: Starting point and category range

Having determined the category at step one, the court should use the corresponding starting point to reach a sentence within the following category range. The starting point applies to all offenders irrespective of plea or previous convictions.

Sentencers should consider whether to ask for psychiatric reports in order to assist in the appropriate sentencing (hospital orders or mental health treatment requirements) of certain offenders to whom this consideration may be relevant.

Harm	Culpability			
	A	**B**	**C**	**D**
Category 1	**Starting point** 5 years' custody	**Starting point** 2 years 6 months' custody	**Starting point** 36 weeks' custody	**Starting point** 12 weeks' custody
	Category range 3 years 6 months'– 8 years' custody	**Category range** 1–4 years' custody	**Category range** 12 weeks–1 year 6 months' custody	**Category range** High-level community order– 36 weeks' custody
Category 2	**Starting point** 2 years 6 months' custody	**Starting point** 36 weeks' custody	**Starting point** 12 weeks' custody	**Starting point** High-level community order
	Category range 1–4 years' custody	**Category range** 12 weeks'–1 year 6 months' custody	**Category range** High-level community order– 36 weeks' custody	**Category range** Low-level community order– 12 weeks' custody
Category 3	**Starting point** 36 weeks' custody	**Starting point** 12 weeks' custody	**Starting point** High-level community order	**Starting point** Low-level community order
	Category range 12 weeks'–1 year 6 months' custody	**Category range** High-level community order– 36 weeks' custody	**Category range** Low-level community order– 12 weeks' custody	**Category range** Band C fine– High-level community order

The court should then consider any adjustment for any aggravating or mitigating factors. The following is a non-exhaustive list of additional factual elements providing the context of the offence and factors relating to the offender.

Identify whether any combination of these, or other relevant factors, should result in an upward or downward adjustment from the starting point.

Factors increasing seriousness	
Statutory aggravating factors:	*Other aggravating factors:*
Previous convictions, having regard to (a) the nature of the offence to which the conviction relates and its relevance to the current offence; and (b) the time that has elapsed since the conviction Offence committed while on bail	Using a position of trust to facilitate the offence Victim is particularly vulnerable (not all vulnerabilities are immediately apparent) Grossly violent or offensive material sent Impact of offence on others, particularly children Exploiting contact arrangements with a child to commit the offence Offence committed against those working in the public sector or providing a service to the public Failure to comply with current court orders Offence committed on licence or post sentence supervision Offences taken into consideration

Factors reducing seriousness or reflecting personal mitigation
No previous convictions or no relevant/recent convictions
Remorse
Good character and/or exemplary conduct
Serious medical condition requiring urgent, intensive, or long-term treatment
Age and/or lack of maturity
Mental disorder or learning disability (where not taken into account at step one)
Sole or primary carer for dependent relatives
Determination and/or demonstration of steps having been taken to address offending behaviour

RACIALLY OR RELIGIOUSLY AGGRAVATED HARASSMENT/ STALKING OFFENCES ONLY

Having determined the category of the basic offence to identify the sentence of a non-aggravated offence, the court should now consider the level of racial or religious aggravation involved and apply an appropriate uplift to the sentence in accordance with the following guidance. The following is a list of factors which the court should consider to determine the level of aggravation. Where there are characteristics present which fall under different levels of aggravation, the court should balance these to reach a fair assessment of the level of aggravation present in the offence.

Maximum sentence for the aggravated offence on indictment is 14 years' custody (maximum for the basic offence is 10 years' custody).

HIGH LEVEL OF RACIAL OR RELIGIOUS AGGRAVATION	SENTENCE UPLIFT
Racial or religious aggravation was the predominant motivation for the offence Offender was a member of, or was associated with, a group promoting hostility based on race or religion (where linked to the commission of the offence) Aggravated nature of the offence caused severe distress to the victim or the victim's family (over and above the distress already considered at step one) Aggravated nature of the offence caused serious fear and distress throughout local community or more widely	Increase the length of custodial sentence if already considered for the basic offence or consider a custodial sentence, if not already considered for the basic offence

MEDIUM LEVEL OF RACIAL OR RELIGIOUS AGGRAVATION	SENTENCE UPLIFT
Racial or religious aggravation formed a significant proportion of the offence as a whole Aggravated nature of the offence caused some distress to the victim or the victim's family (over and above the distress already considered at step one) Aggravated nature of the offence caused some fear and distress throughout local community or more widely	Consider a significantly more onerous penalty of the same type or consider a more severe type of sentence than for the basic offence

LOW LEVEL OF RACIAL OR RELIGIOUS AGGRAVATION	SENTENCE UPLIFT
Aggravated element formed a minimal part of the offence as a whole Aggravated nature of the offence caused minimal or no distress to the victim or the victim's family (over and above the distress already considered at step one)	Consider a more onerous penalty of the same type identified for the basic offence

Magistrates may find that, although the appropriate sentence for the basic offence would be within their powers, the appropriate increase for the aggravated offence would result in a sentence in excess of their powers. If so, they must commit for sentence to the Crown Court.

C8.2.2 Key points

- See the key points in **C8.1.2**
  - It is a defence for a person charged with an offence under s 4 to show that:
    - his course of conduct was pursued for the purpose of preventing or detecting crime. There is a test of rationality to this defence which applies a minimum objective standard to the relevant person's mental processes. It imposes a requirement for good faith and an absence of arbitrariness. Detection or prevention need not be the sole purpose but it must be a dominant purpose of the defendant (*Hayes v Willoughby* [2012] UKSC 17);
    - his course of conduct was pursued under any enactment or rule of law, or to comply with any condition or requirement imposed by any person under any enactment; or
    - the pursuit of his course of conduct was reasonable for the protection of himself or another, or for the protection of his or another's property.
  - The naming of two complainants in one charge under s 4 is not duplicitous, but at least one of the complainants must have feared violence on at least two occasions (*Caurti v Director of Public Prosecutions* [2002] EWHC 867 (Admin)).

See *Blackstone's Criminal Practice 2019* **B2.190–B2.197**

C8.3 Stalking

The offences of stalking mirror the approach of the basic and aggravated forms of the harassment offences set out at **C8.1** and **C8.2**.

The defences in s 1(3) Protection from Harassment Act 1997 are available (see **C8.1**).

C8.3.1 *The basic offence*

Protection from Harassment Act 1997, s 2A

2A Offence of stalking

(1) A person is guilty of an offence if—
    (a) the person pursues a course of conduct in breach of section 1(1), and
    (b) the course of conduct amounts to stalking.
(2) For the purposes of subsection (1)(b) (and section 4A(1)(a)) a person's course of conduct amounts to stalking of another person if—
    (a) it amounts to harassment of that person,
    (b) the acts or omissions involved are ones associated with stalking, and
    (c) the person whose course of conduct it is knows or ought to know that the course of conduct amounts to harassment of the other person.
(3) The following are examples of acts or omissions which, in particular circumstances, are ones associated with stalking—
    (a) following a person,
    (b) contacting, or attempting to contact, a person by any means,
    (c) publishing any statement or other material—
        (i) relating or purporting to relate to a person, or
        (ii) purporting to originate from a person,
    (d) monitoring the use by a person of the internet, email or any other form of electronic communication,
    (e) loitering in any place (whether public or private),
    (f) interfering with any property in the possession of a person,
    (g) watching or spying on a person.
    . . .
(6) This section is without prejudice to the generality of section 2.

SO (Either way if racially or religiously aggravated)

‖‖‖ 6 months' imprisonment and/or fine (2 years if racially or religiously aggravated)

C8.3.2 *Sentencing*

See the sentencing guideline at **C8.1.1**

C8.3.3 *Aggravated stalking*

Protection from Harassment Act 1997, s 4A

4A Stalking involving fear of violence or serious alarm or distress

(1) A person ('A') whose course of conduct—
   (a) amounts to stalking, and
   (b) either—
      (i) causes another ('B') to fear, on at least two occasions, that violence will be used against B, or
      (ii) causes B serious alarm or distress which has a substantial adverse effect on B's usual day-to-day activities,

   is guilty of an offence if A knows or ought to know that A's course of conduct will cause B so to fear on each of those occasions or (as the case may be) will cause such alarm or distress.

(2) For the purposes of this section A ought to know that A's course of conduct will cause B to fear that violence will be used against B on any occasion if a reasonable person in possession of the same information would think the course of conduct would cause B so to fear on that occasion.

(3) For the purposes of this section A ought to know that A's course of conduct will cause B serious alarm or distress which has a substantial adverse effect on B's usual day-to-day activities if a reasonable person in possession of the same information would think the course of conduct would cause B such alarm or distress.

(4) It is a defence for A to show that—
   (a) A's course of conduct was pursued for the purpose of preventing or detecting crime,
   (b) A's course of conduct was pursued under any enactment or rule of law or to comply with any condition or requirement imposed by any person under any enactment, or
   (c) the pursuit of A's course of conduct was reasonable for the protection of A or another or for the protection of A's or another's property.
   ...

(8) This section is without prejudice to the generality of section 4.

EW

ḤḤḤ 6 months' imprisonment and/or fine/10 years' imprisonment (14 years if racially or religiously aggravated)

GC if racially or religiously aggravated

DO

C8.3.4 *Sentencing*

See the sentencing guideline at **C8.2.1**

8.3.4 Key points

In *R v Qosja* [2016] EWCA Crim 1543 it was held that the aggravated offence is made out if a person, whose course of conduct amounts to stalking, causes another to fear on at least two occasions that violence will be used. This is wide enough to cover a person who is caused to fear on a particular occasion that violence will be used on an uncertain future date. This does not need to be a specific threat of violence but the requirement is that they fear that violence will (rather than may be) used.

Section 4A requires no objective conduct on the part of a defendant beyond stalking. The remainder of the statutory test is concerned with the effect on the mind of the complainant, and the knowledge, or constructive knowledge, of the defendant. The question that arises is the actual effect on the mind of the victim. As regards the requirement in s 4A(1)(a)(i) that the person fears, on at least two occasions, that violence will be used against him or her, evidence of a threat to use sexually explicit material was not evidence of a fear of violence. That a complainant feared that she would be 'hunted down' by the appellant was not, unless more was said, evidence of a fear of violence, although it might have been evidence of a fear of stalking or harassment. It is not enough to establish that conditions existed that might reasonably have engendered a fear of violence: that will be so in many stalking cases. The court must be sure that such a fear was actually engendered. The offence requires proof of a specific state of mind on the part of the complainant, not merely proof of circumstances that might reasonably engender that state of mind (*Pendlebury v DPP* [2018] EWHC 3567 (Admin)).

C9 **Immigration and Document Offences**

C9.1 Illegal entry and deception

Immigration Act 1971, ss 24, 24A, and 24B

24 Illegal entry and similar offences

(1) [It is an offence—]

    (a) if contrary to this Act he knowingly enters the United Kingdom in breach of a deportation order or without leave;

    (b) if, having only a limited leave to enter or remain in the United Kingdom, he knowingly either—

    (c) remains beyond the time limited by the leave; or

    (d) (ii) fails to observe a condition of the leave;

    (e) if, having lawfully entered the United Kingdom without leave by virtue of section 8(1) above, he remains without leave beyond the time allowed by section 8(1);

    (f) if, without reasonable excuse, he fails to comply with any requirement imposed on him under Schedule 2 to this Act to report to a medical officer of health, or to attend, or submit to a test or examination, as required by such an officer;

    (g) if, without reasonable excuse, he fails to observe any restriction imposed on him under Schedule 2 or 3 to this Act as to residence, as to his employment or occupation or as to reporting to the police, to an immigration officer or to the Secretary of State;

    (h) if he disembarks in the United Kingdom from a ship or aircraft after being placed on board under Schedule 2 or 3 to this Act with a view to his removal from the United Kingdom;

    (i) if he embarks in contravention of a restriction imposed by or under an Order in Council under section 3(7) of this Act.

(1A) A person commits an offence under subsection (1)(b)(i) above on the day when he first knows that the time limited by his leave has expired and continues to commit it throughout any period during which he is in the United Kingdom thereafter; but a person shall not be prosecuted under that provision more than once in respect of the same limited leave.

(2) The extended time limit for prosecutions which is provided for by section 28 below shall apply to offences under subsection (1)(a) and

(3) (c) above.

(4) In proceedings for an offence against subsection (1)(a) above of entering the United Kingdom without leave—

    (a) any stamp purporting to have been imprinted on a passport or other travel document by an immigration officer on a particular date for the purpose of giving leave shall be presumed to have been duly so imprinted, unless the contrary is proved;

    (b) proof that a person had leave to enter the United Kingdom shall lie on the defence if, but only if, he is shown to have entered within six months before the date when the proceedings were commenced.

24A Deception

(1) A person who is not a British citizen is guilty of an offence if, by means which include deception by him—

    (a) he obtains or seeks to obtain leave to enter or remain in the United Kingdom; or

    (b) he secures or seeks to secure the avoidance, postponement or revocation of enforcement action against him.

---

(2) 'Enforcement action', in relation to a person, means—
  (a) the giving of directions for his removal from the United Kingdom ('directions') under Schedule 2 to this Act or section 10 of the Immigration and Asylum Act 1999;
  (b) the making of a deportation order against him under section 5 of this Act; or
  (c) his removal from the United Kingdom in consequence of directions or a deportation order.

24B Illegal working

(1) A person ('P') who is subject to immigration control commits an offence if—
  (a) P works at a time when P is disqualified from working by reason of P's immigration status, and
  (b) at that time P knows or has reasonable cause to believe that P is disqualified from working by reason of P's immigration status.
(2) For the purposes of subsection (1) a person is disqualified from working by reason of the person's immigration status if—
  (a) the person has not been granted leave to enter or remain in the United Kingdom, or
  (b) the person's leave to enter or remain in the United Kingdom—
    (i) is invalid,
    (ii) has ceased to have effect (whether by reason of curtailment, revocation, cancellation, passage of time or otherwise), or
    (iii) is subject to a condition preventing the person from doing work of that kind...
(8) The reference in subsection (1) to a person who is subject to immigration control is to a person who under this Act requires leave to enter or remain in the United Kingdom.
(9) Where a person is on immigration bail within the meaning of Part 1 of Schedule 10 to the Immigration Act 2016—
  (a) the person is to be treated for the purposes of subsection (2) as if the person had been granted leave to enter the United Kingdom, but
  (b) any condition as to the person's work in the United Kingdom to which the person's immigration bail is subject is to be treated for those purposes as a condition of leave...
(10) The reference in subsection (1) to a person working is to that person working—
  (a) under a contract of employment,
  (b) under a contract of apprenticeship,
  (c) under a contract personally to do work,
  (d) under or for the purposes of a contract for services,
  (e) for a purpose related to a contract to sell goods,
  (f) as a constable,
  (g) in the course of Crown employment,
  (h) as a relevant member of the House of Commons staff, or
  (i) as a relevant member of the House of Lords staff...
(13) In this section 'contract' means a contract whether express or implied and, if express, whether oral or in writing.

SO ss 24 and 25B

EW s 24A

Fine/6 months' imprisonment (ss 24 and 25B)

6 months'/2 years' imprisonment (s 24A)

C9.1.1 Key points

The burden of proving that entry was legal falls upon the defendant in relation to prosecutions commenced within six months of that entry (s 24(4)(b)).

C9.2 Assisting unlawful entry

Immigration Act 1971, ss 25, 25A, and 25B

25 Assisting unlawful immigration to member state

(1) A person commits an offence if he—
  (a) does an act which facilitates the commission of a breach of immigration law by an individual who is not a citizen of the European Union,
  (b) knows or has reasonable cause for believing that the act facilitates the commission of a breach of immigration law by the individual, and
  (c) knows or has reasonable cause for believing that the individual is not a citizen of the European Union.

25A Helping asylum-seeker to enter United Kingdom

(1) A person commits an offence if—
  (a) he knowingly and for gain facilitates the arrival in, or the entry into, the United Kingdom of an individual, and
  (b) he knows or has reasonable cause to believe that the individual is an asylum-seeker.

25B Assisting entry to United Kingdom in breach of deportation or exclusion order

(1) A person commits an offence if he—
  (a) does an act which facilitates a breach of a deportation order in force against an individual who is a citizen of the European Union, and
  (b) knows or has reasonable cause for believing that the act facilitates a breach of the deportation order.

EW

Fine/6 months' imprisonment/14 years' imprisonment

C9.2.1 Key points

Facilitation of a breach of immigration law under s 25 Immigration Act 1971 includes facilitating a breach by an asylum seeker (*R v Bina* [2014] EWCA Crim 1444). *R v Ali* [2013] EWCA Crim 43 confirms that, to prove an offence under s 25 Immigration Act 1971, it is not essential that breach actually occurs, and *R v Boateng* [2016] EWCA Crim 57 confirms that, for there to be an offence of facilitating the illegal entry of a person to the UK, it was not necessary that the person who enters be dishonest or aware of the position.

C9.3 Possessing false passports, work permits, registration cards, etc

Immigration Act 1971, ss 26 and 26A

26 General offences in connection with administration of Act

(1) A person shall be guilty of an offence punishable on summary conviction with a fine or with imprisonment for not more than six months, or with both, in any of the following cases—

   (a) if, without reasonable excuse, he refuses or fails to submit to examination under Schedule 2 to this Act;

   (b) if, without reasonable excuse, he refuses to fails to furnish or produce any information in his possession, or any documents in his possession or control, which he is on an examination under that Schedule required to furnish or produce;

   (c) if on any such examination or otherwise he makes or causes to be made to an immigration officer or other person lawfully acting in the execution of a relevant enactment a return, statement or representation which he knows to be false or does not believe to be true;

   (d) if, without lawful authority, he alters any certificate of entitlement, entry clearance, work permit or other document issued or made under or for the purposes of this Act, or uses for the purposes of this Act, or has in his possession for such use, any passport, certificate of entitlement, entry clearance, work permit or other document which he knows or has reasonable cause to believe to be false;

   (e) if, without reasonable excuse, he fails to complete and produce a landing or embarkation card in accordance with any order under Schedule 2 to this Act;

   (f) if, without reasonable excuse, he fails to comply with any requirement of regulations under section 4(3) or of an order under section 4(4) above;

   (g) if, without reasonable excuse, he obstructs an immigration officer or other person lawfully acting in the execution of this Act.

(2) The extended time limit for prosecutions which is provided for by section 28 below shall apply to offences under subsection (1)(c) and

   (a) above.

26A Registration card

...

(3) A person commits an offence if he—

   (a) makes a false registration card,

   (b) alters a registration card with intent to deceive or to enable another to deceive,

   (c) has a false or altered registration card in his possession without reasonable excuse,

   (d) uses or attempts to use a false registration card for a purpose for which a registration card is issued,

   (e) uses or attempts to use an altered registration card with intent to deceive,

   (f) makes an article designed to be used in making a false registration card,

(g) makes an article designed to be used in altering a registration card with intent to deceive or to enable another to deceive, or

(h) has an article within paragraph (f) or (g) in his possession without reasonable excuse.

(4) In subsection (3) 'false registration card' means a document which is designed to appear to be a registration card.

SO s 26

EW s 26A

s 26 Fine and/or 6 months' imprisonment

on 3s 26A fine/6 months' imprisonment/10 years' imprisonment (ss (3)(a), (b), (d), (e), (f), or (g)), 2 years' imprisonment (ss (3)(c) or (h))

C9.3.1 *Time limits*

The 6-month time limit does not apply to offences under s 26(1)(c) and (d), or s 28(1)(a) and (c).

C9.4 Entering the UK without documentation

Asylum and Immigration (Treatment of Claimants, etc.) Act 2004, s 2

2 Entering United Kingdom without passport, &c.

(1) A person commits an offence if at a leave or asylum interview he does not have with him an immigration document which—
   (a) is in force, and
   (b) satisfactorily establishes his identity and nationality or citizenship.

(2) A person commits an offence if at a leave or asylum interview he does not have with him, in respect of any dependent child with whom he claims to be travelling or living, an immigration document which—
   (a) is in force, and
   (b) satisfactorily establishes the child's identity and nationality or citizenship.

(3) But a person does not commit an offence under subsection (1) or (2) if—
   (a) the interview referred to in that subsection takes place after the person has entered the United Kingdom, and
   (b) within the period of three days beginning with the date of the interview the person provides to an immigration officer or to the Secretary of State a document of the kind referred to in that subsection.

(4) It is a defence for a person charged with an offence under subsection (1)—
   (a) to prove that he is an EEA national,
   (b) to prove that he is a member of the family of an EEA national and that he is exercising a right under the EU Treaties in respect of entry to or residence in the United Kingdom,

(c) to prove that he has a reasonable excuse for not being in possession of a document of the kind specified in subsection (1),

(d) to produce a false immigration document and to prove that he used that document as an immigration document for all purposes in connection with his journey to the United Kingdom, or

(e) to prove that he travelled to the United Kingdom without, at any stage since he set out on the journey, having possession of an immigration document.

(5) It is a defence for a person charged with an offence under subsection (2) in respect of a child—

(a) to prove that the child is an EEA national,

(b) to prove that the child is a member of the family of an EEA national and that the child is exercising a right under the EU Treaties in respect of entry to or residence in the United Kingdom,

(c) to prove that the person has a reasonable excuse for not being in possession of a document of the kind specified in subsection (2),

(d) to produce a false immigration document and to prove that it was used as an immigration document for all purposes in connection with the child's journey to the United Kingdom, or

(e) to prove that he travelled to the United Kingdom with the child without, at any stage since he set out on the journey, having possession of an immigration document in respect of the child.

(6) Where the charge for an offence under subsection (1) or (2) relates to an interview which takes place after the defendant has entered the United Kingdom—

(a) subsections (4)(c) and (5)(c) shall not apply, but

(b) it is a defence for the defendant to prove that he has a reasonable excuse for not providing a document in accordance with subsection (3).

(7) For the purposes of subsections (4) to (6)—

(a) the fact that a document was deliberately destroyed or disposed of is not a reasonable excuse for not being in possession of it or for not providing it in accordance with subsection (3), unless it is shown that the destruction or disposal was—

(i) for a reasonable cause, or

(ii) beyond the control of the person charged with the offence, and

(b) in paragraph (a)(i) "reasonable cause" does not include the purpose of—

(i) delaying the handling or resolution of a claim or application or the taking of a decision,

(ii) increasing the chances of success of a claim or application, or

(iii) complying with instructions or advice given by a person who offers advice about, or facilitates, immigration into the United Kingdom, unless in the circumstances of the case it is unreasonable to expect non-compliance with the instructions or advice.

(8) A person shall be presumed for the purposes of this section not to have a document with him if he fails to produce it to an immigration officer or official of the Secretary of State on request.

...

(12) In this section—

- "EEA national" means a national of a State which is a contracting party to the Agreement on the European Economic Area signed at Oporto on 2nd May 1992 (as it has effect from time to time),

- "immigration document" means—

(a) a passport, and

(b) a document which relates to a national of a State other than the United Kingdom and which is designed to serve the same purpose as a passport, and

- "leave or asylum interview" means an interview with an immigration officer or an official of the Secretary of State at which a person—
  - (a) seeks leave to enter or remain in the United Kingdom, or
  - (b) claims that to remove him from or require him to leave the United Kingdom would breach the United Kingdom's obligations under the Refugee Convention or would be unlawful under section 6 of the Human Rights Act 1998 (c. 42) as being incompatible with his Convention rights.
- (13) For the purposes of this section—
  - (a) a document which purports to be, or is designed to look like, an immigration document, is a false immigration document, and
  - (b) an immigration document is a false immigration document if and in so far as it is used—
    - (i) outside the period for which it is expressed to be valid,
    - (ii) contrary to provision for its use made by the person issuing it, or
    - (iii) by or in respect of a person other than the person to or for whom it was issued.

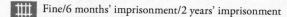 Fine/6 months' imprisonment/2 years' imprisonment

9.4.1 Key points

There is a defence under the Asylum and Immigration (Treatment of Claimants) Act 2004 where the defendant could not obtain a valid immigration document in their own country (*Thet v DPP* [2006] EWHC 2701).

 See *Blackstone's Criminal Practice 2020* **B22**

C9.5 Possession of false identity documents, etc without reasonable excuse

Identity Documents Act 2010, ss 6 and 7

6 Possession of false identity documents, etc without reasonable excuse

(1) It is an offence for a person ('P'), without reasonable excuse, to have in P's possession or under P's control—
  - (a) an identity document that is false,
  - (b) an identity document that was improperly obtained,
  - (c) an identity document that relates to someone else,
  - (d) any apparatus which, to P's knowledge, is or has been specially designed or adapted for the making of false identity documents, or
  - (e) any article or material which, to P's knowledge, is or has been specially designed or adapted to be used in the making of such documents.

...

7 Meaning of 'identity document'

(1) For the purposes of sections 4 to 6 'identity document' means any document that is or purports to be—
   (a) an immigration document,
   (b) a United Kingdom passport (within the meaning of the Immigration Act 1971),
   (c) a passport issued by or on behalf of the authorities of a country or territory outside the United Kingdom or by or on behalf of an international organisation,
   (d) a document that can be used (in some or all circumstances) instead of a passport,
   (e) a licence to drive a motor vehicle granted under Part 3 of the Road Traffic Act 1988 or under Part 2 of the Road Traffic (Northern Ireland) Order 1981, or
   (f) a driving licence issued by or on behalf of the authorities of a country or territory outside the United Kingdom.
(2) In subsection (1)(a) 'immigration document' means—
   (a) a document used for confirming the right of a person under the EU Treaties in respect of entry or residence in the United Kingdom,
   (b) a document that is given in exercise of immigration functions and records information about leave granted to a person to enter or to remain in the United Kingdom, or
   (c) a registration card (within the meaning of section 26A of the Immigration Act 1971).
   (3) In subsection (2)(b) 'immigration functions' means functions under the Immigration Acts (within the meaning of the Asylum and Immigration (Treatment of Claimants, etc.) Act 2004).
(4) References in subsection (1) to the issue of a document include its renewal, replacement or re-issue (with or without modifications).
(5) In this section 'document' includes a stamp or label.
(6) The Secretary of State may by order amend the definition of 'identity document'.

EW

 6 months' imprisonment and/or fine/2 years' imprisonment

C9.5.1 *Sentencing*

Offence seriousness (culpability and harm)		
A. Identify the appropriate starting point		
Starting points based on first-time offender pleading not guilty		
Examples of nature of activity	**Starting point**	**Range**
Single document possessed	Medium-level community order	Band C fine–high-level community order
Small number of documents, no evidence of dealing	12 weeks' custody	6 weeks' custody–Crown Court
Considerable number of documents possessed, evidence of involvement in larger operation	Crown Court	Crown Court

Offence seriousness (culpability and harm)	
B. Consider the effect of aggravating and mitigating factors (other than those within examples above)	
The following may be particularly relevant but these lists are not exhaustive	
Factors indicating higher culpability	**Factors indicating lower culpability**
1. Clear knowledge that documents false	1. Group activity
2. Number of documents possessed (where not in offence descriptions above)	2. Potential impact of use (where not in offence descriptions above)
Factor indicating greater degree of harm	
1. Genuine mistake or ignorance	

C9.5.2 *Defences*

Immigration and Asylum Act 1999, s 31

31 Defences based on Article 31(1) of the Refugee Convention

(1) It is a defence for a refugee charged with an offence to which this section applies to show that, having come to the United Kingdom directly from a country where his life or freedom was threatened (within the meaning of the Refugee Convention), he—
  (a) presented himself to the authorities in the United Kingdom without delay;
  (b) showed good cause for his illegal entry or presence; and
  (c) made a claim for asylum as soon as was reasonably practicable after his arrival in the United Kingdom.

(2) If, in coming from the country where his life or freedom was threatened, the refugee stopped in another country outside the United Kingdom, subsection (1) applies only if he shows that he could not reasonably have expected to be given protection under the Refugee Convention in that other country.

(3) In England and Wales and Northern Ireland the offences to which this section applies are any offence, and any attempt to commit an offence, under—
  (a) Part I of the Forgery and Counterfeiting Act 1981 (forgery and connected offences);
  (b) section 24A of the 1971 Act (deception); or
  (c) section 26(1)(d) of the 1971 Act (falsification of documents).
  ...

(5) A refugee who has made a claim for asylum is not entitled to the defence provided by subsection (1) in relation to any offence committed by him after making that claim.

(6) 'Refugee' has the same meaning as it has for the purposes of the Refugee Convention.

(7) If the Secretary of State has refused to grant a claim for asylum made by a person who claims that he has a defence under subsection (1), that person is to be taken not to be a refugee unless he shows that he is.

C9.5.3 Key points

- Refugees are protected under Article 31 of the UN Convention relating to the status of refugees as recognised by these proivsions

  ...

The defence was considered in *R v Matete* [2013] EWCA Crim 1372.

The requirement that the claim for asylum must be made as soon as was reasonably practicable does not necessarily mean at the earliest possible moment (*Asfaw* [2008] UKHL 31).

It follows that the fact a refugee stopped in a third country in transit is not necessarily fatal and may be explicable: the refugee has some choice as to where he might properly claim asylum. The main touchstones by which exclusion from protection should be judged are the length of the stay in the intermediate country, the reasons for delaying there, and whether or not the refugee sought or found protection de jure or de facto from the persecution from which he or she was seeking to escape (*Asfaw*).The Court of Appeal has found that stays as long as three months in countries where a refugee could not reasonably be expected to seek asylum do not necessarily exclude reliance on the defence. Even where the third country is a signatory to the Refugee Convention, this is not necessarily fatal to the statutory defence. Short stopovers in 'safe' countries have been accepted by the Court of Appeal as falling within the description of 'in transit' for the purposes of the 'come directly' provision in s 31. Examples include:

- stays in Turkey of up to one month (see *Jaddi* [2012] EWCA Crim 2565);
- stays in Greece of up to two weeks (see *Mohamed v R* [2010] EWCA Crim 2400);
- stays in Spain of up to 20 days (see *Mateta v R* [2013] EWCA Crim 1372); and
- stays in France of up to 10 days (*R v Nguidjol (Richard Sohe)* 18 June 2015 unreported).

A short stopover within the UK has also been found to be in transit for the purposes of s 31 where the defendant was in the hands of an agent organizing their journey, and/or had been advised to seek asylum elsewhere, and always intended to do so (*Sadeghi* [2014] EWCA Crim 2933).

The courts will consider the individual circumstances of the case, such as the length of the stay and the reason for delay in coming to the UK. The fact that the defendant has not made an application for asylum immediately on entry to the UK will not necessarily mean a s 31 defence is not available to them. A stay of 13 days in the UK has been found by the Court of Appeal to satisfy the requirements of s 31 for the purposes of making a claim for asylum as soon as reasonably practicable (*Mulugeta v R* [2015] EWCA Crim 6).

The requirement that the refugee demonstrates 'good cause' for his illegal entry or presence in the UK will be satisfied by showing that he was reasonably travelling on false papers (*R v Uxbridge MC ex p Adimi* [2001] QB 667).

If the document itself is false then it is no defence in a case where the document was being used for establishing a registrable fact, that it bore the correct details of the defendant (*R v Jamalov*, The Times, 17 March 2010), but the defendant's ignorance of a document's falsity could amount to a reasonable cause for possessing it (*R v Unah* [2011] EWCA Crim 1837).

In *L; HVN; THN; T v R* [2013] EWCA Crim 991 the court considered that the abuse of process jurisdiction should be used to stay cases where the defendant was the subject of human trafficking and there was a connection with their criminality.

The review by the court was wider than a *Wednesbury* review. The court discharged its responsibilities under the European Parliament and Council Directive 2011/36/EU by:

(i) reviewing decisions to prosecute;
(ii) staying inappropriate prosecutions; and
(iii) discharging defendants when prosecution was appropriate but punishment was not.

It was essential that a court made full enquiries as to the defendant's true age and their involvement in human trafficking—when it may still provide arguments in favour of an abuse of process or at least mitigation (see **A1.1**).

See *Blackstone's Criminal Practice 2019* **B6.58–B6.63**

C10 **Prison Offences**

C10.1 Conveyance of articles into prison

The Prison Act 1952 lists the following prohibited articles (s 40A):

List A articles	List B articles
(a) a controlled drug (as defined for the purposes of the Misuse of Drugs Act 1971);	(a) alcohol (as defined for the purposes of the Licensing Act 2003);
(b) an explosive;	(b) a mobile telephone;
(c) any firearm or ammunition (as defined in s 57 of the Firearms Act 1968);	(c) a camera;
(d) any other offensive weapon (as defined in s 1(9) of the Police and Criminal Evidence Act 1984).	(d) a sound-recording device.
	'Camera' includes any device by means of which a photograph (as defined in s 40E) can be produced; 'sound-recording device' includes any device by means of which a sound-recording (as defined in s 40E) can be made. The reference in paragraph (b), (c), or (d) of List B to a device of any description includes a reference to—
	(a) a component part of a device of that description; or
	(b) an article designed or adapted for use with a device of that description (including any disk, film, or other separate article on which images, sounds, or information may be recorded).

- A List C article is any article or substance proscribed for the purposes of s 40A by prison rules. This includes electronic cigarettes, lighters, and matches

IO (For List A articlés)

SO (For List C articles)

EW (For List B articles)

▦ (For List A articles fine and/or 6 months'/10 years' imprisonment; for List B articles, fine and/or 6 months'/2 years' imprisonment; for List C articles, level 3 fine only)

Prison Act 1952, s 40C

40B Conveyance etc.of List A articles into or out of prison

(1) A person who, without authorisation—

    (a) brings, throws or otherwise conveys a List A article into or out of a prison,

    (b) causes another person to bring, throw or otherwise convey a List A article into or out of a prison,

    (c) leaves a List A article in any place (whether inside or outside a prison) intending it to come into the possession of a prisoner, or

    (d) knowing a person to be a prisoner, gives a List A article to him, is guilty of an offence.

40C Conveyance etc of List B or C articles into or out of prison

(1) A person who, without authorisation—

   (a) brings, throws or otherwise conveys a List B article into or out of a prison,

   (b) causes another person to bring, throw or otherwise convey a List B article into or out of a prison,

   (c) leaves a List B article in any place (whether inside or outside a prison) intending it to come into the possession of a prisoner, or

   (d) knowing a person to be a prisoner, gives a List B article to him, is guilty of an offence.

(2) A person who, without authorisation—

   (a) brings, throws or otherwise conveys a List C article into a prison intending it to come into the possession of a prisoner,

   (b) causes another person to bring, throw or otherwise convey a List C article into a prison intending it to come into the possession of a prisoner,

   (c) brings, throws or otherwise conveys a List C article out of a prison on behalf of a prisoner,

   (d) causes another person to bring, throw or otherwise convey a List C article out of a prison on behalf of a prisoner,

   (e) leaves a List C article in any place (whether inside or outside a prison) intending it to come into the possession of a prisoner, or

   (f) while inside a prison, gives a List C article to a prisoner, is guilty of an offence.

(3) A person who attempts to commit an offence under subsection (2) is guilty of that offence.

(4) In proceedings for an offence under this section it is a defence for the accused to show that—

   (a) he reasonably believed that he had authorisation to do the act in respect of which the proceedings are brought, or

   (b) in all the circumstances there was an overriding public interest which justified the doing of that act.

C10.1.2 Key points

R v Johnson [2017] EWCA Crim 189 confirms that whilst there is no stated mental element for the offence under s 40C, the offence will be made out if the Crown proves that person knew that they had a prohibited item. It was not necessary to prove that they knew the actual nature of the contents of a package.

C10.2 Unauthorized possession of knives, etc in prison

Prison Act 1952, s 40CA

Unauthorised possession in prison of knife or offensive weapon

(1) A person who, without authorisation, is in possession of an article specified in subsection (2) inside a prison is guilty of an offence.

(2) The articles referred to in subsection (1) are—

   (a) any article that has a blade or is sharply pointed;

   (b) any other offensive weapon (as defined in section 1(9) of the Police and Criminal Evidence Act 1984).

(3) In proceedings for an offence under this section it is a defence for the accused to show that—
- (a) he reasonably believed that he had authorisation to be in possession of the article in question, or
- (b) in all the circumstances there was an overriding public interest which justified his being in possession of the article.

(4) In this section 'authorisation' means authorisation given for the purposes of this section; and subsections (1) to (3) of section 40E apply in relation to authorisations so given as they apply to authorisations given for the purposes of section 40D.

EW

 Fine and/or 6 months'/4 years' imprisonment

C10.3 **Throwing articles into prison**

Prison Act 1952, s 40CB

40CB Throwing articles into prison

(1) A person who, without authorisation, throws any article or substance into a prison is guilty of an offence.

(2) For the purposes of subsection (1)—
- (a) the reference to an article or substance does not include a reference to a List A article, a List B article or a List C article (as defined by section 40A);
- (b) the reference to 'throwing' an article or substance into a prison includes a reference to doing anything from outside the prison that results in the article or substance being projected or conveyed over or through a boundary of the prison so as to land inside the prison.

(3) In proceedings for an offence under this section it is a defence for the accused to show that—
- (a) he reasonably believed that he had authorisation to do the act in respect of which the proceedings are brought, or
- (b) in all the circumstances there was an overriding public interest which justified the doing of that act.

(4) In this section 'authorisation' means authorisation given for the purposes of this section; and subsections (1) to (3) of section 40E apply in relation to authorisations so given as they apply to authorisations given for the purposes of section 40D.

EW

Fine and/or 6 months'/2 years' imprisonment

C10.4 **Other offences relating to prison security**

Prison Act 1952, s 40D

40D Other offences relating to prison security

(1) A person who, without authorisation—

    (a) takes a photograph, or makes a sound-recording, inside a prison, or

    (b) transmits, or causes to be transmitted, any image, sound or information from inside a prison by electronic communications for simultaneous reception outside the prison, is guilty of an offence.

(2) It is immaterial for the purposes of subsection (1)(a) where the recording medium is located.

(3) A person who, without authorisation—

    (a) brings or otherwise conveys a restricted document out of a prison or causes such a document to be brought or conveyed out of a prison...

is guilty of an offence.

(3A) A person who, without authorisation, is in possession of any of the items specified in subsection (3B) inside a prison is guilty of an offence.

(3B) The items referred to in subsection (3A) are—

    (a) a device capable of transmitting or receiving images, sounds or information by electronic communications (including a mobile telephone);

    (b) a component part of such a device;

    (c) an article designed or adapted for use with such a device (including any disk, film or other separate article on which images, sounds or information may be recorded).

(4) In proceedings for an offence under this section it is a defence for the accused to show that—

    (a) he reasonably believed that he had authorisation to do the act in respect of which the proceedings are brought, or

    (b) in all the circumstances there was an overriding public interest which justified the doing of that act.

EW

 Fine and/or 6 months'/2 years' imprisonment

C11 **Public Order**

C11.1 **Affray**

Public Order Act 1986, ss 3(1)–(4), 6(2) and (5)

3 Affray

(1) A person is guilty of affray if he uses or threatens unlawful violence towards another and his conduct is such as would cause a person of reasonable firmness present at the scene to fear for his personal safety.

(2) Where 2 or more persons use or threaten the unlawful violence, it is the conduct of them taken together that must be considered for the purposes of subsection (1).

(3) For the purposes of this section a threat cannot be made by the use of words alone.

(4) No person of reasonable firmness need actually be, or be likely to be, present at the scene

...

6 Mental element: miscellaneous

(2) A person is guilty of violent disorder or affray only if he intends to use or threaten violence or is aware that his conduct may be violent or threaten violence.

(5) For the purposes of this section a person whose awareness is impaired by intoxication shall be taken to be aware of that of which he would be aware if not intoxicated, unless he shows either that his intoxication was not self-induced or that it was caused solely by the taking or administration of a substance in the course of medical treatment.

EW

6 months' imprisonment and/or fine/3 years' imprisonment

DO Dangerous offender

C11.1.1 *Sentencing*

Note The Sentencing Council has consulted on a new guideline which is likely to come in to force in late 2019/early 2020

Offence seriousness (culpability and harm)		
A. Identify the appropriate starting point		
Starting points based on first-time offender pleading not guilty		
Example of nature of activity	**Starting point**	**Range**
Brief offence involving low-level violence, no substantial fear created	Low-level community order	Band C fine–medium-level community order
Degree of fighting or violence that causes substantial fear	High-level community order	Medium-level community order–12 weeks' custody
Fight involving a weapon/throwing objects, or conduct causing risk of serious injury	18 weeks' custody	12 weeks' custody–Crown Court

Offence seriousness (culpability and harm)	
B. Consider the effect of aggravating and mitigating factors (other than those within examples in the preceding table)	
the following may be particularly relevant but these lists are not exhaustive	
Factors indicating higher culpability	**Factors indicating lower culpability**
1. Group action	1. Did not start the trouble
2. Threats	2. Provocation
3. Lengthy incident	3. Stopped as soon as police arrived
Factors indicating greater degree of harm	
1. Vulnerable person(s) present	
2. Injuries caused	
3. Damage to property	

C11.1.2 Key points

- Section 6 provides that a threat cannot be made by the use of words alone.
- Affray may be committed in private as well as in public places. However, the fact that a third party could not be present may enable the court to hold that a hypothetical bystander would have viewed the threat as being restricted to the parties involved due to the turbulence of their relationship (*Leeson v Director of Public Prosecutions* [2010] EWHC 994 (Admin) where a conviction was quashed where L, who was drunk, had threatened a person with a knife in the bathroom of a private dwelling).

- In *R v Sanchez* (1996) 160 JP 321, the court approved the following academic commentary:

> The offence of affray envisages at least three persons:(i) the person using or threatening unlawful violence; (ii) a person towards whom the violence or threat is directed; and (iii) a person of reasonable firmness who need not actually be, or be likely to be, present at the scene.

- The definition of 'affray' is very wide, and in *Sanchez* the court agreed that care has to be taken to avoid extending it so widely that it would cover every common assault:

> A common assault may be very trivial, so that it would not cause anyone to fear for his 'personal safety'. But where the assault threatens serious harm to the victim, there may be evidence of affray depending on the circumstances. The person of reasonable firmness present in a small room as in the present case might fear for his personal safety whereas the same person, observing the same conduct in an open space, would not. Thus the question in the present case was not whether a person of reasonable firmness in J's shoes would have feared for his personal safety but whether this hypothetical person, present in the room and seeing D's conduct towards J, would have so feared.
>
> The common law offence which it was intended to replace was, said the Law Commission, 'typically charged in cases of pitched street battles between rival gangs, spontaneous fights in public houses, clubs and at seaside resorts, and revenge attacks on individuals'.

- If a group committed an affray, all taking part in unlawful violence, it was not necessary to attribute particular acts to any individual (*Dragjoshi v Croydon MC* [2017] EWHC 2840 (QB)).
- Reference should also be made to *R v Davison* [1992] Crim LR 31 and *R v Plavecz* [2002] Crim LR 837.
- The fact that a third party who is present does not feel afraid for their own safety is of evidential significance (*R v Blinkhorn* [2006] EWCA Crim 1416).

 See *Blackstone's Criminal Practice 2019* **B11.37–B11.46**

C11.2 Alcohol on coaches and trains

Sporting Events (Control of Alcohol etc) Act 1985, s 1(1)–(5)

1 Offences in connection with alcohol on coaches and trains

(1) This section applies to a vehicle which—
   (a) is a public service vehicle or railway passenger vehicle, and
   (b) is being used for the principal purpose of carrying passengers for the whole or part of a journey to or from a designated sporting event.
(2) A person who knowingly causes or permits alcohol to be carried on a vehicle to which this section applies is guilty of an offence—
   (a) if the vehicle is a public service vehicle and he is the operator of the vehicle or the servant or agent of the operator, or
   (b) if the vehicle is a hired vehicle and he is the person to whom it is hired or the servant or agent of that person.

(3) A person who has alcohol in his possession while on a vehicle to which this section applies is guilty of an offence.

(4) A person who is drunk on a vehicle to which this section applies is guilty of an offence.

(5) In this section 'public service vehicle' and 'operator' have the same meaning as in the Public Passenger Vehicles Act 1981.

SO

 Fine level 4 (s 1(2) offence), 3 months' imprisonment/fine level 3 (s 1(3) offence), fine level 2 (s 1(4) offence)

C11.3 **Begging**

Section 3 Vagrancy Act, as amended by s 70 Criminal Justice Act 1982, provides:

Vagrancy Act, s 3

Every person wandering abroad, or placing himself or herself in any public place, street, highway, court, or passage, to beg or gather alms, or causing or procuring or encouraging any child or children so to do; shall be deemed an idle and disorderly person within the true intent and meaning of this Act; and ... it shall be lawful (to impose a fine).

SO

 Fine level 3

C11.4 **Disorderly behaviour (harassment, alarm, or distress)**

Public Order Act 1986, s 5(1)

5 Harassment, alarm or distress

(1) A person is guilty of an offence if he—
    (a) uses threatening or abusive words or behaviour, or disorderly behaviour, or
    (b) displays any writing, sign or other visible representation which is threatening or abusive,
    within the hearing or sight of a person likely to be caused harassment, alarm or distress thereby.

SO

 Level 3 fine; level 4 fine if racially or religiously aggravated

C11.4.1 *Sentencing*

Note The Sentencing Council has consulted on a new guideline which is likely to come in to force in late 2019/early 2020

Offence seriousness (culpability and harm)		
A. Identify the appropriate starting point		
Starting points based on first-time offender pleading not guilty		
Examples of nature of activity	Starting point	Range
Shouting, causing disturbance for some minutes	Band A fine	Conditional discharge–Band B fine
Substantial disturbance caused	Band B fine	Band A fine–Band C fine

Offence seriousness (culpability and harm)	
B. Consider the effect of aggravating and mitigating factors (other than those within examples in the preceding table)	
The following may be particularly relevant but these lists are not exhaustive	
Factors indicating higher culpability	Factors indicating lower culpability
1. Group action	1. Stopped as soon as police arrived
2. Lengthy incident	2. Brief/minor incident
Factors indicating greater degree of harm	3.Provocation
1. Vulnerable person(s) present	
2. Offence committed at school, hospital, or other place where vulnerable persons may be present	
3. Victim providing public service	

C11.4.2 Key points

Section 5 provides:

Public Order Act 1986, s 5(3)

5 Harassment, alarm or distress

(3) It is a defence for the accused to prove—
  (a) that he had no reason to believe that there was any person within hearing or sight who was likely to be caused harassment, alarm or distress, or
  (b) that he was inside a dwelling and had no reason to believe that the words or behaviour used, or the writing, sign or other visible representation displayed, would be heard or seen by a person outside that or any other dwelling, or
  (c) that his conduct was reasonable.
    • Section 6 provides:

Public Order Act 1986, s 6(4) and (5)

6 Mental element: miscellaneous

(4) A person is guilty of an offence under section 5 only if he intends his words or behaviour, or the writing, sign or other visible representation, to be threatening, abusive or insulting, or is aware that it may be threatening, abusive or insulting or (as the case may be) he intends his behaviour to be or is aware that it may be disorderly.

(5) For the purposes of this section a person whose awareness is impaired by intoxication shall be taken to be aware of that of which he would be aware if not intoxicated, unless he shows either that his intoxication was not self-induced or that it was caused solely by the taking or administration of a substance in the course of medical treatment.

- An offence under s 5 may be committed in a public or a private place, except that no offence is committed where the words or behaviour are used, or the writing, sign, or other visible representation is displayed, by a person inside a dwelling and the other person is also inside that or another dwelling. Subject to particular facts, a dwelling for the purposes of ss 8 and 5(2) does not include a garden to front or rear of a property (*DPP v Distill* [2017] EWHC 2244 (Admin)).
- The offence may be committed against a police officer but they are expected to show a degree of resilience (*Williams v CPS* [2018] EWHC 2869 (Admin) Confirming *DPP v Orum* 1981 1 WLR 88).
- A person can be harassed without emotional upset (*Southard v Director of Public Prosecutions* [2006] EWHC 3449 (Admin)). In *Southard*, the defendant intervened in his brother's arrest, shouting 'fuck off' and 'fuck you' at the officer. The conviction was upheld. The harassment must not, however, be trivial (eg *R (R) v Director of Public Prosecutions* [2006] EWHC 1375 (Admin)—another case involving a police officer where the conviction was quashed).
- *Harvey v DPP* [2011] EWHC 3992 (Admin) confirms that it is not an offence under s 5 Public Order Act to use swear words in the presence of a police officer. The Crown must produce evidence of the likelihood of harassment, alarm, or distress. This cannot be implied for police officers or young people for whom they are a regular feature of life.
- Concealing a video camera in a changing room can amount to disorderly behaviour (*Vigon v Director of Public Prosecutions* (1997) 162 JP 115).
- For considerations under the European Convention on Human Rights (ECHR) (and in particular Art 10 ECHR), see *Abdul and others v Crown Prosecution Service* [2011] EWHC 247 (Admin). The following principles emerge from Article 10 ECHR jurisprudence (para 49 of the judgment):

  (i) The starting point is the importance of the right to freedom of expression.

  (ii) In this regard, it must be recognized that legitimate protest can be offensive at least to some—and on occasions must be, if it is to have impact. Moreover, the right to freedom of expression would be unacceptably devalued if it did no more than protect those holding popular, mainstream views; it must plainly extend beyond that so that minority views can be freely expressed, even if distasteful. [The context of the remarks is a key factor.]

(iii) The justification for interference with the right to freedom of expression must be convincingly established. Accordingly, while Article 10 does not confer an unqualified right to freedom of expression, the restrictions contained in Article 10.2 are to be narrowly construed.

(iv) There is not and cannot be any universal test for resolving when speech goes beyond legitimate protest, so attracting the sanction of the criminal law. The justification for invoking the criminal law is the threat to public order. Inevitably, the context of the particular occasion will be of the first importance.

(v) The relevance of the threat to public order should not be taken as meaning that the risk of violence by those reacting to the protest is, without more, determinative; sometimes it may be that protesters are to be protected. That said, in striking the right balance when determining whether speech is 'threatening, abusive or insulting', the focus on minority rights should not result in overlooking the rights of the majority.

(vi) Even if there is otherwise a prima facie case for contending that an offence has been committed under s 5, it is still for the Crown to establish that prosecution is a proportionate response, necessary for the preservation of public order.

If the line between legitimate freedom of expression and a threat to public order has indeed been crossed, freedom of speech will not have been impaired by 'ruling ... out' threatening, abusive, or insulting speech. Thus a decision to discontinue a s 5 prosecution was not irrational where there was no risk of public disorder and the language was intemperate and offensive. That did not make it abusive under s 5 when read with Art 10 ECHR (*C A A v DPP* [2019[EWHC 9 (Admin))

 See *Blackstone's Criminal Practice 2019* **B11.68–B11.82**

C11.5 **Disorderly behaviour with intent to cause harassment, alarm, or distress**

Public Order Act 1986, s 4A(1)

4A Intentional harassment, alarm or distress

(1) A person is guilty of an offence if, with intent to cause a person harassment, alarm or distress, he—

  (a) uses threatening, abusive or insulting words or behaviour, or disorderly behaviour, or

  (b) displays any writing, sign or other visible representation which is threatening, abusive or insulting,

thereby causing that or another person harassment, alarm or distress.

SO

6 months' imprisonment and/or fine

Note: Racially or religiously aggravated offence is triable either way (2 years on indictment, and the offence then becomes a specified offence for the purposes of the dangerous offender provisions)

C11.5.1 *Sentencing*

Note The Sentencing Council has consulted on a new guideline which is likely to come in to force in late 2019/ early 2020

Offence seriousness (culpability and harm)		
A. Identify the appropriate starting point		
Starting points based on first-time offender pleading not guilty		
Examples of nature of activity	**Starting point**	**Range**
Threats, abuse, or insults made more than once but on same occasion against the same person, eg.while following down the street	Band C fine	Band B fine–low-level community order
Group action or deliberately planned action against targeted victim	Medium-level community order	Low-level community order–12 weeks' custody
Weapon brandished or used or threats against vulnerable victim—course of conduct over longer period	12 weeks' custody	High-level community order–26 weeks' custody

Offence seriousness (culpability and harm)	
B. Consider the effect of aggravating and mitigating factors (other than those within examples in the preceding table)	
The following may be particularly relevant but these lists are not exhaustive	
Factors indicating higher culpability	**Factors indicating lower culpability**
1. High degree of planning	1. Very short period
2. Offender deliberately isolates victim	2. Provocation
Factors indicating greater degree of harm	
1. Offence committed in vicinity of victim's home	
2. Large number of people in vicinity	
3. Actual or potential escalation into violence	
4. Particularly serious impact on victim	

C11.5.2 Key points

Section 4A(3) provides:

Public Order Act 1986, s 4A(3)

4A Intentional harassment, alarm or distress

(3) It is a defence for the accused to prove—
   (a) that he was inside a dwelling and had no reason to believe that the words or behaviour used, or the writing, sign or other visible representation displayed, would be heard or seen by a person outside that or any other dwelling, or
   (b) that his conduct was reasonable.

- An offence under this section may be committed in a public or a private place, except that no offence is committed where the words or behaviour are used, or the writing, sign, or other visible representation is displayed, by a person inside a dwelling and the person who is harassed, alarmed, or distressed is also inside that or another dwelling.
- For considerations under the ECHR (and in particular Art 10 ECHR), see *Abdul and others v Crown Prosecution Service* [2011] EWHC 247 (Admin).

 See *Blackstone's Criminal Practice 2019* **B11.60–11.68**

C11.6 Drunk and disorderly in a public place

Criminal Justice Act 1967, s 91(1), (2), and (4)

91 Drunkenness in a public place

(1) Any person who in any public place is guilty, while drunk, of disorderly behaviour… shall be liable on summary conviction to a fine not exceeding [level 3 on the standard scale].
(2) The foregoing subsection shall have effect instead of any corresponding provision contained in section 12 of the Licensing Act 1872, section 58 of the Metropolitan Police Act 1839, section 37 of the City of London Police Act 1839, and section 29 of the Town Police Clauses Act 1847 (being enactments which authorise the imposition of a short term of imprisonment or of a fine not exceeding £10 or both for the corresponding offence) and instead of any corresponding provision contained in any local Act.
(3) …
(4) In this section 'public place' includes any highway and any other premises or place to which at the material time the public have or are permitted to have access, whether on payment or otherwise.

SO Level 3 fine

SO Summary only

C11.6.1 *Sentencing*

Criminal Justice Act 1967, s 91

Triable only summarily

Maximum: Level 3 fine

Offence range: Conditional discharge–Band C fine

STEPS ONE AND TWO: Determining the offence seriousness

The starting point applies to all offenders irrespective of plea or previous convictions.

Starting point	Range
Band A fine	Conditional discharge–Band C fine

The court should then consider adjustment for any aggravating or mitigating factors. The following is a **non-exhaustive** list of additional factual elements providing the context of the offence and factors relating to the offender. Identify whether any combination of these, or other relevant factors, should result in an upward or downward adjustment from the sentence arrived at so far.

Factors increasing seriousness	Factors reducing seriousness or reflecting personal mitigation
Statutory aggravating factors: • Previous convictions, having regard to (a) the nature of the offence to which the conviction relates and its relevance to the current offence; and (b) the time that has elapsed since the conviction • Offence committed while on bail • Offence motivated by, or demonstrating hostility based on any of the following characteristics or presumed characteristics of the victim: religion, race, disability, sexual orientation, or transgender identity **Other aggravating factors:** • Substantial disturbance caused • Offence ties up disproportionate police resource • Disregard of earlier warning regarding conduct • Failure to comply with current court orders • Offence committed on licence or post sentence supervision • Location of the offence • Timing of the offence • Offence committed against those working in the public sector or providing a service to the public • Presence of others including, especially children or vulnerable people	• Minimal disturbance caused • No previous convictions **or** no relevant/recent convictions • Remorse • Good character and/or exemplary conduct • Age and/or lack of maturity where it affects the responsibility of the offender

C11.6.2 Key points

• In *Carroll v Director of Public Prosecutions* [2009] EWHC 554 (Admin), the court stated that:

> 4. The offence requires proof of three elements, namely that (1) the defendant was drunk; (2) he was in a public place; and (3) he was guilty of disorderly behaviour. Only the first and third elements call for further comment:

...

9. As to the first element in *Neale v E (A Minor)* (1983) 80 Crim App R 20, this court (Robert Goff LJ and Mann J, as they each then were) decided that the word 'drunk' should be given its ordinary and natural meaning. In the end, therefore, whether a defendant was drunk is a simple question of fact in each case. On familiar principles it is the voluntary consumption of alcohol which is the requisite *mens rea*, such as it is, of this most basic offence. If that voluntary consumption results in the defendant becoming drunk then the first element of the offence is proved.

10. As to the third element, there is no requirement for *mens rea* at all. What is required is proof that objectively viewed the defendant was guilty of disorderly behaviour. Specific drunken intent and recklessness are nothing to the point. The words 'disorderly behaviour' are again to be given their ordinary and natural meaning. In the end, therefore, it is a simple question of fact in each case: whether the defendant is guilty of disorderly behaviour.

 See *Blackstone's Criminal Practice 2019* **B11.201–B11.205**

C11.7 Football-related offences

Section 2 Sporting Events (Control of Alcohol etc) Act 1985 concerns possession of alcohol while entering or trying to enter a designated sports ground (s 2(1)), and being drunk in, or while trying to enter, a sports ground (s 2(2)); the Football Offences Act 1991 covers throwing of missiles (s 2), indecent or racialist chanting (s 3), and going onto prohibited areas (s 4); and the Criminal Justice and Public Order Act 1994 deals with the unauthorized sale or attempted sale of tickets (s 166).

Sporting Events (Control of Alcohol etc) Act 1985, s 2(1), (1A), (2), and (3)

2 Offences in connection with alcohol, containers etc at sports grounds

(1) A person who has alcohol or an article to which this section applies in his possession—

    (a) at any time during the period of a designated sporting event when he is in any area of a designated sports ground from which the event may be directly viewed, or

    (b) while entering or trying to enter a designated sports ground at any time during the period of a designated sporting event at that ground, is guilty of an offence.

(1A) Subsection (1)(a) above has effect subject to section 5A(1) of this Act.

(2) A person who is drunk in a designated sports ground at any time during the period of a designated sporting event at that ground or is drunk while entering or trying to enter such a ground at any time during the period of a designated sporting event at that ground is guilty of an offence.

(3) This section applies to any article capable of causing injury to a person struck by it, being—

    (a) a bottle, can or other portable container (including such an article when crushed or broken) which—

      (i) is for holding any drink, and

      (ii) is of a kind which, when empty, is normally discarded or returned to, or left to be recovered by, the supplier, or

(b) part of an article falling within paragraph (a) above; but does not apply to anything that is for holding any medicinal product (within the meaning of the Medicines Act 1968) or any veterinary medicinal product (within the meaning of the Veterinary Medicines Regulations 2006).

Football Offences Act 1991, ss 2, 3, and 4

2 Throwing of missiles

It is an offence for a person at a designated football match to throw anything at or towards—

(a) the playing area, or any area adjacent to the playing area to which spectators are not generally admitted, or
(b) any area in which spectators or other persons are or may be present, without lawful authority or lawful excuse (which shall be for him to prove).

3 Indecent or racialist chanting

(1) It is an offence to engage or take part in chanting of an indecent or racialist nature at a designated football match.
(2) For this purpose—

(a) 'chanting' means the repeated uttering of any words or sounds (whether alone or in concert with one or more others); and
(b) 'of a racialist nature' means consisting of or including matter which is threatening, abusive or insulting to a person by reason of his colour, race, nationality (including citizenship) or ethnic or national origins.

4 Going onto the playing area

It is an offence for a person at a designated football match to go onto the playing area, or any area adjacent to the playing area to which spectators are not generally admitted, without lawful authority or lawful excuse (which shall be for him to prove).

Criminal Justice and Public Order Act 1994, s 166

166 Sale of tickets by unauthorised persons

(1) It is an offence for an unauthorised person to—
(a) sell a ticket for a designated football match, or
(b) otherwise to dispose of such a ticket to another person.
(2) For this purpose—
(a) a person is 'unauthorised' unless he is authorised in writing to sell or otherwise dispose of tickets for the match by the organisers of the match;
(aa) a reference to selling a ticket includes a reference to—
(i) offering to sell a ticket;
(ii) exposing a ticket for sale;
(iii) making a ticket available for sale by another;
(iv) advertising that a ticket is available for purchase; and
(v) giving a ticket to a person who pays or agrees to pay for some other goods or services or offering to do so.
(b) a 'ticket' means anything which purports to be a ticket;
. . .

3 months' imprisonment/level 3 fine (s 2(1) Sporting Events (Control of Alcohol etc) Act 1985 offence), level 2 fine (s 2(2) offence)

Level 3 fine (throwing missile; indecent or racialist chanting; going onto prohibited areas)

Fine (unauthorised sale of tickets) s 166 Criminal Justice and Public Order Act 1994

C11.7.1 *Sentencing*

STEP ONE: Determining the offence category

The court should determine the offence category using the following table.

Category 1	Higher culpability **and** greater harm
Category 2	Higher culpability **and** lesser harm **or** lower culpability **and** greater harm
Category 3	Lower culpability **and** lesser harm

The court should determine the offender's culpability and the harm caused with reference **only** to the following factors. Where an offence does not fall squarely into a category, individual factors may require a degree of weighting before making an overall assessment and determining the appropriate offence category.

CULPABILITY demonstrated by one or more of the following:
Factors indicating higher culpability
• Deliberate or flagrant action • Disregard of warnings • Commercial operation • Inciting others • (Possession of) large quantity of alcohol • Targeted abuse
Factors indicating lower culpability
• All other cases

HARM demonstrated by one or more of the following:
Factors indicating greater harm
• Distress or alarm caused • Actual injury or risk of injury • Significant financial loss to others
Factors indicating lesser harm
• All other cases

STEP TWO: Starting point and category range

Having determined the category at step one, the court should use the starting point to reach a sentence within the appropriate category range in the following table. The starting point applies to all offenders irrespective of plea or previous convictions.

Offence category	Starting point	Range
Category 1	Band C fine	Band C fine
Category 2	Band B fine	Band A fine–Band C fine
Category 3	Band A fine	Conditional discharge–Band B fine

Possession of alcohol only

Offence Category	Starting Point	Range
Category 1	Band C fine	Band C fine–High-level community order
Category 2	Band B fine	Band A fine–Band C fine
Category 3	Band A fine	Conditional discharge–Band B fine

The court should then consider adjustment for any aggravating or mitigating factors. The following is a **non-exhaustive** list of additional factual elements providing the context of the offence and factors relating to the offender. Identify whether any combination of these, or other relevant factors, should result in an upward or downward adjustment from the sentence arrived at so far.

Factors increasing seriousness	Factors reducing seriousness or reflecting personal mitigation
Statutory aggravating factors: • Previous convictions, having regard to (a) the nature of the offence to which the conviction relates and its relevance to the current offence; and (b) the time that has elapsed since the conviction • Offence committed while on bail • Offence motivated by, or demonstrating hostility based on any of the following characteristics or presumed characteristics of the owner/keeper of the animal: religion, race, disability, sexual orientation, or transgender identity **Other aggravating factors:** • Presence of children • Offence committed on licence or post-sentence supervision	• Remorse • Admissions to police in interview • Ready co-operation with authorities • Minimal disturbance caused • No previous convictions **or** no relevant/recent convictions • Good character and/or exemplary conduct • Age and/or lack of maturity where it affects the responsibility of the offender

 See *Blackstone's Criminal Practice 2019* **B11.129–B11.132** and **B11.211–B11.215**

C11.8 Threatening behaviour, fear, or provocation of violence

Public Order Act 1986, ss 4(1), 6(3) and (5)

4 Fear or provocation of violence

(1) A person is guilty of an offence if he—
  (a) uses towards another person threatening, abusive or insulting words or behaviour, or
  (b) distributes or displays to another person any writing, sign or other visible representation which is threatening, abusive or insulting,

with intent to cause that person to believe that immediate unlawful violence will be used against him or another by any person, or to provoke the immediate use of unlawful violence by that person or another, or whereby that person is likely to believe that such violence will be used or it is likely that such violence will be provoked.

...

6 Mental element: miscellaneous

(3) A person is guilty of an offence under section 4 only if he intends his words or behaviour, or the writing, sign or other visible representation, to be threatening, abusive or insulting, or is aware that it may be threatening, abusive or insulting.

...

(5) For the purposes of this section a person whose awareness is impaired by intoxication shall be taken to be aware of that of which he would be aware if not intoxicated, unless he shows either that his intoxication was not self-induced or that it was caused solely by the taking or administration of a substance in the course of medical treatment.

SO (Racially or religiously aggravated offence is triable either way)

▓ 6 months' imprisonment and/or fine. Racially or religiously aggravated offence carries a maximum 2 years' imprisonment on indictment and the offence then becomes a specified offence for the purposes of the dangerous offender provisions

C11.8.1 *Sentencing*

Note The Sentencing Council has consulted on a new guideline which is likely to come in to force in late 2019/ early 2020

Offence seriousness (culpability and harm)		
A. Identify the appropriate starting point		
Starting points based on first-time offender pleading not guilty		
Examples of nature of activity	**Starting point**	**Range**
Fear or threat of low-level immediate unlawful violence such as push, shove, or spit	Low-level community order	Band B fine–medium-level community order
Fear or threat of medium-level immediate unlawful violence such as punch	High-level community order	Low-level community order–12 weeks' custody
Fear or threat of high-level immediate unlawful violence such as use of weapon; missile thrown; gang involvement	12 weeks' custody	6–26 weeks' custody

Offence seriousness (culpability and harm)	
B. Consider the effect of aggravating and mitigating factors (other than those within examples above)	
The following may be particularly relevant but these lists are not exhaustive	
Factors indicating higher culpability	**Factors indicating lower culpability**
1. Planning	1. Impulsive action
2. Offender deliberately isolates victim	2. Short duration
3. Group action	3. Provocation
4. Threat directed at victim because of job	
5. History of antagonism towards victim	
Factors indicating greater degree of harm	
1. Offence committed at school, hospital, or other place where vulnerable persons may be present	
2. Offence committed on enclosed premises such as public transport	
3. Vulnerable victim(s)	
4. Victim needs medical help/counselling	

C11.8.2 Key points

- An offence under s 4 may be committed in a public or a private place, except that no offence is committed where the words or behaviour are used, or the writing, sign, or other visible representation is distributed or displayed, by a person inside a dwelling and the other person is also inside that or another dwelling.

- Subject to the Crown proving the use of threatening, etc words/behaviour and the *mens rea, Winn v DPP* (1992) 156 JP 881 confirmed that there are four ways in which the offence can be committed:
  - by intending to cause the person against whom the conduct is directed to believe that immediate unlawful violence will be used against him or another;
  - by intending to provoke the immediate use of unlawful violence by that person or another;
  - the person against whom the conduct is directed being likely to believe that immediate unlawful violence will be used; or
  - its being likely that immediate unlawful violence will be provoked.
- Actions taken in self-defence do not amount to unlawful violence.
- For the conduct to be used towards another, that other must be physically present (*Atkin v DPP* (1989) 89 Cr App R 199).
- The need for immediate unlawful violence means that it cannot be at some uncertain future time (*Horseferry Road Stipendiary Magistrate, ex p Siadatan* [1991] 1 QB 260), but it does not mean that it has to be instantaneous.
- For considerations under the European Convention on Human Rights (and in particular Art 10 ECHR), see *Abdul and others v Crown Prosecution Service* [2011] EWHC 247 (Admin).

 See *Blackstone's Criminal Practice 2019* **B11.47–B11.59**

C11.9 Taxi touting/soliciting for hire

Criminal Justice and Public Order Act 1994, s 167

 SO

 Sentence level 4 fine

C11.10.1 *Sentencing*

STEP ONE: Determining the offence category

The cCourt should determine the offence category using the following table.

Category 1	Higher culpability **and** greater harm
Category 2	Higher culpability **and** lesser harm **or** lower culpability **and** greater harm
Category 3	Lower culpability **and** lesser harm

The court should determine the offender's culpability and the harm caused with reference **only** to the following factors. Where an offence does not fall squarely into a category, individual factors may require a degree of weighting before making an overall assessment and determining the appropriate offence category.

CULPABILITY demonstrated by one or more of the following:
Factors indicating higher culpability
• Targeting of vulnerable/unsuspecting victim(s) (including tourists) • Commercial business/large scale operation • Offender not licensed to drive • Positive step(s) taken to deceive
Factors indicating lower culpability
• All other cases

HARM demonstrated by one or more of the following:
Factors indicating greater harm
• Passenger safety compromised by vehicle condition • Passenger(s) overcharged
Factors indicating lesser harm
• All other cases

STEP TWO: Starting point and category range

Having determined the category at step one, the court should use the starting point to reach a sentence within the appropriate category range in the following table. The starting point applies to all offenders irrespective of plea or previous convictions.

Offence category	Starting point	Range
Category 1	Band C fine	Band B fine–Band C fine and disqualification 6–12 months
Category 2	Band B fine	Band A fine–Band B fine and consider disqualification 3–6 months
Category 3	Band A fine	Conditional discharge–Band A fine and consider disqualification 1–3 months

Note: Refer to fines for offence committed for 'commercial' purposes.

The court should then consider adjustment for any aggravating or mitigating factors. The following is a **non-exhaustive** list of additional factual elements providing the context of the offence and factors relating to the offender. Identify whether any combination of these, or other relevant factors, should result in an upward or downward adjustment from the sentence arrived at so far.

Factors increasing seriousness	Factors reducing seriousness or reflecting personal mitigation
Statutory aggravating factors: • Previous convictions, having regard to (a) the nature of the offence to which the conviction relates and its relevance to the current offence; and (b) the time that has elapsed since the conviction • Offence committed while on bail • Offence motivated by, or demonstrating hostility based on any of the following characteristics or presumed characteristics of the owner/keeper of the animal: religion, race, disability, sexual orientation, or transgender identity **Other aggravating factors:** • Failure to comply with current court orders • Offence committed on licence or post sentence supervision • PHV licence refused/ineligible	• No previous convictions **or** no relevant/recent convictions • Remorse • Good character and/or exemplary conduct • Mental disorder or learning disability • Sole or primary carer for dependent relatives

C11.9.2 Key points

Touting requires some form of invitation to a prospective hirer (*R (Oddy) v Bugbugs Ltd* [2003] EWHC 2865 (Admin)).

C11.10 Violent disorder

Public Order Act 1986, s 2

(1) Where three or more persons who are present together use or threaten unlawful violence and the conduct of them (taken together) is such as would cause a person of reasonable firmness present at the scene to fear for his personal safety, each of the persons using or threatening unlawful violence is guilty of violent disorder.

(2) It is immaterial whether or not the three or more use or threaten unlawful violence simultaneously.

(3) No person of reasonable firmness need actually be, be likely to be, present at the scene.

(4) Violent disorder may be committed in private as well as in public places.

Public Order Act 1986, s 6

(2) A person is guilty of violent disorder ... only if he intends to use or threatens violence or is aware that his conduct may be violent or threatens violence.

...

(5) A person whose awareness is impaired by intoxication shall be taken to be aware of that of which he would be aware if not intoxicated, unless he shows either that his intoxication was not self-induced or that it was caused solely by the taking or administration of a substance in the course of medical treatment.

6 months/imprisonment and/or a fine; 5 years' imprisonment

C11.10.1 *Sentencing*

Note The Sentencing Council has consulted on a new guideline which is likely to come in to force in late 2019/ early 2020. These offences should normally be dealt with in the Crown Court. However, there may be rare cases involving minor violence or threats of violence leading to no or minor injury, with few people involved and no weapon or missiles, in which a custodial sentence within the jurisdiction of a magistrates' court may be appropriate.

C11.10.2 Key points

- The offence of violent disorder does not require a common purpose and the expression 'present together' means no more than being in the same place at the same time; there is no requirement that there is a degree of cooperation between those who are using or offering violence (*R v NW* [2010] EWCA Crim 404).
- In *Allan v Ireland* (1984) 79 Cr App R 206 the Divisional Court held that a defendant's voluntary presence as part of a crowd engaged in threatening behaviour is capable of raising a prima facie case of participation, but mere voluntary presence is not sufficient to convict a defendant unless the court is satisfied that he at least also gave some overt encouragement to the others who were directly involved in the threatening behaviour. The prosecution must prove that (a) the relevant defendant intended to encourage and did encourage the offence by his presence, and (b) he was aware that his conduct (as opposed to the conduct of the group) might be violent or threatening behaviour (*R v Blackwood* [2002] EWCA Crim 3102).

 See *Blackstone's Criminal Practice 2019* **B11.28–B11.36**

C12 Road Traffic Offences—Definitions

C12.1 Accident

'Accident' is to be given its ordinary meaning (*Chief Constable of West Midlands v Billingham* [1979] 1 WLR 747). A deliberate act can amount to an accident (*Chief Constable of Staffordshire v Lees* [1981] RTR 506). A physical impact is not necessary (*R v Currie* [2007] EWCA Crim 927), but the *de minimis* principle applies (*R v Morris* [1972] 1 WLR 228).

C12.2 Causing

Causing requires a positive act (*Ross Hillman Ltd v Bond* [1974] QB 435) committed with prior knowledge.

C12.3 Driver

Section 192(1) Road Traffic Act 1988 provides:

> **Road Traffic Act 1988, s 192(1)**
>
> **192 General interpretation of Act**
>
> (1)...
>
> > 'driver', where a separate person acts as a steersman of a motor vehicle, includes (except for the purposes of section 1 of this Act) that person as well as any other person engaged in the driving of the vehicle, and 'drive' is to be interpreted accordingly,
>
> ...

A person supervising a driver will not be a driver unless he exercises some control over the vehicle (eg dual controls) (*Evans v Walkden* [1956] 1 WLR 1019).

C12.4 Driving

R v MacDonagh [1974] QB 448 defined 'driving' as use of the driver's controls for the purpose of directing the movement of the vehicle. The court gave the following guidance:

> There are an infinite number of ways in which a person may control the movement of a motor vehicle, apart from the orthodox one of sitting in the driving seat and using the engine for propulsion. He may be coasting down a hill with the gears in neutral and the engine switched off; he may be steering a vehicle which is being towed by another. As has already been pointed out, he may be sitting in the driving seat whilst others push, or half sitting in the driving seat but keeping one foot on the road in order to induce the car to move. Finally, as in the present case, he may be standing in the road and himself pushing the car with or without using the steering wheel to direct it. Although the word 'drive' must be given a wide meaning, the Courts must be alert to see that the net is not thrown so widely that it includes activities which cannot be said to be driving a motor vehicle in any ordinary use of that word in the English language.

As a person may be driving a stationary vehicle, it is a matter of fact to be decided in each case, and factors such as the reason for the vehicle stopping and the duration of the stop will be relevant (*Planton v Director of Public Prosecutions* [2002] RTR 107).

Steering a vehicle being towed would amount to driving where there was an operational braking system (*McQuaid v Anderton* [1981] 1 WLR 154), as would freewheeling a vehicle down a hill while steering (*Saycell v Bool* [1948] 2 All ER 83). A person steering from the passenger seat is driving (*Tyler v Whatmore* [1976] RTR 83).

C12.5 **In charge**

In cases where the matter is not clear, the case of *Director of Public Prosecutions v Watkins* (1989) 89 Cr App R 112 should be considered in detail. The court laid down the following broad guidance:

> Broadly there are two distinct classes of case. (1) If the defendant is the owner or lawful possessor of the vehicle or has recently driven it, he will have been in charge of it, and the question for the Court will be whether he is still in charge or whether he has relinquished his charge. Usually such a defendant will be prima facie in charge unless he has put the vehicle in someone else's charge. However, he would not be so if in all the circumstances he has ceased to be in actual control and there is no realistic possibility of his resuming actual control while unfit: eg if he is at home in bed for the night, if he is a great distance from the car, or if it is taken by another.

> (2) If the defendant is not the owner, the lawful possessor, or recent driver but is sitting in the vehicle or is otherwise involved with it, the question for the Court is, as here, whether he has assumed being in charge of it. In this class of case the defendant will be in charge if, whilst unfit, he is voluntarily in de facto control of the vehicle or if, in the circumstances, including his position, his intentions and his actions, he may be expected imminently to assume control. Usually this will involve his having gained entry to the car and evinced an intention to take control of it. But gaining entry may not be necessary if he has manifested that intention some other way, eg by stealing the keys of a car in circumstances which show he means presently to drive it.

> The circumstances to be taken into account will vary infinitely, but the following will be usually relevant:
> (i) Whether and where he is in the vehicle or how far he is from it.
> (ii) What he is doing at the relevant time.
> (iii) Whether he is in possession of a key that fits the ignition.
> (iv) Whether there is evidence of an intention to take or assert control of the car by driving or otherwise
> (v) Whether any other person is in, at or near the vehicle and if so, the like particulars in respect of that person.

> It will be for the Court to consider all the above factors with any others which may be relevant and reach its decision as a question of fact and degree.

C12.6 **Motor vehicle**

There is no statutory definition of 'vehicle' and therefore its ordinary meaning of a carriage or conveyance should apply. Where the statute uses the phrase 'motor vehicle', the definition to be found in s 185 Road Traffic Act 1988 states that it is a 'mechanically propelled vehicle intended or adapted for use on roads'. The maximum speed of the vehicle is not a relevant factor (*Director of Public Prosecutions v King* [2008] EWHC 447 (Admin)). Section 20(1)(b) Chronically Sick and Disabled Persons Act 1970 means that a mechanically propelled invalid carriage, provided that it complies with the prescribed requirements and is being used in accordance with the prescribed conditions, is not a 'motor vehicle' for all the purposes of the Road Traffic Act 1988 save for the sole and specific exception of s 22A, and is thus excluded from the ambit of the nine sections of the 1988 Act that apply to mechanically propelled vehicles, including offences of driving with excess alcohol (*Croitoru v Crown Prosecution Service* [2016] EWHC 1645 (Admin)).

C12.7 Owner

This includes a person in possession of a vehicle under a hire or hire-purchase agreement.

C12.8 Permitting

A person permits use when he allows or authorizes use, or fails to take reasonable steps to prevent use. For permitting use with no insurance, the prosecution do not need to show that the person knew the driver to be uninsured. If, however, use is conditional (eg on the person having insurance), the outcome would be different (*Newbury v Davis* [1974] RTR 367).

C12.9 Public place

This is a place to which the public have access. However, the law draws a distinction between general public access and access for a defined group of persons. The law in this area is complex and voluminous, and advocates should always seek an adjournment where the answer is not clear. In *Richardson* [2018] EWHC 428 (Admin) the court held that the absence of barriers was not itself enough to make a car park a public place. The majority of the signage suggested otherwise.

C12.10 Road

This is defined as any highway or road to which the public have access. The following have been held to be a road:

- pedestrian pavement (*Randall v Motor Insurers' Bureau* [1968] 1 WLR 1900);
- grass verge at the side of a road (*Worth v Brooks* [1959] Crim LR 855);
- bridges over which a road passes.

It will be a matter of fact and degree as to whether something is a road, and whether or not the public have access. A car park will not generally be a road, even if there are roads running through it. In *Barrett v Director of Public Prosecutions*, 10 February 2009, the court held that a roadway running through a private caravan park, and facilitating entry to a beach, constituted a road.

A vehicle will be 'on' a road when part of the vehicle protrudes over a road (*Avery v Crown Prosecution Service* [2011] EWHC 2388 (Admin)).

C12.11 Highway

This is defined as land over which there is a right of way on foot, by riding, or with vehicles and cattle. A highway includes: bridleways, footpaths, footways, walkways, carriageways, and driftways.

See generally *Blackstone's Criminal Practice 2019* **C1**

C13 Road Traffic Offences

C13.1 Causing death by dangerous driving

Road Traffic Act 1988, s 1

GC

DO

 14 years. Obligatory disqualification for minimum of 2 years. Mandatory retest by way of extended test

IO

C13.1.1 *Sentencing*

Causing death by dangerous driving

Road Traffic Act 1988 (s 1)

Maximum penalty: 14 years' imprisonment minimum disqualification of 2 years with compulsory extended re-test nature of offence	Starting point	Sentencing range
Level 1 The most serious offences encompassing driving that involved a deliberate decision to ignore (or a flagrant disregard for) the rules of the road and an apparent disregard for the great danger being caused to others	8 years' custody	7–14 years' custody
Level 2 Driving that created a *substantial* risk of danger	5 years' custody	4–7 years' custody
Level 3 Driving that created a *significant* risk of danger [*Where the driving is markedly less culpable than for this level, reference should be made to the starting point and range for the most serious level of causing death by careless driving*]	3 years' custody	2–5 years' custody

Additional aggravating factors	Additional mitigating factors
1. Previous convictions for motoring offences, particularly offences that involve bad driving or the consumption of excessive alcohol or drugs before driving 2. More than one person killed as a result of the offence 3. Serious injury to one or more victims, in addition to the death(s) 4. Disregard of warnings 5. Other offences committed at the same time, such as driving other than in accordance with the terms of a valid licence; driving while disqualified; driving without insurance; taking a vehicle without consent; driving a stolen vehicle 6. The offender's irresponsible behaviour such as failing to stop, falsely claiming that one of the victims was responsible for the collision, or trying to throw the victim off the car by swerving in order to escape 7. Driving off in an attempt to avoid detection or apprehension	1. Alcohol or drugs consumed unwittingly 2. Offender was seriously injured in the collision 3. The victim was a close friend or relative 4. Actions of the victim or a third party contributed significantly to the likelihood of a collision occurring and/or death resulting 5. The offender's lack of driving experience contributed to the commission of the offence 6. The driving was in response to a proven and genuine emergency falling short of a defence

C13.1.2 Key points

- One of the tests for dangerous driving as set out in s 2A Road Traffic Act 1988 must be satisfied, producing a causal link to the death. See **C13.6.2**
- CPS policy on prosecuting bad driving can be found on <www.cps.gov.uk>.

See *Blackstone's Criminal Practice 2019* **C3.7**

C13.2 Causing death by careless driving when under the influence of drink or drugs
Road Traffic Act 1988, section 3A

GC

14 years. Obligatory disqualification for minimum of 2 years. Mandatory retest by way of extended test

IO

DO

C13.2.1 *Sentencing*

Road Traffic Act 1988 (s 3A)

Maximum penalty: 14 years' imprisonment;

minimum disqualification of 2 years with compulsory extended re-test

The legal limit of alcohol is 35µg breath (80mg in blood and 107mg in urine)	Careless/ inconsiderate driving arising from momentary inattention with no aggravating factors	Other cases of careless/ inconsiderate driving	Careless/ inconsiderate driving falling not far short of dangerousness
71µ or above of alcohol/ high quantity of drugs OR deliberate non-provision of specimen where evidence of serious impairment	**Starting point:** 6 years' custody Sentencing range: 5–10 years' custody	**Starting point:** 7 years' custody Sentencing range: 6–12 years' custody	**Starting point:** 8 years' custody Sentencing range: 7–14 years' custody
51–70 µg of alcohol/ moderate quantity of drugs OR deliberate non-provision of specimen	**Starting point:** 4 years' custody Sentencing range: 3–7 years' custody	**Starting point:** 5 years' custody Sentencing range: 4–8 years' custody	**Starting point:** 6 years' custody Sentencing range: 5–9 years' custody
35–50 µg of alcohol/ minimum quantity of drugs OR test quantity of drugs OR test refused because of honestly held but unreasonable belief	**Starting point:** 18 months' custody Sentencing range: 26 weeks–4 years' custody	**Starting point:** 3 years' custody Sentencing range: 2–5 years' custody	**Starting point:** 4 years' custody Sentencing range: 3–6 years' custody

Additional aggravating factors	Additional mitigating factors
1. Other offences committed at the same time, such as driving other than in accordance with the terms of a valid licence; driving while disqualified; driving without insurance; taking a vehicle without consent; driving a stolen vehicle 2. Previous convictions for motoring offences, particularly offences that involve bad driving or the consumption of excessive alcohol before driving 3. More than one person was killed as a result of the offence 4. Serious injury to one or more persons in addition to the death(s) 5. Irresponsible behaviour such as failing to stop or falsely claiming that one of the victims was responsible for the collision	1. Alcohol or drugs consumed unwittingly 2. Offender was seriously injured in the collision 3. The victim was a close friend or relative 4. The actions of the victim or a third party contributed significantly to the likelihood of a collision occurring and/or death resulting 5. The driving was in response to a proven and genuine emergency falling short of a defence

C13.2.2 Key points

- The offence can be committed in eight separate ways.
- See **C13.3**, **C13.8**, and **C13.10** for details of constituent offences.

C13.3 Careless driving (drive without due care and attention)

Road Traffic Act 1988, s 3

3 Careless, and inconsiderate, driving

If a person drives a mechanically propelled vehicle on a road or other public place without due care and attention, or without reasonable consideration for other persons using the road or place, he is guilty of an offence.

Fine. Must endorse and may disqualify. If no disqualification, impose 3–9 points

C13.3.1 *Sentencing*

Maximum: Unlimited fine
Offence range: Band A fine–Band C fine

STEP ONE: Determining the offence category

The court should determine the offence category using the following table.

Category 1	Higher culpability **and** greater harm
Category 2	Higher culpability **and** lesser harm **or** lower culpability **and** greater harm
Category 3	Lower culpability **and** lesser harm

The court should determine the offender's culpability and the harm caused with reference only to the following factors. Where an offence does not fall squarely into a category, individual factors may require a degree of weighting before making an overall assessment and determining the appropriate offence category.

CULPABILITY demonstrated by one or more of the following:	
Factors indicating higher culpability	Factors indicating lower culpability
• Excessive speed or aggressive driving • Carrying out other tasks while driving • Vehicle used for the carriage of heavy goods or for the carriage of passengers for reward • Tiredness or driving while unwell • Driving contrary to medical advice (including written advice from the drug manufacturer not to drive when taking any medicine)	• All other cases

HARM demonstrated by one or more of the following:	
Factors indicating greater harm	Factors indicating lesser harm
• Injury to others • Damage to other vehicles or property • High level of traffic or pedestrians in vicinity	• All other cases

STEP TWO: Starting point and category range

Having determined the category at step one, the court should use the appropriate starting point to reach a sentence within the category range in the following table. The starting point applies to all offenders irrespective of plea or previous convictions.

Level of seriousness	Starting point	Range	Disqualification/ points
Category 1	Band C fine	Band C fine	Consider disqualification OR 7–9 points
Category 2	Band B fine	Band B fine	5–6 points
Category 3	Band A fine	Band A fine	3–4 points

 Must endorse and may disqualify. If no disqualification impose 3–9 points

The court should then consider further adjustment for any aggravating or mitigating factors. The following is a **non-exhaustive** list of additional factual elements providing the context of the offence and factors relating to the offender. Identify whether any combination of these, or other relevant factors, should result in an upward or downward adjustment from the sentence arrived at so far.

Factors increasing seriousness	
Statutory aggravating factors:	*Other aggravating factors:*
• Previous convictions, having regard to (a) the nature of the offence to which the conviction relates and its relevance to the current offence; and (b) the time that has elapsed since the conviction • Offence committed while on bail	• Failure to comply with current court orders • Offence committed on licence or post sentence supervision • Contravening a red signal at a level crossing
Factors reducing seriousness or reflecting personal mitigation	
• No previous convictions **or** no relevant/recent convictions • Remorse • Good character and/or exemplary conduct	

C13.3.2 Key points

• Careless driving is defined in the Act.

Section 3ZA(2)–(4) Road Traffic Act 1988 provides:

Road Traffic Act 1988, s 3ZA(2)–(4)

3ZA Meaning of careless, or inconsiderate, driving

...

(2) A person is to be regarded as driving without due care and attention if (and only if) the way he drives falls below what would be expected of a competent and careful driver.

(3) In determining for the purposes of subsection (2) above what would be expected of a careful and competent driver in a particular case, regard shall be had not only to the circumstances of which he could be expected to be aware but also to any circumstances shown to have been within the knowledge of the accused.

(4) A person is to be regarded as driving without reasonable consideration for other persons only if those persons are inconvenienced by his driving.

• Examples of careless or inconsiderate driving:

Careless driving

• overtaking on the inside or driving inappropriately close to another vehicle;
• inadvertent mistakes, such as driving through a red light or emerging from a side road into the path of another vehicle;
• short distractions such as tuning a car radio.

Inconsiderate driving

• flashing of lights to force other drivers in front to give way;
• misuse of any lane to avoid queuing or to gain some other advantage over other drivers;

- driving that inconveniences other road users or causes unnecessary hazards, such as unnecessarily remaining in an overtaking lane, unnecessarily slow driving or braking without good cause, driving with undipped headlights which dazzle oncoming drivers, or driving through a puddle causing pedestrians to be splashed.
- If death has resulted from the driving, any trial should await the conclusion of any inquest (*Smith v Director of Public Prosecutions* [2000] RTR 36).
- Failure to drive in accordance with the Highway Code will generally amount to careless driving.
- An offence of careless driving can be tried alongside an offence of dangerous driving as an alternative. However, it is not clear as to why this is done in the magistrates' court, as the offence is a statutory alternative in any event.
- If the facts are such that in the absence of an explanation put forward by the defendant, or where that explanation is objectively inadequate, the only possible conclusion is that he was careless, he should be convicted (*Director of Public Prosecutions v Cox* (1993) 157 JP 1044).
- A court does not need to consider an alternative inference from facts, such as mechanical defect, without hearing evidence of the same (*Director of Public Prosecutions v Tipton* (1992) 156 JP 172).

 See *Blackstone's Criminal Practice 2019* **C6.1–C6.8**

C13.4 Causing death by disqualified, careless, unlicensed, or uninsured driving

Road Traffic Act 1988, ss 2B, 3ZB, and 3ZC

Causing death by:
- disqualified driving;
- careless or inconsiderate driving;
- unlicensed, or uninsured drivers.

EW but causing death by disqualified driving is triable only on indictment;

Causing death by disqualified driving: 6 months' imprisonment and/or fine/10 years' imprisonment
- Causing death by careless, etc driving: 6 months' imprisonment and/or a fine/5 years' imprisonment;
- Causing death by unlicensed or uninsured driving: 6 months' imprisonment and/or fine/2 years' imprisonment;
- Minimum disqualification of 12 months, discretionary retest, 3–11 penalty points.

C13.4.1 *Sentencing*

Death by careless or inconsiderate driving

Nature of offence	Starting point	Sentencing range
Careless or inconsiderate driving falling not far short of dangerous driving	15 months' custody	36 weeks–3 years' custody
Other cases of careless or inconsiderate driving	36 weeks' custody	Community order (HIGH)–2 years' custody
Careless or inconsiderate driving arising from momentary inattention with no aggravating factors	Community order (MEDIUM)	Community order (LOW)–community order (HIGH)

Additional aggravating factors	Additional mitigating factors
1. Other offences committed at the same time, such as driving other than in accordance with the terms of a valid licence; driving while disqualified; driving without insurance; taking a vehicle without consent; driving a stolen vehicle 2. Previous convictions for motoring offences, particularly offences that involve bad driving 3. More than one person was killed as a result of the offence 4. Serious injury to one or more persons in addition to the death(s) 5. Irresponsible behaviour, such as failing to stop or falsely claiming that one of the victims was responsible for the collision	1. Offender was seriously injured in the collision 2. The victim was a close friend or relative 3. The actions of the victim or a third party contributed to the commission of the offence 4. The offender's lack of driving experience contributed significantly to the likelihood of a collision 5. The driving was in response to a proven and genuine emergency falling short of a defence

Causing death by unlicensed, disqualified, or uninsured drivers

Nature of offence	Starting point	Sentencing range
The offender was disqualified from driving; OR	12 months'	36 weeks–2 years'
The offender was unlicensed or uninsured plus two or more aggravating factors from the list below	custody	custody
The offender was unlicensed or uninsured plus at least one aggravating factor from the list below	26 weeks' custody	Community order (HIGH)–36 weeks' custody
The offender was unlicensed or uninsured—no aggravating factors	Community order (MEDIUM)	Community order (LOW) to community order (HIGH)

Additional aggravating factors	Additional mitigating factors
1. Previous convictions for motoring offences, whether involving bad driving or involving an offence of the same kind that forms part of the present conviction (ie unlicensed, disqualified, or uninsured driving) 2. More than one person was killed as a result of the offence 3. Serious injury to one or more persons in addition to the death(s) 4. Irresponsible behaviour such as failing to stop or falsely claiming that someone else was driving	1. The decision to drive was brought about by a proven and genuine emergency falling short of a defence 2. The offender genuinely believed that he or she was insured or licensed to drive 3. The offender was seriously injured as a result of the collision 4. The victim was a close friend or relative

C13.4.2 Key points

- Death must result from the act of driving but need not occur at the same time as the incident (*R v Jenkins* [2012] EWCA Crim 2909; dangerous parking).
- The driving must be more than a minimal cause of the death.
- Where the driver is faultless and the total responsibility for the death lies with the deceased, no offence is committed under s 3ZB (*R v Hughes* [2013] UKSC 56). *R v MH* [2011] EWCA Crim 1508 suggests it is open to the defence to argue that the defendant's contribution to the death was no more than minimal where, for example, in a stationary car or where the victim would have died anyway, say, because of a new act intervening.

 See *Blackstone's Criminal Practice 2019* **C3**

C13.5 Causing serious injury by dangerous driving or by disqualified driving

Road Traffic Act 1988, s 1A

1A Causing serious injury by dangerous driving

(1) A person who causes serious injury to another person by driving a mechanically pro-pelled vehicle dangerously on a road or other public place is guilty of an offence.

(2) In this section 'serious injury' means—

    (a) in England and Wales, physical harm which amounts to grievous bodily harm for the purposes of the Offences against the Person Act 1861,

    (b) ...

C13.5.1 *Causing serious injury by disqualified driving*

Road Traffic Act 1988, s 3ZD

(1) A person is guilty of an offence under this section if he or she—
    (a) causes serious injury to another person by driving a motor vehicle on a road, and
    (b) at that time, is committing an offence under section 103(1)(b) of this Act (driving while disqualified).

(2) In this section 'serious injury' means—

    (a) in England and Wales, physical harm which amounts to grievous bodily harm for the purposes of the Offences against the Person Act 1861.

EW

- Dangerous driving: 6 months' imprisonment and/or fine/5 years' imprisonment
- Disqualified driving: 6 months' imprisonment and/or fine/4 years' imprisonment

Obligatory disqualification for 12 months (with obligatory retest if dangerous driving). If no disqualification then 3–11 penalty points

C13.5.2 Key points

- Dangerous driving is defined by s 2A Road Traffic Act 1988. See **C13.6.2**.
- There is no specific sentencing guideline, but there have been decisions where there have been convictions under s 20 Offences Against the Person Act 1861.

 See *Blackstone's Criminal Practice 2019* **C3.55**

C13.6 **Dangerous driving**

> **Road Traffic Act 1988, s 2**
>
> **2 Dangerous driving**
>
> A person who drives a mechanically propelled vehicle dangerously on a road or other public place is guilty of an offence.

EW

 6 months' imprisonment and/or fine/2 years' imprisonment. Must endorse and disqualify for a minimum period of 12 months; must order extended retest; must disqualify for at least 2 years if offender has had two or more disqualifications for periods of 56 days or more in preceding 3 years

C13.6.1 *Sentencing*

Offence seriousness (culpability and harm) A. Identify the appropriate starting point Starting points based on first-time offender pleading not guilty		
Example of nature of activity	**Starting point**	**Range**
Single incident where little or no damage or risk of personal injury	Medium-level community order	Low-level community order–high-level community order Disqualify 12–15 months
Incident(s) involving excessive speed or showing off, especially on busy roads or in built-up area; OR	12 weeks' custody	High-level community order–26 weeks' custody
Single incident where little or no damage or risk of personal injury but offender was disqualified driver		Disqualify 15–24 months

Prolonged bad driving involving deliberate disregard for safety of others; OR Incident(s) involving excessive speed or showing off, especially on busy roads or in built-up area, by disqualified driver; OR Driving as described in box above while being pursued by police	Crown Court	Crown Court

Offence seriousness (culpability and harm)
B. Consider the effect of aggravating and mitigating factors (other than those within examplesin the preceding table)
The following may be particularly relevant but these lists are not exhaustive

Factors indicating higher culpability	Factors indicating lower culpability
1. Disregarding warnings of others 2. Evidence of alcohol or drugs 3. Carrying out other tasks while driving 4. Carrying passengers or heavy load 5. Tiredness 6. Aggressive driving, such as driving much too close to vehicle in front, racing, inappropriate attempts to overtake, or cutting in after overtaking 7. Driving when knowingly suffering from a medical condition which significantly impairs the offender's driving skills 8. Driving a poorly maintained or dangerously loaded vehicle, especially where motivated by commercial concerns **Factors indicating greater degree of harm** 1. Injury to others 2. Damage to other vehicles or property	1. Genuine emergency 2. Speed not excessive 3. Offence due to inexperience rather than irresponsibility of driver

C13.6.2 Key points

• Section 2A Road Traffic Act 1988 provides:

Road Traffic Act 1988, s 2A

2A Meaning of dangerous driving

(1) For the purposes of sections 1 and 2 above a person is to be regarded as driving dangerously if (and, subject to subsection (2) below, only if)—
   (a) the way he drives falls far below what would be expected of a competent and careful driver, and
   (b) it would be obvious to a competent and careful driver that driving in that way would be dangerous.
(2) A person is also to be regarded as driving dangerously for the purposes of sections 1 and 2 above if it would be obvious to a competent and careful driver that driving the vehicle in its current state would be dangerous.
(3) In subsections (1) and (2) above 'dangerous' refers to danger either of injury to any person or of serious damage to property; and in determining for the purposes of those subsections what would be expected of, or obvious to, a competent and

> careful driver in a particular case, regard shall be had not only to the circumstances
> of which he could be expected to be aware but also to any circumstances shown to
> have been within the knowledge of the accused.
>
> (4) In determining for the purposes of subsection (2) above the state of a vehicle, regard
> may be had to anything attached to or carried on or in it and to the manner in which it
> is attached or carried.

- The special skill (or indeed lack of skill) of a driver is an irrelevant circumstance when considering whether the driving is dangerous (*R v Bannister* [2009] EWCA Crim 1571).
- The fact that the defendant had consumed alcohol is an admissible factor (*R v Webster* [2006] 2 Cr App R 103). Where drink is a major plank of the prosecution case, advocates should have regard to *R v McBride* [1962] 2 QB 167.
- Where a vehicle's dangerous state is due to its official design and not use, it will not usually be appropriate to prosecute (*R v Marchant* [2004] 1 All ER 1187).
- A vehicle is being driven in a dangerous state if the driver is aware that his ability to control the vehicle might be impaired such that the standard of his driving might fall below the requisite standard (*R v Marison* [1997] RTR 457).

 See *Blackstone's Criminal Practice 2019* **C3.39**

C13.7 **Driving while disqualified**

Road Traffic Act 1988, s 103(1)

103 Obtaining licence, or driving, while disqualified

(1) A person is guilty of an offence if, while disqualified for holding or obtaining a licence, he—
  (a) obtains a licence, or
  (b) drives a motor vehicle on a road.
  ...

SO

 6 months' imprisonment and/or fine. Must endorse and may disqualify. If no disqualification, impose 6 points

C13.7.1 *Sentencing*

Road Traffic Act 1988, s 103
Triable only summarily
Maximum: Unlimited fine and/or 6 months
Offence range: Band C fine–26 weeks' custody

STEP ONE: Determining the offence category

The court should determine the offence category using the following table.

Category 1	Higher culpability **and** greater harm
Category 2	Higher culpability **and** lesser harm **or** lower culpability **and** greater harm
Category 3	Lower culpability **and** lesser harm

The court should determine the offender's culpability and the harm caused with reference **only** to the following factors. Where an offence does not fall squarely into a category, individual factors may require a degree of weighting before making an overall assessment and determining the appropriate offence category.

CULPABILITY demonstrated by one or more of the following:	
Factors indicating higher culpability	**Factors indicating lower culpability**
• Driving shortly after disqualification imposed • Vehicle obtained during disqualification period • Driving for reward	• All other cases

HARM demonstrated by one or more of the following:	
Factors indicating greater harm	**Factors indicating lesser harm**
• Significant distance driven • Evidence of associated bad driving	• All other cases

STEP TWO: Starting point and category range

Having determined the category at step one, the court should use the appropriate starting point to reach a sentence within the category range in the following table. The starting point applies to all offenders irrespective of plea or previous convictions.

Level of seriousness	Starting point	Range	Penalty points/disqualification
Category 1	12 weeks' custody	High-level community order–26 weeks' custody	Disqualify for 12–18 months beyond expiry of current ban (extend if imposing immediate custody)
Category 2	High-level community order	Medium level community order–12 weeks' custody	Disqualify for 6–12 months beyond expiry of current ban (extend if imposing immediate custody)
Category 3	Low-level community order	Band C fine–medium-level community order	Disqualify for 3–6 months beyond expiry of current ban **OR** 6 points

Must endorse and may disqualify. If no disqualification impose 6 points

Extend disqualification if imposing immediate custody

The court should then consider further adjustment for any aggravating or mitigating factors. The following is a **non-exhaustive** list of additional factual elements providing the context of the offence and factors relating to the offender. Identify whether any combination of these, or other relevant factors, should result in an upward or downward adjustment from the sentence arrived at so far.

Factors increasing seriousness	
Statutory aggravating factors:	*Other aggravating factors:*
• Previous convictions, having regard to (a) the **nature** of the offence to which the conviction relates and its **relevance** to the current offence; and (b) the **time** that has elapsed since the conviction **Note** An offender convicted of this offence will always have at least one relevant previous conviction for the offence that resulted in disqualification. The starting points and ranges take this into account; any other previous convictions should be considered in the usual way. • Offence committed while on bail	• Failure to comply with current court orders (not including the current order for disqualification) • Offence committed on licence or post sentence supervision • Carrying passengers • Giving false details

Factors reducing seriousness or reflecting personal mitigation
• No previous convictions **or** no relevant/recent convictions • Good character and/or exemplary conduct • Remorse • Genuine emergency established • Age and/or lack of maturity where it affects the responsibility of the offender • Serious medical condition requiring urgent, intensive or long-term treatment

C13.7.2 Key points

- The prosecution do not need to prove that the defendant was aware of the prosecution that led to his being disqualified (*Taylor v Kenyon* [1952] 2 All ER 726); this is the case even where a driving licence has been returned to the defendant by mistake (*R v Bowsher* [1972] RTR 202). If the defendant was genuinely unaware of the disqualification and had no reason to anticipate one, prosecution is unlikely and an absolute discharge likely if one proceeds.
- Strict proof that the person disqualified by the court is the person now charged is required. This will normally arise from (a) admission, (b) fingerprints, (c) evidence of identity from someone in court when the disqualification was made (*R v Derwentside Justices, ex p Heaviside* [1996] RTR 384). Other evidence such as an unusual name will at least raise a prima facie case that the defendant will need to answer in order to avoid conviction (*Olakunori v Director of Public Prosecutions* [1998] COD 443).

- An admission made while giving evidence is sufficient to prove a disqualification, even in the absence of a certificate of conviction (*Moran v Crown Prosecution Service* (2000) 164 JP 562).
- A defendant's silence in interview (where he did not later rely on any fact) and his general attitude to the management of the case in accordance with the Criminal Procedure Rules, could not provide sufficient proof (*Mills v Director of Public Prosecutions* [2008] EWHC 3304 (Admin)).
- Consistency of personal details will normally be sufficient to raise a prima facie case. If the defendant calls no evidence to contradict that prima facie case, it will be open to the court to be satisfied that identity is proved (*Pattison v Director of Public Prosecutions* [2006] RTR 13).
- A solicitor could be called as a witness to confirm identity, although the practice is discouraged (*R (Howe) v South Durham Magistrates' Court* [2005] RTR 4).
- A mistaken belief by the defendant that he was not driving on a road will not amount to a defence (*R v Miller* [1975] 1 WLR 1222).
- The fact that a disqualification was later quashed on appeal does not provide a defence (*R v Thames Magistrates' Court, ex p Levy*, The Times, 17 July 1997).
- A bad character application in relation to the disqualification is not necessary as it has to do with the alleged facts of the offence (s 98 Criminal Justice Act 2003) (*Director of Public Prosecutions v Agyemang* [2009] EWHC 1542 (Admin)).

 See *Blackstone's Criminal Practice 2019* **C6.40–C6.45**

C13.8 Excess alcohol/Excess drugs

Road Traffic Act 1988, ss 5(1) and 5A

5 Driving or being in charge of a motor vehicle with alcohol concentration above prescribed limit

(1) If a person—
   (a) drives or attempts to drive a motor vehicle on a road or other public place, or
   (b) is in charge of a motor vehicle on a road or other public place, after consuming so much alcohol that the proportion of it in his breath, blood, or urine exceeds the prescribed limit he is guilty of an offence.
   ...

5A Driving or being in charge of a motor vehicle with concentration of specified controlled drug above specified limit.

(1) This section applies where a person ('D')—
   (a) drives or attempts to drive a motor vehicle on a road or other public place, or
   (b) is in charge of a motor vehicle on a road or other public place, and there is in D's body a specified controlled drug.
(2) D is guilty of an offence if the proportion of the drug in D's blood or urine exceeds the specified limit for that drug.

C13 Road Traffic Offences

The legal limit of alcohol in the body is: 35 micrograms (µg) per 100 millilitres of breath. 80 milligrams (mg) per 100 millilitres of blood. 107 milligrams per 100 millilitres of urine

The specified drugs and limits are:

Illicit drugs	
Benzoylecgonine	50 µg per litre of blood
Cocaine	10 µg per litre of blood
Delta–9–tetrahydrocannabinol (cannabis and cannabinol)	2 µg per litre of blood
Ketamine	20 µg per litre of blood
Lysergic acid diethylamide (LSD)	1 µg per litre of blood
Methylamphetamine	10 µg per litre of blood
Methylenedioxymethaphetamine (MDMA– ecstasy)	10 µg per litre of blood
Monoacetylmorphine (6–MAM– heroin and diamorphine)	5 µg per litre of blood)
Amphetamine	250 µg per litre of blood
General prescription drugs	
Clonazepam	50 µg per litre of blood
Diazepam	550 µg per litre of blood
Flunitrazepam	300 µg per litre of blood
Lorazepam	100 µg per litre of blood
Methadone	500 µg per litre of blood
Morphine	80 µg per litre of blood
Oxazepam	300 µg per litre of blood
Temazepam	1000 µg per litre of blood

- For driving: 6 months' imprisonment and/or fine; obligatory disqualification (see below)
- For being in charge: 3 months' imprisonment and/or level 4 fine; Discretionary disqualification, 10 points

See **C13.16** for offence of being unfit through drink or drugs.

C13.8.1 *Sentencing: driving with excess alcohol*

Road Traffic Act 1988, s 5(1)(a)
Triable only summarily
Maximum: Unlimited fine and/or 6 months
Offence range: Band B fine–26 weeks' custody

STEPS ONE AND TWO: Determining the offence seriousness

- Must endorse and disqualify for at least 12 months
- Must disqualify for at least 2 years if offender has had two or more disqualifications for periods of 56 days or more in preceding 3 years—refer to disqualification guidance and consult your legal adviser for further guidance
- Must disqualify for at least 3 years if offender has been convicted of a relevant offence in preceding 10 years—consult your legal adviser for further guidance
- Extend disqualification if imposing immediate custody If there is a delay in sentencing after conviction, consider interim disqualification

The starting point applies to all offenders irrespective of plea or previous convictions.

Level of alcohol			Starting point	Range	Disqualification	Disqual. 2nd offence in 10 years– see note
Breath (µg)	Blood (mg)	Urine (mg)				
120–150 and above	276–345 and above	367–459 and above	12 weeks' custody	High-level community order– 26 weeks' custody	29–36 months (extend if imposing immediate custody)	36–60 months
90–119	207–275	275–366	Medium-level community order	Low-level community order – High-level community order	23–28 months	36–52 months
60–89	138–206	184–274	Band C fine	Band C fine– Low-level community order	17–22 months	36–46 months
36–59	81–137	108–183	Band C fine	Band B fine– Band C fine	12–16 months	36–40 months

Note: When considering the guidance regarding the length of disqualification in the case of a second offence, the period to be imposed in any individual case will depend on an assessment of all the relevant circumstances, including the length of time since the earlier ban was imposed and the gravity of the current offence but disqualification must be for at least three years.

The court should then consider further adjustment for any aggravating or mitigating factors. The following is a **non-exhaustive** list of additional factual elements providing the context of the offence and factors relating to the offender. Identify whether any combination of these, or other relevant factors, should result in an upward or downward adjustment from the sentence arrived at so far.

Factors increasing seriousness	
Statutory aggravating factors:	*Other aggravating factors:*
• Previous convictions, having regard to (a) the **nature** of the offence to which the conviction relates and its **relevance** to the current offence; and (b) the **time** that has elapsed since the conviction • Offence committed while on bail	• Failure to comply with current court orders • Offence committed on licence or post-sentence supervision • LGV, HGV, PSV etc • Poor road or weather conditions • Carrying passengers • Driving for hire or reward • Evidence of unacceptable standard of driving • Involved in accident • High level of traffic or pedestrians in the vicinity

Factors reducing seriousness or reflecting personal mitigation
• No previous convictions **or** no relevant/recent convictions • Genuine emergency established* • Spiked drinks* • Very short distance driven* • Remorse • Good character and/or exemplary conduct • Serious medical condition requiring urgent, intensive or long-term treatment • Age and/or lack of maturity where it affects the responsibility of the offender • Mental disorder or learning disability • Sole or primary carer for dependent relatives

* even where not amounting to special reasons

C13.8.2 *Sentencing*

Being in charge with excess alcohol

Road Traffic Act 1988, s 5(1)(b)
Triable only summarily
Maximum: Level 4 fine and/or 3 months
Offence range: Band A fine – 6 weeks' custody

STEPS ONE AND TWO: Determining the offence seriousness

• Must endorse and may disqualify. If no disqualification impose 10 points
• Extend any disqualification if imposing immediate custody

The starting point applies to all offenders irrespective of plea or previous convictions.

Level of alcohol			Starting point	Range	Disqualification/Points
Breath (μ	Blood (mg)	Urine (mg)			
120–150 and above	276–345 and above	367–459 and above	Medium-level community order	Low-level community order–6 weeks' custody	Disqualify 6–12 months (extend if imposing immediate custody)

Level of alcohol			Starting point	Range	Disqualification/Points
Breath (μ	Blood (mg)	Urine (mg)			
90–119	207–275	275–366	Band C fine	Band C fine–Medium level community order	Consider disqualification up to 6 months **OR** 10 points
60–89	138–206	184–274	Band B fine	Band B fine–Band C fine	Consider disqualification **OR** 10 points
36–59	81–137	108–183	Band B fine	Band A fine – Band B fine	10 points

The court should then consider further adjustment for any aggravating or mitigating factors. The following is a **non-exhaustive** list of additional factual elements providing the context of the offence and factors relating to the offender. Identify whether any combination of these, or other relevant factors, should result in an upward or downward adjustment from the sentence arrived at so far.

Factors increasing seriousness	
Statutory aggravating factors:	*Other aggravating factors:*
• Previous convictions, having regard to (a) the **nature** of the offence to which the conviction relates and its **relevance** to the current offence; and (b) the **time** that has elapsed since the conviction • Offence committed while on bail	• Failure to comply with current court orders • Offence committed on licence or post-sentence supervision • In charge of LGV, HGV, PSV etc • High likelihood of driving • Offering to drive for hire or reward

Factors reducing seriousness or reflecting personal mitigation
• No previous convictions **or** no relevant/recent convictions • Low likelihood of driving • Spiked drinks* • Remorse • Good character and/or exemplary conduct • Serious medical condition requiring urgent, intensive, or long-term treatment • Age and/or lack of maturity where it affects the responsibility of the offender • Mental disorder or learning disability • Sole or primary carer for dependent relatives

* even where not amounting to special reasons

C13.8.3 *Sentencing: excess drugs*

Drug driving: Sentencing Council guidance

Introduction

The limits for illegal drugs are set in line with a zero tolerance approach but ruling out accidental exposure. The limits for drugs that may be medically prescribed are set in line with a road safety risk-based approach, at levels above the normal concentrations found with therapeutic use. This is different from the approach taken when setting the limit for alcohol, where the limit was set at a level where the effect of the alcohol would be expected to have impaired a person's driving ability. For these reasons it would be wrong to rely on the Driving with Excess Alcohol guideline when sentencing an offence under this legislation.

Guidance only

It is important to note that this guidance does not carry the same authority as a sentencing guideline, and sentencers are not obliged to follow it.

C13.8.3.1 Drug driving guidance

- As a guide, where an offence of driving or attempting to drive has been committed and there are no factors that increase seriousness the cCourt should consider a starting point of a **Band C fine**, and a disqualification in the region of 12–22 months.

The list of factors that increase seriousness appears in the following table. This is an exhaustive list and only factors that appear in the list should be considered.

- Where there are factors that increase seriousness the court should consider increasing the sentence on the basis of the level of seriousness.
- The community order threshold is likely to be crossed where there is evidence of one or more factors that increase seriousness. The court should also consider imposing a disqualification in the region of 23–28 months.
- The custody threshold is likely to be crossed where there is evidence of one or more factors that increase seriousness and one or more aggravating factors (see following table). The court should also consider imposing a disqualification in the region of 29–36 months.
- Having determined a starting point, the court should consider additional factors that may make the offence more or less serious. A non-exhaustive list of aggravating and mitigating factors is set out in the following table.

Factors that increase seriousness (this is an exhaustive list)	
<ul><li>Evidence of another specified drug(1) or of alcohol in the body</li><li>Evidence of an unacceptable standard of driving</li><li>Driving (or in charge of) an LGV, HGV or PSV</li><li>Driving (or in charge of) a vehicle driven for hire or reward</li></ul>	
Aggravating and mitigating factors (these are non-exhaustive lists)	
Aggravating factors	Mitigating factors
<ul><li>Previous convictions having regard to (a) the nature of the offence to which the conviction relates and its relevance to the current offence; and (b) the time that has elapsed since the conviction</li><li>Location e.g. near school</li><li>Carrying passengers</li><li>High level of traffic or pedestrians in the vicinity</li><li>Poor road or weather conditions</li></ul>	<ul><li>No previous convictions or no relevant/recent convictions</li><li>Remorse</li><li>Good character and/or exemplary conduct</li><li>Age and/or lack of maturity where it affects the responsibility of the offender</li><li>Mental disorder or learning disability</li><li>Sole or primary carer for dependent relatives</li><li>Very short distance driven</li><li>Genuine emergency established.</li></ul>

Note: (1) For these purposes, cocaine and benzoylecgonine (BZE) shall be treated as one drug as they both occur in the body as a result of cocaine use rather than poly-drug use. Similarly 6-Monoacteylmorphine and Morphine shall be treated as one drug as they both occur in the body as a result of heroin use. Finally, Diazepam and Temazepam shall be treated as one drug as they also both occur in the body as a result of Temazepam use.

C13.8.3.2 *In charge*

- As a guide, where an offence of being in charge has been committed but there are no factors that increase seriousness the court should consider a starting point of a Band B fine, and endorsing the licence with 10 penalty points. The list of factors that increase seriousness appears in the following table. Please note this is an exhaustive list and only factors that appear in the list should be considered.
- Where there are factors that increase seriousness the court should consider increasing the sentence on the basis of the level of seriousness.
- The community order threshold is likely to be crossed where there is evidence of one or more factors that increase seriousness and one or more aggravating factors (see the following table). The court should also consider imposing a disqualification.
- Where there is evidence of one or more factors that increase seriousness and a greater number of aggravating factors (see the following table) the court may consider it appropriate to impose a short custodial sentence of up to 12 weeks. The court should also consider imposing a disqualification.
- Having determined a starting point, the court should consider additional factors that may make the offence more or less serious. A non-exhaustive list of aggravating and mitigating factors is set out in the following table.

Factors that increase seriousness (this is an exhaustive list)	
<ul><li>Evidence of another specified drug(1) or of alcohol in the body</li><li>Evidence of an unacceptable standard of driving</li><li>Driving (or in charge of) an LGV, HGV or PSV</li><li>Driving (or in charge of) a vehicle driven for hire or reward</li></ul>	

Aggravating and mitigating factors (these are non-exhaustive lists)	
Aggravating factors	*Mitigating factors*
<ul><li>Previous convictions having regard to (a) the nature of the offence to which the conviction relates and its relevance to the current offence; and (b) the time that has elapsed since the conviction</li><li>Location eg near school</li><li>Carrying passengers</li><li>High level of traffic or pedestrians in the vicinity</li><li>Poor road or weather conditions</li></ul>	<ul><li>No previous convictions or no relevant/recent convictions</li><li>Remorse</li><li>Good character and/or exemplary conduct</li><li>Age and/or lack of maturity where it affects the responsibility of the offender</li><li>Mental disorder or learning disability</li><li>Sole or primary carer for dependent relatives</li><li>Very short distance driven</li><li>Genuine emergency established</li></ul>

Note: (1) For these purposes, cocaine and benzoylecgonine (BZE) shall be treated as one drug as they both occur in the body as a result of cocaine use rather than poly-drug use. Similarly 6-Monoacteylmorphine and Morphine shall be treated as one drug as they both occur in the body as a result of heroin use. Finally, Diazepam and Temazepam shall be treated as one drug as they also both occur in the body as a result of Temazepam use.

C13.8.4 Key points

- Where there has been no consumption of alcohol between the incidence of driving and the testing, the alcohol reading is conclusive (s 15(2) Road

Traffic Offenders Act 1988, and *Griffiths v Director of Public Prosecutions* [2002] EWHC 792 (Admin)). However, the presumption in s 15(2) applies only to trials and does not extend to a *Newton* hearing (*Goldsmith v Director of Public Prosecutions* [2009] EWHC 3010 (Admin)).

- Where there is post-driving consumption of alcohol, the defendant is able to 'back calculate' to obtain a reading at the time of driving (s 15(3) Road Traffic Offenders Act 1988). The prosecution are also entitled to rely upon back calculations, but in practice rarely do so (*Gumbley v Cunningham* [1989] RTR 49).
- There will be no prosecution unless the alcohol level is at least 40 microgrammes (Home Office Circular 46/1982); it should be noted that this 'allowance' is already built into any blood or urine analysis.

C13.8.5 *Defences*

- Section 5(2)–(3) provides:

Road Traffic Act 1988, s 5(2)–(3)

5 Driving or being in charge of a motor vehicle with alcohol concentration above prescribed limit

(1) It is a defence for a person charged with an offence under subsection (1)(b) above to prove that at the time he is alleged to have committed the offence the circumstances were such that there was no likelihood of his driving the vehicle whilst the proportion of alcohol in his breath, blood or urine remained likely to exceed the prescribed limit.

(2) The court may, in determining whether there was such a likelihood as is mentioned in subsection (2) above, disregard any injury to him and any damage to the vehicle.

- Section 5A (3)–(7) provides:

Road Traffic Act 1988, s 5A(3)–(7)

(3) It is a defence for a person ("D") charged with an offence under this section to show that—
  (a) the specified controlled drug had been prescribed or supplied to D for medical or dental purposes,
  (b) D took the drug in accordance with any directions given by the person by whom the drug was prescribed or supplied, and with any accompanying instructions (so far as consistent with any such directions) given by the manufacturer or distributor of the drug, and
  (c) D's possession of the drug immediately before taking it was not unlawful under section 5(1) of the Misuse of Drugs Act 1971 (restriction of possession of controlled drugs) because of an exemption in regulations made under section 7 of that Act (authorisation of activities otherwise unlawful under foregoing provisions).
(4) The defence in subsection (3) is not available if D's actions were—
  (a) contrary to any advice, given by the person by whom the drug was prescribed or supplied, about the amount of time that should elapse between taking the drug and driving a motor vehicle, or

---

(b) contrary to any accompanying instructions about that matter (so far as consistent with any such advice) given by the manufacturer or distributor of the drug.

(5) If evidence is adduced that is sufficient to raise an issue with respect to the defence in subsection (3), the court must assume that the defence is satisfied unless the prosecution proves beyond reasonable doubt that it is not.

(6) It is a defence for a person ("D") charged with an offence by virtue of subsection (1) (b) to prove that at the time D is alleged to have committed the offence the circumstances were such that there was no likelihood of D driving the vehicle whilst the proportion of the specified controlled drug in D's blood or urine remained likely to exceed the specified limit for that drug.

(7) The court may, in determining whether there was such a likelihood, disregard any injury to D and any damage to the vehicle.

- The burden of proof falls on the defendant (*Sheldrake v Director of Public Prosecutions* [2005] RTR 2).
- Duress is available as a defence. The defence will be available only for as long as the threat is active and a sober and reasonable person would have driven (*Crown Prosecution Service v Brown* [2007] EWHC 3274 (Admin)).
- Automatism is available as a defence.

 See *Blackstone's Criminal Practice 2019* **C5.58**

C13.9 Fail to give information of driver's identity as required

Road Traffic Act 1988, s 172

Duty to give information as to identity of driver etc in certain circumstances

(1) This section applies—
- (a) to any offence under the preceding provisions of this Act except—
  - (i) an offence under Part V, or
  - (ii) an offence under section 13, 16, 51(2), 61(4), 67(9), 68(4), 96 or 120, and to an offence under section 178 of this Act,
- (b) to any offence under sections 25, 26 or 27 of the Road Traffic Offenders Act 1988,
- (c) to any offence against any other enactment relating to the use of vehicles on roads, and
- (d) to manslaughter.

(2) Where the driver of a vehicle is alleged to be guilty of an offence to which this section applies—
- (a) the person keeping the vehicle shall give such information as to the identity of the driver as he may be required to give by or on behalf of a chief officer of police, and
- (b) any other person shall if required as stated above give any information which it is in his power to give and may lead to identification of the driver.

(3) Subject to the following provisions, a person who fails to comply with a requirement under subsection (2) above shall be guilty of an offence.

(4) [see **C13.9.1**]

(5) Where a body corporate is guilty of an offence under this section and the offence is proved to have been committed with the consent or connivance of, or to be

attributable to neglect on the part of, a director, manager, secretary or other similar officer of the body corporate, or a person who was purporting to act in any such capacity, he, as well as the body corporate, is guilty of that offence and liable to be proceeded against and punished accordingly.

(6) Where the alleged offender is a body corporate, or the proceedings are brought against him by virtue of subsection (5) above or subsection (11) below, subsection (4) above shall not apply unless, in addition to the matters there mentioned, the alleged offender shows that no record was kept of the persons who drove the vehicle and that the failure to keep a record was reasonable.

(7) A requirement under subsection (2) may be made by written notice served by post; and where it is so made—

   (a) it shall have effect as a requirement to give the information within the period of 28 days beginning with the day on which the notice is served, and

   (b) the person on whom the notice is served shall not be guilty of an offence under this section if he shows either that he gave the information as soon as reasonably practicable after the end of that period or that it has not been reasonably practicable for him to give it.

(8) Where the person on whom a notice under subsection (7) above is to be served is a body corporate, the notice is duly served if it is served on the secretary or clerk of that body.

(9) For the purposes of section 7 of the Interpretation Act 1978 as it applies for the purposes of this section the proper address of any person in relation to the service on him of a notice under subsection (7) above is—

   (a) in the case of the secretary or clerk of a body corporate, that of the registered or principal office of that body or (if the body corporate is the registered keeper of the vehicle concerned) the registered address, and

   (b) in any other case, his last known address at the time of service.

(10) In this section—

   'registered address', in relation to the registered keeper of a vehicle, means the address recorded in the record kept under the Vehicles Excise and Registration Act 1994 with respect to that vehicle as being that person's address, and

   'registered keeper', in relation to a vehicle, means the person in whose name the vehicle is registered under that Act; and references to the driver of a vehicle include references to the rider of a cycle.

SO 6 points (no endorsement for limited companies)

Level 3 fine

C13.9.1 Key points

• Section 172(4) provides:

Road Traffic Act 1988, s 172(4)

172 Duty to give information as to identity of driver etc in certain circumstances

(4) A person shall not be guilty of an offence by virtue of paragraph (a) of subsection (2) above if he shows that he did not know and could not with reasonable diligence have ascertained who the driver of the vehicle was.

- In *Krishevsky v DPP* [2014] EWHC 1755 (Admin) the court emphasized that the obligations under this provision arose on service and not on receipt.
- In *Duff v Director of Public Prosecutions* [2009] EWHC 675 (Admin), D's wife was served with a notice under s 172 Road Traffic Act 1988 requiring her to identify the name of the driver. D in fact replied to the notice, naming himself as the driver. As a result, a further s 172 notice was then served on D. Following legal advice, D did not respond to that notice and was subsequently convicted of failing to provide information. It was held that the conviction was sound, as the request to which he had in fact responded was a request of D's wife, not D himself.
- *Phiri v DPP* [2017] EWHC 2546 (Admin) confirms that a driver whose response is not received because he relied upon a third party to despatch it, is guilty of the offence.
- A driver is to be judged in relation to 172(4) by the actions he did or did not take only from the time of the police request to ascertain the identity of the driver, not before (*Atkinson v Director of Public Prosecutions* [2011] EWHC 3363 (Admin)). In *Lord Howard of Lympne v Director of Public Prosecutions* [2018] EWHC 100 (Admin) it was held that, although the form had no suitable box when the keeper was not sure who was the driver, a failure or inability to identify the driver constituted a breach of s 172(2)(a), and the keeper had committed an offence under s 172(3) but subject to establishing the defence under s 172(4). In establishing that defence, in a case where either husband or wife was driving (as they indicated in their s 172 replies), the court will be sharp to seek real evidence of diligent attempts to identify which was the driver at the relevant time: *Marshall v CPS* [2015] EWHC 2333 (Admin).
- For the defences available under s 172(7)(b), see *Purnell v Snaresbrook Crown Court* [2011] EWHC 934 (Admin) and *Whiteside v Director of Public Prosecutions* [2011] EWHC 3471 (Admin). *Whiteside* held that a lack of personal knowledge of the request was not itself a defence. But the defendant may be able to show that it was not reasonably practicable for him to have been aware of the notice and to provide the information sought.
- The notice is deemed served under s 1(3) of the Road Traffic Offenders Act 1974 unless the issue is raised by the defence by evidence (*Hall v DPP* [2013] EWHC 2544 (Admin)).

 See *Blackstone's Criminal Practice 2019* **C2.12**

C13.10 Fail to provide specimen for analysis

Road Traffic Act 1988, s 7(6) and (7)

7 Provision of specimens for analysis

(6) A person who, without reasonable excuse, fails to provide a specimen when required to do so in pursuance of this section is guilty of an offence.

(7) A constable must, on requiring any person to provide a specimen in pursuance of this section, warn him that a failure to provide it may render him liable to prosecution.

| SO | Driving/attempting to drive: 6 months' imprisonment and/or fine. Must endorse and disqualify for at least 12 months. Must disqualify for at least 2 years if offender has had two or more disqualifications for periods of 56 days or more in preceding 3 years. Must disqualify for at least 3 years if offender has been convicted of a relevant offence in preceding 10 years |

In-charge: 3 months' imprisonment and/or level 4 fine. Must endorse and may disqualify. If no disqualification, impose 10 points

C13.10.1 *Fail to provide specimen for analysis (drive/attempt to drive)*

The court should determine the offence category using the following table .

Category 1	Higher culpability **and** greater harm
Category 2	Higher culpability **and** lesser harm **or** lower culpability **and** greater harm
Category 3	Lower culpability **and** lesser harm

The court should determine the offender's culpability and the harm caused with reference **only** to the following factors. Where an offence does not fall squarely into a category, individual factors may require a degree of weighting before making an overall assessment and determining the appropriate offence category.

CULPABILITY demonstrated by one or more of the following:	
Factors indicating higher culpability	Factors indicating lower culpability
• Deliberate refusal/failure	• All other cases

HARM demonstrated by one or more of the following:	
Factors indicating greater harm	Factors indicating lesser harm
• High level of impairment	• All other cases

STEP TWO: Starting point and category range

Having determined the category at step one, the court should use the appropriate starting point to reach a sentence within the category range in the following table.

- Must endorse and disqualify for at least 12 months
- Must disqualify for at least 2 years if offender has had two or more disqualifications for periods of 56 days or more in preceding 3 years—refer to the **disqualification guidance** and consult your legal adviser for further guidance
- Must disqualify for at least 3 years if offender has been convicted of a relevant offence in preceding 10 years—consult your legal adviser for further guidance
- **Extend disqualification** if imposing immediate custody

If there is a delay in sentencing after conviction, consider interim disqualification.

The starting point applies to all offenders irrespective of plea or previous convictions.

Level of seriousness	Starting point	Range	Disqualification	Disqual. 2nd offence in 10 years
Category 1	12 weeks' custody	High-level community order–26 weeks' custody	29–36 months (Extend if imposing immediate custody)	36–60 months (Extend if imposing immediate custody)
Category 2	Medium-level community order	Low-level community order–High-level community order	17–28 months	36–52 months
Category 3	Band C fine	Band B fine–Low-level community order	12–16 months	36–40 months

Note: when considering the guidance regarding the length of disqualification in the case of a second offence, the period to be imposed in any individual case will depend on an assessment of all the relevant circumstances, including the length of time since the earlier ban was imposed and the gravity of the current offence but disqualification must be for at least three years.

The court should then consider further adjustment for any aggravating or mitigating factors. The following is a **non-exhaustive** list of additional factual elements providing the context of the offence and factors relating to the offender. Identify whether any combination of these, or other relevant factors, should result in an upward or downward adjustment from the sentence arrived at so far.

Factors increasing seriousness	
Statutory aggravating factors:	*Other aggravating factors:*
• Previous convictions, having regard to a) the **nature** of the offence to which the conviction relates and its **relevance** to the current offence; and b) the **time** that has elapsed since the conviction • Offence committed while on bail	• Failure to comply with current court orders • Offence committed on licence or post sentence supervision • LGV, HGV PSV etc. • Poor road or weather conditions • Carrying passengers • Driving for hire or reward • Evidence of unacceptable standard of driving • Involved in accident • High level of traffic or pedestrians in the vicinity

Factors reducing seriousness or reflecting personal mitigation
• No previous convictions or no relevant/recent convictions • Remorse • Good character and/or exemplary conduct • Serious medical condition requiring urgent, intensive or long-term treatment • Age and/or lack of maturity where it affects the responsibility of the offender • Mental disorder or learning disability • Sole or primary carer for dependent relatives

C13.10.2 *Fail to provide specimen for analysis (in charge)*

STEP ONE: Determining the offence category

The Court should determine the offence category using the following table.

Category 1	Higher culpability **and** greater harm
Category 2	Higher culpability **and** lesser harm **or** lower culpability **and** greater harm
Category 3	Lower culpability **and** lesser harm

The court should determine the offender's culpability and the harm caused with reference **only** to the following factors. Where an offence does not fall squarely into a category, individual factors may require a degree of weighting before making an overall assessment and determining the appropriate offence category.

CULPABILITY demonstrated by one or more of the following:	
Factors indicating higher culpability	**Factors indicating lower culpability**
• Deliberate refusal/failure	• Honestly held belief but unreasonable excuse • Genuine attempt to comply • All other cases

HARM demonstrated by one or more of the following:	
Factors indicating greater harm	**Factors indicating lesser harm**
• High level of impairment	• All other cases

STEP TWO: Starting point and category range

Having determined the category at step one, the court should use the corresponding starting point to reach a sentence within the following category range.

• Must endorse and may disqualify. If no disqualification impose 10 points
• **Extend any disqualification** if imposing immediate custody

The starting point applies to all offenders irrespective of plea or previous convictions.

Level of seriousness	Starting Point	Range	Disqualification/points
Category 1	Medium-level community order	Low-level community order–6 weeks' custody	Disqualify 6–12 months (Extend if imposing immediate custody)
Category 2	Band C fine	Band C fine–Medium level community order	Disqualify up to 6 months **OR** 10 points
Category 3	Band B fine	Band B fine	10 points

The court should then consider further adjustment for any aggravating or mitigating factors. The following is a **non-exhaustive** list of additional factual elements providing the context of the offence and factors relating to the offender. Identify whether any combination of these, or other relevant factors, should result in an upward or downward adjustment from the sentence arrived at so far.

Factors increasing seriousness	
Statutory aggravating factors:	*Other aggravating factors:*
• Previous convictions, having regard to (a) the **nature** of the offence to which the conviction relates and its **relevance** to the current offence; and (b) the **time** that has elapsed since the conviction • Offence committed while on bail	• High likelihood of driving • Failure to comply with current court orders • Offence committed on licence or post sentence supervision • In charge of LGV, HGV, PSV etc • Offering to drive for hire or reward
Factors reducing seriousness or reflecting personal mitigation	
• No previous convictions **or** no relevant/recent convictions • Remorse • Good character and/or exemplary conduct • Serious medical condition requiring urgent, intensive or long-term treatment • Age and/or lack of maturity where it affects the responsibility of the offender • Mental disorder or learning disability • Sole or primary carer for dependent relatives	

C13.10.3 Key points

- A reasonable excuse for failing to provide must relate to inability due to physical or mental issues (*R v Lennard* [1973] RTR 252).
- The suspect need not in fact be the driver if relevant investigation is being conducted by the police.
- Failure to mention a medical reason at the time of refusal does not preclude a court from finding that a reasonable excuse existed, although it was a factor to be taken into account (*Piggott v Director of Public Prosecutions* [2008] RTR 16).
- Once a reasonable excuse is raised, it is for the prosecution to disprove it (*McKeon v Director of Public Prosecutions* [2008] RTR 14) but to require the Crown to disprove a defence of reasonable excuse (here in relation to needle phobia), the defence must lay an evidential basis, ie raise the issue by evidence. An assertion in the police station alone (during the statutory procedure) cannot meet that requirement (*R (Cuns) v Hammersmith Magistrates Court* [2016] EWHC 748 (Admin)).
- A failure to understand the statutory warning relating to prosecution may amount to a reasonable excuse if the accused's understanding of English is poor (*Chief Constable of Avon and Somerset v Singh* [1988] RTR 107); but if an accredited interpreter is present there is an (rebuttable) inference that the warning was understood (*Bielecki v DPP* [2011] EWHC 2245 (Admin)). Failure to understand due to intoxication will not suffice.
- The taking of a specimen does not have to be delayed (over and above a couple of minutes) for the purpose of taking legal advice (*R v Gearing* [2008] EWHC 1695 (Admin)).

See *Blackstone's Criminal Practice 2019* **C5.25**

C13.11 Fail to stop/report road accident

Road Traffic Act 1988, s 170

170 Duty of driver to stop, report accident and give information or documents

(1) This section applies in a case where, owing to the presence of a mechanically propelled vehicle on a road or other public place, an accident occurs by which—
  (a) personal injury is caused to a person other than the driver of that mechanically propelled vehicle, or
  (b) damage is caused—
    (i) to a vehicle other than that mechanically propelled vehicle or a trailer drawn by that mechanically propelled vehicle, or
    (ii) to an animal other than an animal in or on that mechanically propelled vehicle or a trailer drawn by that mechanically propelled vehicle, or
    (iii) to any other property constructed on, fixed to, growing in or otherwise forming part of the land on which the road or place in question is situated or land adjacent to such land.

(2) The driver of the mechanically propelled vehicle must stop and, if required to do so by any person having reasonable grounds for so requiring, give his name and address and also the name and address of the owner and the identification marks of the vehicle.

(3) If for any reason the driver of the mechanically propelled vehicle does not give his name and address under subsection (2) above, he must report the accident.

(4) A person who fails to comply with subsection (2) or (3) above is guilty of an offence.

(5) If, in a case where this section applies by virtue of subsection (1)(a) above, the driver of a motor vehicle does not at the time of the accident produce such a certificate of insurance or security, or other evidence, as is mentioned in section 165(2)(a) of this Act—
  (a) to a constable, or
  (b) to some person who, having reasonable grounds for so doing, has required him to produce it,
  the driver must report the accident and produce such a certificate or other evidence. This subsection does not apply to the driver of an invalid carriage.

(6) To comply with a duty under this section to report an accident or to produce such a certificate of insurance or security, or other evidence, as is mentioned in section 165(2)(a) of this Act, the driver—
  (a) must do so at a police station or to a constable, and
  (b) must do so as soon as is reasonably practicable and, in any case, within twenty-four hours of the occurrence of the accident.

(7) A person who fails to comply with a duty under subsection (5) above is guilty of an offence, but he shall not be convicted by reason only of a failure to produce a certificate or other evidence if, within seven days after the occurrence of the accident, the certificate or other evidence is produced at a police station that was specified by him at the time when the accident was reported.

(8) In this section 'animal' means horse, cattle, ass, mule, sheep, pig, goat or dog.

SO 6 months' imprisonment and/or fine. Must endorse and may disqualify. If no disqualification, impose 5–10 points.

C13.11.1 *Sentencing*

Road Traffic Act 1988, s 170(4)
Triable only summarily
Maximum: Unlimited fine and/or 6 months
Offence range: Band A fine–26 weeks' custody

STEP ONE: Determining the offence category

The court should determine the offence category using the following table.

Category 1	Higher culpability **and** greater harm
Category 2	Higher culpability **and** lesser harm **or** lower culpability **and** greater harm
Category 3	Lower culpability **and** lesser harm

The court should determine the offender's culpability and the harm caused with reference **only** to the following factors. Where an offence does not fall squarely into a category, individual factors may require a degree of weighting before making an overall assessment and determining the appropriate offence category.

| CULPABILITY demonstrated by one or more of the following: | |
Factors indicating higher culpability	Factors indicating lower culpability
• Offence committed in circumstances where a request for a sample of breath, blood or urine would have been made had the offender stopped • Offence committed by offender seeking to avoid arrest for another offence • Offender knew or suspected that personal injury caused and/or left injured party at scene • Giving false details	• All other cases

| HARM demonstrated by one or more of the following: | |
Factors indicating greater harm	Factors indicating lesser harm
• Injury caused • Significant damage	• All other cases

STEP TWO: Starting point and category range

Having determined the category at step one, the court should use the appropriate starting point to reach a sentence within the category range in the following table. The starting point applies to all offenders irrespective of plea or previous convictions.

Level of seriousness	Starting point	Range	Disqualification/points
Category 1	High-level community order	Low-level community order–26 weeks' custody	Disqualify 6–12 months **OR** 9–10 points (extend if imposing immediate custody)

Level of seriousness	Starting point	Range	Disqualification/points
Category 2	Band C fine	Band B fine– Medium-level community order	Disqualify up to 6 months **OR** 7–8 points
Category 3	Band B fine	Band A fine–Band C fine	5–6 points

- Must endorse and may disqualify. If no disqualification impose 3–9 points
- Extend disqualification if imposing immediate custody

The court should then consider further adjustment for any aggravating or mitigating factors. The following is a **non-exhaustive** list of additional factual elements providing the context of the offence and factors relating to the offender. Identify whether any combination of these, or other relevant factors, should result in an upward or downward adjustment from the sentence arrived at so far.

Factors increasing seriousness	
Statutory aggravating factors:	*Other aggravating factors:*
• Previous convictions, having regard to (a) the nature of the offence to which the conviction relates and its relevance to the current offence; and (b) the time that has elapsed since the conviction • Offence committed while on bail	• Little or no attempt made to comply with duty • Evidence of bad driving • Failure to comply with current court orders • Offence committed on licence or post sentence supervision

Factors reducing seriousness or reflecting personal mitigation
• No previous convictions **or** no relevant/recent convictions   • Remorse   • Good character and/or exemplary conduct   • Reasonably believed identity known   • Genuine fear of retribution   • Significant attempt made to comply with duty   • Serious medical condition requiring urgent, intensive, or long-term treatment   • Age and/or lack of maturity where it affects the responsibility of the offender   • Mental disorder or learning disability

C13.11.2 Key points

A driver who is unaware of the accident cannot commit an offence under these provisions (*Harding v Price* [1948] 1 KB 695); but if he later becomes aware of the accident, he must report it personally if he becomes aware within 24 hours (*DPP v Drury* [1989] RTR 165).

If a driver was genuinely unaware that an accident had occurred, or remained of the view that none had occurred (even in circumstances where someone informed that person that there had been an accident), there is no duty to report.

However, if the appellant was unaware of the accident because of her drunken state, she could not rely upon that as a defence where she is voluntarily intoxicated. This is a crime of basic intent (*Magee v Crown Prosecution Service* [2014] EWHC 4089 (Admin)).

C13.11.3 *Power of police to stop vehicles*

> **Road Traffic Act 1988, s 163**
>
> (1) A person driving a mechanically propelled vehicle on a road must stop the vehicle on being required to do so by a constable in uniform or a traffic officer ...
> (3) If a person fails to comply with this section he is guilty of an offence.

SO

Level 3 fine with no endorsement

See *Blackstone's Criminal Practice 2019* **C6.51–C6.55**

C13.12 **No insurance, using, causing, or permitting**

Road Traffic Act 1988, s 143

SO Fine/discretionary disqualification/6–8 penalty points

C13.12.1 *Sentencing*

Road Traffic Act 1988, s 143

Triable only summarily

Maximum: Unlimited fine

Offence range: Band B–Band C fine

STEP ONE: Determining the offence category

The court should determine the offence category using the following table.

Category 1	Higher culpability **and** greater harm
Category 2	Higher culpability **and** lesser harm **or** lower culpability **and** greater harm
Category 3	Lower culpability **and** lesser harm

The court should determine the offender's culpability and the harm caused with reference **only** to the following factors. Where an offence does not fall squarely into a category, individual factors may require a degree of weighting before making an overall assessment and determining the appropriate offence category.

CULPABILITY demonstrated by one or more of the following:	
Factors indicating higher culpability	Factors indicating lower culpability
• Never passed test • Gave false details • Driving LGV, HGV, PSV etc • Driving for hire or reward • Evidence of sustained uninsured use	• All other cases

HARM demonstrated by one or more of the following:	
Factors indicating greater harm	**Factors indicating lesser harm**
• Involved in accident where injury caused • Involved in accident where damage caused	• All other cases

STEP TWO: Starting point and category range

Having determined the category at step one, the court should use the appropriate starting point to reach a sentence within the category range in the following table. The starting point applies to all offenders irrespective of plea or previous convictions.

Level of seriousness	Starting Point	Range	Disqualification/points
Category 1	Band C fine	Band C fine	Disqualify 6–12 months
Category 2	Band C fine	Band C fine	Consider disqualification for up to 6 months **OR** 8 points
Category 3	Band C fine	Band B fine–Band C fine	6–8 points

 • Must endorse and may disqualify. If no disqualification impose 6–8 points

The court should then consider further adjustment for any aggravating or mitigating factors. The following is a **non-exhaustive** list of additional factual elements providing the context of the offence and factors relating to the offender. Identify whether any combination of these, or other relevant factors, should result in an upward or downward adjustment from the sentence arrived at so far.

Factors increasing seriousness	
Statutory aggravating factors:	*Other aggravating factors:*
• Previous convictions, having regard to (a) the **nature** of the offence to which the conviction relates and its **relevance** to the current offence; and (b) the **time** that has elapsed since the conviction • Offence committed while on bail	• Failure to comply with current court orders • Offence committed on licence or post sentence supervision
Factors reducing seriousness or reflecting personal mitigation	
• No previous convictions **or** no relevant/recent convictions • Remorse • Good character and/or exemplary conduct • Responsibility for providing insurance rests with another (where not amounting to a defence) • Genuine misunderstanding • Recent failure to renew or failure to transfer vehicle details where insurance was in existence • Vehicle not being driven	

C13.12.2 Key points

- See **C12** for definitions.
- Proceedings may be brought within six months of a prosecutor forming the opinion that there is sufficient evidence of an offence having been committed (subject to an overall three-year time bar). See **A12.1.2**
- It is for a defendant to show that he was insured, once it is established that a motor vehicle was used on a road or other public place. However, in *DPP v Whittaker* [2015] EWHC 1850 (Admin) it was held that once the defence have proved the existence of a valid insurance policy, it is for the Crown to prove to the normal criminal standard that it does not cover the driving at issue.
- It is not necessary that the vehicle be capable of being driven (*Pumbien v Vines* [1996] RTR 37).
- Employed drivers have the following defence available to them:

Road Traffic Act 1988, s 143(3)

143 Users of motor vehicles to be insured or secured against third-party risks

(3) A person charged with using a motor vehicle in contravention of this section shall not be convicted if he proves—

    (a) that the vehicle did not belong to him and was not in his possession under a contract of hiring or of loan,

    (b) that he was using the vehicle in the course of his employment, and

    (c) that he neither knew nor had reason to believe that there was not in force in relation to the vehicle such a policy of insurance or security as is mentioned in subsection (1) above.

- Where a private hire licence was for a limited area but the defendant held an insurance policy for hire and reward, he was insured wherever he worked as s 148 Road Traffic Act 1988 invalidated any restriction in the policy to a particular area (*Oldham BC v Sajjad* [2016] EWHC 3597 (Admin)).

 See *Blackstone's Criminal Practice 2019* **C6.46–C6.51**

C13.13 Offences concerning the driver

Offence	Maximum	Points	Starting point	Special considerations
Fail to cooperate with preliminary (roadside) breath test	L3	4	B	
Fail to give information of driver's identity as required	L3	6	C	For limited companies, endorsement is not available; a fine is the only available penalty

Offence	Maximum	Points	Starting point	Special considerations
Fail to produce insurance certificate	L4	–	A	Fine per offence, not per document
Fail to produce test certificate	L3	–	A	
Drive otherwise than in accordance with licence (where could be covered)	L3	–	A	
Drive otherwise than in accordance with licence (**C13.17**)	L3	3–6	A	Aggravating factor if no licence ever held

 See *Blackstone's Criminal Practice 2019* **C6**

C13.14 Offences concerning the vehicle

The guidelines for some of the following offences differentiate between three types of offender when the offence is committed in the course of business: driver, owner-driver, and owner-company. For owner-drivers, the starting point is the same as for drivers; however, the court should consider an uplift of at least 25 per cent.

Offence	Maximum	Points	Starting point	Special considerations
No excise licence	L3 or 5 times annual duty, whichever is greater	–	A (1–3 months unpaid) B (4–6 months unpaid) C (7–12 months unpaid)	Add duty lost
Fail to notify change of ownership to DVLA	L3	–	A	If offence committed in course of business: A (driver) A* (owner-driver) B (owner-company)
No test certificate	L3	–	A	If offence committed in course of business: A (driver) A* (owner-driver) B (owner-company)

Offence	Maximum	Points	Starting point	Special considerations
Brakes defective Key points: it is sufficient only to prove that any part of the braking system is defective (*Kennett v British Airports Authority* [1975] Crim LR 106). The fact that everything possible (eg servicing) has been done in order to ensure that the vehicle is in good condition does not amount to a defence (*Hawkins v Holmes* [1974] RTR 436), as maintenance of the braking system is an absolute obligation on the driver (*Green v Burnett* [1954] 3 All ER 273).	L4	3	B	If offence committed in course of business: B (driver) B* (owner-driver) C (owner-company) L5 if goods vehicle
Steering defective	L4	3	B	If offence committed in course of business: B (driver) B* (owner-driver) C (owner-company) L5 if goods vehicle
Tyres defective. It is a defence if the vehicle is not being used and there was no intention to use when the tyres were defective, regardless of the fact that the vehicle was on a road (*Eden v Mitchell* [1975] RTR 425). There is no requirement for the prosecution to have had the tyre examined by an authorized examiner as the issue was a simple question of fact (*Phillips v Thomas* [1974] RTR 28).	L4	3	B	If offence committed in course of business: B (driver) B* (owner-driver) C (owner-company) L5 if goods vehicle Penalty per tyre

Offence	Maximum	Points	Starting point	Special considerations
Condition of vehicle/ accessories/equipment involving danger of injury (Road Traffic Act 1988, s 40A)	L4	3	B	Must disqualify for at least 6 months if offender has one or more previous convictions for same offence within 3 years If offence committed in course of business: B (driver) B* (owner-driver) C (owner-company) L5 if goods vehicle
Exhaust defective	L3	–	A	If offence committed in course of business: A (driver) A* (owner-driver) B (owner-company)
Lights defective	L3	–	A	If offence committed in course of business: A (driver) A* (owner-driver) B (owner-company)

 See *Blackstone's Criminal Practice 2019* **C6**

C13.15 **Speeding**

Road Traffic Regulation Act 1984, s 89(1)

 SO

 Level 3 fine (level 4 if motorway)

C13.15.1 *Sentencing*

Triable only summarily

Maximum: Level 3 fine (Level 4 if motorway)

Offence range: Band A fine–Band C fine

STEPS ONE AND TWO: Determining the offence seriousness

The starting point applies to all offenders irrespective of plea or previous convictions.

Speed limit (mph)	Recorded speed (mph)		
20	41 and above	31–40	21–30
30	51 and above	41–50	31–40
40	66 and above	56–65	41–55
50	76 and above	66–75	51–65
60	91 and above	81–90	61–80
70	101 and above	91–100	71–90
Sentencing range	Band C fine	Band B fine	Band A fine
Points/ disqualification	Disqualify 7–56 days **OR** 6 points	Disqualify 7–28 days **OR** 4–6 points	3 points

- Must endorse and may disqualify. If no disqualification impose 3–6 points
- Where an offender is driving grossly in excess of the speed limit the court should consider a disqualification in excess of 56 days

The court should then consider further adjustment for any aggravating or mitigating factors. The following is a **non-exhaustive** list of additional factual elements providing the context of the offence and factors relating to the offender. Identify whether any combination of these, or other relevant factors, should result in an upward or downward adjustment from the sentence arrived at so far.

Factors increasing seriousness	
Statutory aggravating factors:	*Other aggravating factors:*
• Previous convictions, having regard to (a) the **nature** of the offence to which the conviction relates and its **relevance** to the current offence; and (b) the **time** that has elapsed since the conviction • Offence committed while on bail	• Offence committed on licence or post sentence supervision • Poor road or weather conditions • Driving LGV, HGV, PSV etc • Towing caravan/trailer • Carrying passengers or heavy load • Driving for hire or reward • Evidence of unacceptable standard of driving over and above speed • Location eg near school • High level of traffic or pedestrians in the vicinity
Factors reducing seriousness or reflecting personal mitigation	
• No previous convictions **or** no relevant/recent convictions • Good character and/or exemplary conduct • Genuine emergency established	

C13.15.2 Key points

- Necessity is available as a defence (*Moss v Howdle* [1997] SLT 782).
- Check that a notice of intended prosecution has been served in time.

- Save where the road is a restricted road, there needs to be signage in accordance with the regulations. A failure to provide adequate signage is fatal to any conviction. In *Jones v Director of Public Prosecutions* [2011] EWHC 50 (Admin), the court held that the relevant question to be answered by the court was:

> Whether by the point on the road where the alleged offence took place (the point of enforcement) the driver by reference to the route taken thereto has been given (or drivers generally have been given) adequate guidance of the speed limit to be observed at that point on the road by the signs on the relevant part or parts of the road *in so far as (and thus to the extent that) those traffic signs comply with the 2002 Regulations?*

- In relation to restricted roads (where a 30 mph speed limit applies) there must be a system of street lighting not more than 200 yards apart. If this matter is put in issue (but not otherwise), the prosecution must establish this beyond reasonable doubt.
- The 200-yard rule relates to a 'system of street lighting', so some lights may be more than 200 yards apart, it being a question of fact whether the 'system of lighting' as a whole complies. In *Briere v Hailstone* (1968) 112 SJ 767, a conviction was upheld even though 50 per cent of the lamps were incorrectly distanced. Similarly, the fact that one lamp was in disrepair did not affect a conviction (*Spittle v Kent County Constabulary* [1985] Crim LR 744).

 See *Blackstone's Criminal Practice 2019* **C6.58–C6.62**

C13.16 Unfit through drink or drugs

Road Traffic Act 1988, s 4(1), (2), and (5)

4 Driving, or being in charge, when under influence of drink or drugs

(1) A person who, when driving or attempting to drive a mechanically propelled vehicle on a road or other public place, is unfit to drive through drink or drugs is guilty of an offence.
(2) Without prejudice to subsection (1) above, a person who, when in charge of a mechanically propelled vehicle which is on a road or other public place, is unfit to drive through drink or drugs is guilty of an offence.

...

(5) For the purposes of this section, a person shall be taken to be unfit to drive if his ability to drive properly is for the time being impaired.

SO Drive/attempt to drive: 6 months' imprisonment and/or fine. Must endorse and disqualify for at least 12 months. Must disqualify for at least 2 years if offender has had two or more disqualifications for periods of 56 days or more in preceding years.

Must disqualify for at least 3 years if offender has been convicted of a relevant offence in preceding 10 years.

In-charge: 3 months' imprisonment and/or level 4 fine. Must endorse and may disqualify. If no disqualification, impose 10 points.

C13.16.1 *Sentencing: driving or attempting to drive*

Road Traffic Act 1988, s 4(1)

Triable only summarily

Maximum: Unlimited fine and/or 6 months

Offence range: Band B fine–26 weeks' custody

STEP ONE: Determining the offence category

The court should determine the offence category using the following table.

Category 1	Higher culpability and greater harm
Category 2	Higher culpability and lesser harm or lower culpability and greater harm
Category 3	Lower culpability and lesser harm

The court should determine the offender's culpability and the harm caused with reference **only** to the following factors. Where an offence does not fall squarely into a category, individual factors may require a degree of weighting before making an overall assessment and determining the appropriate offence category.

CULPABILITY demonstrated by one or more of the following:	
Factors indicating higher culpability	Factors indicating lower culpability
• Driving LGV, HGV or PSV etc • Driving for hire or reward	• All other cases

HARM demonstrated by one or more of the following:	
Factors indicating greater harm	Factors indicating lesser harm
• High level of impairment	• All other cases

STEP TWO: Starting point and category range

Having determined the category at step one, the court should use the appropriate starting point to reach a sentence within the category range in the following table .

- Must endorse and disqualify for at least 12 months
- Must disqualify for at least 2 years if offender has had two or more disqualifications for periods of 56 days or more in preceding 3 years—refer to the disqualification guidance and consult your legal adviser for further guidance

- Must disqualify for at least 3 years if offender has been convicted of a relevant offence in preceding 10 years—consult your legal adviser for further guidance
- Extend disqualification if imposing immediate custody

If there is a delay in sentencing after conviction, consider interim disqualification.

The starting point applies to all offenders irrespective of plea or previous convictions.

Level of seriousness	Starting point	Range	Disqualification	Disqual. 2nd offence in 10 years
Category 1	12 weeks' custody	High-level community order– 26 weeks' custody	29–36 months (extend if imposing immediate custody)	36–60 months (extend if imposing immediate custody
Category 2	Medium-level community order	Low-level community order–High-level community order	17–28 months	36–52 months
Category 3	Band C fine	Band B fine–Low-level community order	12–16 months	36–40 months

Note: When considering the guidance regarding the length of disqualification in the case of a second offence, the period to be imposed in any individual case will depend on an assessment of all the relevant circumstances, including the length of time since the earlier ban was imposed and the gravity of the current offence but disqualification must be for at least three years.

The court should then consider further adjustment for any aggravating or mitigating factors. The following is a **non-exhaustive** list of additional factual elements providing the context of the offence and factors relating to the offender. Identify whether any combination of these, or other relevant factors, should result in an upward or downward adjustment from the sentence arrived at so far.

Factors increasing seriousness	
Statutory aggravating factors:	*Other aggravating factors:*
• Previous convictions, having regard to (a) the **nature** of the offence to which the conviction relates and its **relevance** to the current offence; and (b) the **time** that has elapsed since the conviction • Offence committed while on bail	• Failure to comply with current court orders • Offence committed on licence or post sentence supervision • Poor road or weather conditions • Evidence of unacceptable standard of driving • Involved in accident • Carrying passengers • High level of traffic or pedestrians in the vicinity

Factors reducing seriousness or reflecting personal mitigation
• No previous convictions **or** no relevant/recent convictions • Remorse • Good character and/or exemplary conduct • Serious medical condition requiring urgent, intensive, or long-term treatment • Age and/or lack of maturity where it affects the responsibility of the offender • Mental disorder or learning disability • Sole or primary carer for dependent relatives

C13.16.2 *Sentencing: in-charge*

Road Traffic Act, 1988, s 4(2)

Triable only summarily

Maximum: Level 4 fine and/or 3 months

Offence range: Band B fine–12 weeks' custody

STEP 1 – Determining the offence category

The court should determine the offence category using the following table.

Category 1	Higher culpability **and** greater harm
Category 2	Higher culpability **and** lesser harm **or** lower culpability **and** greater harm
Category 3	Lower culpability **and** lesser harm

The court should determine the offender's culpability and the harm caused with reference **only** to the following factors. Where an offence does not fall squarely into a category, individual factors may require a degree of weighting before making an overall assessment and determining the appropriate offence category.

CULPABILITY demonstrated by one or more of the following:	
Factors indicating higher culpability	**Factors indicating lower culpability**
• High likelihood of driving • In charge of LGV, HGV or PSV etc • Offering to drive for hire or reward	• All other cases

HARM demonstrated by one or more of the following:	
Factors indicating greater harm	**Factors indicating lesser harm**
• High level of impairment	• All other cases

STEP TWO: Starting point and category range

Having determined the category at step one, the court should use the appropriate starting point to reach a sentence within the category range in the following table.

- Must endorse and may disqualify. If no disqualification impose 10 points
- Extend disqualification if imposing immediate custody

The starting point applies to all offenders irrespective of plea or previous convictions.

Level of seriousness	Starting point	Range	Disqualification/points
Category 1	High-level community order	Medium-level community order–12 weeks' custody	Consider disqualification (extend if imposing immediate custody) **OR** 10 points

Level of seriousness	Starting point	Range	Disqualification/points
Category 2	Band C fine	Band B fine– Medium-level community order	Consider disqualification **OR** 10 points
Category 3	Band B fine	Band B fine	10 points

The court should then consider further adjustment for any aggravating or mitigating factors. The following is a **non-exhaustive** list of additional factual elements providing the context of the offence and factors relating to the offender. Identify whether any combination of these, or other relevant factors, should result in an upward or downward adjustment from the sentence arrived at so far.

Factors increasing seriousness	
Statutory aggravating factors:	*Other aggravating factors:*
• Previous convictions, having regard to (a) the **nature** of the offence to which the conviction relates and its **relevance** to the current offence; and (b) the **time** that has elapsed since the conviction • Offence committed while on bail	• Failure to comply with current court orders • Offence committed on licence or post sentence supervision

Factors reducing seriousness or reflecting personal mitigation
• No previous convictions **or** no relevant/recent convictions • Remorse • Good character and/or exemplary conduct • Serious medical condition requiring urgent, intensive, or long-term treatment • Age and/or lack of maturity where it affects the responsibility of the offender • Mental disorder or learning disability • Sole or primary carer for dependent relatives

C13.16.3 Key points

• No likelihood of driving while unfit provides a defence in law to the in-charge offence. Section 4(3) and (4) of the Road Traffic Act 1988 provides:

Road Traffic Act 1988, s 4(3) and (4)

4 Driving, or being in charge, when under influence of drink or drugs

(3) For the purposes of subsection (2) above, a person shall be deemed not to have been in charge of a mechanically propelled vehicle if he proves that at the material time the circumstances were such that there was no likelihood of his driving it so long as he remained unfit to drive through drink or drugs.

(4) The court may, in determining whether there was such a likelihood as is mentioned in subsection (3) above, disregard any injury to him and any damage to the vehicle.

• Drugs include normal medicines.
• Evidence of impairment to drive may be provided by both expert and lay witnesses. Note, however, that a lay witness can give evidence as to a

person's demeanour (and how much he drank, for example) but not on the ultimate question of whether the person was 'fit' to drive.

- The results of any evidential specimens are admissible (Road Traffic Offenders Act 1988, ss 15 and 16).

 See *Blackstone's Criminal Practice 2019* **C5.57**

C13.17 Driving otherwise than in accordance with a licence

Road Traffic Act 1988, s 87

C13.17.1 *Sentencing*

Level 3 fine

Disqualification discretionary and endorsement obligatory (3–6 points) in a case where the offender's driving would not have been in accordance with any licence that could have been granted to him.

C13.17.2 *Restrictions applicable to children and young persons*

A person can apply for a driving licence up to three months before they can start driving.

C13.17.2.1 *Aged 16 years*

A person aged 16 years can apply for a provisional moped licence and take compulsory basic training (CBT) to start riding category AM and category Q mopeds. They must take a moped test within two years.

- Category AM mopeds have a maximum speed over 25km/h and no more than 45km/h.
- Category Q mopeds are two- or three-wheeled mopeds with a maximum speed of 25km/h.

C13.17.2.2 *Aged 17 years*

A person aged 17 years can apply for a provisional licence for a small motor-bike (category A1). They then need to complete compulsory basic training (CBT) and take the A1 theory and practical tests within two years to get a full A1 licence.

- Category A1 covers motorbikes not exceeding: 125cc engine size/11kW power output/0.1kW/kg power to weight ratio.

A person aged 17 years can apply for a provisional licence to drive a car subject to the restrictions on that licence.

C13.17.2.3 *Restrictions on the use of a provisional licence*

A provisional licence has certain restrictions on its use.
A person with a provisional licence to drive a moped:

- must not drive a moped that has a maximum speed exceeding 25mph;
- must not drive a motorbike on a public road unless they have taken or are in the process of taking a compulsory basic training course;
- must not carry a passenger on the motorbike;
- must display 'L' plates ('D' plates in Wales) on the front and back of the vehicle;
- must not drive on a motorway.

A person with a provisional licence to drive a motorbike:

- must not drive a motorbike that is above 125cc;
- must not drive a motorbike on a public road unless they have taken or are in the process of taking a compulsory basic training course;
- must not carry a passenger on the motorbike;
- must display 'L' plates ('D' plates in Wales) on the front and back of the vehicle;
- must not drive on a motorway.

A person who has a provisional licence to drive a car or other vehicle (except a motorbike):

- must display 'L' plates on the front and back of the vehicle (or 'D' plates in Wales);
- must not drive on a motorway;
- if the vehicle has more than one seat, must have someone with them whenever they are driving. The person supervising must sit in the front passenger seat and be fit to drive the vehicle, for example, they must not be drunk. They must also be aged 21 or over and have had a full driving licence (for the type of vehicle being driven) for at least three years.

A person who has passed a driving test and is still waiting to receive a full licence is not subject to these restrictions.

C13.17.2.4 *Full driving licence*

In order to obtain a full licence to drive a moped a person must:

- pass the theory test for motorcycles; and
- pass the moped practical test.

In order to obtain a full licence to drive a motorcycle a person must:

- pass the theory test for motorcycles; and
- pass the motorcycle practical test.

In order to obtain a full driving licence to drive a car a person must:

- pass the theory test for cars; and
- pass the practical driving test.

C13.17.2.5 *New driver provisions (see D17.10)*

A person who builds up six or more penalty points within two years of passing their first driving test will automatically lose their licence. They will have to apply and pay for a new provisional licence and pass both theory and practical parts of the driving test again to obtain a full licence.

However, a period of disqualification does not trigger the new driver provisions.

C14 **Sexual Offences**

C14.1 **Definitions**

C14.1.1 *Consent*

The Sexual Offences Act (SOA) 2003 provides:

Sexual Offences Act 2003, ss 74, 75, 76

74 'Consent'

For the purposes of this Part, a person consents if he agrees by choice, and has the freedom and capacity to make that choice.

75 Evidential presumptions about consent

(1) If in proceedings for an offence to which this section applies it is proved–
  (a) that the defendant did the relevant act,
  (b) that any of the circumstances specified in subsection (2) existed, and
  (c) that the defendant knew that those circumstances existed,
  the complainant is to be taken not to have consented to the relevant act unless sufficient evidence is adduced to raise an issue as to whether he consented, and the defendant is to be taken not to have reasonably believed that the complainant consented unless sufficient evidence is adduced to raise an issue as to whether he reasonably believed it.
(2) The circumstances are that—
  (a) any person was, at the time of the relevant act or immediately before it began, using violence against the complainant or causing the complainant to fear that immediate violence would be used against him;
  (b) any person was, at the time of the relevant act or immediately before it began, causing the complainant to fear that violence was being used, or that immediate violence would be used, against another person;
  (c) the complainant was, and the defendant was not, unlawfully detained at the time of the relevant act;
  (d) the complainant was asleep or otherwise unconscious at the time of the relevant act;
  (e) because of the complainant's physical disability, the complainant would not have been able at the time of the relevant act to communicate to the defendant whether the complainant consented;
  (f) any person had administered to or caused to be taken by the complainant, without the complainant's consent, a substance which, having regard to when it was administered or taken, was capable of causing or enabling the complainant to be stupefied or overpowered at the time of the relevant act.
(3) In subsection (2)(a) and (b), the reference to the time immediately before the relevant act began is, in the case of an act which is one of a continuous series of sexual activities, a reference to the time immediately before the first sexual activity began.

76 Conclusive presumptions about consent

(1) If in proceedings for an offence to which this section applies it is proved that the defendant did the relevant act and that any of the circumstances specified in subsection (2) existed, it is to be conclusively presumed—

(a) that the complainant did not consent to the relevant act, and
(b) that the defendant did not believe that the complainant consented to the relevant act.
(2) The circumstances are that—
(a) the defendant intentionally deceived the complainant as to the nature or purpose of the relevant act;
(b) the defendant intentionally induced the complainant to consent to the relevant act by impersonating a person known personally to the complainant.

Only pressure and coercion or two frauds are capable of vitiating consent: fraud as to the nature of the sexual act (which appears to include deception as to gender at birth or is closely associated with the nature and purpose of the act) and fraud as to the identity of the perpetrator through impersonation of husband or partner (*R (on the application of Monica) v DPP* [2018] EWHC 3469 (QB)).

C14.1.2 *Sexual in nature*

Sexual Offences Act 2003, s 78

For the purposes of this Part (except section 71), penetration, touching, or any other activity is sexual if a reasonable person would consider that—

(a) whatever its circumstances or any person's purpose in relation to it, it is because of its nature sexual, or
(b) because of its nature it may be sexual and because of its circumstances or the purpose of any person in relation to it (or both) it is sexual.

Acts which are automatically sexual within the meaning of s 78(a) would include penile penetration or oral sex. Where the act is not automatically sexual it was held in *R v H* [2005] EWCA Crim 732, [2005] 2 Cr App R 9 that two requirements must be satisfied: first, that the touching could reasonably be considered to be sexual; and, secondly, that the touching, because of its circumstances or the purpose of any person in relation to it (or both) was sexual.

C14.2 Assault by penetration

Sexual Offences Act 2003, s 2

(1) A person (A) commits an offence if—
(a) he intentionally penetrates the vagina or anus of another person (B) with a part of his body or anything else,
(b) the penetration is sexual,
(c) B does not consent to the penetration, and
(d) A does not reasonably believe that B consents.
(2) Whether a belief is reasonable is to be determined having regard to all the circumstances, including any steps A has taken to ascertain whether B consents.
(3) Sections 75 and 76 apply to an offence under this section.

GC

IO

DO

⧎	Life

SON

C14.2.1 Key points

- Penetration is a continuing act from entry to withdrawal (s 79(2) SOA 2003).
- For the definition of 'sexual' see and consent see **C14.1.1**.

C14.3 Causing etc a child under 13 to engage in sexual activity

Sexual Offences Act 2003, s 8

8 Causing or inciting a child under 13 to engage in sexual activity

(1) A person commits an offence if—
  (a) he intentionally causes or incites another person (B) to engage in an activity,
  (b) the activity is sexual, and
  (c) B is under 13.
(2) A person guilty of an offence under this section, if the activity caused or incited involved—

  (a) penetration of B's anus or vagina,
  (b) penetration of B's mouth with a person's penis,
  (c) penetration of a person's anus or vagina with a part of B's body or by B with anything else, or
  (d) penetration of a person's mouth with B's penis, is liable, on conviction on indictment, to imprisonment for life.

EW	Save where penetration is involved and the offences become triable only on indictment

⧎	6 months and/or fine/14 years' imprisonment unless penetration involved when Life

DO

IO

C14.3.1 *Sentencing*

STEP ONE: Determining the offence category

The court should determine which categories of harm and culpability the offence falls into by reference only to the following tables.

Harm		Culpability	
		A	**B**
Category 1	The extreme nature of one or more category 2 factors or the extreme impact caused by a combination of category 2 factors may elevate to category 1	Significant degree of planning Offender acts together with others to commit the offence Use of alcohol/drugs on victim to facilitate the offence Grooming behaviour used against victim Abuse of trust Previous violence against victim Offence committed in course of burglary Sexual images of victim recorded, retained, solicited or shared Deliberate isolation of victim Commercial exploitation and/or motivation Offence racially or religiously aggravated Offence motivated by, or demonstrating hostility to the victim based on his or her sexual orientation (or presumed sexual orientation) or transgender identity (or presumed transgender identity) Offence motivated by, or demonstrating, hostility to the victim based on his or her disability (or presumed disability)	Factor(s) in category A not present
Category 2	• Severe psychological or physical harm • Penetration of vagina or anus (using body or object) by, or of, the victim • Penile penetration of mouth by, or of, the victim • Additional degradation/humiliation • Abduction • Prolonged detention/sustained incident • Violence or threats of violence • Forced/uninvited entry into victim's home • Child is particularly vulnerable due to extreme youth and/or personal circumstances		
Category 3	Factor(s) in categories 1 and 2 not present		

STEP TWO: Starting point and category range

Having determined the category, the court should use the corresponding starting points to reach a sentence within the following category range . The starting point applies to all offenders irrespective of plea or previous convictions. Having determined the starting point, step two allows further adjustment for aggravating or mitigating features, set out on the next page.

A case of particular gravity, reflected by multiple features of culpability or harm in step one, could merit upward adjustment from the starting point before further adjustment for aggravating or mitigating features, set out in the table.

	A	B
Category 1	**Starting point** 13 years' custody **Category range** 11–17 years' custody	**Starting point** 11 years' custody **Category range** 10–15 years' custody
Category 2	**Starting point** 8 years' custody Category range 5–10 years' custody	**Starting point** 6 years' custody **Category range** 3–9 years' custody
Category 3	**Starting point** 5 years' custody **Category range** 3–8 years' custody	**Starting point** 2 years' custody **Category range** 1–4 years' custody

The following table contains a **non-exhaustive** list of additional factual elements providing the context of the offence and factors relating to the offender. Identify whether any combination of these, or other relevant factors, should result in an upward or downward adjustment from the starting point. In particular, relevant recent convictions are likely to result in an upward adjustment. In some cases, having considered these factors, it may be appropriate to move outside the identified category range.

Aggravating factors	
Statutory aggravating factors	*Other aggravating factors*
• Previous convictions, having regard to (a) the nature of the offence to which the conviction relates and its relevance to the current offence; and (b) the time that has elapsed since the conviction • Offence committed while on bail	• Specific targeting of a particularly vulnerable child • Ejaculation (where not taken into account at step one) • Blackmail or other threats made (where not taken into account at step one) • Pregnancy or STI as a consequence of offence • Location of offence • Timing of offence • Use of weapon or other item to frighten or injure • Victim compelled to leave their home, school, etc • Failure to comply with current court orders

Aggravating factors	
	• Offence committed while on licence • Exploiting contact arrangements with a child to commit an offence • Presence of others, especially other children • Any steps taken to prevent the victim reporting an incident, obtaining assistance and/or from assisting or supporting the prosecution • Attempts to dispose of or conceal evidence • Commission of offence while offender under the influence of alcohol or drugs • Victim encouraged to recruit others

Mitigating factors
• No previous convictions or no relevant/recent convictions • Remorse • Previous good character and/or exemplary conduct* • Age and/or lack of maturity where it affects the responsibility of the offender • Mental disorder or learning disability, particularly where linked to the commission of the offence • Sexual activity was incited but no activity took place because the offender voluntarily desisted or intervened to prevent it

*Previous good character/exemplary conduct is different from having no previous convictions. The more serious the offence, the less the weight which should normally be attributed to this factor. Where previous good character/exemplary conduct has been used to facilitate the offence, this mitigation should not normally be allowed and such conduct may constitute an aggravating factor.

In the context of this offence, previous good character/exemplary conduct should not normally be given any significant weight and will not normally justify a reduction in what would otherwise be the appropriate sentence.

C14.4 Child sex offences committed by children or young persons

Sexual Offences Act 2003, s 13

Child sex offences committed by children or young person

s 13(1) A person under 18 commits an offence if he does anything which would be an offence under any of ss 9 to 12 if he were aged 18.

 6 months/fine/5 years' imprisonment

SON If the offender is or has been sentenced, in respect of the offence, to imprisonment for a term of at least 12 months

C14.5 Child sexual offences

Sexual Offences Act 2003, s 10

Causing or inciting a child to engage in sexual activity

(1) A person aged 18 or over (A) commits an offence if—

    (a) he intentionally causes or incites another person (B) to engage in an activity,

    (b) the activity is sexual, and

    (c) either—

        (i) B is under 16 and A does not reasonably believe that B is 16 or over, or

        (ii) B is under 13.

EW but indictable only if the activity involves penetration

⊞ 6 months and/or fine: 14 years' imprisonment See **C14.14**

DO

GC

SON

Sexual Offences Act 2003, s 11

Engaging in sexual activity in the presence of a child

(1) A person aged 18 or over (A) commits an offence if—

    (a) he intentionally engages in an activity,

    (b) the activity is sexual,

    (c) for the purpose of obtaining sexual gratification, he engages in it—

        (i) when another person (B) is present or is in a place from which A can be observed, and

        (ii) knowing or believing that B is aware, or intending that B should be aware, that he is engaging in it, and

    (d) either—

        (i) B is under 16 and A does not reasonably believe that B is 16 or over, or

        (ii) B is under 13.

EW

⊞ 6 months and/or fine/ 10 years' imprisonment

DO

SON

Key points *R. v B and L* [2018] EWCA Crim 1439 confirms that the offence under s 11(1) requires there to be a link between the 'purpose of obtaining sexual gratification' and the presence of the child.

C14.5.1 *Sentencing*

This guideline also applies to offences under s 12.

STEP ONE: Determining the offence category

The court should determine which categories of harm and culpability the offence falls into by reference only to the following tables.

Harm		Culpability	
		A	B
Category 1	Causing victim to view extreme pornography Causing victim to view indecent/ prohibited images of children Engaging in, or causing a victim to view live, sexual activity involving sadism/ violence/sexual activity with an animal/a child	Significant degree of planning Offender acts together with others in order to commit the offence Use of alcohol/drugs on victim to facilitate the offence Grooming behaviour used against victim Abuse of trust Use of threats (including blackmail) Specific targeting of a particularly vulnerable child Significant disparity in age Commercial exploitation and/or motivation Offence racially or religiously aggravated Offence motivated by, or demonstrating, hostility to the victim based on his or her sexual orientation (or presumed sexual orientation) or transgender identity (or presumed transgender identity) Offence motivated by, or demonstrating, hostility to the victim based on his or her disability (or presumed disability)	Factor(s) in category A not present
Category 2	Engaging in, or causing a victim to view images of or view live, sexual activity involving: penetration of vagina or anus (using body or object), penile penetration of the mouth, masturbation		
Category 3	Factor(s) in categories 1 and 2 not present		

STEP TWO: Starting point and category range

Having determined the category, the court should use the corresponding starting points to reach a sentence within the following category range The starting point applies to all offenders irrespective of plea or previous convictions. Having determined the starting point, step two allows further adjustment for aggravating or mitigating features, set out on the next page.

A case of particular gravity, reflected by multiple features of culpability or harm in step one, could merit upward adjustment from the starting point before further adjustment for aggravating or mitigating features, set out on the next page.

Where there is a sufficient prospect of rehabilitation, a community order with a sex offender treatment programme requirement under s 202 of the Criminal Justice Act 2003 can be a proper alternative to a short or moderate length custodial sentence.

	A	B
Category 1	**Starting point** 4 years' custody **Category range** 3–6 years' custody	**Starting point** 2 years' custody **Category range** 1–3 years' custody
Category 2	**Starting point** 2 years' custody **Category range** 1–3 years' custody	**Starting point** 1 year's custody **Category range** High-level community order– 18 months' custody
Category 3	**Starting point** 26 weeks' custody **Category range** High-level community order– 1 year's custody	**Starting point** Medium-level community order **Category range** Low-level community order– High-level community order

The following table contains a non-exhaustive list of additional factual elements providing the context of the offence and factors relating to the offender. Identify whether any combination of these, or other relevant factors, should result in an upward or downward adjustment from the starting point. In particular, relevant recent convictions are likely to result in an upward adjustment. In some cases, having considered these factors, it may be appropriate to move outside the identified category range.

When sentencing appropriate category 2 or 3 offences, the court should also consider the custody threshold as follows:

- has the custody threshold been passed?
- if so, is it unavoidable that a custodial sentence be imposed?
- if so, can that sentence be suspended?

Aggravating factors	
Statutory aggravating factors	*Other aggravating factors*
• Previous convictions, having regard to (a) the nature of the offence to which the conviction relates and its relevance to the current offence; and (b) the time that has elapsed since the conviction • Offence committed while on bail	• Location of offence • Timing of offence • Victim compelled to leave their home, school, etc • Failure to comply with current court orders • Offence committed while on licence • Exploiting contact arrangements with a child to commit an offence • Presence of others, especially other children • Any steps taken to prevent the victim reporting an incident, obtaining assistance and/or from assisting or supporting the prosecution • Attempts to dispose of or conceal evidence • Failure of offender to respond to previous warnings • Commission of offence while offender under the influence of alcohol or drugs • Victim encouraged to recruit others
Mitigating factors	
• No previous convictions or no relevant/recent convictions • Remorse • Previous good character and/or exemplary conduct* • Age and/or lack of maturity where it affects the responsibility of the offender • Mental disorder or learning disability, particularly where linked to the commission of the offence • Demonstration of steps taken to address offending behaviour	

* Previous good character/exemplary conduct is different from having no previous convictions. The more serious the offence, the less the weight which should normally be attributed to this factor. Where previous good character/exemplary conduct has been used to facilitate the offence, this mitigation should not normally be allowed and such conduct may constitute an aggravating factor.

Sexual Offences Act 2003, s 12

Causing a child to watch a sexual act

(1) A person aged 18 or over (A) commits an offence if—

    (a) for the purpose of obtaining sexual gratification, he intentionally causes another person (B) to watch a third person engaging in an activity, or to look at an image of any person engaging in an activity,

    (b) the activity is sexual, and

    (c) either—

        (i) B is under 16 and A does not reasonably believe that B is 16 or over, or

        (ii) B is under 13.

EW

 6 months/fine;10 years' imprisonment

DO

STEP ONE: Determining the offence category

The court should determine which categories of harm and culpability the offence falls into by reference only to the following tables.

Harm		Culpability	
		A	B
Category 1	• Causing victim to view extreme pornography • Causing victim to view indecent/prohibited images of children • Engaging in, or causing a victim to view live, sexual activity involving sadism/violence/sexual activity with an animal/a child	• Significant degree of planning • Offender acts together with others in order to commit the offence • Use of alcohol/drugs on victim to facilitate the offence • Grooming behaviour used against victim • Abuse of trust • Use of threats (including blackmail) • Specific targeting of a particularly vulnerable child • Significant disparity in age • Commercial exploitation and/or motivation • Offence racially or religiously aggravated • Offence motivated by, or demonstrating, hostility to the victim based on his or her sexual orientation (or presumed sexual orientation) or transgender identity (or presumed transgender identity) • Offence motivated by, or demonstrating, hostility to the victim based on his or her disability (or presumed disability)	• Factor(s) in category A not present
Category 2	• Engaging in, or causing a victim to view images of or view live, sexual activity involving: • penetration of vagina or anus (using body or object) • penile penetration of the mouth • masturbation		
Category 3	Factor(s) in categories 1 and 2 not present		

STEP TWO: Starting point and category range

Having determined the category, the court should use the corresponding starting points to reach a sentence within the category range on the next page. The starting point applies to all offenders irrespective of plea or previous convictions. Having determined the starting point, step two allows further adjustment for aggravating or mitigating features, set out on the next page.

A case of particular gravity, reflected by multiple features of culpability or harm in step one, could merit upward adjustment from the starting point before further adjustment for aggravating or mitigating features, set out on the next page.

Where there is a sufficient prospect of rehabilitation, a community order with a sex offender treatment programme requirement under s 202 Criminal Justice Act 2003 can be a proper alternative to a short or moderate length custodial sentence.

	A	B
Category 1	• **Starting point** • 4 years' custody • **Category range** • 3–6 years' custody	• **Starting point** • 2 years' custody • **Category range** • 1–3 years' custody
Category 2	• **Starting point** • 2 years' custody • **Category range** • 1–3 years' custody	• **Starting point** • 1 years' custody • **Category range** • High-level community order–18 months' custody
Category 3	• **Starting point** • 26 weeks' custody • **Category range** • High-level community order–1 year's custody	• **Starting point** • Medium-level community order • **Category range** • Low-level community order–High-level community order

The following table contains a non-exhaustive list of additional factual elements providing the context of the offence and factors relating to the offender. Identify whether any combination of these, or other relevant factors, should result in an upward or downward adjustment from the starting point. In particular, relevant recent convictions are likely to result in an upward adjustment. In some cases, having considered these factors, it may be appropriate to move outside the identified category range.

When sentencing appropriate category 2 or 3 offences, the court should also consider the custody threshold as follows:

• has the custody threshold been passed?
• if so, is it unavoidable that a custodial sentence be imposed?
• if so, can that sentence be suspended?

Aggravating factors
Statutory aggravating factors
• Previous convictions, having regard to (a) the nature of the offence to which the conviction relates and its relevance to the current offence; and (b) the time that has elapsed since the conviction • Offence committed while on bail • Other aggravating factors • Location of offence • Timing of offence • Victim compelled to leave their home, school, etc • Failure to comply with current court orders
• Offence committed while on licence • Exploiting contact arrangements with a child to commit an offence • Presence of others, especially other children • Any steps taken to prevent the victim reporting an incident, obtaining assistance and/or from assisting or supporting the prosecution • Attempts to dispose of or conceal evidence • Failure of offender to respond to previous warnings • Commission of offence while offender under the influence of alcohol or drugs • Victim encouraged to recruit others
Mitigating factors
• No previous convictions or no relevant/recent convictions • Remorse • Previous good character and/or exemplary conduct* • Age and/or lack of maturity where it affects the responsibility of the offender • Mental disorder or learning disability, particularly where linked to the commission of the offence • Demonstration of steps taken to address offending behaviour

* Previous good character/exemplary conduct is different from having no previous convictions. The more serious the offence, the less the weight which should normally be attributed to this factor. Where previous good character/exemplary conduct has been used to facilitate the offence, this mitigation should not normally be allowed and such conduct may constitute an aggravating factor.

C14.6 Exploitation of prostitution

Sexual Offences Act 2003, ss 52 and 53

 6 months' imprisonment and/or fine/7 years' imprisonment

C14.6.1 *Sentencing*

CAUSING OR INCITING PROSTITUTION FOR GAIN

Sexual Offences Act 2003, s 52

CONTROLLING PROSTITUTION FOR GAIN

Sexual Offences Act 2003, s 53

STEP ONE: Determining the offence category

The court should determine which categories of harm and culpability the offence falls into by reference only to the following tables.

HARM	
Category 1	• Abduction/detention • Violence or threats of violence • Sustained and systematic psychological abuse • Individual(s) forced or coerced to participate in unsafe/degrading sexual activity • Individual(s) forced or coerced into seeing many 'customers' • Individual(s) forced/coerced/deceived into prostitution
Category 2	Factor(s) in category 1 not present

CULPABILITY		
A	**B**	**C**
• Causing, inciting or controlling prostitution on significant commercial basis • Expectation of significant financial or other gain • Abuse of trust • Exploitation of those known to be trafficked • Significant involvement in limiting the freedom of prostitute(s) • Grooming of individual(s) to enter prostitution including through cultivation of a dependency on drugs or alcohol	• Close involvement with prostitute(s) for example control of finances, choice of clients, working conditions, etc (where offender's involvement is not as a result of coercion)	• Performs limited function under direction • Close involvement but engaged by coercion/intimidation/exploitation

STEP TWO: Starting point and category range

Having determined the category, the court should use the corresponding starting points to reach a sentence within the following category range. The starting point applies to all offenders irrespective of plea or previous convictions. Having determined the starting point, step two allows further adjustment for aggravating or mitigating features, set out [below].

A case of particular gravity, reflected by multiple features of culpability or harm in step one, could merit upward adjustment from the starting point before further adjustment for aggravating or mitigating features, set out [below].

Where there is a sufficient prospect of rehabilitation, a community order with a sex offender treatment programme requirement under s 202 Criminal Justice Act 2003 can be a proper alternative to a short or moderate length custodial sentence.

Category 1	**Starting point** 4 years' custody **Category range** 3–6 years' custody	**Starting point** 2 years 6 months' custody **Category range** 2–4 years' custody	**Starting point** 1 year's custody **Category range** 26 weeks–2 years' custody

Category 2	Starting point 2 years 6 months' custody **Category range** 2–5 years custody	Starting point 1 year's custody **Category range** High-level community order–2 years' custody	Starting point Medium-level community order **Category range** Low-level community order– high-level community order

The following table contains a non-exhaustive list of additional factual elements providing the context of the offence and factors relating to the offender. Identify whether any combination of these, or other relevant factors, should result in an upward or downward adjustment from the starting point. In particular, relevant recent convictions are likely to result in an upward adjustment. In some cases, having considered these factors, it may be appropriate to move outside the identified category range.

When sentencing appropriate category 2 offences, the court should also consider the custody threshold as follows:

- has the custody threshold been passed?
- if so, is it unavoidable that a custodial sentence be imposed?
- if so, can that sentence be suspended?

Aggravating factors	
Statutory aggravating factors	*Other aggravating factors*
• Previous convictions, having regard to (a) the nature of the offence to which the conviction relates and its relevance to the current offence; and (b) the time that has elapsed since the conviction • Offence committed while on bail	• Failure to comply with current court orders • Offence committed while on licence • Deliberate isolation of prostitute(s) • Threats made to expose prostitute(s) to the authorities (for example, immigration or police), family/friends or others • Harm threatened against the family/friends of prostitute(s) • Passport/identity documents removed • Prostitute(s) prevented from seeking medical treatment • Food withheld • Earnings withheld/kept by offender or evidence of excessive wage reduction or debt bondage, inflated travel or living expenses, or unreasonable interest rates • Any steps taken to prevent the reporting of an incident, obtaining assistance, and/or from assisting or supporting the prosecution • Attempts to dispose of or conceal evidence • Prostitute(s) forced or coerced into pornography • Timescale over which operation has been run
Mitigating factors	
• No previous convictions **or** no relevant/recent convictions • Remorse • Previous good character and/or exemplary conduct* • Age and/or lack of maturity where it affects the responsibility of the offender • Mental disorder or learning disability, particularly where linked to the commission of the offence • Demonstration of steps taken to address offending behaviour	

* Previous good character/exemplary conduct is different from having no previous convictions. The more serious the offence, the less weight which should normally be attributed to this factor. Where previous good character/exemplary conduct has been used to facilitate the offence, this mitigation should not normally be allowed and such conduct may constitute an aggravating factor.

See *Blackstone's Criminal Practice 2019* **B3.250–B3.264**

C14.7 Engaging in sexual activity

Sexual Offences Act 2003, s 4

4 Causing a person to engage in sexual activity without consent

(1) A person (A) commits an offence if—
    (a) he intentionally causes another person (B) to engage in an activity,
    (b) the activity is sexual,
    (c) B does not consent to engaging in the activity, and
    (d) A does not reasonably believe that B consents.
(2) Whether a belief is reasonable is to be determined having regard to all the circumstances, including any steps A has taken to ascertain whether B consents.
(3) Sections 75 and 76 apply to an offence under this section.
(4) A person guilty of an offence under this section, if the activity caused involved—
    (a) penetration of B's anus or vagina,
    (b) penetration of B's mouth with a person's penis,
    (c) penetration of a person's anus or vagina with a part of B's body or by B with anything else, or
    (d) penetration of a person's mouth with B's penis,
is liable, on conviction on indictment, to imprisonment for life.

⟊ 6 months' imprisonment and/or fine/10 years imprisonment (or life when penetration involved)

EW save when penetration involved when indictable only

DO

IO When penetration involved

STEP ONE: Determining the offence category

The court should determine which categories of harm and culpability the offence falls into by reference only to the following tables.

C14 Sexual Offences

HARM		CULPABILITY	
		A	**B**
Category 1	The extreme nature of one or more category 2 factors or the extreme impact caused by a combination of category 2 factors may elevate to category 1	• Significant degree of planning • Offender acts together with others to commit the offence • Use of alcohol/drugs on victim to facilitate the offence • Abuse of trust • Previous violence against victim • Offence committed in course of burglary • Recording of the offence • Commercial exploitation and/or motivation • Offence racially or religiously aggravated • Offence motivated by, or demonstrating, hostility to the victim based on his or her sexual orientation (or presumed sexual orientation) or transgender identity (or presumed transgender identity) • Offence motivated by, or demonstrating, hostility to the victim based on his or her disability (or presumed disability)	Factor(s) in category A not present
Category 2	• Severe psychological or physical harm • Penetration using large or dangerous object(s) • Pregnancy or STI as a consequence of offence • Additional degradation/humiliation • Abduction • Prolonged detention/sustained incident • Violence or threats of violence • Forced/uninvited entry into victim's home • Victim is particularly vulnerable due to personal circumstances*		
Category 3	Factor(s) in categories 1 and 2 not present		

* for children under 13 please refer to the [separate] guideline

STEP TWO: Starting point and category range

Having determined the category, the court should use the corresponding starting points to reach a sentence within the category range on the next page. The starting point applies to all offenders irrespective of plea or previous convictions. Having determined the starting point, step two allows further adjustment for aggravating or mitigating features, set out on the next page.

A case of particular gravity, reflected by multiple features of culpability or harm in step one, could merit upward adjustment from the starting point before further adjustment for aggravating or mitigating features, set out on the next page.

Where there is a sufficient prospect of rehabilitation, a community order with a sex offender treatment programme requirement under s 202 Criminal Justice Act 2003 can be a proper alternative to a short or moderate length custodial sentence.

Where offence involved penetration:

	A	B
Category 1	**Starting point** 15 years' custody **Category range** 13–19 years' custody	**Starting point** 12 years' custody **Category range** 10–15 years' custody
Category 2	**Starting point** 8 years' custody **Category range** 5–13 years' custody	**Starting point** 6 years' custody **Category range** 4–9 years' custody
Category 3	**Starting point** 4 years' custody **Category range** 2–6 years' custody	**Starting point** 2 years' custody **Category range** High-level community order–4 years' custody

Where offence did not involve penetration:

	A	B
Category 1	**Starting point** 4 years' custody **Category range** 3–7 years' custody	**Starting point** 2 years 6 months' custody **Category range** 2–4 years' custody
Category 2	**Starting point** 2 years' custody **Category range** 1–4 years' custody	**Starting point** 1 year's custody **Category range** High-level community order–2 years' custody
Category 3	**Starting point** 26 weeks' custody **Category range** High-level community order–1 year's custody	**Starting point** High-level community order **Category range** Medium-level community order–26 weeks' custody

The following table contains a **non-exhaustive** list of additional factual elements providing the context of the offence and factors relating to the offender. Identify whether any combination of these, or other relevant factors, should result in an upward or downward adjustment from the starting point. In particular, relevant recent convictions are likely to result in an upward adjustment. In some cases, having considered these factors, it may be appropriate to move outside the identified category range.

When sentencing appropriate category 2 or 3 offences, the court should also consider the custody threshold as follows:

- has the custody threshold been passed?
- if so, is it unavoidable that a custodial sentence be imposed?
- if so, can that sentence be suspended?

Aggravating factors	
Statutory aggravating factors	*Other aggravating factors*
• Previous convictions, having regard to (a) the nature of the offence to which the conviction relates and its relevance to the current offence; and (b) the time that has elapsed since the conviction • Offence committed while on bail	• Specific targeting of a particularly vulnerable victim • Ejaculation (where not taken into account at step one) • Blackmail or other threats made (where not taken into account at step one) • Location of offence • Timing of offence • Use of weapon or other item to frighten or injure • Victim compelled to leave their home (including victims of domestic violence) • Failure to comply with current court orders • Offence committed while on licence • Exploiting contact arrangements with a child to commit an offence • Presence of others, especially children • Any steps taken to prevent the victim reporting an incident, obtaining assistance and/or from assisting or supporting the prosecution • Attempts to dispose of or conceal evidence • Commission of offence while under the influence of alcohol or drugs
Mitigating factors	
No previous convictions or no relevant/recent convictions Remorse Previous good character and/or exemplary conduct* Age and/or lack of maturity where it affects the responsibility of the offender Mental disorder or learning disability, particularly where linked to the commission of the offence	

* Previous good character/exemplary conduct is different from having no previous convictions. The more serious the offence, the less the weight which should normally be attributed to this factor. Where previous good character/exemplary conduct has been used to facilitate the offence, this mitigation should not normally be allowed and such conduct may constitute an aggravating factor. In the context of this offence, previous good character/exemplary conduct should not normally be given any significant weight and will not normally justify a reduction in what would otherwise be the appropriate sentence.

C14.8 Exposure

> ### Sexual Offences Act 2003, s 66(1)
>
> **66 Exposure**
>
> (1) A person commits an offence if—
>
>   (a) he intentionally exposes his genitals, and
>   (b) he intends that someone will see them and be caused alarm or distress.

 6 months' imprisonment and/or fine/2 years' imprisonment

If—

(a) where the offender was under 18, he is or has been sentenced in respect of the offence to imprisonment for a term of at least 12 months;

(b) in any other case—

    (i) the victim was under 18, or
    (ii) the offender, is—

        (a) sentenced to a term of imprisonment,
        (b) detained in a hospital, or
        (c) made the subject of a community sentence of at least 12 months.

C14.8.1 *Sentencing*

STEP ONE: Determining the offence category

The court should determine the offence category using the following table.

Category 1	Raised harm **and** raised culpability
Category 2	Raised harm **or** raised culpability
Category 3	Exposure **without** raised harm or culpability factors present

The court should determine culpability and harm caused or intended, by reference only to the following factors, which comprise the principal factual elements of the offence. Where an offence does not fall squarely into a category, individual factors may require a degree of weighting before making an overall assessment and determining the appropriate offence category.

Factors indicating raised harm
• Victim followed/pursued • Offender masturbated

Factors indicating raised culpability
• Specific or previous targeting of a particularly vulnerable victim
• Abuse of trust
• Use of threats (including blackmail)
• Offence racially or religiously aggravated
• Offence motivated by, or demonstrating, hostility to the victim based on his or her sexual orientation (or presumed sexual orientation) or transgender identity (or presumed transgender identity)
• Offence motivated by, or demonstrating, hostility to the victim based on his or her disability (or presumed disability)

STEP TWO: Starting point and category range

Having determined the category, the court should use the corresponding starting points to reach a sentence within the category range [below]. The starting point applies to all offenders irrespective of plea or previous convictions. Having determined the starting point, step two allows further adjustment for aggravating or mitigating features, set out [below].

A case of particular gravity, reflected by multiple features of culpability or harm in step one, could merit upward adjustment from the starting point before further adjustment for aggravating or mitigating features, set out [below].

Where there is a sufficient prospect of rehabilitation, a community order with a sex offender treatment programme requirement under s 202 Criminal Justice Act 2003 can be a proper alternative to a short or moderate length custodial sentence.

Category 1	**Starting point** 26 weeks' custody **Category range** 12 weeks'–1 year's custody
Category 2	**Starting point** High-level community order **Category range** Medium-level community order–26 weeks' custody
Category 3	**Starting point** Medium-level community order **Category range** Band A fine–high-level community order

The following table contains a non-exhaustive list of additional factual elements providing the context of the offence and factors relating to the offender. Identify whether any combination of these, or other relevant factors, should result in an upward or downward adjustment from the starting point. In particular, relevant recent convictions are likely to result in an upward adjustment. In some cases, having considered these factors, it may be appropriate to move outside the identified category range.

When sentencing category 2 offences, the court should also consider the custody threshold as follows:

- has the custody threshold been passed?
- if so, is it unavoidable that a custodial sentence be imposed?
- if so, can that sentence be suspended?

When sentencing category 3 offences, the court should also consider the community order threshold as follows:

- has the community order threshold been passed?

Aggravating factors	
Statutory aggravating factors	*Other aggravating factors*
• Previous convictions, having regard to (a) the nature of the offence to which the conviction relates and its relevance to the current offence; and (b) the time that has elapsed since the conviction • Offence committed while on bail	• Location of the offence • Timing of the offence • Any steps taken to prevent the victim reporting an incident, obtaining assistance, and/or from assisting or supporting the prosecution • Failure to comply with current court orders • Offence committed while on licence • Commission of offence while under the influence of alcohol or drugs • Presence of others, especially children
Mitigating factors	
• No previous convictions **or** no relevant/recent convictions • Remorse • Previous good character and/or exemplary conduct* • Age and/or lack of maturity where it affects the responsibility of the offender • Mental disorder or learning disability, particularly where linked to the commission of the offence • Demonstration of steps taken to address offending behaviour	

* Previous good character/exemplary conduct is different from having no previous convictions. The more serious the offence, the less the weight which should normally be attributed to this factor. Where previous good character/exemplary conduct has been used to facilitate the offence, this mitigation should not normally be allowed and such conduct may constitute an aggravating factor.

C14.8.2 Key points

- This offence is committed where an offender intentionally exposes his or her genitals and intends that someone will see them and be caused alarm or distress. It is gender-neutral, covering exposure of male or female genitalia to a male or female witness.
- This guideline may be relevant by way of analogy to conduct charged as the common law offence of outraging public decency. That offence is triable either way and has a maximum penalty of a fine and/or 6 months' imprisonment when tried summarily.

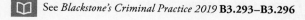 See *Blackstone's Criminal Practice 2019* **B3.293–B3.296**

C14.9 Extreme pornography

Criminal Justice and Immigration Act 2008, ss 63, 65–66

63 Possession of extreme pornographic images

(1) It is an offence for a person to be in possession of an extreme pornographic image.

(2) An 'extreme pornographic image' is an image which is both—
   (a) pornographic, and
   (b) an extreme image.

(3) An image is 'pornographic' if it is of such a nature that it must reasonably be assumed to have been produced solely or principally for the purpose of sexual arousal.

(4) Where (as found in the person's possession) an image forms part of a series of images, the question whether the image is of such a nature as is mentioned in subsection (3) is to be determined by reference to—
   (a) the image itself, and
   (b) (if the series of images is such as to be capable of providing a context for the image) the context in which it occurs in the series of images.

(5) So, for example, where—
   (a) an image forms an integral part of a narrative constituted by a series of images, and
   (b) having regard to those images as a whole, they are not of such a nature that they must reasonably be assumed to have been produced solely or principally for the purpose of sexual arousal,
   the image may, by virtue of being part of that narrative, be found not to be pornographic, even though it might have been found to be pornographic if taken by itself.

(5A) In relation to possession of an image in . . . an 'extreme image' is an image which—
   (a) falls within subsection (7) or (7A), and
   (b) is grossly offensive, disgusting or otherwise of an obscene character.

(7) An image falls within this subsection if it portrays, in an explicit and realistic way, any of the following—
   (a) an act which threatens a person's life,
   (b) an act which results, or is likely to result, in serious injury to a person's anus, breasts or genitals,
   (c) an act which involves sexual interference with a human corpse, or
   (d) a person performing an act of intercourse or oral sex with an animal (whether dead or alive), and a reasonable person looking at the image would think that any such person or animal was real.

(7A) An image falls within this subsection if it portrays, in an explicit and realistic way, either of the following—
   (a) an act which involves the non-consensual penetration of a person's vagina, anus or mouth by another with the other person's penis, or
   (b) an act which involves the non-consensual sexual penetration of a person's vagina or anus by another with a part of the other person's body or anything else, and a reasonable person looking at the image would think that the persons were real.

(7B) For the purposes of subsection (7A)—
   (a) penetration is a continuing act from entry to withdrawal;
   (b) 'vagina' includes vulva.

(8) In this section 'image' means—
   (a) a moving or still image (produced by any means); or

    (b) data (stored by any means) which is capable of conversion into an image within paragraph (a).

 (9) In this section references to a part of the body include references to a part surgically constructed (in particular through gender reassignment surgery).

(10) Proceedings for an offence under this section may not be instituted—

    (a) in England and Wales, except by or with the consent of the Director of Public Prosecutions;

...

65 Defences: general

(1) Where a person is charged with an offence under section 63, it is a defence for the person to prove any of the matters mentioned in subsection (2).

(2) The matters are—

    (a) that the person had a legitimate reason for being in possession of the image concerned;

    (b) that the person had not seen the image concerned and did not know, nor had any cause to suspect, it to be an extreme pornographic image;

    (c) that the person—

       (i) was sent the image concerned without any prior request having been made by or on behalf of the person, and

       (ii) did not keep it for an unreasonable time.

(3) In this section 'extreme pornographic image' and 'image' have the same meanings as in section 63.

66 Defence: participation in consensual acts

(A1) Subsection (A2) applies where in England and Wales—

    (a) a person ('D') is charged with an offence under section 63, and

    (b) the offence relates to an image that portrays an act or acts within subsection (7)(a) to (c) or (7A) of that section (but does not portray an act within subsection (7)(d) of that section).

(A2) It is a defence for D to prove—

    (a) that D directly participated in the act or any of the acts portrayed, and

    (b) that the act or acts did not involve the infliction of any non-consensual harm on any person, and

    (c) if the image portrays an act within section 63(7)(c), that what is portrayed as a human corpse was not in fact a corpse, and

    (d) if the image portrays an act within section 63(7A), that what is portrayed as non-consensual penetration was in fact consensual, and

(A3) For the purposes of this section harm inflicted on a person is 'non-consensual' harm if—

    (a) the harm is of such a nature that the person cannot, in law, consent to it being inflicted on himself or herself; or

    (b) where the person can, in law, consent to it being so inflicted, the person does not in fact consent to it being so inflicted.

EW

 6 months' imprisonment and/or fine/3 years' imprisonment (2 years if the offence relates to an image that does not portray any act within s 63(7)(a) or (b))

SON

If the offender—
- (a) was 18 or over, and
- (b) is sentenced to imprisonment for a term of at least 2 years

C14.9.1 Key points

Section 63(3) means was the image produced for the purpose of sexually arousing anyone who comes to have it, be that the producer himself, a distributor, or an ultimate recipient. The section is designed to prevent the possession of such images by any person. The purpose of the subsection is to identify the types of image that are pornographic. The word 'pornographic' here deals with the assumed purpose of the image. The identity or purpose of the producer is immaterial; the circumstances in which the images are received are immaterial (*R v DB* [2016] EWCA Crim 474).There are two elements to be made out in order for an individual to have possession:

(1) the images must have been within the defendant's custody or control, ie so that he was capable of accessing them; and
(2) he must have known that he possessed an image or a group of images. Knowledge of the content of those images is not required to make out the basic ingredients of the offence; instead that issue is dealt with by the statutory defence under s 65(2) (*R v Okoro* [2019] EWCA Crim 1929).

 See *Blackstone's Criminal Practice 2019* **B3.342–B3.347**

C14.10 Familial child sexual offences

Sexual Offences Act 2003, ss 25 and 26

25 Sexual activity with a child family member

(1) A person (A) commits an offence if—
   (a) he intentionally touches another person (B),
   (b) the touching is sexual,
   (c) the relation of A to B is within section 27,
   (d) A knows or could reasonably be expected to know that his relation to B is of a description falling within that section, and
   (e) either—
      (i) B is under 18 and A does not reasonably believe that B is 18 or over, or
      (ii) B is under 13.
(2) Where in proceedings for an offence under this section it is proved that the other person was under 18, the defendant is to be taken not to have reasonably believed that that person was 18 or over unless sufficient evidence is adduced to raise an issue as to whether he reasonably believed it.
(3) Where in proceedings for an offence under this section it is proved that the relation of the defendant to the other person was of a description falling within section 27, it is to be taken that the defendant knew or could reasonably have been expected to know that his relation to the other person was of that description unless sufficient evidence is adduced to raise an issue as to whether he knew or could reasonably have been expected to know that it was.

...

(6) This subsection applies where the touching involved–

    (a) penetration of B's anus or vagina with a part of A's body or anything else,

    (b) penetration of B's mouth with A's penis,

    (c) penetration of A's anus or vagina with a part of B's body, or

    (d) penetration of A's mouth with B's penis.

26 Inciting a child family member to engage in sexual activity

(1) A person (A) commits an offence if—

    (a) he intentionally incites another person (B) to touch, or allow himself to be touched by, A,

    (b) the touching is sexual,

    (c) the relation of A to B is within section 27,

    (d) A knows or could reasonably be expected to know that his relation to B is of a description falling within that section, and

    (e) either—

        (i) B is under 18 and A does not reasonably believe that B is 18 or over, or

        (ii) B is under 13.

(2) Where in proceedings for an offence under this section it is proved that the other person was under 18, the defendant is to be taken not to have reasonably believed that that person was 18 or over unless sufficient evidence is adduced to raise an issue as to whether he reasonably believed it.

(3) Where in proceedings for an offence under this section it is proved that the relation of the defendant to the other person was of a description falling within section 27, it is to be taken that the defendant knew or could reasonably have been expected to know that his relation to the other person was of that description unless sufficient evidence is adduced to raise an issue as to whether he knew or could reasonably have been expected to know that it was.

...

(6) This subsection applies where the touching to which the incitement related involved—

    (a) penetration of B's anus or vagina with a part of A's body or anything else,

    (b) penetration of B's mouth with A's penis,

    (c) penetration of A's anus or vagina with a part of B's body, or

    (d) penetration of A's mouth with B's penis.

EW but indictable only if the activity involves penetration

GC

▦ 6 months' imprisonment/fine; 14 years' imprisonment

SON

If the offender—

(a) was 18 or over, or

(b) is or has been sentenced in respect of the offence to imprisonment for a term of at least 12 months

C14.10.1 *Sentencing*

STEP ONE: Determining the offence category

The court should determine which categories of harm and culpability the offence falls into by reference only to the following tables. This offence involves those who have a family relationship with the victim and it should be assumed that the greater the abuse of trust within this relationship the more grave the offence.

Harm		Culpability	
		A	B
Category 1	Penetration of vagina or anus (using body or object) Penile penetration of mouth In either case by, or of, the victim	Significant degree of planning Offender acts together with others to commit the offence Use of alcohol/drugs on victim to facilitate the offence Grooming behaviour used against victim Use of threats (including blackmail) Sexual images of victim recorded, retained, solicited or shared Specific targeting of a particularly vulnerable child Significant disparity in age Commercial exploitation and/or motivation Offence racially or religiously aggravated Offence motivated by, or demonstrating, hostility to the victim based on his or her sexual orientation (or presumed sexual orientation) or transgender identity (or presumed transgender identity) Offence motivated by, or demonstrating, hostility to the victim based on his or her disability (or presumed disability)	Factor(s) in category A not present
Category 2	Touching of naked genitalia or naked breasts by, or of, the victim		
Category 3	Other sexual activity		

STEP TWO: Starting point and category range

Having determined the category, the court should use the corresponding starting points to reach a sentence within the following category range. The starting point applies to all offenders irrespective of plea or previous convictions. Having determined the starting point, step two allows further adjustment for aggravating or mitigating features, set out on the next page.

A case of particular gravity, reflected by multiple features of culpability or harm in step one, could merit upward adjustment from the starting point before further adjustment for aggravating or mitigating features, set out on the next page.

Where there is a sufficient prospect of rehabilitation, a community order with a sex offender treatment programme requirement under s 202 Criminal Justice Act 2003 can be a proper alternative to a short or moderate length custodial sentence.

	A	B
Category 1	**Starting point** 6 years' custody **Category range** 4–10 years' custody	**Starting point** 3 years 6 months' custody **Category range** 2 years 6 months–5 years' custody
Category 2	**Starting point** 4 years' custody **Category range** 2–6 years' custody	**Starting point** 18 months' custody **Category range** 26 weeks'–2 years 6 months' custody
Category 3	**Starting point** 1 year's custody **Category range** High-level community order– 3 years' custody	**Starting point** Medium-level community order **Category range** Low-level community order– High-level community

The following table contains a **non-exhaustive** list of additional factual elements providing the context of the offence and factors relating to the offender. Identify whether any combination of these, or other relevant factors, should result in an upward or downward adjustment from the starting point. In particular, relevant recent convictions are likely to result in an upward adjustment. In some cases, having considered these factors, it may be appropriate to move outside the identified category range.

When sentencing appropriate category 3 offences, the court should also consider the custody threshold as follows:

- has the custody threshold been passed?
- if so, is it unavoidable that a custodial sentence be imposed?
- if so, can that sentence be suspended?

Aggravating factors	
Statutory aggravating factors	*Other aggravating factors*

Aggravating factors	
• Previous convictions, having regard to (a) the nature of the offence to which the conviction relates and its relevance to the current offence; and (b) the time that has elapsed since the conviction • Offence committed while on bail	• Severe psychological or physical harm • Ejaculation • Pregnancy or STI as a consequence of offence • Location of offence • Timing of offence • Victim compelled to leave their home, school, etc • Failure to comply with current court orders • Offence committed while on licence • Exploiting contact arrangements with a child to commit an offence • Presence of others, especially other children • Any steps taken to prevent the victim reporting an incident, obtaining assistance and/or from assisting or supporting the prosecution • Attempts to dispose of or conceal evidence • Failure of offender to respond to previous warnings • Commission of offence while under the influence of alcohol or drugs • Victim encouraged to recruit others • Period over which offence committed

Mitigating factors

- No previous convictions or no relevant/recent convictions
- Remorse
- Previous good character and/or exemplary conduct*
- Age and/or lack of maturity where it affects the responsibility of the offender
- Mental disorder or learning disability, particularly where linked to the commission of the offence
- Sexual activity was incited but no activity took place because the offender voluntarily desisted or intervened to prevent it

* Previous good character/exemplary conduct is different from having no previous convictions. The more serious the offence, the less the weight which should normally be attributed to this factor. Where previous good character/exemplary conduct has been used to facilitate the offence, this mitigation should not normally be allowed and such conduct may constitute an aggravating factor.

In the context of this offence, previous good character/exemplary conduct should not normally be given any significant weight and will not normally justify a reduction in what would otherwise be the appropriate sentence.

C14.11 Indecent photographs of children

Protection of Children Act 1978, s 1(1)–(4)

1 Indecent photographs of children

(1) Subject to sections 1A and 1B, it is an offence for a person—
  (a) to take, or permit to be taken or to make, any indecent photograph or pseudo-photograph of a child; or
  (b) to distribute or show such indecent photographs or pseudo-photographs; or
  (c) to have in his possession such indecent photographs or pseudo-photographs, with a view to their being distributed or shown by himself or others; or
  (d) to publish or cause to be published any advertisement likely to be understood as conveying that the advertiser distributes or shows such indecent photographs or pseudo-photographs, or intends to do so.

(2) For purposes of this Act, a person is to be regarded as distributing an indecent photograph or pseudo-photograph if he parts with possession of it to, or exposes or offers it for acquisition by, another person.

(3) Proceedings for an offence under this Act shall not be instituted except by or with the consent of the Director of Public Prosecutions.

(4) Where a person is charged with an offence under subsection (1)(b) or (c), it shall be a defence for him to prove—

    (a) that he had a legitimate reason for distributing or showing the photographs or pseudo-photographs or (as the case may be) having them in his possession; or

    (b) that he had not himself seen the photographs or pseudo-photographs and did not know, nor had any cause to suspect, them to be indecent.

...

Criminal Justice Act 1988, s 160

160 Possession of indecent photograph of child

(1) Subject to section 160A, it is an offence for a person to have any indecent photograph or pseudo-photograph of a child in his possession.

(2) Where a person is charged with an offence under subsection (1) above, it shall be a defence for him to prove—

    (a) that he had a legitimate reason for having the photograph or pseudo-photograph in his possession; or

    (b) that he had not himself seen the photograph or pseudo-photograph and did not know, nor had any cause to suspect, it to be indecent; or

    (c) that the photograph or pseudo-photograph was sent to him without any prior request made by him or on his behalf and that he did not keep it for an unreasonable time.

EW

⊞ 6 months' imprisonment and/or fine/10 years' imprisonment (5 years if s 160)

DO

SON

If—

(a) the indecent photographs or pseudo-photographs showed persons under 16, and

(b) the offender—

    (i) was 18 or over, or

    (ii) is sentenced in respect of the offence to imprisonment for a term of at least 12 months.

STEP ONE: Determining the offence category

The court should determine the offence category using the following table.

	Possession	Distribution*	Production**
Category A	• Possession of images involving penetrative sexual activity • Possession of images involving sexual activity with an animal or sadism	• Sharing images involving penetrative sexual activity • Sharing images involving sexual activity with an animal or sadism	• Creating images involving penetrative sexual activity • Creating images involving sexual activity with an animal or sadism
Category B	• Possession of images involving non-penetrative sexual activity	• Sharing of images involving non-penetrative sexual activity	• Creating images involving non-penetrative sexual activity
Category C	• Possession of other indecent images not falling within categories A or B	• Sharing of other indecent images not falling within categories A or B	• Creating other indecent images not falling within categories A or B

* Distribution includes possession with a view to distributing or sharing images.

** Production includes the taking or making of any image at source, for instance the original image. Making an image by simple downloading should be treated as possession for the purposes of sentencing.

In most cases the intrinsic character of the most serious of the offending images will initially determine the appropriate category. If, however, the most serious images are unrepresentative of the offender's conduct a lower category may be appropriate. A lower category will not, however, be appropriate if the offender has produced or taken (for example photographed) images of a higher category.

STEP TWO: Starting point and category range

Having determined the category, the court should use the corresponding starting points to reach a sentence within the following category range. The starting point applies to all offenders irrespective of plea or previous convictions. Having determined the starting point, step two allows further adjustment for aggravating or mitigating features, set out on the next page.

Where there is a sufficient prospect of rehabilitation, a community order with a sex offender treatment programme requirement under s 202 Criminal Justice Act 2003 can be a proper alternative to a short or moderate length custodial sentence.

	Possession	Distribution	Production
Category A	**Starting point** 1 year's custody **Category range** 26 weeks'–3 years' custody	**Starting point** 3 years' custody **Category range** 2–5 years' custody	**Starting point** 6 years' custody **Category range** 4–9 years' custody
Category B	**Starting point** 26 weeks' custody **Category range** High-level community order–18 months' custody	**Starting point** 1 year's custody **Category range** 26 weeks–2 years' custody	**Starting point** 2 years' custody **Category range** 1–4 years' custody

	Possession	Distribution	Production
Category C	**Starting point** High-level community order **Category range** Medium-level community order–26 weeks' custody	**Starting point** 13 weeks' custody **Category range** High-level community order–26 weeks' custody	**Starting point** 18 months' custody **Category range** 1–3 years' custody

The following table contains a non-exhaustive list of additional factual elements providing the context of the offence and factors relating to the offender. Identify whether any combination of these, or other relevant factors, should result in an upward or downward adjustment from the starting point. In particular, relevant recent convictions are likely to result in an upward adjustment. In some cases, having considered these factors, it may be appropriate to move outside the identified category range.

When sentencing appropriate category B or C offences, the court should also consider the custody threshold as follows:

- has the custody threshold been passed?
- if so, is it unavoidable that a custodial sentence be imposed?
- if so, can that sentence be suspended?

Aggravating factors	
Statutory aggravating factors	*Other aggravating factors*
• Previous convictions, having regard to (a) the nature of the offence to which the conviction relates and its relevance to the current offence; and (b) the time that has elapsed since the conviction • Offence committed while on bail	• Failure to comply with current court orders • Offence committed while on licence • Age and/or vulnerability of the child depicted+ • Discernible pain or distress suffered by child depicted • Period over which images were possessed, distributed or produced • High volume of images possessed, distributed, or produced • Placing images where there is the potential for a high volume of viewers
	• Collection includes moving images • Attempts to dispose of or conceal evidence • Abuse of trust • Child depicted known to the offender • Active involvement in a network or process that facilitates or commissions the creation or sharing of indecent images of children • Commercial exploitation and/or motivation • Deliberate or systematic searching for images portraying young children, category A images, or the portrayal of familial sexual abuse • Large number of different victims • Child depicted intoxicated or drugged
	+Age and/or vulnerability of the child should be given significant weight. In cases where the actual age of the victim is difficult to determine sentencers should consider the development of the child (infant, pre-pubescent, post-pubescent)

Mitigating factors
• No previous convictions **or** no relevant/recent convictions
• Remorse
• Previous good character and/or exemplary conduct*
• Age and/or lack of maturity where it affects the responsibility of the offender
• Mental disorder or learning disability, particularly where linked to the commission of the offence
• Demonstration of steps taken to address offending behaviour

* Previous good character/exemplary conduct is different from having no previous convictions. The more serious the offence, the less the weight which should normally be attributed to this factor. Where previous good character/exemplary conduct has been used to facilitate the offence, this mitigation should not normally be allowed and such conduct may constitute an aggravating factor.

C14.11.1 Key points

- There were two types of *mens rea* required to prove an offence under s 1(1)(a) Protection of Children Act 1978. One was when making by downloading to a computer or telephone. The other was by photographing or filming the image. The former alone required proof of an awareness as to what was being downloaded (*R v PW* [2016] EWCA Crim 745).
- Under s 160 Criminal Justice Act 1988 there are two elements to be made out in order for an individual to have possession:
  (1) the images must have been within the defendant's custody or control, ie so that he was capable of accessing them; and
  (2) he must have known that he possessed an image or a group of images. Knowledge of the content of those images is not required to make out the basic ingredients of the offence; instead that issue is dealt with by the statutory defence under s 160(2) (*R v Okoro* [2019] EWCA Crim 1929).
- Photograph includes tracing or other image derived in whole or part from a photograph or pseudo-photograph.
- Whether a photograph is indecent depends on normally recognized standards of propriety.
- The age of the child may be relevant to the issue of indecency (*R v Owen* (1988) 88 Cr App R 291).
- The opening of an email or viewing of an image on the screen would amount to the making of an image if the defendant has the requisite knowledge of what he is doing.
- A person is not in possession of images if they have been deleted, if he is not able to recover those images (*R v Porter* [2006] EWCA Crim 560).
- A child is a person under 18 years of age (Sexual Offences Act 2003, s 45).

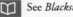 See *Blackstone's Criminal Practice 2019* **B3.318–B3.329**

C14.12 Keeping a brothel used for prostitution

Sexual Offences Act 1956, s 33

33 Keeping a brothel

It is an offence for a person to keep a brothel, or to manage, or act or assist in the management of, a brothel.

 3 months' imprisonment and/or level 3 fine. If previous conviction: 6 months' imprisonment and/or level 4 fine

Sexual Offences Act 1956, s 33A

33A Keeping a brothel used for prostitution

(1) It is an offence for a person to keep, or to manage, or act or assist in the management of, a brothel to which people resort for practices involving prostitution (whether or not also for other practices).

 6 months' imprisonment and/or fine/7 years' imprisonment

C14.12.1 *Sentencing*

STEP ONE: Determining the offence category

The court should determine which categories of harm and culpability the offence falls into by reference only to the following tables .

Harm	
Category 1	• Under-18-year-olds working in brothel • Abduction/detention • Violence or threats of violence • Sustained and systematic psychological abuse • Those working in brothel forced or coerced to participate in unsafe/degrading sexual activity • Those working in brothel forced or coerced into seeing many 'customers' • Those working in brothel forced/coerced/deceived into prostitution • Established evidence of community impact
Category 2	Factor(s) in category 1 not present

Culpability		
A	**B**	**C**
• Keeping brothel on significant commercial basis • Involvement in keeping a number of brothels • Expectation of significant financial or other gain • Abuse of trust • Exploitation of those known to be trafficked • Significant involvement in limiting freedom of those working in brothel • Grooming of a person to work in the brothel including through cultivation of a dependency on drugs or alcohol	• Keeping/managing premises • Close involvement with those working in brothel eg control of finances, choice of clients, working conditions, etc (where offender's involvement is not as a result of coercion)	• Performs limited function under direction • Close involvement but engaged by coercion/ intimidation/ exploitation

STEP TWO: Starting point and category range

Having determined the category, the court should use the corresponding starting points to reach a sentence within the category range [below]. The starting point applies to all offenders irrespective of plea or previous convictions. Having determined the starting point, step two allows further adjustment for aggravating or mitigating features, set out [below].

A case of particular gravity, reflected by multiple features of culpability or harm in step one, could merit upward adjustment from the starting point before further adjustment for aggravating or mitigating features, set out [below].

Where there is a sufficient prospect of rehabilitation, a community order with a sex offender treatment programme requirement under s 202 Criminal Justice Act 2003 can be a proper alternative to a short or moderate length custodial sentence.

	A	**B**	**C**
Category 1	**Starting point** 5 years' custody **Category range** 3–6 years' custody	**Starting point** 3 years' custody **Category range** 2–5 years custody	**Starting point** 1 year's custody **Category range** High-level community order– 18 months' custody
Category 2	**Starting point** 3 years' custody **Category range** 2–5 years custody	**Starting point** 12 months' custody **Category range** 26 weeks–2 years' custody	**Starting point** Medium-level community order **Category range** Low-level community order– high-level community order

The following table contains a non-exhaustive list of additional factual elements providing the context of the offence and factors relating to the offender. Identify whether any combination of these, or other relevant factors, should result in an upward or downward adjustment from the starting point. In particular, relevant recent convictions are likely to result in an upward adjustment. In some cases, having considered these factors, it may be appropriate to move outside the identified category range.

When sentencing appropriate category 1 offences, the court should also consider the custody threshold as follows:

- has the custody threshold been passed?
- if so, is it unavoidable that a custodial sentence be imposed?
- if so, can that sentence be suspended?

Aggravating factors	
Statutory aggravating factors	*Other aggravating factors*
• Previous convictions, having regard to (a) the nature of the offence to which the conviction relates and its relevance to the current offence; and (b) the time that has elapsed since the conviction • Offence committed while on bail	• Failure to comply with current court orders • Offence committed while on licence • Deliberate isolation of those working in brothel • Threats made to expose those working in brothel to the authorities (for example, immigration or police), family/friends, or others • Harm threatened against the family/friends of those working in brothel • Passport/identity documents removed. • Those working in brothel prevented from seeking medical treatment • Food withheld • Those working in brothel passed around by offender and moved to other brothels • Earnings of those working in brothel withheld/kept by offender, or evidence of excessive wage reduction or debt bondage, inflated travel or living expenses, or unreasonable interest rates
	• Any steps taken to prevent those working in brothel reporting an incident, obtaining assistance, and/or from assisting or supporting the prosecution • Attempts to dispose of or conceal evidence • Those working in brothel forced or coerced into pornography • Timescale over which operation has been run
Mitigating factors	
• No previous convictions **or** no relevant/recent convictions • Remorse • Previous good character and/or exemplary conduct* • Age and/or lack of maturity where it affects the responsibility of the offender • Mental disorder or learning disability, particularly where linked to the commission of the offence • Demonstration of steps taken to address offending behaviour	

* Previous good character/exemplary conduct is different from having no previous convictions. The more serious the offence, the less the weight which should normally be attributed to this factor. Where previous good character/exemplary conduct has been used to facilitate the offence, this mitigation should not normally be allowed and such conduct may constitute an aggravating factor.

 See *Blackstone's Criminal Practice 2019* **B3.354–B3.369**

C14.13 **Kerb crawling, paying for sexual services, loitering, and soliciting**

Sexual Offences Act 2003, ss 51A and 53A

51A Soliciting

51A(1) It is an offence for a person in a street or public place to solicit another (B) for the purpose of obtaining B's sexual services as a prostitute.

(2) The reference to a person in a street or public place includes a person in a vehicle in a street or public place.

. . .

(4) In this section 'street' has the meaning given by section 1(4) of the Street Offences Act 1959.

53A Paying for sexual services of a prostitute subjected to force etc

53A(1) A person (A) commits an offence if—

    (a) A makes or promises payment for the sexual services of a prostitute (B),

    (b) a third person (C) has engaged in exploitative conduct of a kind likely to induce or encourage B to provide the sexual services for which A has made or promised payment, and

    (c) C engaged in that conduct for or in the expectation of gain for C or another person (apart from A or B).

(2) The following are irrelevant—

    (a) where in the world the sexual services are to be provided and whether those services are provided,

    (b) whether A is, or ought to be, aware that C has engaged in exploitative conduct.

(3) C engages in exploitative conduct if—

    (a) C uses force, threats (whether or not relating to violence) or any other form of coercion, or

    (b) C practises any form of deception.

Street Offences Act 1959, s 1(1)

1 Loitering or soliciting for purposes of prostitution

(1) It shall be an offence for a person aged 18 or over (whether male or female) persistently to loiter or solicit in a street or public place for the purpose of prostitution.

 Fine level 3 (for a first offence under Street Offences Act 1959, s 1, the fine is level 2)

 See *Blackstone's Criminal Practice 2019* **B3.250–B3.317**

C14.14 Offences against child under 13

There are three offences under ss 5–7 SOA 2003. It is not necessary to prove that the defendant knew that the complainant was under the age of 13 (*R v G* [2008] UKHL 37, [2009] 1 AC 92). For s7 **see C14.12**

C14.14.1 *Rape of child under 13*

Sexual Offences Act 2003, s 5

(1) A person commits an offence if—

    (a) he intentionally penetrates the vagina, anus, or mouth of another person with his penis, and

    (b) the other person is under 13.

 GC

IO

DO

Life

For youths see the *Handbook of Youths in the Criminal Courts*

SON

C14.14.2 *Assault by penetration of a child under 13*

Sexual Offences Act 2003, s 6

(1) A person commits an offence if—

    (a) he intentionally penetrates the vagina or anus of another person with a part of his body or anything else,

    (b) the penetration is sexual, and

    (c) the other person is under 13.

GC

IO

Life

For youths see the *Handbook of Youths in the Criminal Courts*

SON

C14.15 **Possession of paedophile manual**

Serious Crime Act 2015, s 69

69 Possession of paedophile manual

(1) It is an offence to be in possession of any item that contains advice or guidance about abusing children sexually.

(2) It is a defence for a person (D) charged with an offence under this section—

    (a) to prove that D had a legitimate reason for being in possession of the item;

    (b) to prove that—

        (i) D had not read, viewed or (as appropriate) listened to the item, and

        (ii) D did not know, and had no reason to suspect, that it contained advice or guidance about abusing children sexually; or

    (c) to prove that—

        (i) the item was sent to D without any request made by D or on D's behalf, and

        (ii) D did not keep it for an unreasonable time.

...

(4) Proceedings for an offence under this section may be brought—

    (a) in England and Wales, only by or with the consent of the Director of Public Prosecutions;

C14.15.1 Key points

Serious Crime Act 2015, s 69

(8) In this section—,

    'abusing children sexually' means doing anything that constitutes—

    (a) an offence under Part 1 of the Sexual Offences Act 2003, or under Part 2, 3, against a person under 16, or

    (b) an offence under section 1 of the Protection of Children Act 1978 involving indecent photographs (but not pseudo-photographs), or doing anything outside England and Wales that would constitute such an offence if done in England and Wales;

    'item' includes anything in which information of any description is recorded;

    'prohibited item' means an item within subsection (1).

EW

 6 months' imprisonment and/or a fine/2 years' imprisonment

 SON

If the offender—

(a) was 18 or over, or

(b) is sentenced in respect of the offence to imprisonment for a term of at least 12 months

---

C14.16 Prohibited images of children

Coroners and Justice Act 2009, s 62

62 Possession of prohibited images of children

(1) It is an offence for a person to be in possession of a prohibited image of a child.

(2) A prohibited image is an image which—

    (a) is pornographic,

    (b) falls within subsection (6), and

    (c) is grossly offensive, disgusting or otherwise of an obscene character.

(3) An image is 'pornographic' if it is of such a nature that it must reasonably be assumed to have been produced solely or principally for the purpose of sexual arousal.

(4) Where (as found in the person's possession) an image forms part of a series of images, the question whether the image is of such a nature as is mentioned in subsection (3) is to be determined by reference to—

    (a) the image itself, and

    (b) (if the series of images is such as to be capable of providing a context for the image) the context in which it occurs in the series of images.

(5) So, for example, where—

    (a) an image forms an integral part of a narrative constituted by a series of images, and

    (b) having regard to those images as a whole, they are not of such a nature that they must reasonably be assumed to have been produced solely or principally for the purpose of sexual arousal,

    the image may, by virtue of being part of that narrative, be found not to be pornographic, even though it might have been found to be pornographic if taken by itself.

(6) An image falls within this subsection if it—

    (a) is an image which focuses solely or principally on a child's genitals or anal region, or

    (b) portrays any of the acts mentioned in subsection (7).

(7) Those acts are—

    (a) the performance by a person of an act of intercourse or oral sex with or in the presence of a child;

    (b) an act of masturbation by, of, involving or in the presence of a child;

    (c) an act which involves penetration of the vagina or anus of a child with a part of a person's body or with anything else;

    (d) an act of penetration, in the presence of a child, of the vagina or anus of a person with a part of a person's body or with anything else;

    (e) the performance by a child of an act of intercourse or oral sex with an animal (whether dead or alive or imaginary);

    (f) the performance by a person of an act of intercourse or oral sex with an animal (whether dead or alive or imaginary) in the presence of a child.

(8) For the purposes of subsection (7), penetration is a continuing act from entry to withdrawal.

(9) Proceedings for an offence under subsection (1) may not be instituted—

    (a) in England and Wales, except by or with the consent of the Director of Public Prosecutions;

. . .

EW

6 months' imprisonment and/or fine/3 years' imprisonment

SON

If the offender—
(a) was 18 or over, and
(b) is sentenced to imprisonment for a term of at least 2 years

C14.16.1 Key points

- Section 64 of the Coroners and Justice Act 2009 provides for the following defence:

Coroners and Justice Act 2009, s 64(1)

64 Defences

(1) Where a person is charged with an offence under section 62(1), it is a defence for the person to prove any of the following matters—

  (a) that the person had a legitimate reason for being in possession of the image concerned;

  (b) that the person had not seen the image concerned and did not know, nor had any cause to suspect, it to be a prohibited image of a child;

  (c) that the person—

    (i) was sent the image concerned without any prior request having been made by or on behalf of the person, and

    (ii) did not keep it for an unreasonable time.

- Section 63 of the Act defines the meaning of 'image' and 'child'.

 See *Blackstone's Criminal Practice 2019* **B3.330–B3.335**

C14.17 Rape

Sexual Offences Act 2003, s 1

(1) A person (A) commits an offence if—

  (a) he intentionally penetrates the vagina, anus, or mouth of another person (B) with his penis,

  (b) B does not consent to the penetration, and

  (c) A does not reasonably believe that B consents.

(2) Whether a belief is reasonable is to be determined having regard to all the circumstances, including any steps A has taken to ascertain whether B consents.

(3) Sections 75 and 76 apply to an offence under this section.

GC

DO

卌 Life

IO

SON

C14.17.1 *Sentencing*

For youths see the *Handbook of Youths in the Criminal Courts*

C14.17.2 Key points

• Penetration is a continuing act from entry to withdrawal (s 79(2) SOA 2003).
• For consent see **C14.1.1**.

C14.18 Sexual activity in a public lavatory

Sexual Offences Act 2003, s 71(1) and (2)

71 Sexual activity in a public lavatory

(1) A person commits an offence if—
  (a) he is in a lavatory to which the public or a section of the public has or is permitted to have access, whether on payment or otherwise,
  (b) he intentionally engages in an activity, and,
  (c) the activity is sexual.
(2) For the purposes of this section, an activity is sexual if a reasonable person would, in all the circumstances but regardless of any person's purpose, consider it to be sexual.

SO 6 months' imprisonment and/or fine

C14.18.1 *Sentencing*
STEP ONE: Determining the offence category

The court should determine the offence category using the following table.

Category 1	Higher culpability **and** greater harm
Category 2	Higher culpability **and** lesser harm **or** lower culpability **and** greater harm
Category 3	Lower culpability **and** lesser harm

The court should determine the offender's culpability and the harm caused with reference only to the following factors. Where an offence does not fall squarely into a category, individual factors may require a degree of weighting before making an overall assessment and determining the appropriate offence category.

CULPABILITY demonstrated by one or more of the following:	
Factors indicating higher culpability	Factors indicating lower culpability
• Intimidating behaviour/threats of violence to member(s) of the public • Blatant behaviour	• All other cases
HARM demonstrated by one or more of the following:	
Factors indicating greater harm	Factors indicating lesser harm
• Distress suffered by members of the public • Children or young persons present	• All other cases

STEP TWO: Starting point and category range

Having determined the category at step one, the court should use the starting point to reach a sentence within the appropriate category range in the following table. The starting point applies to all offenders irrespective of plea or previous convictions.

Offence category	Starting point	Range
Category 1	Low-level community order	Band C fine–High-level community order
Category 2	Band C fine	Band B fine–Low-level community order
Category 3	Band B fine	Band A fine–Band C fine

Persistent offending of this nature may justify an upward adjustment outside the category range and may cross the community threshold even though the offence otherwise warrants a lesser sentence.

The court should then consider adjustment for any aggravating or mitigating factors. The following is a non-exhaustive list of additional factual elements providing the context of the offence and factors relating to the offender. Identify whether any combination of these, or other relevant factors, should result in an upward or downward adjustment from the sentence arrived at so far.

Factors increasing seriousness	
Statutory aggravating factors:	Other aggravating factors:
• Previous convictions, having regard to (a) the nature of the offence to which the conviction relates and its relevance to the current offence; and (b) the time that has elapsed since the conviction • Offence committed while on bail	• Failure to comply with current court orders • Offence committed on licence or post sentence supervision • Offences taken into consideration • Location • Presence of children • Established evidence of community/wider impact
Factors reducing seriousness or reflecting personal mitigation	
• No previous convictions **or** no relevant/recent convictions • Remorse • Good character and/or exemplary conduct • Serious medical condition requiring urgent, intensive or long-term treatment • Age and/or lack of maturity where it affects the responsibility of the offender	

C14.18.2 Key points

- This offence is committed where an offender intentionally engages in sexual activity in a public lavatory. It was introduced to give adults and children the freedom to use public lavatories for the purpose for which they are designed, without the fear of being an unwilling witness to overtly sexual behaviour of a kind that most people would not expect to be conducted in public. It is primarily a public order offence rather than a sexual offence.
- This guideline may be relevant by way of analogy to conduct charged as the common law offence of outraging public decency. That offence is triable either way and has a maximum penalty of a fine and/or six months' imprisonment when tried summarily.

📖 See *Blackstone's Criminal Practice 2019* **B3.310–B3.312**

C14.19 Sexual activity with a child

Sexual Offences Act 2003, s 9

9 Sexual activity with a child

(2) A person aged 18 or over (A) commits an offence if—
    (a) he intentionally touches another person (B),
    (b) the touching is sexual, and
    (c) either—
        (i) B is under 16 and A does not reasonably believe that B is 16 or over, or
        (ii) B is under 13.
(3) A person guilty of an offence under this section, if the touching involved—
    (a) penetration of B's anus or vagina with a part of A's body or anything else,
    (b) penetration of B's mouth with A's penis,
    (c) penetration of A's anus or vagina with a part of B's body, or
    (d) penetration of A's mouth with B's penis.

EW Save where penetration is involved and the offences become triable only on indictment

 6 months' imprisonment and/or fine/14 years' imprisonment

 DO

Note the following guideline also applies to offences under s 10 SOA 2003.

STEP ONE: Determining the offence category

The court should determine which categories of harm and culpability the offence falls into by reference only to the following tables. This guideline also applies to offences committed remotely/online.

Harm		Culpability	
		A	**B**
Category 1	• Penetration of vagina or anus (using body or object) • Penile penetration of mouth In either case by, or of, the victim	• Significant degree of planning • Offender acts together with others to commit the offence • Use of alcohol/drugs on victim to facilitate the offence • Grooming behaviour used against victim • Abuse of trust • Use of threats (including blackmail) • Sexual images of victim recorded, retained, solicited or shared	Factor(s) in category A not present
		• Specific targeting of a particularly vulnerable child • Offender lied about age • Significant disparity in age • Commercial exploitation and/or motivation • Offence racially or religiously aggravated • Offence motivated by, or demonstrating, hostility to the victim based on his or her sexual orientation (or presumed sexual orientation) or transgender identity (or presumed transgender identity) • Offence motivated by, or demonstrating, hostility to the victim based on his or her disability (or presumed disability)	
Category 2	• Touching, or exposure, of naked genitalia or naked breasts by, or of, the victim		
Category 3	Other sexual activity		

STEP TWO: Starting point and category range

Having determined the category, the court should use the corresponding starting points to reach a sentence within the following category range. The starting point applies to all offenders irrespective of plea or previous convictions. Having determined the starting point, step two allows further adjustment for aggravating or mitigating features, set out on the next page.

A case of particular gravity, reflected by multiple features of culpability or harm in step one, could merit upward adjustment from the starting point before further adjustment for aggravating or mitigating features, set out in the table.

Where there is a sufficient prospect of rehabilitation, a community order with a sex offender treatment programme requirement under s 202 Criminal Justice Act 2003 can be a proper alternative to a short or moderate length custodial sentence.

	A	B
Category 1	**Starting point** 5 years' custody **Category range** 4–10 years' custody	**Starting point** 1 year's custody **Category range** High-level community order–2 years' custody
Category 2	**Starting point** 3 years' custody **Category range** 2–6 years' custody	**Starting point** 26 weeks' custody **Category range** High-level community order–1 year's custody
Category 3	**Starting point** 26 weeks' custody **Category range** High-level community order–3 years' custody	**Starting point** Medium-level community order **Category range** Low-level community order–High-level community order

The following table contains a non-exhaustive list of additional factual elements providing the context of the offence and factors relating to the offender. Identify whether any combination of these, or other relevant factors, should result in an upward or downward adjustment from the starting point. In particular, relevant recent convictions are likely to result in an upward adjustment. In some cases, having considered these factors, it may be appropriate to move outside the identified category range. When sentencing appropriate category 2 or 3 offences, the court should also consider the custody threshold as follows:

- has the custody threshold been passed?
- if so, is it unavoidable that a custodial sentence be imposed?
- if so, can that sentence be suspended?

Aggravating factors	
Statutory aggravating factors	*Other aggravating factors*
• Previous convictions, having regard to (a) the nature of the offence to which the conviction relates and its relevance to the current offence; and b) the time that has elapsed since the conviction • Offence committed while on bail	• Severe psychological or physical harm • Ejaculation • Pregnancy or STI as a consequence of offence • Location of offence • Timing of offence • Victim compelled to leave their home, school, etc • Failure to comply with current court orders • Offence committed while on licence • Exploiting contact arrangements with a child to commit an offence

Aggravating factors	
	• Presence of others, especially other children • Any steps taken to prevent the victim reporting an incident, obtaining assistance and/or from assisting or supporting the prosecution • Attempts to dispose of or conceal evidence • Failure of offender to respond to previous warnings • Commission of offence while under the influence of alcohol or drugs • Victim encouraged to recruit others • Period over which offence committed

Mitigating factors
• No previous convictions or no relevant/recent convictions • Remorse • Previous good character and/or exemplary conduct* • Age and/or lack of maturity where it affects the responsibility of the offender • Mental disorder or learning disability, particularly where linked to the commission of the offence • Sexual activity was incited but no activity took place because the offender voluntarily desisted or intervened to prevent it

* Previous good character/ exemplary conduct is different from having no previous convictions. The more serious the offence, the less the weight which should normally be attributed to this factor. Where previous good character/ exemplary conduct has been used to facilitate the offence, this mitigation should not normally be allowed and such conduct may constitute an aggravating factor.

 See Blackstone's Criminal Practice 2019 B3.60–B3.67 and B3.85–B3.92

C14.20 **Sexual assault**

Sexual Offences Act 2003, s 3(1)–(3)

3 Sexual assault

(1) A person (A) commits an offence if—
  (a) he intentionally touches another person (B),
  (b) the touching is sexual,
  (c) B does not consent to the touching, and
  (d) A does not reasonably believe that B consents.
(2) Whether a belief is reasonable is to be determined having regard to all the circumstances, including any steps A has taken to ascertain whether B consents.
(3) Sections 75 and 76 apply to an offence under this section.

EW

 6 months' imprisonment and/or fine/10 years' imprisonment

(a) where the offender was under 18, he is or has been sentenced, in respect of the offence, to imprisonment for a term of at least 12 months;

(b) in any other case—

    (i) if the victim was under 18, or

    (ii) the offender is—

        (a) sentenced to a term of imprisonment,

        (b) detained in a hospital, or

        (c) made the subject of a community sentence of at least 12 months.

C14.20.1 *Sentencing*

SOA 2003, s 3

STEP ONE: Determining the offence category

The court should determine which categories of harm and culpability the offence falls into by reference only to the following tables.

Harm		Culpability	
		A	**B**
Category 1	• Severe psychological or physical harm • Abduction • Violence or threats of violence • Forced/uninvited entry into victim's home	• Significant degree of planning • Offender acts together with others to commit the offence • Use of alcohol/drugs on victim to facilitate the offence • Abuse of trust • Previous violence against victim • Offence committed in course of burglary • Recording of offence • Commercial exploitation and/or motivation • Offence racially or religiously aggravated • Offence motivated by, or demonstrating, hostility to the victim based on his or her sexual orientation (or presumed sexual orientation) or transgender identity (or presumed transgender identity) • Offence motivated by, or demonstrating, hostility to the victim based on his or her disability (or presumed disability)	Factor(s) in category A not present

Harm		Culpability	
		A	B
Category 2	• Touching of naked genitalia or naked breasts • Prolonged detention/ sustained incident • Additional degradation/ humiliation • Victim is particularly vulnerable due to personal circumstances		
Category 3	• Factor(s) in categories 1 and 2 not present		

STEP TWO: Starting point and category range

Having determined the category, the court should use the corresponding starting points to reach a sentence within the category range [below]. The starting point applies to all offenders irrespective of plea or previous convictions. Having determined the starting point, step two allows further adjustment for aggravating or mitigating features, set out on the next page.

A case of particular gravity, reflected by multiple features of culpability or harm in step one, could merit upward adjustment from the starting point before further adjustment for aggravating or mitigating features, set out [below].

Where there is a sufficient prospect of rehabilitation, a community order with a sex offender treatment programme requirement under s 202 Criminal Justice Act 2003 can be a proper alternative to a short or moderate length custodial sentence.

	A	B
Category 1	**Starting point** 4 years' custody **Category range** 3–7 years custody	**Starting point** 2 years 6 months' custody **Category range** 2–4 years custody
Category 2	**Starting point** 2 years' custody **Category range** 1–4 years' custody	**Starting point** 1 year's custody **Category range** High-level community order–2 years' custody
Category 3	**Starting point** 26 weeks' custody **Category range** High-level community order–1 year's custody	**Starting point** High-level community order **Category range** Medium-level community order–26 weeks' custody

The following table contains a non-exhaustive list of additional factual elements providing the context of the offence and factors relating to the offender.

Identify whether any combination of these, or other relevant factors, should result in an upward or downward adjustment from the starting point. In particular, relevant recent convictions are likely to result in an upward adjustment. In some cases, having considered these factors, it may be appropriate to move outside the identified category range.

When sentencing appropriate category 2 or 3 offences, the court should also consider the custody threshold as follows:

- has the custody threshold been passed?
- if so, is it unavoidable that a custodial sentence be imposed?
- if so, can that sentence be suspended?

Aggravating factors	
Statutory aggravating factors	*Other aggravating factors*
• Previous convictions, having regard to (a) the nature of the offence to which the conviction relates and its relevance to the current offence; and (b) the time that has elapsed since the conviction • Offence committed while on bail	• Specific targeting of a particularly vulnerable victim • Blackmail or other threats made (where not taken into account at step one) • Location of offence • Timing of offence • Use of weapon or other item to frighten or injure • Victim compelled to leave their home (including victims of domestic violence) • Failure to comply with current court orders • Offence committed while on licence • Exploiting contact arrangements with a child to commit an offence • Presence of others, especially children
	• Any steps taken to prevent the victim reporting an incident, obtaining assistance, and/or from assisting or supporting the prosecution • Attempts to dispose of or conceal evidence • Commission of offence while under the influence of alcohol or drugs
Mitigating factors	
• No previous convictions **or** no relevant/recent convictions • Remorse • Previous good character and/or exemplary conduct* • Age and/or lack of maturity where it affects the responsibility of the offender • Mental disorder or learning disability, particularly where linked to the commission of the offence • Demonstration of steps taken to address offending behaviour	

* Previous good character/exemplary conduct is different from having no previous convictions. The more serious the offence, the less the weight which should normally be attributed to this factor. Where previous good character/exemplary conduct has been used to facilitate the offence, this mitigation should not normally be allowed and such conduct may constitute an aggravating factor.

C14.20.2 Key points

- A belief in consent arising from delusional psychotic illness must be objectively judged but the personality or disability of the defendant may be relevant to whether the belief was reasonably held where for instance it involved the reading of subtle social signals. An irrational belief can never meet the reasonableness test (*R v B* [2013] EWCA Crim 3).

C14.21 Sexual assault of a child under 13

Sexual Offences Act 2003, s 7

Sexual assault of a child under 13

(1) A person commits an offence if—

    (a) he intentionally touches another person,

    (b) the touching is sexual, and

    (c) the other person is under 13.

 6 months' imprisonment and/or fine/14 years' imprisonment

If the offender—

(a) was 18 or over, or

(b) is or has been sentenced in respect of the offence to imprisonment for a term of at least 12 months

STEP ONE: Determining the offence category

The court should determine which categories of harm and culpability the offence falls into by reference only to the following tables.

Harm		Culpability	
		A	**B**
Category 1	• Severe psychological or physical harm • Abduction • Violence or threats of violence • Forced/uninvited entry into victim's home	• Significant degree of planning • Offender acts together with others to commit the offence • Use of alcohol/drugs on victim to facilitate the offence • Grooming behaviour used against victim • Abuse of trust	Factor(s) in category A not present

Harm		Culpability	
		A	**B**
Category 2	• Touching of naked genitalia or naked breast area • Prolonged detention/ sustained incident • Additional degradation/ humiliation • Child is particularly vulnerable due to extreme youth and/or personal circumstances	• Previous violence against victim • Offence committed in course of burglary • Sexual images of victim recorded, retained, solicited, or shared • Deliberate isolation of victim • Commercial exploitation and/or motivation • Offence racially or religiously aggravated • Offence motivated by, or demonstrating, hostility to the victim based on his or her sexual orientation (or presumed sexual orientation) or transgender identity (or presumed transgender identity) • Offence motivated by, or demonstrating, hostility to the victim based on his or her disability (or presumed disability)	
Category 3	Factor(s) in categories 1 and 2 not present		

STEP TWO: Starting point and category range

Having determined the category, the court should use the corresponding starting points to reach a sentence within the category range [below]. The starting point applies to all offenders irrespective of plea or previous convictions. Having determined the starting point, step two allows further adjustment for aggravating or mitigating features, set out [below].

A case of particular gravity, reflected by multiple features of culpability or harm in step one, could merit upward adjustment from the starting point before further adjustment for aggravating or mitigating features, set out [below].

Where there is a sufficient prospect of rehabilitation, a community order with a sex offender treatment programme requirement under s 202 Criminal Justice Act 2003 can be a proper alternative to a short or moderate length custodial sentence.

	A	**B**
Category 1	**Starting point** 6 years' custody **Category range** 4–9 years' custody	**Starting point** 4 years' custody **Category range** 3–7 years' custody
Category 2	**Starting point** 4 years' custody **Category range** 3–7 years' custody	**Starting point** 2 years' custody **Category range** 1–4 years' custody

	A	B
Category 3	**Starting point** 1 year's custody **Category range** 26 weeks'–2 years' custody	**Starting point** 26 weeks' custody **Category range** High-level community order–1 year's custody

The following table contains a non-exhaustive list of additional factual elements providing the context of the offence and factors relating to the offender. Identify whether any combination of these, or other relevant factors, should result in an upward or downward adjustment from the starting point. In particular, relevant recent convictions are likely to result in an upward adjustment. In some cases, having considered these factors, it may be appropriate to move outside the identified category range.

Aggravating factors	
Statutory aggravating factors	*Other aggravating factors*
• Previous convictions, having regard to (a) the nature of the offence to which the conviction relates and its relevance to the current offence; and (b) the time that has elapsed since the conviction • Offence committed while on bail	• Specific targeting of a particularly vulnerable child • Blackmail or other threats made (where not taken into account at step one) • Location of offence • Timing of offence • Use of weapon or other item to frighten or injure • Victim compelled to leave their home, school, etc • Failure to comply with current court orders • Offence committed while on licence • Exploiting contact arrangements with a child to commit an offence
	• Presence of others, especially other children • Any steps taken to prevent the victim reporting an incident, obtaining assistance, and/or from assisting or supporting the prosecution • Attempts to dispose of or conceal evidence • Commission of offence while under the influence of alcohol or drugs • Victim encouraged to recruit others

Mitigating factors
• No previous convictions **or** no relevant/recent convictions • Remorse • Previous good character and/or exemplary conduct* • Age and/or lack of maturity where it affects the responsibility of the offender • Mental disorder or learning disability, particularly where linked to the commission of the offence

* Previous good character/exemplary conduct is different from having no previous convictions. The more serious the offence, the less the weight which should normally be attributed to this factor. Where previous good character/exemplary conduct has been used to facilitate the offence, this mitigation should not normally be allowed and such conduct may constitute an aggravating factor. In the context of this offence, previous good character/exemplary conduct should not normally be given any significant weight and will not normally justify a reduction in what would otherwise be the appropriate sentence.

C14.22 Sexual communications with a child

 6 months' imprisonment and/or a fine/2 years' imprisonment

C14.23 Sex offenders register—fail to comply with notification requirements

 Fine and/or 6 months'/5 years' imprisonment

C14.23.1 *Sentencing*
STEP ONE: Determining the offence category

The court should determine the offence category with reference only to the factors listed in the following tables. In order to determine the category the court should assess **culpability** and **harm**.

Culpability	In assessing culpability, the court should consider the intention and motivation of the offender in committing any breach.
A	Determined attempts to avoid detection Long period of non compliance
B	Deliberate failure to comply with requirement
C	Minor breach Breach just short of reasonable excuse

Harm
The level of harm is determined by weighing up all the factors of the case to determine the harm that has been caused or was at risk of being caused. In assessing any risk of harm posed by the breach, consideration should be given to the original offence(s) for which the order was imposed and the circumstances in which the breach arose.

Category 1	Breach causes or risks very serious harm or distress
Category 2	Cases falling between categories 1 and 3
Category 3	Breach causes or risks little or no harm or distress

STEP TWO: Starting point and category range

Having determined the category at step one, the court should use the corresponding starting point to reach a sentence within the category range from the following appropriate sentence table. The starting point applies to all offenders irrespective of plea or previous convictions.

Harm	Culpability		
	A	**B**	**C**
Category 1	**Starting point** 2 years' custody	**Starting point** 1 year's custody	**Starting point** 36 weeks' custody
	Category range 1–4 years' custody	**Category range** 26 weeks'–2 years' custody	**Category range** 26 weeks'–1 year 6 months' custody
Category 2	**Starting point** 1 year's custody	**Starting point** 36 weeks' custody	**Starting point** High level community order
	Category range 26 weeks'–2 years' custody	**Category range** 26 weeks'–1 year 6 months' custody	**Category range** Medium-level community order–36 weeks' custody
Category 3	**Starting point** 36 weeks' custody	**Starting point** High-level community order	**Starting point** Low-level community order
	Category range 26 weeks'–1 year 6 months' custody	**Category range** Medium-level community order–36 weeks' custody	**Category range** Band B fine–Medium level community order

The following table contains a non-exhaustive list of additional factual elements providing the context of the offence and factors relating to the offender. Identify whether any combination of these, or other relevant factors, should result in an upward or downward adjustment from the starting point.

In some cases, having considered these factors, it may be appropriate to move outside the identified category range.

Factors increasing seriousness	
Statutory aggravating factors:	*Other aggravating factors:*
• Previous convictions, having regard to a) the nature of the offence to which the conviction relates and its relevance to the current offence; and b) the time that has elapsed since the conviction • Offence committed while on bail	• Breach committed shortly after order made • History of disobedience of court orders (where not already taken into account as a previous conviction) • Breach constitutes a further offence (where not separately prosecuted) • Offence committed on licence or while subject to post-sentence supervision

Factors reducing seriousness or reflecting personal mitigation
• Breach committed after long period of compliance • Prompt voluntary surrender/admission of breach or failure • Age and/or lack of maturity where it affects the responsibility of the offender • Mental disorder or learning disability where linked to the commission of the offence • Sole or primary carer for dependent relatives

C14.23.2 Key points

- A person who is subject to the notification requirements commits a criminal offence if he fails, without reasonable excuse, to:
  - make an initial notification, in accordance with s 83(1), of those matters set out in the Sexual Offences Act 2003 (Notification Requirements) (England and Wales) Regulations 2012;
  - notify a change of details in accordance with s 84(1);
  - make a renotification in accordance with s 85(1);
  - comply with any requirement imposed by regulations concerned with the notification of foreign travel (s 86(1));
  - notify the fact that a change did not happen as predicted when it had been notified in advance in accordance with s 84(4)(b);
  - allow a police officer to take his photograph or fingerprints (s 87(4));
  - ensure that a young offender on whose behalf he is required by a parental direction to comply with the notification requirements attends a police station when a notification is made (s 89(2)(b));
  - in the first four cases set out above, if he knowingly provides false information;
  - the prescribed information includes names, addresses, date of birth, National Insurance number, bank accounts, debit and credit card details, and details of passports or other identity documents.

- The offence occurs on the first day of breach and continues—only one breach can be prosecuted in such circumstances.
- A conditional discharge cannot be imposed on breach.

 See *Blackstone's Criminal Practice 2019* **E23**

C14.24 Voyeurism

Sexual Offences Act 2003, ss 67 and 67A

67 Voyeurism

(1) A person commits an offence if—
- (a) for the purpose of obtaining sexual gratification, he observes another person doing a private act, and
- (b) he knows that the other person does not consent to being observed for his sexual gratification.

(2) A person commits an offence if—
- (a) he operates equipment with the intention of enabling another person to observe, for the purpose of obtaining sexual gratification, a third person (B) doing a private act, and
- (b) he knows that B does not consent to his operating equipment with that intention.

(3) A person commits an offence if—
- (a) he records another person (B) doing a private act,
- (b) he does so with the intention that he or a third person will, for the purpose of obtaining sexual gratification, look at an image of B doing the act, and
- (c) he knows that B does not consent to his recording the act with that intention.

(4) A person commits an offence if he installs equipment, or constructs or adapts a structure or part of a structure, with the intention of enabling himself or another person to commit an offence under subsection (1).

67A Voyeurism: additional offences

(1) A person (A) commits an offence if—
- (a) A operates equipment beneath the clothing of another person (B),
- (b) A does so with the intention of enabling A or another person (C), for a purpose mentioned in subsection (3), to observe—
  - (i) B's genitals or buttocks (whether exposed or covered with underwear), or
  - (ii) the underwear covering B's genitals or buttocks,

  in circumstances where the genitals, buttocks or underwear would not otherwise be visible,

  and
- (c) A does so—
  - (i) without B's consent, and
  - (ii) without reasonably believing that B consents.

(2) A person (A) commits an offence if—
- (a) A records an image beneath the clothing of another person (B),
- (b) the image is of—
  - (i) B's genitals or buttocks (whether exposed or covered with underwear), or
  - (ii) the underwear covering B's genitals or buttocks,

in circumstances where the genitals, buttocks or underwear would not otherwise be visible,

(c) A does so with the intention that A or another person (C) will look at the image for a purpose mentioned in subsection (3), and

(d) A does so—

(i) without B's consent, and

(ii) without reasonably believing that B consents.

(3) The purposes referred to in subsections (1) and (2) are—

(a) obtaining sexual gratification (whether for A or C);

(b) humiliating, alarming or distressing B.

 6 months' imprisonment and/or fine/2 years' imprisonment

If—

(a) where the offender was under 18, he is or has been sentenced in respect of the offence to imprisonment for a term of at least 12 months;

(b) in any other case—

(i) the victim was under 18, or

(ii) the offender is or has been—

(a) sentenced to a term of imprisonment,

(b) detained in a hospital, or

(c) made the subject of a community sentence of at least 12 months.

And in relation to s 67A the offence was committed for the purpose mentioned in s 67A(3)(a) (sexual gratification),

C14.24.1 *Sentencing*

SOA 2003, s 67

STEP ONE: Determining the offence category

The court should determine the offence category using the following table.

Category 1	Raised harm **and** raised culpability
Category 2	Raised harm **or** raised culpability
Category 3	Voyeurism **without** raised harm or culpability factors present

The court should determine culpability and harm caused or intended, by reference only to the following factors, which comprise the principal factual elements of the offence. Where an offence does not fall squarely into a category, individual factors may require a degree of weighting before making an overall assessment and determining the appropriate offence category.

Factors indicating raised harm
• Image(s) available to be viewed by others • Victim observed or recorded in their own home or residence

Factors indicating raised culpability
• Significant degree of planning • Image(s) recorded • Abuse of trust • Specific or previous targeting of a particularly vulnerable victim • Commercial exploitation and/or motivation • Offence racially or religiously aggravated • Offence motivated by, or demonstrating, hostility to the victim based on his or her sexual orientation (or presumed sexual orientation) or transgender identity (or presumed transgender identity) • Offence motivated by, or demonstrating, hostility to the victim based on his or her disability (or presumed disability)

STEP TWO: Starting point and category range

Having determined the category, the court should use the corresponding starting points to reach a sentence within the category range [below]. The starting point applies to all offenders irrespective of plea or previous convictions. Having determined the starting point, step two allows further adjustment for aggravating or mitigating features, set out [below].

A case of particular gravity, reflected by multiple features of culpability or harm in step one, could merit upward adjustment from the starting point before further adjustment for aggravating or mitigating features, set out [below].

Where there is a sufficient prospect of rehabilitation, a community order with a sex offender treatment programme requirement under s 202 Criminal Justice Act 2003 can be a proper alternative to a short or moderate length custodial sentence.

Category 1	**Starting point** 26 weeks' custody **Category range** 12 weeks'–18 months' custody
Category 2	**Starting point** High-level community order **Category range** Medium-level community order–26 weeks' custody
Category 3	**Starting point** Medium-level community order **Category range** Band A fine–high-level community order

The following table contains a non-exhaustive list of additional factual elements providing the context of the offence and factors relating to the offender. Identify whether any combination of these, or other relevant factors, should result in an upward or downward adjustment from the starting point. In particular, relevant recent convictions are likely to result in an upward

adjustment. In some cases, having considered these factors, it may be appropriate to move outside the identified category range.

When sentencing category 2 offences, the court should also consider the custody threshold as follows:

- has the custody threshold been passed?
- if so, is it unavoidable that a custodial sentence be imposed?
- if so, can that sentence be suspended?

When sentencing category 3 offences, the court should also consider the community order threshold as follows:

- has the community order threshold been passed?

Aggravating factors	
Statutory aggravating factors	*Other aggravating factors*
• Previous convictions, having regard to (a) the nature of the offence to which the conviction relates and its relevance to the current offence; and (b) the time that has elapsed since the conviction • Offence committed while on bail	• Location of offence • Timing of offence • Failure to comply with current court orders • Offence committed while on licence • Distribution of images, whether or not for gain • Placing images where there is the potential for a high volume of viewers • Period over which victim observed • Period over which images were made or distributed • Any steps taken to prevent victim reporting an incident, obtaining assistance, and/or from assisting or supporting the prosecution • Attempts to dispose of or conceal evidence
Mitigating factors	
• No previous convictions **or** no relevant/recent convictions • Remorse • Previous good character and/or exemplary conduct* • Age and/or lack of maturity where it affects the responsibility of the offender • Mental disorder or learning disability, particularly where linked to the commission of the offence • Demonstration of steps taken to address offending behaviour	

* Previous good character/exemplary conduct is different from having no previous convictions. The more serious the offence, the less weight which should normally be attributed to this factor. Where previous good character/exemplary conduct has been used to facilitate the offence, this mitigation should not normally be allowed and such conduct may constitute an aggravating factor.

C14.24.2 Key points

- Section 68 provides for the interpretation of key phrases:

Sexual Offences Act 2003, s 68

68 Voyeurism: interpretation

(1) For the purposes of section 67, a person is doing a private act if the person is in a place which, in the circumstances, would reasonably be expected to provide privacy, and—

(a) the person's genitals, buttocks or breasts are exposed or covered only with underwear,

(b) the person is using a lavatory, or

(c) the person is doing a sexual act that is not of a kind ordinarily done in public.

(1A) For the purposes of sections 67 and 67A, operating equipment includes enabling or securing its activation by another person without that person's knowledge.

(2) In section 67, 'structure' includes a tent, vehicle or vessel or other temporary or movable structure.

- Consent is defined under s 74 of the Act:

Sexual Offences Act 2003, s 74

74 'Consent' see C14.1.1

 See *Blackstone's Criminal Practice 2019* **B3.297–B3.305**

C15 Dishonesty and Offences against Property

C15.1 Aggravated burglary

Theft Act 1968, s 10

(1) A person is guilty of aggravated burglary if he commits any burglary and at the time has with him any firearm or imitation firearm, any weapon of offence, or any explosive; and for this purpose—

(a) 'firearm' includes an airgun or air pistol, and 'imitation firearm' means anything which has the appearance of being a firearm, whether capable of being discharged or not; and

(b) 'weapon of offence' means any article made or adapted for use for causing injury to or incapacitating a person, or intended by the person having it with him for such use; and

(c) 'explosive' means any article manufactured for the purpose of producing a practical effect by explosion, or intended by the person having it with him for that purpose.

 Life

C15.1.1 *Sentencing*

The court should determine the offence category using the following table.

Category 1	Greater harm and higher culpability
Category 2	Greater harm and lower culpability or lesser harm and higher culpability
Category 3	Lesser harm and lower culpability

The court should determine culpability and harm caused or intended, by reference only to the following factors, which comprise the principal factual elements of the offence. Where an offence does not fall squarely into a category, individual factors may require a degree of weighting before making an overall assessment and determining the appropriate offence category.

Harm		Culpability	
Factors indicating greater harm	**Factors indicating lesser harm**	**Factors indicating higher culpability**	**Factors indicating lower culpability**
Theft of/damage to property causing a significant degree of loss to the victim (whether economic, commercial, sentimental, or personal value)	No physical or psychological injury or other significant trauma to the victim No violence used or threatened and a weapon is not produced	Victim or premises deliberately targeted (eg, due to vulnerability or hostility based on disability, race, sexual orientation)	Offender exploited by others Mental disorder or learning disability, where linked to the commission of the offence
Soiling, ransacking or vandalism of property Victim at home or on the premises (or returns) while offender present Significant physical or psychological injury or other significant trauma to the victim Violence used or threatened against victim, particularly involving a weapon Context of general public disorder		A significant degree of planning or organization Equipped for burglary (eg, implements carried and/or use of vehicle) Weapon present on entry Member of a group or gang	

STEP TWO: Starting point and category range

Having determined the category, the court should use the corresponding starting points to reach a sentence within the following category range. The starting point applies to all offenders irrespective of plea or previous convictions. A case of particular gravity, reflected by multiple features of culpability or harm in step one, could merit upward adjustment from the starting point before further adjustment for aggravating or mitigating features, set out on the next page.

Offence category	Starting point (applicable to all offenders)	Category range (applicable to all offenders)
Category 1	10 years' custody	9–13 years' custody
Category 2	6 years' custody	4–9 years' custody
Category 3	2 years' custody	1–4 years' custody

The following table contains a **non-exhaustive** list of additional factual elements providing the context of the offence and factors relating to the offender. Identify whether any combination of these, or other relevant factors, should result in an upward or downward adjustment from the starting point. In particular, relevant recent convictions are likely to result in an upward adjustment. In some cases, having considered these factors, it may be appropriate to move outside the identified category range.

Factors increasing seriousness	Factors reducing seriousness or reflecting personal mitigation
Statutory aggravating factors: Previous convictions, having regard to (a) the nature of the offence to which the conviction relates and its relevance to the current offence; and (b) the time that has elapsed since the conviction Offence committed while on bail *Other aggravating factors include:* Child at home (or returns home) when offence committed Offence committed at night Abuse of power and/or position of trust Gratuitous degradation of victim Any steps taken to prevent the victim reporting the incident or obtaining assistance and/or from assisting or supporting the prosecution Victim compelled to leave their home (in particular victims of domestic violence) Established evidence of community impact Commission of offence while under the influence of alcohol or drugs Failure to comply with current court orders Offence committed while on licence Offences Taken Into Consideration (TICs)	Subordinate role in a group or gang Injuries caused recklessly Nothing stolen or only property of very low value to the victim (whether economic, commercial, sentimental, or personal) Offender has made voluntary reparation to the victim No previous convictions or no relevant/recent convictions Remorse Good character and/or exemplary conduct Determination, and/or demonstration of steps taken to address addiction or offending behaviour Serious medical conditions requiring urgent, intensive, or long-term treatment Age and/or lack of maturity where it affects the responsibility of the offender Lapse of time since the offence where this is not the fault of the offender Mental disorder or learning disability, where not linked to the commission of the offence Sole or primary carer for dependent relatives

15.1.2 Key points

The relevant time for consideration of an intent in relation to a 'weapon of offence' (not made or adapted to cause injury to the person) is the time of the theft and not of the entry (*R v Eletu and White* [2018] EWCA Crim 599).

C15.2 Aggravated vehicle-taking

Theft Act 1968, s 12A(1)–(3)

12A Aggravated vehicle-taking

(1) Subject to subsection (3) below, a person is guilty of aggravated taking of a vehicle if—

    (a) he commits an offence under section 12(1) above (in this section referred to as a 'basic offence') in relation to a mechanically propelled vehicle; and

    (b) it is proved that, at any time after the vehicle was unlawfully taken (whether by him or another) and before it was recovered, the vehicle was driven, or injury or damage was caused, in one or more of the circumstances set out in paragraphs (a) to (d) of subsection (2) below.

(2) The circumstances referred to in subsection (1)(b) above are—
  (a) that the vehicle was driven dangerously on a road or other public place;
  (b) that, owing to the driving of the vehicle, an accident occurred by which injury was caused to any person;
  (c) that, owing to the driving of the vehicle, an accident occurred by which damage was caused to any property, other than the vehicle;
  (d) that damage was caused to the vehicle.

(3) A person is not guilty of an offence under this section if he proves that, as regards any such proven driving, injury or damage as is referred to in subsection (1)(b) above, either—
  (a) the driving, accident or damage referred to in subsection (2) above occurred before he committed the basic offence; or
  (b) he was neither in nor on nor in the immediate vicinity of the vehicle when that driving, accident or damage occurred.

EW Summary only if damage only and under £5,000

⧓ s 12A(2)(a) and (b): 6 months and/or fine/2 years' imprisonment (14 years' if accident caused death when the offence becomes a specified offence for the dangerous offender provisions and **IO**). Must endorse and disqualify for at least 12 months. Must disqualify for at least 2 years if offender has had two or more disqualifications for periods of 56 days or more in preceding 3 years.

⧓ s 12A(2)(c) and (d): 6 months' imprisonment and/or fine/2 years' imprisonment. Must endorse and disqualify for at least 12 months. Must disqualify for at least 2 years if offender has had two or more disqualifications for periods of 56 days or more in preceding 3 years.

C15.2.1 *Sentencing: dangerous driving or accident causing injury*

Offence seriousness (culpability and harm)		
A. Identify the appropriate starting point		
Starting points based on first-time offender pleading not guilty		
Example of nature of activity	**Starting point**	**Range**
Taken vehicle involved in single incident of bad driving where little or no damage or risk of personal injury	High-level community order	Medium-level community order–12 weeks' custody
Taken vehicle involved in incident(s) involving excessive speed or showing off, especially on busy roads or in built-up area	18 weeks' custody	12–26 weeks' custody
Taken vehicle involved in prolonged bad driving involving deliberate disregard for safety of others	Crown Court	Crown Court

Offence seriousness (culpability and harm)
B. Consider the effect of aggravating and mitigating factors (other than those within examples in the preceding table)
The following may be particularly relevant but these lists are not exhaustive

Factors indicating higher culpability
1. Disregarding warnings of others
2. Evidence of alcohol or drugs
3. Carrying out other tasks while driving
4. Tiredness
5. Trying to avoid arrest
6. Aggressive driving, such as driving much too close to vehicle in front, inappropriate attempts to overtake, or cutting in after overtaking
Factors indicating greater degree of harm
1. Injury to others
2. Damage to other vehicle or property

C15.2.2 *Sentencing: damage caused*

Offence seriousness (culpability and harm)

A. Identify the appropriate starting point

Starting points based on first-time offender pleading not guilty

Examples of nature of activity	Starting point	Range
Exceeding authorised use of, eg employer's or relative's, vehicle; retention of hire car beyond return date; minor damage to taken vehicle	Medium-level community order	Low-level community order–high level community order
Greater damage to taken vehicle and/or moderate damage to another vehicle and/or moderate damage to another vehicle and/or property	High-level community order	Medium-level community order–12 weeks' custody
Vehicle taken as part of burglary or from private premises; severe damage	18 weeks' custody	12–26 weeks' custody (Crown Court if damage over £5,000)

Offence seriousness (culpability and harm)

B. Consider the effect of aggravating and mitigating factors (other than those within examples in the preceding table)

The following may be particularly relevant but these lists are not exhaustive

Factors indicating higher culpability	Factors indicating lower culpability
1. Vehicle deliberately damaged/destroyed 2. Offender under influence of alcohol/drugs **Factors indicating greater degree of harm** 1. Passenger(s) carried 2. Vehicle belonging to elderly or disabled person 3. Emergency service vehicle 4. Medium to large goods vehicle 5. Damage caused in moving traffic accident	1. Misunderstanding with owner 2. Damage resulting from actions of another (where this does not provide a defence)

C15.2.3 `Key points`

- A magistrates' court can convict a defendant of the alternative offence of vehicle taking if it does not find the aggravating feature(s) (*H v Liverpool Youth Court* [2001] Crim LR 897).
- The allegation under s 12A Theft Act 1968 that there has been a taking and 'owing to the driving of the vehicle, an accident occurred by which injury was caused to any person' requires an element of fault in the driving. There must have been at least some act or omission in the control of the car which involved some element of fault and which contributed in some more than minimal way (*R v Taylor* [2016] UKSC 5). This will apply equally to an accident in which damage is caused.

 See *Blackstone's Criminal Practice 2018* **B4.127–B4.134**

C15.3 Alcohol/tobacco etc., fraudulently evade duty

Customs and Excise Management Act 1979, section 170

EW

 6 months' imprisonment and/or £20,000/7 years' imprisonment

C15.3.1 *Sentencing*

See **Appendix 3**.

 if for adult offender prohibited goods include indecent photographs of children under 16.

C15.3.2 `Key points`

- It is not sufficient for the prosecution to show that the defendant was merely reckless (*R v Panayi* [1989] 1 WLR 187).
- It is irrelevant that the defendant does not know the precise nature of the goods being imported (*R v Shivpuri* [1987] AC 1).
- The burden of proving that duty has been paid falls on the defendant (s 154).
- The prosecution have the right to appeal sentence (*Customs and Excise Commissioners v Brunt* (1998) 163 JP 161).

 See *Blackstone's Criminal Practice 2018* **B16.42–B16.56**

C15.4 **Blackmail**

Theft Act 1968, s 21

(1) A person is guilty of blackmail if, with a view to gain for himself or another or with intent to cause loss to another, he makes any unwarranted demand with menaces; and for this purpose a demand with menaces is unwarranted unless the person making it does so in the belief—

(a) that he has reasonable grounds for making the demand; and

(b) that the use of the menaces is a proper means of reinforcing the demand.

(2) The nature of the act or omission demanded is immaterial, and it is also immaterial whether the menaces relate to action to be taken by the person making the demand.

GC

 14 years' imprisonment

IO

C15.5 **Burglary**

Theft Act 1968, s 9(1) and (2)

9 Burglary

(1) A person is guilty of burglary if—

(a) he enters any building or part of a building as a trespasser and with intent to commit any such offence as is mentioned in subsection (2) below; or

(b) having entered any building or part of a building as a trespasser he steals or attempts to steal anything in the building or that part of it or inflicts or attempts to inflict on any person therein any grievous bodily harm.

(2) The offences referred to in subsection (1)(a) above are offences of stealing anything in the building or part of a building in question, of inflicting on any person therein any grievous bodily harm therein, and of doing unlawful damage to the building or anything therein.

IO If either the offence compromises the commission of, or an intention to commit, grievous bodily harm or in a dwelling if any person in the dwelling was subjected to violence or the threat of violence (Sch 1 para 28 Magistrates' Courts Act 1980).

Or if the offender:

- was 18 or over when he committed the offence,
- had previously been convicted of two other domestic burglary offences in England and Wales; one of those offences has been committed after conviction for the other and both of the previous domestic burglaries had been committed on or after 1 December 1999;

EW in other cases

DO Where the burglary is committed with intent to inflict grievous bodily harm or do unlawful damage

░░░░ 6 months' imprisonment and/or fine/10 years' imprisonment (14 years if dwelling)

C15.5.1 *Sentencing: non-dwelling*

STEP ONE: Determine the offence category

Category 1	Greater harm and higher culpability
Category 2	Greater harm and lower culpability or lesser harm and higher culpability
Category 3	Lesser harm and lower culpability

Factors indicating greater harm	Factors indicating higher culpability
Theft of/damage to property causing a significant degree of loss to the victim (whether economic, commercial, or personal value)	Premises or victim deliberately targeted (to include pharmacy or doctor's surgery and targeting due to vulnerability of victim or hostility based on disability, race, sexual orientation, and so forth)
Soiling, ransacking, or vandalism of property	
Victim on the premises (or returns) while offender present	A significant degree of planning or organization
Trauma to the victim, beyond the normal inevitable consequence of intrusion and theft	Knife or other weapon carried (where not charged separately)
Violence used or threatened against victim	Equipped for burglary (eg implements carried and/or use of vehicle)
Context of general public disorder	Member of a group or gang
Factors indicating lower harm	**Factors indicating lower culpability**
Nothing stolen or only property of very low value to the victim (whether economic, commercial, or personal)	Offence committed on impulse, with limited intrusion into property
Limited damage or disturbance to property	Offender exploited by others
	Mental disorder or learning disability, where linked to the commission of the offence

STEP TWO: Starting point and category range

Offence category	Starting point	Category range
Category 1	2 years custody	1–5 years custody
Category 2	18 weeks' custody	Low-level community order to Crown Court (51 weeks' custody)
Category 3	Medium-level community order	Band B fine–18 weeks' custody

Factors increasing seriousness	Factors reducing seriousness or reflecting personal mitigation
Statutory aggravating factors: Previous convictions, having regard to (a) the nature of the offence to which the conviction relates and its relevance to the current offence; and (b) the time that has elapsed since the conviction Offence committed while on bail **Other aggravating factors include:** Offence committed at night, particularly where staff present or likely to be present Abuse of a position of trust Gratuitous degradation of the victim Any steps taken to prevent the victim reporting the incident or obtaining assistance and/or from assisting or supporting the prosecution Established evidence of community impact Commission of offence while under the influence of alcohol or drugs Failure to comply with current court orders Offence committed while on licence Offences taken into consideration (TICs)	Offender has made voluntary reparation to the victim Subordinate role in a group or gang No previous convictions or no relevant/recent convictions Remorse Good character and/or exemplary conduct Determination and/or demonstration of steps taken to address addiction or offending behaviour Serious medical conditions requiring urgent, intensive, or long-term treatment Age and/or lack of maturity where it affects the responsibility of the offender Lapse of time since the offence where this is not the fault of the offender Mental disorder or learning disability, where not linked to the commission of the offence Sole or primary carer for dependent relatives

C15.5.2 *Sentencing: dwelling*

Because of its significance in present or future sentencing it is important that every case is correctly classified. Whether premises are a dwelling for these purposes is essentially a matter of fact and degree. The term does not require that the building to be occupied on the date of the entry if it is still furnished and ready for use as a home even if owned on a buy-to-let basis (*Hudson v CPS* [2017] EWHC 841 (Admin)). Entry to a communal lobby area in flats is not a domestic burglary (*R v Ogungbile* [2017] EWCA Crim 1826).

STEP ONE: Determine the offence category

Category 1	Greater harm and higher culpability
Category 2	Greater harm and lower culpability or lesser harm and higher culpability
Category 3	Lesser harm and lower culpability

Factors indicating greater harm	Factors indicating higher culpability
Theft of/damage to property causing a significant degree of loss to the victim (whether economic, sentimental, or personal value) Soiling, ransacking, or vandalism of property Occupier at home (or returns home) while offender present Trauma to the victim beyond the normal inevitable consequence of intrusion and theft Violence used or threatened against victim Context of general public disorder	Victim or premises deliberately targeted (eg due to vulnerability or hostility based on disability, race, or sexual orientation) A significant degree of planning or organization Knife or other weapon carried (where not charged separately) Equipped for burglary (eg implements carried and/or use of vehicle) Member of a group or gang

Factors indicating lesser harm	Factors indicating lower culpability
Nothing stolen or only property of very low value to the victim (whether economic, sentimental, or personal) Limited damage or disturbance to property	Offence committed on impulse, with limited intrusion into property Offender exploited by others Mental disorder or learning disability, where linked to the commission of the offence

STEP TWO: Starting point and category range

Where the defendant is dependent on or has a propensity to misuse drugs and there is sufficient prospect of success, a community order with a drug rehabilitation requirement under s 209 Criminal Justice Act 2003 may be a proper alternative to a short or moderate length custodial sentence.

Offence category	Starting point	Category range
Category 1	3 years' custody	2–6 years custody
Category 2	1 year's custody	High-level community order–Crown Court (2 years' custody)
Category 3	High-level community order	Low-level community order–26 weeks' custody

Factors increasing seriousness	Factors reducing seriousness or reflecting personal mitigation
Statutory aggravating factors: Previous convictions, having regard to (a) the nature of the offence to which the conviction relates and its relevance to the current offence; and (b) the time that has elapsed since the conviction* Offence committed while on bail	Offender has made voluntary reparation to the victim Subordinate role in a group or gang No previous convictions or no relevant/recent convictions Remorse Good character and/or exemplary conduct
Other aggravating factors include: Child at home (or returns home) when offence committed Offence committed at night Gratuitous degradation of the victim Any steps taken to prevent the victim reporting the incident or obtaining assistance and/or from assisting or supporting the prosecution Victim compelled to leave their home (in particular victims of domestic violence) Established evidence of community impact Commission of offence while under the influence of alcohol or drugs Failure to comply with current court orders Offence committed while on licence Offences taken into consideration (TICs)	Determination and/or demonstration of steps taken to address addiction or offending behaviour Serious medical conditions requiring urgent, intensive, or long-term treatment Age and/or lack of maturity where it affects the responsibility of the offender Lapse of time since the offence where this is not the fault of the offender Mental disorder or learning disability, where not linked to the commission of the offence Sole or primary carer for dependent relatives

* Where sentencing an offender for a qualifying third domestic burglary, the court must apply section 111 of the Powers of the Criminal Courts (Sentencing) Act 2000 and impose a custodial term of at least 3 years, unless it is satisfied that there are particular circumstances which relate to any of the offences or to the offender, which would make it unjust to do so.

C15.5.4 Key points

- Entry can be partial (*R v Brown* [1985] Crim LR 212), and may be effected without any part of the body entering the building (eg cane and hook burglaries).
- 'Building' is a factual not a legal issue, and will depend on all of the circumstances (*Caurti v Cozens* [1973] AC 854).
- Trespass can be committed knowingly or recklessly (*R v Collins* [1973] QB 100).

 See *Blackstone's Criminal Practice 2019* **B4.75–B4.95**

C15.6 Electricity—abstract/use without authority

Theft Act 1968, s 13

13 Abstracting of electricity

A person who dishonestly uses without due authority, or dishonestly causes to be wasted or diverted, any electricity shall be guilty of an offence.

 EW

 6 months' imprisonment and/or fine/5 years' imprisonment

C15.6.1 *Sentencing*

STEP ONE: Determine the offence category

The court should determine the offence category with reference only to the factors identified in the following tables. In order to determine the category the court should assess culpability and harm.

The level of culpability is determined by weighing up all the factors of the case to determine the offender's role and the extent to which the offending was planned and the sophistication with which it was carried out.

CULPABILITY demonstrated by one or more of the following:
A—High culpability
A leading role where offending is part of a group activity Involvement of others through coercion, intimidation, or exploitation Sophisticated nature of offence/significant planning Abuse of position of power or trust or responsibility Commission of offence in association with or to further other criminal activity

B—Medium culpability
A significant role where offending is part of a group activity All other cases where characteristics for categories A or C are not present

C—Lesser culpability
Performed limited function under direction Involved through coercion, intimidation, or exploitation Limited awareness or understanding of offence

Where there are characteristics present which fall under different levels of culpability, the court should balance these characteristics to reach a fair assessment of the offender's culpability.

The level of harm is assessed by weighing up all the factors of the case to determine the level of harm caused.

Greater harm
A significant risk of, or actual injury to persons or damage to property Significant volume of electricity extracted as evidenced by length of time of offending and/or advanced type of illegal process used

Lesser harm
All other cases

STEP TWO: Starting point and category range

Having determined the category at step one, the court should use the starting point to reach a sentence within the appropriate category range in the following table .

The starting point applies to all offenders irrespective of plea or previous convictions.

Harm	Culpability		
	A	B	C
Greater	**Starting point** 12 weeks' custody	**Starting point** Medium-level community order	**Starting point** Band C fine
	Category range High-level community order–1 year's custody	**Category range** Low-level community order–12 weeks' custody	**Category range** Band B fine–low-level community order
Lesser	**Starting point** High-level community order	**Starting point** Low-level community order	**Starting point** Band A fine
	Category range Medium-level community order–12 weeks' custody	**Category range** Band C fine–medium-level community order	**Category range** Discharge–Band C fine

The court should then consider further adjustment for any aggravating or mitigating factors. The following table contains a non-exhaustive list of additional factual elements providing the context of the offence and factors relating to the offender. Identify whether any combination of these, or other relevant factors, should result in an upward or downward adjustment from the starting point.

Factors increasing seriousness	
Statutory aggravating factors	*Other aggravating factors*
Previous convictions, having regard to (a) the **nature** of the offence to which the conviction relates and its **relevance** to the current offence; and (b) the **time** that has elapsed since the conviction Offence committed while on bail	Electricity abstracted from another person's property Attempts to conceal/dispose of evidence Failure to comply with current court orders
Factors reducing seriousness or reflecting personal mitigation	
No previous convictions or no relevant/recent convictions Good character and/or exemplary conduct Serious medical condition requiring urgent, intensive, or long-term treatment Age and/or lack of maturity where it affects the responsibility of the offender Mental disorder or learning disability Sole or primary carer for dependent relatives Determination and/or demonstration of steps having been taken to address addiction or offending behaviour	

 See *Blackstone's Criminal Practice 2019* **B4.140–B4.145**

C15.7 **False accounting**

Theft Act 1968, s 17(1)

17 False accounting

(1) Where a person dishonestly, with a view to gain for himself or another or with intent to cause loss to another,—
   (a) destroys, defaces, conceals or falsifies any account or any record or document made or required for any accounting purpose; or
   (b) in furnishing information for any purpose produces or makes use of any account, or any such record or document as aforesaid, which to his knowledge is or may be misleading, false or deceptive in a material particular,
   (c) he shall on conviction...

EW

 6 months' imprisonment and/or fine/7 years' imprisonment

C15.7.1 *Sentencing*

See Appendix 3.

 See *Blackstone's Criminal Practice 2019* **B6.3–B6.14**

C15.8 False statement/representation to obtain social security benefit

Social Security Administration Act 1992, ss 111A and 112

111A Dishonest representations for obtaining benefit etc

(1) If a person dishonestly—
  (a) makes a false statement or representation; or
  (b) produces or furnishes, or causes or allows to be produced or furnished, any document or information which is false in a material particular;
with a view to obtaining any benefit or other payment or advantage under the relevant social security legislation (whether for himself or for some other person), he shall be guilty of an offence.

(1A) A person shall be guilty of an offence if—
  (a) there has been a change of circumstances affecting any entitlement of his to any benefit or other payment or advantage under any provision of the relevant social security legislation;
  (b) the change is not a change that is excluded by regulations from the changes that are required to be notified;
  (c) he knows that the change affects an entitlement of his to such a benefit or other payment or advantage; and
  (d) he dishonestly fails to give a prompt notification of that change in the prescribed manner to the prescribed person.

(1B)A person shall be guilty of an offence if—
  (a) there has been a change of circumstances affecting any entitlement of another person to any benefit or other payment or advantage under any provision of the relevant social security legislation;
  (b) the change is not a change that is excluded by regulations from the changes that are required to be notified;
  (c) he knows that the change affects an entitlement of that other person to such a benefit or other payment or advantage; and
  (d) he dishonestly causes or allows that other person to fail to give a prompt notification of that change in the prescribed manner to the prescribed person.

(1C) This subsection applies where—
  (a) there has been a change of circumstances affecting any entitlement of a person ('the claimant') to any benefit or other payment or advantage under any provision of the relevant social security legislation;
  (b) the benefit, payment, or advantage is one in respect of which there is another person ('the recipient') who for the time being has a right to receive payments to which the claimant has, or (but for the arrangements under which they are payable to the recipient) would have, an entitlement; and
  (c) the change is not a change that is excluded by regulations from the changes that are required to be notified.

(1D) In a case where subsection (1C) above applies, the recipient is guilty of an offence if—

   (a) he knows that the change affects an entitlement of the claimant to a benefit or other payment or advantage under a provision of the relevant social security legislation;

   (b) the entitlement is one in respect of which he has a right to receive payments to which the claimant has, or (but for the arrangements under which they are payable to the recipient) would have, an entitlement; and

   (c) he dishonestly fails to give a prompt notification of that change in the prescribed manner to the prescribed person.

(1E) In a case where that subsection applies, a person other than the recipient is guilty of an offence if—

   (a) he knows that the change affects an entitlement of the claimant to a benefit or other payment or advantage under a provision of the relevant social security legislation;

   (b) the entitlement is one in respect of which the recipient has a right to receive payments to which the claimant has, or (but for the arrangements under which they are payable to the recipient) would have, an entitlement; and

   (c) he dishonestly causes or allows the recipient to fail to give a prompt notification of that change in the prescribed manner to the prescribed person.

(1F) In any case where subsection (1C) above applies but the right of the recipient is confined to a right, by reason of his being a person to whom the claimant is required to make payments in respect of a dwelling, to receive payments of housing benefit—

   (a) a person shall not be guilty of an offence under subsection (1D) or (1E) above unless the change is one relating to one or both of the following—

      (i) the claimant's occupation of that dwelling;

      (ii) the claimant's liability to make payments in respect of that dwelling; but

   (b) subsections (1D)(a) and (1E)(a) above shall each have effect as if after 'knows' there were inserted 'or could reasonably be expected to know'.

(1G) For the purposes of subsections (1A) to (1E) above a notification of a change is prompt if, and only if, it is given as soon as reasonably practicable after the change occurs.

112 False representations for obtaining benefit etc

(1) If a person for the purpose of obtaining any benefit or other payment under the relevant social security legislation whether for himself or some other person, or for any other purpose connected with that legislation—

   (a) makes a statement or representation which he knows to be false; or

   (b) produces or furnishes, or knowingly causes or knowingly allows to be produced or furnished, any document or information which he knows to be false in a material particular, he shall be guilty of an offence.

(1A) A person shall be guilty of an offence if—

   (a) there has been a change of circumstances affecting any entitlement of his to any benefit or other payment or advantage under any provision of the relevant social security legislation;

   (b) the change is not a change that is excluded by regulations from the changes that are required to be notified;

   (c) he knows that the change affects an entitlement of his to such a benefit or other payment or advantage; and

   (d) he fails to give a prompt notification of that change in the prescribed manner to the prescribed person.

(1B) A person is guilty of an offence under this section if—

(a) there has been a change of circumstances affecting any entitlement of another person to any benefit or other payment or advantage under any provision of the relevant social security legislation;

(b) the change is not a change that is excluded by regulations from the changes that are required to be notified;

(c) he knows that the change affects an entitlement of that other person to such a benefit or other payment or advantage; and

(d) he causes or allows that other person to fail to give a prompt notification of that change in the prescribed manner to the prescribed person.

(1C) In a case where subsection (1C) of section 111A above applies, the recipient is guilty of an offence if—

(a) he knows that the change affects an entitlement of the claimant to a benefit or other payment or advantage under a provision of the relevant social security legislation;

(b) the entitlement is one in respect of which he has a right to receive payments to which the claimant has, or (but for the arrangements under which they are payable to the recipient) would have, an entitlement; and

(c) he fails to give a prompt notification of that change in the prescribed manner to the prescribed person.

(1D) In a case where that subsection applies, a person other than the recipient is guilty of an offence if—

(a) he knows that the change affects an entitlement of the claimant to a benefit or other payment or advantage under a provision of the relevant social security legislation;

(b) the entitlement is one in respect of which the recipient has a right to receive payments to which the claimant has, or (but for the arrangements under which they are payable to the recipient) would have, an entitlement; and

(c) he causes or allows the recipient to fail to give a prompt notification of that change in the prescribed manner to the prescribed person.

(1E) Subsection (1F) of section 111A above applies in relation to subsections (1C) and (1D) above as it applies in relation to subsections (1D) and (1E) of that section.

(1F) For the purposes of subsections (1A) to (1D) above a notification of a change is prompt if, and only if, it is given as soon as reasonably practicable after the change occurs.

Section 111A:

6 months' imprisonment and/or fine/7 years' imprisonment Section 112:

3 months' imprisonment and/or level 3 fine

C15.8.1 *Sentencing*

For offences under s 111A, refer to the 'Fraud Guideline' at **Appendix 3**. For s 112:

Offence seriousness (culpability and harm)		
A. Identify the appropriate starting point		
Starting points based on first-time offender pleading not guilty		
Examples of nature of activity	**Starting point**	**Range**
Claim fraudulent from the start, up to £5,000 obtained (s 111A or s 112)	Medium-level community order	Band B fine–high-level community order
Claim fraudulent from the start, more than £5,000 but less than £20,000 obtained	12 weeks' custody	Medium-level community order to Crown Court
Claim fraudulent from the start, large-scale, professional offending	Crown Court	Crown Court

Offence seriousness (culpability and harm)	
B. Consider the effect of aggravating and mitigating factors (other than those within examples in the previous table)	
The following may be particularly relevant but these lists are not exhaustive	
Factors indicating higher culpability 1. Offending carried out over a long period 2. Offender acting in unison with one or more others 3. Planning 4. Offender motivated by greed or desire to live beyond his/her means 5. False identities or other personal details used 6. False or forged documents used 7. Official documents altered or falsified	**Factors indicating lower culpability** 1. Pressurized by others 2. Claim initially legitimate **Factor indicating lesser degree of harm** 1. Voluntary repayment of amounts overpaid

R v Noel [2012] EWCA Crim 956 confirmed that a custodial sentence was not appropriate for an offence under s 112(1A)(2) (failing to notify change of circumstances) of the Social Security Amendment Act 1982 by a woman of good character, involving £12,500 over nearly 5 years. The committal to the Crown Court had been only for the purposes of confiscation. *R v Vitorio Condomiti* [2015] EWCA Crim 806 held that a legitimate entitlement to benefits not claimed is also a mitigating factor and is a form of set-off based against what the applicant would have received, had a claim been made.

C15.8.2 Key points

Allocation

In guidance published by the CPS, including guidance on diversion from prosecution, it is suggested that administrative penalties may be suitable (subject to an absence of aggravating factors) for offences to a value of £2,000, and that summary jurisdiction may be accepted (subject to mitigating and aggravating factors) to the sum of £35,000. By the Social Security (Penalty as Alternative to Prosecution) (Maximum Amount) Order 2015 the maximum amount of the penalty that may be offered as an alternative to prosecution is set at £5,000 for matters occurring wholly on or after 1 April 2015.

- In *R v Laku* [2008] EWCA Crim 1748, L made false representations in order to claim benefits and was prosecuted under ss 111A and 111A(1A) of the Social Security Administration Act 1992. On subsequent claims he did not correct the falsehoods. Held: convictions under s 111A(1A) quashed; he had not failed to notify a change in circumstances as the same false circumstances that founded the convictions under s 111A continued.
- An offence under s 111A(1B) requires a positive act on the part of the defendant. Sitting back and doing nothing does not amount to (allowing) an offence (*R v Tilley* [2009] EWCA Crim 1426).
- The offence under s 112(1A) Social Security Administration Act 1992 was interpreted in *Coventry City Council v Vassell* [2011] EWHC 1542 (Admin), and is committed if:
  - there is a change of circumstances affecting entitlement to benefit;
  - that change is not excluded from reporting by regulations; and
  - the defendant knows that change affects his entitlement to benefit; the court held this meant 'would' affect (not 'could' affect) that entitlement;
  - in relation to the requirement that the defendant fails to give prompt notification in the prescribed manner to the prescribed person the court held that whether there was prompt notice is a matter of fact. In considering who is the prescribed person, the court confirmed that the DWP will not suffice if the regulations specify the local authority. However, the defendant must *know* who is the correct person for the offence to be committed. In considering that aspect, relevant issues include the information provided by the local authority and the unexpected continuation of benefit.

C15.8.3 *Time limits for prosecution*

The normal six-month time limit for summary-only offences is extended in relation to s 112 by s 116(2): On time limits see **A12.1.2**.

Social Security Administration Act 1992, s 116(2)–(3)

116 Legal proceedings

(2) Notwithstanding anything in any Act—
  (a) proceedings for an offence under this Act (other than proceedings to which paragraph (b) applies), or for an offence under the Jobseekers Act 1995, may be begun at any time within the period of 3 months from the date on which evidence, sufficient in the opinion of the Secretary of State to justify a prosecution for the offence, comes to his knowledge or within a period of 12 months from the commission of the offence, whichever period last expires; and
  (b) proceedings brought by the appropriate authority for an offence under this Act relating to housing benefit or council tax benefit may be begun at any time within the period of 3 months from the date on which evidence, sufficient in the opinion of the appropriate authority to justify a prosecution for the offence, comes to the authority's knowledge or within a period of 12 months from the commission of the offence, whichever period last expires.

(2A) Subsection (2) above shall not be taken to impose any restriction on the time when proceedings may be begun for an offence under section 111A above.

(3) For the purposes of subsection (2) above—

(a) a certificate purporting to be signed by or on behalf of the Secretary of State as to the date on which such evidence as is mentioned in paragraph (a) of that subsection came to his knowledge shall be conclusive evidence of that date; and.

(b) a certificate of the appropriate authority as to the date on which such evidence as is mentioned in paragraph (b) of that subsection came to the authority's knowledge shall be conclusive evidence of that date.

See *Blackstone's Criminal Practice 2019* **B5.8** and **B16.58–B16.66**

C15.9 **Found on enclosed premises**

Vagrancy Act 1824, s 4

4 Persons committing certain offences to be deemed rogues and vagabonds

[The following is an abbreviated version of the original]... [E]very person wandering abroad and lodging in any barn or outhouse, or in any deserted or unoccupied building, or in the open air, or under a tent, or in any cart or waggon, and not giving a good account of himself or herself; every person being found in or upon any dwelling house, warehouse, coach-house, stable, or outhouse, or in any inclosed yard, garden, or area, for any unlawful purpose;... is guilty of an offence.

C15.9.1 Key points

An unlawful purpose is to commit an offence. Hiding from the police is therefore not enough (*L v CPS* [2007] EWHC 1843 (Admin)).

SO

Level 3 fine/3 months' imprisonment

See *Blackstone's Criminal Practice 2019* **B4.95**

C15.10 **Fraud**

Fraud Act 2006, ss 1(1) and (2), 2, 3, 4, and 5

1 Fraud

(1) A person is guilty of fraud if he is in breach of any of the sections listed in subsection (2) (which provide for different ways of committing the offence).

(2) The sections are—

(a) section 2 (fraud by false representation),

(b) section 3 (fraud by failing to disclose information), and

(c) section 4 (fraud by abuse of position).

2 Fraud by false representation

(1) A person is in breach of this section if he—
   (a) dishonestly makes a false representation, and
   (b) intends, by making the representation—
      (i) to make a gain for himself or another, or
      (ii) to cause loss to another or to expose another to a risk of loss.

(2) A representation is false if—
   (a) it is untrue or misleading, and
   (b) the person making it knows that it is, or might be, untrue or misleading.

(3) 'Representation' means any representation as to fact or law, including a representation as to the state of mind of—
   (a) the person making the representation, or
   (b) any other person.

(4) A representation may be express or implied.

(5) For the purposes of this section a representation may be regarded as made if it (or anything implying it) is submitted in any form to any system or device designed to receive, convey or respond to communications (with or without human intervention).

3 Fraud by failing to disclose information

A person is in breach of this section if he—
(a) dishonestly fails to disclose to another person information which he is under a legal duty to disclose, and
(b) intends, by failing to disclose the information—
   (i) to make a gain for himself or another, or
   (ii) to cause loss to another or to expose another to a risk of loss.

4 Fraud by abuse of position

(1) A person is in breach of this section if he—
   (a) occupies a position in which he is expected to safeguard, or not to act against, the financial interests of another person,
   (b) dishonestly abuses that position, and
   (c) intends, by means of the abuse of that position—
      (i) to make a gain for himself or another, or
      (ii) to cause loss to another or to expose another to a risk of loss.

(2) A person may be regarded as having abused his position even though his conduct consisted of an omission rather than an act.

5 'Gain' and 'loss'

(1) The references to gain and loss in sections 2 to 4 are to be read in accordance with this section.

(2) 'Gain' and 'loss'—
   (a) extend only to gain or loss in money or other property;
   (b) include any such gain or loss whether temporary or permanent;
   and 'property' means any property whether real or personal (including things in action and other intangible property).

(3) 'Gain' includes a gain by keeping what one has, as well as a gain by getting what one does not have.

(4) 'Loss' includes a loss by not getting what one might get, as well as a loss by parting with what one has.

EW

 6 months' imprisonment and/or fine/10 years' imprisonment

C15.10.1 *Sentencing*

See **Appendix 3**.

C15.10.2 Key points

The offence under s 2 requires that the defendant know that the representation was or might have been misleading. This is a subjective test. It is not a test of reasonableness or of what the defendant ought to have known. However, a defendant cannot close their eyes to obvious doubts about the genuineness of the representations (*R v Augunas* [2013] EWCA Crim 2046).

The facts must be considered in each case under s 3 to identify the relevant legal duty. *R v D* [2019] EWCA Crim 209 confirmed that here is no 'legal duty to disclose' within the meaning of s 3 Fraud Act 2006 to notify a change of circumstance in relation to council tax under the Local Government Finance Act 1992.

While an offence under s 4 does not require a fiduciary relationship, there must be something akin to one. The test is objective and does not depend on the views of the defendant. In *R v Valujevs* [2014] EWCA Crim 2888 it was held that gang-masters might meet the test where there is an interference by them with the payment of wages due.

 See *Blackstone's Criminal Practice 2019* **B5.4–B5.20**

C15.11 **Going equipped for theft**

> **Theft Act 1968, s 25(1)–(3), (5)**
>
> **25 Going equipped for stealing etc**
>
> (1) A person shall be guilty of an offence if, when not at his place of abode, he has with him any article for use in the course of or in connection with any burglary or theft.
> (2) A person guilty of an offence under this section shall on conviction on indictment be liable to imprisonment for a term not exceeding three years.
> (3) Where a person is charged with an offence under this section, proof that he had with him any article made or adapted for use in committing a burglary or theft shall be evidence that he had it with him for such use.
> (4) ...
> (5) For purposes of this section an offence under section 12(1) of this Act of taking a conveyance shall be treated as theft.

EW

 6 months' imprisonment and/or fine/3 years' imprisonment

C15.11.1 *Sentencing*

STEP ONE: Determining the offence category

The court should determine the offence category with reference only to the factors identified in the following tables. In order to determine the category the court should assess culpability and harm.

The level of culpability is determined by weighing up all the factors of the case to determine the offender's role and the extent to which the offending was planned and the sophistication with which it was carried out.

CULPABILITY demonstrated by one or more of the following:
A—High culpability
A leading role where offending is part of a group activity Involvement of others through coercion, intimidation, or exploitation Significant steps taken to conceal identity and/or avoid detection Sophisticated nature of offence/significant planning Offender equipped for robbery or domestic burglary
B—Medium culpability
A significant role where offending is part of a group activity All other cases where characteristics for categories A or C are not present
C—Lesser culpability
Involved through coercion, intimidation, or exploitation Limited awareness or understanding of offence Little or no planning

Where there are characteristics present which fall under different levels of culpability, the court should balance these characteristics to reach a fair assessment of the offender's culpability.

HARM

This guideline refers to preparatory offences where no theft has been committed. The level of harm is determined by weighing up all the factors of the case to determine the harm that would be caused if the item(s) were used to commit a substantive offence.

Greater harm
Possession of item(s) which have the potential to facilitate an offence affecting a large number of victims Possession of item(s) which have the potential to facilitate an offence involving high-value items
Lesser harm
All other cases

STEP TWO: Starting point and category range

Having determined the category at step one, the court should use the starting point to reach a sentence within the appropriate category range in the following table.

The starting point applies to all offenders irrespective of plea or previous convictions.

Harm	Culpability		
	A	B	C
Greater	**Starting point** 1 year's custody	**Starting point** 18 weeks' custody	**Starting point** Medium-level community order
	Category range 26 weeks'–1 year 6 months' custody	**Category range** High-level community order–36 weeks' custody	**Category range** Low-level community order–high-level community order
Lesser	**Starting point** 26 weeks' custody	**Starting point** High-level community order	**Starting point** Band C fine
	Category range 12 weeks'–36 weeks' custody	**Category range** Medium-level community order–12 weeks' custody	**Category range** Discharge–medium-level community order

Consecutive sentences for multiple offences may be appropriate—please refer to the *Offences Taken into Consideration* and *Totality* guidelines.

The court should then consider further adjustment for any aggravating or mitigating factors. The following is a non-exhaustive list of additional factual elements providing the context of the offence and factors relating to the offender. Identify whether any combination of these, or other relevant factors, should result in an upward or downward adjustment from the starting point.

Factors increasing seriousness	
Statutory aggravating factors	*Other aggravating factors*
Previous convictions, having regard to (a) the **nature** of the offence to which the conviction relates and its **relevance** to the current offence; and (b) the **time** that has elapsed since the conviction Offence committed while on bail	Attempts to conceal/dispose of evidence Established evidence of community/ wider impact Failure to comply with current court orders Offence committed on licence Offences taken into consideration

Factors reducing seriousness or reflecting personal mitigation
No previous convictions or no relevant/recent convictions Good character and/or exemplary conduct Serious medical condition requiring urgent, intensive, or long-term treatment Age and/or lack of maturity where it affects the responsibility of the offender Mental disorder or learning disability Sole or primary carer for dependent relatives Determination and/or demonstration of steps having been taken to address addiction or offending behaviour

C15.11.2

The article need not be intended for immediate use but it must be intended for future use (see *R v Ellames* [1974] 1 WLR 1391). Proof of intent is required and not mere contemplation of an offence (see *R v Hargreaves* [1985] Crim LR 243).

 See *Blackstone's Criminal Practice 2019* **B4.150–4.158**

C15.12 **Handling stolen goods**

> **Theft Act 1968, s 22(1)**
>
> **22 Handling stolen goods**
>
> (1) A person handles stolen goods if (otherwise than in the course of the stealing) knowing or believing them to be stolen goods he dishonestly receives the goods, or dishonestly undertakes or assists in their retention, removal, disposal or realisation by or for the benefit of another person, or if he arranges to do so.

EW

 6 months' imprisonment and/or fine/14 years' imprisonment

C15.12.1 *Sentencing*

STEP ONE: Determine the offence category

The court should determine the offence category with reference only to the factors identified in the following tables. In order to determine the category the court should assess culpability and harm.

The level of culpability is determined by weighing up all the factors of the case to determine the offender's role and the extent to which the offending was planned and the sophistication with which it was carried out.

CULPABILITY demonstrated by one or more of the following:
A—High culpability
A leading role where offending is part of a group activity   Involvement of others through coercion, intimidation, or exploitation   Abuse of position of power, or trust, or responsibility   Professional and sophisticated offence   Advance knowledge of the primary offence   Possession of very recently stolen goods from a domestic burglary or robbery
B—Medium culpability
A significant role where offending is part of a group activity   Offender acquires goods for resale   All other cases where characteristics for categories A or C are not present

CULPABILITY demonstrated by one or more of the following:
C—Lesser culpability
Performed limited function under direction Involved through coercion, intimidation, or exploitation Little or no planning Limited awareness or understanding of offence Goods acquired for offender's personal use

Where there are characteristics present which fall under different levels of culpability, the court should balance these characteristics to reach a fair assessment of the offender's culpability.

HARM

Harm is assessed by reference to the financial value (to the loser) of the handled goods and any significant additional harm to the victim or others associated with the underlying offence—examples of additional harm may include but are not limited to:

Property stolen from a domestic burglary or a robbery (unless this has already been taken into account in assessing culpability)

Items stolen were of substantial value to the loser, regardless of monetary worth

Metal theft causing disruption to infrastructure

Damage to heritage assets

Category 1	Very high value goods stolen (above £100,000) or high value with significant additional harm to the victim or others
Category 2	High-value goods stolen (£10,000 to £100,000) and no significant additional harm or medium-value with significant additional harm to the victim or others
Category 3	Medium-value goods stolen (£1,000 to £10,000) and no significant additional harm or low-value with significant additional harm to the victim or others
Category 4	Low-value goods stolen (up to £1,000) and little or no significant additional harm to the victim or others

STEP TWO: Starting point and category range

Having determined the category at step one, the court should use the starting point to reach a sentence within the appropriate category range in the following table.

The starting point applies to all offenders irrespective of plea or previous convictions.

Harm	Culpability		
	A	**B**	**C**
Category 1 Where the value greatly exceeds £100,000, it may be appropriate to move outside the identified range. Adjustment should be made for any significant additional harm where very high value stolen goods are handled.	**Starting point** 5 years' custody **Category range** 3–8 years' custody	**Starting point** 3 years' custody **Category rang** 1 year 6 months' – 4 years' custody	**Starting point** 1 year's custody **Category range** 26 weeks'–1 year 6 months' custody
Category 2	**Starting point** 3 years' custody **Category range** 1 year 6 months'– 4 years' custody	**Starting point** 1 year's custody **Category range** 26 weeks'–1 year 6 months' custody	**Starting point** High-level community order **Category range** Low-level community order–26 weeks' custody
Category 3	**Starting point** 1 year's custody **Category range** 26 weeks'–2 years' custody	**Starting point** High-level community order **Category range** Low-level community order–26 weeks' custody	**Starting point** Band C fine **Category range** Band B fine–low-level community order
Category 4	**Starting point** High-level community order **Category range** Medium-level community order–26 weeks' custody	**Starting point** Low-level community order **Category range** Band C fine–high-level community order	**Starting point** Band B fine **Category range** Discharge–Band C fine

Consecutive sentences for multiple offences may be appropriate—please refer to the *Offences Taken into Consideration* and *Totality* guidelines.

The court should then consider further adjustment for any aggravating or mitigating factors. The following is a non-exhaustive list of additional factual elements providing the context of the offence and factors relating to the offender. Identify whether any combination of these, or other relevant factors, should result in an upward or downward adjustment from the starting point.

Factors increasing seriousness	
Statutory aggravating factors	*Other aggravating factors*
Previous convictions, having regard to (a) the nature of the offence to which the conviction relates and its relevance to the current offence; and (b) the time that has elapsed since the conviction Offence committed while on bail	Seriousness of the underlying offence, for example, armed robbery Deliberate destruction, disposal, or defacing of stolen property Damage to a third party Failure to comply with current court orders Offence committed on licence Offences taken into consideration Established evidence of community/ wider impact
Factors reducing seriousness or reflecting personal mitigation	
No previous convictions or no relevant/recent convictions Good character and/or exemplary conduct Serious medical condition requiring urgent, intensive, or long-term treatment Age and/or lack of maturity where it affects the responsibility of the offender Mental disorder or learning disability Sole or primary carer for dependent relatives Determination and/or demonstration of steps having been taken to address addiction or offending behaviour	

C15.12.2 Key points

- Mere suspicion that goods are stolen will not suffice.
- In *R v Hall* (1985) 81 Cr App R 260, belief was said to be present when someone thought: 'I cannot say for certain that those goods are stolen, but there can be no other reasonable conclusion in the light of all the circumstances of all I have heard and seen.' Similarly if the person admits that 'my brain is telling me [they are stolen] despite what I have heard'.
- If the defendant argues that he has paid an adequate consideration for the goods, it falls upon the prosecution to disprove (*Hogan v Director of Public Prosecutions* [2007] EWHC 978 (Admin)).

 See *Blackstone's Criminal Practice 2019* **B4.159–B4.183**

C15.13 Making, adapting, supplying, or offering to supply articles for fraud

Fraud Act 2006, s 7

7 Making or supplying articles for use in frauds

(1) A person is guilty of an offence if he makes, adapts, supplies or offers to supply any article—
   (a) knowing that it is designed or adapted for use in the course of or in connection with fraud, or
   (b) intending it to be used to commit, or assist in the commission of, fraud.

 Fine/6 months'/10 years' imprisonment

C15.13.1 *Sentencing*

See **Appendix 3**.

C15.13.2 Key points

For definition of an 'article', see **C15.17.2**.

See *Blackstone's Criminal Practice 2019* **B5.24 and B5.25**

C15.14 Making off without payment

Theft Act 1978, s 3

3 Making off without payment

(1) Subject to subsection (3) below, a person who, knowing that payment on the spot for any goods supplied or service done is required or expected from him, dishonestly makes off without having paid as required or expected and with intent to avoid payment of the amount due shall be guilty of an offence.

(2) For purposes of this section 'payment on the spot' includes payment at the time of collecting goods on which work has been done or in respect of which service has been provided.

(3) Subsection (1) above shall not apply where the supply of the goods or the doing of the service is contrary to law, or where the service done is such that payment is not legally enforceable.

EW

 6 months' imprisonment and/or fine/2 years' imprisonment

C15.14.1 *Sentencing*

STEP ONE: Determining the offence category

The court should determine the offence category with reference only to the factors identified in the following tables. In order to determine the category the court should assess culpability and harm.

The level of culpability is determined by weighing up all the factors of the case to determine the offender's role and the extent to which the offending was planned and the sophistication with which it was carried out.

CULPABILITY demonstrated by one or more of the following:
A—High culpability
A leading role where offending is part of a group activity Involvement of others through coercion, intimidation, or exploitation Sophisticated nature of offence/significant planning Offence involving intimidation or the use or threat of force Deliberately targeting victim on basis of vulnerability

CULPABILITY demonstrated by one or more of the following:
B—Medium culpability
A significant role where offending is part of a group activity Some degree of planning involved All other cases where characteristics for categories A or C are not present
C—Lesser culpability
Performed limited function under direction Involved through coercion, intimidation or exploitation Little or no planning Limited awareness or understanding of offence

Where there are characteristics present which fall under different levels of culpability, the court should balance these characteristics to reach a fair assessment of the offender's culpability.

HARM

Harm is assessed by reference to the actual loss that results from the offence and any significant additional harm suffered by the victim—examples of additional harm may include but are not limited to:

A high level of inconvenience caused to the victim	
Emotional distress	
Fear/loss of confidence caused by the crime	
A greater impact on the victim due to the size or type of their business	
Category 1	Goods or services obtained above £200 **or** goods/services up to £200 with significant additional harm to the victim
Category 2	Goods or services obtained up to £200 **and** little or no significant additional harm to the victim

STEP TWO: Starting point and category range

Having determined the category at step one, the court should use the starting point to reach a sentence within the appropriate category range in the following table.

The starting point applies to all offenders irrespective of plea or previous convictions.

Harm	Culpability		
	A	B	C

Harm	Culpability		
Category 1 Where the value greatly exceeds £200, it may be appropriate to move outside the identified range. Adjustment should be made for any significant additional harm for offences above £200.	**Starting point** 12 weeks' custody **Category range** High-level community order–36 weeks' custody	**Starting point** Low-level community order **Category range** Band C fine–high-level community order	**Starting point** Band B fine **Category range** Band A fine–low-level community order
Category 2	**Starting point** Medium-level community order **Category range** Low-level community order–12 weeks' custody	**Starting point** Band C fine **Category range** Band B fine–low-level community order	**Starting point** Band A fine **Category range** Discharge–band B fine

Consecutive sentences for multiple offences may be appropriate—please refer to the *Offences Taken into Consideration* and *Totality* guidelines.

The court should then consider further adjustment for any aggravating or mitigating factors. The following list is a non-exhaustive list of additional factual elements providing the context of the offence and factors relating to the offender. Identify whether any combination of these, or other relevant factors, should result in an upward or downward adjustment from the starting point.

Factors increasing seriousness	
Statutory aggravating factors	*Other aggravating factors*
Previous convictions, having regard to (a) the **nature** of the offence to which the conviction relates and its relevance to the current offence; and (b) the **time** that has elapsed since the conviction Offence committed while on bail Offence motivated by, or demonstrating hostility based on any of the following characteristics or presumed characteristics of the victim: religion, race, disability, sexual orientation, or transgender identity	Steps taken to prevent the victim reporting or obtaining assistance and/or from assisting or supporting the prosecution Attempts to conceal/dispose of evidence Failure to comply with current court orders Offence committed on licence Offences taken into consideration Established evidence of community/wider impact
Factors reducing seriousness or reflecting personal mitigation	
No previous convictions or no relevant/recent convictions Remorse, particularly where evidenced by voluntary reparation to the victim Good character and/or exemplary conduct Serious medical condition requiring urgent, intensive, or long-term treatment Age and/or lack of maturity where it affects the responsibility of the offender Mental disorder or learning disability Sole or primary carer for dependent relatives Determination and/or demonstration of steps having been taken to address addiction or offending behaviour	

C15.14.2 Key points

The intention to avoid making payment means a permanent intention not to pay, so a person who genuinely disputes a bill and challenges someone to bring legal action cannot be said to have committed an offence.

 See *Blackstone's Criminal Practice 2019* **B5.38–B5.45**

C15.15 Money laundering

Proceeds of Crime Act 2002, ss 327–329

327 Concealing etc

(1) A person commits an offence if he—
   (a) conceals criminal property;
   (b) disguises criminal property;
   (c) converts criminal property;
   (d) transfers criminal property;
   (e) removes criminal property from England and Wales or from Scotland or from Northern Ireland.
(2) But a person does not commit such an offence if—
   (a) he makes an authorised disclosure under section 338 and (if the disclosure is made before he does the act mentioned in subsection (1)) he has the appropriate consent;
   (b) he intended to make such a disclosure but had a reasonable excuse for not doing so;
   (c) the act he does is done in carrying out a function he has relating to the enforcement of any provision of this Act or of any other enactment relating to criminal conduct or benefit from criminal conduct.
(2A) Nor does a person commit an offence under subsection (1) if—
   (a) he knows, or believes on reasonable grounds, that the relevant criminal conduct occurred in a particular country or territory outside the United Kingdom, and
   (b) the relevant criminal conduct—
      (i) was not, at the time it occurred, unlawful under the criminal law then applying in that country or territory, and
      (ii) is not of a description prescribed by an order made by the Secretary of State.
(2B) In subsection (2A) 'the relevant criminal conduct' is the criminal conduct by reference to which the property concerned is criminal property.
(2C) A deposit-taking body that does an act mentioned in paragraph (c) or (d) of subsection (1) does not commit an offence under that subsection if—
   (a) it does the act in operating an account maintained with it, and
   (b) the value of the criminal property concerned is less than the threshold amount determined under section 339A for the act.
(3) Concealing or disguising criminal property includes concealing or disguising its nature, source, location, disposition, movement or ownership or any rights with respect to it.

328 Arrangements

(1) A person commits an offence if he enters into or becomes concerned in an arrangement which he knows or suspects facilitates (by whatever means) the acquisition, retention, use or control of criminal property by or on behalf of another person.

(2) But a person does not commit such an offence if—
- (a) he makes an authorised disclosure under section 338 and (if the disclosure is made before he does the act mentioned in subsection (1)) he has the appropriate consent;
- (b) he intended to make such a disclosure but had a reasonable excuse for not doing so;
- (c) the act he does is done in carrying out a function he has relating to the enforcement of any provision of this Act or of any other enactment relating to criminal conduct or benefit from criminal conduct.

329 Acquisition, use and possession

(1) A person commits an offence if he—
- (a) acquires criminal property;
- (b) uses criminal property;
- (c) has possession of criminal property.

(2) But a person does not commit such an offence if—
- (a) he makes an authorised disclosure under section 338 and (if the disclosure is made before he does the act mentioned in subsection (1)) he has the appropriate consent;
- (b) he intended to make such a disclosure but had a reasonable excuse for not doing so;
- (c) he acquired or used or had possession of the property for adequate consideration;
- (d) the act he does is done in carrying out a function he has relating to the enforcement of any provision of this Act or of any other enactment relating to criminal conduct or benefit from criminal conduct.

(3) For the purposes of this section—
- (a) a person acquires property for inadequate consideration if the value of the consideration is significantly less than the value of the property;
- (b) a person uses or has possession of property for inadequate consideration if the value of the consideration is significantly less than the value of the use or possession;
- (c) the provision by a person of goods or services which he knows or suspects may help another to carry out criminal conduct.

The critical definitions for these offences are contained in s 340 Proceeds of Crime Act 2002:

Proceeds of Crime Act 2002, s 340(2)–(4)(b)

340 Interpretation

(2) Criminal conduct is conduct which—
- (a) constitutes an offence in any part of the United Kingdom, or
- (b) would constitute an offence in any part of the United Kingdom if it occurred there.

(3) Property is criminal property if—
- (a) it constitutes a person's benefit from criminal conduct or it represents such a benefit (in whole or part and whether directly or indirectly), and
- (b) the alleged offender knows or suspects that it constitutes or represents such a benefit.

(4) It is immaterial—
  (a) who carried out the conduct;
  (b) who benefited from it;
...

 6 months' imprisonment and/or fine/14 years' imprisonment

C15.15.1 *Sentencing*

STEP ONE: Determining the offence category

The court should determine the offence category with reference to the following tables. In order to determine the category the court should assess culpability and harm.

The level of **culpability** is determined by weighing up all the factors of the case to determine the offender's role and the extent to which the offending was planned and the sophistication with which it was carried out	Harm A Harm is initially assessed by the value of the money laundered
Culpability demonstrated by one or more of the following:	
A—High culpability	**Category 1** £10 million or more Starting point based on £30 million
A leading role where offending is part of a group activity	**Category 2** £2 million–£10 million Starting point based on £5 million
Involvement of others through pressure, influence	**Category 3** £500,000–£2 million Starting point based on £1 million
Abuse of position of power, or trust, or responsibility	**Category 4** £100,000–£500,000 Starting point based on £300,000
Sophisticated nature of offence/significant planning	**Category 5** £10,000–£100,000 Starting point based on £50,000
Criminal activity conducted over sustained period of time	**Category 6** Less than £10,000 Starting point based on £5,000

B—Medium culpability	Harm B
Other cases where characteristics for categories A or C are not present A significant role where offending is part of a group activity	Money laundering is an integral component of much serious criminality To complete the assessment of harm, the court should take into account the level of harm associated with the underlying offence to determine whether it warrants
C—Lesser culpability	upward adjustment of the starting point within the range, or in appropriate cases,
Performed limited function under direction Involved through coercion, intimidation, or exploitation Not motivated by personal gain Opportunistic 'one-off' offence; very little or no planning Limited awareness or understanding of extent of criminal activity	outside the range Where it is possible to identify the underlying offence, regard should be given to the relevant sentencing levels for that offence

STEP TWO: Starting point and category range

Having determined the category at step one, the court should use the appropriate starting point (as adjusted in accordance with step one) to reach a sentence within the category range in the following table. The starting point applies to all offenders irrespective of plea or previous convictions.

Where the value is larger or smaller than the amount on which the starting point is based, this should lead to upward or downward adjustment as appropriate.

Where the value greatly exceeds the amount of the starting point in category 1, it may be appropriate to move outside the identified range.

Section 327 Proceeds of Crime Act 2002: Concealing/disguising/converting/transferring/removing criminal property from England & Wales

Section 328 Proceeds of Crime Act 2002: Entering into arrangements concerning criminal property

Section 329 Proceeds of Crime Act 2002: Acquisition, use and possession of criminal property

Maximum: 14 years' custody

Categories 1 to 3 refer to sums in excess of £500,000 and guideline sentencing levels are beyond the jurisdiction of the magistrates' court.

Harm	Culpability		
	A	**B**	**C**
Category 4 £100,000–£500,000 Starting point based on £300,000	**Starting point** 5 years' custody	**Starting point** 3 years' custody	**Starting point** 18 months' custody
	Category range 3– 6 years' custody	**Category range** 18 months'–4 years' custody	**Category range** 26 weeks'–3 years' custody

Harm	Culpability		
	A	B	C
Category 5 £10,000–£100,000 Starting point based on £50,000	**Starting point** 3 years' custody	**Starting point** 18 months' custody	**Starting point** 26 weeks' custody
	Category range 18 months'–4 years' custody	**Category range** 26 weeks'–3 years' custody	**Category range** Medium-level community order–1 year's custody
Category 6 Less than £10,000 Starting point based on £5,000	**Starting point** 1 year's custody	**Starting point** High-level community order	**Starting point** Low-level community order
	Category range 26 weeks'–2 years' custody	**Category range** Low-level community order–1 year's custody	**Category range** Band B fine–medium-level community order

The following table contains a non-exhaustive list of additional factual elements providing the context of the offence and factors relating to the offender.

Identify whether any combination of these or other relevant factors should result in an upward or downward adjustment of the sentence arrived at thus far.

Consecutive sentences for multiple offences may be appropriate where large sums are involved.

Factors increasing seriousness	
Statutory aggravating factors:	*Other aggravating factors:*
Previous convictions, having regard to (a) the nature of the offence to which the conviction relates and its relevance to the current offence; and (b) the time that has elapsed since the conviction Offence committed while on bail	Attempts to conceal/dispose of evidence Established evidence of community/wider impact Failure to comply with current court orders Offence committed on licence Offences taken into consideration Failure to respond to warnings about behaviour Offences committed across borders Blame wrongly placed on others Damage to third party, for example loss of employment by legitimate employees

Factors reducing seriousness or reflecting personal mitigation
No previous convictions or no relevant/recent convictions Remorse Little or no prospect of success Good character and/or exemplary conduct Serious medical conditions requiring urgent, intensive, or long-term treatment Age and/or lack of maturity where it affects the responsibility of the offender Lapse of time since apprehension where this does not arise from the conduct of the offender Mental disorder or learning disability Sole or primary carer for dependent relatives Offender cooperated with investigation, made early admissions, and/or voluntarily reported offending Determination and/or demonstration of steps having been taken to address addiction or offending behaviour Activity originally legitimate

C15.15.2 Key points

- For there to be criminal property, there must be an intent or a suspicion that there is a benefit from criminal conduct.
- Knowledge of a potential breach of trust was not of itself the same as knowledge or suspicion of crime. That the defendant ought to have known is not enough (*Holt v Attorney General* [2014] UKPC 4).
- In *Wilkinson v DPP* [2006] EWHC 3012 (Admin), the court discouraged the use of this offence (with its requirement only for suspicion rather than belief) when a handling charge would adequately have reflected the seriousness of the offence.
- For there to be an offence there must be actual criminal conduct and the proceeds must already be the product of that crime (*R v Gabriel* [2006] EWCA Crim 229). However, a court might decide that 'clean' money had changed its nature and become 'criminal property' because it was obtained by fraud (*R v GH* [2015] UKSC 24). This case also confirmed that the money need not be 'criminal property' at the moment the parties come to a prohibited arrangement, but it must amount to 'criminal property' at the time the arrangement begins to operate upon it.
- *R v Ogden* [2016] EWCA Crim 6 confirms that an offence of conspiracy to convert criminal property (s 327 Proceeds of Crime Act 2000) is committed when A, who is in possession of controlled drugs, agrees to supply B with what B is aware is a controlled drug. The drugs are criminal property.
- There are two ways in which the Crown can prove that the property derives from crime. Either:
  - by showing that it derives from criminal conduct of a specific kind; or
  - by proving that the circumstances in which it was handled create an irresistible inference that it can only have derived from crime (*Kuchhadia v R* [2015] EWCA Crim 1252).
- *R v Rogers (Bradley)* [2014] EWCA Crim 1680 confirms that payments into a Spanish bank account by reason of frauds committed in England are amenable to the jurisdiction of the English courts, as ss 327–329 Proceeds of Crime Act 2002 have extraterritorial effect.

 See *Blackstone's Criminal Practice 2019* **B21**

C15.16 Obtaining services dishonestly

Fraud Act 2006, s 11(1) and (2)

11 Obtaining services dishonestly

(1) A person is guilty of an offence under this section if he obtains services for himself or another—
   (a) by a dishonest act, and
   (b) in breach of subsection (2).

(2) A person obtains services in breach of this subsection if—
  (a) they are made available on the basis that payment has been, is being or will be made for or in respect of them,
  (b) he obtains them without any payment having been made for or in respect of them or without payment having been made in full, and
  (c) when he obtains them, he knows—
    (i) that they are being made available on the basis described in paragraph (a), or
    (ii) that they might be, but intends that payment will not be made, or will not be made in full.

 6 months' imprisonment and/or fine/5 years' imprisonment

C15.16.1 *Sentencing*

The offence of *obtaining services dishonestly* may be committed in circumstances that otherwise could be charged as an offence contrary to s 1 Fraud Act 2006, or may be more akin to *making off without payment*, contrary to s 3 Theft Act 1978. For this reason, it has not been included specifically within any of the guidelines for fraud, and one of the following approaches should be used:

- where it involves conduct which can be characterized as a fraud offence (such as obtaining credit through fraud or payment card fraud), the court should apply the guideline for the relevant type of fraud (see **Appendix 3**); or
- where the conduct could be characterized as *making off without payment* (ie where an offender, knowing that payment on the spot for any goods supplied or service done is required or expected, dishonestly makes off without having paid and with intent to avoid payment), the guideline for that offence should be used (see **C15.14.1**).

 See *Blackstone's Criminal Practice 2019* **B5.31–B5.37**

C15.17 **Possession of articles for fraud**

Fraud Act 2006, s 6

6 Possession etc of articles for use in frauds

(1) A person is guilty of an offence if he has in his possession or under his control any article for use in the course of or in connection with any fraud.

 Fine/6 months'/5 years' imprisonment

C15.17.1 *Sentencing*

See **Appendix 3**.

C15.17.2 Key points

Section 8 provides:

> **Fraud Act 2006, s 8**
>
> **8 'Article'**
>
> (1) For the purposes of—
>
>   (a) sections 6 and 7, and
>   (b) the provisions listed in subsection (2), so far as they relate to articles for use in the course of or in connection with fraud, 'article' includes any program or data held in electronic form.

R v Sakalauskas [2013] EWCA Crim 2278 confirms that an 'article' in s 6 Fraud Act 2006 (as was the case under s 25 Theft Act 1968) meant any article that the defendant had with him for the purposes of fraud but not articles which he had possessed for that purpose in the past.

See *Blackstone's Criminal Practice 2019* **B5.21 and B5.22**

C15.18 Railway fare evasion

Regulation of Railways Act 1889, s 5(1) and (3)

 Level 3 fine or 3 months' imprisonment (s 5(3)); level 2 fine (s 5(1))

C15.18.1 *Sentencing*

Regulation of Railways Act 1889, s 5(3) (travelling on railway without paying fare, with intent to avoid payment); s 5(1) (failing to produce ticket)

Triable only summarily:

Maximum:

Level 2 fine (s 5(1) failing to produce ticket) Level 3 fine and/or 3 months (s 5(3) travelling on railway with intent to avoid payment)

Offence range:

Conditional Discharge—Band C fine (s 5(1))

Conditional Discharge—Low-level community order (s 5(3))

STEP ONE: Determining the offence category

The court should determine the offence category using the following table.

Category 1	Higher culpability and greater harm
Category 2	Higher culpability and lesser harm or lower culpability and greater harm
Category 3	Lower culpability and lesser harm

The court should determine the offender's culpability and the harm caused with reference only to the following factors. Where an offence does not fall squarely into a category, individual factors may require a degree of weighting before making an overall assessment and determining the appropriate offence category.

| CULPABILITY demonstrated by one or more of the following: |
| **Factors indicating higher culpability** |
| • Aggressive, abusive or disruptive behaviour |
| **Factors indicating lower culpability** |
| • All other cases |
| HARM demonstrated by one or more of the following: |
| **Factors indicating greater harm** |
| • High revenue loss |
| **Factors indicating lesser harm** |
| • All other cases |

STEP TWO: Starting point and category range

Having determined the category at step one, the court should use the corresponding starting point to reach a sentence within the following category range. The starting point applies to all offenders irrespective of plea or previous convictions.

Travelling on railway without paying fare, with intent

Offence category	Starting point	Range
Category 1	Band C fine	Band B fine–Low-level community order
Category 2	Band B fine	Band A fine–Band C fine
Category 3	Band A fine	Conditional discharge–Band B fine

Failing to produce a ticket

Offence category	Starting point	Range
Category 1	Band B fine	Band B fine–Band C fine
Category 2	Band A fine	Band A fine–Band B fine
Category 3	Band A fine	Conditional discharge–Band B fine

The court should then consider adjustment for any aggravating or mitigating factors. The following is a non-exhaustive list of additional factual elements providing the context of the offence and factors relating to the offender. Identify whether any combination of these, or other relevant factors, should result in an upward or downward adjustment from the sentence arrived at so far.

Factors increasing seriousness	
Statutory aggravating factors:	*Other aggravating factors:*
• Previous convictions, having regard to (a) the **nature** of the offence to which the conviction relates and its **relevance** to the current offence; and (b) the **time** that has elapsed since the conviction • Offence committed while on bail • Offence motivated by, or demonstrating hostility based on, any of the following characteristics or presumed characteristics of the victim: religion, race, disability, sexual orientation, or transgender identity	• Offence has avoided paying any of the fare • Offence produces incorrect ticket or document to pass as legitimate fare payer • Failure to comply with current court orders • Abuse to staff • Offence committed on licence or post-sentence supervision
Factors reducing seriousness or reflecting personal mitigation	
• No previous convictions **or** no relevant/recent convictions • Remorse • Good character and/or exemplary conduct • Serious medical condition requiring urgent, intensive, or long-term treatment • Age and/or lack of maturity where it affects the responsibility of the offender • Mental disorder or learning disability	

C15.19 **Robbery and assault with intent to rob**

Theft Act 1968, s 8

(1) A person is guilty of robbery if he steals, and immediately before or at the time of doing so, and in order to do so, he uses force on any person or puts or seeks to put any person in fear of being then and there subjected to force.

(2) A person guilty of robbery, or of an assault with intent to rob, shall on conviction on indictment be liable to imprisonment for life.

GC

DO

▦ Life

IO

C15.19.1 *Sentencing*

A separate guideline applies for children and young people and appears in the *Handbook for youths in the criminal courts*.

C15.19.2 Key points

- Force may be used indirectly, for example wrenching a bag from a victim's hand: *R v Clouden* [1987] Crim LR 56. Snatching a cigarette from the victim's hand was not robbery in *P v DPP* [2012] EWHC 1657 (Admin).
- Force must be used or threatened immediately before or at the time of stealing: *R v Vinall* [2011] EWCA Crim 6252.
- The force must be connected to the stealing: *R v Shendley* [1970] Crim LR 49.
- The elements of theft must be present: dishonesty, an intention to deprive permanently, and appropriation. See **C15.21**
- There must be intention or at least recklessness as to the use of force.

See *Blackstone's Criminal Practice 2019* **B4.66–B4.74**

C15.20 Tax credit fraud

Tax Credits Act 2002, s 35

35 Offence of fraud

A person commits an offence if he is knowingly concerned in any fraudulent activity undertaken with a view to obtaining payments of a tax credit by him or any other person.

 EW

 6 months' imprisonment and/or fine/7 years' imprisonment

C15.20.1 *Sentencing*
See **Appendix 3**.

C15.20.2 Key points

- Disposing of the proceeds of fraud amounts to a fraudulent activity (*R v Kolapo* [2009] EWCA Crim 545).
- *R v Nolan and Howard* [2012] EWCA Crim 671 confirmed that the passive receipt of moneys and failure to report did not amount to 'fraudulent activity', which requires a positive act of misrepresentation with a view to gain. The statute requires behaviour calculated to achieve, rather than to capitalize on what had already been achieved.
- This is an offence of specific intention, requiring proof by the prosecution of 'knowledge'. Knowing connotes something more than mere recklessness (*R v Godir* [2018] EWCA Crim 2294).

 See *Blackstone's Criminal Practice 2019* **B16.7**

C15.21 Theft

Theft Act 1968, s 1(1) and (2)

1 Basic definition of theft

(1) A person is guilty of theft if he dishonestly appropriates property belonging to another with the intention of permanently depriving the other of it; and 'thief' and 'steal' shall be construed accordingly.

(2) It is immaterial whether the appropriation is made with a view to gain, or is made for the thief's own benefit.

EW

 6 months' imprisonment and/or fine/7 years' imprisonment; low value theft from a shop tried summarily 6 months and/or a fine

C15.21.1 *Sentencing*

General theft: Theft Act 1968, s 1

Including:
> Theft from the person
> Theft in a dwelling
> Theft in breach of trust
> Theft from a motor vehicle
> Theft of a motor vehicle
> Theft of a pedal bicycle
> and all other s 1 Theft Act 1968 offences, but excluding theft from a shop or stall.

STEP ONE: Determining the offence category

The court should determine the offence category with reference only to the factors identified in the following tables. In order to determine the category the court should assess culpability and harm.

The level of culpability is determined by weighing up all the factors of the case to determine the offender's role and the extent to which the offending was planned and the sophistication with which it was carried out.

CULPABILITY demonstrated by one or more of the following:
A—High culpability
A leading role where offending is part of a group activity Involvement of others through coercion, intimidation, or exploitation Breach of a high degree of trust or responsibility Sophisticated nature of offence/significant planning Theft involving intimidation or the use or threat of force Deliberately targeting victim on basis of vulnerability

B—Medium culpability
A significant role where offending is part of a group activity
Some degree of planning involved
Breach of some degree of trust or responsibility
All other cases where characteristics for categories A or C are not present

C—Lesser culpability
Performed limited function under direction
Involved through coercion, intimidation, or exploitation
Little or no planning
Limited awareness or understanding of offence

Where there are characteristics present which fall under different levels of culpability, the court should balance these characteristics to reach a fair assessment of the offender's culpability.

HARM

Harm is assessed by reference to the financial loss that results from the theft and any significant additional harm suffered by the victim or others—examples of significant additional harm may include but are not limited to:
    Items stolen were of substantial value to the loser—regardless of monetary worth
    High level of inconvenience caused to the victim or others
    Consequential financial harm to victim or others
    Emotional distress
    Fear/loss of confidence caused by the crime
    Risk of or actual injury to persons or damage to property
    Impact of theft on a business
    Damage to heritage assets
    Disruption caused to infrastructure
    Intended loss should be used where actual loss has been prevented.

Category 1	Very-high-value goods stolen (above £100,000) **or** high-value with significant additional harm to the victim or others
Category 2	High-value goods stolen (£10,000 to £100,000) **and** no significant additional harm **or** medium-value with significant additional harm to the victim or others
Category 3	Medium-value goods stolen (£500 to £10,000) **and** no significant additional harm **or** low-value with significant additional harm to the victim or others
Category 4	Low-value goods stolen (up to £500) **and** little or no significant additional harm to the victim or others

STEP TWO: Starting point and category range

Having determined the category at step one, the court should use the starting point to reach a sentence within the appropriate category range in the following table.

The starting point applies to all offenders irrespective of plea or previous convictions.

Harm	Culpability		
	A	**B**	**C**
Category 1 Adjustment should be made for any significant additional harm factors where very high value goods are stolen	**Starting point** 3 years 6 months' custody	**Starting point** 2 years' custody	**Starting point** 1 year's custody
	Category range 2 years 6 months'–6 years' custody	**Category range** 1–3 years 6 months' custody	**Category range** 26 weeks'–2 years' custody
Category 2	**Starting point** 2 years' custody	**Starting point** 1 year's custody	**Starting point** High-level community order
	Category range 1 year–3 years 6 months' custody	**Category range** 26 weeks'–2 years' custody	**Category range** Low-level community order–36 weeks' custody
Category 3	**Starting point** 1 year's custody	**Starting point** High-level community order	**Starting point** Band C fine
	Category range 26 weeks'–2 years' custody	**Category range** Low-level community order–36 weeks' custody	**Category range** Band B fine–low-level community order
Category 4	**Starting point** High-level community order	**Starting point** Low-level community order	**Starting point** Band B fine
	Category range Medium-level community order–36 weeks' custody	**Category range** Band C fine–medium-level community order	**Category range** Discharge–band C fine

The preceding table refers to single offences. Where there are multiple offences, consecutive sentences may be appropriate: please refer to the *Offences Taken into Consideration* and *Totality* guidelines.

Where multiple offences are committed in circumstances which justify consecutive sentences, and the total amount stolen is in excess of £1 million, then an aggregate sentence in excess of 7 years may be appropriate.

Where the offender is dependent on or has a propensity to misuse drugs or alcohol and there is sufficient prospect of success, a community order with a drug rehabilitation requirement under s 209, or an alcohol treatment requirement under s 212 Criminal Justice Act 2003, may be a proper alternative to a short or moderate custodial sentence.

Where the offender suffers from a medical condition that is susceptible to treatment but does not warrant detention under a hospital order, a community order with a mental health treatment requirement under s 207 Criminal Justice Act 2003 may be a proper alternative to a short or moderate custodial sentence.

The court should then consider further adjustment for any aggravating or mitigating factors. The following is a non-exhaustive list of additional factual elements providing the context of the offence and factors relating to the offender. Identify whether any combination of these, or other relevant factors, should result in an upward or downward adjustment from the sentence arrived at so far.

Factors increasing seriousness	
Statutory aggravating factors:	*Other aggravating factors:*
Previous convictions, having regard to (a) the nature of the offence to which the conviction relates and its relevance to the current offence; and (b) the time that has elapsed since the conviction Offence committed while on bail Offence motivated by, or demonstrating hostility based on, any of the following characteristics or presumed characteristics of the victim: religion, race, disability, sexual orientation, or transgender identity	Stealing goods to order Steps taken to prevent the victim reporting or obtaining assistance and/or from assisting or supporting the prosecution Offender motivated by intention to cause harm or revenge Offence committed over sustained period of time Attempts to conceal/dispose of evidence Failure to comply with current court orders Offence committed on licence Offences taken into consideration Established evidence of community/wider impact (for issues other than prevalence) Prevalence—see **C15.21.1.1**
Factors reducing seriousness or reflecting personal mitigation	
No previous convictions or no relevant/recent convictions Remorse, particularly where evidenced by voluntary reparation to the victim Good character and/or exemplary conduct Serious medical condition requiring urgent, intensive, or long-term treatment Age and/or lack of maturity where it affects the responsibility of the offender Mental disorder or learning disability Sole or primary carer for dependent relatives Determination and/or demonstration of steps having been taken to address addiction or offending behaviour Inappropriate degree of trust or responsibility	

C15.21.1.1 *Prevalence*

There may be exceptional local circumstances that arise which may lead a court to decide that prevalence should influence sentencing levels. The pivotal issue in such cases will be the harm caused to the community. It is essential that the court, before taking account of prevalence:

- has supporting evidence from an external source, for example, community impact statements, to justify claims that a particular crime is prevalent in their area, and is causing particular harm in that community, and
- is satisfied that there is a compelling need to treat the offence more seriously than elsewhere.

C15.21.1.2 *Theft from a shop or stall*

STEP ONE: Determining the offence category

The court should determine the offence category with reference only to the factors identified in the following tables. In order to determine the category the court should assess culpability and harm.

The level of culpability is determined by weighing up all the factors of the case to determine the offender's role and the extent to which the offending was planned and the sophistication with which it was carried out.

A—High culpability
A leading role where offending is part of a group activity Involvement of others through coercion, intimidation, or exploitation Sophisticated nature of offence/significant planning Significant use or threat of force Offender subject to a banning order from the relevant shop or stall Child accompanying offender is actively used to facilitate the offence (not merely present when offence is committed)
B—Medium culpability
A significant role where offending is part of a group activity Some degree of planning involved Limited use or threat of force All other cases where characteristics for categories A or C are not present
C—Lesser culpability
Performed limited function under direction Involved through coercion, intimidation, or exploitation Little or no planning Mental disorder/learning disability where linked to commission of the offence

Where there are characteristics present which fall under different levels of culpability, the court should balance these characteristics to reach a fair assessment of the offender's culpability.

HARM

Harm is assessed by reference to the financial loss that results from the theft and any significant additional harm suffered by the victim—examples of significant additional harm may include but are not limited to:

Emotional distress

Damage to property

Effect on business

A greater impact on the victim due to the size or type of their business

A particularly vulnerable victim

Intended loss should be used where actual loss has been prevented.

Category 1	High-value goods stolen (above £1,000) **or** medium-value with significant additional harm to the victim
Category 2	Medium-value goods stolen (£200 to £1,000) **and** no significant additional harm **or** low-value with significant additional harm to the victim
Category 3	Low-value goods stolen (up to £200) **and** little or no significant additional harm to the victim

STEP TWO: Starting point and category range

Having determined the category at step one, the court should use the starting point to reach a sentence within the appropriate category range in the following table.

The starting point applies to all offenders irrespective of plea or previous convictions.

Harm	Culpability		
	A	B	C
Category 1 Where the value greatly exceeds £1,000 it may be appropriate to move outside the identified range. Adjustment should be made for any significant additional harm where high value goods are stolen.	**Starting point** 26 weeks' custody	**Starting point** Medium-level community order	**Starting point** Band C fine
	Category range 12 weeks'–3 years' custody	**Category range** Low-level community order–26 weeks' custody	**Category range** Band B fine–low-level community order
Category 2	**Starting point** 12 weeks' custody	**Starting point** Low-level community order	**Starting point** Band B fine
	Category range High-level community order–26 weeks' custody	**Category range** Band C fine–medium-level community order	**Category range** Band A fine–band C fine
Category 3	**Starting point** High-level community order	**Starting point** Band C fine	**Starting point** Band A fine
	Category range Low-level community order–12 weeks' custody	**Category range** Band B fine–low-level community order	**Category range** Discharge–band B fine

Consecutive sentences for multiple offences may be appropriate—please refer to the *Offences Taken into Consideration* and *Totality* guidelines. Previous diversionary work with an offender does not preclude the court from considering this type of sentencing option again if appropriate.

Where the offender is dependent on or has a propensity to misuse drugs or alcohol and there is sufficient prospect of success, a community order with a drug rehabilitation requirement under s 209, or an alcohol treatment requirement under s 212 Criminal Justice Act 2003, may be a proper alternative to a short or moderate length custodial sentence.

Where the offender suffers from a medical condition that is susceptible to treatment but does not warrant detention under a hospital order, a community order with a mental health treatment requirement under s 207 Criminal Justice Act 2003 may be a proper alternative to a short or moderate length custodial sentence.

The court should then consider further adjustment for any aggravating or mitigating factors. The following is a non-exhaustive list of additional factual elements providing the context of the offence and factors relating to the offender. Identify whether any combination of these, or other relevant factors, should result in an upward or downward adjustment from the sentence arrived at so far.

Factors increasing seriousness	
Statutory aggravating factors:	*Other aggravating factors:*
Previous convictions, having regard to (a) the nature of the offence to which the conviction relates and its relevance to the current offence; and (b) the time that has elapsed since the conviction. Relevant recent convictions may justify an upward adjustment, including outside the category range In cases involving significant persistent offending, the community and custodial thresholds may be crossed even though the offence otherwise warrants a lesser sentence. Any custodial sentence must be kept to the necessary minimum Offence committed while on bail Offence motivated by, or demonstrating hostility based on, any of the following characteristics or presumed characteristics of the victim: religion, race, disability, sexual orientation, or transgender identity	Stealing goods to order Steps taken to prevent the victim reporting or obtaining assistance and/or from assisting or supporting the prosecution Attempts to conceal/dispose of evidence Offender motivated by intention to cause harm or revenge Failure to comply with current court orders Offence committed on licence Offences taken into consideration Established evidence of community/wider impact (for issues other than prevalence) Prevalence—see **C15.21.1.1**

Factors reducing seriousness or reflecting personal mitigation
No previous convictions or no relevant/recent convictions
Remorse, particularly where evidenced by voluntary reparation to the victim
Good character and/or exemplary conduct
Serious medical condition requiring urgent, intensive, or long-term treatment
Age and/or lack of maturity where it affects the responsibility of the offender
Mental disorder or learning disability (where not linked to the commission of the offence)
Sole or primary carer for dependent relatives.
Determination and/or demonstration of steps having been taken to address addiction or offending behaviour.
Offender experiencing exceptional financial hardship.

C15.21.1.3 On prevalence see C15.21.1.1 and particularly R v Bondzie 2016 EWCA Crim 552

C15.21.2 Key points

Dishonesty is interpreted in accordance with *Ivey v Genting Casinos (UK) Ltd* (t/a Crockfords) [2017] UKSC 67.

The court must first ascertain (subjectively) the actual state of the individual's knowledge or belief as to the facts. Once the actual state of mind as to knowledge or belief as to facts is established, the question whether his conduct was honest or dishonest is to be determined by the fact-finder by applying the (objective) standards of ordinary decent people. There is no requirement that the defendant must appreciate that what he has done is, by those standards, dishonest.

'Dishonestly' is considered in s 2 Theft Act 1968:

Theft Act 1968, s 2

2 'Dishonestly'

(1) A person's appropriation of property belonging to another is not to be regarded as dishonest—
   (a) if he appropriates the property in the belief that he has in law the right to deprive the other of it, on behalf of himself or of a third person; or
   (b) if he appropriates the property in the belief that he would have the other's consent if the other knew of the appropriation and the circumstances of it; or
   (c) (except where the property came to him as trustee or personal representative) if he appropriates the property in the belief that the person to whom the property belongs cannot be discovered by taking reasonable steps.
(2) A person's appropriation of property belonging to another may be dishonest notwithstanding that he is willing to pay for the property. 'Appropriation' means the assumption of any of the rights of an owner (*R v Gomez* [1993] AC 442).

The intention permanently to deprive is also considered in s 6 Theft Act 1968:

Theft Act 1968, s 6

6 'With the intention of permanently depriving the other of it'

(1) A person appropriating property belonging to another without meaning the other permanently to lose the thing itself is nevertheless to be regarded as having the intention of permanently depriving the other of it if his intention is to treat the thing as his own to dispose of regardless of the other's rights; and a borrowing or lending of it may amount to so treating it if, but only if, the borrowing or lending is for a period and in circumstances making it equivalent to an outright taking or disposal.
(2) Without prejudice to the generality of subsection (1) above, where a person, having possession or control (lawfully or not) of property belonging to another, parts with the property under a condition as to its return which he may not be able to perform, this (if done for purposes of his own and without the other's authority) amounts to treating the property as his own to dispose of regardless of the other's rights.

C15.21.3 Low-value shoplifting

Low-value shoplifting is triable only summarily unless an adult defendant elects for trial on indictment.

Magistrates' Courts Act 1980, s 22A

(3) 'Low-value shoplifting' means an offence under section 1 of the Theft Act 1968 in circumstances where—
  (a) the value of the stolen goods does not exceed £200,
  (b) the goods were being offered for sale in a shop or any other premises, stall, vehicle or place from which there is carried on a trade or business, and
  (c) at the time of the offence, the person accused of low-value shoplifting was, or was purporting to be, a customer or potential customer of the person offering the goods for sale.
(4) For the purposes of subsection (3)(a)—
  (a) the value of the stolen goods is the price at which they were being offered for sale at the time of the offence, and
  (b) where the accused is charged on the same occasion with two or more offences of low-value shoplifting, the reference to the value involved has effect as if it were a reference to the aggregate of the values involved . . .

It is possible in law to attempt this offence (Criminal Attempts Act 1981, s 1(5)).

SO 6 months' imprisonment and/or a fine. In the Crown Court if the defendant elects 7 years but should not normally exceed 12 months (*R v Chamberlin* [2017] EWCA Crim 39)

,,,,,,,,,,,,

C15.22 **Trespass against property**

C15.22.1 *Squatting*

Legal Aid, Sentencing and Punishment of Offenders Act 2012, s 144

144 Offence of squatting in a residential building

(1) A person commits an offence if—
  (a) the person is in a residential building as a trespasser having entered it as a trespasser,
  (b) the person knows or ought to know that he or she is a trespasser, and
  (c) the person is living in the building or intends to live there for any period.
(2) The offence is not committed by a person holding over after the end of a lease or licence (even if the person leaves and re-enters the building).
(3) For the purposes of this section—
  (a) 'building' includes any structure or part of a structure (including a temporary or moveable structure), and

---

(b) a building is 'residential' if it is designed or adapted, before the time of entry, for use as a place to live.

(4) For the purposes of this section the fact that a person derives title from a trespasser, or has the permission of a trespasser, does not prevent the person from being a trespasser.

SO

6 months' imprisonment and/or fine

C15.22.2 Key points

It will be necessary to check that there was not even an informal licence; and whether a person intends to 'live' rather than stay temporarily will be a matter of fact in each case.

See *Blackstone's Criminal Practice 2019* **B13.31**

C15.22.3 *Aggravated trespass*

Criminal Justice and Public Order Act 1994, s 68(1) and (2)

68 Offence of aggravated trespass

(1) A person commits the offence of aggravated trespass if he trespasses on land and, in relation to any lawful activity which persons are engaging in or are about to engage in on that or adjoining land, does there anything which is intended by him to have the effect—
  (a) of intimidating those persons or any of them so as to deter them or any of them from engaging in that activity,
  (b) of obstructing that activity, or
  (c) of disrupting that activity.
(2) Activity on any occasion on the part of a person or persons on land is 'lawful' for the purposes of this section if he or they may engage in the activity on the land on that occasion without committing an offence or trespassing on the land.

SO

3 months' imprisonment and/or level 4 fine

C15.22.4 Key points

- There are four elements to the offence (*Richardson v DPP* [2014] UKSC 8; *Barnard v DPP* [2000] Crim LR 371):
  - trespass on land,
  - where a lawful activity is engaged,
  - the intention to have any one of the three effects specified (*Tilly v DPP* [2001] EWHC 821 (Admin)),
  - an act done towards that end. This must be distinct from the act of trespass (*Peppersharp v DPP* [2012] EWHC 474 (Admin)). However, a mass

entry and demonstration would, on particular facts, meet this need if there was an intimidatory affect to prevent people from engaging in a lawful activity (*Bauer and others* [2013] EWHC 634 (Admin)).

- Actual disruption is not required if the necessary intention is proved (*Winder v DPP* (1996) 160 JP 713).
- Activity takes place only if there is someone on the land who is not allowed to go on with what he is entitled to do (*Tilly v DPP* [2001] EWHC 821 (Admin)). An activity will only be unlawful if it involves a criminal offence that is integral to the core activity carried on but not where the criminality is incidental, collateral, or remote.

The defence must by evidence raise the issue of such a specific criminal offence in English law, by the landowner. If that is done the burden passes to the Crown to disprove that proposition to the criminal standard (*Richardson v DPP* [2014] UKSC 8).

 See *Blackstone's Criminal Practice 2019* **B13.45**

C15.23 TWOC (vehicle-taking without consent)

Theft Act 1968, s 12(1), (5), (6), and (7)

12 Taking motor vehicle or other conveyance without authority

(1) Subject to subsections (5) and (6) below, a person shall be guilty of an offence if, without having the consent of the owner or other lawful authority, he takes any conveyance for his own or another's use or knowing that any conveyance has been taken without such authority, drives it or allows himself to be carried in or on it.

...

(5) Subsection (1) above shall not apply in relation to pedal cycles; but, subject to subsection (6) below, a person who, without having the consent of the owner or other lawful authority, takes a pedal cycle for his own or another's use, or rides a pedal cycle knowing it to have been taken without such authority, shall on summary conviction be liable to a fine not exceeding level 3 on the standard scale.

(6) A person does not commit an offence under this section by anything done in the belief that he has lawful authority to do it or that he would have the owner's consent if the owner knew of his doing it and the circumstances of it.

(7) For purposes of this section—

(a) 'conveyance' means any conveyance constructed or adapted for the carriage of a person or persons whether by land, water or air, except that it does not include a conveyance constructed or adapted for use only under the control of a person not carried in or on it, and 'drive' shall be construed accordingly; and

(b) 'owner', in relation to a conveyance which is the subject of a hiring agreement or hire-purchase agreement, means the person in possession of the conveyance under that agreement.

SO

 6 months' imprisonment and/or fine

C15.23.1 *Sentencing*

Theft Act 1968, s 12

Triable only summarily:
  Maximum: Unlimited fine and/or 6 months
  Offence range: Band B fine–26 weeks' custody

STEP ONE: Determining the offence category

The court should determine the offence category using the following table.

Category 1	Higher culpability **and** greater harm
Category 2	Higher culpability **and** lesser harm **or** lower culpability **and** greater harm
Category 3	Lower culpability **and** lesser harm

The court should determine the offender's culpability and the harm caused with reference only to the following factors. Where an offence does not fall squarely into a category, individual factors may require a degree of weighting before making an overall assessment and determining the appropriate offence category.

CULPABILITY demonstrated by one or more of the following:	
Factors indicating higher culpability	**Factors indicating lower culpability**
• A leading role where offending is part of a group activity • Involvement of others through coercion, intimidation, or exploitation • Sophisticated nature of offence/significant planning • Abuse of position of power or trust or responsibility • Commission of offence in association with or to further other criminal activity	• Performed limited function under direction • Involved through coercion, intimidation or exploitation • Limited awareness or understanding of offence • Exceeding authorised use of eg employer's or relative's vehicle • Retention of hire car for short period beyond return date
HARM demonstrated by one or more of the following:	
Factors indicating greater harm	**Factors indicating lesser harm**
• Vehicle later burnt • Vehicle belonging to elderly/disabled person • Emergency services vehicle • Medium to large goods vehicle • Passengers carried • Damage to lock/ignition • Vehicle taken from private premises	• All other cases

STEP TWO: Starting point and category range

Having determined the category at step one, the court should use the appropriate starting point to reach a sentence within the category range in the following table. The starting point applies to all offenders irrespective of plea or previous convictions.

Level of seriousness	Starting point	Range	Disqualification
Category 1	High-level community order	Medium-level community order–26 weeks' custody	Consider disqualification 9–12 months (extend if imposing immediate custody)
Category 2	Medium-level community order	Low-level community order–High-level community order	Consider disqualification 5–8 months
Category 3	Low-level community order	Band B fine–Medium-level community order	Consider disqualification

- **Extend any disqualification if imposing immediate custody**

The court should then consider further adjustment for any aggravating or mitigating factors. The following is a non-exhaustive list of additional factual elements providing the context of the offence and factors relating to the offender. Identify whether any combination of these, or other relevant factors, should result in an upward or downward adjustment from the sentence arrived at so far.

Factors increasing seriousness	
Statutory aggravating factors:	*Other aggravating factors:*
• Previous convictions, having regard to (a) the **nature** of the offence to which the conviction relates and its **relevance** to the current offence; and (b) the **time** that has elapsed since the conviction • Offence committed while on bail	• Failure to comply with current court orders • Offence committed on licence or post-sentence supervision
Factors reducing seriousness or reflecting personal mitigation	
• No previous convictions **or** no relevant/recent convictions • Remorse • Good character and/or exemplary conduct • Age and/or lack of maturity where it affects the responsibility of the offender • Mental disorder or learning disability • Sole or primary carer for dependent relatives • Cooperation with the investigation	

C15.23.2 Key points

This offence is summary only, but subject to the following exception in relation to limitation period. On time limits see **A12.1.2**. Section 12(4A)–(4C) of the Act provides:

Theft Act 1968, s 12(4A)–(4C)

(4A) Proceedings for an offence under subsection (1) above (but not proceedings of a kind falling within subsection (4) above) in relation to a mechanically propelled vehicle—
    (a) shall not be commenced after the end of the period of three years beginning with the day on which the offence was committed; but
    (b) subject to that, may be commenced at any time within the period of six months beginning with the relevant day.

(4B) In subsection (4A)(b) above 'the relevant day' means—
  (a) in the case of a prosecution for an offence under subsection (1) above by a public prosecutor, the day on which sufficient evidence to justify the proceedings came to the knowledge of any person responsible for deciding whether to commence any such prosecution;
  (b) in the case of a prosecution for an offence under subsection (1) above which is commenced by a person other than a public prosecutor after the discontinuance of a prosecution falling within paragraph (a) above which relates to the same facts, the day on which sufficient evidence to justify the proceedings came to the knowledge of the person who has decided to commence the prosecution or (if later) the discontinuance of the other prosecution;
  (c) in the case of any other prosecution for an offence under subsection (1) above, the day on which sufficient evidence to justify the proceedings came to the knowledge of the person who has decided to commence the prosecution.
(4C) For the purposes of subsection (4A)(b) above a certificate of a person responsible for deciding whether to commence a prosecution of a kind mentioned in subsection (4B)(a) above as to the date on which such evidence as is mentioned in the certificate came to the knowledge of any person responsible for deciding whether to commence any such prosecution shall be conclusive evidence of that fact.

- There must be movement for a vehicle to be taken (*R v Bogacki* [1973] QB 832). The vehicle must be taken as a conveyance (*R v Stokes* [1983] RTR 59). The burden of proving that the defendant did not have a belief that he had the authority of the owner lies on the Crown once the defendant has raised the issue by evidence (*R v Gannon* (1987) 87 Cr App R 254). The belief must exist at the time of the taking (*R v Ambler* [1979] RTR 217).
- Formal evidence of ownership may not be necessary where it is possible to infer from the facts that the cycle had not been abandoned: *Sturrock v DPP* [1996] RTR 216.

 See *Blackstone's Criminal Practice 2019* **B4.116–B4.126**

C15.24 Unauthorized use of trade mark, etc

Trade Marks Act 1994, s 92(1)–(4)

92 Unauthorised use of trade mark, etc in relation to goods

(1) A person commits an offence who with a view to gain for himself or another, or with intent to cause loss to another, and without the consent of the proprietor—
  (a) applies to goods or their packaging a sign identical to, or likely to be mistaken for, a registered trade mark, or
  (b) sells or lets for hire, offers or exposes for sale or hire or distributes goods which bear, or the packaging of which bears, such a sign, or
  (c) has in his possession, custody or control in the course of a business any such goods with a view to the doing of anything, by himself or another, which would be an offence under paragraph (b).
(2) A person commits an offence who with a view to gain for himself or another, or with intent to cause loss to another, and without the consent of the proprietor—

(a) applies a sign identical to, or likely to be mistaken for, a registered trade mark to material intended to be used—
   (i) for labelling or packaging goods,
   (ii) as a business paper in relation to goods, or
   (iii) for advertising goods, or

(b) uses in the course of a business material bearing such a sign for labelling or packaging goods, as a business paper in relation to goods, or for advertising goods, or

(c) has in his possession, custody or control in the course of a business any such material with a view to the doing of anything, by himself or another, which would be an offence under paragraph (b).

(3) A person commits an offence who with a view to gain for himself or another, or with intent to cause loss to another, and without the consent of the proprietor—

(a) makes an article specifically designed or adapted for making copies of a sign identical to, or likely to be mistaken for, a registered trade mark, or

(b) has such an article in his possession, custody or control in the course of a business,

knowing or having reason to believe that it has been, or is to be, used to produce goods, or material for labelling or packaging goods, as a business paper in relation to goods, or for advertising goods.

(4) A person does not commit an offence under this section unless—

(a) the goods are goods in respect of which the trade mark is registered, or

(b) the trade mark has a reputation in the United Kingdom and the use of the sign takes or would take unfair advantage of, or is or would be detrimental to, the distinctive character or the repute of the trade mark.

(5) It is a defence for a person charged with an offence under this section to show that he believed on reasonable grounds that the use of the sign in the manner in which it was used, or was to be used, was not an infringement of the registered trade mark.

 6 months' imprisonment and/or fine/10 years' imprisonment

C15.24.1 *Sentencing*

Offence seriousness (culpability and harm)		
A. Identify the appropriate starting point		
Starting points based on first-time offender pleading not guilty		
Examples of nature of activity	**Starting point**	**Range**
Small number of counterfeit items	Band C fine	Band B fine–low-level community order
Larger number of counterfeit items but no involvement in wider operation	Medium-level community order, plus fine*	Low-level community order–12 weeks' custody, plus fine*
Examples of nature of activity	**Starting point**	**Range**
High number of counterfeit items or involvement in wider operation, eg manufacture or distribution	12 weeks' custody	6 weeks' custody to Crown Court
Central role in large-scale operation	Crown Court	Crown Court

* This may be an offence where it is appropriate to combine a fine with a community order.

Offence seriousness (culpability and harm)	
B. Consider the effect of aggravating and mitigating factors (other than those within examples in the preceding table)	
The following may be particularly relevant but these lists are not exhaustive	
Factors indicating higher culpability 1. High degree of professionalism 2. High level of profit **Factor indicating greater degree of harm** 1. Purchasers at risk of harm, eg from counterfeit drugs	**Factor indicating lower culpability** 1. Mistake or ignorance about provenance of goods

C15.24.2 Key points

It is a defence for a person charged with an offence under s 92 to show that he believed on reasonable grounds that the use of the sign in the manner in which it was used, or was to be used, was not an infringement of the registered trade mark. In order to be able to satisfy the statutory defence under s 95(2) Trade Marks Act 1994, the defendant must show not only that he had an honest belief that the trade marks did not infringe registered trade marks, but also that he had reasonable grounds for so believing. Section 97 makes provision for the forfeiture of counterfeit goods and packaging.

R v C and Others [2017] UKSC 58 holds that a criminal offence can be committed where the proprietor of the registered trade mark has given his consent to the application of the sign that is its registered trade mark, or has itself applied its own registered trade mark, to the goods, but has not given his consent to the sale, distribution, or possession of them.

 See *Blackstone's Criminal Practice 2019* **B6.105**

C15.25 Use of threat or violence for the purpose of securing entry to premises

Criminal Law Act 1977, s 6

6 Violence for securing entry

(1) Subject to the following provisions of this section, any person who, without lawful authority, uses or threatens violence for the purpose of securing entry into any premises for himself or for any other person is guilty of an offence, provided that—

   (a) there is someone present on those premises at the time who is opposed to the entry which the violence is intended to secure; and

   (b) the person using or threatening the violence knows that that is the case.

(1A) Subsection (1) above does not apply to a person who is a displaced residential occupier or a protected intending occupier of the premises in question or who is acting on behalf of such an occupier; and if the accused adduces sufficient evidence that he was, or was acting on behalf of, such an occupier he shall be presumed to be, or to be acting on behalf of, such an occupier unless the contrary is proved by the prosecution.

(2) Subject to subsection (1A) above, the fact that a person has any interest in or right to possession or occupation of any premises shall not for the purposes of subsection (1) above constitute lawful authority for the use or threat of violence by him or anyone else for the purpose of securing his entry into those premises.

(3) (repealed).

(4) It is immaterial for the purposes of this section—

    (a) whether the violence in question is directed against the person or against property; and

    (b) whether the entry which the violence is intended to secure is for the purpose of acquiring possession of the premises in question or for any other purpose.

SO

6 months' imprisonment and/or fine

C15.25.1 Key points

The terms premises, displaced residential occupier, and protected intending occupier are defined by ss 12 and 12A Criminal Law Act 1977.

C15.26 Vehicle interference

Criminal Attempts Act 1981, s 9(1) and (2)

9 Interference with vehicles

(1) A person is guilty of the offence of vehicle interference if he interferes with a motor vehicle or trailer or with anything carried in or on a motor vehicle or trailer with the intention that an offence specified in subsection (2) below shall be committed by himself or some other person.

(2) The offences mentioned in subsection (1) above are—

    (a) theft of the motor vehicle or trailer or part of it;

    (b) theft of anything carried in or on the motor vehicle or trailer; and

    (c) an offence under section 12(1) of the Theft Act 1968 (taking and driving away without consent);

    and, if it is shown that a person accused of an offence under this section intended that one of those offences should be committed, it is immaterial that it cannot be shown which it was.

SO

3 months' imprisonment and/or level 4 fine

C15.26.1 Sentencing

Criminal Attempts Act 1981, s 9

Triable only summarily:
    Maximum: Level 4 fine and/or 3 months
    Offence range: Band A fine–12 weeks' custody

STEP ONE: Determining the offence category

The court should determine the offence category using the following table.

Category 1	Higher culpability **and** greater harm
Category 2	Higher culpability **and** lesser harm **or** lower culpability **and** greater harm
Category 3	Lower culpability **and** lesser harm

The court should determine the offender's culpability and the harm caused with reference **only** to the following factors. Where an offence does not fall squarely into a category, individual factors may require a degree of weighting before making an overall assessment and determining the appropriate offence category.

CULPABILITY demonstrated by one or more of the following:	
Factors indicating higher culpability	**Factors indicating lower culpability**
• Leading role where offending is part of a group activity • Targeting of particular vehicles and/or contents • Planning	• All other cases

HARM demonstrated by one or more of the following:	
Factors indicating greater harm	**Factors indicating lesser harm**
• Damage caused significant financial loss, inconvenience or distress to victim • Vehicle left in a dangerous condition	• All other cases

STEP TWO: Starting point and category range

Having determined the category at step one, the court should use the corresponding starting point to reach a sentence within the category range in the following table. The starting point applies to all offenders irrespective of plea or previous convictions.

Offence category	Starting point	Range
Category 1	High-level community order	Medium level community order–12 weeks' custody
Category 2	Medium-level community order	Band C fine–High-level community order
Category 3	Band C fine	Band A fine–Low-level community order

The court should then consider adjustment for any aggravating or mitigating factors. The following is a non-exhaustive list of additional factual elements providing the context of the offence and factors relating to the offender. Identify whether any combination of these, or other relevant factors, should result in an upward or downward adjustment from the sentence arrived at so far.

Factors increasing seriousness	
Statutory aggravating factors:	*Other aggravating factors:*
• Previous convictions, having regard to (a) the **nature** of the offence to which the conviction relates and its **relevance** to the current offence; and (b) the **time** that has elapsed since the conviction • Offence committed while on bail	• Failure to comply with current court orders • Offence committed on licence or post-sentence supervision • Part of a spree • Offence against emergency services vehicle

Factors reducing seriousness or reflecting personal mitigation
• No previous convictions **or** no relevant/recent convictions • Good character and/or exemplary conduct • Age and/or lack of maturity where it affects the responsibility of the offender • Mental disorder or learning disability • Sole or primary carer for dependent relatives

 See *Blackstone's Criminal Practice 2019* **B4.136–B4.139**

C15.27 Vehicle licence/registration fraud

Vehicle Excise and Registration Act 1994, s 44(1) and (2)

44 Forgery and fraud

(1) A person is guilty of an offence if he forges, fraudulently alters, fraudulently uses, fraudulently lends or fraudulently allows to be used by another person anything to which subsection (2) applies

(2) This subsection applies to—
  (a) a vehicle licence,
  (b) a trade licence,
  (c) a nil licence,
  (d) a registration mark,
  (e) a registration document, and
  (f) a trade plate (including a replacement trade plate).

 EW

 Fine/2 years' imprisonment

Note: There are offences carrying the same penalties under s 173 (forgery, etc, of licences, counterparts of Community licences, test certificates, certificates of insurance and other documents and things) and s 174 (making certain false statements, etc, and withholding certain material information) Road Traffic Act 1988.

C15.27.1 *Sentencing*

Offence seriousness (culpability and harm)		
A. Identify the appropriate starting point		
Starting points based on first-time offender pleading not guilty		
Examples of nature of activity	**Starting point**	**Range**
Use of unaltered licence from another vehicle	Band B fine	Band B fine
Forged licence bought for own use, or forged/altered for own use	Band C fine	Band C fine
Use of number plates from another vehicle; OR licence/number plates forged or altered for sale to another	High-level community order (in Crown Court)	Medium-level community order to Crown Court (Note: community order and custody available only in Crown Court)

Offence seriousness (culpability and harm)	
B. Consider the effect of aggravating and mitigating factors (other than those within examples in the preceding table)	
The following may be particularly relevant but these lists are not exhaustive	
Factors indicating higher culpability 1. LGV, PSV, taxi, etc 2. Long-term fraudulent use **Factors indicating greater degree of harm** 1. High financial gain 2. Innocent victim deceived 3. Legitimate owner inconvenienced	**Factors indicating lower culpability** 1. Licence/registration mark from another vehicle owned by defendant 2. Short-term use

 See *Blackstone's Criminal Practice 2019* **C4.10**

C16 Offences against the Person

C16.1 Assault occasioning actual bodily harm

> ### Offences Against the Person Act 1861, s 47
>
> #### 47 Assault occasioning bodily harm
>
> Whosoever shall be convicted ... of any assault occasioning actual bodily harm shall be liable ...

Fine and/or 6 months'/5 years' imprisonment (7 years if racially aggravated)

C16.1.1 *Sentencing*

STEP ONE: Determining the offence category

Category 1	Greater harm (serious injury must normally be present) and higher culpability
Category 2	Greater harm (serious injury must normally be present) and lower culpability or lesser harm and higher culpability
Category 3	Lesser harm and lower culpability

Factors indicating greater harm	Factors indicating higher culpability
Injury (which includes disease transmission and/or psychological harm) which is serious in the context of the offence (must normally be present) Victim is particularly vulnerable because of personal circumstances Sustained or repeated assault on the same victim	**Statutory aggravating factors:** Offence motivated by, or demonstrating, hostility to, the victim based on his or her sexual orientation (or presumed sexual orientation) Offence motivated by, or demonstrating, hostility to, the victim based on the victim's disability (or presumed disability)
	Other aggravating factors: A significant degree of premeditation Deliberately causes more harm than is necessary for commission of offence Deliberate targeting of vulnerable victim Leading role in group or gang Offence motivated by, or demonstrating, hostility based on the victim's age, sex, gender identity (or presumed gender identity)
Factors indicating lesser harm	**Factors indicating lower culpability**
Injury which is less serious in the context of the offence	Subordinate role in group or gang A greater degree of provocation than normally expected Lack of premeditation Mental disorder or learning disability, where linked to commission of the offence Excessive self-defence

A person could be seen as particularly vulnerable because he was intoxicated even where he struck the first blow, if there is an excessive response (*R v Halane* [2014] EWCA Crim 477). Not every victim of domestic violence is to be treated as particularly vulnerable for the purpose of the guideline. Serious injury must be interpreted in the context of the particular offence. It means not on the margins and more substantial injury (*R v Thomas* [2014] EWCA Crim 1715). In *R v Maloney (James)* [2015] EWCA Crim 798 the Crown alleged the deliberate targeting of a vulnerable victim, acknowledging that this may involve an element of double counting, thus increasing both harm and culpability. The court found that there was not enough evidence that the defendant targeted the victim *because* she was vulnerable; rather, he was angry with her and she happened to be vulnerable. On the facts in *R v Wilson* [2019] EWCA Crim 468, there being two blows could not properly be described as a repeated assault.

STEP TWO: Starting point and category range

Offence category	Starting point	Category range
Category 1	1 year 6 months' custody	1 year–3 years' custody
Category 2	26 weeks' custody	Low-level community order–51 weeks' custody
Category 3	Medium-level community order	Band A fine–high-level community order

Factors increasing seriousness	
Statutory aggravating factors	*Other aggravating factors*
Previous convictions, having regard to (a) the nature of the offence to which the conviction relates and its relevance to the current offence; and (b) the time that has elapsed since the conviction Offence committed while on bail	Location of the offence Timing of the offence Ongoing effect upon the victim Offence committed against those working in the public sector or providing a service to the public Presence of others including relatives, especially children or partner of the victim Gratuitous degradation of victim In domestic violence cases, victim forced to leave their home Failure to comply with current court orders Offence committed while on licence Attempt to conceal or dispose of evidence Failure to respond to warnings or concerns expressed by others about the offender's behaviour Commission of offence while under the influence of alcohol or drugs Abuse of power and/or position of trust Exploiting contact arrangements with a child to commit an offence Established evidence of community impact Any steps taken to prevent the victim reporting an incident, obtaining assistance, and/or from assisting or supporting the prosecution Offences taken into consideration (TICs)

Factors increasing seriousness
Factors reducing seriousness or reflecting personal mitigation
No previous convictions or no relevant/recent convictions
Single blow
Remorse
Good character and/or exemplary conduct
Determination and/or demonstration of steps taken to address addiction or offending behaviour
Serious medical conditions requiring urgent, intensive, or long-term treatment
Isolated incident
Age and/or lack of maturity where it affects the responsibility of the offender
Lapse of time since the offence where this is not the fault of the offender
Mental disorder or learning disability, where not linked to the commission of the offence
Sole or primary carer for dependent relatives

C16.1.2 Key points

- Action or words causing the person to apprehend imminent unlawful force. A conditional threat amounts to an assault, as does a threat to do something in the future (how far into the future is a matter of debate: see *R v Constanza* [1997] 2 Cr App R 492). Words in themselves could suffice, as could a gesture (eg using fingers to imitate a gun being fired, or a slashing action across the throat). An extreme example can be found in *R v Ireland* [1998] AC 147, a case where the appellant made silent phone calls to the victim. Conditional actions—for example, 'get out of my house or I will hurt you'—will amount to an assault. The words may also indicate that no assault is going to happen, as in *Tuberville v Savage* (1669) 1 Mod Rep 3 ('if it were not assize time, I would not take such language from you'). Creating a danger can amount to an assault; for example if a prisoner knows that he has a needle secreted on him and dishonestly does not inform a police officer carrying out a search, he may be liable if the officer injures himself on that needle, such a risk being reasonably foreseeable (*Director of Public Prosecutions v Santana-Bermudez* [2003] EWHC 2908 (Admin)).
- A battery involves the use of actual force being applied to the victim.
- Harm, which must be more than merely transient or trifling, encompasses not only injury but also hurt and damage. The concept of bodily harm is wide-ranging, and includes the cutting off of someone's hair (*DPP v Smith* [2006] 2 Cr App R 1). Psychiatric injury, in a medically diagnosed form, can amount to bodily harm, but anything short of this, for example upset or distress, will not.
- *Mens rea* is intention or recklessness. Note that the *mens rea* relates to the act of assault or battery; there is no requirement to prove that harm was intended, or that the defendant was reckless as to whether or not harm would be caused.

C16.1.3 *Defences*

The following defences should be considered:

- Consent, although *R v Brown* [1994] 1 AC 212 limits the application of this defence in sado-masochistic situations. It remains available, for instance, in sport or medical treatment, or where a wife agrees to be 'branded' (*R v Wilson* [1996] 2 Cr App R 241).
- Lawful correction or chastisement, but subject to s 58 Children Act 2004:

Children Act 2004, s 58(1)–(2)

58 Reasonable punishment

1. In relation to any offence specified in subsection (2), battery of a child cannot be justified on the ground that it constituted reasonable punishment.
2. The offences referred to in subsection (1) are—
   (a) an offence under section 18 or 20 of the Offences against the Person Act 1861 (c. 100) (wounding and causing grievous bodily harm);
   (b) an offence under section 47 of that Act (assault occasioning actual bodily harm);
   (c) an offence under section 1 of the Children and Young Persons Act 1933 (c. 12) (cruelty to persons under 16).

- Self-defence. Because there must be an unlawful act, a person acting in self-defence cannot be guilty of an assault; and once the issue has been raised by the defence in evidence, the Crown must prove that the defendant was not acting in self-defence. Householders enjoy a wider definition of self-defence under the amended s 76 Criminal Justice and Immigration Act 2008. The 'householder' version of self-defence (was the act grossly disproportionate) applies to all lawful occupiers of a property and not just to the owner (*R v Day* [2015] EWCA Crim 1646). It applies against all trespassers whether or not an intruder (*R v Cheeseman* [2019] EWCA Crim199).
- Defence of property.
- Prevention of crime.
- Horseplay. Consent to rough and undisciplined play where there is no intention to harm is a defence to a charge of assault including where, consent being absent, there is a genuine (however unreasonable) belief by a defendant that consent was present (*R v Jones and others* (1986) 83 Cr App R 375).

 See *Blackstone's Criminal Practice 2019* **B2.27–B2.36**

C16.2 Assault with intent to resist arrest

Offences Against the Person Act 1861, s 38

38 Assault with intent to resist apprehension, etc

Whosoever shall assault any person with intent to resist or prevent the lawful apprehension or detainer of himself or of any other person for any offence, shall be guilty of an offence.

 6 months' imprisonment and/or fine/2 years' imprisonment

C16.2.1 *Sentencing*

STEP ONE: Determining the offence category

Category 1	Greater harm and higher culpability
Category 2	Greater harm and lower culpability; or lesser harm and higher culpability
Category 3	Lesser harm and lower culpability

Factors indicating greater harm	Factors indicating higher culpability
Sustained or repeated assault on the same victim	**Statutory aggravating factors:** Offence racially or religiously aggravated Offence motivated by, or demonstrating, hostility to the victim based on his or her sexual orientation (or presumed sexual orientation) Offence motivated by, or demonstrating, hostility to the victim based on the victim's disability (or presumed disability) **Other aggravating factors:** A significant degree of premeditation Use of weapon or weapon equivalent (eg shod foot, head-butting, use of acid, use of animal) Intention to commit more serious harm than actually resulted from the offence Deliberately causes more harm than is necessary for commission of offence Leading role in group or gang Offence motivated by, or demonstrating, hostility based on the victim's age, sex, gender identity (or presumed gender identity)
Factors indicating lesser harm	**Factors indicating lower culpability**
Injury that is less serious in the context of the offence	Subordinate role in group or gang Lack of premeditation Mental disorder or learning disability, where linked to commission of the offence

STEP TWO: *Starting point and category range*

Offence category	Starting point	Category range
Category 1	26 weeks' custody	12 weeks' custody to Crown Court (51 weeks' custody)
Category 2	Medium-level community order	Low-level community order–high-level community order
Category 3	Band B fine	Band A fine–band C fine

Factors increasing seriousness	
Statutory aggravating factors:	*Other aggravating factors:*
Previous convictions, having regard to (a) the **nature** of the offence to which the conviction relates and its relevance to the current offence; and (b) the **time** that has elapsed since the conviction Offence committed while on bail	Location of the offence Timing of the offence Ongoing effect upon the victim Gratuitous degradation of victim Failure to comply with current court orders Offence committed while on licence Attempt to conceal or dispose of evidence Failure to respond to warnings or concerns expressed by others about the offender's behaviour Commission of offence while under the influence of alcohol or drugs Established evidence of community impact Any steps taken to prevent the victim reporting an incident, obtaining assistance, and/or assisting or supporting the prosecution Offences taken into consideration (TICs)

Factors reducing seriousness or reflecting personal mitigation
No previous convictions or no relevant/recent convictions Single blow Remorse Good character and/or exemplary conduct Determination and/or demonstration of steps taken to address addiction or offending behaviour Serious medical conditions requiring urgent, intensive, or long-term treatment Isolated incident Age and/or lack of maturity where it affects the responsibility of the defendant Lapse of time since the offence where this is not the fault of the offender Mental disorder or learning disability, where not linked to the commission of the offence Sole or primary carer for dependent relatives

C16.2.2 Key points

- The arrest must be a lawful one, and the defendant's honest but mistaken belief in that regard does not afford a defence (*R v Lee* (2001) 165 JP 344).
- The prosecution do not need to prove that the defendant knew that the person was a police officer (*R v Brightling* [1991] Crim LR 364).

 See *Blackstone's Criminal Practice 2019* **B2.22–B2.26**

C16.3 Assaulting a police constable or resisting or obstructing a police constable

Police Act 1996, s 89(1)–(2)

89 Assaults on constables

(1) Any person who assaults a constable in the execution of his duty, or a person assisting a constable in the execution of his duty, shall be guilty of an offence...
(2) Any person who resists or wilfully obstructs a constable in the execution of his duty, or a person assisting a constable in the execution of his duty, shall be guilty of an offence ...

SO

 6 months' imprisonment and/or fine (assaults), and/or 1 month imprisonment/level 3 fine/(resist/obstruct)

C16.3.1 *Sentencing, s 89(1) Assault*

STEP ONE: Determining the offence category

Category 1	Greater harm and higher culpability
Category 2	Greater harm and lower culpability; or lesser harm and higher culpability
Category 3	Lesser harm and lower culpability

Factors indicating greater harm	Factors indicating higher culpability
Sustained or repeated assault on the same victim	**Statutory aggravating factors:** Offence racially or religiously aggravated Offence motivated by, or demonstrating, hostility to the victim based on his or her sexual orientation (or presumed sexual orientation) Offence motivated by, or demonstrating, hostility to the victim based on the victim's disability (or presumed disability) **Other aggravating factors:** A significant degree of premeditation Use of weapon or weapon equivalent (eg shod foot, headbutting, use of acid, use of animal) Intention to commit more serious harm than actually resulted from the offence Deliberately causes more harm than is necessary for commission of offence Leading role in group or gang Offence motivated by, or demonstrating, hostility based on the victim's age, sex, gender identity (or presumed gender identity)
Factors indicating lesser harm	**Factors indicating lower culpability**
Injury which is less serious in the context of the offence	Subordinate role in group or gang Lack of premeditation Mental disorder or learning disability, where linked to commission of the offence

STEP TWO: Starting point and category range

Offence category	Starting point	Category range
Category 1	12 weeks' custody	Low-level community order–26 weeks' custody
Category 2	Medium-level community order	Low-level community order–high-level community order
Category 3	Band B fine	Band A fine–band C fine

Factors increasing seriousness	
Statutory aggravating factors:	*Other aggravating factors:*
Previous convictions, having regard to (a) the nature of the offence to which the conviction relates and its relevance to the current offence; and (b) the time that has elapsed since the conviction Offence committed while on bail	Location of the offence Timing of the offence Ongoing effect upon the victim Gratuitous degradation of victim Failure to comply with current court orders Offence committed while on licence Attempt to conceal or dispose of evidence Failure to respond to warnings or concerns expressed by others about the offender's behaviour Commission of offence while under the influence of alcohol or drugs Established evidence of community impact Any steps taken to prevent the victim reporting an incident, obtaining assistance, and/or assisting or supporting the prosecution Offences taken into consideration (TICs)

Factors reducing seriousness or reflecting personal mitigation
No previous convictions or no relevant/recent convictions Single blow Remorse Good character and/or exemplary conduct Determination and/or demonstration of steps taken to address addiction or offending behaviour Serious medical conditions requiring urgent, intensive, or long-term treatment Isolated incident Age and/or lack of maturity where it affects the responsibility of the offender Lapse of time since the offence where this is not the fault of the offender Mental disorder or learning disability, where not linked to the commission of the offence Sole or primary carer for dependent relatives

C16.3.1.1 *Sentencing (s 89(2)) Wilful Obstruction*

Police Act 1996, s 89(2)

Triable only summarily:
 Maximum: Level 3 fine and/or one month
 Offence range: Conditional Discharge–Medium-level community order

STEP ONE: Determining the offence category

The court should determine the offence category using the following table.

Category 1	Higher culpability and greater harm
Category 2	Higher culpability and lesser harm or lower culpability and greater harm
Category 3	Lower culpability and lesser harm

The court should determine the offender's culpability and the harm caused with reference only to the following factors. Where an offence does not fall squarely into a category, individual factors may require a degree of weighting before making an overall assessment and determining the appropriate offence category.

CULPABILITY demonstrated by one or more of the following:	
Factors indicating higher culpability	**Factors indicating lower culpability**
• Deliberate obstruction or interference • Use of force, aggression or intimidation • Group action	• All other cases

HARM demonstrated by one or more of the following:	
Factors indicating greater harm	**Factors indicating lesser harm**
• Offender's actions significantly increase risk to officer or other(s) • Offender's actions result in a suspect avoiding arrest • Offender's actions result in a significant waste of resources	• All other cases

STEP TWO: Starting point and category range

Having determined the category at step one, the court should use the corresponding starting point to reach a sentence within the following category range. The starting point applies to all offenders irrespective of plea or previous convictions.

Offence category	Starting point	Range
Category 1	Low-level community order	Band C fine–Medium-level community order
Category 2	Band B fine	Band A fine–Band C fine
Category 3	Band A fine	Conditional discharge–Band B fine

The court should then consider adjustment for any aggravating or mitigating factors. The following is a non-exhaustive list of additional factual elements providing the context of the offence and factors relating to the offender. Identify whether any combination of these, or other relevant factors, should result in an upward or downward adjustment from the sentence arrived at so far.

Factors increasing seriousness	
Statutory aggravating factors:	*Other aggravating factors:*
• Previous convictions, having regard to (a) the **nature** of the offence to which the conviction relates and its **relevance** to the current offence; and (b) the **time** that has elapsed since the conviction • Offence committed while on bail • Offence motivated by, or demonstrating hostility based on any of the following characteristics or presumed characteristics of the victim: religion, race, disability, sexual orientation, or transgender identity	• Failure to comply with current court orders • Offence committed on licence or post-sentence supervision • Blame wrongly placed on others • Injury caused to an officer/another • Giving false details
Factors reducing seriousness or reflecting personal mitigation	
• No previous convictions **or** no relevant/recent convictions • Remorse • Brief incident • Acting under direction or coercion of another • Genuinely held belief if coming to the aid of another, that the other was suffering severe medical difficulty • Good character and/or exemplary conduct • Serious medical condition requiring urgent, intensive, or long-term treatment • Age and/or lack of maturity where it affects the responsibility of the offender • Mental disorder or learning disability	

C16.3.2 Key points

- The constable must be acting lawfully (ie in execution of his duty).
- Self-defence may be raised as a defence to both assault and obstruction of a police officer, even one acting in the execution of their duty (*Wheeldon v CPS* [2018] EWHC 247 (Admin); *Oraki v DPP* [2018] EWHC 115 (Admin)). So in *Dixon v CPS* [2018] EWHC 3154 (Admin), where two officers unlawfully detained the defendant who was entitled to use reasonable force to resist but the court held that a third officer intervened lawfully because he feared the defendant had a weapon, there was a defence if the defendant honestly believed the officer was assaulting him. However the force must be reasonable—a bite was not.
- The prosecution do not need to prove that the defendant knew that the person was a police officer (*R v Brightling* [1991] Crim LR 364).
- If officer A is not acting lawfully in arresting a suspect, officer B who in good faith seeks to assist officer A will not be acting lawfully (*Cumberbatch v Crown Prosecution Service* [2009] EWHC 3353 (Admin)).
- If a suspect is accused of trying to impede the arrest of a third party, it must be shown that the arrest of that third party was lawful (*Riley v Director of Public Prosecutions* (1990) 91 Cr App R 14).
- Where the defendant interfered with the lawful detention by a police officer of another, an officer pushing the defendant away cannot
  (i) legitimize an earlier obstruction by the defendant of an officer in execution of his duty; or
  (ii) provide an indemnity against all further actions of the defendant including a continuing obstruction. This is a different scenario to that

when the only issue is whether the officer was touching the person without any intention to arrest. In any event the officer's push was a lawful act in accordance with s 3 Criminal Law Act 1967 (*Metcalfe v CPS* [2015] EWHC 1091 (Admin)).

- For the lawfulness of a police officer entering premises to save life or limb, see *Baker v Crown Prosecution Service* [2009] EWHC 299 (Admin). An officer may enter premises to prevent a potential breach of the peace (*Laporte v MPC* [2014] EWHC 3574 (QB)).

- For the situation where a police officer has had a licence to remain on property revoked, see *R (Fullard) v Woking Magistrates' Court* [2005] EWHC 2922 (Admin).

- An officer who had not yet established grounds for arrest was acting unlawfully in restraining a suspect (*Wood v Director of Public Prosecutions* [2008] EWHC 1056 (Admin)). It was unlawful to take hold of a woman to question her (*Collins v Wilcock* [1984] 1 WLR 1172), but not every interference with a citizen's liberty will be sufficient to take the officer outside the course of his duty. A police officer may take hold of a person's arm to attract his attention and calm him down (*Mepstead v DPP* (1996) 160 JP 175).

- While a police officer may touch someone to gain their attention, if they are told to desist, a further touching will take the officer outside the execution of their duty (*R (Shah) v Central Criminal Court* [2013] EWHC 1747 (Admin)). A police officer may not detain a person, beyond acceptable conduct by any member of the public, even for one second, without intending to exercise a power of arrest. This included the use of an implied threat of force if the person did not remain (*Walker v Commissioner of the Metropolitan Police* [2014] EWCA Civ 897). However where an officer seeks to have the defendant stop but does not use or threaten violence the action is lawful notwithstanding that he may have had an unlawful intent to detain without an arrest. It is what is said and done and not what is intended that is critical (*Tester v DPP* 2015 EWHC 1353 (Admin)).

- The powers of the police to stop and search, and of entry under the Police and Criminal Evidence Act 1984, are interpreted strictly (see *R v Bristol* [2007] EWCA Crim 3214 and *B v Director of Public Prosecutions* [2008] EWHC 1655 (Admin)).

- A police officer who had a mere belief in the existence of a search warrant was not acting in the execution of their duty. But the existence of a warrant could be inferred by the court from other facts proved such as evidence that it was a planned raid by a specialist unit (*Sykes v CPS* [2013] EWHC 3600 (Admin)).

- An arrest is lawful if the factual grounds are explained. It is not necessary to identify the statute creating the offence (*McCann v CPS* [2015] EWHC 2461 (Admin)).

See *Blackstone's Criminal Practice 2019* **B2.37–B2.47**

C16.4 **Common assault**

Criminal Justice Act 1988, s 39

1) Common assault and battery shall be ... offences

Assaults on Emergency Workers (Offences) Act 2018

1 Common assault and battery

(1) The section applies to an offence of common assault, or battery, that is committed against an emergency worker acting in the exercise of functions as such a worker.

(3) For the purposes of subsection (1), the circumstances in which an offence is to be taken as committed against a person acting in the exercise of functions as an emergency worker include circumstances where the offence takes place at a time when the person is not at work but is carrying out functions which, if done in work time, would have been in the exercise of functions as an emergency worker.

2 Aggravating factor

(1) This section applies where—
  (a) the court is considering for the purposes of sentencing the seriousness of an offence listed in subsection (3), and
  (b) the offence was committed against an emergency worker acting in the exercise of functions as such a worker.

(2) The court—
  (a) must treat the fact mentioned in subsection (1)(b) as an aggravating factor (that is to say, a factor that increases the seriousness of the offence), and
  (b) must state in open court that the offence is so aggravated.

(3) The offences referred to in subsection (1)(a) are—
  (a) an offence under any of the following provisions of the Offences against the Person Act 1861—
    (i) section 16 (threats to kill);
    (ii) section 18 (wounding with intent to cause grievous bodily harm);
    (iii) section 20 (malicious wounding);
    (iv) section 23 (administering poison etc);
    (v) section 28 (causing bodily injury by gunpowder etc);
    (vi) section 29 (using explosive substances etc with intent to cause grievous bodily harm);
    (vii) section 47 (assault occasioning actual bodily harm);
  (b) an offence under section 3 of the Sexual Offences Act 2003 (sexual assault);
  (c) manslaughter;
  (d) kidnapping;
  (e) an ancillary offence in relation to any of the preceding offences.

(4) For the purposes of subsection (1)(b), the circumstances in which an offence is to be taken as committed against a person acting in the exercise of functions as an emergency worker include circumstances where the offence takes place at a time when the person is not at work but is carrying out functions which, if done in work time, would have been in the exercise of functions as an emergency worker.

(5) In this section—
'ancillary offence', in relation to an offence, means any of the following—
  (a) aiding, abetting, counselling or procuring the commission of the offence;
  (b) an offence under Part 2 of the Serious Crime Act 2007 (encouraging or assisting crime) in relation to the offence;
  (c) attempting or conspiring to commit the offence;
  'emergency worker' has the meaning given by section 3.

(6) Nothing in this section prevents a court from treating the fact mentioned in subsection (1)(b) as an aggravating factor in relation to offences not listed in subsection (3).

3 Meaning of 'emergency worker'

(1) In sections 1 and 2, 'emergency worker' means—
  (a) a constable;
  (b) a person (other than a constable) who has the powers of a constable or is otherwise employed for police purposes or is engaged to provide services for police purposes;
  (c) a National Crime Agency officer;
  (d) a prison officer;
  (e) a person (other than a prison officer) employed or engaged to carry out functions in a custodial institution of a corresponding kind to those carried out by a prison officer;
  (f) a prisoner custody officer, so far as relating to the exercise of escort functions;
  (g) a custody officer, so far as relating to the exercise of escort functions;
  (h) a person employed for the purposes of providing, or engaged to provide, fire services or fire and rescue services;
  (i) a person employed for the purposes of providing, or engaged to provide, search services or rescue services (or both);
  (j) a person employed for the purposes of providing, or engaged to provide—
      (i) NHS health services, or
      (ii) services in the support of the provision of NHS health services, and whose general activities in doing so involve face to face interaction with individuals receiving the services or with other members of the public.
(2) It is immaterial for the purposes of subsection (1) whether the employment or engagement is paid or unpaid.
(3) In this section—
'custodial institution' means any of the following—
  (a) a prison;
  (b) a young offender institution, secure training centre, secure college or remand centre;
  (c) a removal centre, a short-term holding facility or pre-departure accommodation, as defined by section 147 of the Immigration and Asylum Act 1999;
  (d) services custody premises, as defined by section 300(7) of the Armed Forces Act 2006;
      'custody officer' has the meaning given by section 12(3) of the Criminal Justice and Public Order Act 1994;
      'escort functions'—
  (a) in the case of a prisoner custody officer, means the functions specified in section 80(1) of the Criminal Justice Act 1991;
  (b) in the case of a custody officer, means the functions specified in paragraph 1 of Schedule 1 to the Criminal Justice and Public Order Act 1994;
      'NHS health services' means any kind of health services provided as part of the health service continued under section 1(1) of the National Health Service Act 2006 and under section 1(1) of the National Health Service (Wales) Act 2006;
      'prisoner custody officer' has the meaning given by section 89(1) of the Criminal Justice Act 1991.

SO Common assault and battery

EW Assault on emergency workers and racially aggravated common assault

- 6 months' and/or fine (common assault and battery)
- 6 months and/ or fine/12 months (assaults on emergency workers)
- 6 months and/or a fine/ 2 years (if racially or religiously aggravated) '

> **DO** (Racially or religiously aggravated: common assault)

C16.4.1 *Sentencing (basic common assault)*

R v McGarrick [2019] EWCA Crim 530 confirms that the basic guideline cannot be carried across to the <u>Assaults on Emergency Workers (Offences) Act 2018</u>. The General guideline the Sentencing Council states that care should be taken to avoid double counting factors including those already taken into account in assessing culpability or harm or those inherent in the offence.

STEP ONE: Determining the offence category

Category 1	Greater harm (injury or fear of injury must normally be present) and higher culpability
Category 2	Greater harm (injury or fear of injury must normally be present) and lower culpability; or lesser harm and higher culpability
Category 3	Lesser harm and lower culpability

Factors indicating greater harm	Factors indicating higher culpability
Injury or fear of injury which is serious in the context of the offence (must normally be present) Victim is particularly vulnerable because of personal circumstances Sustained or repeated assault on the same victim	**Statutory aggravating factors:** Offence motivated by, or demonstrating, hostility to the victim based on his or her sexual orientation (or presumed sexual orientation) Offence motivated by, or demonstrating, hostility to the victim based on the victim's disability (or presumed disability) **Other aggravating factors:** A significant degree of premeditation Threatened or actual use of weapon or weapon equivalent (eg shod foot, head-butting, use of acid, use of animal) Intention to commit more serious harm than actually resulted from the offence Deliberately causes more harm than is necessary for commission of offence Deliberate targeting of vulnerable victim Leading role in group or gang Offence motivated by, or demonstrating, hostility based on the victim's age, sex, gender identity (or presumed gender identity)
Factors indicating lesser harm	**Factors indicating lower culpability**
Injury which is less serious in the context of the offence	Subordinate role in group or gang A greater degree of provocation than normally expected Lack of premeditation Mental disorder or learning disability, where linked to commission of the offence Excessive self-defence

STEP TWO: Starting point and category range

Offence category	Starting point	Category range
Category 1	High-level community order	Low-level community order–23 weeks' custody
Category 2	Medium-level community order	Band A fine–high-level community order
Category 3	Band A fine	Discharge–band C fine

Factors increasing seriousness	
Statutory aggravating factors	*Other aggravating factors*
Previous convictions, having regard to (a) the nature of the offence to which the conviction relates and its relevance to the current offence; and (b) the time that has elapsed since the conviction Offence committed while on bail	Location of the offence Timing of the offence Ongoing effect upon the victim Offence committed against those working in the public sector or providing a service to the public Presence of others including relatives, especially children or partner of the victim Gratuitous degradation of victim In domestic violence cases, victim forced to leave their home Failure to comply with current court orders Offence committed while on licence Attempt to conceal or dispose of evidence Failure to respond to warnings or concerns expressed by others about the offender's behaviour Commission of offence while under the influence of alcohol or drugs Abuse of power and/or position of trust. Exploiting contact arrangements with a child to commit an offence Established evidence of community impact. Any steps taken to prevent the victim reporting an incident, obtaining assistance, and/or assisting or supporting the prosecution Offences taken into consideration (TICs)

Factors reducing seriousness or reflecting personal mitigation
No previous convictions or no relevant/recent convictions Single blow Remorse Good character and/or exemplary conduct Determination and/or demonstration of steps taken to address addiction or offending behaviour Serious medical conditions requiring urgent, intensive, or long-term treatment Isolated incident Age and/or lack of maturity where it affects the responsibility of the offender Lapse of time since the offence where this is not the fault of the offender Mental disorder or learning disability, where not linked to the commission of the offence Sole or primary carer for dependent relative

Racially aggravated offences: the court should determine the appropriate sentence for the offence without taking account of the element of aggravation and then make an addition to the sentence, considering the level of aggravation involved. It may be appropriate to move outside the identified category range, taking into account the increased statutory maximum.

C16.4.2 Key points

- Common assault comprises both assault (where 'assault' means the intentional or reckless causing of another to apprehend immediate unlawful violence) and assault by beating (battery—the intentional or reckless inflicting of unlawful force).

The element of assault described as 'hostility' conveys that some non-hostile contact is an ordinary incident of life to which there is implied consent. A genuine belief that an assault is necessary to save a life or prevent a third party attack is a defence but a wish to do good is not. Forced feeding is an offence. (*R v B* [2013] EWCA Crim 3).

- Defences (see **C16.1.3**):
  - Consent: evidence of a lack of consent can be inferred from evidence in the case and need not come from the complainant (see *Director of Public Prosecutions v Shabbir* [2009] EWHC 2754 (Admin)).
  - Lawful correction or chastisement: this defence survives the implementation of s 58 Children Act 2004.
  - Self-defence.
  - Defence of property.
  - Prevention of crime.

 See *Blackstone's Criminal Practice 2019* **B2.1–B2.21**

C16.5 **Child neglect, etc**

Children and Young Persons Act 1933, s 1(1)

1 Cruelty to persons under 16

(1) If any person who has attained the age of sixteen years and has responsibility for any child or young person under that age, wilfully assaults, ill-treats, (whether physically or mentally), neglects, abandons, or exposes him, or causes or procures him to be assaulted, ill-treated (whether physically or mentally), neglected, abandoned, or exposed, in a manner likely to cause him unnecessary suffering or injury to health (whether the suffering or injury is of a physical or a psychological nature), that person shall be guilty of an offence.

---

 6 months' imprisonment and/or fine/10 years' imprisonment

C16.5.1 *Sentencing*

STEP ONE: Determining the offence category

The court should determine the offence category with reference only to the factors listed in the following tables. In order to determine the category the court should assess culpability and harm.

The court should weigh all the following factors in determining the offender's culpability.

Where there are characteristics present which fall under different levels of culpability, the court should balance these characteristics to reach a fair assessment of the offender's culpability.

Culpability demonstrated by one or more of the following:
A—High culpability: Prolonged and/or multiple incidents of serious cruelty, including serious neglect Gratuitous degradation of victim and/or sadistic behaviour Use of very significant force Use of a weapon Deliberate disregard for the welfare of the victim Failure to take any steps to protect the victim from offences in which the above factors are present Offender with professional responsibility for the victim (where linked to the commission of the offence)
B—Medium culpability: Use of significant force Prolonged and/or multiple incidents of cruelty, including neglect Limited steps taken to protect victim in cases with category A factors present Other cases falling between A and C because: Factors in both high and lesser categories are present which balance each other out; and/or The offender's culpability falls between the factors as described in high and lesser culpability
C—Lesser culpability: Offender's responsibility substantially reduced by mental disorder or learning disability or lack of maturity Offender is victim of domestic abuse, including coercion and/or intimidation (where linked to the commission of the offence) Steps taken to protect victim but fell just short of what could reasonably be expected Momentary or brief lapse in judgement including in cases of neglect Use of some force or failure to protect the victim from an incident involving some force Low level of neglect

HARM

The court should consider the following factors to determine the level of harm that has been caused or was intended to be caused to the victim.

Psychological, developmental or emotional harm: A finding that the psychological, developmental or emotional harm is serious may be based on a clinical diagnosis but the court may make such a finding based on other evidence from or on behalf of the victim that serious psychological, developmental or emotional harm exists. It is important to be clear that the absence of such a finding does not imply that the psychological, developmental, or emotional harm suffered by the victim is minor or trivial.

Harm	
The level of harm is assessed by weighing up all the factors of the case.	
Category 1	• Serious psychological, developmental, and/or emotional harm • Serious physical harm (including illnesses contracted due to neglect)
Category 2	• Cases falling between categories 1 and 3 • A high likelihood of category 1 harm being caused
Category 3	• Little or no psychological, developmental, and/or emotional harm • Little or no physical harm

STEP TWO: Starting point and category range

Having determined the category at step one, the court should use the corresponding starting point to reach a sentence within the following category range. The starting point applies to all offenders irrespective of plea or previous convictions.

Where a case does not fall squarely within a category, adjustment from the starting point may be required before adjustment for aggravating or mitigating features.

Harm	Culpability		
	A	**B**	**C**
Category 1	**Starting point** 6 years' custody	**Starting point** 3 years' custody	**Starting point** 1 year's custody
	Category range 4–8 years' custody	**Category range** 2–6 years' custody	**Category range** High-level community order–2 years 6 months' custody
Category 2	**Starting point** 3 years' custody	**Starting point** 1 year's custody	**Starting point** High-level community order
	Category range 2–6 years' custody	**Category range** High-level community order–2 years 6 months' custody	**Category range** Medium-level community order–1 year's custody
Category 3	**Starting point** 1 year's custody	**Starting point** High-level community order	**Starting point** Medium-level community order
	Category range High-level community order–2 years 6 months' custody	**Category range** Medium-level community order–1 year's custody	**Category range** Low-level community order–6 months' custody

The following table contains a non-exhaustive list of additional factual elements providing the context of the offence and factors relating to the offender. Identify whether any combination of these, or other relevant factors, should result in an upward or downward adjustment from the sentence arrived at so far. In particular, relevant recent convictions are likely to result in an upward

adjustment. In some cases, having considered these factors, it may be appropriate to move outside the identified category range.

Factors increasing seriousness	Factors reducing seriousness or reflecting personal mitigation
Statutory aggravating factors: Previous convictions, having regard to (a) the nature of the offence to which the conviction relates and its relevance to the current offence; and (b) the time that has elapsed since the conviction Offence committed while on bail	No previous convictions or no relevant/recent convictions Remorse Determination and demonstration of steps having been taken to address addiction or offending behaviour, including co-operation with agencies working for the welfare of the victim
Other aggravating factors: Failure to seek medical help (where not taken into account at step one) Commission of offence while under the influence of alcohol or drugs Deliberate concealment and/or covering up of the offence Blame wrongly placed on others Failure to respond to interventions or warnings about behaviour Threats to prevent reporting of the offence Failure to comply with current court orders Offence committed on licence or post sentence supervision Offences taken into consideration Offence committed in the presence of another child	Sole or primary carer for dependent relatives (see step five for further guidance on parental responsibilities) Good character and/or exemplary conduct (where previous good character/exemplary conduct has been used to facilitate or conceal the offence, this should not normally constitute mitigation and such conduct may constitute aggravation) Serious medical condition requiring urgent, intensive, or long-term treatment Mental disorder, learning disability, or lack of maturity (where not taken into account at step one) Co-operation with the investigation

... STEP FIVE: Parental responsibilities of sole or primary carers

In the majority of child cruelty cases the offender will have parental responsibility for the victim.

When considering whether to impose custody the court should step back and review whether this sentence will be in the best interests of the victim (as well as other children in the offender's care). This must be balanced with the seriousness of the offence and all sentencing options remain open to the court but careful consideration should be given to the effect that a custodial sentence could have on the family life of the victim and whether this is proportionate to the seriousness of the offence. This may be of particular relevance in lower culpability cases or where the offender has otherwise been a loving and capable parent/carer.

Where custody is unavoidable consideration of the impact on the offender's children may be relevant to the length of the sentence imposed. For more serious offences where a substantial period of custody is appropriate, this consideration will carry less weight.

C16.5.2 Key points

- Section 1(2) Children and Young Persons Act 1933 provides that:
  - a parent or other person legally liable to maintain a child or young person, or the legal guardian of a child or young person, shall be deemed to have neglected him in a manner likely to cause injury to his health if he has failed to provide adequate food, clothing, medical aid, or lodging for him, or if, having been unable otherwise to provide such food, clothing, medical aid, or lodging, he has failed to take steps to procure it to be provided under the enactments applicable in that behalf;
  - where it is proved that the death of an infant under three years of age was caused by suffocation (not being suffocation caused by disease or the presence of any foreign body in the throat or air passages of the infant) while the infant was in bed, or lying next to an adult in or on any kind of furniture or surface being used by the adult for the purpose of sleeping, with some other person who has attained the age of 16 years, that other person shall, if he was, when he went to bed, under the influence of drink or drugs, be deemed to have neglected the infant in a manner likely to cause injury to its health.
- Section 1(3) provides that a person may be convicted of an offence under this section:
  - notwithstanding that actual suffering or injury to health, or the likelihood of actual suffering or injury to health, was obviated by the action of another person;
  - notwithstanding the death of the child or young person in question.

R v Turbill and Broadway [2012] EWCA Crim 1422 confirms that offences requiring wilful neglect require more than carelessness (even gross carelessness) or negligence. The neglect must be wilful. The definition in *Shepherd* (1981) AC 394 applies to child neglect and to neglect under the Mental Capacity Act 2005.

 See *Blackstone's Criminal Practice 2019* **B2.138–B2.149**

C16.6 Domestic abuse

Serious Crime Act 2015, s 76

Controlling or coercive behaviour in an intimate or family relationship

(1) A person (A) commits an offence if—
   (a) A repeatedly or continuously engages in behaviour towards another person (B) that is controlling or coercive,
   (b) at the time of the behaviour, A and B are personally connected,
   (c) the behaviour has a serious effect on B, and
   (d) A knows or ought to know that the behaviour will have a serious effect on B.
(2) A and B are 'personally connected' if—
   (a) A is in an intimate personal relationship with B, or
   (b) A and B live together and—
      (i) they are members of the same family, or
      (ii) they have previously been in an intimate personal relationship with each other.

(3) But A does not commit an offence under this section if at the time of the behaviour in question—

(a) A has responsibility for B, for the purposes of Part 1 of the Children and Young Persons Act 1933 (see section 17 of that Act), and

(b) B is under 16.

(4) A's behaviour has a 'serious effect' on B if—

(a) it causes B to fear, on at least two occasions, that violence will be used against B, or

(b) it causes B serious alarm or distress which has a substantial adverse effect on B's usual day-to-day activities.

(5) For the purposes of subsection (1)(d) A 'ought to know' that which a reasonable person in possession of the same information would know.

(6) For the purposes of subsection (2)(b)(i) A and B are members of the same family if—

(a) they are, or have been, married to each other;

(b) they are, or have been, civil partners of each other;

(c) they are relatives;

(d) they have agreed to marry one another (whether or not the agreement has been terminated);

(e) they have entered into a civil partnership agreement (whether or not the agreement has been terminated);

(f) they are both parents of the same child;

(g) they have, or have had, parental responsibility for the same child.

(7) In subsection (6)—

'civil partnership agreement' has the meaning given by section 73 of the Civil Partnership Act 2004;

'child' means a person under the age of 18 years;

'parental responsibility' has the same meaning as in the Children Act 1989;

'relative' has the meaning given by section 63(1) of the Family Law Act 1996.

(8) In proceedings for an offence under this section it is a defence for A to show that—

(a) in engaging in the behaviour in question, A believed that he or she was acting in B's best interests, and

(b) the behaviour was in all the circumstances reasonable.

(9) A is to be taken to have shown the facts mentioned in subsection (8) if—

(a) sufficient evidence of the facts is adduced to raise an issue with respect to them, and

(b) the contrary is not proved beyond reasonable doubt.

(10) The defence in subsection (8) is not available to A in relation to behaviour that causes B to fear that violence will be used against B.

 6 months' imprisonment and/or a fine/5 years' imprisonment.

C16.6.1 *Sentencing*

Also refer to the Overarching principles: Domestic abuse guideline See **Appendix 5**.

STEP ONE: Determining the offence category

The court should determine the offence category with reference only to the factors in the following tables. In order to determine the category the court should assess culpability and harm.

The level of culpability is determined by weighing up all the factors of the case. Where there are characteristics present which fall under different levels of culpability, the court should balance these characteristics to reach a fair assessment of the offender's culpability

Culpability demonstrated by one or more of the following:
A—Higher culpability   • Conduct intended to maximize fear or distress   • Persistent action over a prolonged period   • Use of multiple methods of controlling or coercive behaviour   • Sophisticated offence   • Conduct intended to humiliate and degrade the victim
B—Medium culpability   • Conduct intended to cause some fear or distress   • Scope and duration of offence that falls between categories A and C   • All other cases that fall between categories A and C
C—Lesser culpability   • Offender's responsibility substantially reduced by mental disorder or learning disability   • Offence was limited in scope and duration

HARM	
The level of harm is assessed by weighing up all the factors of the case.	
Category 1	• Fear of violence on many occasions • Very serious alarm or distress which has a substantial adverse effect on the victim • Significant psychological harm
Category 2	• Fear of violence on at least two occasions • Serious alarm or distress which has a substantial adverse effect on the victim

STEP TWO: Starting point and category range

Having determined the category at step one, the court should use the corresponding starting point to reach a sentence within the following category range. The starting point applies to all offenders irrespective of plea or previous convictions

Harm	Culpability		
	A	B	C
Category 1	**Starting point** 2 years 6 months' custody	**Starting point** 1 year's custody	**Starting point** 26 weeks' custody
	Category range 1–4 years' custody	**Category range** 26 weeks'–2 years 6 months' custody	**Category range** High-level community order–1 year's custody
Category 2	**Starting point** 1 year's custody	**Starting point** 26 weeks' custody	**Starting point** Medium-level community order
	Category range 26 weeks'–2 years 6 months' custody	**Category range** High-level community order–1 year's custody	**Category range** Low-level community order–26 weeks' custody

The court should then consider any adjustment for any aggravating or mitigating factors. The following is a non-exhaustive list of additional factual elements providing the context of the offence and factors relating to the offender.

Identify whether any combination of these, or other relevant factors, should result in an upward or downward adjustment from the starting point.

Factors increasing seriousness	
Statutory aggravating factors:	*Other aggravating factors:*
Previous convictions, having regard to (a) the nature of the offence to which the conviction relates and its relevance to the current offence; and (b) the time that has elapsed since the conviction Offence committed while on bail Offence motivated by, or demonstrating hostility based on any of the following characteristics or presumed characteristics of the victim: religion, race, disability, sexual orientation, or transgender identity	Steps taken to prevent the victim reporting an incident Steps taken to prevent the victim obtaining assistance A proven history of violence or threats by the offender in a domestic context Impact of offence on others particularly children Exploiting contact arrangements with a child to commit the offence Victim is particularly vulnerable (not all vulnerabilities are immediately apparent) Victim left in debt, destitute, or homeless Failure to comply with current court orders Offence committed on licence or post sentence supervision Offences taken into consideration

Factors reducing seriousness or reflecting personal mitigation
No previous convictions or no relevant/recent convictions Remorse Good character and/or exemplary conduct Serious medical condition requiring urgent, intensive, or long-term treatment Age and/or lack of maturity Mental disorder or learning disability (where not taken into account at step one) Sole or primary carer for dependent relatives Determination and/or demonstration of steps having been taken to address offending behaviour

C16.6.2 Key points

In the definitive guideline on domestic abuse (see **Appendix 5**)

The following definitions are included:

- Controlling behaviour is a range of acts designed to make a person subordinate and/or dependent by isolating them from sources of support, exploiting their resources and capabilities for personal gain, depriving them of the means needed for independence, resistance, and escape and/or regulating their everyday behaviour.
- Coercive behaviour is an act or pattern of acts of assault, threats, humiliation (whether public or private) and intimidation or other abuse that is used to harm, punish, or frighten the victim. Abuse may take place through person to person contact, or through other methods, including but not limited to, telephone calls, text, email, social networking sites, or use of GPS tracking devices

C16.7 False imprisonment

A common law offence—the unlawful and intentional or reckless restraint of a victim's freedom of movement from a particular place (*R v Rahman* (1985) 81 Cr App R 349).

GC

DO

IO

Life

C16.7.1 Key points

- The requisite *mens rea* is intention or subjective recklessness.
- This is an offence of basic intent. Voluntary intoxication is not a defence.

C16.8 Grievous bodily harm/unlawful wounding

Offences Against the Person Act 1861, s 20

20 Inflicting bodily injury, with or without weapon

Whosoever shall unlawfully and maliciously wound or inflict any grievous bodily harm upon any other person, either with or without any weapon or instrument, shall be guilty of an offence.

EW

6 months' imprisonment and/or fine/5 years' imprisonment (7 years if racially or religiously aggravated)

GC

DO

C16.8.1 *Sentencing*

STEP ONE: Determine the offence category

Category 1	Greater harm (serious injury must normally be present) and higher culpability
Category 2	Greater harm (serious injury must normally be present) and lower culpability; or lesser harm and higher culpability
Category 3	Lesser harm and lower culpability

Factors indicating greater harm	Factors indicating higher culpability
Injury (which includes disease transmission and/or psychological harm) which is serious in the context of the offence (must normally be present) Victim is particularly vulnerable because of personal circumstances Sustained or repeated assault on the same victim	*Statutory aggravating factors:* Offence motivated by, or demonstrating, hostility to the victim based on his or her sexual orientation (or presumed sexual orientation) Offence motivated by, or demonstrating, hostility to the victim based on the victim's disability (or presumed disability) *Other aggravating factors:* A significant degree of premeditation Use of weapon or weapon equivalent (eg shod foot, head-butting, use of acid, use of animal) Intention to commit more serious harm than actually resulted from the offence Deliberately causes more harm than is necessary for commission of offence
	Deliberate targeting of vulnerable victim Leading role in group or gang Offence motivated by, or demonstrating, hostility based on the victim's age, sex, gender identity (or presumed gender identity
Factors indicating lesser harm	
Injury which is less serious in the context of the offence	

STEP TWO: Starting point and category range

Offence category	Starting point	Category range
Category 1	3 years' custody	2 years 6 months–4 years' custody
Category 2	1 year 6 months' custody	1–3 years' custody
Category 3	High-level community order	Low-level community order–51 weeks' custody

Factors increasing seriousness	
Statutory aggravating factors:	*Other aggravating factors:*

Factors increasing seriousness	
Previous convictions, having regard to (a) the **nature** of the offence to which the conviction relates and its relevance to the current offence; and (b) the **time** that has elapsed since the conviction Offence committed while on bail	Location of the offence Timing of the offence Ongoing effect upon the victim Offence committed against those working in the public sector or providing a service to the public Presence of others including relatives, especially children or partner of the victim Gratuitous degradation of victim In domestic violence cases, victim forced to leave their home Failure to comply with current court orders Offence committed while on licence. Attempt to conceal or dispose of evidence Failure to respond to warnings or concerns expressed by others about the offender's behaviour Commission of offence while under the influence of alcohol or drugs Abuse of power and/or position of trust Exploiting contact arrangements with a child to commit an offence Established evidence of community impact Any steps taken to prevent the victim reporting an incident, obtaining assistance, and/or assisting or supporting the prosecution Offences taken into consideration (TICs)
Factors reducing seriousness or reflecting personal mitigation	
No previous convictions or no relevant/recent convictions Single blow Remorse Good character and/or exemplary conduct Determination and/or demonstration of steps taken to address addiction or offending behaviour Serious medical conditions requiring urgent, intensive, or long-term treatment Isolated incident Age and/or lack of maturity where it affects the responsibility of the offender Lapse of time since the offence where this is not the fault of the offender Mental disorder or learning disability, where not linked to the commission of the offence Sole or primary carer for dependent relatives	

C16.8.2 Key points

Wounding requires the breaking of the continuity of the whole of the skin. Although this may include relatively minor injuries, charging standards indicate that this offence should not be used in such cases.

Harm can be inflicted without the need for an assault. Grievous bodily harm has no statutory definition but the harm must be really serious (*DPP v Smith* [1961] AC 290). It may include psychiatric injury but only if both causation and extent of the disorder is established by expert psychiatric evidence (*R v Ireland* [1998] AC 147).

To be malicious there must be intention or subjective recklessness to inflict some kind of bodily harm, but the harm foreseen need not be serious. (*R v Mowatt* [1968] 1 QB 421).

This is a crime of basic intent.

C16.8.3 *Defences*

For defences see **C16.1.3**.

 See *Blackstone's Criminal Practice 2019* **B2.48–B2.63**

C16.9 **Kidnapping**

Common law offence—the taking or carrying away of one person by another by force or fraud, without the consent of that person and without lawful excuse.

 Life

Harassment—putting people in fear of violence

C16.10 **Threats to kill**

> ### Offences Against the Person Act 1861, s 16
>
> **16 Threats to kill**
>
> A person who without lawful excuse makes to another a threat, intending that that other would fear it would be carried out, to kill that other or a third person shall be guilty of an offence.

 6 months' imprisonment and/or fine/10 years' imprisonment

C16.10.1 *Sentencing*

Where offence committed in a domestic context, also refer to the Overarching principles: Domestic abuse guideline See **Appendix 5**.

STEP ONE: Determining the offence category

The court should determine the offence category with reference only to the factors in the following tables. In order to determine the category the court should assess culpability and harm.

The level of culpability is determined by weighing up all the factors of the case. Where there are characteristics present which fall under different levels of culpability, the court should

balance these characteristics to reach a fair assessment of the offender's culpability.

Culpability demonstrated by one or more of the following:
A—Higher culpability   Significant planning and/or sophisticated offence   Visible weapon   Threat(s) made in the presence of children   History of and/or campaign of violence towards the victim   Threat(s) with significant violence
B—Medium culpability   Cases that fall between categories A and C because: Factors are present in A and C which balance each other out and/or   The offender's culpability falls between the factors described in A and C
C—Lesser culpability   Offender's responsibility substantially reduced by mental disorder or learning disability   Offence was limited in scope and duration

HARM	
The level of harm is assessed by weighing up all the factors of the case.	
Category 1	Very serious distress caused to the victim Significant psychological harm caused to the victim Offence has a considerable practical impact on the victim
Category 2	Harm that falls between categories 1 and 3, and in particular: Some distress caused to the victim Some psychological harm caused to the victim Offence has some practical impact on the victim
Category 3	Little or no distress or harm caused to the victim

STEP TWO: Starting point and category range

Having determined the category at step one, the court should use the corresponding starting point to reach a sentence within the following category range. The starting point applies to all offenders irrespective of plea or previous convictions

Harm	Culpability		
	A	**B**	**C**
Category 1	**Starting point** 4 years' custody	**Starting point** 2 years' custody	**Starting point** 1 year's custody
	Category range 2–7 years' custody	**Category range** 1–4 years' custody	**Category range** 26 weeks'–2 years 6 months' custody
Category 2	**Starting point** 2 years' custody	**Starting point** 1 year's custody	**Starting point** 26 weeks' custody
	Category range 1–4 years' custody	**Category range** 26 weeks'–2 years 6 months' custody	**Category range** High-level community order–1 year's custody
Category 3	**Starting point** 1 year's custody	**Starting point** 26 weeks' custody	**Starting point** Medium-level community order
	Category range 26 weeks'–2 years 6 months' custody	**Category range** High-level community order–1 year's custody	**Category range** Low-level community order–High-level community order

The court should then consider any adjustment for any aggravating or mitigating factors. The following is a non-exhaustive list of additional factual elements providing the context of the offence and factors relating to the offender.

Identify whether any combination of these, or other relevant factors, should result in an upward or downward adjustment from the starting point.

Factors increasing seriousness	Factors reducing seriousness or reflecting personal mitigation
Statutory aggravating factors: Previous convictions, having regard to (a) the nature of the offence to which the conviction relates and its relevance to the current offence; and (b) the time that has elapsed since the conviction Offence committed while on bail Offence motivated by, or demonstrating hostility based on any of the following characteristics or presumed characteristics of the victim: religion, race, disability, sexual orientation, or transgender identity	No previous convictions or no relevant/recent convictions Remorse Good character and/or exemplary conduct Serious medical condition requiring urgent, intensive or long-term treatment Age and/or lack of maturity Mental disorder or learning disability (where not taken into account at step one)
Other aggravating factors: Offence committed against those working in the public sector or providing a service to the public Impact of offence on others, particularly children Victim is particularly vulnerable (not all vulnerabilities are immediately apparent) Failure to comply with current court orders Offence committed on licence or post sentence supervision Offences taken into consideration	Sole or primary carer for dependent relatives Determination and/or demonstration of steps having been taken to address offending behaviour

Where offence committed in a domestic context, also refer to the Overarching principles: Domestic abuse guideline (see **Appendix 5**)

 See *Blackstone's Criminal Practice 2019* **B1.149–B1.153**

C16.11 Wounding or inflicting grievous bodily harm with intent

Offences Against the Person Act 1861, s 18

Whosoever shall unlawfully and maliciously by any means whatsoever wound or cause any grievous bodily harm to any person, with intent, to do some grievous bodily harm to any person, or with intent to resist or prevent the lawful apprehension or detainer of any person, shall be guilty of [an offence].

 for life

C16.11.1 *Sentencing*

STEP ONE: Determining the offence category

The court should determine the offence category using the following table .

Category 1	Greater harm (serious injury must normally be present) **and** higher culpability
Category 2	Greater harm (serious injury must normally be present) **and** lower culpability;or lesser harm **and** higher culpability
Category 3	Lesser harm **and** lower culpability

The court should determine the offender's culpability and the harm caused, or intended, by reference only to the following factors (as demonstrated by the presence of one or more). These factors comprise the principal factual elements of the offence and should determine the category.

Factors indicating greater harm	Factors indicating higher culpability
Injury (which includes disease transmission and/or psychological harm) which is serious in the context of the offence (must normally be present) Victim is particularly vulnerable because of personal circumstances Sustained or repeated assault on the same victim	Statutory aggravating factors: Offence racially or religiously aggravated Offence motivated by, or demonstrating, hostility to the victim based on his or her sexual orientation (or presumed sexual orientation) Offence motivated by, or demonstrating, hostility to the victim based on the victim's disability (or presumed disability) Other aggravating factors: A significant degree of premeditation Use of weapon or weapon equivalent (for example, shod foot, headbutting, use of acid, use of animal) Intention to commit more serious harm than actually resulted from the offence Deliberately causes more harm than is necessary for commission of offence Deliberate targeting of vulnerable victim Leading role in group or gang Offence motivated by, or demonstrating, hostility based on the victim's age, sex, gender identity (or presumed gender identity)
Factors indicating lesser harm	**Factors indicating lower culpability**
Injury which is less serious in the context of the offence	Subordinate role in group or gang A greater degree of provocation than normally expected Lack of premeditation Mental disorder or learning disability, where linked to commission of the offence Excessive self defence

STEP TWO: Starting point and category range

Having determined the category, the court should use the corresponding starting points to reach a sentence within the following category range. The starting point applies to all offenders irrespective of plea or previous convictions. A case of particular gravity, reflected by multiple features of culpability in step one, could merit upward adjustment from the starting point before further adjustment for the following aggravating or mitigating features.

Offence category	Starting point (applicable to all offenders)	Category range (applicable to all offenders)
Category 1	12 years' custody	9–16 years' custody
Category 2	6 years' custody	5–9 years' custody
Category 3	4 years' custody	3–5 years' custody

The following table contains a non-exhaustive list of additional factual elements providing the context of the offence and factors relating to the offender. Identify whether any combination of these, or other relevant factors, should result in an upward or downward adjustment from the starting point. In some cases, having considered these factors, it may be appropriate to move outside the identified category range.

Factors increasing seriousness	
Statutory aggravating factors:	*Other aggravating factors:*
Previous convictions, having regard to (a) the nature of the offence to which the conviction relates and its relevance to the current offence; and (b) the time that has elapsed since the conviction Offence committed while on bail	Location of the offence Timing of the offence Ongoing effect upon the victim Offence committed against those working in the public sector or providing a service to the public Presence of others including relatives, especially children or partner of the victim Gratuitous degradation of victim In domestic violence cases, victim forced to leave their home Failure to comply with current court orders Offence committed while on licence An attempt to conceal or dispose of evidence Failure to respond to warnings or concerns expressed by others about the offender's behaviour Commission of offence while under the influence of alcohol or drugs Abuse of power and/or position of trust
	Exploiting contact arrangements with a child to commit an offence Previous violence or threats to the same victim Established evidence of community impact Any steps taken to prevent the victim reporting an incident, or obtaining assistance and/or from assisting or supporting the prosecution Offences taken into consideration (TICs)
Factors reducing seriousness or reflecting personal mitigation	
No previous convictions or no relevant/recent convictions Single blow Remorse Good character and/or exemplary conduct Determination, and/or demonstration of steps taken to address addiction or offending behaviour Serious medical conditions requiring urgent, intensive, or long-term treatment Isolated incident Age and/or lack of maturity where it affects the responsibility of the offender Lapse of time since the offence where this is not the fault of the offender Mental disorder or learning disability, where not linked to the commission of the offence Sole or primary carer for dependent relatives	

C16.11.2 Key points

For the definitions of wound and grievous bodily harm see **C16.8.2**

A knee may be 'weapon equivalent' for the purposes of the guideline (*R v JDL* [2018] EWCA Crim 1766.

C17 **Weapons Offences**

C17.1 **Firearms—general**

C17.1.1 *Definitions*

Firearm—defined by the Firearms Act 1968, s 57(1)

57

(1) In this Act, the expression 'firearm' means—
  (a) a lethal barrelled weapon (see subsection (1B));
  (b) a prohibited weapon;
  (c) a relevant component part in relation to a lethal barrelled weapon or a prohibited weapon (see subsection (1D));
  (d) an accessory to a lethal barrelled weapon or a prohibited weapon where the accessory is designed or adapted to diminish the noise or flash caused by firing the weapon;
  and so much of section 1 of this Act as excludes any description of firearm from the category of firearms to which that section applies shall be construed as also excluding component parts of, and accessories to, firearms of that description.

(1A) ...

(1B) In subsection (1)(a), 'lethal barrelled weapon' means a barrelled weapon of any description from which a shot, bullet or other missile, with kinetic energy of more than one joule at the muzzle of the weapon, can be discharged.

(1C) Subsection (1) is subject to section 57A (exception for airsoft guns).

(1D) For the purposes of subsection (1)(c), each of the following items is a relevant component part in relation to a lethal barrelled weapon or a prohibited weapon—
  (a) a barrel, chamber or cylinder,
  (b) a frame, body or receiver,
  (c) a breech block, bolt or other mechanism for containing the pressure of discharge at the rear of a chamber,
  but only where the item is capable of being used as a part of a lethal barrelled weapon or a prohibited weapon.

(2) In this Act, the expression 'ammunition' means ammunition for any firearm and includes grenades, bombs and other like missiles, whether capable of use with a firearm or not, and also includes prohibited ammunition.

(2A) In this Act 'self-loading' and 'pump-action' in relation to any weapon mean respectively that it is designed or adapted (otherwise than as mentioned in section 5(1)(a)) so that it is automatically re-loaded or that it is so designed or adapted that it is re-loaded by the manual operation of the fore-end or forestock of the weapon.

(2B) In this Act 'revolver', in relation to a smooth-bore gun, means a gun containing a series of chambers which revolve when the gun is fired.

57A Exception for airsoft guns

(1) An 'airsoft gun' is not to be regarded as a firearm for the purposes of this Act.

(2) An 'airsoft gun' is a barrelled weapon of any description which—
  (a) is designed to discharge only a small plastic missile (whether or not it is also capable of discharging any other kind of missile), and
  (b) is not capable of discharging a missile (of any kind) with kinetic energy at the muzzle of the weapon that exceeds the permitted level.

---

(3) 'Small plastic missile' means a missile that—
    (a) is made wholly or partly from plastics,
    (b) is spherical, and
    (c) does not exceed 8 millimetres in diameter.
(4) The permitted kinetic energy level is—

    (a) in the case of a weapon which is capable of discharging two or more missiles successively without repeated pressure on the trigger, 1.3 joules;
    (b) in any other case, 2.5 joules.

Imitation firearm—defined by the Firearms Act 1968, s 57(4).

57(4)

'imitation firearm' means any thing which has the appearance of being a firearm (other than such a weapon as is mentioned in section 5(1)(b) of this Act) whether or not it is capable of discharging any shot, bullet or other missile;...

An item is an imitation firearm if it 'looked like' a firearm at the time of its use (*R v Morris and King* (1984) 149 JP 60).

An imitation firearm has to be a thing which was separate and distinct from the defendant; putting one's hand inside a jacket pocket and using the fingers to give the impression of a firearm was not enough (*R v Bentham* [2005] UKHL 18).

Ammunition—defined by the Firearms Act 1968, s 57(2).

57(2)

In this Act, the expression 'ammunition' means ammunition for any firearm and includes grenades, bombs and other like missiles, whether capable of use with a firearm or not, and also includes prohibited ammunition.

C17.1.2 *Sentencing*

A sentencing guideline has not been issued in relation to firearms offences. The Court of Appeal decision in *R v Avis* [1998] 1 Cr App R 420 therefore remains the guideline case. This provides the following general guidance:

The unlawful possession and use of firearms is generally recognised as a grave source of danger to society. The reasons are obvious. Firearms may be used to take life or cause serious injury. They are used to further the commission of other serious crimes. Often the victims will be those charged with the enforcement of the law or the protection of persons or property. In the conflicts which occur between competing criminal gangs, often related to the supply of drugs, the use and possession of firearms provoke an escalating spiral of violence.

Where imitation firearms are involved, the risk to life and limb is absent, but such weapons can be and often are used to frighten and intimidate victims in order to reinforce unlawful demands. Such imitation weapons are often very hard to distinguish from the real thing—for practical purposes, impossible in the circumstances in which they are used—and the victim is usually as much frightened and intimidated as if a genuine firearm had been used. Such victims are often isolated and vulnerable.

Sometimes the firearm involved, although genuine, has been disabled from firing, or cannot be fired for want of ammunition. In such cases again the risk to life and limb is absent, but the risk of use to frighten or intimidate remains, and the weapon may be used in earnest on another occasion.

The appropriate level of sentence for a firearms offence, as for any other offence, will depend on all the facts and circumstances relevant to the offence and the offender, and it would be wrong for this Court to seek to prescribe unduly restrictive sentencing guidelines. It will, however, usually be appropriate for the sentencing court to ask itself a series of questions:

(1) What sort of weapon is involved? Genuine firearms are more dangerous than imitation firearms. Loaded firearms are more dangerous than unloaded firearms. Unloaded firearms for which ammunition is available are more dangerous than firearms for which no ammunition is available. Possession of a firearm which has no lawful use (such as a sawn-off shotgun) will be viewed even more seriously than possession of a firearm which is capable of lawful use.

(2) What (if any) use has been made of the firearm? It is necessary for the court, as with any other offence, to take account of all circumstances surrounding any use made of the firearm: the more prolonged and premeditated and violent the use, the more serious the offence is likely to be.

(3) With what intention (if any) did the defendant possess or use the firearm? Generally speaking, the most serious offences under the Act are those which require proof of a specific criminal intent (to endanger life, to cause fear of violence, to resist arrest, to commit an indictable offence). The more serious the act intended, the more serious the offence.

(4) What is the defendant's record? The seriousness of any firearms offence is inevitably increased if the offender has an established record of committing firearms offences or crimes of violence.

The offence under s 5(1)(b) is used to prosecute those in possession of CS gas.

C17.1.3 *Mandatory minimum sentence (see D20)*

C17.1.4 *Possessing firearm or ammunition without firearm certificate*

Firearms Act 1968, s 1

1.— Requirement of firearms certificate

(1) Subject to any exemption under this Act, it is an offence for a person—

(a) to have in his possession, or to purchase or acquire, a firearm to which this section applies without holding a firearm certificate in force at the time, or otherwise than as authorised by such a certificate;

(b) to have in his possession, or to purchase or acquire, any ammunition to which this section applies without holding a firearm certificate in force at the time, or otherwise than as authorised by such a certificate, or in quantities in excess of those so authorised.

(2) It is an offence for a person to fail to comply with a condition subject to which a firearm certificate is held by him.

(3) This section applies to every firearm except—

(a) a shot gun within the meaning of this Act, that is to say a smooth-bore gun (not being an air gun) which—
  (i) has a barrel not less than 24 inches in length and does not have any barrel with a bore exceeding 2 inches in diameter;
  (ii) either has no magazine or has a non-detachable magazine incapable of holding more than two cartridges; and
  (iii) is not a revolver gun; and
(b) an air weapon (that is to say, an air rifle, air gun or air pistol which does not fall within section 5(1) and which is not of a type declared by rules made by the Secretary of State under section 53 of this Act to be specially dangerous).

(3A) A gun which has been adapted to have such a magazine as is mentioned in subsection (3)(a)(ii) above shall not be regarded as falling within that provision unless the magazine bears a mark approved by the Secretary of State for denoting that fact and that mark has been made, and the adaptation has been certified in writing as having been carried out in a manner approved by him, either by one of the two companies mentioned in section 58(1) of this Act or by such other person as may be approved by him for that purpose.

(4) This section applies to any ammunition for a firearm, except the following articles, namely:—
  (a) cartridges containing five or more shot, none of which exceeds. 36 inch in diameter;
  (b) ammunition for an air gun, air rifle or air pistol; and
  (c) blank cartridges not more than one inch in diameter measured immediately in front of the rim or cannelure of the base of the cartridge.

EW

---

6 months and/or fine /

(i) where the offence is committed in an aggravated form within the meaning of section 4(4) of this Act, 7 years or a fine; or both,

4 (4) A person who commits an offence under section 1 of this Act by having in his possession, or purchasing or acquiring, a shotgun which has been shortened contrary to subsection (1) above or a firearm which has been converted as mentioned in subsection (3) above (whether by a registered firearms dealer or not), without holding a firearm certificate authorising him to have it in his possession, or to purchase or acquire it, shall be treated for the purposes of provisions of this Act relating to the punishment of offences as committing that offence in an aggravated form.

(ii) in any other case, 5 years and /or fine;

C17.1.4.1 *Sentencing*

For general guidance on sentencing firearms offences see **C17.1.2**.

C17.1.4.2 Key points

- Possession contrary to s 1 is established if the prosecution can prove the defendant knowingly had in his possession an article which was in fact a firearm (*R v Hussain* (1981) 72 Cr App R 143).
- Section 1(1) of the Firearms Act 1982 applies to any article which has the appearance of being a firearm to which s 1 Firearms Act 1968 applies and is readily convertible into such a firearm. In such cases it will be an offence

under s 1 1968 Act to possess the article without a firearms certificate. It shall be a defence for the accused to show that he did not know and had no reason to suspect that the imitation firearm was so constructed or adapted as to be readily converted into a firearm to which s 1 1968 Act applies (s 1(5) Firearms Act 1982).

C17.1.5 *Offences relating to air weapons*

Firearms Act 1968, s 22(4), s 23

It is an offence for a person under the age of eighteen to have with him an air weapon or ammunition for an air weapon.

23

(1) It is not an offence under section 22(4) of this Act for a person to have with him an air weapon or ammunition while he is under the supervision of a person of or over the age of twenty-one; but where a person has with him an air weapon on any premises in circumstances where he would be prohibited from having it with him but for this subsection, it is an offence for the person under whose supervision he is to allow him to use it for firing any missile beyond those premises.

(1A) In proceedings against a person for an offence under subsection (1) it shall be a defence for him to show that the only premises into or across which the missile was fired were premises the occupier of which had consented to the firing of the missile (whether specifically or by way of a general consent).

(2) It is not an offence under section 22(4) of this Act for a person to have with him an air weapon or ammunition at a time when—

   (a) being a member of a rifle club or miniature rifle club for the time being approved by the Secretary of State for the purposes of this section or section 15 of the Firearms (Amendment) Act 1988, he is engaged as such a member in connection with target shooting; or

   (b) he is using the weapon or ammunition at a shooting gallery where the only firearms used are either air weapons or miniature rifles not exceeding .23 inch calibre.

(3) It is not an offence under section 22(4) of this Act for a person of or over the age of fourteen to have with him an air weapon or ammunition on private premises with the consent of the occupier.

Firearms Act 1968, s 21A

21A Firing an air weapon beyond premises

(1) A person commits an offence if—

   (a) he has with him an air weapon on any premises; and

   (b) he uses it for firing a missile beyond those premises.

(2) In proceedings against a person for an offence under this section it shall be a defence for him to show that the only premises into or across which the missile was fired were premises the occupier of which had consented to the firing of the missile (whether specifically or by way of a general consent).

SO Note other provisions of s 22 are either-way offences with heavier penalties available to the court

⊞ Level 3 fine

C17.1.5.1 Key points

- Some barrelled air or gas weapons are capable of being firearms within the meaning of s 57(1) Firearms Act 1968.
- Air weapons are not subject to the certification requirements of s 1 Firearms Act 1968 unless the device has been declared 'specially dangerous' under the Firearms (Dangerous Air Weapons) Rules 1969 or it falls within the definition of a prohibited weapon (see **C17.1.6**).

 See *Blackstone's Criminal Practice 2019* **B12.17, B12.48–B12.52**

C17.1.6 *Possessing prohibited weapons or ammunition*

Firearms Act 1968, s 5

5. — Weapons subject to general prohibition

(1) A person commits an offence if, without authority, he has in his possession, or purchases or acquires,

    (a) any firearm which is so designed or adapted that two or more missiles can be successively discharged without repeated pressure on the trigger;

    (ab) any self-loading or pump-action rifled gun other than one which is chambered for .22 rim-fire cartridges;

    (aba) any firearm which either has a barrel less than 30 centimetres in length or is less than 60 centimetres in length overall, other than an air weapon, a muzzle-loading gun or a firearm designed as signalling apparatus;

    (ac) any self-loading or pump-action smooth-bore gun which is not an air weapon or chambered for .22 rim-fire cartridges and either has a barrel less than 24 inches in length or is less than 40 inches in length overall;

    (ad) any smooth-bore revolver gun other than one which is chambered for 9 mm. rim-fire cartridges or a muzzle-loading gun;

    (ae) any rocket launcher, or any mortar, for projecting a stabilised missile, other than a launcher or mortar designed for line-throwing or pyrotechnic purposes or as signalling apparatus;

    (af) any air rifle, air gun or air pistol which uses, or is designed or adapted for use with, a self-contained gas cartridge system;

    (ag) any rifle with a chamber from which empty cartridge cases are extracted using—

        (i) energy from propellant gas, or

        (ii) energy imparted to a spring or other energy storage device by propellant gas, other than a rifle which is chambered for .22 rim-fire cartridges;.

    (b) any weapon of whatever description designed or adapted for the discharge of any noxious liquid, gas or other thing; and

    (c) any cartridge with a bullet designed to explode on or immediately before impact, any ammunition containing or designed or adapted to contain any such noxious thing as is mentioned in paragraph (b) above and, if capable of being used with a firearm of any description, any grenade, bomb (or other like missile), or rocket or shell designed to explode as aforesaid.

(1A) Subject to section 5A of this Act, a person commits an offence if, without the authority, he has in his possession, or purchases or acquires, or sells or transfers—

    (a) any firearm which is disguised as another object;

(b) any rocket or ammunition not falling within paragraph (c) of subsection (1) of this section which consists in or incorporates a missile designed to explode on or immediately before impact and is for military use;

'(ba) any device (commonly known as a bump stock) which is designed or adapted so that—

(i) it is capable of forming part of or being added to a selfloading lethal barrelled weapon (as defined in section 57(1B) and (2A)), and

(ii) if it forms part of or is added to such a weapon, it increases the rate of fire of the weapon by using the recoil from the weapon to generate repeated pressure on the trigger; and'

(c) any launcher or other projecting apparatus not falling within paragraph (ae) of that subsection which is designed to be used with any rocket or ammunition falling within paragraph (b) above or with ammunition which would fall within that paragraph but for its being ammunition falling within paragraph (c) of that subsection;

(d) any ammunition for military use which consists in or incorporates a missile designed so that a substance contained in the missile will ignite on or immediately before impact;

(e) any ammunition for military use which consists in or incorporates a missile designed, on account of its having a jacket and hard-core, to penetrate armour plating, armour screening or body armour;

(f) any ammunition which incorporates a missile designed or adapted to expand on impact;

(g) anything which is designed to be projected as a missile from any weapon and is designed to be, or has been, incorporated in—

(i) any ammunition falling within any of the preceding paragraphs; or

(ii) any ammunition which would fall within any of those paragraphs but for its being specified in subsection (1) of this section.

(2) The weapons and ammunition specified in subsections (1) and (1A) of this section (including, *'in the case of weapons, any devices falling within subsection (1)(ba) of this section and,'#.* in the case of ammunition, any missiles falling within subsection (1A)(g) of this section) are referred to in this Act as 'prohibited weapons' and 'prohibited ammunition' respectively.

(2A) A person commits an offence if without authority—

(a) he manufactures any weapon device or ammunition specified in subsection (1) of this section,

(b) he sells or transfers any prohibited weapon or prohibited ammunition,

(c) he has in his possession for sale or transfer any prohibited weapon or prohibited ammunition, or

(d) he purchases or acquires for sale or transfer any prohibited weapon or prohibited ammunition.

(3) In this section 'authority' means an authority given in writing by—

(a) the Secretary of State (in or as regards England and Wales),

(4) An authority shall be subject to conditions specified in it, including such as the Secretary of State or the Scottish Ministers (as appropriate), having regard to the circumstances of each particular case, think fit to impose for the purpose of securing that the prohibited weapon or ammunition to which the authority relates will not endanger the public safety or the peace.

(5) It is an offence for a person to whom an authority is given under this section to fail to comply with any condition of the authority.

...

(7) For the purposes of this section and section 5A of this Act—

   (a) any rocket or ammunition which is designed to be capable of being used with a military weapon shall be taken to be for military use;

   (b) references to a missile designed so that a substance contained in the missile will ignite on or immediately before impact include references to any missile containing a substance that ignites on exposure to air; and

   (c) references to a missile's expanding on impact include references to its deforming in any predictable manner on or immediately after impact.

(8) For the purposes of subsection (1)(aba) and (ac) above, any detachable, folding, retractable or other movable butt-stock shall be disregarded in measuring the length of any firearm.

(9) Any reference in this section to a muzzle-loading gun is a reference to a gun which is designed to be loaded at the muzzle end of the barrel or chamber with a loose charge and a separate ball (or other missile).

 (unless mandatory minimum sentence (D20)—

Section 5(1)(a), (ab), (aba), (ac), (ad), (ae), (af) or (c)	Possessing ... prohibited weapons or ammunition.	On indictment	10 years or a fine, or both.
Section 5(1)(b)	Possessing. prohibited weapon designed for discharge of noxious liquid etc.	(a) Summary (b) On indictment	6 months or a fine of the statutory maximum, or both. 10 years or a fine or both.
Section 5(1)(a), (ab), (aba), (ac), (ad), (ae), (af), (ag), (ba), or (c), Section 5(1A)(a)	Possessing ... prohibited weapons or ammunition Possessing... firearm disguised as other object.	On indictment On indictment	10 years or a fine, or both. 10 years or a fine. Or both
Section 5(1A)(b), (c), (d), (e), (f), or (g)	Possessing... other prohibited weapons.	(a) Summary (b) On indictment	6 months or a fine of the statutory maximum, or both. 10 years or a fine, or both.
Section 5(2A)	Manufacturing or distributing, or possessing for distribution, prohibited weapons or ammunition	On indictment	Imprisonment for life.[GC]
Section 5(5) ...	Non-compliance with condition of Defence Council authority.	Summary ...	6 months or a fine of level 5 on the standard scale; or both.

C17.1.6.1 *Allocation*

Where the statutory minimum sentence under s 51A applies (see **C17.1.3**) the court must send for trial (see **D20**).

C17.1.6.2 Key points

- To prove possession contrary to s 5 the prosecution merely had to prove possession of the object and that it was a prohibited weapon. It did not have to prove that the defendant either knew, or could have known, that the object was a weapon prohibited by the 1968 Act (*R v Deyemi* [2007] EWCA 2060, [2008] 1 Cr App R 25).
- It was not a defence to possession of a CS gas canister contrary to s 5(1)(b) that the defendant did not know or could not reasonably have been expected to know that the canister contained CS gas (*R v Bradish* (1990) 90 Cr App R 271).
- A person found in possession of a sawn-off shotgun inside a plastic bag is still in possession of the firearm even if he thought the bag contained a crowbar (*R v Waller* [1991] Crim LR 381).
- Momentary handling of a firearm by the accused followed by his immediate rejection of it, did not constitute possession of it within the meaning of s 5 (*R v T* [2011] EWCA Crim 1646).

C17.1.7 *Possession of firearm with intent to endanger life*

Firearms Act 1968, s 16

It is an offence for a person to have in his possession any firearm or ammunition with intent by means thereof to endanger life or cause serious injury to property, or to enable another person by means thereof to endanger life or cause serious injury to property, whether any injury to person or property has been caused or not.

GC

DO

▦ Life

IO

C17.1.7.1 *Sentencing*

A mandatory minimum sentence applies in the case of certain prohibited weapons specified in s 51A.

For general guidance on sentencing firearms offences see **C17.1.2**.

C17.1.7.2 Key points

- There is no requirement that the firearm or ammunition is prohibited under s 5 Firearms Act 1968 (*R v Salih* [2008] 1 WLR 2627).
- Section 16 does not extend to imitation firearms.
- The prosecution are not required to prove an immediate or unconditional intention to endanger life. The intention may last as long as the possession

lasts and to possess a firearm ready for use if and when an occasion arises is an offence within s 16 (*R v Bentham* [1973] QB 357).

- It is possible to raise self-defence (*R v Georgiades* [1989] 1 WLR 759) but for the issue to be left to a jury there must be evidence of fear of imminent attack (*R v Stubbs* [2007] EWCA Crim 1714).

C17.1.8 *Possession of firearm with intent to cause fear of violence*

> **Firearms Act 1968, s 16A**
>
> It is an offence for a person to have in his possession any firearm or imitation firearm with intent—
> (a) by means thereof to cause, or
> (b) to enable another person by means thereof to cause, any person to believe that unlawful violence will be used against him or another person.

fine/10 years imprisonment

C17.1.8.1 *Sentencing*

A mandatory minimum sentence applies in the case of certain prohibited weapons specified in s 51A. There is no sentencing guideline for this offence. For general guidance on sentencing firearms offences see **C17.1.2**.

C17.1.8.2 Key points

- For the meaning of firearm and imitation firearm see **C17.1.1**.
- The requirement that the violence must be 'unlawful' allows the defendant to raise the fact that he was acting in self-defence.
- As long as the defendant intends to cause a fear of unlawful violence, it does not matter that the victim is aware that the item is in fact an imitation firearm (*K v DPP* [2006] EWHC 2183 (Admin)).

C17.1.9 *Use of firearm to resist arrest*

> **Firearms Act 1968, s 17**
>
> (1) It is an offence for a person to make or attempt to make any use whatsoever of a firearm or imitation firearm with intent to resist or prevent the lawful arrest or detention of himself or another person.

(2) If a person, at the time of his committing or being arrested for an offence specified in Schedule 1 to this Act, has in his possession a firearm or imitation firearm, he shall be guilty of an offence under this subsection unless he shows that he had it in his possession for a lawful object....

(4) For purposes of this section, the definition of 'firearm' in section 57(1) of this Act shall apply without paragraphs (b) and (c) of that subsection, and 'imitation firearm' shall be construed accordingly.

 Life

 Where the statutory minimum sentence under s 51A applies the court must send for trial

C17.1.9.1 *Sentencing*

A mandatory minimum sentence applies in the case of certain prohibited weapons specified in s 51A. There is no sentencing guideline for this offence. For general guidance on sentencing firearms offences see **C17.1.2**.

C17.1.10 *Possessing firearm while committing an indictable offence*

Firearms Act 1968, s 17(2) and (4)

(2) If a person, at the time of his committing or being arrested for an offence specified in Schedule 1 to this Act, has in his possession a firearm or imitation firearm, he shall be guilty of an offence under this subsection unless he shows that he had it in his possession for a lawful object.

(4) For purposes of this section, the definition of 'firearm' in section 57(1) of this Act shall apply without paragraphs (b) and (c) of that subsection, and 'imitation firearm' shall be construed accordingly

 Life

C17.1.10.1 *Sentencing*

A mandatory minimum sentence applies in the case of certain prohibited weapons specified in s 51A. There is no sentencing guideline for this offence. For general guidance on sentencing firearms offences see **C17.1.2**.

C17.1.10.2 Key points

- For the definition of firearm and imitation firearm see **C17.1.1**.
- Possession for the purposes of s 17(2) is satisfied by custody and control of the firearm and does not require that the defendant has the firearm with him at the time of his arrest (*R v North* [2001] EWCA Crim 544).
- Sch 1 Firearms Act 1968 contains the following offences:
  (a) Offences under s 1 Criminal Damage Act 1971;
  (b) Offences under any of the following provisions of the Offences Against the Person Act 1861: ss 20 to 22 (inflicting bodily injury; garrotting; criminal use of stupefying drugs); s 30 (laying explosive to building etc); s 32 (endangering railway passengers by tampering with track); s 38 (assault with intent to commit felony or resist arrest); s 47 (criminal assaults);
  (c) Offences under Part I of the Child Abduction Act 1984 (abduction of children);
  (d) Theft, robbery, burglary, blackmail, and any offence under s 12(1) Theft Act 1968;
  (e) Offence under s 89(1) Police Act 1996 (assaulting constable in execution of his duty);
  (f) Offences under s 90(1) Criminal Justice Act 1991 (assaulting prisoner custody officer);
  (g) Offences under s 12(1) Criminal Justice and Public Order Act 1994 (assaulting secure training centre officer);
  (h) Offences under Sch 11 para 4 Immigration and Asylum Act 1999 (assaulting a detainee custody officer);
  (i) Offences under the Sexual Offences Act 2003: ss 1 (rape); s 2 (assault by penetration); s 4 (causing a person to engage in sexual activity involving penetration without consent); s 5 (rape of child under 13); s 6 (assault by penetration of child under 13); s 30 (sexual activity involving penetration with a person with a mental disorder impeding choice); and s 31 (causing or inciting a person with a mental disorder impeding choice to engage in sexual activity involving penetration);
  (j) Aiding and abetting the commission of any such offence; and
  (k) Attempting to commit any such offence.
- An offence specified in Sch 1 need not have been committed but the defendant must have been lawfully arrested for one of the offences specified (*R v Nelson* [2001] 1 QB 55).

C17.1.11 *Possession of firearm with intent to commit indictable offence*

Firearms Act 1968, s 18

(1) It is an offence for a person to have with him a firearm or imitation firearm with intent to commit an indictable offence, or to resist arrest or prevent the arrest of another, in either case while he has the firearm or imitation firearm with him.

(2) In proceedings for an offence under this section proof that the accused had a firearm or imitation firearm with him and intended to commit an offence, or to resist or prevent arrest, is evidence that he intended to have it with him while doing so.

GC

DO

 Life

IO

C17.1.11.1 *Sentence*

A mandatory minimum sentence applies in the case of certain prohibited weapons specified in s 51A. For general guidance on sentencing firearms offences see **C17.1.2**.

C17.1.11.2 Key points

• For the definition of firearm and imitation firearm see **C17.1.1**.

• In *R v Stoddart* [1998] 2 Cr App R 25 the Court of Appeal held that there are three elements to an offence under s 18:

    (a) that the defendant had with him a firearm or imitation firearm;

    (b) that he intended to have it with him; and

    (c) that at the same time he had the intention to commit an indictable offence or to resist or prevent arrest.

The prosecution must prove that the firearm or imitation firearm was with the defendant as opposed to being under his control somewhere else. He may have the firearm with him if it is readily accessible to him at the time of the offence (*R v Pawlicki* [1992] 1 WLR 827).

C17.1.12 *Carrying firearm in public place*

Firearms Act 1968, s 19

19 Carrying a firearm in a public place

A person commits an offence if, without lawful authority or reasonable excuse (the proof whereof lies on him) he has with him in a public place—

(a) a loaded shot gun,

(b) an air weapon (whether loaded or not),

(c) any other firearm (whether loaded or not) together with ammunition suitable for use in that firearm, or

(d) an imitation firearm.

 (Summary only if an air weapon; indictable only if the firearm is a firearm specified in s 5(1)(a), (ab), (aba), (ac), (ad), (ae) (af) (ag) (ba), and s 5(1A)(a))

6 months' imprisonment and/or fine/7 years' imprisonment (12 months if imitation weapon)

C17.1.12.1 *Sentencing*

Offence seriousness (culpability and harm)		
A. Identify the appropriate starting point		
Starting points based on first-time offender pleading not guilty		
Examples of nature of activity	Starting point	Range
Carrying an unloaded air weapon	Low-level community order	Band B fine to medium-level community order
Carrying loaded air weapon/imitation firearm/unloaded shot gun without ammunition	High-level community order	Medium-level community order to 26 weeks' custody (air weapon) Medium-level community order to Crown Court (imitation firearm, unloaded shot gun)
Carrying loaded shot gun/carrying shot gun or any other firearm together with ammunition for it	Crown Court	Crown Court

Offence seriousness (culpability and harm)
B. Consider the effect of aggravating and mitigating factors (other than those within examples in the preceding table)
The following may be particularly relevant but these lists are not exhaustive

Factors indicating higher culpability	Factors indicating lower culpability
1. Brandishing firearm	1. Firearm not in sight
2. Carrying firearm in a busy place	2. No intention to use firearm
3. Planned illegal use	3. Firearm to be used for lawful
Factors indicating greater degree of harm	purpose (not amounting to
1. Person or people put in fear	defence)
2. Offender participating in violent incident	

C17.1.12.2 Key points

- It is not necessary to show that the defendant knew that a gun was loaded (*R v Harrison* [1996] Crim LR 200).
- An item is an imitation firearm if it 'looked like' a firearm at the time of its use (*R v Morris and King* (1984) 149 JP 60).

- A part of the body (eg fingers pointed under clothing) could not constitute an imitation firearm (*R v Bentham* [2005] UKHL 18).
- For the definition of firearm and imitation firearm see **C17.1.1**.
- Public place includes any highway and any other premises or place to which at the material time the public have or are permitted to have access, whether on payment or otherwise (s 57(4) Firearms Act 1968).

 See *Blackstone's Criminal Practice 2019* **B12.108**

C17.2 Possession of bladed article or offensive weapon

Obligatory minimum sentences will apply to those committing second offences on or after 17 July 2015 (see **D20**).

Criminal Justice Act 1988, s 139(1)–(5) and (7)

139 Offence of having article with blade or point in public place

(1) Subject to subsections (4) and (5) below, any person who has an article to which this section applies with him in a public place shall be guilty of an offence.

(2) Subject to subsection (3) below, this section applies to any article which has a blade or is sharply pointed except a folding pocketknife.

(3) This section applies to a folding pocketknife if the cutting edge of its blade exceeds 3 inches.

(4) It shall be a defence for a person charged with an offence under this section to prove that he had good reason or lawful authority for having the article with him in a public place.

(5) Without prejudice to the generality of subsection (4) above, it shall be a defence for a person charged with an offence under this section to prove that he had the article with him—

(a) for use at work;

(b) for religious reasons; or

(c) as part of any national costume.

...

(7) In this section 'public place' includes any place to which at the material time the public have or are permitted access, whether on payment or otherwise.

Prevention of Crime Act 1953, s 1(1) and (4)

1 Prohibition of the carrying of offensive weapons without lawful authority or reasonable excuse

(1) Any person who without lawful authority or reasonable excuse, the proof whereof shall lie on him, has with him in any public place any offensive weapon shall be guilty of an offence...

(4) In this section 'public place' includes any highway and any other premises or place to which at the material time the public have or are permitted to have access whether on payment or otherwise and 'offensive weapon' means any article made or adapted for use for causing injury to the person, or intended by the person having it with him for such use by him or some other person.

Criminal Justice Act 1988, s 139A(1) and (2)

139A Offence of having article with blade or point (or offensive weapon) on school *[educational]* premises

(1) Any person who has an article to which section 139 of this Act applies with him on school premises *or further education premises* shall be guilty of an offence.

(2) Any person who has an offensive weapon within the meaning of section 1 of the Prevention of Crime Act 1953 with him on school premises *or further education premises*

shall be guilty of an offence. It shall be a defence for a person charged with an offence under this section to prove that he had good reason or lawful authority for having the article with him in a public place.

EW 6 months' imprisonment and/or fine/4 years' imprisonment

Criminal Justice Act 1988, s 141

141 Possession of certain offensive weapons in private

(1A) *Any person who possesses a weapon to which this section applies in private is guilty of an offence ...*

(1C) *For the purposes of subsection (1A) as it has effect in relation to England and Wales, a person possesses a weapon to which this section applies in private if the person possesses the weapon in a place other than—*

   (a) *a public place,*

   (b) *school premises,*

   (c) *further education premises, or*

   (d) *a prison ...*

(7A) *It is a defence for a person charged with an offence under subsection (1A) to show that the weapon in question is one of historical importance*

(11ZA) *It is a defence for a person charged with an offence under subsection (1A) to show that they possessed the weapon in question for educational purposes only.*

SO *6 months and/or a fine*

Note: These provisions are likely on implementation to apply to weapons specified in the Criminal Justice Act 1988 (Offensive Weapons) Order 1988 as amended. Specific defences apply to Sikh curved swords for use in a religious or ceremonial ceremony.

C17.2.1 *Sentencing (see Appendix 4)*

Note: A separate guideline applies for children and young people and appears in the *Handbook* for youths in the criminal courts.

C17.2.2 Key points

Has with him

- The Crown must prove that the person had the item with him and that it falls within the definition in the section. Only then must the defence establish a defence to the civil standard.
- It is necessary to show that the person knew that he was in possession of the offensive weapon (*R v Cugullere* [1961] 2 All ER 343).
- A court should not approach the issue of 'good reason' (and thus 'reasonable excuse') wholly objectively, nor hold that an angry, intoxicated, or traumatized state of mind could not contribute to good reason. A fear of attack can constitute good reason, the defendant's state of mind was relevant, and 'good reason' should be allowed a natural meaning. In *R v Clancy* [2012] EWCA Crim 8 (a decision under s 139 Criminal Justice Act 1988) the distorted thinking of the defendant following a sexual assault had to be considered. Only if the view was wholly unreasonable in all the circumstances as perceived by her should a court dismiss the defence.
- While *Ohlson v Hylton* [1975] 1 WLR 724 confirms that an offence does not occur if a person lawfully in possession of an article, which is not offensive per se, suddenly uses it in the heat of an altercation, an offence does occur if a person leaves the scene to collect a weapon (*R v Tucker* [2016] EWCA Crim 13).

Public place

- A public place is defined by both statutes. A landing in a block of flats is a public place if it could be reached without hindrance (*Knox v Anderson* [1982] 76 Cr App R 156) but not if access was restricted by key, access code, or intercom (*Williams v DPP* [1992] 95 Crim App R 415). Unimpeded access does not necessarily make it a public place. Public access must be implied or tolerated (*Harriott v DPP* [2005] EWHC 965 (Admin)).

Offensive weapon

- Weapons held by the appellate courts to be offensive per se include: a bayonet, a stiletto, a handgun, a butterfly knife, and a flick knife. Items that are inherently dangerous but manufactured for a lawful purpose are not offensive per se (eg razor blades, baseball bats, kitchen knives). It is likely that items prohibited for sale in England and Wales by virtue of the Criminal Justice Act 1988 (Offensive Weapons) (Amendment) Order 1988 (SI 1988/2019) are offensive per se.
- A belt buckle that comprises a knuckleduster but has additional items to secure the belt closed is not necessarily offensive per se, rather the court must make findings of fact whether the buckle had been made (as a knuckleduster) for the purpose of causing injury, and had then been adapted by the belt manufacturer, or whether it had in fact been manufactured as a buckle for a belt as a fashion item (*R v Christof* [2015] EWHC 4096 (Admin)).

Bladed article

- A lock knife is not a folding knife, irrespective of the blade length (*Harris v Director of Public Prosecutions* [1993] 1 WLR 82).

- A blade capable of being locked, however weakly, was not a folding pocket-knife as it was not immediately foldable by simply applying pressure to the blade (*Sharma v DPP* [2018] EWHC 3330 (Admin)).
- A cut-throat razor, less than 3" in length, does not fall within the definition of a folding pocket knife as it is a razor and not a knife (*R v D* [2019] EWCA Crim 45).
- A screwdriver is not a bladed article (*R v Davis* [1998] Crim LR 564).
- A blade does not need to be sharp—a butter knife can be a bladed article (*Brooker v Director of Public Prosecutions* [2005] EWHC 1132 (Admin)).

Reasonable excuse / good reason

- 'Good reason' has been interpreted to mean the same as 'reasonable excuse' under the 1953 Act.
- The fact that a defendant's employment was only casual was not a relevant consideration to prevent it being a good reason (*Chalal v Director of Public Prosecutions* [2010] EWHC 439 (Admin)).
- While mere forgetfulness cannot amount to a reasonable excuse (or good reason) (*R v Glidewell* [1999] EWCA Crim 1221), the court must consider all the circumstances in which the forgetfulness arose (*R v Jolie* [2003] EWCA Crim 543).
- Fear of attack may amount to a reasonable excuse if the risk is imminent (*R v McAuley* [2009] EWCA Crim 2130).
- An innocent purpose for having a weapon, offensive per se, in a public place does not equate to a reasonable excuse. Rather the court is entitled to consider whether there is a necessity or immediate temporal connection between possession and the purpose for which it is carried (*Garry v CPS* [2019] EWHC 636 (Admin)).

Criminal Justice Act 1988, s 139A

- school premises extend to surrounding land, playing fields, and yards;
- the offence can be committed when the school is closed;
- private schools' premises fall within the Act.

 See *Blackstone's Criminal Practice 2019* **B12.141–B12.191**

C17.3 Aggravated possession of bladed articles and offensive weapons (threats)

Prevention of Crime Act 1953, s 1A

1A Offence of threatening with offensive weapon in public

(1) A person is guilty of an offence if that person—
  (a) has an offensive weapon with him or her in a public place,
  (b) unlawfully and intentionally threatens another person (A) with the weapon, and

---

(c) does so in such a way that there [is an immediate risk of serious physical harm to that other person.] *a reasonable person (B) who was exposed to the same threat as A would think there was an immediate risk of physical harm to B*

[(2) For the purposes of this section physical harm is serious if it amounts to grievous bodily harm for the purposes of the Offences against the Person Act 1861.]

(3) In this section 'public place' and 'offensive weapon' have the same meaning as in section 1.

...

(12) If on a person's trial for an offence under this section (whether on indictment or not) the person is found not guilty of that offence but it is proved that the person committed an offence under section 1, the person may be convicted of the offence under that section.

Criminal Justice Act 1988, s 139AA

139AA Offence of threatening with article with blade or point or offensive weapon

(1) A person is guilty of an offence if that person—
  (a) has an article to which this section applies with him or her in a public place or on school premises,
  (b) unlawfully and intentionally threatens another person *(A)* with the article, and
  (c) does so in such a way that there [is an immediate risk of serious physical harm to that other person.] *a reasonable person (B) who was exposed to the same threat as A would think there was an immediate risk of physical harm to B*

(1A) A person is guilty of an offence if that person—
  (a) has an article to which this section applies with them on further education premises,
  (b) unlawfully and intentionally threatens another person ('A') with the article, and
  (c) does so in such a way that a reasonable person ('B') who was exposed to the same threat as A would think that there was an immediate risk of physical harm to B.

(2) In relation to a public place this section applies to an article to which section 139 applies.

(3) In relation to school premises this section applies to each of these—
  (a) an article to which section 139 applies;
  (b) an offensive weapon within the meaning of section 1 of the Prevention of Crime Act 1953.

(3A) In relation to further education premises this section applies to each of these—
  (a) an article to which section 139 applies;
  (b) an offensive weapon within the meaning of section 1 of the Prevention of Crime Act 1953.

(4) For the purposes of this section physical harm is serious if it amounts to grievous bodily harm for the purposes of the Offences against the Person Act 1861.

(5) In this section—
  'public place' has the same meaning as in section 139; 'school premises' has the same meaning as in section 139A.

(12) If on a person's trial for an offence under this section (whether on indictment or not) the person is found not guilty of that offence but it is proved that the person committed an offence under section 139 or 139A, the person may be convicted of the offence under that section.

EW 6 months' imprisonment and/or fine/4 years' imprisonment *but* with a minimum obligatory sentence unless it would be unjust in all the circumstances. In that situation community penalties may be imposed (s 305(4) Criminal Justice Act 2003). A 20 per cent reduction on that obligatory sentence is available for an early guilty plea, and there appears to be no statutory reason why a sentence on an adult should not be suspended. See **D20**.

Offensive Weapons Act 2019, s 52

52 Offence of threatening with an offensive weapon etc in a private place

(1) A person ('A') commits an offence if—
   (a) while A is in a private place, A unlawfully and intentionally threatens another person ('B') with an article or substance to which this subsection applies, and
   (b) A does so in such a way that there is an immediate risk of serious physical harm to B.
(2) Subsection (1) applies to an article or substance if it is—
   (a) an offensive weapon within the meaning of section 1 of the Prevention of Crime Act 1953,
   (b) an article to which section 139 of the Criminal Justice Act 1988 (offence of having article with blade or point in public place) applies, or
   (c) a corrosive substance.
(3) In the application of subsection (1) to an article within subsection (2)(a) or (b), 'private place' means a place other than—
   (a) a public place,
   (b) a place which is part of school premises, or
   (c) a place which is part of further education premises.
(4) In the application of subsection (1) to a corrosive substance, 'private place' means a place other than a public place.
(5) For the purposes of subsection (1) physical harm is serious if it amounts to grievous bodily harm for the purposes of the Offences against the Person Act 1861.
(8) In this section and section 53—
   'corrosive substance' means a substance that is capable of burning human skin by corrosion; 'further education premises' means land used solely for the purposes of—
   (a) an institution within the further education sector (within the meaning of section 91 of the Further and Higher Education Act 1992), or
   (b) a 16 to 19 Academy (within the meaning of section 1B of the Academies Act 2010), excluding any land occupied solely as a dwelling by a person employed at the institution or the 16 to 19 Academy;

EW *6 months and/or a fine/4 years*

C17.3.1 *Sentencing (see Appendix 5)*

Note: A separate guideline applies for children and young people and appears in the *Handbook* for youths in the criminal courts.

C17.3.2 Key points

The defences available to the aggravated offences do not replicate those for the basic crimes

C17.4 Offences in relation to corrosive substances

C17.4.1 *Offence of having a corrosive substance in a public place*

(1) *A person commits an offence if they have a corrosive substance with them in a public place.*

(2) *It is a defence for a person charged ... with an offence under subsection (1) to prove that they had good reason or lawful authority for having the corrosive substance with them in a public place.*

(3) *Without prejudice to the generality of subsection (2), it is a defence for a person charged .. with an offence under subsection (1) to prove that they had the corrosive substance with them for use at work.*

(7) *A person guilty of an offence under subsection (1) is liable—*

EW *6 months' imprisonment and/or fine/4 years' imprisonment but with a minimum obligatory sentence unless it would be unjust in all the circumstances. In that situation community penalties may be imposed (s 305(4) Criminal Justice Act 2003). A 20 per cent reduction on that obligatory sentence is available for an early guilty plea, and there appears to be no statutory reason why a sentence on an adult should not be suspended. See D26*

C17.4.2 Key points

- *'corrosive substance' means a substance which is capable of burning human skin by corrosion;*
- *'public place', in relation to England and Wales or Northern Ireland, includes any place to which, at the time in question, the public have or are permitted access, whether on payment or otherwise; see C17.2.2.*

Part D
Sentencing

D1 Alteration of Sentence

D1.1 Section 142 Magistrates' Courts Act 1980

Section 142 Magistrates' Courts Act 1980 gives the court power to reopen sentence. There are no time restrictions, but a court must have regard to the principle of finality of sentence, meaning that in many cases it will not be proper to interfere (*R (Trigger) v Northampton Magistrates' Court* [2011] EWHC 149 (Admin)). For case law see **A6.2**. Section 142(1) provides:

> **Magistrates' Courts Act 1980, s 142(1)**
>
> **142 Power of magistrates' court to re-open cases to rectify mistakes etc**
>
> (1) A magistrates' court may vary or rescind a sentence or other order imposed or made by it when dealing with an offender if it appears to the court to be in the interests of justice to do so, and it is hereby declared that this power extends to replacing a sentence or order which for any reason appears to be invalid by another which the court has power to impose or make.

 See *Blackstone's Criminal Practice 2019* **D23.23–D23.28**

D2 Banning Orders (Football)

Banning orders are imposed under s 14A Football Spectators Act 1989.

D2.1 Criteria and effect

Banning orders must be imposed when an offender is convicted of a relevant offence, and if the court is satisfied that there are reasonable grounds to believe that making a banning order would help to prevent violence or disorder at or in connection with any regulated football matches.

The core requirements of such an order are to prohibit the offender from attending regulated football matches in England and Wales. When matches are being played abroad, the order will require the offender to report to a police station and surrender his passport (unless there are exceptional circumstances certified by the court as to why this should not be done). Other requirements can be imposed, for example not to go within a certain distance of a football ground.

The order must be for a period of between 3 and 5 years, or 6 and 10 years if a custodial sentence (including a sentence of detention) is imposed for the original offence. A banning order cannot be limited to matches between particular teams (*Commissioner of Police of the Metropolis v Thorpe* [2015] EWHC 3339 (Admin)).

In *Newman v Commissioner of Police of the Metropolis* [2009] EWHC 1642 (Admin), the court held that the police were entitled to rely upon compilation witness statements and compilation video footage, and had no duty to disclose the underlying material from which they were drawn. There is no statutory disclosure regime applicable to the making of banning orders and a court should apply normal principles of 'fairness'. Advocates seeking disclosure should be careful to specify the material that they wish to view and the reasons why. An application that amounts to nothing more than a 'fishing expedition' ought to be refused.

D2.2 Relevant offences

Relevant offences are listed in Sch 1 to the 1989 Act. For some offences, the court will need to make a declaration of relevance (see **D2.3**).

Football Spectators Act 1989, Sch 1

1. This Schedule applies to the following offences:

    (a) any offence under section 14J(1) or 21C(2) of this Act,

    (b) any offence under section 2 or 2A of the Sporting Events (Control of Alcohol etc) Act 1985 (alcohol, containers, and fireworks) committed by the accused at any football match to which this Schedule applies or while entering or trying to enter the ground,

    (c) any offence under section 4A or 5 of the Public Order Act 1986 (harassment, alarm, or distress) or any provision of Part III of that Act (racial hatred) committed during a period relevant to a football match to which this Schedule applies at any premises while the accused was at, or was entering or leaving or trying to enter or leave, the premises,

(d) any offence involving the use or threat of violence by the accused towards another person committed during a period relevant to a football match to which this Schedule applies at any premises while the accused was at, or was entering or leaving or trying to enter or leave, the premises,

(e) any offence involving the use or threat of violence towards property committed during a period relevant to a football match to which this Schedule applies at any premises while the accused was at, or was entering or leaving or trying to enter or leave, the premises,

(f) any offence involving the use, carrying or possession of an offensive weapon or a firearm committed during a period relevant to a football match to which this Schedule applies at any premises while the accused was at, or was entering or leaving or trying to enter or leave, the premises,

(g) any offence under section 12 of the Licensing Act 1872 (persons found drunk in public places, etc) of being found drunk in a highway or other public place committed while the accused was on a journey to or from a football match to which this Schedule applies being an offence as respects which the court makes a declaration that the offence related to football matches,

(h) any offence under section 91(1) of the Criminal Justice Act 1967 (disorderly behaviour while drunk in a public place) committed in a highway or other public place while the accused was on a journey to or from a football match to which this Schedule applies being an offence as respects which the court makes a declaration that the offence related to football matches, ...

(j) any offence under section 1 of the Sporting Events (Control of Alcohol etc) Act 1985 (alcohol on coaches or trains to or from sporting events) committed while the accused was on a journey to or from a football match to which this Schedule applies being an offence as respects which the court makes a declaration that the offence related to football matches,

(k) any offence under section 4A or 5 of the Public Order Act 1986 (harassment, alarm, or distress) or any provision of Part III of that Act (racial hatred) committed while the accused was on a journey to or from a football match to which this Schedule applies being an offence as respects which the court makes a declaration that the offence related to football matches,

(l) any offence under section 4 or 5 of the Road Traffic Act 1988 (driving etc when under the influence of drink or drugs or with an alcohol concentration above the prescribed limit) committed while the accused was on a journey to or from a football match to which this Schedule applies being an offence as respects which the court makes a declaration that the offence related to football matches,

(m) any offence involving the use or threat of violence by the accused towards another person committed while one or each of them was on a journey to or from a football match to which this Schedule applies being an offence as respects which the court makes a declaration that the offence related to football matches,

(n) any offence involving the use or threat of violence towards property committed while the accused was on a journey to or from a football match to which this Schedule applies being an offence as respects which the court makes a declaration that the offence related to football matches,

(o) any offence involving the use, carrying or possession of an offensive weapon or a firearm committed while the accused was on a journey to or from a football match to which this Schedule applies being an offence as respects which the court makes a declaration that the offence related to football matches,

(p) any offence under the Football (Offences) Act 1991,

(q) any offence under section 4A or 5 of the Public Order Act 1986 (harassment, alarm, or distress) or any provision of Part 3 or 3A of that Act (hatred by reference to race etc)—

(i) which does not fall within paragraph (c) or (k) above,

(ii) which was committed during a period relevant to a football match to which this Schedule applies, and

(iii) as respects which the court makes a declaration that the offence related to that match or to that match and any other football match which took place during that period,

(r) any offence involving the use or threat of violence by the accused towards another person—

(i) which does not fall within paragraph (d) or (m) above,

(ii) which was committed during a period relevant to a football match to which this Schedule applies, and

(iii) as respects which the court makes a declaration that the offence related to that match or to that match and any other football match which took place during that period,

(s) any offence involving the use or threat of violence towards property—

(i) which does not fall within paragraph (e) or (n) above,

(ii) which was committed during a period relevant to a football match to which this Schedule applies, and

(iii) as respects which the court makes a declaration that the offence related to that match or to that match and any other football match which took place during that period,

(t) any offence involving the use, carrying or possession of an offensive weapon or a firearm—

(i) which does not fall within paragraph (f) or (o) above,

(ii) which was committed during a period relevant to a football match to which this Schedule applies, and

(iii) as respects which the court makes a declaration that the offence related to that match or to that match and any other football match which took place during that period.

(u) any offence under section 166 of the Criminal Justice and Public Order Act 1994 (sale of tickets by unauthorised persons) which relates to tickets for a football match.

D2.3 **Declaration of relevance**

The prosecution must give 5 days' notice that they intend to invite a court to make a declaration of relevance. That notice period may be waived by the defence; it can also be dispensed with by the court if the interests of justice do not require a longer notice period to be given. Note that the court can grant an adjournment to facilitate the 5-day notice period.

The declaration is that the offence related to that match, or to that match and any other football match which took place during that period.

Each of the following periods is 'relevant to' a football match to which Sch 1 applies:

- in the case of a match which takes place on the day on which it is advertised to take place, the period:
  - beginning 24 hours before whichever is the earlier of the start of the match and the time at which it was advertised to start, and
  - ending 24 hours after it ends;
- in the case of a match which does not take place on the day on which it was advertised to take place, the period:
  - beginning 24 hours before the time at which it was advertised to start on that day, and
  - ending 24 hours after that time....

In *R v Arbery* [2008] EWCA Crim 702, the offenders were drinking in a public house following a football match, waiting for their train home, when violence broke out with rival supporters. A football banning order was quashed on appeal, as the court held that the offence arose out of a disagreement in the pub, completely unrelated to football.

In *R v Eliot* [2007] EWCA Crim 1002, the court gave a helpful insight into how the issue of 'relevance' might be approached:

> Did the offences committed in the present case relate to the match? Clearly, the presence of the applicants in London and indeed at Leicester Square related to the match. But it is not their presence, or their allegiance, which is the touchstone of the declaration; it is the relationship between the offence and the match. Here, the offences were sparked by the presence of a group of football supporters in London. The spark, however, had nothing to do with the match itself on the facts as found by the judge. The violence took place, not because of anything that had happened at the football match, or between supporters but because of disparaging remarks made to a lady who had nothing to do with the football match and remarks which had nothing to do with the football match. In those circumstances, we do not consider that, in this case, the statutory requirement was satisfied.

In *Director of Public Prosecutions v Beaumont* [2008] EWHC 523 (Admin), the court rejected an argument that there was a temporal limit to the making of a banning order. In that case the violence erupted more than one hour after the end of the match.

Reviewing the law in *R v Doyle* [2012] EWCA Crim 1869, the court said that two requirements must be met in order to require the mandatory imposition of an order:

- Conviction of a relevant offence (Sch 1—see **D2.2**). These offences must 'relate' to football matches, which is an issue of fact—one match will suffice. Merely being on a journey to a match is not enough. Groups of fans will more easily meet the test. It is not enough that the violence would not have occurred 'but for' the journey to the football match.
- There are reasonable grounds to believe that the making of an order would help to prevent violence or disorder at or in connection with a regulated football match. One match can raise an inquiry, but there must be a risk of repetition.
- In *R v Irving* [2013] EWCA Crim 1932, the court confirmed:
  - Where the particular offence in Sch 1 Football Spectators Act 1989 requires a declaration that the offence related to a particular football match, the

failure to make such a declaration meant that no order could be made.

- An offence could relate to a football match even though the defendant supported neither team and did not go to the game, as where there is an ambush of supporters.
- The court must also find that there are reasonable grounds for believing that such an order would help to prevent violence or disorder. This required specific reasoning.
- Requirements attached to the order must be considered individually and be proportionate.

D2.4 Sentencing

In sentencing [for this offence], the court should refer to the sentencing approach in step one of the guideline for breach of a criminal behaviour order to determine culpability and harm, and determine an appropriate sentence bearing in mind the maximum penalty for the offence.

D2.5 Appeals

An appeal lies to the Crown Court in respect to the making of a banning order or dismissal of prosecution application (Football Spectators Act 1989, s 14D).

See *Blackstone's Criminal Practice 2019* **E21.3–E21.7**

D3 Breach of Prison Licence Supervision; Return to Custody

Under s 256AA Criminal Justice Act (CJA) 2003, if a person is sentenced to under 2 years in custody, they will be subject to supervision for a year from the date of their actual release 'for the purposes of rehabilitation'.

Similar arrangements are made for 'youths' who are 18 on the date of their release from post-January 2015 sentences of detention and training, or detention, under s 91 Powers of Criminal Courts (Sentencing) Act 2000, extending their period of supervision in these cases.

D3.1 Breach of supervision requirements imposed under section 256AA

A new application for legal aid may be made under s 14(b) Legal Aid Sentencing and Punishment of Offenders Act 2012.

Criminal Justice Act 2003, s 256AC

(4) If it is proved to the satisfaction of the court that the person has failed without reasonable excuse to comply with a supervision requirement imposed under section 256AA, the court may—
  (a) order the person to be committed to prison for a period not exceeding 14 days (subject to subsection (7)),
  (b) order the person to pay a fine not exceeding level 3 on the standard scale, or
  (c) make an order (a 'supervision default order') imposing on the person—
    (i) an unpaid work requirement (as defined by section 199), or
    (ii) a curfew requirement (as defined by section 204).
(5) Section 177(3) (obligation to impose electronic monitoring requirement) applies in relation to a supervision default order that imposes a curfew requirement as it applies in relation to a community order that imposes such a requirement.
(6) If the court deals with the person under subsection (4), it must revoke any supervision default order which is in force at that time in respect of that person.
(7) Where the person is under the age of 21—
  (a) an order under subsection (4)(a) in respect of the person must be for committal to a young offender institution instead of to prison,
(8) A person committed to prison or a young offender institution by an order under subsection (4)(a) is to be regarded as being in legal custody.
(9) A fine imposed under subsection (4)(b) is to be treated, for the purposes of any enactment, as being a sum adjudged to be paid by a conviction.
(10) In Schedule 19A (supervision default orders)—
  (a) Part 1 makes provision about requirements of supervision default orders, and
  (b) Part 2 makes provision about the breach, revocation and amendment of supervision default orders.
(11) A person dealt with under this section may appeal to the Crown Court against the order made by the court.

D3.2 Breach of a supervision default order

Breach of a supervision default order, without reasonable excuse, can be dealt with by using either:

- up to 14 days' custody;
- up to level 3 fine; or
- amended supervision default orders, taking account of what has already been done.

Supervision default orders are to be revoked if custody is later imposed (Sch 19A CJA 2003).

D3.3 Sentencing

D3.3.1 *Breach of post-sentence supervision*

The definitive guideline is as follows:

> Where the court determines a penalty is appropriate for a breach of a post sentence supervision requirement it must take into account the extent to which the offender has complied with all of the requirements of the post-sentence supervision or supervision default order when imposing a penalty.

In assessing the level of compliance with the order the court should consider:

(i)   the offender's overall attitude and engagement with the order as well as the proportion of elements completed;

(ii) the impact of any completed or partially completed requirements on the offender's behaviour;

(iii) the proximity of the breach to the imposition of the order; and

(iv) evidence of circumstances or offender characteristics, such as disability, mental health issues, or learning difficulties which have impeded offender's compliance with the order.

Level of compliance	Penalty
Low	Up to 7 days' committal to custody **or** Supervision default order in range of 30–40 hours' unpaid work **or** 8–12 hour curfew for minimum of 20 days
Medium	Supervision default order in range of 20–30 hours' unpaid work **or** 4–8 hour curfew for minimum of 20 days **or** Band B fine
High	Band A fine

D3.3.2 *Breach of supervision default order*

Level of compliance	Penalty
Low	Revoke supervision default order and order up to 14 days' committal to custody
Medium	Revoke supervision default order and impose new order in range of 40–60 hours' unpaid work **or** 8–16 hour curfew for minimum of 20 days
High	Band B fine

(i) A supervision default order must include either:
an unpaid work requirement of between 20 and 60 hours, or a curfew requirement for between 2 and 16 hours for a minimum of 20 days and no longer than the end of the post-sentence supervision period.
(ii) The maximum fine which can be imposed is £1,000.

D3.4 Return to custody

This power has ceased to exist and it should be noted that s 265 CJA 2003 means a new sentence cannot be made consecutive to a sentence following recall (following *R v Kerrigan* [2014] EWCA Crim 2348) and a sentence cannot be artificially increased to allow for this (see *Costello* [2010] EWCA Crim 371).

D4 **Committal for Sentence**

D4.1 **Criteria**

See also **A4**.

A magistrates' court may commit an offender for sentence for an either-way offence following a conviction (Powers of Criminal Courts (Sentencing) Act 2000 (PCC(S)A 2000), s 3) or guilty plea (s 4)

A magistrates' court will commit for sentence if the court is of the opinion:

- that the offence or the combination of the offence and one or more offences associated with it was so serious that greater punishment should be inflicted for the offence than the court has power to impose; or
- in the case of a violent or sexual offence, that a custodial sentence for a term longer than the court has power to impose is necessary to protect the public from serious harm from the offender.

Additional committal powers in relation to other offences are provided for under s 6 PCC(S)A 2000. The powers of the Crown Court depend on the use of the correct section to commit the defendant.

Powers of Criminal Courts (Sentencing) Act 2000, ss 3–6

3 Committal for sentence on summary trial of offence triable either way

(1) Subject to subsection (4) below, this section applies where on the summary trial of an offence triable either way a person aged 18 or over is convicted of the offence.

(2) If the court is of the opinion—

    (a) that the offence or the combination of the offence and one or more offences associated with it was so serious that the Crown Court should, in the court's opinion, have the power to deal with the offender in any way it could deal with him if he had been convicted on indictment the court may commit the offender in custody or on bail to the Crown Court for sentence in accordance with section 5(1) below.

(3) Where the court commits a person under subsection (2) above, section 6 below (which enables a magistrates' court, where it commits a person under this section in respect of an offence, also to commit him to the Crown Court to be dealt with in respect of certain other offences) shall apply accordingly.

(4) This section does not apply in relation to an offence as regards which this section is excluded by section 17D or 33 of the Magistrates' Courts Act 1980 (certain offences where value involved is small).

(5) The preceding provisions of this section shall apply in relation to a corporation as if—

    (a) the corporation were an individual aged 18 or over; and

    (b) in subsection (2) above, the words 'in custody or on bail' were omitted.

4 Committal for sentence on indication of guilty plea to offence triable either way

(1) This section applies where—

(a) a person aged 18 or over appears or is brought before a magistrates' court ('the court') on an information charging him with an offence triable either way ('the offence');

(b) he or his representative indicates that he would plead guilty if the offence were to proceed to trial; and

he or (where applicable) his representative indicates under section 17A, 17B or 20(7) of the Magistrates' Courts Act 1980 that he would plead guilty if the offence were to proceed to trial; and

(c) proceeding as if section 9(1) of the Magistrates' Courts Act 1980 were complied with and he pleaded guilty under it, the court convicts him of the offence.

(1A) But this section does not apply to an offence as regards which this section is excluded by section 17D of that Act (certain offences where value involved is small).

(2) If the court has sent the offender to the Crown Court for trial for one or more related offences, that is to say, one or more offences which, in its opinion, are related to the offence, it may commit him in custody or on bail to the Crown Court to be dealt with in respect of the offence in accordance with section 5(1) below.

(3) If the power conferred by subsection (2) above is not exercisable but the court is still to inquire, as examining justices, into one or more related offences—

(a) it shall adjourn the proceedings relating to the offence until after the conclusion of its inquiries; and

(b) if it commits the offender to the Crown Court for trial for one or more related offences, it may then exercise that power.

If the power conferred by subsection (2) above is not exercisable but the court is still to determine to, or to determine whether to, send the offender to the Crown Court for trial under section 51 or 51A of the Crime and Disorder Act 1998 for one or more related offences—

(a) it shall adjourn the proceedings relating to the offence until after it has made those determinations; and

(b) if it sends the offender to the Crown Court for trial for one or more related offences, it may then exercise that power.

(4) Where the court—

(a) under subsection (2) above commits the offender to the Crown Court to be dealt with in respect of the offence, and

(b) does not state that, in its opinion, it also has power so to commit him under section 3(2) or, as the case may be, section 3A(2) above, section 5(1) below shall not apply unless he is convicted before the Crown Court of one or more of the related offences.

(5) Where section 5(1) below does not apply, the Crown Court may deal with the offender in respect of the offence in any way in which the magistrates' court could deal with him if it had just convicted him of the offence.

(6) Where the court commits a person under subsection (2) above, section 6 below (which enables a magistrates' court, where it commits a person under this section in respect of an offence, also to commit him to the Crown Court to be dealt with in respect of certain other offences) shall apply accordingly.

(7) For the purposes of this section one offence is related to another if, were they both to be prosecuted on indictment, the charges for them could be joined in the same indictment.

(8) In reaching any decision under or taking any step contemplated by this section—

(a) the court shall not be bound by any indication of sentence given in respect of the offence under section 20 of the Magistrates' Courts Act 1980 (procedure where summary trial appears more suitable); and

(b) nothing the court does under this section may be challenged or be the subject of any appeal in any court on the ground that it is not consistent with an indication of sentence.

6 Committal for sentence in certain cases where offender committed in respect of another offence

(1) This section applies where a magistrates' court ('the committing court') commits a person in custody or on bail to the Crown Court under any enactment mentioned in subsection (4) below to be sentenced or otherwise dealt with in respect of an offence ('the relevant offence').

(2) Where this section applies and the relevant offence is an indictable offence, the committing court may also commit the offender, in custody or on bail as the case may require, to the Crown Court to be dealt with in respect of any other offence whatsoever in respect of which the committing court has power to deal with him (being an offence of which he has been convicted by that or any other court).

(3) Where this section applies and the relevant offence is a summary offence, the committing court may commit the offender, in custody or on bail as the case may require, to the Crown Court to be dealt with in respect of—

(a) any other offence of which the committing court has convicted him, being either—
   (i) an offence punishable with imprisonment; or
   (ii) an offence in respect of which the committing court has a power or duty to order him to be disqualified under section 34, 35 or 36 of the Road Traffic Offenders Act 1988 (disqualification for certain motoring offences); or
(b) any suspended sentence in respect of which the committing court has under paragraph 11(1) of Schedule 12 to the Criminal Justice Act 2003 power to deal with him.

(4) The enactments referred to in subsection (1) above are—

(a) the Vagrancy Act 1824 (incorrigible rogues);
(b) sections 3 to 4A above (committal for sentence for offences triable either way);
(c) section 13(5) below (conditionally discharged person convicted of further offence);
(d) paragraph 11(2) of Schedule 12 to the Criminal Justice Act 2003 (committal to Crown Court where offender convicted during operational period of suspended sentence).

Where a summary-only offence has been committed in breach of a Crown Court suspended sentence the new offence may (Sch 12 para 11 CJA 2003) be committed, under s 6, to the Crown Court (*R v Jepson* [2013] EWCA Crim 1362). However, where a summary-only offence is committed in breach of a Crown Court community order, there is no such power to commit the new offence when the breach is committed under Sch 8 para 22 CJA 2003 (*R v De Bitto* [2013] EWCA Crim 1134.

 See *Blackstone's Criminal Practice 2019* **D23.29**

D5 Community Orders

Imposition and Breach

D5.1 Criteria for imposition

Note: A sentencing decision flow chart appears inside the back cover.

Section 148 of the Criminal Justice Act (CJA) 2003 (as amended) provides:

> **Criminal Justice Act 2003 s 148**
>
> **148 Restrictions on imposing community sentences**
>
> (1) A court must not pass a community sentence on an offender unless it is of the opinion that the offence, or the combination of the offence and one or more offences associated with it, was serious enough to warrant such a sentence.
>
> (2) Where a court passes a community sentence which consists of or includes a community order—
>
>   (a) the particular requirement or requirements forming part of the community order must be such as, in the opinion of the court, is, or taken together are, the most suitable for the offender, and
>
>   (b) the restrictions on liberty imposed by the order must be such as in the opinion of the court are commensurate with the seriousness of the offence, or the combination of the offence and one or more offences associated with it.
>
> (3) Subsections (1) and (2) (b) have effect subject to section 151(2).
>
> (4) The fact that by virtue of any provision of this section—
>
>   (a) a community sentence may be passed in relation to an offence; or
>
>   (b) particular restrictions on liberty may be imposed by a community order or youth rehabilitation order,
>
> does not require a court to pass such a sentence or to impose those restrictions.

Because a court is not required to impose a community sentence in cases where the offence is serious enough to justify such a sentence, there is a wider discretion to impose financial penalties.

Section 150A CJA 2003 restricts community orders for those aged 18 or above to offences that are punishable with imprisonment.

D5.2 Reports

The court must obtain a report unless the court is of the view that one is unnecessary. (See **D25**.)

No custodial sentence or community sentence is invalidated by the failure of a court to obtain and consider a pre-sentence report (s 156(6) CJA 2003).

D5.3 Sentencing guidelines

The Sentencing Council's definitive guideline on the imposition of community and custodial sentences provides that sentencers must consider all available disposals at the time of sentence; even where the threshold for a community sentence has been passed, a fine or discharge may be an appropriate penalty. In particular, a Band D fine may be an appropriate alternative to a community order.

The guideline provides that the seriousness of the offence should be the initial factor in determining which requirements to include in a community order. It establishes three sentencing ranges within the community order band based on offence seriousness (low, medium, and high), and identifies non-exhaustive examples of requirements that might be appropriate in each. These are set out in the table following. The examples focus on punishment in the community; other requirements of a rehabilitative nature may be more appropriate in some cases.

The particular requirements imposed within the range must be suitable for the individual offender and will be influenced by a wide range of factors, including the stated purpose(s) of the sentence, the risk of reoffending, the ability of the offender to comply, and the availability of the requirements in the local area. The court must ensure that the restriction on the offender's liberty is commensurate with the seriousness of the offence and that the requirements imposed are the most suitable for the offender.

Sentences should not necessarily escalate from one community order range to the next on each sentencing occasion. The decision as to the appropriate range of community order should be based upon the seriousness of the new offence(s) (which will take into account any previous convictions).

Low	Medium	High
Offences only just cross community order threshold, where the seriousness of the offence or the nature of the offender's record means that a discharge or fine is inappropriate	Offences that obviously fall within the communit y order band	Offences only just fall below the custody threshold or the custody threshold is crossed but a community order is more appropriate in the circumstances
In general, only one requirement will be appropriate and the length may be curtailed if additional requirements are necessary		More intensive sentences which combine two or more requirements may be appropriate

Low	Medium	High
Suitable requirements might include: • Any appropriate rehabilitative 40–80 hours' unpaid work • curfew requirement within the lowest range (eg up to 16 hours per day for a few weeks) • exclusion requirement, for a few months • prohibited activity requirement • attendance centre requirement (where available)	Suitable requirements might include: • Any appropriate rehabilitative • greater number of hours of unpaid work (eg 80–150 hours) • curfew requirement within the middle range (eg up to 16 hours per day for 2–3 months) • exclusion requirement lasting in the region of 6 months • prohibited activity requirement	Suitable requirements might include: • Any appropriate rehabilitative 150–300 hours' unpaid work • curfew requirement up to 12 hours per day for 4–12 months • exclusion order lasting in the region of 12 months

If order does not contain a punitive requirement, suggested fine levels are indicated below:		
BAND A FINE	BAND B FINE	BAND C FINE

D5.4 Requirements

Criminal Justice Act 2003, s 177(2A)–(2B)

Obligations when imposing a community order)

177 (2A) Where the court makes a community order, the court must—
  (a) include in the order at least one requirement imposed for the purpose of punishment, or
  (b) impose a fine for the offence in respect of which the community order is made, or
  (c) comply with both of paragraphs (a) and (b).
(2B) Subsection (2A) does not apply where there are exceptional circumstances which—
  (a) relate to the offence or to the offender,
  (b) would make it unjust in all the circumstances for the court to comply with subsection (2A)(a) in the particular case, and a fine for the offence concerned.

It is a matter for the court to decide which requirements amount to a punishment in each case. When imposing requirements on the offender as part of the community order, a court should balance the requirements, or combination of requirements, with the offender's personal circumstances, and avoid conflict with work, schooling, or religious beliefs.

The available requirements are:

- unpaid work of between 40 and 300 hours to be completed within 12 months;
- rehabilitation activity requirement (the court does not prescribe the activities to be included but will specify the maximum number of activity days the offender must complete);
- a programme (the court must specify the initial length (*R v Price* [2013] EWCA Crim 1283));
- prohibited activity;
- curfew of 2–16 hours in any 24 hours for up to 12 months;
- exclusion, normally with electronic monitoring; such a requirement to exclude the offender from the UK is unlawful (*R (Dragoman) v Camberwell Green Magistrates' Court* [2012] EWHC 4105 (Admin)), maximum 2 years;
the exclusion may be continuous or during specified periods;
- residence;
- mental health treatment;
- drug rehabilitation;
- alcohol treatment;
- (if under 25) attendance centre; for 12–36 hours;
- foreign travel restriction for up to 12 months;

- alcohol abstinence and monitoring (not fully in force), if alcohol an element of the offence or a factor contributing to it and the offender is not dependent on alcohol;
- electronic monitoring.

 See *Blackstone's Criminal Practice 2019* **E8**

D5.5 Community order made after a remand in custody or on a qualifying curfew

In *R v Hemmings* [2008] 1 Cr App R (S) 106, the court held:

> A sentence of a community order, and all the more so one coupled with requirements which have a real impact on the offender's liberty, is a form of punishment. It does not seem to us to be right that the appellant should receive a substantial further punishment in circumstances where he has already received what was in practice the maximum punishment by way of imprisonment which the law could have imposed. That reasoning seems to us to be in line with the reasoning in [earlier cases where] ... the court took the course of imposing a conditional discharge.

In *R v Rakib* [2011] EWCA Crim 870, the court, considering *Hemmings*, held that time spent in custody was not a determinative factor, and the rehabilitative aims of sentencing (s 142(1) CJA 2003) may in some cases justify a community penalty even if the offender had served on remand the equivalent of the maximum custodial sentence.

Where the time spent on a qualifying curfew meant that there would be immediate release from the appropriate prison sentence, it was not improper to impose a community order with requirements to address the underlying cause of offending. The court would not have imposed a punitive unpaid work requirement in addition (*R v Pereira-Lee* [2016] EWCA Crim 1705).

D5.6 Breach of and offences while on a community order

D5.6.1 Key points

Breach of community orders imposed under the CJA 2003 is dealt with in accordance with Sch 8 to that Act (as amended). There is no power to remand a person alleged to be in breach on bail, save on a committal to the Crown Court. Bail Act issues cannot therefore arise. Proceedings for breach can be issued after the community order has expired: para 20(1) Sch 8 CJA 2003 as interpreted in *National Probation Service v Blackfriars Crown Court* [2019] EWHC 529 (Admin).

A general defence of reasonable excuse is open to the defendant. The fact that a person is appealing against a community order does not give him a reasonable excuse not to comply (*West Midlands Probation Board v Sutton Coldfield Magistrates' Court* [2008] EWHC 15 (Admin)).

On breach of a community order due to the offender having failed to comply with the terms of the order, the court must act in one of the following ways:

- impose a fine of up to £2,500;
- impose more onerous requirements than the original order (having taken into account the offender's level of cooperation with the order) and let the order continue (including, on one occasion, lengthening the order by up to six months beyond its original date);
- if the order was made by the Crown Court, commit the offender for sentence;
- revoke the order and deal with the offender in any manner in which it could deal with him if he had just been convicted by the court of the offence (having taken into account the offender's level of cooperation with the order).

It should be noted that, with respect to an offender aged 18 years or older, imprisonment for a term of up to 6 months can be imposed following a wilful and persistent failure to comply, even if the original offence is not in itself imprisonable.

A court must be 'satisfied' that a breach has occurred to the criminal standard of proof (*West Yorkshire Probation Board v Boulter* (2005) 169 JP 601).

If the breach has occurred due to the offender's ill-health, a court should not resentence (*R v Bishop* [2004] EWCA Crim 2956).

If a person breaches an order that does not already include an unpaid work requirement, and the court is minded to impose such a requirement, the minimum hours to be worked shall be 20 (Sch 8, para 9(3A) CJA 2003).

There is no power to commence breach proceedings once the operational period has expired (*West Yorkshire Probation Board v Cruickshanks* [2010] EWHC 615 (Admin)).

Putting an offender, subject to a community order, before the court for breach was an important tool available to the probation service to ensure that orders work effectively. Critical was whether there had been any reoffending; whether the risk had reduced and whether the probation service felt the order could usefully continue (*R v Aslam (Aqib)* [2016] EWCA Crim 845).

D5.6.2 *Sentencing*

The definitive Guideline on breach offences states the following.

Breach of community order by failing to comply with requirements

The court must take into account the extent to which the offender has complied with the requirements of the community order when imposing a penalty.

In assessing the level of compliance with the order the court should consider:

(i) the overall attitude and engagement with the order as well as the proportion of elements completed;
(ii) the impact of any completed or partially completed requirements on the offender's behaviour;
(iii) the proximity of breach to imposition of order; and
(iv) evidence of circumstances or offender characteristics, such as disability, mental health issues, or learning difficulties which have impeded the offender's compliance with the order.

Overall compliance with order	Penalty
Wilful and persistent non-compliance	Revoke the order and resentence imposing custodial sentence (even where the offence seriousness did not originally merit custody)
Low level of compliance	Revoke the order and resentence original offence **or** Add curfew requirement 20–30 days* **or** 30–50 hours' additional unpaid work/extend length of order/add additional requirement(s) **or** Band C fine
Medium level of compliance	Revoke the order and resentence original offence **or** Add curfew requirement 10–20 days* **or** 20–30 hours additional unpaid work/extend length of order/add additional requirement(s) **or** Band B fine
High level of compliance	Add curfew requirement 6–10 days* **or** 10–20 hours' additional unpaid work/extend length of order/add additional requirement(s) **or** Band A fine

* Curfew days do not have to be consecutive and may be distributed over particular periods, for example at weekends, as the court deems appropriate. The period of the curfew should not exceed the duration of the community order and cannot be for longer than 12 months.

Technical guidance

(a) If imposing more onerous requirements the length of the order may be extended up to three years or six months longer than the previous length, which ever is longer (but only once).

(b) If imposing unpaid work as a more onerous requirement and an unpaid work requirement was not previously included, the minimum number of hours that can be imposed is 20.

(c) The maximum fine that can be imposed is £2,500.

(d) If resentencing, a suspended sentence MUST NOT be imposed as a more severe alternative to a community order. A suspended sentence may only be imposed if it is fully intended that the offender serve a custodial sentence in accordance with the Imposition of Community and Custodial Sentences guideline.

(e) Where the order was imposed by the Crown Court, magistrates should consider their sentencing powers in dealing with a breach. Where the judge imposing the order reserved any breach proceedings commit the breach for sentence.

D5.6.3 *Further offences whilst subject to a community order (Sch 8, para 21)*

If the offender has committed a further offence during the life of the community order and is convicted whilst that order is in force, the court has three options open to it in respect to the original order:

• do nothing, and sentence for the new offence; or
• if the order was made by the Crown Court, commit the offender for sentence; or

- revoke the order and deal with the offender in any manner in which it could deal with him if he had just been convicted by the court of the offence (having taken into account the offender's level of cooperation with the order).

D5.6.4 *Sentencing*

The Definitive Guideline on breach offences states:

Powers of the court following a subsequent conviction

A conviction for a further offence does not constitute a breach of a community order. However, in such a situation, the court should consider the ... guidance [in] the Offences Taken into Consideration and Totality guideline: (**D2.1**)

Offender convicted of an offence while serving a community order

The power to deal with the offender depends on his being convicted whilst the order is still in force; it does not arise where the order has expired, even if the additional offence was committed whilst it was still current.

If an offender, in respect of whom a community order made by a magistrates' court is in force, is convicted by a magistrates' court of an additional offence, the magistrates' court should ordinarily revoke the previous community order and sentence afresh for both the original and the additional offence.

Where an offender, in respect of whom a community order made by a Crown Court is in force, is convicted by a magistrates' court, the magistrates' court may, and ordinarily should, commit the offender to the Crown Court, in order to allow the Crown Court to resentence for the original offence and the additional offence.

The sentencing court should consider the overall seriousness of the offending behaviour taking into account the additional offence and the original offence. The court should consider whether the combination of associated offences is sufficiently serious to justify a custodial sentence.

If the court does not consider that custody is necessary, it should impose a single community order that reflects the overall totality of criminality. The court must take into account the extent to which the offender complied with the requirements of the previous order.

D5.6.5 *Approach to be taken by the court*

The Sentencing Council provided guidance in *Guideline: New Sentences: Criminal Justice Act 2003*, paras 1.1.44–1.1.47):

- When increasing the onerousness of requirements, the court must consider the impact on the offender's ability to comply and the possibility of precipitating a custodial sentence for further breach. For that reason, and particularly where the breach occurs towards the end of the sentence, the court should take account of compliance to date and may consider that extending the supervision or operational periods will be more sensible; in other cases it might choose to add punitive or rehabilitative requirements instead. In making these changes the court must be mindful of the legislative restrictions on the overall length of community sentences and on the supervision and operational periods allowed for each type of requirement.

- The court dealing with breach of a community sentence should have as its primary objective ensuring that the requirements of the sentence are finished, and this is important if the court is to have regard to the statutory purposes of sentencing. A court that imposes a custodial sentence for breach without giving adequate consideration to alternatives is in danger of imposing a sentence that is not commensurate with the seriousness of the original offence and is solely a punishment for breach. This risks undermining the purposes it has identified as being important. Nonetheless, courts will need to be vigilant to ensure that there is a realistic prospect of the purposes of the order being achieved.

- A court sentencing for breach must take account of the extent to which the offender has complied with the requirements of the community order, the reasons for breach, and the point at which the breach has occurred. Where a breach takes place towards the end of the operational period and the court is satisfied that the offender's appearance before the court is likely to be sufficient in itself to ensure future compliance, then given that it is not open to the court to make no order, an approach that the court might wish to adopt could be to resentence in a way that enables the original order to be completed properly—for example, a differently constructed community sentence that aims to secure compliance with the purposes of the original sentence. (Note the restriction on making no order has now been removed.)

- If the court decides to make the order more onerous, it must give careful consideration, with advice from the Probation Service, to the offender's ability to comply. A custodial sentence should be the last resort, where all reasonable efforts to ensure that an offender completes a community sentence have failed.

See *Blackstone's Criminal Practice 2019* **E8.30**

D6 **Compensation Order**

D6.1 Criteria

Powers of Criminal Courts (Sentencing) Act 2000, s 130(1)–(10)

130 Compensation orders against convicted persons

(1) A court by or before which a person is convicted of an offence, instead of or in addition to dealing with him in any other way, may, on application or otherwise, make an order (in this Act referred to as a 'compensation order') requiring him—

    (a) to pay compensation for any personal injury, loss or damage resulting from that offence or any other offence which is taken into consideration by the court in determining sentence; or

    (b) to make payments for funeral expenses or bereavement in respect of a death resulting from any such offence, other than a death due to an accident arising out of the presence of a motor vehicle on a road; but this is subject to the following provisions of this section and to section 131 below.

(2) Where the person is convicted of an offence the sentence for which is fixed by law or falls to be imposed under 110(2) or 111(2) above, section 51A(2) of the Firearms Act 1968, section 225, 226, 227 or 228 of the Criminal Justice Act 2003 or section 29(4) or (6) of the Violent Crime Reduction Act 2006, subsection (1) above shall have effect as if the words 'instead of or' were omitted.

(2A) A court must consider making a compensation order in any case where this section empowers it to do so.

(3) A court shall give reasons, on passing sentence, if it does not make a compensation order in a case where this section empowers it to do so.

(4) Compensation under subsection (1) above shall be of such amount as the court considers appropriate, having regard to any evidence and to any representations that are made by or on behalf of the accused or the prosecutor.

(5) In the case of an offence under the Theft Act 1968 or Fraud Act 2006, where the property in question is recovered, any damage to the property occurring while it was out of the owner's possession shall be treated for the purposes of subsection (1) above as having resulted from the offence, however and by whomever the damage was caused.

(6) A compensation order may only be made in respect of injury, loss or damage (other than loss suffered by a person's dependants in consequence of his death) which was due to an accident arising out of the presence of a motor vehicle on a road, if—

    (a) it is in respect of damage which is treated by subsection (5) above as resulting from an offence under the Theft Act 1968 or Fraud Act 2006; or

    (b) it is in respect of injury, loss or damage as respects which—

        (i) the offender is uninsured in relation to the use of the vehicle; and

        (ii) compensation is not payable under any arrangements to which the Secretary of State is a party.

(7) Where a compensation order is made in respect of injury, loss or damage due to an accident arising out of the presence of a motor vehicle on a road, the amount to be paid may include an amount representing the whole or part of any loss of or reduction in preferential rates of insurance attributable to the accident.

(8) A vehicle the use of which is exempted from insurance by section 144 of the Road Traffic Act 1988 is not uninsured for the purposes of subsection (6) above.

(9) A compensation order in respect of funeral expenses may be made for the benefit of any one who incurred the expenses.

(10) A compensation order in respect of bereavement may be made only for the benefit of a person for whose benefit a claim for damages for bereavement could be made under section 1A of the Fatal Accidents Act 1976; and the amount of compensation in respect of bereavement shall not exceed the amount for the time being specified in section 1A (3) of that Act.

D6.2 Principles

A magistrates' court can order compensation for each offence without limit of amount, and may also award compensation in relation to offences taken into consideration. If there is a compensation order, a victim surcharge is not obligatory.

The principles are set out in *R v York* [2018] EWCA Crim 2754

1   an offender must give details of her means
2   a judge must enquire about, and make clear findings about the offender's means
3   the court must take into account an offender's means
4   an order should not be made unless it is realistic, in the sense the court is satisfied that the offender has or will have the means to pay within a reasonable time. In general, excessively long repayment periods should be avoided
5   a court should not make an order on the assumption that it will be paid by somebody else
6   it is wrong to fix an amount of compensation without regard to the instalments which are capable of being paid by the offender and the period over which they should be paid

In relation to motor vehicle damage, the maximum payable will generally be the excess not paid by the Motor Insurers Bureau (MIB) (£300 in untraced driver cases with significant personal injury; otherwise nil), save where it is in respect of a vehicle stolen or taken without consent and there is damage to that vehicle, or the claim is not covered by the MIB.

If the amount of compensation is not agreed, the prosecution must be in a position to call evidence. In cases where the loss is unclear or subject to complex argument, the best course of action is to leave the matter to the civil courts to resolve (*R v Horsham Justices, ex p Richards* [1985] 2 All ER 1114; *R v Bewick* [2007] EWCA Crim 3297). A court can, however, make a common-sense determination (eg £50 for a small broken window).

D6.3 Assessment of means

In determining whether to make a compensation order against any person, and in determining the amount to be paid by any person under such an order, the court shall have regard to his means so far as they appear or are known to the court. An order made in the absence of a means inquiry is at risk of being ruled unlawful (*R v Gray* [2011] EWCA Crim 225).

Where the court considers:

- that it would be appropriate both to impose a fine and to make a compensation order, but
- that the offender has insufficient means to pay both an appropriate fine and appropriate compensation,

the court shall give preference to compensation (though it may impose a fine as well).

Save where a sentence of custody impacts on the offender's ability to pay, there is nothing wrong in principle with imposing compensation in addition to a custodial penalty.

D6.4 Time for payment

Whilst payment within a year is often required, and the defendant's means are relevant to the amount of an order, the time for payment must be proportionate. A one-year period was inappropriate and was increased on the facts in *R v Campbell (Natalie)* [2015] EWCA Crim 1876.

D6.5 Suggested levels of compensation

The Magistrates' Court Sentencing Guidelines set out the following scales for the award of compensation:

Physical injury		
Type of injury	**Description**	**Starting point**
Graze	Depending on size	£75
Bruise	Depending on size	£100
Cut: no permanent scar	Depending on size and whether stitched	£100–300
Black eye		£125
Eye	Blurred or double vision lasting up to 6 weeks	£500
	Blurred or double vision lasting for 6–13 weeks	£1,000
	Blurred or double vision lasting for more than 13 weeks (recovery expected)	£1,500
Brain	Concussion lasting 1 week	£1,500
Nose	Undisplaced fracture of nasal bone	£1,000
	Displaced fracture requiring manipulation	£2,000
	Deviated nasal septum requiring septoplasty	£2,000
Loss of non-front tooth	Depending on cosmetic effect	£750 per tooth
Loss of front tooth	Depending on cosmetic effect	£1,500 per tooth
Facial scar	Minor disfigurement (permanent)	£1,000
Arm	Fractured humerus, radius, ulna (substantial recovery)	£1,500
Shoulder	Dislocated (substantial recovery)	£90

D6 Compensation Order

Physical injury		
Type of injury	**Description**	**Starting point**
Wrist	Dislocated/fractured—including scaphoid fracture (substantial recovery)	£2,400
	Fractured—colles type (substantial recovery)	£2,400
Sprained wrist, ankle	Disabling for up to 6 weeks	£500
	Disabling for 6–13 weeks	£800
	Disabling for more than 13 weeks	£2,500
Finger	Fractured finger other than index finger (substantial recovery)	£300
	Fractured index finger (substantial recovery)	£1,200
	Fractured thumb (substantial recovery)	£1,750
Leg	Fractured fibula (substantial recovery)	£1,000
	Fractured femur, tibia (substantial recovery)	£1,800
Abdomen	Injury requiring laparotomy	£1,800

Mental injury	
Description	**Starting point**
Temporary mental anxiety (including terror, shock, distress), not medically verified	£500
Disabling mental anxiety, lasting more than 6 weeks, medically verified	£1,000
Disability mental illness, lasting up to 28 weeks, confirmed by psychiatric diagnosis	£1,500

Physical and sexual abuse		
Type of abuse	**Description**	**Starting point**
Physical abuse of adult	Intermittent physical assaults resulting in accumulation of healed wounds, burns, or scalds, but with no appreciable disfigurement	£2,000
Physical abuse of child	Isolated or intermittent assault(s) resulting in weals, hair pulled from scalp, etc	£1,000
	Intermittent physical assaults resulting in accumulation of healed wounds, burns, or scalds, but with no appreciable disfigurement	£1,000
Sexual abuse of adult	Non-penetrative indecent physical acts over clothing	£1,000
	Non-penetrative indecent act(s) under clothing	£2,000
Sexual abuse of child (under 18)	Non-penetrative indecent physical act(s) over clothing	£1,000
	Non-penetrative frequent assaults over clothing or non-penetrative indecent act under clothing	£1,500 or £2,000
	Repetitive indecent acts under clothing	£3,300

 See *Blackstone's Criminal Practice 2019* **E16**

D7 Confiscation

Proceeds of Crime Act 2002

D7.1 Criteria

A magistrates' court has no power to make a confiscation order. However, in some cases it will be appropriate to accept jurisdiction for an offence but find that the prosecution or court later consider that confiscation proceedings are appropriate (a common example is in relation to counterfeit goods). A magistrates' court may commit an offender to the Crown Court for the purposes of activating the confiscation regime under the Proceeds of Crime Act 2002, even where a discharge is considered the proper sentence (see *R v Varma* [2012] UKSC 42 and **D14**) or the offence is summary only (*R v Sumal & Sons (Properties) Limited* 2012 EWCA Crim 1840).

In the event that the prosecution wish to proceed with confiscation proceedings, the court *must* commit the offender to the Crown Court for sentence.

Proceeds of Crime Act 2002, s 70

70 Committal by magistrates' court

(1) This section applies if—
   (a) defendant is convicted of an offence by a magistrates' court, and
   (b) the prosecutor asks the court to commit the defendant to the Crown Court with a view to a confiscation order being considered under section 6.
(2) In such a case the magistrates' court—
   (a) must commit the defendant to the Crown Court in respect of the offence, and
   (b) may commit him to the Crown Court in respect of any other offence falling within subsection (3).
(3) An offence falls within this subsection if—
   (a) the defendant has been convicted of it by the magistrates' court or any other court, and
   (b) the magistrates' court has power to deal with him in respect of it.
(4) If a committal is made under this section in respect of an offence or offences—
   (a) section 6 applies accordingly, and
   (b) the committal operates as a committal of the defendant to be dealt with by the Crown Court in accordance with section 71.
(5) If a committal is made under this section in respect of an offence for which (apart from this section) the magistrates' court could have committed the defendant for sentence under section 3(2) of the Sentencing Act (offences triable either way) the court must state whether it would have done so.
(6) A committal under this section may be in custody or on bail.

Particular note should be made of s 70(5), with the court being invited to confirm that it would not otherwise have committed for sentence. Later clarification cannot be relied upon and it is therefore essential that a full contemporaneous note is taken (*R v Blakeburn* [2007] EWCA Crim 1803).

The process of appeal against conviction is complex when a case is committed under these provisons. It seems that such an appeal should be lodged within 21 days under the Criminal Procedure Rules Part 34(2)(b).

 See *Blackstone's Criminal Practice 2019* **E19**

D8 **Criminal Behaviour Orders**

D8.1 **Notice**

Criminal Procedure rule 31.3 requires prosecutors to give notice as soon as practicable, on a prescribed form, of their intention to apply for a criminal behaviour order (CBO). A defence lawyer should not feel pressurized into dealing with what can be a complex area of law without adequate notice.

D8.2 **Criteria**

Criminal behaviour orders are made following conviction.

Anti-social Behaviour Crime and Policing Act 2014, Pt 2, ss 22 and 25

22 Power to make orders

(1) This section applies where a person ('the offender') is convicted of an offence.

(2) The court may make a criminal behaviour order against the offender if two conditions are met.

(3) The first condition is that the court is satisfied, beyond reasonable doubt, that the offender has engaged in behaviour that caused or was likely to cause harassment, alarm or distress to any person.

(4) The second condition is that the court considers that making the order will help in preventing the offender from engaging in such behaviour.

(5) A criminal behaviour order is an order which, for the purpose of preventing the offender from engaging in such behaviour—
  (a) prohibits the offender from doing anything described in the order;
  (b) requires the offender to do anything described in the order.

(6) The court may make a criminal behaviour order against the offender only if it is made in addition to—
  (a) a sentence imposed in respect of the offence, or
  (b) an order discharging the offender conditionally.

(7) The court may make a criminal behaviour order against the offender only on the application of the prosecution.

(8) The prosecution must find out the views of the local youth offending team before applying for a criminal behaviour order to be made if the offender will be under the age of 18 when the application is made.

(9) Prohibitions and requirements in a criminal behaviour order must, so far as practicable, be such as to avoid—

  (a) any interference with the times, if any, at which the offender normally works or attends school or any other educational establishment;
  (b) any conflict with the requirements of any other court order or injunction to which the offender may be subject.

...

25 Duration of order etc

(1) A criminal behaviour order takes effect on the day it is made, subject to subsection (2).

---

(2) If on the day a criminal behaviour order ('the new order') is made the offender is subject to another criminal behaviour order ('the previous order'), the new order may be made so as to take effect on the day on which the previous order ceases to have effect.

(3) A criminal behaviour order must specify the period ('the order period') for which it has effect.

(4) In the case of a criminal behaviour order made before the offender has reached the age of 18, the order period must be a fixed period of—
   (a) not less than 1 year, and
   (b) not more than 3 years.

(5) In the case of a criminal behaviour order made after the offender has reached the age of 18, the order period must be—
   (a) a fixed period of not less than 2 years, or
   (b) an indefinite period (so that the order has effect until further order).

(6) A criminal behaviour order may specify periods for which particular prohibitions or requirements have effect.

D8.3 Relevant case law

DPP v Bulmer [2015] EWHC 2323 (Admin) confirms that there is no burden of proof as such. It is an evaluative exercise. However such orders are not to be lightly imposed. The issue is not one of pure discretion. Whilst the availability of positive requirements is important their absence does not mean that an order cannot be made. A failure to comply with past orders is a relevant consideration but not of itself a reason for refusing an order—variation of the existing order or imposition of a new one may assist. Any requirement must be proportionate and tailored to the specific circumstances. The ordinary power to arrest may not be sufficient, without an order, for the police to prevent anti-social behaviour in advance.

The earlier case law in relation to anti-social behaviour orders (ASBOs) has been adopted for CBOs by *R v Khan* [2018] EWCA Crim1472.. CBOs can impose positive as well as negative obligations and can apply to members of the same household.

Evidence of post-complaint behaviour is admissible to show whether a person has acted in an anti-social manner (and whether an order is necessary) (*Birmingham City Council v Dixon* [2009] EWHC 761 (Admin)).

That conduct was likely to cause harassment, alarm, or distress does not require evidence that the conduct was actually witnessed as long as there were people in the vicinity (street drug dealing) who were likely to see it, and thereby be caused harassment, etc (*R v Hashi* [2014] EWCA Crim 2119).

Many of the principles established in the leading case, *R v Boness* [2005] EWCA Crim 2395, and other cases (notably *R v P (Shane Tony)* [2004] EWCA Crim 287, *R v McGrath* [2005] EWCA Crim 353, and *W v Director of Public Prosecutions* [2005] EWCA Civ 1333), continue to apply to CBOs.

- The requirement that a prohibition was necessary (helpful) to protect persons from further anti-social acts by the defendant means that the use of an ASBO to punish a defendant is unlawful.

- Each separate prohibition must be targeted at the individual and the specific form of anti-social behaviour it is intended to prevent. The order must be tailored to the defendant and not designed on a word processor for generic use. Therefore the court must ask itself when considering a specific order, 'Is this order necessary (helpful) to protect persons in any place in England and Wales from further anti-social acts by the defendant?'

- Each prohibition must be precise and capable of being understood by the defendant. Therefore the court should ask itself before making an order: 'Are the terms of this order clear so that the defendant will know precisely what it is that he is prohibited from doing?' (So unfamiliar words like 'curtilage' and 'environs' should be avoided, as should vague ones like 'implement' or 'paraphernalia'.) For example, a prohibition should clearly delineate any exclusion zone by reference to a map and clearly identify those whom the defendant must not contact or associate with.

- The terms of the order must be proportionate in the sense that they must be commensurate with the risk to be guarded against. This is particularly important where an order may interfere with a Convention right protected by the Human Rights Act 1998, for example Articles 8, 10, and 11 ECHR.

- There is no requirement that the prohibited acts should by themselves give rise to harassment, alarm, or distress.

- An ASBO should not be used merely to increase the sentence of imprisonment which an offender is liable to receive.

- Different considerations may apply if the maximum sentence is only a fine, but the court must still go through all the steps to make sure that an ASBO is necessary (helpful).

The fact that an order prohibits a defendant from committing a specified criminal offence does not automatically invalidate it. However, the court should not make such an order if the sentence which could be passed following conviction for the offence would be a sufficient deterrent. In addition, the Court of Appeal has indicated that prohibiting behaviour that is in any event a crime does not necessarily address the aim of an ASBO, which is to prevent anti-social behaviour. The better course is to make an anticipatory form of order, namely an order which prevents a defendant from doing an act preparatory to the commission of the offence, thereby helping to prevent the criminal offence from being committed in the first place. For example, an order might prevent a defendant from entering a shopping centre rather than stealing from shops; or possessing a can of spray paint rather than causing criminal damage.

If a court wishes to make an order prohibiting a group of youngsters from racing cars or motorbikes on an estate or driving at excessive speed then the order should not (normally) prohibit driving whilst disqualified. It should prohibit, for example, the offender whilst on the estate from taking part in, or encouraging, racing or driving at an excessive speed. It might also prevent the group from congregating with named others in a particular area of the estate.

In *R (Cooke) v Director of Public Prosecutions* [2008] EWHC 2703 (Admin), the court held that an order was not appropriate in relation to an offender who due to mental incapacity was not able to understand its terms, as such an order would fail to protect the public and could therefore not be said to be necessary to protect others. It is suggested that this will apply all the more forcefully under the CBO regime as an order cannot help to prevent antisocial behaviour where the defendant does not understand its terms or his obligations.

A condition not to cause harassment, alarm, or distress was too imprecise; conditions had to be clear as to what behaviour the order was seeking to discourage (*Heron v Plymouth City Council* [2009] EWHC 3562 (Admin)).

D8.4 Alternative orders

The flexibility of CBOs has removed the need for orders such as those under the Licensed Premises (Exclusion of Certain Persons) Act 1980 when crimes involving violence occurred on licensed premises.

Knife Crime Prevention orders will be available, first in pilot areas, on the implementation of part 2 of the Offensive Weapons Act 2019.

 See *Blackstone's Criminal Practice 2019* **D25.1–D25.47**

D9 **Custodial Sentences**

D9.1 **Criteria**

Note: A sentencing decision flow chart appears inside the back cover.

The court must not pass a custodial sentence unless it is of the opinion that the offence, or the combination of the offence and one or more offences associated with it, was so serious that neither a fine alone nor a community sentence can be justified for the offence.

The Sentencing Council's definitive guideline on the imposition of community and custodial sentences sets out four questions for consideration:

(1) Has the custody threshold been passed?
(2) Is it unavoidable that a sentence of imprisonment be imposed?
(3) What is the shortest term commensurate with the seriousness of the offence?
(4) Can the sentence be suspended?

It confirms that:

- The clear intention of the threshold test is to reserve prison as a punishment for the most serious offences.
- Passing the custody threshold does not mean that a custodial sentence should be deemed inevitable.
- For offenders on the cusp of custody, imprisonment should not be imposed where there would be an impact on dependants which would make a custodial sentence disproportionate to achieving the aims of sentencing.
- Sentencers should be clear that they would impose an immediate custodial sentence if the power to suspend were not available (see **D31**).

Nothing prevents the court from passing a custodial sentence on the offender if:

- he fails to express his willingness to comply with a requirement which is proposed by the court to be included in a community order and which requires an expression of such willingness; or
- he fails to comply with an order under s 161(2) Criminal Justice Act 2003 (pre-sentence drug testing *when in force*).

The custodial sentence must be for the shortest term (not exceeding the permitted maximum) that in the opinion of the court is commensurate with the seriousness of the offence, or the combination of the offence and one or more offences associated with it.

D9.2 **Minima and maxima sentences**

Type of sentence	Age requirement	Notes
Detention in young offender institution	18–20 years	Minimum sentence of 21 days. Maximum 6 months for any one offence. Maximum 12 months for two or more either-way offences. Subject always to the statutory maximum for the offences in question **s 97 Powers of Criminal Courts (Sentencing) Act 2000** See **D14**
Imprisonment	21 years+	Minimum 5 days save for detention imposed under ss 135 and 136 Magistrates' Courts Act 1980. Maximum 6 months for any one offence. Maximum 12 months for two or more either-way offences. Subject always to the statutory maximum for the offences in question; **s 78 Powers of Criminal Courts (Sentencing) Act 2000 and s 133(2) Magistrates' Courts Act 2000**

 See *Blackstone's Criminal Practice 2019* **E2**

D10 **Dangerous Offenders**

D10.1 **Criteria**

Generally speaking, the dangerous offender provisions are of concern to the magistrates' court only when determining venue. The only sentence now available is an extended sentence, and this is available for those who commit a specified violent or sexual offence, where the court is of the opinion that 'there is a significant risk to members of the public of serious harm occasioned by the commission by him of further specified offences' (s 227 Criminal Justice Act (CJA) 2003). If new information becomes available during a summary trial, there is a residuary power to commit for sentence under these dangerous offender provisions (s 3A Powers of Criminal Courts (Sentencing) Act 2000).

D10.2 **Specified offences**

Specified offences are those listed in Sch 15 CJA 2003.

 See *Blackstone's Criminal Practice 2019* **D24.38–D24.41**

D11 Deferment of Sentence

D11.1 Criteria

The magistrates' court can defer sentence, on one occasion, for a maximum period of 6 months, to enable the court to assess the offender's capacity to change or carry out reparation to the victim. Such cases are simply adjourned (not on bail), and a warrant can be issued (s 1(7)(b) Powers of Criminal Courts (Sentencing) Act (PCC(S)A) 2000) if the offender fails to attend for sentence (the court also has the option of issuing a summons, and the court should be invited to try this option first). If the offender reoffends before the period of deferment has expired, he may be dealt with for the deferred matter.

The power to defer shall be exercisable only if:

- the offender consents;
- the offender undertakes to comply with any requirements as to his conduct during the period of the deferment that the court considers it appropriate to impose; and
- the court is satisfied, having regard to the nature of the offence and the character and circumstances of the offender, that it would be in the interests of justice to exercise the power.

D11.2 The legislative framework

Sections 1–1D PCC(S)A

D11.3 Sentencing Council: deferred sentences: definitive guideline on new sentences (Criminal Justice Act 2003), paragraphs 1.2.6–1.2.9

A deferred sentence enables the court to review the conduct of the defendant before passing sentence, having first prescribed certain requirements. It also provides several opportunities for an offender to have some influence as to the sentence passed—

(a) it tests the commitment of the offender not to re-offend;
(b) it gives the offender an opportunity to do something where progress can be shown within a short period;
(c) it provides the offender with an opportunity to behave or refrain from behaving in a particular way that will be relevant to sentence.

The decision to defer sentence should be predominantly for a small group of cases at either the custody threshold or the community sentence threshold, where the sentencer feels that there would be particular value in giving the offender the opportunities listed because, if the offender complies with the requirements, a different sentence will be justified at the end of the deferment period.

This could be a community sentence instead of a custodial sentence, or a fine or discharge instead of a community sentence. It may, rarely, enable a custodial sentence to be suspended rather than imposed immediately.

A court may impose any conditions during the period of deferment that it considers appropriate. These could be specific requirements as set out in the provisions for community sentences, or requirements that are drawn more widely. The requirements may include restorative justice requirements. These should be specific, measurable conditions so that the offender knows exactly what is required and the court can assess compliance; the restriction on liberty should be limited to ensure that the offender has a reasonable expectation of being able to comply whilst maintaining his or her social responsibilities.

Given the need for clarity in the mind of the offender and the possibility of sentence by another court, the court should give a clear indication (and make a written record) of the type of sentence it would be minded to impose if it had not decided to defer and ensure that the offender understands the consequences of failure to comply with the court's wishes during the deferral period.

 See *Blackstone's Criminal Practice 2019* **D20.103–D20.110**

D12 **Deprivation Order**

D12.1 **Criteria**

Orders of this kind should not be made without warning the defendant in advance and inviting representations, otherwise they are liable to be quashed on appeal (*R v Ball* [2002] EWCA Crim 2777). The court should not proceed without first ascertaining the value of the property, and should also ensure that an order made against just one offender does not result in an overly disproportionate sentence (*Ball*). Such an order will be invalid if the financial consequences and the value of the property have not been considered (*Trans Berckx BVBA v North Avon and Swindon Magistrates' Court* [2011] EWHC 2605 (Admin)).

The power can be used to deprive the defendant of their interest in property intended to be used for any offence, not just the particular offence before the court (*R v O'Farrell* [1988] Crim LR 387). Deprivation orders are intended only for straightforward cases involving unencumbered property (*R v Troth* [1980] Crim LR 249). In connection with child pornography the order should be proportionate in the particular circumstances (*R v Connelly* [2012] EWCA Crim 2049). An order may be made if, following proper procedures allowing the defendant and any relevant third party to give evidence, cash found at the home of a defendant convicted of drugs offences is identified as the proceeds of, or working capital for, drug dealing (*R v Rowan Jones* [2017] EWCA Crim 2192).

Powers of Criminal Courts (Sentencing) Act 2000, s 143

143 Powers to deprive offenders of property used etc for purposes of crime

(1) Where a person is convicted of an offence and the court by or before which he is convicted is satisfied that any property which has been lawfully seized from him, or which was in his possession or under his control at the time when he was apprehended for the offence or when a summons in respect of it was issued—
  (a) has been used for the purpose of committing, or facilitating the commission of, any offence, or
  (b) was intended by him to be used for that purpose, the court may (subject to subsection (5) below) make an order under this section in respect of that property.
(2) Where a person is convicted of an offence and the offence, or an offence which the court has taken into consideration in determining his sentence, consists of unlawful possession of property which—
  (a) has been lawfully seized from him, or
  (b) was in his possession or under his control at the time when he was apprehended for the offence of which he has been convicted or when a summons in respect of that offence was issued, the court may (subject to subsection (5) below) make an order under this section in respect of that property.
(3) An order under this section shall operate to deprive the offender of his rights, if any, in the property to which it relates, and the property shall (if not already in their possession) be taken into the possession of the police ...

(5) In considering whether to make an order under this section in respect of any property, a court shall have regard—

    (a) to the value of the property; and

    (b) to the likely financial and other effects on the offender of the making of the
order (taken together with any other order that the court contemplates making).

(6) Where a person commits an offence to which this subsection applies by—

    (a) driving, attempting to drive, or being in charge of a vehicle, or

    (b) failing to comply with a requirement made under section 7 or 7A of the Road
Traffic Act 1988 (failure to provide specimen for analysis or laboratory test or to
give permission for such a test) in the course of an investigation into whether the
offender had committed an offence while driving, attempting to drive or being
in charge of a vehicle, or

    (c) failing, as the driver of a vehicle, to comply with subsection (2) or (3) of section
170 of the Road Traffic Act 1988 (duty to stop and give information or report
accident),

the vehicle shall be regarded for the purposes of subsection (1) above (and section
144(1)(b) below) as used for the purpose of committing the offence (and for the
purpose of committing any offence of aiding, abetting, counselling or procuring the
commission of the offence).

(7) Subsection (6) above applies to—

    (a) an offence under the Road Traffic Act 1988 which is punishable with
imprisonment;

    (b) an offence of manslaughter; and

    (c) an offence under section 35 of the Offences Against the Person Act 1861
(wanton and furious driving).

  See *Blackstone's Criminal Practice 2019* **E18**

D13 Detention in Young Offender Institution

D13.1 Criteria

The general requirements for the imposition of a custodial sentence (see **D9**) must be met. A minimum sentence of 21 days must be imposed.

A suspended sentence order (see **D31**) may be imposed.

D13.2 Breach of YOI licence

A new application for legal aid may be made under s 14(b) Legal Aid Sentencing and Punishment of Offenders Act 2012.

Section 256C Criminal Justice Act 2003 provides:

Criminal Justice Act 2003, s 256C

256C(4) Breach of supervision requirements

(4) If it is proved to the satisfaction of the court that the offender has failed to comply with requirements under section 256B(6) (the supervision requirements), the court may—

    (a) order the offender to be detained, in prison or such youth detention accommodation as the Secretary of State may determine, for such period, not exceeding 30 days, as the court may specify, or

    (b) impose on the offender a fine not exceeding level 3 on the standard scale.

If returned to custody the offender serves the whole of the period involved and the supervision period is reduced by the time served.

 See *Blackstone's Criminal Practice 2019* **E7.4**

D14 Discharges

Conditional and Absolute

D14.1 Criteria

A discharge can be imposed where it is inexpedient to inflict any punishment. A conditional discharge can be for up to three years. Only the orders mentioned in s 12(7) Powers of Criminal Courts (Sentencing) Act 2000 can be made alongside a discharge, but a magistrates' court may commit an offender to the Crown Court for the purposes of activating the confiscation regime under the Proceeds of Crime Act 2002 even where a discharge is considered the proper sentence (*R v Varma* [2012] UKSC 42). Thus, ancillary orders may be made including disqualifications but a discharge may not be linked, for a single offence, with a fine, community order, or custodial sentence.

> **Powers of Criminal Courts (Sentencing) Act 2000, s 12(7)**
>
> **12 Absolute and conditional discharge**
>
> (7) Nothing in this section shall be construed as preventing a court, on discharging an offender absolutely or conditionally in respect of any offence, from making an order for costs against the offender or imposing any disqualification on him or from making in respect of the offence an order under section 130, 143 or 148 below (compensation orders, deprivation orders and restitution orders).

Where a person who has received a youth caution is convicted of an offence committed within 2 years of the caution, the court by or before which he is so convicted:

- shall not impose a conditional discharge in respect of the offence unless it is of the opinion that there are exceptional circumstances relating to the offence or the offender which justify its doing so; and
- where it does so, shall state in open court that it is of that opinion and why it is.

A person convicted of breaching a Criminal Behaviour Order may not receive a conditional discharge (s 30(3) Anti-social Behaviour Crime and Policing Act 2014). The same rule applies to those who breach a Sexual Harm Prevention Order (s 103I(4) Sexual Offences Act 2003; a Sexual Risk Order (s 122H(4));breach a Slavery and Trafficking Protection or Risk Order (s 30(4) Modern Slavery Act 2015); breach of a stalking protection order (s 3 Stalking Protection Act 2019); *or for breach of a knife crime prevention order (s29(4) Offensive Weapons Act 2019)*.

If a person commits an offence during the life of a conditional discharge, he may be resentenced for that original offence even if the period of discharge has expired at the date of sentence. The offender will be sentenced with reference to his age at the date of resentence, not the date of the previous offence, and can be sentenced in any way as if he had just been convicted of the offence. If the conditional discharge was imposed by the Crown Court, the offender may be committed to that court for resentence.

There is no requirement to resentence, and a court could sentence for a new offence and leave the conditional discharge in place if it saw fit to do so.

 See *Blackstone's Criminal Practice 2019* **E12**

D15 Discounts for Early Plea

The Sentencing Council has issued a guideline that is now the key point of reference.

D15.1 Criteria

A court must discount a sentence in return for a guilty plea. A magistrates' court may impose a maximum sentence as an alternative to committing the case for sentence to the Crown Court. A full discount must be given even if the prosecution case is overwhelming. The amount of discount will depend upon the timing of the plea. A one-third reduction is only available, subject to exceptions, when a guilty plea is indicated at the first hearing whether the case proceeds in the magistrates' or Crown court. Thereafter the maximum is one-quarter, reducing to 10 per cent if the plea is entered at the time of trial. The discount is separate from any other reduction, for instance for remorse, which should be taken in to account before the discount for guilty plea is applied:

> The reduction has no impact on sentencing decisions in relation to ancillary orders, including disqualification.

B. KEY PRINCIPLES ...

Factors such as admissions at interview, co-operation with the investigation and demonstrations of remorse should not be taken into account in determining the level of reduction. Rather, they should be considered separately and prior to any guilty plea reduction, as potential mitigating factors.

D. DETERMINING THE LEVEL OF REDUCTION

The maximum level of reduction in sentence for a guilty plea is one-third

D1. Plea indicated at the first stage of the proceedings

Where a guilty plea is indicated at the first stage of proceedings a reduction of one-third should be made (subject to the exceptions in section F). The first stage will normally be the first hearing at which a plea or indication of plea is sought and recorded by the court.

D2. Plea indicated after the first stage of proceedings – maximum one quarter –sliding scale of reduction thereafter

After the first stage of the proceedings the maximum level of reduction is one-quarter (subject to the exceptions in section F).

The reduction should be decreased from one-quarter to a maximum of one-tenth on the first day of trial having regard to the time when the guilty plea is first indicated to the court relative to the progress of the case and the trial date (subject to the exceptions in section F). The reduction should normally be decreased further, even to zero, if the guilty plea is entered during the course of the trial.

For the purposes of this guideline a trial will be deemed to have started when pre-recorded cross-examination has begun.

Note: In cases where (in accordance with the Criminal Procedure Rules) a defendant is given the opportunity to enter a guilty plea without attending a court hearing, doing so within the required time limits will constitute a plea at the first stage of proceedings.

E. APPLYING THE REDUCTION

E1. Imposing one type of sentence rather than another

The reduction in sentence for a guilty plea can be taken into account by imposing one type of sentence rather than another; for example:

by reducing a custodial sentence to a community sentence, or by reducing a community sentence to a fine.

Where a court has imposed one sentence rather than another to reflect the guilty plea there should normally be no further reduction on account of the guilty plea. Where, however, the less severe type of sentence is justified by other factors, the appropriate reduction for the plea should be applied in the normal way.

E2. More than one summary offence

When dealing with more than one summary offence, the aggregate sentence is limited to a maximum of six months. Allowing for a reduction for each guilty plea, consecutive sentences might result in the imposition of the maximum six-month sentence. Where this is the case, the court may make a modest additional reduction to the overall sentence to reflect the benefits derived from the guilty pleas.

E3. Keeping an either way case in the magistrates' court to reflect a guilty plea

Reducing a custodial sentence to reflect a guilty plea may enable a magistrates' court to retain jurisdiction of an either way offence rather than committing the case for sentence to the Crown Court.

In such cases a magistrates' court should apply the appropriate reduction to the sentence for the offence(s) arrived at in accordance with any offence specific sentencing guideline and if the resulting sentence is then within its jurisdiction it should go on to sentence.

F. EXCEPTIONS

F1. Further information, assistance or advice necessary before indicating plea

Where the sentencing court is satisfied that there were particular circumstances which significantly reduced the defendant's ability to understand what was alleged or otherwise made it unreasonable to expect the defendant to indicate a guilty plea sooner than was done, a reduction of one-third should still be made.

In considering whether this exception applies, sentencers should distinguish between cases in which it is necessary to receive advice and/or have sight of evidence in order to understand whether the defendant is in fact and law guilty of the offence(s) charged, and cases in which a defendant merely delays guilty plea(s) in order to assess the strength of the prosecution evidence and the prospects of conviction or acquittal.

F2. Newton hearings and special reasons hearings

In circumstances where an offender's version of events is rejected at a Newton hearing or special reasons hearing, the reduction which would have been available at the stage of proceedings the plea was indicated should normally be halved. Where witnesses are called during such a hearing, it may be appropriate further to decrease the reduction.

F3. Offender convicted of a lesser or different offence

If an offender is convicted of a lesser or different offence from that originally charged, and has earlier made an unequivocal indication of a guilty plea to this lesser or different offence to the prosecution and the court, the court should give the level of reduction that is appropriate to the stage in the proceedings at which this indication of plea (to the lesser or different offence) was made taking into account any other of these exceptions that apply. In the Crown Court where the offered plea is a permissible alternative on the indictment as charged, the offender will not be treated as having made an unequivocal indication unless the offender has entered that plea.

F4. Minimum sentence under section 51A of the Firearms Act 1968

There can be no reduction for a guilty plea if the effect of doing so would be to reduce the length of sentence below the required minimum term.

F5. Appropriate custodial sentences for persons aged 18 or over when convicted under the Prevention of Crime Act 1953 and Criminal Justice Act 1988 and prescribed custodial sentences under the Power of Criminal Courts (Sentencing) Act 2000

In circumstances where:

an appropriate custodial sentence of at least six months falls to be imposed on a person aged 18 or over who has been convicted under sections 1 or 1A of the Prevention of Crime Act 1953; or sections 139, 139AA or 139A of the Criminal Justice Act 1988 (certain possession of knives or offensive weapon offences) or a prescribed custodial sentence falls to be imposed under section 110 of the Powers of Criminal Courts (Sentencing) Act 2000 (drug trafficking offences) or section 111 of the Powers of Criminal Courts (Sentencing) Act 2000 (burglary offences).

the court may impose any sentence in accordance with this guideline which is not less than 80 per cent of the appropriate or prescribed custodial period.

D15.1.1 *Case law decisions*

A 25 per cent discount was appropriate where the defence awaited medical evidence as to fitness to plead but had made no admissions about the evidence and had not raised that issue on the better case management (BCM) form in the magistrates' court (*R v Clarke* [2018] EWCA Crim1845). An indication that there is likely to be a guilty plea, on a basis, is not enough to earn a full discount (*R v Davis* [2019] EWCA Crim 553) but an indication of a guilty plea to an indictable-only offence on a BCM form, at the sending of the case, is sufficient (*R v Hewison* [2019] EWCA Crim 1278).

R v Joy [2014] EWCA Crim 2321 confirmed that the fact that on charge the defendant had said not guilty was not a relevant factor. Whilst the number of similar previous convictions goes to seriousness and so the sentence to be imposed, it cannot impact on the discount for guilty plea (*R v Darkwa* [2015] EWCA Crim 260).

In *R v Butt* [2017] EWCA Crim 352, where the defendant had seen initial details of the prosecution case and, at the police station, the CCTV, discount was lost when he delayed so that defence lawyers could view the CCTV. Not having seen the body worn video is not a reason to preserve the discount until it has been viewed (*R v Powlett* [2019] EWCA Crim 440). Admissions in interview but a not guilty indication on the BCM form at sending, will result in only a 25 per cent discount if the plea is entered at the plea and trial preparation hearing. It was not entered at the first opportunity. The admission may however add other mitigation such as remorse (*R v Price* [2018] EWCA Crim1784).

D16 **Disqualification from Driving**

D16.1 **Criteria**

Disqualification (or in the fifth example, a revocation) may arise in one of five ways:

(1) Offence carrying obligatory disqualification (see **D16.4**).
(2) Offence carrying discretionary disqualification (see **D16.6**).
(3) As a result of accumulating 12 or more penalty points (see **D16.7**).
(4) As a result of conviction for any offence, or an offence where a vehicle was used for crime (ss 146 and 147 Powers of Criminal Courts (Sentencing) Act (PCC(S)A) 2000) (see **D16.9**).
(5) As a result of a 'new driver' accumulating six penalty points (see **D16.10**)

If a mandatory disqualification is imposed then the licence should be endorsed but not with any penalty points. Section 44(1) Road Traffic Offenders Act (RTOA) 1988 (*R v Usaceva* [2015] EWCA Crim 166). Section 39 RTOA 1988 allows for applications to suspend a disqualification pending appeal.

D16.2 **Interim disqualification**

An interim disqualification can be imposed when the court commits an offender for sentence to the Crown Court, remits the case to another court, or defers or adjourns sentence (s 26 RTOA 1988). More than one interim disqualification may be imposed, but the total term must not exceed 6 months. An interim disqualification should not be imposed when the length of the disqualification will be extended because an immediate prison sentence will be imposed (*R v Needham and others* [2016] EWCA Crim 455 below).

 See *Blackstone's Criminal Practice 2019* **C7.11**

D16.3 **Disqualification with an immediate custodial sentence**

A period of disqualification has to be extended by the time actually served in custody in accordance with ss 35A and 35B RTOA 1988.

Road Traffic Offenders Act 1988, ss 35A and 35B

35A Extension of disqualification where custodial sentence also imposed

(1) This section applies where a person is convicted in England and Wales of an offence for which the court—
   (a) imposes a custodial sentence, and
   (b) orders the person to be disqualified under section 34 or 35.
(2) The order under section 34 or 35 must provide for the person to be disqualified for the appropriate extension period, in addition to the discretionary disqualification period.
(3) The discretionary disqualification period is the period for which, in the absence of this section, the court would have disqualified the person under section 34 or 35.

---

(4) The appropriate extension period is—

...

(h) a period equal to half the custodial sentence imposed ...

(5) If a period determined under subsection (4) includes a fraction of a day, that period is to be rounded up to the nearest number of whole days.

(6) This section does not apply where—

(a) the custodial sentence was a suspended sentence.

35B Effect of custodial sentence in other cases

(1) This section applies where a person is convicted in England and Wales of an offence for which a court proposes to order the person to be disqualified under section 34 or 35 and—

(a) the court proposes to impose on the person a custodial sentence (other than a suspended sentence) for another offence, or

(b) at the time of sentencing for the offence, a custodial sentence imposed on the person on an earlier occasion has not expired.

(2) In determining the period for which the person is to be disqualified under section 34 or 35, the court must have regard to the consideration in subsection (3) if and to the extent that it is appropriate to do so.

(3) The consideration is the diminished effect of disqualification as a distinct punishment if the person who is disqualified is also detained in pursuance of a custodial sentence.

(4) If the court proposes to order the person to be disqualified under section 34 or 35 and to impose a custodial sentence for the same offence, the court may not in relation to that disqualification take that custodial sentence into account for the purposes of subsection (2).

Similar provisions apply where the sentence is imposed under s 146 or 147 PCC(S)A 2000.

These provisions were given detailed consideration in *R v Needham and others* [2016] EWCA Crim 455 which offered the following staged guidance:

Step 1—Does the court intend to impose a 'discretionary' disqualification under section 34 or section 35 for any offence?

YES—go to step 2

Step 2—Does the court intend to impose a custodial term for that same offence?

YES—section 35A applies and the court must impose an extension period (see section 35A(4)(h) for that same offence and consider step 3.

NO—section 35A does not apply at all—go on to consider section 35B and step 4

Step 3—Does the court intend to impose a custodial term for another offence (which is longer or consecutive) or is the defendant already serving a custodial sentence?

YES—then consider what increase ('uplift') in the period of 'discretionary disqualification' is required to comply with section 35B(2) and (3). In accordance with section 35B(4) ignore any custodial term imposed for an offence involving disqualification under section 35A.

Discretionary period + extension period + uplift = total period of disqualification

NO—no need to consider section 35B at all

Discretionary period + extension period = total period of disqualification

Step 4—Does the court intend to impose a custodial term for another offence or is the defendant already serving a custodial sentence?

YES—then consider what increase ('uplift') in the period of 'discretionary disqualification' is required to comply with section 35B(2) and (3).

Discretionary period + uplift = total period of disqualification

The total length of the disqualification should be reduced to allow for the time spent on remand (*R v Gregory* [2017] EWCA Crim 2045; *R v Mascarenas*. [2018] EWCA Crim 1467).

D16.4 Obligatory disqualification

Where a person is convicted of an offence involving obligatory disqualification, the court must order him to be disqualified for such period not less than 12 months as the court thinks fit, unless the court for special reasons (see **D16.5**) thinks fit to order him to be disqualified for a shorter period or not to order him to be disqualified at all (s 34 RTOA 1988).

A person disqualified for dangerous driving must also be ordered to undertake an extended driving test.

A mandatory disqualification does not have the effect of removing any penalty points existing on the licence.

There are certain exceptions to the minimum 12-month period that are applicable to those sentenced in the magistrates' court, as set out in **D16.4.1–D16.4.3**.

D16.4.1 *Minimum three-year disqualification*

A minimum 3-year disqualification follows where, within the 10 years immediately preceding the commission of the offence, a person has been convicted of any such offence, and is again convicted of an offence under any of the following provisions of the Road Traffic Act 1988, that is:

- s 3A (causing death by careless driving when under the influence of drink or drugs);
- s 4(1) (driving or attempting to drive while unfit);
- s 5(1)(a) (driving or attempting to drive with excess alcohol);
- s 7(6) (failing to provide a specimen) where that is an offence involving obligatory disqualification;
- s 7A(6) (failing to allow a specimen to be subjected to laboratory test) where that is an offence involving obligatory disqualification.

D16.4.2 *Minimum 2-year disqualification*

A minimum 2-year disqualification follows in relation to a person on whom more than one disqualification for a fixed period of 56 days or more has been imposed within the three years immediately preceding the commission of the offence.

D16.4.3 *Minimum 6-months' disqualification*

A minimum 6-months' disqualification follows where a person convicted of an offence under s 40A of the Road Traffic Act 1988 (using vehicle in dangerous condition, etc) has, within the 3 years immediately preceding the commission of the offence, been convicted of any such offence.

D16.5 Special reasons

There is no statutory definition of 'special reasons', but it must not amount to a defence in law, must be directly connected with the offence in question (not the offender), and must be a mitigating or extenuating circumstance. The burden (civil standard) falls on the defendant. Good character, personal service to the community (eg being a doctor), financial hardship as a result of a disqualification, and the fact the offence was not particularly serious have all been held not to amount to special reasons.

It should be noted that under the guideline on discount for guilty plea, in circumstances where an offender's version of events is rejected at a special reasons hearing, the reduction which would have been available at the stage of proceedings the plea was indicated should normally be halved. Where witnesses are called during such a hearing, it may be appropriate further to decrease the reduction.

An ignorance of the terms of motor insurance cannot generally amount to special reasons (*Rennison v Knowler* [1947] 1 All ER 302), unless the person was misled or there is a particularly good reason for the ignorance (eg illness, confusion brought about by others).

If special reasons are found, the court has a discretion not to endorse points, and to reduce or not impose a mandatory period of disqualification. Note, however, that for an offence involving mandatory disqualification, where special reasons are found and the court does not disqualify, it must impose points, unless it finds special reasons also for not doing so.

Common special reasons are:

- spiked drinks or mistake as to item drunk;
- shortness of distance driven;
- medical or other emergencies.

In *Warring-Davies v Director of Public Prosecutions* [2009] EWHC 1172 (Admin), the court emphasized the need to find a causal link between any alleged medical condition and the driving in question.

In *Director of Public Prosecutions v Harrison* [2007] EWHC 556 (Admin), the court held it wrong to find special reasons where a drunken person drove 446 yards in order to find youths who had harassed him earlier.

In *Director of Public Prosecutions v Oram* [2005] EWHC 964 (Admin), the court held that special reasons would not be arguable to a drunk driver who relied upon shortness of distance driven alone.

Taylor v Rajan [1974] RTR 304 deals with the principles involved in 'emergency' cases:

> This is not the first case in which the court has had to consider whether driving in an emergency could justify a conclusion that there are special reasons for not disqualifying the driver. If a man, in the well-founded belief that he will not drive

again, puts his car in the garage, goes into his house and has a certain amount to drink in the belief that he is not going to drive again, and if thereafter is an emergency which requires him in order to deal with it to take his car out despite his intention to leave it in the garage, then that is a situation which can in law amount to a special reason for not disqualifying a driver. On the other hand, Justices who are primarily concerned with dealing with this legislation should approach the exercise of the resulting discretion with great care. The mere fact that the facts disclose a special reason does not mean that the driver is to escape disqualification as a matter of course. There is a very serious burden upon the Justices, even when a special reason has been disclosed, to decide whether in their discretion they should decline to disqualify a particular case. The Justices should have very much in mind that if a man deliberately drives when he knows he has consumed a considerable quantity of drink, he presents a potential source of danger to the public which no private crisis can likely excuse. One of the most important matters which Justices have to consider in the exercise of this discretion is whether the emergency (and I call it such for want of a more convenient word) was sufficiently acute to justify the driver taking his car out. The Justices should only exercise a discretion in favour of the driver in clear and compelling circumstances ... The Justices therefore must consider the whole of the circumstances. They must consider the nature and degree of the crisis or emergency which has caused the defendant to take the car out. They must consider with particular care whether there were alternative means of transport or methods of dealing with the crisis other than and alternative to the use by the defendant of his own car. They should have regard to the manner in which the defendant drove ... and they should generally have regard to whether the defendant acted responsibly or otherwise ... The matter must be considered objectively and the quality and gravity of the crisis must be assessed in that way. Last, but by no means least, if the alcohol content in the defendant's blood and body is very high, that is a powerful reason for saying that the discretion should not be exercised in his favour. Indeed, if the alcohol content exceeds 100 milligrammes per hundred millilitres of blood, the Justices should rarely, if ever, exercise this discretion in favour of the defendant driver....

In *DPP v Heathcote* [2011] EWHC 2536 (Admin), it was held that in deciding whether an 'emergency' justified driving, the court should ask whether a sober, reasonable, and responsible friend would have advised the defendant to drive. Relevant factors included:

- amount drunk;
- threat to others;
- state of the roads;
- distance to be driven;
- nature of the emergency;
- what alternatives were available.

The court confirmed that the use of an emergency as a special reason was not limited to life and limb cases; but, on the facts, to chase the thieves of a relative's car was not acceptable.

Chatters v Burke [1986] 3 All ER 168 details the seven factors relevant to a 'shortness of distance driven' argument:

- distance;
- manner of driving;
- state of the vehicle;
- whether there was an intention to drive further;

- road and traffic conditions;
- possibility of danger to road users and pedestrians;
- reason for the driving.

In order to establish a spiked drinks defence, it will be necessary to prove that the drink was laced, that the defendant did not know it was laced, and that but for the lacing of the drink his alcohol level would not have exceeded the legal limit. It will normally be necessary to call expert evidence in relation to the last point. The higher the reading, the less likely it is that a defendant will be able to prove he had no knowledge. If a court is of the view that the defendant ought to have realized his drink was spiked, it will not find special reasons (*Pridige v Grant* [1985] RTR 196).

McCormick and Hitchins [1988] RTR 182 held that special reasons could be available not to endorse points, where the allegation was of failing to provide a specimen when in charge, if the court was satisfied there was no intention to drive and that the defendant could not have been a danger on the road.

 See *Blackstone's Criminal Practice 2019* **C7.8** and **C7.55**

D16.6 Discretionary disqualification

Where an offence carries discretionary disqualification, the court must consider disqualification before it considers the imposition of penalty points. This is the case even if the offender would be liable to disqualification under the 'totting-up' provisions.

Practitioners will consider the tactical considerations of inviting a court to impose a discretionary disqualification as opposed to points that could trigger a totting-up disqualification. The benefit of a discretionary disqualification is that it can be for as short a period as the court directs; the negative side is that any previous points remain on the licence. If a totting-up disqualification were imposed, all the points would be removed but the defendant would face a minimum six-month period of disqualification. This applies only if the court is minded to impose a shorter period, as a defendant may prefer to tot up and clear his licence after a 6-month disqualification, rather than have, say, 4 months disqualified and still have the existing points hanging over him. If a court disqualifies then no additional penalty points are imposed. The period of disqualification can be for any period the court thinks proper.

D16.7 As a result of accumulating 12 or more penalty points

Under s 35 RTOA 1988 (see **D16.8**), if a driver has accumulated 12 or more points on his licence, the court must order him to be disqualified for not less than the minimum period, unless it is satisfied, having regard to all the circumstances, that there are grounds for disqualifying him for a shorter period or not to disqualify him. In calculating the points on the licence ('totting up'), the court will have regard to:

- the points to be imposed for the new offence, and
- any points on the licence for offences committed no longer than three years from the date of commission of the new offence (therefore, points run from the date of the old offence to the date of new offence) (s 29 RTOA 1988).

If there has been in the 3-year period a disqualification under the totting-up provisions, then points imposed prior to that disqualification would be disregarded.

The minimum period of disqualification is:

- 6 months if no previous disqualification;
- 12 months if one previous disqualification (for 56 days or more);
- 2 years if two or more previous disqualifications (for 56 days or more).

The previous disqualifications must have been imposed within 3 years of the date of the new offence to count.

D16.8 Mitigating circumstances

'Mitigating circumstances' may be argued in order to escape disqualification as a result of totting-up (see **D16.7**).

Section 35 RTOA 1988 provides:

Road Traffic Offenders Act 1988, s 35

35 Disqualification for repeated offences

(1) Where—
  (a) a person is convicted of an offence to which this subsection applies, and
  (b) the penalty points to be taken into account on that occasion number twelve or more,
  the court must order him to be disqualified for not less than the minimum period unless the court is satisfied, having regard to all the circumstances, that there are grounds for mitigating the normal consequences of the conviction and thinks fit to order him to be disqualified for a shorter period or not to order him to be disqualified.
(1A) Subsection (1) above applies to—
  (a) an offence involving discretionary disqualification and obligatory endorsement, and
  (b) an offence involving obligatory disqualification in respect of which no order is made under section 34 of this Act.
(2) The minimum period referred to in subsection (1) above is—
  (a) six months if no previous disqualification imposed on the offender is to be taken into account, and
  (b) one year if one, and two years if more than one, such disqualification is to be taken into account;
  and a previous disqualification imposed on an offender is to be taken into account if it was for a fixed period of 56 days or more and was imposed within the three years immediately preceding the commission of the latest offence in respect of which penalty points are taken into account under section 29 of this Act.
(3) Where an offender is convicted on the same occasion of more than one offence to which subsection (1) above applies—

(a) not more than one disqualification shall be imposed on him under subsection (1) above,

(b) in determining the period of the disqualification the court must take into account all the offences, and

(c) for the purposes of any appeal any disqualification imposed under subsection (1) above shall be treated as an order made on the conviction of each of the offences.

(4) No account is to be taken under subsection (1) above of any of the following circumstances—

(a) any circumstances that are alleged to make the offence or any of the offences not a serious one,

(b) hardship, other than exceptional hardship, or

(c) any circumstances which, within the three years immediately preceding the conviction, have been taken into account under that subsection in ordering the offender to be disqualified for a shorter period or not ordering him to be disqualified.

(5) References in this section to disqualification do not include a disqualification imposed under section 26 of this Act or section 147 of the Powers of Criminal Courts (Sentencing) Act 2000 or section 223A or 436A of the Criminal Procedure (Scotland) Act 1975 (offences committed by using vehicles) or a disqualification imposed in respect of an offence of stealing a motor vehicle, an offence under section 12 or 25 of the Theft Act 1968, an offence under section 178 of the Road Traffic Act 1988, or an attempt to commit such an offence.

(5A) The preceding provisions of this section shall apply in relation to a conviction of an offence committed by aiding, abetting, counselling, procuring, or inciting to the commission of, an offence involving obligatory disqualification as if the offence were an offence involving discretionary disqualification.

The burden of establishing mitigating circumstances is on the defendant; and those circumstances will generally need to be proved by way of evidence as opposed to submission. If hardship is argued as a mitigating circumstance it must be exceptional but hardship is not a prerequisite for finding mitigating circumstances in all the circumstances of a particular case (*R v Preston* [1986] RTR 136).

 See *Blackstone's Criminal Practice 2019* **C7.28**

D16.9 As a result of conviction for any offence, or an offence where a vehicle was used for crime

Section 146 PCC(S)A 2000 gives a court the power to disqualify an offender from holding a driving licence following a conviction for any offence. There need be no nexus between driving and the offence in question, and nothing additional should be written into the statute over and above what is already present; this allows a court to use the provision whenever it feels it to be appropriate in all of the circumstances (*R v Sofekun* [2008] EWCA Crim 2035).

Section 147 PCC(S)A 2000 gives courts a narrower power to disqualify where a motor vehicle was involved in the commission of the offence. In the magistrates' court the power is limited solely to the offences of assault:

Powers of Criminal Courts (Sentencing) Act 2000, s 147(1) and (3)

147 Driving disqualification when vehicle used for purposes of crime

(1) This section ... applies where a person is convicted by or before any court of common assault or of any other offence involving an assault (including an offence of aiding, abetting, counselling or procuring, or inciting to the commission of, an offence).

(2) ...

(3) If, in a case to which this section applies by virtue of subsection (2) above, the court is satisfied that the assault was committed by driving a motor vehicle, the court may order the person convicted to be disqualified, for such period as the court thinks fit, for holding or obtaining a driving licence.

 See *Blackstone's Criminal Practice 2019* **E21.11** and **E21.12**

D16.10 Road Traffic (New Drivers) Act 1995

Newly qualified drivers are subject to a 2-year probationary period. If at any time during that period the points to be endorsed on a driving licence amount to six or more, the licence will be automatically revoked. The relevant date is the date of offence not conviction, so revocation cannot be avoided by delaying court proceedings.

In appropriate cases, advocates may seek to invite courts to disqualify instead of endorse points, in order to try to avoid the draconian consequences of accumulating six or more penalty points.

 See *Blackstone's Criminal Practice 2019* **C7.44**

D16.11 Disqualification in the offender's absence

Section 11(4) Magistrates' Courts Act 1980 provides that there can be no disqualification in absence except on the resumption of a hearing after adjournment. Disqualification should not be imposed in absence where there is evidence that the defendant has an acceptable reason for not attending or where there are reasons to believe it would be contrary to the interests of justice to do so.

D16.12 Return of driving licence

D16.12.1 *Overview*

Section 42 RTOA 1988 and r 29(2) Crim PR provide for a disqualified driver to apply to the court for the return of his driving licence, prior to the expiry of the disqualification period. These proceedings may be funded at the magistrates' court by way of a means-tested representation order.

Period of disqualification	Minimum period of disqualification that must have elapsed before court can consider an application
Less than 4 years	2 years
4 years, but less than 10 years	One half of the disqualification period
10 years or more	5 years

If a disqualification is imposed by virtue of s 36(1) of the Act (disqualification until test is passed), there is no power to return a licence under s 43.

D16.12.2 *Criteria to be applied*

On any such application the court may, as it thinks proper having regard to:

- the character of the person disqualified and his conduct subsequent to the order;
- the nature of the offence; and
- any other circumstances of the case,

either by order remove the disqualification as from such date as may be specified in the order, or refuse the application.

D16.12.3 *Further application following refusal*

Where an application is refused, a further application shall not be entertained if made within three months after the date of the refusal.

 See *Blackstone's Criminal Practice 2019* **C7.42**

D17 Fines

D17.1 Criteria

Maximum fine levels

For offences committed on or after 12 March 2015 there is no upper limit to the level of fine at Level 5 that may be imposed in a magistrates' court. The Legal Aid Sentencing and Punishment of Offenders Act 2012 (Fines on summary conviction) Regulations 2015 contain detailed exceptions to this rule. The Criminal Practice Direction XIII Annex 3 contains provisions requiring certain serious offences to be identified by the Crown so that an authorized district judge may be appointed to deal with the case.

Fine band starting points and ranges; fine levels

These appear inside the front cover of this edition.

The Magistrates' Court Sentencing Guideline contains the following guidance:

Approach to the assessment of fines—introduction

The amount of a fine must reflect the seriousness of the offence (Criminal Justice Act ('CJA') 2003, s 164(2)).

The court must also take into account the financial circumstances of the offender; this applies whether it has the effect of increasing or reducing the fine (CJA 2003, s164(3) and 164(4)).

The aim is for the fine to have an equal impact on offenders with different financial circumstances; it should be a hardship but should not force the offender below a reasonable 'subsistence' level. Normally a fine should be of an amount that is capable of being paid within 12 months though there may be exceptions to this.

The guidance in this section aims to establish a clear, consistent and principled approach to the assessment of fines that will apply fairly in the majority of cases. However, it is impossible to anticipate every situation that may be encountered and in each case the court will need to exercise its judgement to ensure that the fine properly reflects the seriousness of the offence and takes into account the financial circumstances of the offender.

Definition of relevant weekly income

The seriousness of an offence determines the choice of fine band and the position of the offence within the range for that band. The offender's financial circumstances are taken into account by expressing that position as a proportion of the offender's relevant weekly income.

Where:

- an offender is in receipt of income from employment or is self- employed **and**
- that income is more than £120 per week after deduction of tax and national insurance (or equivalent where the offender is self-employed),— the actual income is the relevant weekly income.

Where:

- an offender's only source of income is state benefit (including where there is relatively low additional income as permitted by the benefit regulations), or

---

- the offender is in receipt of income from employment or is self-employed but the amount of income after deduction of tax and national insurance is £120 per week or less,

the relevant weekly income is deemed to be £120.

Additional information about the basis for this approach is set out in Approach to offenders on low income.

In calculating relevant weekly income no account should be taken of tax credits, housing benefit, child benefit or similar.

No reliable information

Where an offender has failed to provide information, or the court is not satisfied that it has been given sufficient reliable information, it is entitled to make such determination as it thinks fit regarding the financial circumstances of the offender (CJA 2003, s 164(5)). Any determination should be clearly stated on the court records for use in any subsequent variation or enforcement proceedings. In such cases, a record should also be made of the applicable fine band and the court's assessment of the position of the offence within that band based on the seriousness of the offence.

Where there is no information on which a determination can be made, the court should proceed on the basis of an assumed relevant weekly income of £440. This is derived from national median pre-tax earnings;* a gross figure is used as, in the absence of financial information from the offender, it is not possible to calculate appropriate deductions.

Where there is some information that tends to suggest a significantly lower or higher income than the recommended £440 default sum, the court should make a determination based on that information.

A court is empowered to remit a fine in whole or part if the offender subsequently provides information as to means (CJA 2003, s 165(2)). The assessment of offence seriousness and, therefore, the appropriate fine band and the position of the offence within that band are not affected by the provision of this information.* (This figure is a projected estimate based upon the 2012–13 Survey of Personal Incomes using economic assumptions consistent with the Office for Budget Responsibility's March 2015 economic and fiscal outlook. The latest actual figure available is for 2012–13, when median pre-tax income was £404 per week.)

Assessment of financial circumstances

While the initial consideration for the assessment of a fine is the offender's relevant weekly income, the court is required to take account of the offender's financial circumstances including assets more broadly. Guidance on important parts of this assessment is set out below.

An offender's financial circumstances may have the effect of increasing or reducing the amount of the fine; however, they are not relevant to the assessment of offence seriousness. They should be considered separately from the selection of the appropriate fine band and the court's assessment of the position of the offence within the range for that band.

Out of the ordinary expenses

In deciding the proportions of relevant weekly income that are the starting points and ranges for each fine band, account has been taken of reasonable living expenses. Accordingly, no further allowance should normally be made for these. In addition, no allowance should normally be made where the offender has dependants.

Outgoings will be relevant to the amount of the fine only where the expenditure is out of the ordinary and substantially reduces the ability to pay a financial penalty so that the requirement to pay a fine based on the standard approach would lead to undue hardship.

Unusually low outgoings

Where the offender's living expenses are substantially lower than would normally be expected, it may be appropriate to adjust the amount of the fine to reflect this. This may apply, for example, where an offender does not make any financial contribution towards his or her living costs.

Savings

Where an offender has savings, these will not normally be relevant to the assessment of the amount of a fine although they may influence the decision on time to pay.

However, where an offender has little or no income but has substantial savings, the court may consider it appropriate to adjust the amount of the fine to reflect this.

Household has more than one source of income

Where the household of which the offender is a part has more than one source of income, the fine should normally be based on the income of the offender alone.

However, where the offender's part of the income is very small (or the offender is wholly dependent on the income of another), the court may have regard to the extent of the household's income and assets which will be available to meet any fine imposed on the offender (*R v Engen* [2004] EWCA Crim 1536 (CA)).

Potential earning capacity

Where there is reason to believe that an offender's potential earning capacity is greater than his or her current income, the court may wish to adjust the amount of the fine to reflect this (*R v Little* (unreported) 14 April 1976 (CA)). This may apply, for example, where an unemployed offender states an expectation to gain paid employment within a short time. The basis for the calculation of fine should be recorded in order to ensure that there is a clear record for use in variation or enforcement proceedings.

High-income offenders

Where the offender is in receipt of very high income, a fine based on a proportion of relevant weekly income may be disproportionately high when compared with the seriousness of the offence. In such cases, the court should adjust the fine to an appropriate level; as a general indication, in most cases the fine for a first time offender pleading not guilty should not exceed 75 per cent of the maximum fine. In the case of fines which are unlimited the court should decide the appropriate level with the guidance of the legal adviser.

Approach to offenders on low income

An offender whose primary source of income is state benefit will generally receive a base level of benefit (for example, jobseeker's allowance, a relevant disability benefit or income support) and may also be eligible for supplementary benefits depending on his or her individual circumstances (such as child tax credits, housing benefit, council tax benefit and similar). In some cases these benefits may have been replaced by Universal Credit.

If relevant weekly income were defined as the amount of benefit received, this would usually result in higher fines being imposed on offenders with a higher level of need; in most circumstances that would not properly balance the seriousness of the offence with the financial circumstances of the offender. While it might be possible to exclude from the calculation any allowance above the basic entitlement of a single person, that could be complicated and time consuming.

Similar issues can arise where an offender is in receipt of a low earned income since this may trigger eligibility for means related benefits such as working tax credits and housing benefit depending on the particular circumstances. It will not always be possible to determine with any confidence whether such a person's financial circumstances are significantly different from those of a person whose primary source of income is state benefit.

For these reasons, a simpler and fairer approach to cases involving offenders in receipt of low income (whether primarily earned or as a result of benefit) is to identify an amount that is deemed to represent the offender's relevant weekly income.

While a precise calculation is neither possible nor desirable, it is considered that an amount that is approximately half-way between the base rate for jobseeker's allowance and the net weekly income of an adult earning the minimum wage for 30 hours per week represents a starting point that is both realistic and appropriate; this is currently **£120**. The calculation is based on a 30-hour working week in recognition of the fact that many of those on minimum wage do not work a full 37 hour week and that lower minimum wage rates apply to younger people.

With effect from 1 October 2014, the minimum wage is £6.50 per hour for an adult aged 21 or over. Based on a 30-hour week, this equates to approximately £189 after deductions for tax and national insurance. To ensure equivalence of approach, the level of jobseeker's allowance for a single person aged 18 to 24 has been used for the purpose of calculating the mid-point; this is currently £57.90. The figure will be updated in due course in accordance with any changes to benefit and minimum wage levels.

Offence committed for 'commercial' purposes

Some offences are committed with the intention of gaining a significant commercial benefit. These often occur where, in order to carry out an activity lawfully, a person has to comply with certain processes which may be expensive. They include, for example, 'taxi-touting' (where unauthorised persons seek to operate as taxi drivers) and 'fly-tipping' (where the cost of lawful disposal is considerable).

In some of these cases, a fine based on the standard approach set out above may not reflect the level of financial gain achieved or sought through the offending. Accordingly:

a. where the offender has generated income or avoided expenditure to a level that can be calculated or estimated, the court may wish to consider that amount when determining the financial penalty;

b. where it is not possible to calculate or estimate that amount, the court may wish to draw on information from the enforcing authorities about the general costs of operating within the law.

Multiple offences

Where an offender is to be fined for two or more offences that arose out of the same incident, it will often be appropriate to impose on the most serious offence a fine which reflects the totality of the offending where this can be achieved within the maximum penalty for that offence. 'No separate penalty' should be imposed for the other offences.

Where compensation is being ordered, that will need to be attributed to the relevant offence as will any necessary ancillary orders.

Imposition of fines with custodial sentences

A fine and a custodial sentence may be imposed for the same offence although there will be few circumstances in which this is appropriate, particularly where the custodial sentence is to be served immediately. One example might be where an offender has profited financially from an offence but there is no obvious victim to whom compensation can be awarded. Combining these sentences is most likely to be appropriate only where the custodial sentence is short and/or the offender clearly has, or will have, the means to pay.

Care must be taken to ensure that the overall sentence is proportionate to the seriousness of the offence and that better off offenders are not able to 'buy themselves out of custody'.

Payment

A fine is payable in full on the day on which it is imposed. The offender should always be asked for immediate payment when present in court and some payment on the day should be required wherever possible. Where that is not possible, the court may, in certain circumstances, require the offender to be detained (see section 82 of the Magistrates' Courts Act 1980 for restrictions on the power to impose imprisonment on default). More commonly, a court will allow payments to be made over a period set by the court:

a. if periodic payments are allowed, the fine should normally be payable within a maximum of 12 months.
b. compensation should normally be payable within 12 months. However, in exceptional circumstances it may be appropriate to allow it to be paid over a period of up to three years.

Where fine bands D, E and F apply, it may be appropriate for the fine to be of an amount that is larger than can be repaid within 12 months. In such cases, the fine should normally be payable within a maximum of 18 months (band D) or two years (bands E and F).

When allowing payment by instalments payments should be set at a realistic rate taking into account the offender's disposable income. The following approach may be useful:

Net weekly income	Suggested starting point for weekly payment
£60	£5
£120	£10
£200	£25
£300	£50
£400	£80

If the offender has dependants or larger than usual commitments, the weekly payment is likely to be decreased.

The payment terms must be included in any collection order made in respect of the amount imposed.

Collection orders

The Courts Act 2003 created a fines collection scheme which provides for greater administrative enforcement of fines.[editorial note: collection orders are not available against youths (Sch 5 para 1 Courts Act 2003)]

Attachment of earnings orders/applications for benefit deductions

Unless it would be impracticable or inappropriate to do so, the court must make an attachment of earnings or (AEO) or application for benefit deductions (ABD) whenever:

- compensation is imposed (Courts Act 2003, schedule 5, paragraph 7A); or
- the court concludes that the offender is an existing defaulter and that the existing default(s) cannot be disregarded (Courts Act 2003, schedule 5, paragraph 8).

In other cases, the court may make an AEO or ABD with the offender's consent (Courts Act 2003, schedule 5, paragraph 9).

The court must make a collection order in every case in which a fine or compensation order is imposed unless this would be impracticable or inappropriate (Courts Act 2003, schedule 5, paragraph 12). The collection order must state:

- the amount of the sum due, including the amount of any fine, compensation order or other sum;
- whether the court considers the offender to be an existing defaulter;
- whether an AEO or ABD has been made and information about the effect of the order;
- if the court has not made an AEO or ABD; the payment terms
- if an AEO or ABD has been made, the reserve terms (in other words, the payment terms that will apply if the AEO or ABD fails). It will often be appropriate to set a reserve term of payment in full within 14 days.

The rate of payment for fines in bands D and E was approved in *R (Purnell) v South Western Magistrates' Court* [2013] EWHC 64 (Admin), which confirmed also that the responsibility to advise the court of other fines outstanding falls upon the offender. *R v Rance* [2012] EWCA Crim 2023 confirmed that it was for the defendant to provide the court with all relevant financial information, but that fines must have regard only to the means of the offender—there is no concept of a 'tainted gift'.

If the defendant fails to put all relevant information before the court, he cannot later complain that the court has failed to take account of financial circumstances as required by s 164 Criminal Justice Act 2003.

R v Rance also held that whilst the court should have regard to any financial benefit from the crime, this is merely one consideration and does not mean that an equivalent or large proportion of the amount should be included in the fine.

D17.2 The detention alternative

Section 135 Magistrates' Courts Act 1980 provides:

Magistrates' Courts Act 1980, s 135

135 Detention of offender for one day in court-house or police station

(1) A magistrates' court that has power to commit to prison a person convicted of an offence, or would have that power but for section 82 or 88 above, may order him to be detained within the precincts of the courthouse or at any police station until such hour, not later than 8 o'clock in the evening of the day on which the order is made, as the court may direct, and, if it does so, shall not, where it has power to commit him to prison [or detention if aged 18–20 years], exercise that power.

(2) A court shall not make such an order under this section as will deprive the offender of a reasonable opportunity of returning to his abode on the day of the order.

D17.3 Enforcement of fines and confiscation orders

Separate representation orders should be obtained for these proceedings when appropriate

D17.3.1 *Principles*

The principles are set out in *R (Woolcock) v Secretary of State for Communities and Local Government and others* [2018] EWHC 17 (Admin), which was concerned with council tax enforcement, but the same principles apply to all fines and to the enforcement of confiscation orders (*R (Sanghera) v Birmingham MC* [2017] EWHC 3323 (Admin):

i)   The power to commit is coercive: it is intended to be used to extract payment of the debt from those who are able to pay, not to punish the debtor.

ii) Because the liberty of the subject is at issue, even where the subject has been deliberately disobedient and/or has ignored the enforcement process brought against him, it is vital that the magistrates conduct committal proceedings strictly in accordance with the applicable regulations and case law. If they do not, any committal will be unlawful.

...

vi) Before making a committal order, the magistrates' court must conduct a means inquiry in the presence of the debtor. This inquiry is important in respect of a number of issues which the magistrates will or may need to consider, eg whether to make a committal order at all, the conditions upon which such an order may be postponed or suspended (eg the appropriate rate at which arrears should be paid), and whether to remit all or part of the debt.

vii) The court must also consider, and determine, whether the failure to pay is the result of wilful refusal or culpable neglect, as any committal order (including a suspended order) can only be made if it is. Furthermore, even where the magistrates are satisfied that the failure to pay is the result of wilful refusal or culpable neglect, they will need to consider the degree of culpability, as that will be a factor that may be relevant to (eg) the period of imprisonment imposed.

...

ix) Before making any committal order (including a suspended order), the magistrates' court must consider enforcement options to secure payment, other than imprisonment.

...

xii) At the hearing for committal, the subject of the summons has the right to be legally represented. Usually, he will be represented by the duty solicitor. Magistrates should not proceed unless and until they have ascertained whether the subject wishes to be represented; and, if he does, that his representative has had a proper opportunity to take the subject's instructions and give him advice before the hearing commences.

xiii) It is usual, although not obligatory, for magistrates to suspend at least a first committal order on condition that the subject makes regular instalment payments towards the arrears. However, they cannot make any unreasonable order for repayment. Therefore, each instalment to be paid must be reasonable in amount, given the assessment of means that has been conducted. Furthermore, the period for which instalments are to be paid must be reasonable....; but, generally, where the period is two or three years, an order will be reasonable. Cases will be rare in which an instalment period of over three years will be appropriate. In no case has an instalment period of over five years been considered appropriate.

xiv) Where instalments are made a condition of a suspended committal order, the appropriate course is for the magistrates' court to remit such part of the arrears as will reduce the total sum in respect of which the order is made to a sum which can be met by the instalments envisaged within the reasonable period as assessed by the court.

D17.3.2 *Available procedures*

The court may allow further time or further instalment payments.

Magistrates' Courts Act 1980, s 75

Power to dispense with immediate payment

(1) A magistrates' court by whose conviction or order a sum is adjudged to be paid may, instead of requiring immediate payment, allow time for payment, or order payment by instalments.
(2) Where a magistrates' court has allowed time for payment, the court may, on application by or on behalf of the person liable to make the payment, allow further time or order payment by instalments.

The court may, in appropriate circumstances, remit a fine.

Magistrates' Courts Act 1980, s 85

85 Power to remit fine

(1) Where a fine has been imposed on conviction of an offender by a magistrates' court, the court may at any time remit the whole or any part of the fine, but only if it thinks it just to do so having regard to a change of circumstances which has occurred—
    (a) where the court is considering whether to issue a warrant of commitment after the issue of such a warrant in respect of the fine has been postponed under subsection (2) of section 77 above, since the relevant time as defined in subsection (4) of that section; and
    (b) in any other case, since the date of the conviction

At a means enquiry, the powers of the court to impose imprisonment in default is set out in s 82 Magistrates' Courts Act 1980.

D17.3.3 *Powers in default*

Magistrates' Courts Act 1980, s 82

Restriction on power to impose imprisonment for default

(1) A magistrates' court shall not on the occasion of convicting an offender of an offence issue a warrant of commitment for a default in paying any sum adjudged to
be paid by the conviction unless—
   (a) in the case of an offence punishable with imprisonment, he appears to the court
   to have sufficient means to pay the sum forthwith;
   (b) it appears to the court that he is unlikely to remain long enough at a place of
   abode in the United Kingdom to enable payment of the sum to be enforced by
   other methods; or
   (c) on the occasion of that conviction the court sentences him to immediate imprisonment, youth custody or detention in a detention centre for that or another
   offence or he is already serving a sentence of custody for life, or a term of imprisonment, youth custody, detention under section 9 of the Criminal Justice Act
   1982 or detention in a detention centre.

...

(4) Where a magistrates' court is required... to inquire into a person's means, the court
may not on the occasion of the inquiry or at any time thereafter issue a warrant of
commitment for a default in paying any such sum unless—
   (a) in the case of an offence punishable with imprisonment, the offender appears to
   the court to have sufficient means to pay the sum forthwith; or
   (b) the court—
      (i) is satisfied that the default is due to the offender's wilful refusal or culpable
      neglect; and
      (ii) has considered or tried all other methods of enforcing payment of the sum
      and it appears to the court that they are inappropriate or unsuccessful.

(4A) The methods of enforcing payment mentioned in subsection (4)(b)(ii) above are—
   (a) a warrant of distress under section 76 above;
   (b) an application to the High Court or county court for enforcement under section
   87 below;
   (c) an order under section 88 below;
   (d) an attachment of earnings order; and
   (e) if the offender is under the age of 25, an order under section 17 of the Criminal
   Justice Act 1982 (attendance centre orders).

(4B) The cases in which the offender's default may be regarded for the purposes of subsection (4)(b)(i) as being attributable to his wilful refusal or culpable neglect include any
case in which—

   (a) he has refused, otherwise than on reasonable grounds, to consent to a work
   order proposed to be made under Schedule 6 to the Courts Act 2003 (discharge
   of fines by unpaid work), or
   (b) he has without reasonable excuse failed to comply with such an order.

Under Sch5 Courts Act 2003, where an offender is in receipt of Income
Support, income-based Jobseeker's Allowance, income-related Employment
and Support Allowance, Pension Credit or Universal Credit, the court can,
with the offender's consent, order weekly direct deductions to be taken from
the benefit to pay the fine. The deduction rate is £5 per week, but for Universal

Credit only, the deduction can be up to £25 each week. If the benefit is contribution-based Jobseeker's Allowance or contribution-based Employment and Support Allowance, the deduction can be more. Consent is not required where there is a compensation order or there has been default on a collection order unless it would be impractical or inappropriate.

Procedures for fine enforcement appear in the Criminal Procedure Rules Part 30.

 See *Blackstone's Criminal Practice 2019* **E15**

D18 Forfeiture Order

D18.1 Criteria

Section 27 Misuse of Drugs Act 1971 provides:

> ### Misuse of Drugs Act 1971, s 27
>
> **27 Forfeiture**
>
> (1) Subject to subsection (2) below, the court by or before which a person is convicted of an offence under this Act or an offence falling within subsection (3) below or an offence to which section 1 of the Criminal Justice (Scotland) Act 1987 relates may order anything shown to the satisfaction of the court to relate to the offence, to be forfeited and either destroyed or dealt with in such other manner as the court may order.
>
> (2) The court shall not order anything to be forfeited under this section, where a person claiming to be the owner of or otherwise interested in it applies to be heard by the court, unless an opportunity has been given to him to show cause why the order should not be made.
>
> (3) An offence falls within this subsection if it is an offence which is specified in—
>
>   (a) paragraph 1 of Schedule 2 to the Proceeds of Crime Act 2002 (drug trafficking offences), or
>
>   (b) so far as it relates to that paragraph, paragraph 10 of that Schedule.

There are also powers of forfeiture in other statutes, such as the Knives Act 1997 and the Obscene Publications Act 1959.

Section 1 Prevention of Crime Act 1953 provides that, where any person is convicted of an offence under that section, the court may make an order for the forfeiture or disposal of any weapon in respect of which the offence was committed. See also **D12** on deprivation orders.

 See *Blackstone's Criminal Practice 2019* **E18.7** and, in relation to deprivation orders, **D12**

D19 **Mental Health Disposals**

Mental health procedures are dealt with at A20.

D19.1 **Guardianship and hospital orders**

Section 37 Mental Health Act 1983 provides:

Mental Health Act 1983, s 37

37 Powers of court to order hospital admission or guardianship

(1) Where a person is convicted ... by a magistrates' court of an offence punishable on summary conviction with imprisonment, and the conditions mentioned in subsection (2) below are satisfied, the court may by order authorise his admission to and detention in such hospital as may be specified in the order or, as the case may be, place him under the guardianship of a local social services authority or of such other person approved by a local social services authority as may be so specified.

(1A) ...

(1B)...

(2) The conditions referred to in subsection (1) above are that—

   (a) the court is satisfied, on the written or oral evidence of two registered medical practitioners, that the offender is suffering from mental illness, psychopathic disorder, severe mental impairment or mental impairment and that either—

      (i) the mental disorder from which the offender is suffering is of a nature or degree which makes it appropriate for him to be detained in a hospital for medical treatment and, in the case of psychopathic disorder or mental impairment, that such treatment is likely to alleviate or prevent a deterioration of his condition; or

      (ii) in the case of an offender who has attained the age of 16 years, the mental disorder is of a nature or degree which warrants his reception into guardianship under this Act; and

   (b) the court is of the opinion, having regard to all the circumstances including the nature of the offence and the character and antecedents of the offender, and to the other available methods of dealing with him, that the most suitable method of disposing of the case is by means of an order under this section.

(3) Where a person is charged before a magistrates' court with any act or omission as an offence and the court would have power, on convicting him of that offence, to make an order under subsection (1) above in his case as being a person suffering from mental illness or severe mental impairment, then, if the court is satisfied that the accused did the act or made the omission charged, the court may, if it thinks fit, make such an order without convicting him.

(4) An order for the admission of an offender to a hospital (in this Act referred to as 'a hospital order') shall not be made under this section unless the court is satisfied on the written or oral evidence of the registered medical practitioner who would be in charge of his treatment or of some other person representing the managers of the hospital that arrangements have been made for his admission to that hospital, and for his admission to it within the period of 28 days beginning with the date of

---

the making of such an order; and the court may, pending his admission within that period, give such directions as it thinks fit for his conveyance to and detention in a place of safety ...

(8) Where an order is made under this section, the court shall not—

    (a) pass sentence of imprisonment or impose a fine or make a community order (within the meaning of Part 12 of the Criminal Justice Act 2003) in respect of the offence,

    (b) if the order under this section is a hospital order, make a referral order (within the meaning of the Powers of Criminal Courts (Sentencing) Act 2000) in respect of the offence, or

    (c) make in respect of the offender an order under section 150 of that Act (binding over of parent or guardian),

but the court may make any other order which it has power to make apart from this section; and for the purposes of this subsection 'sentence of imprisonment' includes any sentence or order for detention.

 See *Blackstone's Criminal Practice 2019* **E22**

D19.2 Remand to hospital for reports and committal for sentence

Section 35 Mental Health Act 1983 provides:

Mental Health Act 1983, s 35

35 Remand to hospital for report on accused's mental condition

(1) Subject to the provisions of this section, the Crown Court or a magistrates' court may remand an accused person to a hospital specified by the court for a report on his mental condition.

(2) For the purposes of this section an accused person is—

    (a) ...

    (b) in relation to a magistrates' court, any person who has been convicted by the court of an offence punishable on summary conviction with imprisonment and any person charged with such an offence if the court is satisfied that he did the act or made the omission charged or he has consented to the exercise by the court of the powers conferred by this section.

(3) Subject to subsection (4) below, the powers conferred by this section may be exercised if—

    (a) the court is satisfied, on the written or oral evidence of a registered medical practitioner, that there is reason to suspect that the accused person is suffering from mental disorder; and

    (b) the court is of the opinion that it would be impracticable for a report on his mental condition to be made if he were remanded on bail; but those powers shall not be exercised by the Crown Court in respect of a person who has been convicted before the court if the sentence for the offence of which he has been convicted is fixed by law.

(4) The court shall not remand an accused person to a hospital under this section unless satisfied, on the written or oral evidence of the registered medical practitioner who would be responsible for making the report or of some other person representing the managers of the hospital, that arrangements have been made for his admission

to that hospital and for his admission to it within the period of seven days beginning with the date of the remand; and if the court is so satisfied it may, pending his admission, give directions for his conveyance to and detention in a place of safety.

(5) Where a court has remanded an accused person under this section it may further remand him if it appears to the court, on the written or oral evidence of the approved clinician responsible for making the report, that a further remand is necessary for completing the assessment of the accused person's mental condition.

(6) The power of further remanding an accused person under this section may be exercised by the court without his being brought before the court if he is represented by an authorised person who is given an opportunity of being heard.

(7) An accused person shall not be remanded or further remanded under this section for more than 28 days at a time or for more than 12 weeks in all; and the court may at any time terminate the remand if it appears to the court that it is appropriate to do so.

Section 43 Mental Health Act 1983 provides:

Mental Health Act 1983, s 43

43 Power of magistrates' courts to commit for restriction order

(1) If in the case of a person of or over the age of 14 years who is convicted by a magistrates' court of an offence punishable on summary conviction with imprisonment—

   (a) the conditions which under section 37(1) above are required to be satisfied for the making of a hospital order are satisfied in respect of the offender; but

   (b) it appears to the court, having regard to the nature of the offence, the antecedents of the offender and the risk of his committing further offences if set at large, that if a hospital order is made a restriction order should also be made,

the court may, instead of making a hospital order or dealing with him in any other manner, commit him in custody to the Crown Court to be dealt with in respect of the offence. .

(4) The powers of a magistrates' court under section 3 or 3B of the Powers of Criminal Courts (Sentencing) Act 2000 (which enable such a court to commit an offender to the Crown Court where the court is of the opinion, or it appears to the court, as mentioned in the section in question) shall also be exercisable by a magistrates' court where it is of that opinion (or it so appears to it) unless a hospital order is made in the offender's case with a restriction order.

 See *Blackstone's Criminal Practice 2019* **D20.74**

D20 **Minimum Sentences**

D20.1 **Criteria**

Burglary[+]	• Latest offence committed on or after 1 December 1999. • Offender aged 18 or over at date of this offence. • Convicted of two previous domestic burglaries, both of which occurred after 1 December 1999, and had been convicted of the first burglary before he committed the second. Must have been sentenced to a penalty greater than a discharge. On the meaning of a dwelling **see C15.3.1** • Minimum 3-year sentence (discount of 20% permissible for guilty plea). • The case must be sent to the Crown Court.
Drug trafficking[+]	• Latest offence committed on or after 1 October 1997. • Offender aged 18 or over at date of this offence. • Convicted of two previous drug trafficking offences and had been convicted of the first offence before he committed the second but the dates of conviction are not relevant. Must have been sentenced to a penalty greater than a discharge. • 7-year sentence (discount of 20% permissible for guilty plea). • The case must be sent to the Crown Court.

Firearms[#]	Minimum 5 years if 18 or over on the date of conviction, or 3 years if 16 or over but under 18 on that date. **Firearms Act 1968, s 51A**
	(1) This section applies where—
	   (a) an individual is convicted of—
	      (i) an offence under section 5(1)(a), (ab), (aba), (ac), (ad), (ae), (af) or (c) of this Act,
	      (ii) an offence under section 5(1A)(a) of this Act, or
	      (iii) an offence under any of the provisions of this Act listed in subsection (1A) in respect of a firearm or ammunition specified in section 5(1)(a), (ab), (aba), (ac), (ad), (ae), (af) or (c) or section 5(1A)(a) of this Act, and
	   (b) the offence was committed after the commencement of this section and at a time when he was aged 16 or over.
	(1A) The provisions are—
	   (za) section 5(1A) (manufacture, sale, or transfer of firearm or possession etc for sale or transfer);
	   (a) section 16 (possession of firearm with intent to injure);
	   (b) section 16A (possession of firearm with intent to cause fear of violence);
	   (c) section 18 (carrying firearm with criminal intent);
	   (d) section 19 (carrying a firearm in a public place);
	   (e) section 20(1) (trespassing in a building with firearm).
	(2) The court shall impose an appropriate custodial sentence (or order for detention) for a term of at least the required minimum term (with or without a fine) unless the court is of the opinion that there are exceptional circumstances relating to the offence or to the offender which justify its not doing so.

	The relevant date for the section 51(1A) offences is 6 April 2007. For all other offences, it is 22 January 2004.

Aggravated possession of weapons+ Prevention of Crime Act 1953, s 1A; Criminal Justice Act 1988, s 139AA)+*	• Offence committed on or after 3 December 2012. • Minimum 6-month sentence (or 4 months DTO for those of 16 or 17 on the date of conviction with a 20% discount available for a guilty plea.(which makes a DTO impossible) • A suspended sentence is available under s 189 CJA 2003 for those of 18 or over but discouraged by *R v Whyte* [2018] EWCA Crim 2437. The court must have regard to its duty under s 44 Children and Young Persons Act 1933 for those under 18
Second offence under any of s 1 Prevention of Crime Act 1953, s 139 and s 139A Criminal Justice+* Act 1988 *or s 6 Offensive Weapons Act 2019*+	• Offence committed on or after 17 July 2015 (*or date to be confirmed for s6 offensive weapons Act 2019*) • Already convicted when over 16 of any of these offences. • Minimum 6-month sentence or 4 months DTO for those of 16 or 17 on the date of conviction with a 20% discount available for a guilty plea (which makes a DTO impossible) • A suspended sentence is available under s 189 CJA 2003 for those of 18 or over but discouraged by *R v Whyte* [2018] EWCA Crim 2437. The court must have regard to its duty under s 44 Children and Young Persons Act 1933 for those under 18

+ Unless it would be unjust in all the circumstances

Unless there are exceptional circumstances

* The Sentencing Council guideline on Bladed Articles and offensive weapons confirms:

Unjust in all of the circumstances:

In considering whether a statutory minimum sentence would be 'unjust in all of the circumstances' the court must have regard to the particular circumstances of the offence and the offender. If th[ose] circumstances ..the court must impose either a shorter custodial sentence than the statutory minimum provides or an alternative sentence.

The offence:

Having reached this stage of the guideline the court should have made a provisional assessment of the seriousness of the offence. Where the court has determined that the offence seriousness falls far below the custodial threshold the court may consider it unjust to impose the statutory minimum sentence.

The offender:

The court should consider the following factors to determine whether it would be unjust to impose the statutory minimum sentence;

any strong personal mitigation;

whether there is a realistic prospect of rehabilitation;

whether custody will result in significant impact on others.

 See *Blackstone's Criminal Practice 2019* **E5** and **B12.171**

D21 *Newton* Hearings

D21.1 The rule in *Newton*

The rule in *R v Newton* (1982) 77 Cr App R 13 indicates that an offender will be sentenced on the prosecution's version of the facts unless the defence make clear that they are pleading on an alternative basis. In that situation, the Crown must prove its version of the facts by admissible evidence to the criminal standard of proof.

The purpose of a *Newton* hearing is to establish the factual basis for sentence in a case where there is a factual dispute and that dispute is material to sentence. Once a *Newton* hearing takes place the defendant is at risk of findings conflicting with an earlier basis of plea (*Nicholls v DPP* [2013] EWHC 4365 (Admin)).

D21.2 Procedure

In the magistrates' and youth court it was not proper for the trial of one defendant and a *Newton* in relation to the other to take place at the same time. It meant that the inadmissible evidence of the defendant who had pleaded guilty was used at the trial of the co-defendant. (*KK v DPP* [2016] EWHC 1976 (Admin)).

D21.3 Criteria

R v Cairns [2013] EWCA Crim 467 confirmed that there is no obligation to hold a *Newton* hearing:

   (a) if the difference between the two versions of fact is immaterial to sentence (in which event the defendant's version must be adopted: *R v Hall* (1984) 6 Cr App R (S) 321);
   (b) where the defence version can be described as 'manifestly false' or 'wholly implausible': *R v Hawkins* (1985) Cr App R (S) 351; or
   (c) where the matters put forward by the defendant do not contradict the prosecution case but constitute extraneous mitigation where the court is not bound to accept the truth of the matters put forward whether or not they are challenged by the prosecution: *R v Broderick* (1994) 15 Cr App R (S) 476.

Guidance in relation to the holding of *Newton* hearings was set down in *R v Underwood* [2004] EWCA Crim 2256:

   (1) The starting point has to be the defendant's instructions. His advocate will appreciate whether any significant facts about the prosecution evidence are disputed and the factual basis on which the defendant intends to plead guilty. Responsibility for taking initiative and alerting the prosecutor to the disputed areas rests with the defence.
   (2) Where the Crown accepts the defendant's account of the disputed facts, the agreement should be written down and signed by both advocates. It should then be made available to the judge. If pleas have already been accepted and approved then it should be available before the sentencing hearing begins. If the agreed basis of plea is not signed by both advocates, the judge is entitled to ignore it. The Crown might reject the defendant's version. If so, the areas of dispute should be identified in writing, focusing the court's attention on the precise facts in dispute.
   (3) The prosecution's position might be that they have no evidence to contradict the defence's assertions. In those circumstances, particularly if the facts relied on by

the defendant arise from his personal knowledge and depend on his own account of the facts, the Crown should not normally agree the defendant's account unless supported by other material. The court should be notified at the outset in writing of the points in issue and the Crown's responses.

(4) After submissions, the judge will decide how to proceed. If not already decided, he would address the question of whether he should approve the Crown's acceptance of pleas. Then he would address the proposed basis of plea. It should be emphasized that whether or not the basis of plea is agreed, the judge is not bound by any such agreement and is entitled of his own motion to insist that any evidence relevant to the facts in dispute should be called before him, paying appropriate regard to any agreement reached by the advocates and any reasons which the Crown, in particular, might advance to justify him proceeding immediately to sentence. The judge is responsible for the sentencing decision and may order a *Newton* hearing to ascertain the truth about disputed facts.

(5) Relevant evidence should be called by prosecution and defence, particularly where the issue arises from facts which are within the exclusive knowledge of the defendant. If the defendant is willing to give evidence he should be called and, if not, subject to any explanation offered, the judge may draw such inference as he sees fit. The judge can reject the evidence called by the prosecution or by the defendant or his witnesses even if the Crown has not called contradictory evidence. The judge's conclusions should be explained in the judgment.

...

(7) Normally, matters of mitigation are not dealt with by way of a *Newton* hearing but it is always open to the court to allow a defendant to give evidence on matters of mitigation which are within his own knowledge. The judge is entitled to decline to hear evidence about disputed facts if the case advanced is, for good reason, to be regarded as absurd or obviously untenable.

(8) If the issues at the *Newton* hearing are wholly resolved in the defendant's favour, mitigation for guilty pleas should not be reduced. If the defendant is disbelieved or obliges the prosecution to call evidence from the victim, who is then subjected to cross-examination which, because it is entirely unfounded, causes unnecessary and inappropriate distress, or if the defendant conveys that he has no insight into the consequences of his offence, and no genuine remorse, the judge might reduce the discount for the guilty pleas.

The guideline on discount for guilty plea states that if the offender's version of events is rejected at a *Newton* hearing the reduction which would have been available at the stage the plea was indicated should normally be halved. Where witnesses are called during a hearing it may be appropriate further to decrease the reduction.

In *R v Abbas* [2017] EWCA Crim 251 it was confirmed that where an unrealistic basis of plea was put forward and a *Newton* listed, discount could be reduced even though the *Newton* was not pursued. A realistic basis should have been proposed.

See *Blackstone's Criminal Practice 2019* **D20.8–D20.29**

D22 **Notification Requirements**

Notification requirements under the Sexual Offences Act 2003; the Stalking Protection Act 2019; *and the Offensive Weapons Act 2019* are considered in this section.

D22.1 **Sexual Offences Act 2003**

Note that for children and young offenders reference should also be made to Chapter J 21.

Breach is dealt with at **C2.4**.

It is not a requirement that a court 'orders' a notification requirement, as this will follow automatically as a result of a qualifying conviction (ie those offences specified in Sch 3 to the Sexual Offences Act 2003).

An offender will be given a notice to sign and be provided with his own copy that sets down the requirements to be satisfied. For some offences a specific sentence is required before the liability arises. In relation to offences under s 1 Indecency with Children Act 1978, the notification regime only applies if the child is under 16 and the court should if necessary make a determination on that issue (*R v George 2018 EWCA Crim 417*). In *R v Davison* [2008] EWCA Crim 2795, D was ordered to complete 220 hours of unpaid work within a 12-month period. D submitted that a community order which contains solely an unpaid work requirement to be completed within 12 months is not a community sentence of at least 12 months' duration, as it is open to the offender to complete the work within the 12-month period and on completion of the work the community order ceases. The court held:

> the length of a community order must be capable of being determined on the date it is made. In our judgment the period specified under section 177(5) of the Criminal Justice Act 2003 by a court when imposing a community order is the relevant period for the purpose of determining the duration of the order under paragraph 18(b)(ii)(c) of Schedule 3 to the Sexual Offences Act 2003 however long it in fact takes the offender to carry out the requirements under the order.

Penalty	Notification period for an adult (Sexual Offences Act 2003, s 82)
Conditional discharge	Period of discharge
A person sentenced otherwise than as mentioned elsewhere	5 years
Imprisonment for a term of 6 months or less	7 years
Imprisonment for a minimum term of 6 months but less than 30 months	10 years
A person sentenced to imprisonment for life or for 30 months or more	Indeterminate

Note: Where the registration is indeterminate there is a power to apply for removal once 15 years has been served and then every 8 years.

 See *Blackstone's Criminal Practice 2019* **E23**

D22.2 s 9 Stalking Protection Act 2019

While a person is subject to a stalking protection order, or interim order, and is not subject to the notification arrangements set out above, they must within three days notify their names and address.

D22.3 s 24 Offensive Weapons Act 2019

While a person is subject to a knife crime protection order, or interim order, they must within three days notify their names and address.

D23 Offences Taken into Consideration (TICs) and the Totality Principle

D23.1 Criteria for TICs

In *R v Miles* [2006] EWCA Crim 256, the court made the following observations:

[T]he sentence is intended to reflect a defendant's overall criminality. Offences cannot be taken into consideration without the express agreement of the offender. That is an essential prerequisite. The offender is pleading guilty to the offences. If they are to be taken into account (and the court is not obliged to take them into account) they have relevance to the overall criminality. When assessing the significance of TICs, as they are often called, of course the court is likely to attach weight to the demonstrable fact that the offender has assisted the police, particularly if they are enabled to clear up offences which might not otherwise be brought to justice. It is also true that cooperative behaviour of that kind will often provide its own very early indication of guilt, and usually means that no further proceedings at all need be started. They may also serve to demonstrate a genuine determination by the offender (and we deliberately use the colloquialism) to wipe the slate clean, so that when he emerges from whatever sentence is imposed on him, he can put his past completely behind him, without having worry or concern that offences may be revealed and that he is then returned to court. As in so many aspects of sentencing, of course, the way in which the court deals with offences to be taken into consideration depends on context. In some cases the offences taken into consideration will end up by adding nothing or nothing very much to the sentence which the court would otherwise impose. On the other hand, offences taken into consideration may aggravate the sentence and lead to a substantial increase in it. For example, the offences may show a pattern of criminal activity which suggests careful planning or deliberate rather than casual involvement in a crime. They may show an offence or offences committed on bail, after an earlier arrest. They may show a return to crime immediately after the offender has been before the court and given a chance that, by committing the crime, he has immediately rejected. There are many situations where similar issues may arise. One advantage to the defendant, of course, is that if once an offence is taken into consideration, there is no likely risk of any further prosecution for it. If, on the other hand, it is not, that risk remains. In short, offences taken into consideration are indeed taken into consideration. They are not ignored or expunged or disregarded.

The Sentencing Council has issued a definitive guideline in relation to TICs, which was intended to reflect the existing law. It confirms that, when sentencing an offender who requests offences to be taken into consideration, courts should pass a total sentence which reflects all the offending behaviour. The sentence must be just and proportionate, and must not exceed the statutory maximum for the conviction offence.

The court is likely to consider that the fact that the offender has assisted the police (particularly if the offences would not otherwise have been detected) and avoided the need for further proceedings demonstrates a genuine determination by the offender to wipe the slate clean.

The sentence imposed on the offender should, in most circumstances, be increased to reflect the fact that other offences have been taken into consideration. The court should:

- determine the sentencing starting point for the conviction offence;
- consider aggravating and mitigating circumstances. The presence of TICs should generally be treated as an aggravating feature that justifies an upward adjustment from the starting point. Where there is a large number of TICs, it may be appropriate to move outside the category range, although this must be considered in the context of the case and subject to the principle of totality. The court is limited to the statutory maximum for the conviction offence;
- consider whether the frank admission of a number of offences is an indication of a defendant's remorse or determination and/or demonstration of steps taken to address addiction or offending behaviour.

Any reduction for guilty plea should be applied to the total sentence, as should the totality principle.

Ancillary orders may take account of TICs to the limit allowed by the offences for which there is a conviction.

D23.2 Totality principle

The principle of totality comprises two elements:

(1) all courts, when sentencing for more than a single offence, should pass a total sentence which reflects all the offending behaviour before it and is just and proportionate. This is so whether the sentences are structured as concurrent or consecutive. Therefore, concurrent sentences will ordinarily be longer than a single sentence for a single offence.

(2) it is usually impossible to arrive at a just and proportionate sentence for multiple offending simply by adding together notional single sentences. It is necessary to address the offending behaviour, together with the factors personal to the offender as a whole.

D23.2.1 *Concurrent/consecutive sentences*

There is no inflexible rule governing whether sentences should be structured as concurrent or consecutive components. The overriding principle is that the overall sentence must be just and proportionate.

D23.3 Specific applications—custodial sentences

For an existing determinate sentence, where determinate sentence is still to be passed:

Circumstance	Approach
Offender serving a determinate sentence (offence(s) committed before original sentence imposed)	Consider what the sentence length would have been if the court had dealt with the offences at the same time and ensure that the totality of the sentence is just and proportionate in all the circumstances. If it is not, an adjustment should be made to the sentence imposed for the latest offence.
Offender serving a determinate sentence (offence(s) committed after original sentence imposed)	Generally the sentence will be consecutive as it will have arisen out of an unrelated incident. The court must have regard to the totality of the offender's criminality when passing the second sentence, to ensure that the total sentence to be served is just and proportionate. Where a prisoner commits acts of violence in prison, any reduction for totality is likely to be minimal.
Offender serving a determinate sentence but released from custody	The new sentence should start on the day it is imposed: s 265 Criminal Justice Act 2003 prohibits a sentence of imprisonment running consecutively to a sentence from which a prisoner has been released. The sentence for the new offence will take into account the aggravating feature that it was committed on licence. However, it must be commensurate with the new offence and cannot be artificially inflated with a view to ensuring that the offender serves a period in custody additional to the recall period (which will be an unknown quantity in most cases) this is so even if the new sentence will, in consequence, add nothing to the period actually served.
Offender sentenced to a determinate term and subject to an existing suspended sentence order	Where an offender commits an additional offence during the operational period of a suspended sentence and the court orders the suspended sentence to be activated, the additional sentence will generally be consecutive to the activated suspended sentence, as it will arise out of unrelated facts.

 See *Blackstone's Criminal Practice 2019* **D20**

D24 Penalty Points for Driving Offences

(See ss 28 *et seq* Road Traffic Offenders Act (RTOA) 1988)

D24.1 Criteria

Penalty points must be imposed for all offences that are subject to obligatory endorsement, unless the court finds special reasons for not imposing points (see s 44(2) RTOA 1988 and **D16.5**).

A person who acts as a secondary party to an offence carrying obligatory disqualification is liable to 10 penalty points.

If a person is found guilty, on one or more occasions, of more than one offence committed on the same occasion, the range of penalty points is taken as being whichever is the highest available for any one offence (eg a person convicted of speeding (3–6 points) and no insurance (6–8 points) is liable to receive up to 6 or 8 points respectively). A court does, however, have discretion to disapply this rule if reasons are given (s 28 Road Traffic Act 1988).

Where a court orders obligatory disqualification and there are further offences to be sentenced, it should not order points for the further offences.

 See *Blackstone's Criminal Practice 2019* **C7.16–C7.24**

D25 Pre-Sentence Reports

D25.1 Criteria

Section 156 Criminal Justice Act 2003 provides:

> **Criminal Justice Act 2003, s 156**
>
> **156 Pre-sentence reports and other requirements ...**
>
> (3) Subject to subsection (4), a court must obtain and consider a presentence report before—
>
>   (a) in the case of a custodial sentence, forming any such opinion as is mentioned in section 152(2)[so serious], section 153(2)[commensurate term], section 225(1)
>   (b) significant risk of serious harm]), section 226(1)(b[the same]), section 227(1)
>   (b)[the same] or section 228(1)(b)(i)[the same], or
>
>   (b) in the case of a community sentence, forming any such opinion as is mentioned in section 148(1)[serious enough] or (2)(b)[commensurate requirements], or in section 1(4)(b) or
>
>   (c) of the Criminal Justice and Immigration Act 2008[youth rehabilitation orders with intensive supervision and surveillance or fostering], or any opinion as to the suitability for the offender of the particular requirement or requirements to be imposed by the community order or youth rehabilitation order.
>
> (4) Subsection (3) does not apply if, in the circumstances of the case, the court is of the opinion that it is unnecessary to obtain a pre-sentence report.
>
> (5) In a case where the offender is aged under 18, the court must not form the opinion mentioned in subsection (4) unless—
>
>   (a) there exists a previous pre-sentence report obtained in respect of the offender, and
>
>   (b) the court has had regard to the information contained in that report, or, if there is more than one such report, the most recent report.

D25.2 Reports in anticipated guilty plea cases when sending cases to the Crown Court

D25.2.1 *Criminal Practice Direction 3A9*

Where a magistrates' court is considering committal for sentence or the defendant has indicated an intention to plead guilty in a matter which is to be sent to the Crown Court, the magistrates' court should request the preparation of a pre-sentence report for the Crown Court's use if the magistrates' court considers that:

(a) there is a realistic alternative to a custodial sentence; or
(b) the defendant may satisfy the criteria for classification as a dangerous offender; or
(c) there is some other appropriate reason for doing so.

D25.2.2 In addition it will usually be appropriate to order a report where

- the defendant is 17 and under;
- the defendant is under 21 and is a first time offender or has not served a prison sentence (*R v Townsend* [2018] EWCA Crim 875).

D25.3 Sentencing Council General Guideline

Sentencing Council General Guidance states that whenever the court reaches the provisional view that:

- the custody threshold has been passed; and, if so
- the length of imprisonment which represents the shortest term commensurate with the seriousness of the offence;
- the court should obtain a pre-sentence report, whether verbal or written, unless the court considers a report to be unnecessary. Ideally a pre-sentence report should be completed on the same day to avoid adjourning the case.

 See *Blackstone's Criminal Practice 2019* **E1.26** and **E1.27**

D26 Prevention Orders

D26.1 Sexual Harm Prevention Orders

Following conviction for an offence specified in Sch 3 (in some cases dependent on the sentence imposed) or 5 to the Sexual Offences Act 2003, the court may go on to consider whether or not to make a sexual harm prevention order. Schedule 5 contains a wide range of non-sexual offences.

D26.1.1 *Grounds for application*

Sexual Offences Act 2003, ss 103A–D

103A Sexual harm prevention orders: applications and grounds

(1) A court may make an order under this section (a 'sexual harm prevention order') in respect of a person ('the defendant') where subsection (2)or (3) applies to the defendant.

(2) This subsection applies to the defendant where—

(a) the court deals with the defendant in respect of—
(i) an offence listed in Schedule 3 or 5, or
(ii) a finding that the defendant is not guilty of an offence listed in Schedule 3 or 5 by reason of insanity, or
(iii) a finding that the defendant is under a disability and has done the act charged against the defendant in respect of an offence listed in Schedule 3 or 5,

and

(b) the court is satisfied that it is necessary to make a sexual harm prevention order, for the purpose of—
(i) protecting the public or any particular members of the public from sexual harm from the defendant, or
(ii) protecting children or vulnerable adults generally, or any particular children or vulnerable adults, from sexual harm from the defendant outside the United Kingdom.

103B Section 103A: supplemental

(1) In section 103A—

'child' means a person under 18;
'the public' means the public in the United Kingdom;
'sexual harm' from a person means physical or psychological harm caused—
(a) by the person committing one or more offences listed in Schedule 3, or
(b) (in the context of harm outside the United Kingdom) by the person doing, outside the United Kingdom, anything which would constitute an offence listed in Schedule 3 if done in any part of the United Kingdom;
'vulnerable adult' means a person aged 18 or over whose ability to protect himself or herself from physical or psychological harm is significantly impaired through physical or mental disability or illness, through old age or otherwise.

103C SHPOs: effect

(1) A sexual harm prevention order prohibits the defendant from doing anything described in the order.

(2) Subject to section 103D(1), a prohibition contained in a sexual harm prevention order has effect—
   (a) for a fixed period, specified in the order, of at least 5 years, or
   (b) until further order.

(3) A sexual harm prevention order—
   (a) may specify that some of its prohibitions have effect until further order and some for a fixed period;
   (b) may specify different periods for different prohibitions.

(4) The only prohibitions that may be included in a sexual harm prevention order are those necessary for the purpose of—
   (a) protecting the public or any particular members of the public from sexual harm from the defendant, or
   (b) protecting children or vulnerable adults generally, or any particular children or vulnerable adults, from sexual harm from the defendant outside the United Kingdom.

(5) In subsection (4) 'the public', 'sexual harm', 'child' and 'vulnerable adult' each has the meaning given in section 103B(1).

(6) Where a court makes a sexual harm prevention order in relation to a person who is already subject to such an order (whether made by that court or another), the earlier order ceases to have effect.

103D SHPOs: prohibitions on foreign travel

(1) A prohibition on foreign travel contained in a sexual harm prevention order must be for a[n initial] fixed period of not more than 5 years ...

D26.1.2. Key points

- There is nothing in these provisions to indicate that a court must believe a defendant to be 'dangerous' (within the meaning of the sentencing regime) before it can make such an order (*R v Richards* [2006] EWCA Crim 2519).
- Notice of at least two working days of an application for a sexual harm prevention order should always be given under Part 31 of the Criminal Procedure Rules.
- Cases on the predecessor order would appear to remain valid.

The burden of proof for obtaining such an order is the criminal standard (*MPC v Ebanks* [2012] EWHC 2368 (Admin)).

The order must be capable of being complied with without unreasonable difficulty, and free of the risk of unintended breach (*R v Hemsley* [2012] EWCA Crim 225). It must be clear and necessary, and avoid a total ban on the use of the internet, though it can require a history of use of the internet to be kept (*R v Smith* [2012] EWCA Crim 1772; *Mortimer* [2010] EWCA Crim 1303).

R v Smith [2011] EWCA Crim 3142 confirms that if it is intended to allow access to children under 16 only with the consent of their parent/guardian, provision should be made for accidental or inadvertent contact: *Smith* [2012] EWCA Crim 1772 held that following convictions for possession of child pornography, each order must be individually considered with two days' notice. There can be no standard clauses. Contact with children and supervisory requirements should only be prevented when there was a real risk that the offending would progress to contact offences—safety first is not enough. See also *R v Jackson* [2012] EWCA Crim 2602, confirming that to order that the police have access at all times to any computer is too great an invasion of privacy.

In *R v Christopher James* [2012] EWCA Crim 81, where a defendant was convicted of offences of making indecent photographs, it was not on the facts necessary, while controlling the use of the internet, to insert non-contact provisions with children as there was no identified risk, and a 10-year order substituted for lifetime control.

R v NC [2016] EWCA Crim 1448 identified the issues as:

(1) Is the making of the order necessary to protect the public from sexual harm through the commission of schedules offences?
(2) If the order is necessary, are the terms oppressive?
(3) Overall, are the terms proportionate?

R v Sokolowski and *R v Pickard* [2017] EWCA Crim 1903 sets out the following principles:

(i) it is essential that a written draft of the proposed SHPO is both served on the defendant and lodged with the court. The draft should set out the proposed terms, including the proposed duration of the order or, at the very least, flag the question of duration for consideration by the defendant and the court.

(ii) Before it is imposed, the court must be satisfied that an SHPO is necessary for the statutory purpose of protecting the public or any particular members of the public from sexual harm from the defendant. The court has to be satisfied that the prohibitions sought are necessary, and neither oppressive nor disproportionate.

(iii) Particular care must be taken when considering whether prohibitions on contact with children are really necessary; although such orders may be necessary to prevent the defendant from seeking out children for sexual purposes. Where a defendant is convicted of viewing child pornography, then an SHPO should only contain provisions preventing contact, or permitting only supervised contact, with children where there is a real risk that the offending will progress to contact offences. It is not enough for the prosecution to assert, or for the court to assume, that such provisions are necessary on the safety first principle, irrespective of how remote or fanciful the risk of such progression might be. Even when provisions are necessary, they must still be proportionate in their scope.

(iv) It is not normally a legitimate use of an SHPO to use it simply to extend the notification requirements prescribed by law. It does not follow that the duration of an SHPO must be the same as or no longer than the period of the notification requirements.

(v) An SHPO should not be made for an indefinite period, unless the court is satisfied of the need to do so.

Further consideration to modern circumstances was considered in *R v Parsons and Morgan* [2017] EWCA Crim 2163.

 See *Blackstone's Criminal Practice 2019* **E21.22–E21.31**

D26.2 Knife crime prevention orders

Offensive Weapons Act 2019

> **19 Knife crime prevention order made on conviction**
>
> (1) This section applies where—
>   (a) a person aged 12 or over (the "defendant") is convicted of an offence which was committed after the coming into force of this section, and
>   (b) a court dealing with the defendant in respect of the offence is satisfied on the balance of probabilities that the offence is a relevant offence.
> (2) The court may make a knife crime prevention order under this section in respect of the defendant if the following conditions are met.
> (3) The first condition is that the prosecution applies for a knife crime prevention order to be made under this section.
> (4) The second condition is that the court thinks that it is necessary to make the order—
>   (a) to protect the public in England and Wales from the risk of harm involving a bladed article,
>   (b) to protect any particular members of the public in England and Wales (including the defendant) from such risk, or
>   (c) to prevent the defendant from committing an offence involving a bladed article.
> (5) A knife crime prevention order under this section is an order which, for a purpose mentioned in subsection (4)—
>   (a) requires the defendant to do anything described in the order;
>   (b) prohibits the defendant from doing anything described in the order.
> (6) See also—
>   (a) section 21 (which makes further provision about the requirements and prohibitions that may be imposed by a knife crime prevention order under this section),
>   (b) section 22 (which makes further provision about the inclusion of requirements in a knife crime prevention order under this section), and
>   (c) section 23 (which makes provision about the duration of a knife crime prevention order under this section).
> (7) The court may make a knife crime prevention order under this section in respect of the defendant only if it is made in addition to—
>   (a) a sentence imposed in respect of the offence, or
>   (b) an order discharging the offender conditionally.
> (8) For the purposes of deciding whether to make a knife crime prevention order under this section the court may consider evidence led by the prosecution and evidence led by the defendant.
> (9) It does not matter whether the evidence would have been admissible in the proceedings in which the defendant was convicted.
> (10) For the purposes of this section an offence is a relevant offence if—
>   (a) the offence involved violence,
>   (b) a bladed article was used, by the defendant or any other person, in the commission of the offence, or

(c) *the defendant or another person who committed the offence had a bladed article with them when the offence was committed.*

(11) *In subsection (10) "violence" includes a threat of violence*

20 Requirement to consult on application for order under section 19

(1) *This section applies if the prosecution proposes to apply for a knife crime prevention order under section 19 in respect of a defendant who—*
   (a) *is under the age of 18, and*
   (b) *will be under that age when the application is made.*

(2) *Before making the application, the prosecution must consult the youth offending team established under section 39 of the Crime and Disorder Act 1998 in whose area it appears to the prosecution that the defendant lives.*

(3) *If it appears to the prosecution that the defendant lives in the area of two or more youth offending teams, the obligation in subsection (2) is to consult such of those teams as the prosecution thinks appropriate*

21 Provisions of knife crime prevention order

(1) *The only requirements and prohibitions that may be imposed on a defendant by a knife crime prevention order are those which the court making the order thinks are necessary—*
   (a) *to protect the public in England and Wales from the risk of harm involving a bladed article,*
   (b) *to protect any particular members of the public in England and Wales (including the defendant) from such risk, or*
   (c) *to prevent the defendant from committing an offence involving a bladed article.*

(2) *The requirements imposed by a knife crime prevention order on a defendant may, in particular, have the effect of requiring the defendant to—*
   (a) *be at a particular place between particular times on particular days;*
   (b) *be at a particular place between particular times on any day;*
   (c) *present themselves to a particular person at a place where they are required to be between particular times on particular days;*
   (d) *participate in particular activities between particular times on particular days.*

(3) *Section 22 makes further provision about the inclusion of requirements in a knife crime prevention order.*

(4) *The prohibitions imposed by a knife crime prevention order on a defendant may, in particular, have the effect of prohibiting the defendant from—*
   (a) *being in a particular place;*
   (b) *being with particular persons;*
   (c) *participating in particular activities;*
   (d) *using particular articles or having particular articles with them;*
   (e) *using the internet to facilitate or encourage crime involving bladed articles.*

(5) *References in subsection (4) to a particular place or particular persons, activities or articles include a place, persons, activities or articles of a particular description.*

(6) *A knife crime prevention order which imposes prohibitions on a defendant may include exceptions from those prohibitions.*

(7) *Nothing in subsections (2) to (6) affects the generality of section 14(7) or section 19(5).*

(8) *The requirements or prohibitions which are imposed on the defendant by a knife crime prevention order must, so far as practicable, be such as to avoid—*
   (a) *any conflict with the defendant's religious beliefs, and*
   (b) *any interference with the times, if any, at which the defendant normally works or attends any educational establishment.*

22 Requirements included in knife crime prevention order etc

(1) *A knife crime prevention order or interim knife crime prevention order which imposes a requirement on a defendant must specify a person who is to be responsible for supervising compliance with the requirement.*

(2) *That person may be an individual or an organisation.*

(3) *Before including a requirement, the court must receive evidence about its suitability and enforceability from—*

    (a) *the individual to be specified under subsection (1), if an individual is to be specified;*

    (b) *an individual representing the organisation to be specified under subsection (1), if an organisation is to be specified.*

(4) *Before including two or more requirements, the court must consider their compatibility with each other.*

(5) *It is the duty of a person specified under subsection (1)—*

    (a) *to make any necessary arrangements in connection with the requirements for which the person has responsibility (the "relevant requirements");*

    (b) *to promote the defendant's compliance with the relevant requirements;*

    (c) *if the person considers that the defendant—*

        (i) *has complied with all of the relevant requirements, or*

        (ii) *has failed to comply with a relevant requirement,*

        to inform the appropriate chief officer of police.

(6) *In subsection (5)(c) "the appropriate chief officer of police" means—*

    (a) *the chief officer of police for the police area in which it appears to the person specified under subsection (1) that the defendant lives, or*

    (b) *if it appears to that person that the defendant lives in more than one police area, whichever of the chief officers of police of those areas the person thinks it is most appropriate to inform.*

(7) *A defendant subject to a requirement in a knife crime prevention order or interim knife crime prevention order must—*

    (a) *keep in touch with the person specified under subsection (1) in relation to that requirement, in accordance with any instructions given by that person from time to time, and*

    (b) *notify that person of any change of the defendant's home address.*

(8) *The obligations mentioned in subsection (7) have effect as if they were requirements imposed on the defendant by the order.*

23 Duration of knife crime prevention order etc

(1) *A knife crime prevention order or an interim knife crime prevention order under section 18 takes effect on the day on which it is made, subject to subsections (6) and (7).*

(2) *An interim knife crime prevention order under section 17 takes effect when it is served on the defendant, subject to subsections (6) and (7).*

(3) *A knife crime prevention order must specify the period for which it has effect, which must be a fixed period of at least 6 months, and not more than 2 years, beginning with the day on which it takes effect.*

(4) *An interim knife crime prevention order under section 17 has effect until the determination of the application mentioned in subsection (1) of that section, subject to section 27 (variation, renewal or discharge).*

(5) *An interim knife crime prevention order under section 18 has effect until the determination of the application mentioned in subsection (1) of that section, subject to section 27.*

(6) *Subsection (7) applies if a knife crime prevention order or an interim knife crime prevention order is made in respect of—*

    (a) *a defendant who has been remanded in or committed to custody by an order of a court,*

    (b) *a defendant on whom a custodial sentence has been imposed or who is serving or otherwise subject to such a sentence, or*

    (c) *a defendant who is on licence for part of the term of a custodial sentence.*

(7) *The order may provide that it does not take effect until—*

    (a) *the defendant is released from custody,*

    (b) *the defendant ceases to be subject to a custodial sentence, or*

    (c) *the defendant ceases to be on licence.*

(8) *A knife crime prevention order or an interim knife crime prevention order may specify periods for which particular prohibitions or requirements have effect.*

(9) *Where a court makes a knife crime prevention order or an interim knife crime prevention order in respect of a defendant who is already subject to such an order, the earlier order ceases to have effect.*

(10) *In this section "custodial sentence" means—*

    (a) *a sentence of imprisonment or any other sentence or order mentioned in section 76(1) of the Powers of Criminal Courts (Sentencing) Act 2003, or*

    (b) *a sentence or order which corresponds to a sentence or order within paragraph (a) and which was imposed or made under an earlier enactment.*

D27 Prosecution Costs

D27.1 Criteria

The following principles may be derived from the Criminal Practice Direction Division X Part 3 and *R v Northallerton Magistrates' Court, ex p Dove* [2000] 1 Cr App R (S) 136:

(1) An order to pay costs to the prosecutor should never exceed the sum which, having regard to the defendant's means and any other financial order imposed upon him, the defendant was able to pay and which it was reasonable to order the defendant to pay.

(2) Such an order should never exceed the sum that the prosecutor had actually and reasonably incurred (or was liable to a third party to pay, for example when that third party commissions a report on behalf of the prosecution).

(3) The purpose of such an order was to compensate the prosecutor and not punish the defendant. Where the defendant had by his conduct put the prosecutor to avoidable expense he might, subject to his means, be ordered to pay some or all of that sum to the prosecutor. However, he was not to be punished for exercising his constitutional right to defend himself.

(4) While there was no requirement that any sum ordered by justices to be paid to a prosecutor by way of costs should stand in any arithmetical relationship to any fine imposed, the costs ordered to be paid should not in any ordinary way be grossly disproportionate to the fine. Justices should ordinarily begin by deciding on the appropriate fine to reflect the criminality of the defendant's offence, always bearing in mind his means and ability to pay, and then consider what, if any, costs he should be ordered to pay to the prosecutor. If, when the costs sought by the prosecutor were added to the proposed fine, the total exceeded the sum which in the light of the defendant's means and all other relevant circumstances the defendant could reasonably be ordered to pay, it was preferable to achieve an acceptable total by reducing the sum of costs which the defendant was ordered to pay rather than by reducing the fine.

(5) If the offender fails to disclose properly his means to the court, reasonable inferences can be drawn as to his means from evidence they had heard and all the circumstances of the case.

In determining the amount of costs to be paid by an offender, consideration should be given to any time that the offender has spent in custody on remand, if the court is to go on to impose any further punishment (eg a community order) (*R v Rakib* [2011] EWCA Crim 870).

D27.2 Specific costs

The costs of housing an animal pending appeal cannot be classified as prosecution costs but the powers under s 41 Animal Welfare Act 2006 are wide enough to make such a provision (*R (Donovan) v Burnley CC* [2014] EWHC 742 (Admin)).

See **C1.1.5** and *Blackstone's Criminal Practice 2019* **D33.21**

D28 Racially and Religiously Aggravated Crimes

D28.1 Meaning of 'racially aggravated'

Crime and Disorder Act 1998, s 28

28 Meaning of racially or religiously aggravated

(1) An offence is racially or religiously aggravated for the purposes of sections 29 to 32 below if—
   (a) at the time of committing the offence, or immediately before or after doing so, the offender demonstrates towards the victim of the offence hostility based on the victim's membership (or presumed membership) of a racial or religious group; or
   (b) the offence is motivated (wholly or partly) by hostility towards members of a racial or religious group based on their membership of that group.

(2) In subsection (1)(a) above—
'membership', in relation to a racial or religious group, includes association with members of that group;
'presumed' means presumed by the offender.

(3) It is immaterial for the purposes of paragraph (a) or (b) of subsection(1) above whether or not the offender's hostility is also based, to any extent, on any other factor not mentioned in that paragraph.

(4) In this section 'racial group' means a group of persons defined by reference to race, colour, nationality (including citizenship) or ethnic or national origins.

(5) In this section 'religious group' means a group of persons defined by reference to religious belief or lack of religious belief.

D28.2 Specific racially aggravated offences

The Crime and Disorder Act 1988 (CDA 1998) provides for increased sentences for specific offences that are racially or religiously aggravated:

- ss 20 **(C16.8)**, 39 **(C16.4)**, and 47 **(C16.1)** Offences Against the Person Act 1861; (s 29 CDA1998)
- criminal damage **(C6.1.4)** (s 30 CDA 1998)
- ss 4 **(C11.8)**, 4A **(C11.5)**, and 5 **(C11.4)** Public Order Act 1986; (s 31 CDA 1998) and
- harassment offences under the Protection from Harassment Act 1997 (s 2 **(C8.1)**; s 4 **(C8.2)**; s 2A **(C8.3.1)**; s 4A **(C8.3.2)**) (s 32 CDA 1998).

D28.3 Criteria for other offences

Section 145 Criminal Justice Act 2003 provides:

Criminal Justice Act 2003, s 145

145 Increase in sentences for racial or religious aggravation

(1) This section applies where a court is considering the seriousness of an offence other than one under sections 29 to 32 of the Crime and Disorder Act 1998 (c 37) (racially or religiously aggravated assaults, criminal damage, public order offences and harassment etc).

(2) If the offence was racially or religiously aggravated, the court—
   (a) must treat that fact as an aggravating factor, and
   (b) must state in open court that the offence was so aggravated.

(3) Section 28 of the Crime and Disorder Act 1998 (meaning of 'racially or religiously aggravated') applies for the purposes of this section as it applies for the purposes of sections 29 to 32 of that Act. An offence is racially or religiously aggravated if—

   (a) at the time of committing the offence, or immediately before or after doing so, the offender demonstrates towards the victim of the offence hostility based on the victim's membership (or presumed membership) of a racial or religious group; or
   (b) the offence is motivated (wholly or partly) by hostility towards members of a racial or religious group based on their membership of that group.

Following the guidance given by the court in *R v Kelly and Donnelly* [2001] 2 Cr App R (S) 73, the court should follow a two-stage process, identifying first the sentence it would have passed if the offence had not been racially aggravated and then adding an appropriate uplift to reflect the racial element, so that the sentencing process is transparent and the public can see to what extent the racial element has been reflected. There is no fixed uplift, but in *Kelly and Donnelly*, an uplift of 50 per cent was applied.

When sentencing a judge may take account of matters relating to racial, etc aggravation where there had been no acquittal of the aggravated offence, such an allegation had not been deleted, and the issue had been addressed in evidence: *R v O'Leary* [2015] EWCA Crim 1306.

For other aggravating factors, see **D30**.

 See *Blackstone's Criminal Practice 2019* **B11.148–B11.156** and **E1.16**

D29 **Restraining Order**

D29.1 **Criteria**

Under the Protection from Harassment Act 1997, a court may impose a re-straining order following conviction or acquittal (*Kalpotra* [2011] EWCA Crim 1843 and *Brough* [2011] EWCA Crim 2802 confirm that an acquittal includes where the prosecution offer no evidence on a charge). Section 5 provides:

Protection from Harassment Act 1997, s 5(2)–(6)

5 Restraining orders

(1) . . .
(2) The order may, for the purpose of protecting the victim or victims of the offence, or any other person mentioned in the order, from further conduct which—
   (a) amounts to harassment, or
   (b) will cause a fear of violence, prohibit the defendant from doing anything de-scribed in the order.
(3) The order may have effect for a specified period or until further order.
(4) The prosecutor, the defendant or any other person mentioned in the order may apply to the court which made the order for it to be varied or discharged by a further order.
(5) If without reasonable excuse the defendant does anything which he is prohibited from doing by an order under this section, he is guilty of an offence.
(6) A person guilty of an offence under this section is liable—
   (a) on conviction on indictment, to imprisonment for a term not exceeding five years, or a fine, or both, or
   (b) on summary conviction, to imprisonment for a term not exceeding six months, or a fine not exceeding the statutory maximum, or both.

D29.2 **Procedural requirements**

When a prosecutor seeks a restraining order, Criminal Procedure Rules (Crim PR) Part 31.3 requires the following.

(6) Where a restraining order [is] proposed, the prosecutor must—

   (a) serve a draft order on the court officer and on the defendant as soon as practicable (without waiting for the verdict);
   (b) in the draft order specify—
     (i) those prohibitions which, if the defendant is convicted, the pros-ecutor proposes for the purpose of protecting a person from conduct which amounts to harassment or will cause fear of violence, or
     (ii) those prohibitions which, if the defendant is acquitted, the pros-ecutor proposes as necessary to protect a person from harassment by the defendant.

D29.3 Key points on conviction

R v Herrington [2017] EWCA Crim 889, following *R v Brown* [2012] EWCA Crim 1152 but qualifying *R v Khellaf* [2016] EWCA Crim 1297, confirms that a restraining order should not be used to prevent an offender living with the adult victim of an assault who wishes, in a freely given decision, to live with him. Protection of any children should be left to the family court. In the definitive guideline on domestic abuse (see **Appendix 5**) it is confirmed:

> Orders can be made on the initiative of the court; the views of the victim should be sought, but their consent is not required.
>
> The order may prohibit the offender from doing anything for the purpose of protecting the victim of the offence, or any other person mentioned in the order, from further conduct which amounts to harassment or will cause a fear of violence.
>
> If the parties are to continue or resume a relationship, courts may consider a prohibition within the restraining order not to molest the victim (as opposed to a prohibition on contacting the victim).

The terms of the order must be proportionate and not violate the offender's human rights. However, a person can harass someone by publishing truthful things (eg that someone is gay), and an order may be made preventing publication of information that is the truth; such an order will not violate a person's right to freedom of expression under the European Convention (*R v Debnath* [2006] 2 Cr App R (S) 25).

Even though the defendant had been convicted of an offence against a neighbour under s 3 Sexual Offences Act 2003, an order excluding him from his home, where he cared for elderly parents, for five years, could not be justified. The order already prevented him from contacting the neighbour directly or indirectly. Neither the fact of knowing he was living next door nor anxiety from knowing there might be a sighting of him, made this part of the order necessary for the protection of the victim from conduct of the defendant which would cause fear of violence (see *R v M* [2012] EWCA Crim 1144).

An order must name the person it is seeking to protect (*R v Mann*, The Times, 11 April 2000), but there is no reason in principle why an order cannot be made to protect a group of individuals or a company (*R v Buxton* [2010] EWCA Crim 2023).

D29.4 Restraining orders on acquittal

Section 5A of the Protection from Harassment Act 1997 provides:

Protection from Harassment Act 1997, s 5A(1), (2), and (5)

5A Restraining orders on acquittal

(1) A court before which a person ('the defendant') is acquitted of an offence may, if it considers it necessary to do so to protect a person from harassment by the defendant, make an order prohibiting the defendant from doing anything described in the order.

(2) Subsections (3) to (7) of section 5 apply to an order under this section as they apply to an order under that one.

(3) ...

(4) ...

(5) A person made subject to an order under this section has the same right of appeal against the order as if—

    (a) he had been convicted of the offence in question before the court which made the order, and

    (b) the order had been made under section 5.

In relation to restraining orders after acquittal, a new legal aid order may be sought from the court and the matter billed separately (as a CRM 7 non-standard claim).

D29.5 Key points on acquittal

The following points emerge from *R v Major* [2010] EWCA Crim 3016:

- it was not Parliament's intention that orders be made only when the facts are uncontested, nor that orders should be made only rarely;
- the civil standard of proof applies;
- there is no contradiction in making an order post-acquittal, as the standard of proof required for a conviction is higher than that for making a restraining order;
- the evidence did not have to establish on the balance of probabilities that there had been harassment; it was enough if the evidence established conduct which fell short of harassment but which might well, if repeated in the future, amount to harassment and so make an order necessary;
- the court should set out the factual basis for making an order.

In making an order on acquittal, the court must ensure that the defendant is not denied the opportunity to make submissions on the propriety and the terms of an order. See *R v Trott* [2011] EWCA Crim 2395, following *R v Kapotra* [2011] EWCA Crim 1843 (see also Crim PR Part 31). In *R v M J Smith* [2012] EWCA Crim 2566, the court quashed an order on acquittal following a finding that the defendant was not guilty by reason of insanity, as that meant there was no sufficient intent and it unnecessarily criminalized acts that were otherwise lawful; and held that the order was not for the benefit of a sufficiently identifiable group of persons.

The statute requires that the order be necessary and the word is not to be diluted (*R v David Taylor* [2017] EWCA Crim 2209)

See *Blackstone's Criminal Practice 2019* **E21.34** and **E21.38**

D30 Sexual Orientation, Disability, or Transgender Identity

Section 146 Criminal Justice Act 2003 provides:

Criminal Justice Act 2003, s 146

146 Increase in sentences for aggravation related to disability or sexual orientation

(1) This section applies where the court is considering the seriousness of an offence committed in any of the circumstances mentioned in subsection (2).

(2) Those circumstances are—

    (a) that, at the time of committing the offence, or immediately before or after doing so, the offender demonstrated towards the victim of the offence hostility based on—

        (i) the sexual orientation (or presumed sexual orientation) of the victim, or

        (ii) a disability (or presumed disability) of the victim,

        (iii) the victim being or being presumed to be transgender; or

    (b) that the offence is motivated (wholly or partly)—

        (i) by hostility towards persons who are of a particular sexual orientation, or

        (ii) by hostility towards persons who have a disability or a particular disability,

        (iii) by hostility to persons who are transgender.

(3) The court—

    (a) must treat the fact that the offence was committed in any of those circumstances as an aggravating factor, and

    (b) must state in open court that the offence was committed in such circumstances.

(4) It is immaterial for the purposes of paragraph (a) or (b) of subsection (2) whether or not the offender's hostility is also based, to any extent, on any other factor not mentioned in that paragraph.

(5) In this section 'disability' means any physical or mental impairment.

(6) In this section references to being transgender include references to being transsexual, or undergoing, proposing to undergo or having undergone a process or part of a process of gender reassignment.

 See *Blackstone's Criminal Practice 2019* **E1.17**

D31 Suspended Sentences

See s 189 Criminal Justice Act (CJA) 2003.

D31.1 Principles for imposition

The Sentencing Council's definitive guideline on the imposition of community and custodial sentences confirms that 'a suspended sentence must not be imposed as a more severe form of community order. A suspended sentence is a custodial sentence. Sentencers should be clear that they would impose an immediate custodial sentence if the power to suspend were not available. If not, a non-custodial sentence should be imposed.'

The following factors should be weighed in considering whether it is possible to suspend the sentence:

Factors indicating that it would not be appropriate to suspend a custodial sentence	Factors indicating that it may be appropriate to suspend a custodial sentence
Offender presents a risk/danger to the public	Realistic prospect of rehabilitation
Appropriate punishment can only be achieved by immediate custody	Strong personal mitigation
History of poor compliance with court orders	Immediate custody will result in significant harmful impact upon others

D31.2 Length of suspended sentences

A magistrates' court may suspend a sentence of not less than 14 days and not more than 6 months (s 189 CJA 2003). A custodial sentence that is suspended should be for the same term that would have applied if the sentence was to be served immediately. Where a person has served such time on remand that a custodial sentence would result in immediate release, it may not be appropriate to impose a suspended sentence order (*R v Waters and Young* [2008] EWCA Crim 2538).

The court may suspend the sentence for between 6 months and 2 years, and may add appropriate requirement(s) to be completed as part of the order. The time for which a sentence is suspended should reflect the length of the sentence. For sentences up to 12 months, it might normally be appropriate for a sentence to be suspended for 6 months.

D31.3 Requirements

The list of requirements available to a court as part of a suspended sentence appear at **D5.4**.

D31.4 Breach of suspended sentence order

D31.4.1 *Principles*

See Sch 12 to the CJA 2003.

An order will be breached if the offender does not comply with any community requirement during the period of suspension, or commits a further offence during the operational period. Following conviction for a new offence, a magistrates' court has no jurisdiction to deal with breach of a suspended sentence order imposed by the Crown Court; it must either commit the offender for sentence upon conviction for the new offence, or notify the Crown Court of the breach so that that court can take action if it so wishes. A Crown Court order will specify whether or not any breach of its requirements should result in a return to the Crown Court or be left to the magistrates' court (it is the norm for a Crown Court to order any breach be reserved to itself).

There will generally be some reduction of the term of the suspended sentence if there has been substantial compliance with an unpaid work requirement, although there will sometimes be a case in which it is nevertheless appropriate in all the circumstances to activate the suspended sentence in full (*R v McDonagh* [2017] EWCA Crim 2193).

A suspended sentence is a single sentence which, if activated, cannot be activated a second time in respect of a constituent element of the original sentence (*R v Bostan* [2018] EWCA Crim 494)

D31.4.2 *Powers*

Upon a breach being proved the court has the following options open to it:

- order the sentence to take effect (ie send the offender to prison); or
- order the sentence to take effect but with a reduced term of imprisonment; or with an extended operational period; or
- impose more onerous community requirements or extend the supervision or operational period; or
- impose a fine of up to £2,500.
- if no requirements extend operational period.

Note: The court must order one of the first two options unless it would be unjust to do so in all the circumstances. A court must give reasons for so ordering.

D31.4.3 *Sentencing guideline*

Conviction for further offence committed during operational period of order

The court must activate the custodial sentence unless it would be unjust in all the circumstances to do so. The predominant factor in determining whether activation is unjust relates to the level of compliance with the suspended sentence order and the facts/nature of any new offence. These factors are already provided for in the penalties below, which are determined by the nature of the new offence and level of compliance but permit a reduction to the custodial term for relevant completed or partially completed requirements where appropriate.

The facts/nature of the new offence is the primary consideration in assessing the action to be taken on the breach.

Where the breach is in the second or third category below, the prior level of compliance is also relevant. In assessing the level of compliance with the order the court should consider:

(i)   the overall attitude and engagement with the order as well as the proportion of elements completed;

(ii) the impact of any completed or partially completed requirements on the offender's behaviour;

(iii) the proximity of breach to imposition of order; and

(iv) evidence of circumstances or offender characteristics, such as disability, mental health issues, or learning difficulties which have impeded offender's compliance with the order.

Breach involves	Penalty
Multiple and/or more serious new offence(s) committed	Full activation of original custodial term
New offence similar in type and gravity to offence for which suspended sentence order imposed and: (a) No/low level of compliance with suspended sentence order **or** (b) Medium or high level of compliance with suspended sentence order	(a) Full activation of original custodial term (b) Activate sentence but apply appropriate reduction* to original custodial term taking into consideration any unpaid work or curfew requirements completed
New offence less serious than original offence but requires a custodial sentence and: (a) No/low level of compliance with suspended sentence order or (b) Medium or high level of compliance with suspended sentence order	(a) Full activation of original custodial term (b) Activate sentence but apply appropriate reduction* to original custodial term taking into consideration any unpaid work or curfew requirements completed
New offence does not require custodial sentence	Activate sentence but apply reduction* to original custodial term taking into consideration any unpaid work or curfew requirements completed **or** Impose more onerous requirement(s) and/or extend supervision period and/ or extend operational period and/or impose fine

* It is for the court dealing with the breach to identify the appropriate proportionate reduction depending on the extent of any compliance with the requirements specified.

Unjust in all the circumstances

The court dealing with the breach should remember that the court imposing the original sentence determined that a custodial sentence was appropriate in the original case.

In determining if there are other factors which would cause activation to be unjust, the court may consider all factors including:

• any strong personal mitigation;
• whether there is a realistic prospect of rehabilitation;
• whether immediate custody will result in significant impact on others.

Only new and exceptional factors/circumstances not present at the time the suspended sentence order was imposed should be taken into account.

In cases where the court considers that it would be unjust to order the custodial sentence to take effect, it must state its reasons and it must deal with the offender in one of the following ways:

(a) impose a fine not exceeding £2,500; or

(b) extend the operational period (to a maximum of 2 years from date of original sentence); or

(c) if the SSO imposes community requirements, do one or more of the following:
  (i) impose more onerous community requirements;
  (ii) extend the supervision period (to a maximum of 2 years from date of original sentence);
  (iii) extend the operational period (to a maximum of 2 years from date of original sentence.

 See *Blackstone's Criminal Practice 2019* **E6**

D32 Time on Remand or Qualifying Curfew

D32.1 Criteria

Section 240ZA Criminal Justice Act (CJA) 2003 provides that any immediate custodial sentence shall be reduced automatically by any time spent on remand in custody.

Section 240A CJA 2003 requires the sentencing court to direct that time spent on bail under an electronically monitored curfew should be credited against an immediate custodial sentence in a similar way. A person will receive credit at the rate of a half a day for every day spent subject to a qualifying electronically monitored curfew (ie a curfew of nine hours a day or more). There is no general discretion to disallow this time and deductions may only be made in accordance with s 240A(3A and 3B) (eg if already serving another sentence) (*R v Lord* [2015] EWCA Crim 1545). Section 240ZA means that time spent on remand in relation to a new offence cannot count if it coincides with a recall. There would have to be an excessive delay to reduce an otherwise appropriate sentence (*R v Phillips (Nathan)* [2015] EWCA Crim 427).

The section sets out the procedure as follows:

Criminal Justice Act 2003, s 240A

240A Crediting periods of remand on bail: terms of imprisonment and detention

(3) The credit period is calculated by taking the following steps.

Step 1

Add—
- (a) the day on which the offender's bail was first subject to the relevant conditions (and for this purpose a condition is not prevented from being a relevant condition by the fact that it does not apply for the whole of the day in question), and
- (b) the number of other days on which the offender's bail was subject to those conditions (but exclude the last of those days if the offender spends the last part of it in custody).

Step 2

Deduct the number of days on which the offender, whilst on bail subject to the relevant conditions, was also—
- (a) subject to any requirement imposed for the purpose of securing the electronic monitoring of the offender's compliance with a curfew requirement, or
- (b) on temporary release under rules made under section 47 of the Prison Act 1952.

Step 3

From the remainder, deduct the number of days during that remainder on which the offender has broken either or both of the relevant conditions.

Step 4

Divide the result by 2.

Step 5

If necessary, round up to the nearest whole number.

(3A) A day of the credit period counts as time served—
    (a) in relation to only one sentence, and
    (b) only once in relation to that sentence.
(3B) A day of the credit period is not to count as time served as part of any period of
    28 days served by the offender before automatic release (see section 255B(1)).

If there is a dispute as to the time to be allowed, the burden to the criminal standard is on the Crown but the strict rules of evidence do not apply (*R v Hoggard* (2013) EWCA Crim 1024). The matter was further examined in *R v Marshall and others* [2015] EWCA Crim 1999, which emphasized that approved wording should be used so that any error could be corrected administratively under s 142 Magistrates' Courts Act 1980 **(A6.2.1)**:

The defendant will receive full credit for half the time spent under curfew if the curfew qualified under the provisions of section 240A. On the information before me the total period is ... days (subject to the deduct of ... days that I have directed under the Step(s) 2 and/or 3 making a total of ... days), but if this period is mistaken, this court will order an amendment of the record for the correct period to be recorded.

D33 **Victim Surcharge Order**

D33.1 **Criteria**

In any case relating to an offence committed on or after 1 October 2012, the court must impose a surcharge order in accordance with the following table (s 161A Criminal Justice Act 2003 and the Criminal Justice Act 2003 (Surcharge) Order 2012 (SI 2012/1696)). For offences wholly committed on or after 8 April 2016 the figures are increased as shown below (Criminal Justice Act 2003 (Surcharge) (Amendment) Order 2016 (SI 2016/389)).

The charge may be ignored or reduced if the offender would not be able to pay both the surcharge and compensation. If the offender would not be able to pay both a surcharge and a fine, the surcharge takes precedence and the fine should be reduced.

D33.2 **The charges**

Sentence	Adult		Youths		Company	
	Before 28.06.19	**On or after 28.06.19**	**Before 28.06.19**	**On or after 28.06.19**	**Before 28.06.19**	**On or after 28.06.19**
Conditional discharge	£20	£21	£15	£16	£20	£21
Fine	10% in range £30 to £170	10% in range £32 to £181	£20	£21	10% in range £30 to £170	10% in range £32 to £181
YRO/Referral order			£20	£21		
Community order	£85	£90		£21		
Suspended or immediate custodial sentence	£115 if 6 months or less £140 if 6 months to 2 years and suspended sentence over 6 months £170 if immediate sentence over 2 years	£122 if 6 months or less £149 if 6 months to 2 years and supended sentences over 6 months £181 if immediate custodial sentence over 2 years	£30 for all custodial sentences	£32 for all custodial sentences		

One surcharge (at the highest rate) is payable if more than one sentence (including more than one fine) is imposed.

If any one offence was committed as a youth then the youth court figures apply.

TICs are not relevant to the calculation of the surcharge (*R v Bailey; R v Kirk; R v Tote* [2013] EWCA Crim 1551).

R v George (Michael) [2015] EWCA Crim 1096 confirms that a second surcharge is not payable on sentence for breach of an order. Liability stems from conviction and the 'notional' existence of a 'victim'.

See *Blackstone's Criminal Practice 2019* **E15.24**

Appendices

Appendix 1

Preparation for Effective Trial

These notes are prepared by reference to questions for the defence raised by the current Preparation for trial forms in the Magistrates' Court and when a case is sent to the crown court for trial

1.1 Preparation for trial in a magistrates court: relevant questions

6 Advice on plea and absence/7 Partial or different guilty plea

The current law on discount for guilty plea is summarized at **D15**.

The law on trials in the absence of a defendant is at **A2.2.2**.

The law on disclosure of the initial details of the prosecution case is set out in Rule 8 of the Criminal Procedure Rules.

8.3. Initial details of the prosecution case must include—
(a) where, immediately before the first hearing in the magistrates' court, the defendant was in police custody for the offence charged—
  (i) a summary of the circumstances of the offence, and
  (ii) the defendant's criminal record, if any;
(b) where paragraph (a) does not apply—
  (i) a summary of the circumstances of the offence,
  (ii) any account given by the defendant in interview, whether contained in that summary or in another document,
  (iii) any written witness statement or exhibit that the prosecutor then has available and considers material to plea, or to the allocation of the case for trial, or to sentence,
  (iv) the defendant's criminal record, if any, and
  (v) any available statement of the effect of the offence on a victim, a victim's family or others.

8.4. Use of initial details
(1) This rule applies where—
  (a) the prosecutor wants to introduce information contained in a document listed in rule 8.3; and
  (b) the prosecutor has not—
    (i) served that document on the defendant, or
    (ii) made that information available to the defendant.
(2) The court must not allow the prosecutor to introduce that information unless the court first allows the defendant sufficient time to consider it.

The Law Society has given guidance on entering a plea when there is insufficient disclosure fully to advise:

4 Meeting your professional obligation
If your client is unsure about how to plead to the charge/s but you require further information in order to meet your professional obligations in providing adequate advice, you should make both the court and your client aware of any problems this may present.

4.1 Providing advice

You should advise your client about the sentencing discount they will be entitled to if they plead guilty at the first opportunity.

If you advise the client to enter a not guilty plea, or to enter no plea, to protect his or her position due to the lack of information, you should ask the court to make a note of the circumstances and the reasons for pleading so.

To help your client retain the maximum credit for any subsequent guilty plea, you should both:

advise your client about the situation

inform the court of the predicament you face due to the lack of disclosure.

There is a risk that any admission of a lesser offence may be used in evidence to prove ingredients of the greater. However, consideration should be given to *R v Newell* [2012] EWCA Crim 650:

Whilst an answer by a lawyer on a case management form may be admissible as hearsay under the agency rule, a discretion should be exercised to exclude the answer from evidence under section 78 of the Police and Criminal Evidence Act 1984, provided that the case is conducted in accordance with the letter and spirit of the Criminal Procedure Rules. It would be otherwise if there was an ambush.

The *Newton* principles in relation to a basis of plea appear at **D21**.

8 Case management information

8.1 Agreed facts

Facts agreed in section 9 may be used in evidence by the Crown. Great care should be taken before admissions are made, and specific authority obtained from the client.

There was again a risk that other responses in this section 8 might also be used by the Crown in evidence, but that risk has been largely removed by the decision in *R v Newell* (above). However the material can amount to admissible hearsay if the defence have obtained an unfair advantage and a properly constituted hearsay application is made (*Valiati v DPP* [2018] EWHC 2908 (Admin) and *Randell v DPP* [2018] EWHC 1048 (Admin). See **A10.12**)

The tape summary cannot be agreed unless the solicitor was present or the tape has been played. Obtaining a copy of the tape or disc of interview is often problematic. The court has a jurisdiction to order production to the defence under PACE Code E paragraph 3.21.

3.21 The suspect shall be handed a notice which explains:
- how the audio recording will be used;
- the arrangements for access to it;
- that if they are charged or informed they will be prosecuted, a copy of the audio recording will be supplied as soon as practicable or as otherwise agreed between the suspect and the police or on the order of a court.

Information about the defendant's previous convictions held by a solicitor is confidential and must not be disclosed to the client's detriment, but great care must be taken not to mislead the court. It is for the Crown to prove to the criminal standard the existence of previous convictions if they are not agreed.

Note that a Streamlined Forensic Report (SFR) may provide no detail of how the findings have been arrived at or the conditions under which the tests were commissioned. Individuals who are not scientific experts can also produce them: for example, a DNA match report could have been generated and reported automatically as part of an administration process. Test results may not have been generated using accredited procedures. In combination, this can mean that it may not be easy for the Defence to discover whether the evidence is robust or identify if they should challenge it. A Form SFR1 is inadmissible hearsay (*Hunt v CPS* [2018] EWHC 3341 (Admin)).

8.2 Disputed issues

Generally the areas in dispute should be identified. However, a defendant is entitled to put the Crown to proof. In that situation the form should indicate that the defence put the Crown to proof and do not raise any positive defence. Care should be taken, as the absence of a defence may be used in cross-examination should the defendant later raise a specific issue. The law is set out in *R v Rochford* [2010] EWCA Crim 1928. The words in square brackets are so marked because defence statements are not obligatory in the magistrates' court:

> What is the duty of the lawyer if the defendant has no positive case to advance at trial but declines to plead guilty? That is a realistic (if rare) practical possibility. It may occur in at least two situations. It might happen that a defendant within the cloak of privilege confides in his lawyer that he is in fact guilty of the offence charged but refuses to plead guilty. He cannot be prevented from taking that course and his instructions to his lawyer are covered by privilege. He is entitled in those circumstances to sit through the trial and to see whether the Crown can prove the case or not. What he is not entitled to do is to conduct the trial by the putting in issue of specific matters and advancing either evidence or argument towards them without giving notice [in his defence statement] that he is going to do it. A less extreme but equally possible example is the defendant who refuses to give instructions either at all or on specific points. That too can occur. In neither of those situations can it possibly be the obligation of the defendant to put in [to his defence statement] an admission of guilt or a refusal to give instructions. What are the lawyers to do? It seems to us that we can give an answer only in general terms because it would be unhelpful for us to attempt the impossible task of foreseeing every factual scenario that might occur in future. They will have to be dealt with as they arise, case by case. But in general terms our answer is this. The defence [statement] must say that the defendant does not admit the offence or the relevant part of it as the case may be, and calls for the Crown to prove it. But it must also say that he advances no positive case because if he is going to advance a positive case [that must appear in the defence statement and] notice of it must be given.

In its guidance on the Criminal Procedure Rules, the Law Society states:

> Your client is entitled to put the prosecution to proof and you are not required by the CPR to cease acting simply because you are unable to assist the court further. However, you will note the consequent limitation on your client's ability to raise any positive case at his trial.

Thus whilst entitled to put the prosecution to proof, care should be taken in the preparation of the effective trial form because Direction 24B.4 of the Criminal Practice Directions confirms that:

> The identification of issues at the case management stage will have been made without the risk that they would be used at trial as statement of the defendant admissible in

evidence against the defendant, provided the advocate follows the letter and the spirit of the Criminal Procedure Rules. The court may take the view that a party is not acting in the spirit of the Criminal Procedure Rules in seeking to ambush the other party or raising late and technical legal arguments that were not previously raised as issues. No party that seeks to ambush the other at trial should derive an advantage from such a course of action. The court may also take the view that a defendant is not acting in the spirit of the Criminal Procedure Rules if he or she refuses to identify the issues and puts the prosecutor to proof at the case management stage. In both such circumstances the court may limit the proceedings on the day of trial in accordance with CrimPR 3.11(d). In addition any significant divergence from the issues identified at case management at this late stage may well result in the exercise of the court's powers under CrimPR 3.5(6), the powers to impose sanctions.

8.3 Defence statements

These are not obligatory in the magistrates' court but will be required if there are disclosure issues, and such issues cannot be raised without one. A defence statement cannot be filed without the defendant's consent. *R v Rochford* (above) has made clear that compliance with the requirement for a defence statement cannot require a breach of privilege.

9 Admissions

These are formal admissions that will be admitted at trial and on which a defendant can be cross-examined.

10 Application for directions

Check that you will be able to comply with the standard time limits, or apply to vary them. Consider particularly issues around disclosure, if this was served prior to the first hearing and it is intended to serve a defence statement, expert evidence, CCTV, and tapes. Under 2010/64/EU a defendant who does not speak English is entitled to an interpreter and translation of 'essential documents'. Consideration should also be given to special measures required for the defendant or defence witnesses. See and **A27**.

11 Prosecution witnesses

Appropriate assistance should be given in identifying the relevant witnesses and witnesses whose evidence can be read, but this should always be checked with the client. Nothing that is said, including by the court, can make hearsay evidence admissible upon the completion of the form. Either there must be agreement under section 10 of the Criminal Justice Act 1967, or there must be compliance with section 9 of the Criminal Justice Act 1967 or section 114(1) (d) of the Criminal Justice Act 2003. The latter is likely to be used unless the defence identifies the grounds on which the witness is required to attend. (See **A10.10** and **A17.3**.)

The form seeks to identify the time needed to examine and cross-examine each witness. Generous estimates should be given particularly if time is needed to establish a picture to enable effective cross-examination. However, whilst courts will seek to set (*Drinkwater v Solihull MC* [2012] EWHC 765 (Admin)) and enforce a timetable, the resulting trial must be fair. In *R v Jisl* [2004] EWCA

Crim 296 the court said:

> The starting point is simple. Justice must be done. The judge should consider whether to direct a timetable to cover pre-trial steps, and eventually the conduct of the trial itself, not rigid, nor immutable, and fully recognising that during the trial at any rate the unexpected must be treated as normal, and making due allowance for it in the interests of justice. To enable the trial judge to manage the case in a way which is fair to every participant, pre-trial, the potential problems as well as the possible areas for time saving, should be canvassed. In short, a sensible informed discussion about the future management of the case and the most convenient way to present the evidence, whether disputed or not, and where appropriate, with admissions by one or other or both *sides*, should enable the judge to make a fully informed analysis of the future timetable, and the proper conduct of the trial. The objective is not haste and rush, but greater efficiency and better use of limited resources by closer identification of and focus on critical rather than peripheral issues.

In principle, the trial judge should exercise firm control over the timetable, where necessary, making clear in advance and throughout the trial that the timetable will be subject to appropriate constraints, with such necessary even-handedness and flexibility as the interests of the justice require as the case unfolds (*R v Chabban* [2003] EWCA Crim 1012).

12 Expected defence witnesses

An estimate of the number of defence witnesses and details of known witnesses can be given, though there is no obligation to do so and it is unlikely that they have been proofed at this stage. The defence comply with their obligations to notify the details of witnesses if they do so once there is an intention to call them (see **A10.8**). Evidence of general reputation is admissible from character witnesses and particularly when the defendant's credibility was central to the defence. A good character direction was insufficient (*R v Grimes* 2017 NICA 19)

1.2 Case management questionnaire where a case is sent to the crown court for trial

The key question is concisely to identify the **real issues** in the case. This can have a major impact on discount for guilty plea if a guilty plea is later entered. **See D15** There will be cases falling within the exception in paragraph F1 of the Guideline as the case for the prosecution is not yet clear. However admissions as to any facts that are not in dispute are encouraged, even if other issues remain. The crown may be put to proof but the client should understand the implications on any later discount

Appendix 2

Extracts from the Criminal Procedure Rules

Extracts from the following rules are reproduced in this appendix:
- Rule 1 (the overriding objective); and
- Rule 3 (case management).

Part 1 The Overriding Objective

The overriding objective

1.1—(1) The overriding objective of this new code is that criminal cases be dealt with justly.

(2) Dealing with a criminal case justly includes—

    (a) acquitting the innocent and convicting the guilty;

    (b) dealing with the prosecution and the defence fairly;

    (c) recognising the rights of a defendant, particularly those under Article 6 of the European Convention on Human Rights;

    (d) respecting the interests of witnesses, victims and jurors and keeping them informed of the progress of the case;

    (e) dealing with the case efficiently and expeditiously;

    (f) ensuring that appropriate information is available to the court when bail and sentence are considered; and

    (g) dealing with the case in ways that take into account—

        (i) the gravity of the offence alleged,

        (ii) the complexity of what is in issue,

        (iii) the severity of the consequences for the defendant and others affected, and

        (iv) the needs of other cases.

The duty of the participants in a criminal case

1.2—(1) Each participant, in the conduct of each case, must—

    (a) prepare and conduct the case in accordance with the overriding objective;

    (b) comply with these Rules, practice directions and directions made by the court; and

    (c) at once inform the court and all parties of any significant failure (whether or not that participant is responsible for that failure) to take any procedural step required by these Rules, any practice direction or any direction of the court. A failure is significant if it might hinder the court in furthering the overriding objective.

(2) Anyone involved in any way with a criminal case is a participant in its conduct for the purposes of this rule.

The application by the court of the overriding objective

1.3 The court must further the overriding objective in particular when—

    (a) exercising any power given to it by legislation (including these Rules);

    (b) applying any practice direction; or

    (c) interpreting any rule or practice direction.

Part 3 Case Management

The duty of the court

3.2—(1) The court must further the overriding objective by actively managing the case.

(2) Active case management includes—

(a) the early identification of the real issues;

(b) the early identification of the needs of witnesses;

(c) achieving certainty as to what must be done, by whom, and when, in particular by the early setting of a timetable for the progress of the case;

(d) monitoring the progress of the case and compliance with directions;

(e) ensuring that evidence, whether disputed or not, is presented in the shortest and clearest way;

(f) discouraging delay, dealing with as many aspects of the case as possible on the same occasion, and avoiding unnecessary hearings;

(g) encouraging the participants to co-operate in the progression of the case; and

(h) making use of technology.

(3) The court must actively manage the case by giving any direction appropriate to the needs of that case as early as possible.

Fraud Sentencing Guideline (Note: The Sentencing

Council has also published a guideline for corporate defendants accused of fraud, bribery, and money laundering offences, which will usually be handled at the Crown Court.)

GROUP A: General fraud offences

Fraud by false representation, fraud by failing to disclose information, fraud by abuse of position
Fraud Act 2006 (section 1)
Triable either way
Maximum: 10 years' custody
Offence range: Discharge – 8 years' custody

False accounting
Theft Act 1968 (section 17)
Triable either way
Maximum: 7 years' custody
Offence range: Discharge – 6 years and 6 months' custody

STEP ONE Determining the offence category

The court should determine the offence category with reference to the tables below. In order to determine the category the court should assess culpability and harm.

> The level of **culpability** is determined by weighing up all the factors of the case to determine the offender's role and the extent to which the offending was planned and the sophistication with which it was carried out.

Culpability demonstrated by one or more of the following:
A—High culpability
A leading role where offending is part of a group activity
Involvement of others through pressure, influence
Abuse of position of power or trust or responsibility
Sophisticated nature of offence/significant planning
Fraudulent activity conducted over sustained period of time
Large number of victims
Deliberately targeting victim on basis of vulnerability

Culpability demonstrated by one or more of the following:
B—Medium culpability
Other cases where characteristics for categories A or C are not present
A significant role where offending is part of a group activity
C—Lesser culpability
Involved through coercion, intimidation or exploitation
Not motivated by personal gain
Peripheral role in organised fraud
Opportunistic 'one-off' offence; very little or no planning
Limited awareness or understanding of the extent of fraudulent activity

Where there are characteristics present which fall under different levels of culpability, the court should balance these characteristics to reach a fair assessment of the offender's culpability.

Harm is initially assessed by the actual, intended, or risked loss as may arise from the offence.

The values in the table below are to be used for **actual** or **intended** loss only.

Intended loss relates to offences where circumstances prevent the actual loss that is intended to be caused by the fraudulent activity.

Risk of loss (for instance in mortgage frauds) involves consideration of both the likelihood of harm occurring and the extent of it if it does. Risk of loss is less serious than actual or intended loss. Where the offence has caused risk of loss but no (or much less) actual loss the normal approach is to move down to the corresponding point in the next category. This may not be appropriate if either the likelihood or extent of risked loss is particularly high.

Harm A—Loss caused or intended		
Category 1	£500,000 or more	Starting point based on £1 million
Category 2	£100,000–£500,000 or Risk of category 1 harm	Starting point based on £300,000
Category 3	£20,000–£100,000 or Risk of category 2 harm	Starting point based on £50,000
Category 4	£5,000–£20,000 or Risk of category 3 harm	Starting point based on £12,500
Category 5	Less than £5,000 or Risk of category 4 harm	Starting point based on £2,500
Risk of category 5 harm, move down the range within the category		

Harm B—Victim impact demonstrated by one or more of the following:
The court should then take into account the level of harm caused to the victim(s) or others to determine whether it warrants the sentence being moved up to the corresponding point in the next category or further up the range of the initial category.

Harm B—Victim impact demonstrated by one or more of the following:
High impact—move up a category; if in category 1 move up the range
Serious detrimental effect on the victim whether financial or otherwise, for example substantial damage to credit rating
Victim particularly vulnerable (due to factors including but not limited to their age, financial circumstances, mental capacity)
Medium impact—move upwards within the category range
Considerable detrimental effect on the victim whether financial or otherwise
Lesser impact—no adjustment
Some detrimental impact on victim, whether financial or otherwise

STEP TWO Starting point and category range

Having determined the category at step one, the court should use the appropriate starting point (as adjusted in accordance with step one above) to reach a sentence within the category range in the table below. The starting point applies to all offenders irrespective of plea or previous convictions.

Where the value is larger or smaller than the amount on which the starting point is based, this should lead to upward or downward adjustment as appropriate.

Where the value greatly exceeds the amount of the starting point in category 1, it may be appropriate to move outside the identified range.

TABLE 1

Section 1 Fraud Act 2006: Conspiracy to defraud

Maximum: 10 years' custody

Culpability			
Harm	A	B	C
Category 1 £500,000 or more Starting point based on £1 million	**Starting point** 7 years' custody **Category range** 5–8 years' custody	**Starting point** 5 years' custody **Category range** 3–6 years' custody	**Starting point** 3 years' custody **Category range** 18 months' – 4 years' custody
Category 2 £100,000–£500,000 Starting point based on £300,000	**Starting point** 5 years' custody **Category range** 3–6 years' custody	**Starting point** 3 years' custody **Category range** 18 months'– 4 years' custody	**Starting point** 18 months' custody **Category range** 26 weeks'– 3 years' custody
Category 3 £20,000–£100,000 Starting point based on £50,000	**Starting point** 3 years' custody **Category range** 18 months'– 4 years' custody	**Starting point** 18 months' custody **Category range** 26 weeks'– 3 years' custody	**Starting point** 26 weeks' custody **Category range** Medium-level community order– 1 year's custody

Culpability			
Category 4 £5,000–£20,000 Starting point based on £12,500	**Starting point** 18 months' custody **Category range** 26 weeks'–3 years' custody	**Starting point** 26 weeks' custody **Category range** Medium-level community order–1 year's custody	**Starting point** Medium-level community order **Category range** Band B fine– high-level community order
Category 5 Less than £5,000 Starting point based on £2,500	**Starting point** 36 weeks' custody **Category range** High-level community order– 1 year's custody	**Starting point** Medium-level community order **Category range** Band B fine–26 weeks' custody	**Starting point** Band B fine **Category range** Discharge– medium-level community order

TABLE 2

Section 17 Theft Act 1968: False accounting

Maximum: 7 years' custody

Culpability			
Harm	**A**	**B**	**C**
Category 1 £500,000 or more Starting point based on £1 million	**Starting point** 5 years 6 months' custody **Category range** 4 years'– 6 years 6 months' custody	**Starting point** 4 years' custody **Category range** 2 years 6 months' – 5 years' custody	**Starting point** 2 years 6 months' custody **Category range** 15 months'– 3 years 6 months' custody
Category 2 £100,000–£500,000 Starting point based on £300,000	**Starting point** 4 years' custody **Category range** 2 years 6 months'– 5 years' custody	**Starting point** 2 years 6 months' custody **Category range** 15 months'–3 years 6 months' custody	**Starting point** 15 months' custody **Category range** 26 weeks'– 2 years 6 months' custody
Category 3 £20,000–£100,000 Starting point based on £50,000	**Starting point** 2 years 6 months' custody **Category range** 15 months'–3 years 6 months' custody	**Starting point** 15 months' custody **Category range** High-level community order – 2 years 6 months' custody	**Starting point** High-level community order **Category range** Low-level community order – 36 weeks' custody
Category 4 £5,000–£20,000 Starting point based on £12,500	**Starting point** 15 months' custody **Category range** High-level community order– 2 years 6 months' custody	**Starting point** High-level community order **Category range** Low-level community order– 36 weeks' custody	**Starting point** Low-level community order **Category range** Band B fine–medium-level community order

Appendix 3

Culpability			
Category 5 Less than £5,000 Starting point based on £2,500	**Starting point** 26 weeks' custody **Category range** Medium-level community order–36 weeks' custody	**Starting point** Low-level community order **Category range** Band B fine–medium-level community order	**Starting point** Band B fine **Category range** Discharge– low-level community order

The table below contains a non-exhaustive list of additional factual elements providing the context of the offence and factors relating to the offender.

Identify whether any combination of these or other relevant factors should result in an upward or downward adjustment from the sentence arrived at so far.

> Consecutive sentences for multiple offences may be appropriate where large sums are involved.

Factors increasing seriousness	Factors reducing seriousness or reflecting personal mitigation
Statutory aggravating factors:	No previous convictions or no relevant/recent convictions
Previous convictions, having regard to (a) the nature of the offence to which the conviction relates and its relevance to the current offence; and (b) the time that has elapsed since the conviction	Remorse
Offence committed whilst on bail	Good character and/or exemplary conduct
Other aggravating factors:	Little or no prospect of success
Steps taken to prevent the victim reporting or obtaining assistance and/or from assisting or supporting the prosecution	Serious medical conditions requiring urgent, intensive or long-term treatment
Attempts to conceal/dispose of evidence	Age and/or lack of maturity where it affects the responsibility of the offender
Established evidence of community/wider impact	Lapse of time since apprehension where this does not arise from the conduct of the offender
Failure to comply with current court orders	Mental disorder or learning disability
Offence committed on licence	Sole or primary carer for dependent relatives
Offences taken into consideration	Offender co-operated with investigation, made early admissions and/or voluntarily reported offending
Failure to respond to warnings about behaviour	Determination and/or demonstration of steps having been taken to address addiction or offending behaviour
Offences committed across borders	Activity originally legitimate
Blame wrongly placed on others	

GROUP B: Articles for fraud

Possessing, making or supplying articles for use in fraud
Possession of articles for use in frauds
Fraud Act 2006 (section 6)
Triable either way
Maximum: 5 years' custody
Offence range: Band A fine–3 years' custody

Making or supplying articles for use in frauds
Fraud Act 2006 (section 7)
Triable either way
Maximum: 10 years' custody
Offence range: Band C fine–7 years' custody

STEP ONE Determining the offence category

The court should determine the offence category with reference to the tables below. In order to determine the category the court should assess **culpability** and **harm**.

> The level of **culpability** is determined by weighing up all the factors of the case to determine the offender's role and the extent to which the offending was planned and the sophistication with which it was carried out.

Culpability demonstrated by one or more of the following:
A—High culpability
A leading role where offending is part of a group activity
Involvement of others through pressure, influence
Abuse of position of power or trust or responsibility
Sophisticated nature of offence/significant planning
Fraudulent activity conducted over sustained period of time
Articles deliberately designed to target victims on basis of vulnerability
B—Medium culpability
Other cases where characteristics for categories A or C are not present
A significant role where offending is part of a group activity
C—Lesser culpability
Performed limited function under direction
Involved through coercion, intimidation or exploitation
Not motivated by personal gain
Opportunistic 'one-off' offence; very little or no planning
Limited awareness or understanding of extent of fraudulent activity

Appendix 3

Where there are characteristics present which fall under different levels of culpability, the court should balance these characteristics to reach a fair assessment of the offender's culpability.

Harm
This guideline refers to preparatory offences where no substantive fraud has been committed. The level of harm is determined by weighing up all the factors of the case to determine the harm that would be caused if the article(s) were used to commit a substantive offence.
Greater harm
Large number of articles created/supplied/in possession
Article(s) have potential to facilitate fraudulent acts affecting large number of victims
Article(s) have potential to facilitate fraudulent acts involving significant sums
Use of third party identities
Offender making considerable gain as result of the offence
Lesser harm
All other offences

STEP TWO Starting point and category range

Having determined the category at step one, the court should use the appropriate starting point to reach a sentence within the category range in the table below. The starting point applies to all offenders irrespective of plea or previous convictions.

Section 6 Fraud Act 2006: Possessing articles for use in fraud

Maximum: 5 years' custody

Culpability			
Harm	A	B	C
Greater	**Starting point** 18 months' custody	**Starting point** 36 weeks' custody	**Starting point** High-level community order
	Category range 36 weeks' custody–3 years' custody	**Category range** High-level community order–2 years' custody	**Category range** Medium-level community order–26 weeks' custody
Lesser	**Starting point** 26 weeks' custody	**Starting point** Medium-level community order	**Starting point** Band B fine
	Category range High-level community order–18 months' custody	**Category range** Low-level community order–26 weeks' custody	**Category range** Band A fine–medium-level community order

Section 7 Fraud Act 2006: Making or adapting or supplying articles for use in fraud

Maximum: 10 years' custody

Culpability			
Harm	A	B	C
Greater	**Starting point** 4 years 6 months' custody	**Starting point** 2 years 6 months' custody	**Starting point** 1 year's custody
	Category range 3–7 years' custody	**Category range** 18 months'–5 years' custody	**Category range** High-level community order–3 years' custody
Lesser	**Starting point** 2 years' custody	**Starting point** 36 weeks' custody	**Starting point** Medium-level community order
	Category range 26 weeks'–4 years' custody	**Category range** Low-level community order–2 years' custody	**Category range** Band C fine–26 weeks' custody

The table below contains a non-exhaustive list of additional factual elements providing the context of the offence and factors relating to the offender.

Identify whether any combination of these or other relevant factors should result in an upward or downward adjustment from the starting point.

Consecutive sentences for multiple offences may be appropriate where large sums are involved.

Factors increasing seriousness	Factors reducing seriousness or reflecting personal mitigation
Statutory aggravating factors:	No previous convictions or no relevant/recent convictions
Previous convictions, having regard to (a) the nature of the offence to which the conviction relates and its relevance to the current offence; and (b) the time that has elapsed since the conviction	Remorse Good character and/or exemplary conduct
Offence committed whilst on bail	Little or no prospect of success
Other aggravating factors:	Serious medical conditions requiring urgent, intensive or long-term treatment
Steps taken to prevent the victim reporting or obtaining assistance and/or from assisting or supporting the prosecution	Age and/or lack of maturity where it affects the responsibility of the offender
Attempts to conceal/dispose of evidence	Lapse of time since apprehension where this does not arise from the conduct of the offender
Established evidence of community/wider impact	Mental disorder or learning disability
Failure to comply with current court orders	Sole or primary carer for dependent relatives
Offence committed on licence	Offender co-operated with investigation, made early admissions and/or voluntarily reported offending

Factors increasing seriousness	Factors reducing seriousness or reflecting personal mitigation
Offences taken into consideration	Determination and/or demonstration of steps having been taken to address addiction or offending behaviour
Failure to respond to warnings about behaviour	Activity originally legitimate
Offences committed across borders	
Blame wrongly placed on others	

GROUP C: Revenue fraud

Fraud
Conspiracy to defraud (common law)
Triable on indictment only

Fraud Act 2006 (section 1)
Triable either way
Maximum: 10 years' custody
Offence range: Low-level community order–8 years' custody
False accounting
Theft Act 1968 (section 17)
Fraudulent evasion of VAT; False statement for VAT purposes; Conduct amounting to an offence
Value Added Tax Act 1994 (section 72)
Fraudulent evasion of income tax
Taxes Management Act 1970 (section 106A)
Fraudulent evasion of excise duty; Improper importation of goods
Customs and Excise Management Act 1979 (sections 50, 170 and 170B)
Triable either way
Maximum: 7 years' custody
Offence range: Band C fine–6 years and 6 months' custody

Fraud
Cheat the public revenue (common law)
Triable on indictment only
Maximum: Life imprisonment
Offence range: 3–17 years' custody

STEP ONE Determining the offence category

The court should determine the offence category with reference to the tables below. In order to determine the category the court should assess **culpability** and **harm**.

> The level of **culpability** is determined by weighing up all the factors of the case to determine the offender's role and the extent to which the offending was planned and the sophistication with which it was carried out.
>
> **Harm**—Gain/intended gain to offender or loss/intended loss to HMRC.

Culpability demonstrated by one or more of the following:	Category 1 £50 million or more Starting point based on £80 million
A—High culpability	Category 2 £10 million–£50 million Starting point based on £30 million
A leading role where offending is part of a group activity	Category 3 £2 million–£10 million Starting point based on £5 million
Involvement of others through pressure/influence	Category 4 £500,000–£2 million Starting point based on £1 million
Abuse of position of power or trust or responsibility	Category 5 £100,000–£500,000 Starting point based on £300,000
Sophisticated nature of offence/significant planning	Category 6 £20,000–£100,000 Starting point based on £50,000
Fraudulent activity conducted over sustained period of time	Category 7 Less than £20,000 Starting point based on £12,500
B—Medium culpability	
Other cases where characteristics for categories A or C are not present	
A significant role where offending is part of a group activity	
C—Lesser culpability	
Involved through coercion, intimidation or exploitation	
Not motivated by personal gain	
Opportunistic 'one-off' offence; very little or no planning	
Performed limited function under direction	
Limited awareness or understanding of extent of fraudulent activity	

Where there are characteristics present which fall under different levels of culpability, the court should balance these characteristics to reach a fair assessment of the offender's culpability.

STEP TWO Starting point and category range

Having determined the category at step one, the court should use the appropriate starting point to reach a sentence within the category range in the table below. The starting point applies to all offenders irrespective of plea or previous convictions.

Where the value is larger or smaller than the amount on which the starting point is based, this should lead to upward or downward adjustment as appropriate.

Appendix 3

Where the value greatly exceeds the amount of the starting point in category 1, it may be appropriate to move outside the identified range.

TABLE 1

Section 1 Fraud Act 2006: Conspiracy to defraud (common law)

Maximum: 10 years' custody

For offences where the value of the fraud is over £2 million refer to the corresponding category in Table 3 subject to the maximum sentence of 10 years for this offence.

Culpability			
Harm	**A**	**B**	**C**
Category 4 £500,000–£2 million Starting point based on £1 million	**Starting point** 7 years' custody **Category range** 5–8 years' custody	**Starting point** 5 years' custody **Category range** 3–6 years' custody	**Starting point** 3 years' custody **Category range** 18 months' – 4 years' custody
Category 5 £100,000–£500,000 Starting point based on £300,000	**Starting point** 5 years' custody **Category range** 3–6 years' custody	**Starting point** 3 years' custody **Category range** 18 months'– 4 years' custody	**Starting point** 18 months' custody **Category range** 26 weeks'– 3 years' custody
Category 6 £20,000–£100,000 Starting point based on £50,000	**Starting point** 3 years' custody **Category range** 18 months'– 4 years' custody	**Starting point** 18 months' custody **Category range** 26 weeks'– 3 years' custody	**Starting point** 26 weeks' custody **Category range** Medium-level community order– 1 year's custody
Category 7 Less than £20,000	**Starting point** 18 months' custody	**Starting point** 36 weeks' custody	**Starting point** Medium-level community order
Starting point based on £12,500	**Category range** 36 weeks'– 3 years' custody	**Category range** Medium-level community order– 18 months' custody	**Category range** Low-level community order–high-level community order

TABLE 2

Section 17 Theft Act 1968: False Accounting

Section 72(1) Value Added Tax Act 1994: Fraudulent evasion of VAT

Section 72(3) Valued Added Tax Act 1994: False statement for VAT purposes

Section 72(8) Value Added Tax Act 1994: Conduct amounting to an offence

Section 106(a) Taxes Management Act 1970: Fraudulent evasion of income tax

Section 170(1)(a)(i), (ii), (b), 170(2)(a), 170B Customs and Excise Management Act 1979: Fraudulent evasion of excise duty

Section 50(1)(a), (2) Customs and Excise Management Act 1979: Improper importation of goods

Maximum: 7 years' custody

Culpability			
Harm	**A**	**B**	**C**
Category 4 £500,000–£2 million Starting point based on £1 million	**Starting point** 5 years 6 months' custody **Category range** 4 years'– 6 years 6 months' custody	**Starting point** 4 years' custody **Category range** 2 years 6 months'–5 years' custody	**Starting point** 2 years 6 months' custody **Category range** 15 months'– 3 years 6 months' custody
Category 5 £100,000–£500,000 Starting point based on £300,000	**Starting point** 4 years' custody **Category range** 2 years 6 months' – 5 years' custody	**Starting point** 2 years 6 months' custody **Category range** 15 months'–3 years 6 months' custody	**Starting point** 15 months' custody **Category range** 26 weeks'– 2 years 6 months' custody
Category 6 £20,000–£100,000 Starting point based on £50,000	**Starting point** 2 years 6 months' custody **Category range** 15 months'– 3 years 6 months' custody	**Starting point** 15 months' custody **Category range** High-level community order– 2 years 6 months' custody	**Starting point** High-level community order **Category range** Low-level community order – 36 weeks' custody
Category 7 Less than £20,000 Starting point based on £12,500	**Starting point** 15 months' custody **Category range** 26 weeks'–2 years 6 months' custody	**Starting point** 26 weeks' custody **Category range** Medium-level community order– 15 months' custody	**Starting point** Medium-level community order **Category range** Band C fine–high-level community order

TABLE 3

Cheat the Revenue (common law)

Maximum: Life imprisonment

Where the offending is on the most serious scale, involving sums significantly higher than the starting point in category 1, sentences of 15 years and above may be appropriate depending on the role of the offender. In cases involving sums below £2 million the court should refer to Table 1.

Culpability			
Harm	**A**	**B**	**C**
Category 1 £50 million or more Starting point based on £80 million	**Starting point** 12 years' custody **Category range** 10–17 years' custody	**Starting point** 8 years' custody **Category range** 7–12 years' custody	**Starting point** 6 years' custody **Category range** 4–8 years' custody

Culpability			
Category 2 £10 million–£50 million	**Starting point** 10 years' custody	**Starting point** 7 years' custody	**Starting point** 5 years' custody
Starting point based on £30 million	**Category range** 8–13 years' custody	**Category range** 5–9 years' custody	**Category range** 3–6 years' custody
Category 3 £2 million–£10 million	**Starting point** 8 years' custody	**Starting point** 6 years' custody	**Starting point** 4 years' custody
Starting point based on £5 million	**Category range** 6–10 years' custody	**Category range** 4–7 years' custody	**Category range** 3–5 years' custody

The table below contains a non-exhaustive list of additional factual elements providing the context of the offence and factors relating to the offender.

Identify whether any combination of these or other relevant factors should result in any further upward or downward adjustment from the starting point.

Consecutive sentences for multiple offences may be appropriate where large sums are involved.

Factors increasing seriousness	Factors reducing seriousness or reflecting personal mitigation
Statutory aggravating factors:	No previous convictions or no relevant/recent convictions
Previous convictions, having regard to (a) the nature of the offence to which the conviction relates and its relevance to the current offence; and (b) the time that has elapsed since the conviction	Remorse
Offence committed whilst on bail	Good character and/or exemplary conduct
Other aggravating factors:	Little or no prospect of success
Involves multiple frauds	Serious medical condition requiring urgent, intensive or long-term treatment
Number of false declarations	Age and/or lack of maturity where it affects the responsibility of the offender
Attempts to conceal/dispose of evidence	Lapse of time since apprehension where this does not arise from the conduct of the offender
Failure to comply with current court orders	Mental disorder or learning disability
Offence committed on licence	Sole or primary carer for dependent relatives
Offences taken into consideration	Offender co-operated with investigation, made early admissions and/or voluntarily reported offending
Failure to respond to warnings about behaviour	Determination and/or demonstration of steps having been taken to address addiction or offending behaviour

Factors increasing seriousness	Factors reducing seriousness or reflecting personal mitigation
Blame wrongly placed on others	Activity originally legitimate
Damage to third party (for example as a result of identity theft)	
Dealing with goods with an additional health risk	
Disposing of goods to under age purchasers	

GROUP D: Benefit fraud

Dishonest representations for obtaining benefit etc
Social Security Administration Act 1992 (section 111A)
Tax Credit fraud
Tax Credits Act 2002 (section 35)
False accounting
Theft Act 1968 (section 17)
Triable either way
Maximum: 7 years' custody
Offence range: Discharge–6 years 6 months' custody

False representations for obtaining benefit etc
Social Security Administration Act 1992 (section 112)
Triable summarily only
Maximum: Level 5 fine and/or 3 months' custody
Offence range: Discharge–12 weeks' custody

Fraud by false representation, fraud by failing to disclose information, fraud by abuse of position
Fraud Act 2006 (section 1)
Triable either way

Conspiracy to defraud
Common law
Triable on indictment only
Maximum: 10 years' custody
Offence range: Discharge–8 years' custody

STEP ONE Determining the offence category

The court should determine the offence category with reference to the tables below. In order to determine the category the court should assess **culpability** and **harm**.

The level of **culpability** is determined by weighing up all the factors of the case to determine the offender's role and the extent to which the offending was planned and the sophistication with which it was carried out.

Harm—Amount obtained or intended to be obtained

Culpability demonstrated by one or more of the following:	Category 1 £500,000–£2 million Starting point based on £1 million
A—High culpability	Category 2 £100,000–£500,000 Starting point based on £300,000
A leading role where offending is part of a group activity	Category 3 £50,000–£100,000 Starting point based on £75,000
Involvement of others through pressure/influence	Category 4 £10,000–£50,000 Starting point based on £30,000
Abuse of position of power, or trust, or responsibility	Category 5 £2,500–£10,000 Starting point based on £5,000
Sophisticated nature of offence/significant planning	Category 6 Less than £2,500 Starting point based on £1,000
B—Medium culpability	
Other cases where characteristics for categories A or C are not present	
Claim not fraudulent from the outset	
A significant role where offending is part of a group activity	
C—Lesser culpability	
Involved through coercion, intimidation, or exploitation	
Performed limited function under direction	

Where there are characteristics present which fall under different levels of culpability, the court should balance these characteristics to reach a fair assessment of the offender's culpability.

STEP TWO Starting point and category range

Having determined the category at step one, the court should use the appropriate starting point to reach a sentence within the category range in the table below. The starting point applies to all offenders irrespective of plea or previous convictions.

Where the value is larger or smaller than the amount on which the starting point is based, this should lead to upward or downward adjustment as appropriate.

Where the value greatly exceeds the amount of the starting point in category 1, it may be appropriate to move outside the identified range.

TABLE 1

Section 111A Social Security Administration Act 1992: Dishonest representations to obtain benefit etc

Section 35 Tax Credits Act 2002: Tax Credit fraud

Section 17 Theft Act 1968: False accounting

Maximum: 7 years' custody

Culpability			
Harm	**A**	**B**	**C**
Category 1 £500,000 or more Starting point based on £1 million	**Starting point** 5 years 6 months' custody **Category range** 4 years'– 6 years 6 months' custody	**Starting point** 4 years' custody **Category range** 2 years 6 months'– 5 years' custody	**Starting point** 2 years 6 months' custody **Category range** 15 months'– 3 years 6 months' custody
Category 2 £100,000–£500,000 Starting point based on £300,000	**Starting point** 4 years' custody **Category range** 2 years 6 months'– 5 years' custody	**Starting point** 2 years 6 months' custody **Category range** 15 months'–3 years 6 months' custody	**Starting point** 1 year's custody **Category range** 26 weeks'– 2 years 6 months' custody
Category 3 £50,000–£100,000 Starting point based on £75,000	**Starting point** 2 years 6 months' custody **Category range** 2 years'– 3 years 6 months' custody	**Starting point** 1 year's custody **Category range** 26 weeks'– 2 years 6 months' custody	**Starting point** 26 weeks' custody **Category range** High-level community order– 36 weeks' custody
Category 4 £10,000–£50,000 Starting point based on £30,000	**Starting point** 18 months' custody **Category range** 36 weeks'–2 years 6 months' custody	**Starting point** 36 weeks' custody **Category range** Medium-level community order– 21 months' custody	**Starting point** Medium-level community order **Category range** Low-level community order – 26 weeks' custody
Category 5 £2,500–£10,000 Starting point based on £5,000	**Starting point** 36 weeks' custody **Category range** Medium-level community order– 18 months' custody	**Starting point** Medium-level community order **Category range** Low-level community order– 26 weeks' custody	**Starting point** Low-level community order **Category range** Band B fine–medium-level community order
Category 6 Less than £2,500 Starting point based on £1,000	**Starting point** Medium-level community order **Category range** Low-level community order– 26 weeks' custody	**Starting point** Low-level community order **Category range** Band A fine–medium-level community order	**Starting point** Band A fine **Category range** Discharge–Band B fine

Appendix 3

TABLE 2

Section 112

Social Security Administration Act 1992: False representations for obtaining benefit etc

Maximum: Level 5 fine and/or 3 months' custody

Culpability			
Harm	A	B	C
Category 5 Above £2,500 Starting point based on £5,000	**Starting point** High-level community order **Category range** Medium-level community order–12 weeks' custody	**Starting point** Medium-level community order **Category range** Band B fine– high-level community order	**Starting point** Low-level community order **Category range** Band A fine–medium-level community order
Category 6 Less than £2,500 Starting point based on £1,000	**Starting point** Medium-level community order **Category range** Low-level community order–high-level community order	**Starting point** Band B fine **Category range** Band A fine–Band C fine	**Starting point** Band A fine **Category range** Discharge– Band B fine

TABLE 3

Section 1 Fraud Act 2006

Conspiracy to defraud (common law)

Maximum: 10 years' custody

Culpability			
Harm	A	B	C
Category 1 £500,000 or more Starting point based on £1 million	**Starting point** 7 years' custody **Category range** 5–8 years' custody	**Starting point** 5 years' custody **Category range** 3–6 years' custody	**Starting point** 3 years' custody **Category range** 18 months'– 4 years' custody
Category 2 £100,000–£50w0,000 Starting point based on £300,000	**Starting point** 5 years' custody **Category range** 3–6 years' custody	**Starting point** 3 years' custody **Category range** 18 months'–4 years' custody	**Starting point** 15 months' custody **Category range** 26 weeks'– 3 years' custody
Category 3 £50,000–£100,000 Starting point based on £75,000	**Starting point** 3 years' custody **Category range** 2 years 6 months'– 4 years' custody	**Starting point** 15 months' custody **Category range** 36 weeks'– 3 years' custody	**Starting point** 36 weeks' custody **Category range** 26 weeks'–1 year's custody

Culpability			
Category 4 £10,000–£50,000 Starting point based on £30,000	**Starting point** 21 months' custody **Category range** 1 year's– years' custody	**Starting point** 1 year's custody **Category range** High-level community order–2 years' custody	**Starting point** High-level community order **Category range** Low-level community order– 26 weeks' custody
Category 5 £2,500–£10,000 Starting point based on £5,000	**Starting point** 1 year's custody **Category range** High-level community order–2 years' custody	**Starting point** High-level community order **Category range** Low-level community order– 26 weeks' custody	**Starting point** Medium-level community order **Category range** Band C fine– high-level community order
Category 6 Less than £2,500 Starting point based on £1,000	**Starting point** High-level community order **Category range** Low-level community order–26 weeks' custody	**Starting point** Low-level community order **Category range** Band B fine– medium-level community order	**Starting point** Band B fine **Category range** Discharge– Band C fine

The table below contains a non-exhaustive list of additional factual elements providing the context of the offence and factors relating to the offender.

Identify whether any combination of these or other relevant factors should result in any further upward or downward adjustment from the starting point.

Consecutive sentences for multiple offences may be appropriate where large sums are involved.

Factors increasing seriousness	Factors reducing seriousness or reflecting personal mitigation
Statutory aggravating factors:	No previous convictions or no relevant/recent convictions
Previous convictions, having regard to (a) the nature of the offence to which the conviction relates and its relevance to the current offence; and (b) the time that has elapsed since the conviction	Remorse
Offence committed whilst on bail	Good character and/or exemplary conduct
Other aggravating factors:	Serious medical condition requiring urgent, intensive, or long-term treatment
Claim fraudulent from the outset	Legitimate entitlement to benefits not claimed
Proceeds of fraud funded lavish lifestyle	Little or no prospect of success
Length of time over which the offending was committed	Age and/or lack of maturity where it affects the responsibility of the offender
Number of false declarations	Age and/or lack of maturity where it affects the responsibility of the offender

Appendix 3

Factors increasing seriousness	Factors reducing seriousness or reflecting personal mitigation
Attempts to conceal/dispose of evidence Failure to comply with current court orders	Lapse of time since apprehension where this does not arise from the conduct of the offender
Offence committed on licence	Mental disorder or learning disability
Offences taken into consideration	Sole or primary carer for dependent relatives
Failure to respond to warnings about behaviour	Offender co-operated with investigation, made early admissions and/or voluntarily reported offending
Blame wrongly placed on others	Determination and/or demonstration of steps having been taken to address addiction or offending behaviour
Damage to third party (for example as a result of identity theft)	Offender experiencing significant financial hardship or pressure at time fraud was committed due to exceptional circumstances

Appendix 4

Bladed Articles and Offensive Weapons—Sentencing Guideline

Possession of an offensive weapon in a public place
Prevention of Crime Act 1953 (section 1(1))
Possession of an article with blade/point in a public place
Criminal Justice Act 1988 (section 139(1))
Possession of an offensive weapon on school premises
Criminal Justice Act 1988 (section 139A(2))
Possession of an article with blade/point on school premises
Criminal Justice Act 1988 (section 139A(1))
Unauthorised possession in prison of a knife or offensive weapon
Prison Act 1952 (section 40CA)
This offence is subject to statutory minimum sentencing provisions.

STEP ONE: Determining the offence category

The court should determine the offence category with reference only to the factors listed in the tables below. In order to determine the category, the court should assess culpability and harm.

The court should weigh all the factors set out below in determining the offender's culpability.

Where there are characteristics present which fall under different levels of culpability, the court should balance these characteristics to reach a fair assessment of the offender's culpability.

Culpability demonstrated by one or more of the following:

A Possession of a bladed article
   • Possession of a highly dangerous weapon*
   • Offence motivated by, or demonstrating hostility based on any of the following characteristics or presumed characteristics of the victim: religion, race, disability, sexual orientation or transgender identity
B Possession of weapon (other than a bladed article or a highly dangerous weapon) – used to threaten or cause fear
C Possession of weapon (other than a bladed article or a highly dangerous weapon) – not used to threaten or cause fear
D Possession of weapon falls just short of reasonable excuse

*N B an offensive weapon is defined in legislation as 'any article made or adapted for use for causing injury, or is intended by the person having it with him for such use'. A highly dangerous weapon is, therefore, a weapon, including a corrosive substance (such as acid), whose dangerous nature must be substantially above and beyond this. The court must determine whether the weapon is highly dangerous on the facts and circumstances of the case.

Harm

The court should consider the factors set out below to determine the level of harm that has been caused or was risked

Category 1	• Offence committed at a school or other place where vulnerable people are likely to be present • Offence committed in prison • Offence committed in circumstances where there is a risk of serious disorder • Serious alarm/distress caused to the victim • Prolonged incident
Category 2	• All other cases

STEP TWO: Starting point and category range

Having determined the category at step one, the court should use the corresponding starting point to reach a sentence within the category range below. The starting point applies to all offenders irrespective of plea or previous convictions. A case of particular gravity, reflected by multiple features of culpability or harm in step one, could merit upward adjustment from the starting point before further adjustment for aggravating or mitigating features, set out on the next page.

Culpability				
Harm	**A**	**B**	**C**	**D**
Category 1	**Starting point** 1 year 6 months' custody	**Starting point** 9 months' custody	**Starting point** 3 months' custody	**Starting point** High-level community order
	Category range 1–2 years' 6 months' custody	**Category range** 6 months'–1 year 6 months' custody	**Category range** High-level community order– 6 months' custody	**Category range** Medium-level community order– 3 months' custody
Category 2	**Starting point** 6 months' custody	**Starting point** High-level community order	**Starting point** Medium-level community order	**Starting point** Low-level community order
	Category range 3 months'–1 year's custody	**Category range** Medium-level community order– 6 months' custody	**Category range** Low-level community order–High-level community order	**Category range** Band C fine– Medium-level community order

The table below contains a non-exhaustive list of additional factual elements providing the context of the offence and factors relating to the offender. Identify whether any combination of these, or other relevant factors, should result in an upward or downward adjustment from the sentence arrived at so far. In particular, relevant recent convictions are likely to result in an upward

adjustment. In some cases, having considered these factors, it may be appropriate to move outside the identified category range.

Factors increasing seriousness	
Statutory aggravating factors	*Other aggravating factors*
Previous convictions, having regard to a) the nature of the offence to which the conviction relates and its relevance to the current offence; and b) the time that has elapsed since the conviction (unless the convictions will be relevant for the purposes of the statutory minimum sentencing provisions—see step three) Offence committed whilst on bail	Offence was committed as part of a group or gang Attempts to conceal identity Commission of offence whilst under the influence of alcohol or drugs Attempts to conceal/dispose of evidence Failure to comply with current court orders Offence committed on licence or post sentence supervision Offences taken into consideration Failure to respond to warnings about behaviour
Factors reducing seriousness or reflecting personal mitigation	
No previous convictions or no relevant/recent convictions Good character and/or exemplary conduct Serious medical condition requiring urgent, intensive or long-term treatment Age and/or lack of maturity where it affects the responsibility of the offender Mental disorder or learning disability Sole or primary carer for dependent relatives Co-operation with the police	

Bladed Articles and Offensive Weapons – Threats

Threatening with an offensive weapon in a public place

Prevention of Crime Act 1953 (section 1A)

Threatening with an article with blade/point in a public place

Criminal Justice Act 1988 (section 139AA(1))

Threatening with an article with blade/point or offensive weapon on school premises

Criminal Justice Act 1988 (section 139AA(1))

This offence is subject to statutory minimum sentencing provisions.

STEP ONE: Determining the offence category

The court should determine the offence category with reference only to the factors listed in the tables below. In order to determine the category, the court should assess culpability and harm.

The court should weigh all the factors set out below in determining the offender's culpability.

Where there are characteristics present which fall under different levels of culpability, the court should balance these characteristics to reach a fair assessment of the offender's culpability.

Culpability demonstrated by one or more of the following:

A—Higher culpability	• Offence committed using a bladed article • Offence committed using a highly dangerous weapon* • Offence motivated by, or demonstrating hostility based on any of the following characteristics or presumed characteristics of the victim: religion, race, disability, sexual orientation or transgender identity • Significant degree of planning or premeditation
B—Lower culpability	• All other cases

*NB an offensive weapon is defined in legislation as 'any article made or adapted for use for causing injury, or is intended by the person having it with him for such use'. A highly dangerous weapon is, therefore, a weapon, including a corrosive substance (such as acid), whose dangerous nature must be substantially above and beyond this. The court must determine whether the weapon is highly dangerous on the facts and circumstances of the case.

Harm

The court should consider the factors set out below to determine the level of harm that has been caused or was intended to be caused to the victim.

Category 1	• Offence committed at a school or other place where vulnerable people are likely to be present • Offence committed in prison • Offence committed in circumstances where there is a risk of serious disorder • Serious alarm/distress caused to the victim • Prolonged incident
Category 2	• All other cases

STEP TWO: Starting point and category range

Having determined the category at step one, the court should use the corresponding starting point to reach a sentence within the category range below. The starting point applies to all offenders irrespective of plea or previous convictions. A case of particular gravity, reflected by multiple features of culpability or harm in step one, could merit upward adjustment from the starting point before further adjustment for aggravating or mitigating features, set out on the next page.

Culpability		
Harm	A	B
Category 1	**Starting point** 2 years' custody	**Starting point** 1 year 6 months' custody
	Category range 1 year 6 months'–3 years' custody	**Category range** 1–2 years' custody
Category 2	**Starting point** 15 months' custody	**Starting point** 6 months' custody
	Category range 9 months'–2 years' custody	**Category range** 6 months'–1 year 6 months' custody

The table below contains a non-exhaustive list of additional factual elements providing the context of the offence and factors relating to the offender. Identify whether any combination of these, or other relevant factors, should result in an upward or downward adjustment from the sentence arrived at so far. In particular, relevant recent convictions are likely to result in an upward adjustment. In some cases, having considered these factors, it may be appropriate to move outside the identified category range.

Factors increasing seriousness	
Statutory aggravating factors	*Other aggravating factors*
Previous convictions, having regard to (a) the nature of the offence to which the conviction relates and its relevance to the current offence; and (b) the time that has elapsed since the conviction Offence committed whilst on bail	Victim is targeted due to a vulnerability (or a perceived vulnerability) Offence was committed as part of a group or gang Attempts to conceal identity Commission of offence whilst under the influence of alcohol or drugs Attempts to conceal/dispose of evidence Offence committed against those working in the public sector or providing a service to the public Steps taken to prevent the victim reporting or obtaining assistance and/or from assisting or supporting the prosecution Failure to comply with current court orders Offence committed on licence or post sentence supervision Offences taken into consideration Failure to respond to warnings about behaviour
Factors reducing seriousness or reflecting personal mitigation	
No previous convictions or no relevant/recent convictions Good character and/or exemplary conduct Serious medical condition requiring urgent, intensive or long-term treatment Age and/or lack of maturity where it affects the responsibility of the offender Mental disorder or learning disability (where not linked to the commission of the offence) Little or no planning Sole or primary carer for dependent relatives Co-operation with the police	

Domestic Abuse: Definitive Guideline

Extracted Sections

Definitions

Domestic abuse includes so-called 'honour' based abuse, female genital mutilation (FGM) and forced marriage and

> Any incident or pattern of incidents of controlling, coercive, threatening behaviour, violence or abuse between those aged 16 or over who are, or have been, intimate partners or family members regardless of gender or sexuality. The abuse can encompass, but is not limited to: psychological, physical, sexual, financial, or emotional.

Controlling behaviour is a range of acts designed to make a person subordinate and/or dependent by isolating them from sources of support, exploiting their resources and capabilities for personal gain, depriving them of the means needed for independence, resistance and escape and/or regulating their everyday behaviour.

Coercive behaviour is an act or pattern of acts of assault, threats, humiliation (whether public or private) and intimidation or other abuse that is used to harm, punish, or frighten the victim. Abuse may take place through person to person contact, or through other methods, including but not limited to, telephone calls, text, email, social networking sites or use of GPS tracking devices.

Assessing Seriousness

The domestic context of the offending behaviour makes the offending more serious because it represents a violation of the trust and security that normally exists between people in an intimate or family relationship. Additionally, there may be a continuing threat to the victim's safety, and in the worst cases a threat to their life or the lives of others around them.

Aggravating And Mitigating Factors

The following list of non-exhaustive aggravating and mitigating factors are of particular relevance to offences committed in a domestic context, and should be considered alongside offence specific factors.

Aggravating Factors

- Abuse of trust and abuse of power
- Victim is particularly vulnerable (all victims of domestic abuse are potentially vulnerable due to the nature of the abuse, but some victims of domestic abuse may be more vulnerable than others, and not all vulnerabilities are immediately apparent)

- Steps taken to prevent the victim reporting an incident
- Steps taken to prevent the victim obtaining assistance
- Victim forced to leave home, or steps have to be taken to exclude the offender from the home to ensure the victim's safety
- Impact on children (children can be adversely impacted by both direct and indirect exposure to domestic abuse)
- Using contact arrangements with a child to instigate an offence
- A proven history of violence or threats by the offender in a domestic context
- A history of disobedience to court orders (such as, but not limited to, Domestic Violence Protection Orders, non-molestation orders, restraining orders)

Mitigating Factors

Positive good character – as a general principle of sentencing, a court will take account of an offender's positive good character. However, it is recognised that one of the factors that can allow domestic abuse to continue unnoticed for lengthy periods is the ability of the perpetrator to have a public and a private face. In respect of offences committed within a domestic context, an offender's good character in relation to conduct outside these offences should generally be of no relevance where there is a proven pattern of behaviour

Evidence of genuine recognition of the need for change, and evidence of obtaining help or treatment to effect that change

Other Factors Influencing Sentence

The following points of principle should be considered by a court when imposing sentence for any offences committed in a domestic context:

A sentence imposed for an offence committed within a domestic context should be determined by the seriousness of the offence, not by any expressed wishes of the victim ...

Provocation is no mitigation to an offence within a domestic context, except in rare circumstances.

The offender or the victim may ask the court to consider the interests of any children by imposing a less severe sentence. The court should consider not only the effect on the children if the relationship is disrupted but also the likely effect of any further incidents of domestic abuse. The court should take great care with such requests, as the sentence should primarily be determined by the seriousness of the offence.

Offences involving serious violence, or where the emotional/psychological harm caused is severe, will warrant a custodial sentence in the majority of cases.

Passing the custody threshold does not mean that a custodial sentence should be deemed inevitable. Where the custody threshold is only just crossed, the court will wish to consider whether the better option is instead to impose a community order, including a requirement to attend an accredited domestic abuse programme or domestic abuse specific intervention. Such an option will normally only be appropriate where the court is satisfied that the offender genuinely intends to reform his or her behaviour and that there is a real prospect of rehabilitation being successful ...

Appendix 6

Rehabilitation Periods

A Basic Criminal Record Certificates

Offences are only disclosed during the rehabilitation period

Rehabilitation of Offenders Act 1974 as amended

The rehabilitation 'period' for a sentence is the period listed in the following table

Sentence	End of rehabilitation period for adult offenders	End of rehabilitation period for offenders under 18 at date of conviction
A custodial sentence of more than 30 months and up to, or consisting of, 48 months	The end of the period of 7 years beginning with the day on which the sentence (including any licence period) is completed	The end of the period of 42 months beginning with the day on which the sentence (including any licence period) is completed
A custodial sentence of more than 6 months and up to, or consisting of, 30 months	The end of the period of 48 months beginning with the day on which the sentence (including any licence period) is completed	The end of the period of 24 months beginning with the day on which the sentence (including any licence period) is completed
A custodial sentence of 6 months or less	The end of the period of 24 months beginning with the day on which the sentence (including any licence period) is completed	The end of the period of 18 months beginning with the day on which the sentence (including any licence period) is completed
Removal from Her Majesty's service	The end of the period of 12 months beginning with the date of the conviction in respect of which the sentence is imposed	The end of the period of 6 months beginning with the date of the conviction in respect of which the sentence is imposed
A sentence of service detention	The end of the period of 12 months beginning with the day on which the sentence is completed	The end of the period of 6 months beginning with the day on which the sentence is completed
A fine	The end of the period of 12 months beginning with the date of the conviction in respect of which the sentence is imposed	The end of the period of 6 months beginning with the date of the conviction in respect of which the sentence is imposed
A compensation order	The date on which the payment is made in full	The date on which the payment is made in full

Sentence	End of rehabilitation period for adult offenders	End of rehabilitation period for offenders under 18 at date of conviction
A community or youth rehabilitation order	The end of the period of 12 months beginning with the day provided for by or under the order as the last day on which the order is to have effect	The end of the period of 6 months beginning with the day provided for by or under the order as the last day on which the order is to have effect
A relevant order e.g. conditional discharge	The day provided for by or under the order as the last day on which the order is to have effect	The day provided for by or under the order as the last day on which the order is to have effect
Conditional caution	The day 3 months from the date of imposition	The day 3 months from the date of imposition
Absolute discharges and other alternatives to prosecution including cautions	Immediately rehabilitated	Immediately rehabilitated

Note 1. Where no provision is made by or under a community or youth rehabilitation order or a relevant order for the last day on which the order is to have effect, the rehabilitation period for the order is to be the period of 24 months beginning with the date of conviction

Note 2. Endorsements on driving licences are excluded from rehabilitation.

B Standard Criminal Record Certificates

Only offences during the rehabilitation period and 'unprotected convictions' and 'unprotected cautions' will be disclosed.

The effect of the Regulations in relation to convictions and cautions is that

C Enhanced Criminal Record Certificates (s 115 Police Act 1997)

In defined circumstances, an enhanced certificate may be sought which enables the police to disclose additional information held by them as being relevant and proportionate to the particular application. This may include spent and protected data and background information in relation to acquittals, harassment warnings, and other intelligence held by the police (s 113B Police Act 1997).

Appendix 7

General Sentencing Guideline and Expanded Explanations of Aggravating and Mitigating Factors

The Sentencing Council has published general sentencing guidelines for offences with no individual guidelines and expanded definitions of aggravating and mitigating factors. These can be found at https://www.sentencingcouncil.org.uk/the-magistrates-court-sentencing-gb.

General sentencing guidelines

The seriousness of the offence is assessed by considering:

- the **culpability** of the offender
  Culpability is assessed with reference to the offender's role, level of intention and/or premeditation and the extent and sophistication of planning.
  - The court should balance these factors to reach a fair assessment of the offender's overall culpability in all the circumstances of the case and the offender.
  - The mere presence of a factor that is inherent in the offence should not be used in assessing culpability.
  - Deliberate or gratuitous violence or damage to property, over and above what is needed to carry out the offence will normally indicate a higher level of culpability.
  - For offences where there is no requirement for the offender to have any level of intention, recklessness, negligence, dishonesty, knowledge, understanding or foresight for the offence to be made out, the range of culpability **may** be inferred from the circumstances of the offence as follows:

Highest level	Deliberate - intentional act or mission
⇓	Reckless - acted or failed to act regardless of the foreseeable risk
	Negligent - failed to take steps to guard against the act or omission
Lowest level	Low/no culpability - act or omission with none of the above features

- For offences that require some level of culpability (eg intention, recklessness or knowledge) to be made out, the range of culpability will be narrower. Relevant factors **may** typically include but are not limited to:

Highest level	High level of planning/ sophistication/ leading role
⇓	Some planning/ significant role
Lowest level	Little or no planning/ minor role

  - These models of assessing culpability will not be applicable to all offences and

- the **harm** caused by the offending.

  Harm - which the offence caused, was intended to case or might foreseeably have caused
  - There may be primary and secondary victims of an offence and, depending on the offence, victims may include one or more individuals, a community, the general public, the state, the environment and/or animal(s). In some cases there may not be an identifiable victim.
  - An assessment of harm should generally reflect the overall impact of the offence upon the victim(s) and may include direct harm (including physical injury, psychological harm and financial loss) and consequential harm.
  - When considering the value of property lost or damaged the court should also take account of any sentimental value to the victim(s) and any disruption caused to a victim's life, activities or business.
  - When considering harm to animals or the environment relevant considerations will include the impact on rare or endangered species or sensitive locations, and any suffering caused.
  - Where harm was intended but no harm or a lower level of harm resulted – the sentence will normally be assessed with reference to the level of harm intended.
  - Where the harm caused is greater than that intended - the sentence will normally be assessed with reference to the level of harm suffered by the victim.
  - Dealing with a risk of harm involves consideration of both the likelihood of harm occurring and the extent of it if it does.
  - Risk of harm is less serious than the same actual harm. Where the offence has caused risk of harm but no (or less) actual harm the normal approach is to move down to the next category of harm. This may not be appropriate if either the likelihood or extent of potential harm is particularly high.
  - A Victim Personal Statement (VPS) or other impact statement may assist the court in assessing harm, but the absence of a VPS or other impact statement should not be taken to indicate the absence of harm.
  - The court should balance these characteristics to reach a fair assessment of harm in the context of the circumstances of the offence.

Highest level ⇓ Lowest level	Very serious harm caused to individual victim(s) or to wider public/ environment etc
	Serious harm caused OR high risk of very serious harm
	Significant harm caused OR high risk of serious harm
	Low/ no harm caused OR high risk significant harm

The table should be used in conjunction with the notes above and may not be applicable to all offences.

c) The initial assessment of harm and culpability should take no account of plea or previous convictions.

> The court should consider which of the five purposes of sentencing (below) it is seeking to achieve through the sentence that is imposed. More than one purpose might be relevant and the importance of each must be weighed against the particular offence and offender characteristics when determining sentence.
> - The punishment of offenders
> - The reduction of crime (including its reduction by deterrence)
> - The reform and rehabilitation of offenders
> - The protection of the public
> - The making of reparation by offenders to persons affected by their offences

The expanded definitions are listed under the following subject headings. In applying these factors **Effective from:** 01 October 2019

> Care should be taken to avoid double counting factors including those already taken into account in assessing culpability or harm or those inherent in the offence

Statutory aggravating factors

Previous convictions,**Effective from:** 01 October 2019 having regard to a) the **nature** of the offence to which the conviction relates and its **relevance** to the current offence; and b) the **time** that has elapsed since the conviction

> Care should be taken to avoid double counting factors including those already taken into account in assessing culpability or harm or those inherent in the offence

Guidance on the use of previous convictions

The following guidance should be considered when seeking to determine the degree to which previous convictions should aggravate sentence:

Section 143 of the Criminal Justice Act states that:

In considering the seriousness of an offence ("the current offence") committed by an offender who has one or more previous convictions, the court must treat each previous conviction as an aggravating factor if (in the case of that conviction) the court considers that it can reasonably be so treated having regard, in particular, to—

(a) the nature of the offence to which the conviction relates and its relevance to the current offence, and

(b) the time that has elapsed since the conviction.

1. Previous convictions are considered at step two in the Council's offence-specific guidelines.

2. The primary significance of previous convictions (including convictions in other jurisdictions) is the extent to which they indicate trends in offending behaviour and possibly the offender's response to earlier sentences.

3. Previous convictions are normally **relevant** to the current offence when they are of a similar type.

4. Previous convictions of a type different from the current offence **may** be relevant where they are an indication of persistent offending or escalation and/or a failure to comply with previous court orders.

5. Numerous and frequent previous convictions might indicate an underlying problem (for example, an addiction) that could be addressed more effectively in the community and will not necessarily indicate that a custodial sentence is necessary.

6. If the offender received a non-custodial disposal for the previous offence, a court should not necessarily move to a custodial sentence for the fresh offence.

7. In cases involving significant persistent offending, the community and custody thresholds may be crossed even though the current offence normally warrants a lesser sentence. If a custodial sentence is imposed it should be proportionate and kept to the necessary minimum.

8. The aggravating effect of relevant previous convictions reduces with the passage of time; **older convictions are less relevant** to the offender's

culpability for the current offence and less likely to be predictive of future offending.

9. Where the previous offence is particularly old it will normally have little relevance for the current sentencing exercise.
10. The court should consider the time gap since the previous conviction and the reason for it. Where there has been a significant gap between previous and current convictions or a reduction in the frequency of offending this may indicate that the offender has made attempts to desist from offending in which case the aggravating effect of the previous offending will diminish.
11. Where the current offence is significantly less serious than the previous conviction (suggesting a decline in the gravity of offending), the previous conviction may carry less weight.
12. When considering the totality of previous offending a court should take a rounded view of the previous crimes and not simply aggregate the individual offences.
13. Where information is available on the context of previous offending this may assist the court in assessing the relevance of that prior offending to the current offence

• Offence committed whilst on bail

Effective from: 01 October 2019

Care should be taken to avoid double counting factors including those already taken into account in assessing culpability or harm or those inherent in the offence

S143 (3) Criminal Justice Act 2003 states:

In considering the seriousness of any offence committed while the offender was on bail, the court must treat the fact that it was committed in those circumstances as an aggravating factor.

• Offence motivated by, or demonstrating hostility based on the characteristics or presumed characteristics of the victim**Effective from:** 01 October 2019

Care should be taken to avoid double counting factors including those already taken into account in assessing culpability or harm or those inherent in the offence

See below for the statutory provisions.

o **Note the requirement for the court to state that the offence has been aggravated by the relevant hostility.**
o **Where the element of hostility is core to the offending, the aggravation will be higher than where it plays a lesser role.**

Increase in sentences for racial or religious aggravation
s145(2) of the Criminal Justice Act 2003 states:

If the offence was racially or religiously aggravated, the court—
(a) *must treat that fact as an aggravating factor, and*
(b) *must state in open court that the offence was so aggravated.*

An offence is racially or religiously aggravated for these purposes if—

o at the time of committing the offence, or immediately before or after doing so, the offender demonstrates towards the victim of the offence, hostility based on the victim's membership (or presumed membership) of a racial or religious group; **or** o the offence is motivated (wholly or partly) by hostility towards members of a racial or religious group based on their membership of that group.

"membership", in relation to a racial or religious group, includes association with members of that group;

"presumed" means presumed by the offender.

It is immaterial whether or not the offender's hostility is also based, to any extent, on any other factor not mentioned above.

"racial group" means a group of persons defined by reference to race, colour, nationality (including citizenship) or ethnic or national origins.

"religious group" means a group of persons defined by reference to religious belief or lack of religious belief.

Increase in sentences for aggravation related to disability, sexual orientation or transgender identity

s146 of the Criminal Justice Act 2003 states:

(1) This section applies where the court is considering the seriousness of an offence committed in any of the circumstances mentioned in subsection (2).

(2) Those circumstances are—

    (a) that, at the time of committing the offence, or immediately before or after doing so, the offender demonstrated towards the victim of the offence hostility based on—

        (i) the sexual orientation (or presumed sexual orientation) of the victim,

        (ii) a disability (or presumed disability) of the victim, or

        (iii) the victim being (or being presumed to be) transgender, or

    (b) that the offence is motivated (wholly or partly)—

        (i) by hostility towards persons who are of a particular sexual orientation,

        (ii) by hostility towards persons who have a disability or a particular disability or

        (iii) by hostility towards persons who are transgender.

(3) The court—

    (a) must treat the fact that the offence was committed in any of those circumstances as an aggravating factor, and

    (b) must state in open court that the offence was committed in such circumstances.

(4) It is immaterial for the purposes of paragraph (a) or (b) of subsection (2) whether or not the offender's hostility is also based, to any extent, on any other factor not mentioned in that paragraph.

(5) In this section "disability" means any physical or mental impairment.

(6) In this section references to being transgender include references to being transsexual, or undergoing, proposing to undergo or having undergone a process or part of a process of gender reassignment.

- Offence was committed against an emergency worker acting in the exercise of functions as such a worker

Effective from: 01 October 2019

Care should be taken to avoid double counting factors including those already taken into account in assessing culpability or harm or those inherent in the offence

See below for the statutory provisions.

- o **Note the requirement for the court to state that the offence has been so aggravated.**
- o **Note this statutory factor only applies to certain violent or sexual offences as listed below which were committed on or after 13 November 2018.**
- o **For other offences the factor 'Victim was providing a public service or performing a public duty at the time of the offence' can be applied where relevant.**

The Assaults on Emergency Worker (Offences) Act 2018 states:

2 Aggravating factor

(1) This section applies where—

    (a) the court is considering for the purposes of sentencing the seriousness of an offence listed in subsection (3), and

    (b) the offence was committed against an emergency worker acting in the exercise of functions as such a worker.

(2) The court—

    (a) must treat the fact mentioned in subsection (1)(b) as an aggravating factor (that is to say, a factor that increases the seriousness of the offence), and

    (b) must state in open court that the offence is so aggravated.

(3) The offences referred to in subsection (1)(a) are—

    (a) an offence under any of the following provisions of the Offences against the Person Act 1861—

        (i) section 16 (threats to kill);

        (ii) section 18 (wounding with intent to cause grievous bodily harm);

        (iii) section 20 (malicious wounding);

        (iv) section 23 (administering poison etc);

        (v) section 28 (causing bodily injury by gunpowder etc);

        (vi) section 29 (using explosive substances etc with intent to cause grievous bodily harm);

        (vii) section 47 (assault occasioning actual bodily harm);

    (b) an offence under section 3 of the Sexual Offences Act 2003 (sexual assault);

    (c) manslaughter;

    (d) kidnapping;

    (e) an ancillary offence in relation to any of the preceding offences.

(4) For the purposes of subsection (1)(b), the circumstances in which an offence is to be taken as committed against a person acting in the exercise of functions as an emergency worker include circumstances where the offence takes place at a time when the person is not at work but is carrying out functions which, if done in work time, would have been in the exercise of functions as an emergency worker.

(5) In this section—

"ancillary offence", in relation to an offence, means any of the following—

    (a) aiding, abetting, counselling or procuring the commission of the offence;

    (b) an offence under Part 2 of the Serious Crime Act 2007 (encouraging or assisting crime) in relation to the offence;

    (c) attempting or conspiring to commit the offence;

"emergency worker" has the meaning given by section 3.

(6) Nothing in this section prevents a court from treating the fact mentioned in subsection (1)(b) as an aggravating factor in relation to offences not listed in subsection (3).

(7) This section applies only in relation to offences committed on or after the day it comes into force.

3 Meaning of "emergency worker"

(1) In sections 1 and 2, "emergency worker" means—
   (a) a constable;
   (b) a person (other than a constable) who has the powers of a constable or is otherwise employed for police purposes or is engaged to provide services for police purposes;
   (c) a National Crime Agency officer;
   (d) a prison officer;
   (e) a person (other than a prison officer) employed or engaged to carry out functions in a custodial institution of a corresponding kind to those carried out by a prison officer;
   (f) a prisoner custody officer, so far as relating to the exercise of escort functions;
   (g) a custody officer, so far as relating to the exercise of escort functions;
   (h) a person employed for the purposes of providing, or engaged to provide, fire services or fire and rescue services;
   (i) a person employed for the purposes of providing, or engaged to provide, search services or rescue services (or both);
   (j) a person employed for the purposes of providing, or engaged to provide—
      (i) NHS health services, or
      (ii) services in the support of the provision of NHS health services, and whose general activities in doing so involve face to face interaction with individuals receiving the services or with other members of the public.

(2) It is immaterial for the purposes of subsection (1) whether the employment or engagement is paid or unpaid.

(3) In this section—
   "custodial institution" means any of the following—
      (a) a prison;
      (b) a young offender institution, secure training centre, secure college or remand centre;
      (c) a removal centre, a short-term holding facility or pre-departure accommodation, as defined by section 147 of the Immigration and Asylum Act 1999;
      (d) services custody premises, as defined by section 300(7) of the Armed Forces Act 2006;
   "custody officer" has the meaning given by section 12(3) of the Criminal Justice and Public Order Act 1994;
   "escort functions"—
      (a) in the case of a prisoner custody officer, means the functions specified in section 80(1) of the Criminal Justice Act 1991;
      (b) in the case of a custody officer, means the functions specified in paragraph 1 of Schedule 1 to the Criminal Justice and Public Order Act 1994;

"NHS health services" means any kind of health services provided as part of the health service continued under section 1(1) of the National Health Service Act 2006 and under section 1(1) of the National Health Service (Wales) Act 2006;

"prisoner custody officer" has the meaning given by section 89(1) of the Criminal Justice Act 1991.

Other aggravating factors

- Commission of offence whilst under the influence of alcohol or drugs

Effective from: 01 October 2019

Care should be taken to avoid double counting factors including those already taken into account in assessing culpability or harm or those inherent in the offence

The fact that an offender is **voluntarily** intoxicated at the time of the offence will tend to increase the seriousness of the offence provided that the intoxication has **contributed to the offending**.

This applies regardless of whether the offender is under the influence of legal or illegal substance(s).

In the case of a person addicted to drugs or alcohol the intoxication may be considered not to be voluntary, but the court should have regard to the extent to which the offender has sought help or engaged with any assistance which has been offered or made available in dealing with the addiction.

An offender who has voluntarily consumed drugs and/or alcohol must accept the consequences of the behaviour that results, even if it is out of character.

- Offence was committed as part of a group

Effective from: 01 October 2019

Care should be taken to avoid double counting factors including those already taken into account in assessing culpability or harm or those inherent in the offence

The mere membership of a group (two or more persons) should not be used to increase the sentence, but where the offence was committed as part of a group this will normally make it more serious because:
- o the **harm** caused (both physical or psychological) or the potential for harm may be greater and/or
- o the **culpability** of the offender may be higher (the role of the offender within the group will be a relevant consideration).

Culpability based on role in group offending could range from:
- o Higher culpability indicated by a leading role in the group and/or the involvement by the offender of others through coercion, intimidation or exploitation, to
- o Lower culpability indicated by a lesser or subordinate role under direction and/or involvement of the offender through coercion, intimidation or exploitation.

Courts should be alert to factors that suggest that an offender may have been the subject of coercion, intimidation or exploitation (including as a result of domestic abuse, trafficking or modern slavery) which the offender may find difficult to articulate, and where appropriate ask for this to be addressed in a PSR.

Where the offending is part of an organised criminal network, this will make it more serious, and the role of the offender in the organisation will also be relevant.

When sentencing young adult offenders (typically aged 18-25), consideration should also be given to the guidance on the mitigating factor relating to age and/or lack of maturity when considering the significance of group offending.

- Offence involved use or threat of a weapon

Effective from: 01 October 2019

Care should be taken to avoid double counting factors including those already taken into account in assessing culpability or harm or those inherent in the offence

- o A 'weapon' can take many forms
- o The use or production of a weapon has relevance
  - to the **culpability** of the offender where it indicates planning or intention to cause harm; and
  - to the **harm** caused (both physical or psychological) or the potential for harm.
- o Relevant considerations will include:
  - the dangerousness of the weapon;
  - whether the offender brought the weapon to the scene, or just used what was available on impulse;
  - whether the offender made or adapted something for use as a weapon;
  - the context in which the weapon was threatened, used or produced.

When sentencing young adult offenders (typically aged 18-25), consideration should also be given to the guidance on the mitigating factor relating to age and/or lack of maturity when assessing the relevance of this factor to culpability.

- Planning of an offence

Effective from: 01 October 2019

Care should be taken to avoid double counting factors including those already taken into account in assessing culpability or harm or those inherent in the offence

- o Evidence of planning normally indicates a higher level of intention and pre-meditation which increases the level of culpability.
- o Planning may be inferred from the scale and sophistication of the offending and/or the role of the offender.
- o The greater the degree of planning the greater the culpability

- Commission of the offence for financial gain

Effective from: 01 October 2019

Care should be taken to avoid double counting factors including those already taken into account in assessing culpability or harm or those inherent in the offence

- o Where an offence (which is not one which by its nature is an acquisitive offence) has been committed wholly or in part for financial gain or the avoidance of cost, this will increase the seriousness.
- o Where the offending is committed in a commercial context for financial gain or the avoidance of costs, this will normally indicate a higher level of culpability.

- o examples would include, but are not limited to, dealing in unlawful goods, failing to disclose relevant matters to an authority or regulator, failing to comply with a regulation or failing to obtain the necessary licence or permission in order to avoid costs.
- o offending of this type can undermine legitimate businesses.
- o See the guidance on fines if considering a financial penalty.

- High level of profit from the offence

Effective from: 01 October 2019

Care should be taken to avoid double counting factors including those already taken into account in assessing culpability or harm or those inherent in the offence

- o A high level of profit is likely to indicate:
  - high culpability in terms of planning and
  - a high level of harm in terms of loss caused to victims or the undermining of legitimate businesses
- o In most situations a high level of gain will be a factor taken in to account at step one – care should be taken to avoid double counting.
- o See the guidance on fines if considering a financial penalty

- Abuse of trust or dominant position

Effective from: 01 October 2019

Care should be taken to avoid double counting factors including those already taken into account in assessing culpability or harm or those inherent in the offence

- o A close examination of the facts is necessary and a clear justification should be given if abuse of trust is to be found.
- o In order for an abuse of trust to make an offence more serious the relationship between the offender and victim(s) must be one that would give rise to the offender having a significant level of responsibility towards the victim(s) on which the victim(s) would be entitled to rely.
- o Abuse of trust may occur in many factual situations. Examples may include relationships such as teacher and pupil, parent and child, employer and employee, professional adviser and client, or carer (whether paid or unpaid) and dependant. It may also include ad hoc situations such as a late-night taxi driver and a lone passenger. These examples are not exhaustive and do not necessarily indicate that abuse of trust is present.
- o Additionally an offence may be made more serious where an offender has abused their position to facilitate and/or conceal offending.
- o Where an offender has been given an inappropriate level of responsibility, abuse of trust is unlikely to apply.

- Restraint, detention or additional degradation of the victim

Effective from: 01 October 2019

Care should be taken to avoid double counting factors including those already taken into account in assessing culpability or harm or those inherent in the offence

Where an offender deliberately causes **additional** harm to a victim over and above that which is an essential element of the offence - this will increase seriousness. Examples may include, but are not limited to, posts of images on social media designed to cause additional distress to the victim.

Where any such actions are the subject of separate charges, this should be taken into account when assessing totality.

When sentencing young adult offenders (typically aged 18-25), consideration should also be given to the guidance on the mitigating factor relating to age and/or lack of maturity when considering the significance of this factor.

- Vulnerable victim

  Effective from: 01 October 2019

  Care should be taken to avoid double counting factors including those already taken into account in assessing culpability or harm or those inherent in the offence

  o An offence is more serious if the victim is vulnerable because of personal circumstances such as (but not limited to) age, illness or disability (unless the vulnerability of the victim is an element of the offence).

  o Other factors such as the victim being isolated, incapacitated through drink or being in an unfamiliar situation may lead to a court considering that the offence is more serious.

  o The extent to which any vulnerability may impact on the sentence is a matter for the court to weigh up in each case.

  o Culpability will be increased if the offender targeted a victim because of an actual or perceived vulnerability.

  o Culpability will be increased if the victim is made vulnerable by the actions of the offender (such as a victim who has been intimidated or isolated by the offender).

  o Culpability is increased if an offender persisted in the offending once it was obvious that the victim was vulnerable (for example continuing to attack an injured victim).

  o The level of harm (physical, psychological or financial) is likely to be increased if the victim is vulnerable.

- Victim was providing a public service or performing a public duty at the time of the offence

  Effective from: 01 October 2019

  Care should be taken to avoid double counting factors including those already taken into account in assessing culpability or harm or those inherent in the offence

  This reflects:

  o the fact that people in public facing roles are more exposed to the possibility of harm and consequently more vulnerable and/or

  o the fact that someone is working in the public interest merits the additional protection of the courts.

  This applies whether the victim is a public or private employee or acting in a voluntary capacity.

  Care should be taken to avoid double counting where the statutory aggravating factor relating to emergency workers applies.

- Other(s) put at risk of harm by the offending

  Effective from: 01 October 2019

  Care should be taken to avoid double counting factors including those already taken into account in assessing culpability or harm or those inherent in the offence

- o Where there is risk of harm to other(s) not taken in account at step one and not subject to a separate charge, this makes the offence more serious.
- o Dealing with a risk of harm involves consideration of both the likelihood of harm occurring and the extent of it if it does.

Where any such risk of harm is the subject of separate charges, this should be taken into account when assessing totality.

When sentencing young adult offenders (typically aged 18-25), consideration should also be given to the guidance on the mitigating factor relating to age and/or lack of maturity when considering the significance of this factor.

- Offence committed in the presence of other(s) (especially children)

Effective from: 01 October 2019

Care should be taken to avoid double counting factors including those already taken into account in assessing culpability or harm or those inherent in the offence

- o This reflects the psychological harm that may be caused to those who witnessed the offence.
- o The presence of one or more children may in some situations make the primary victim more vulnerable – for example an adult may be less able to resist the offender if concerned about the safety or welfare of children present.
- o When sentencing young adult offenders (typically aged 18-25), consideration should also be given to the guidance on the mitigating factor relating to age and/or lack of maturity when considering the significance of this factor.

- Actions after the event including but not limited to attempts to cover up/ conceal evidence

Effective from: 01 October 2019

Care should be taken to avoid double counting factors including those already taken into account in assessing culpability or harm or those inherent in the offence

The more sophisticated, extensive or persistent the actions after the event, the more likely it is to increase the seriousness of the offence.

When sentencing young adult offenders (typically aged 18-25), consideration should also be given to the guidance on the mitigating factor relating to age and lack of maturity when considering the significance of such conduct.

Where any such actions are the subject of separate charges, this should be taken into account when assessing totality.

- Blame wrongly placed on other(s)

Effective from: 01 October 2019

Care should be taken to avoid double counting factors including those already taken into account in assessing culpability or harm or those inherent in the offence

- o Where the investigation has been hindered and/or other(s) have suffered as a result of being wrongly blamed by the offender, this will make the offence more serious.
- o This factor will **not** be engaged where an offender has simply exercised his or her right not to assist the investigation or accept responsibility for the offending.

When sentencing young adult offenders (typically aged 18-25), consideration should also be given to the guidance on the mitigating factor relating to age and lack of maturity when considering the significance of such conduct.

- Failure to respond to warnings or concerns expressed by others about the offender's behaviour

Effective from: 01 October 2019

Care should be taken to avoid double counting factors including those already taken into account in assessing culpability or harm or those inherent in the offence

Where an offender has had the benefit of warnings or advice about their conduct but has failed to heed it, this would make the offender more blameworthy.

This may particularly be the case when:

- o such warning(s) or advice were of an official nature or from a professional source and/or
- o the warning(s) were made at the time of or shortly before the commission of the offence.

When sentencing young adult offenders (typically aged 18-25), consideration should also be given to the guidance on the mitigating factor relating to age and/or lack of maturity when considering the significance of this factor.

- Offence committed on licence or while subject to court order(s)

Effective from: 01 October 2019

Care should be taken to avoid double counting factors including those already taken into account in assessing culpability or harm or those inherent in the offence

- o An offender who is subject to licence or post sentence supervision is under a particular obligation to desist from further offending.
- o Commission of an offence while subject to a relevant court order makes the offence more serious.
- o The extent to which the offender has complied with the conditions of a licence or order (including the time that has elapsed since its commencement) will be a relevant consideration.
- o Where the offender is dealt with separately for a breach of a licence or order regard should be had to totality
- o Care should be taken to avoid double counting matters taken into account when considering previous convictions.

When sentencing young adult offenders (typically aged 18-25), consideration should also be given to the guidance on the mitigating factor relating to age and/or lack of maturity when considering the significance of this factor.

- Offence committed in custody

Effective from: 01 October 2019

Care should be taken to avoid double counting factors including those already taken into account in assessing culpability or harm or those inherent in the offence

- o Offences committed in custody are more serious because they undermine the fundamental need for control and order which is necessary for the running of prisons and maintaining safety.
- o Generally the sentence for the new offence will be consecutive to the sentence being served as it will have arisen out of an unrelated incident. The

court must have regard to the totality of the offender's criminality when passing the second sentence, to ensure that the total sentence to be served is just and proportionate. Refer to the Totality guideline for detailed guidance.

o Care should be taken to avoid double counting matters taken into account when considering previous convictions.

- Offences taken into consideration (see **D23**)

Effective from: 01 October 2019

Care should be taken to avoid double counting factors including those already taken into account in assessing culpability or harm or those inherent in the offence

Taken from the Offences Taken into Consideration Definitive Guideline:

General principles

When sentencing an offender who requests offences to be taken into consideration (TICs), courts should pass a total sentence which reflects all the offending behaviour. The sentence must be just and proportionate and must not exceed the statutory maximum for the conviction offence.

Offences to be Taken into Consideration

The court has discretion as to whether or not to take TICs into account. In exercising its discretion the court should take into account that TICs are capable of reflecting the offender's overall criminality. The court is likely to consider that the fact that the offender has assisted the police (particularly if the offences would not otherwise have been detected) and avoided the need for further proceedings demonstrates a genuine determination by the offender to 'wipe the slate clean'.

It is generally **undesirable** for TICs to be accepted in the following circumstances:

o where the TIC is likely to attract a greater sentence than the conviction offence;
o where it is in the public interest that the TIC should be the subject of a separate charge;
o where the offender would avoid a prohibition, ancillary order or similar consequence which it would have been desirable to impose on conviction. For example:
  ▪ where the TIC attracts mandatory disqualification or endorsement and the offence(s) for which the defendant is to be sentenced do not;
o where the TIC constitutes a breach of an earlier sentence;
o where the TIC is a specified offence for the purposes of section 224 of the Criminal Justice Act 2003, but the conviction offence is non-specified; or
o where the TIC is not founded on the same facts or evidence or part of a series of offences of the same or similar character (unless the court is satisfied that it is in the interests of justice to do so).

Jurisdiction

The magistrates' court cannot take into consideration an indictable only offence.

The Crown Court can take into account summary only offences provided the TICs are founded on the same facts or evidence as the indictable charge, or are part of a series of offences of the same or similar character as the indictable conviction offence

Procedural safeguards

A court should generally only take offences into consideration if the following procedural provisions have been satisfied:

o the police or prosecuting authorities have prepared a schedule of offences (TIC schedule) that they consider suitable to be taken into consideration. The TIC schedule should set out the nature of each offence, the date of the offence(s), relevant detail about the offence(s) (including, for example, monetary values of items) and any other brief details that the court should be aware of;

o a copy of the TIC schedule must be provided to the defendant and his representative (if he has one) before the sentence hearing. The defendant should sign the TIC schedule to provisionally admit the offences;

o at the sentence hearing, the court should ask the defendant in open court whether he admits each of the offences on the TIC schedule and whether he wishes to have them taken into consideration;

o if there is any doubt about the admission of a particular offence, it should not be accepted as a TIC. Special care should be taken with vulnerable and/or unrepresented defendants;

o if the defendant is committed to the Crown Court for sentence, this procedure must take place again at the Crown Court even if the defendant has agreed to the schedule in the magistrates' court.

Application

The sentence imposed on an offender should, in most circumstances, be increased to reflect the fact that other offences have been taken into consideration. The court should:

12. Determine the sentencing starting point for the conviction offence, referring to the relevant definitive sentencing guidelines. No regard should be had to the presence of TICs at this stage.

13. Consider whether there are any aggravating or mitigating factors that justify an upward or downward adjustment from the starting point.

The presence of TICs should generally be treated as an aggravating feature that justifies an adjustment from the starting point. Where there is a large number of TICs, it may be appropriate to move outside the category range, although this must be considered in the context of the case and subject to the principle of totality. The court is limited to the statutory maximum for the conviction offence.

o Continue through the sentencing process including:

o consider whether the frank admission of a number of offences is an indication of a defendant's remorse or determination and/ or demonstration of steps taken to address addiction or offending behaviour;

o any reduction for a guilty plea should be applied to the overall sentence;

o the principle of totality;

o when considering ancillary orders these can be considered in relation to any or all of the TICs, specifically:

■ compensation orders;

■ restitution orders

• Offence committed in a domestic context (see **Appendix 5**)

Effective from: 01 October 2019

Care should be taken to avoid double counting factors including those already taken into account in assessing culpability or harm or those inherent in the offence

Refer to the Overarching Principles: Domestic Abuse Definitive Guideline

- Offence committed in a terrorist context

Effective from: 01 October 2019

Care should be taken to avoid double counting factors including those already taken into account in assessing culpability or harm or those inherent in the offence

Where there is a terrorist element to the offence, refer also to the Terrorism Offences Definitive Guideline

- Location and/or timing of offence

Effective from: 01 October 2019

Care should be taken to avoid double counting factors including those already taken into account in assessing culpability or harm or those inherent in the offence

- o In general, an offence is not made more serious by the location and/or timing of the offence except in ways taken into account by other factors in this guideline (such as planning, vulnerable victim, offence committed in a domestic context, maximising distress to victim, others put at risk of harm by the offending, offence committed in the presence of others). Care should be taken to avoid double counting.
- o Courts should be cautious about aggravating an offence by reason of it being committed for example at night, or in broad daylight, in a crowded place or in an isolated place unless it also indicates increased harm or culpability not already accounted for.
- o An offence may be more serious when it is committed in places in which there is a particular need for discipline or safety such as prisons, courts, schools or hospitals.

- Established evidence of community/wider impact (see **C15.21.1.1**)

Effective from: 01 October 2019

Care should be taken to avoid double counting factors including those already taken into account in assessing culpability or harm or those inherent in the offence

- o This factor should increase the sentence only where there is clear evidence of wider harm not already taken into account elsewhere. A community impact statement will assist the court in assessing the level of impact.
- o For issues of prevalence see the separate guidance.

- Prevalence (see **C15.21.1.1**)

Effective from: 01 October 2019

Care should be taken to avoid double counting factors including those already taken into account in assessing culpability or harm or those inherent in the offence

- o Sentencing levels in offence specific guidelines take account of collective social harm. Accordingly offenders should normally be sentenced by straightforward application of the guidelines without aggravation for the fact that their activity contributed to a harmful social effect upon a neighbourhood or community.

- o It is not open to a sentencer to increase a sentence for prevalence in ordinary circumstances or in response to a personal view that there is 'too much of this sort of thing going on in this area'.
- o First, there must be evidence provided to the court by a responsible body or by a senior police officer.
- o Secondly, that evidence must be before the court in the specific case being considered with the relevant statements or reports having been made available to the Crown and defence in good time so that meaningful representations about that material can be made.
- o Even if such material is provided, a sentencer will only be entitled to treat prevalence as an aggravating factor if satisfied
  - o that the level of harm caused in a particular locality is significantly higher than that caused elsewhere (and thus already inherent in the guideline levels);
  - o that the circumstances can properly be described as exceptional; **and**
  - o that it is just and proportionate to increase the sentence for such a factor in the particular case being sentenced.
- o **mitigating factors reducing se**

- No previous convictions or no relevant/recent convictions
  Effective from: 01 October 2019

  Care should be taken to avoid double counting factors including those already taken into account in assessing culpability or harm

  - o First time offenders usually represent a lower risk of reoffending. Reoffending rates for first offenders are significantly lower than rates for repeat offenders. In addition, first offenders are normally regarded as less blameworthy than offenders who have committed the same crime several times already. For these reasons first offenders receive a mitigated sentence.
  - o Where there are previous offences but these are old and /or are for offending of a different nature, the sentence will normally be reduced to reflect that the new offence is not part of a pattern of offending and there is therefore a lower likelihood of reoffending.
  - o When assessing whether a previous conviction is 'recent' the court should consider the time gap since the previous conviction and the reason for it.
  - o Previous convictions are likely to be 'relevant' when they share characteristics with the current offence (examples of such characteristics include, but are not limited to: dishonesty, violence, abuse of position or trust, use or possession of weapons, disobedience of court orders). In general the more serious the previous offending the longer it will retain relevance.

- Good character and/or exemplary conduct
  Effective from: 01 October 2019

  Care should be taken to avoid double counting factors including those already taken into account in assessing culpability or harm

  This factor may apply whether or not the offender has previous convictions. Evidence that an offender has demonstrated positive good character through, for example, charitable works may reduce the sentence.

  However, this factor is less likely to be relevant where the offending is very serious. Where an offender has used their good character or status to facilitate or conceal the offending it could be treated as an aggravating factor.

- Remorse

  Effective from: 01 October 2019

  Care should be taken to avoid double counting factors including those already taken into account in assessing culpability or harm

  The court will need to be satisfied that the offender is genuinely remorseful for the offending behaviour in order to reduce the sentence (separate from any guilty plea reduction).

  Lack of remorse should never be treated as an aggravating factor.

- Self-reporting

  Effective from: 01 October 2019

  Care should be taken to avoid double counting factors including those already taken into account in assessing culpability or harm

  Where an offender has self-reported to the authorities, particularly in circumstances where the offence may otherwise have gone undetected, this should reduce the sentence (separate from any guilty plea reduction).

- Cooperation with the investigation/ early admissions

  Effective from: 01 October 2019

  Care should be taken to avoid double counting factors including those already taken into account in assessing culpability or harm

  Assisting or cooperating with the investigation and /or making pre-court admissions may ease the effect on victims and witnesses and save valuable police time justifying a reduction in sentence (separate from any guilty plea reduction).

- Little or no planning

  Effective from: 01 October 2019

  Care should be taken to avoid double counting factors including those already taken into account in assessing culpability or harm

  Where an offender has committed the offence with little or no prior thought, this is likely to indicate a lower level of culpability and therefore justify a reduction in sentence.

  However, impulsive acts of unprovoked violence or other types of offending may indicate a propensity to behave in a manner that would not normally justify a reduction in sentence.

- The offender was in a lesser or subordinate role if acting with others/performed limited role under direction

  Effective from: 01 October 2019

  Care should be taken to avoid double counting factors including those already taken into account in assessing culpability or harm

  Whereas acting as part of a group may make an offence more serious, if the offender's role was minor this may indicate lower culpability and justify a reduction in sentence.

- Involved through coercion, intimidation or exploitation

  Effective from: 01 October 2019

  Care should be taken to avoid double counting factors including those already taken into account in assessing culpability or harm

- o Where this applies it will reduce the culpability of the offender.
- o This factor may be of particular relevance where the offender has been the victim of domestic abuse, trafficking or modern slavery, but may also apply in other contexts.
- o Courts should be alert to factors that suggest that an offender may have been the subject of coercion, intimidation or exploitation which the offender may find difficult to articulate, and where appropriate ask for this to be addressed in a PSR.
- o This factor **may** indicate that the offender is vulnerable and would find it more difficult to cope with custody or to complete a community order.

- Limited awareness or understanding of the offence

  Effective from: 01 October 2019

  Care should be taken to avoid double counting factors including those already taken into account in assessing culpability or harm

  The factor may apply to reduce the culpability
  - o of an offender acting alone who has not appreciated the seriousness of the offence **or**
  - o of an offender who is acting with others and does not appreciate the extent of the overall offending.

  If the offender had genuinely failed to understand or appreciate the seriousness of the offence, the sentence may be reduced from that which would have applied if the offender had understood the full extent of the offence and the likely harm that would be caused.

  Where an offender lacks capacity to understand the full extent of the offending see the guidance under 'Mental disorder or learning disability'.

- Little or no financial gain

  Effective from: 01 October 2019

  Care should be taken to avoid double counting factors including those already taken into account in assessing culpability or harm

  Where an offence (which is not one which by its nature is an acquisitive offence) is committed in a context where financial gain could arise, the culpability of the offender may be reduced where it can be shown that the offender **did not seek to gain financially** from the conduct and did not in fact do so.

- Delay since apprehension

  Effective from: 01 October 2019

  Care should be taken to avoid double counting factors including those already taken into account in assessing culpability or harm

  Where there has been an unreasonable delay in proceedings since apprehension which is not the fault of the offender, the court may take this into account by reducing the sentence **if this has had a detrimental effect on the offender.**

  Note: No fault should attach to an offender for not admitting an offence and/ or putting the prosecution to proof of its case.

- Activity originally legitimate

  Effective from: 01 October 2019

  Care should be taken to avoid double counting factors including those already taken into account in assessing culpability or harm

Where the offending arose from an activity which was originally legitimate, but became unlawful (for example because of a change in the offender's circumstances or a change in regulations), this **may** indicate lower culpability and thereby a reduction in sentence.

This factor will not apply where the offender has used a legitimate activity to mask a criminal activity.

• Age and/or lack of maturity

Effective from: 01 October 2019

Care should be taken to avoid double counting factors including those already taken into account in assessing culpability or harm

Age and/or lack of maturity can affect:
o the offender's responsibility for the offence and
o the effect of the sentence on the offender.

Either or both of these considerations may justify a reduction in the sentence.

The emotional and developmental age of an offender is of at least equal importance to their chronological age (if not greater).

In particular young adults (typically aged 18-25) are still developing neurologically and consequently may be less able to:
o evaluate the consequences of their actions
o limit impulsivity
o limit risk taking

Young adults are likely to be susceptible to peer pressure and are more likely to take risks or behave impulsively when in company with their peers.

Immaturity can also result from atypical brain development. Environment plays a role in neurological development and factors such as adverse childhood experiences including deprivation and/or abuse may affect development.

An immature offender may find it particularly difficult to cope with custody and therefore may be more susceptible to self-harm in custody.

An immature offender may find it particularly difficult to cope with the requirements of a community order without appropriate support.

There is a greater capacity for change in immature offenders and they may be receptive to opportunities to address their offending behaviour and change their conduct.

Many young people who offend either stop committing crime, or begin a process of stopping, in their late teens and early twenties. Therefore a young adult's previous convictions may not be indicative of a tendency for further offending.

Where the offender is a care leaver the court should enquire as to any effect a sentence may have on the offender's ability to make use of support from the local authority. (Young adult care leavers are entitled to time limited support. Leaving care services may change at the age of 21 and cease at the age of 25, unless the young adult is in education at that point). See also the Sentencing Children and Young People Guideline (paragraphs 1.16 and 1.17).

Where an offender has turned 18 between the commission of the offence and conviction the court should take as its starting point the sentence likely to have been imposed on the date at which the offence was committed, but applying the purposes of sentencing adult offenders. See also the Sentencing Children and Young People Guideline (paragraphs 6.1 to 6.3).

When considering a custodial or community sentence for a young adult the National Probation Service should address these issues in a PSR.

• Sole or primary carer for dependent relatives

Effective from: 01 October 2019

Care should be taken to avoid double counting factors including those already taken into account in assessing culpability or harm

This factor is particularly relevant where an offender is on the cusp of custody or where the suitability of a community order is being considered. See also the Imposition of community and custodial sentences guideline.

For offenders on the cusp of custody, imprisonment should not be imposed where there would be an impact on dependants which would make a custodial sentence disproportionate to achieving the aims of sentencing.

Where custody is unavoidable consideration of the impact on dependants may be relevant to the length of the sentence imposed and whether the sentence can be suspended.

For more serious offences where a substantial period of custody is appropriate, this factor will carry less weight.

When imposing a community sentence on an offender with primary caring responsibilities the effect on dependants must be considered in determining suitable requirements.

In addition when sentencing an offender who is pregnant relevant considerations may include:
o any effect of the sentence on the health of the offender and
o any effect of the sentence on the unborn child

The court should ensure that it has all relevant information about dependent children before deciding on sentence.

When an immediate custodial sentence is necessary, the court must consider whether proper arrangements have been made for the care of any dependent children and if necessary consider adjourning sentence for this to be done.

When considering a community or custodial sentence for an offender who has, or may have, caring responsibilities the court should ask the National Probation Service to address these issues in a PSR.

Useful information can be found in the Equal Treatment Bench Book (see in particular Chapter 6 paragraphs 94-100)

• Physical disability or serious medical condition requiring urgent, intensive or long-term treatment

Effective from: 01 October 2019

Care should be taken to avoid double counting factors including those already taken into account in assessing culpability or harm or those inherent in the offence

o The court can take account of physical disability or a serious medical condition by way of mitigation as a reason for reducing the length of the sentence, either on the ground of the greater impact which imprisonment will have on the offender, or as a matter of generally expressed mercy in the individual circumstances of the case.

o However, such a condition, even when it is difficult to treat in prison, will not automatically entitle the offender to a lesser sentence than would otherwise be appropriate.

o There will always be a need to balance issues personal to an offender against the gravity of the offending (including the harm done to victims), and the public interest in imposing appropriate punishment for serious offending.

o A terminal prognosis is not in itself a reason to reduce the sentence even further. The court must impose a sentence that properly meets the aims of sentencing even if it will carry the clear prospect that the offender will die in custody. The prospect of death in the near future will be a matter considered by the prison authorities and the Secretary of State under the early release on compassionate grounds procedure (ERCG).

o But, an offender's knowledge that he will likely face the prospect of death in prison, subject only to the ERCG provisions, is a factor that can be considered by the sentencing judge when determining the sentence that it would be just to impose.

- Mental disorder or learning disability

Effective from: 01 October 2019

Care should be taken to avoid double counting factors including those already taken into account in assessing culpability or harm or those inherent in the offence

Mental disorders and learning disabilities are different things, although an individual may suffer from both. A **learning disability** is a permanent condition developing in childhood, whereas **mental illness** (or a mental health problem) can develop at any time, and is not necessarily permanent; people can get better and resolve mental health problems with help and treatment.

In the context of sentencing a broad interpretation of the terms 'mental disorder' and learning disabilities' should be adopted to include:

o Offenders with an intellectual impairment (low IQ);

o Offenders with a cognitive impairment such as (but not limited to) dyslexia, attention deficit hyperactivity disorder (ADHD);

o Offenders with an autistic spectrum disorder (ASD) including Asperger's syndrome;

o Offenders with a personality disorder;

o Offenders with a mental illness.

Offenders may have a combination of the above conditions.

Sentencers should be alert to the fact that not all mental disorders or learning disabilities are visible or obvious.

A mental disorder or learning disability can affect both:

6. the offender's responsibility for the offence and

7. the impact of the sentence on the offender.

The court will be assisted by a PSR and, where appropriate, medical reports (including from court mental health teams) in assessing:

8. the degree to which a mental disorder or learning disability has reduced the offender's responsibility for the offence. This may be because the condition had an impact on the

offender's ability to understand the consequences of their actions, to limit impulsivity and/or to exercise self-control.

- ○
  - ■ a relevant factor will be the degree to which a mental disorder or learning disability has been exacerbated by the actions of the offender (for example by the **voluntary** abuse of drugs or alcohol or by **voluntarily** failing to follow medical advice);
  - ■ in considering the extent to which the offender's actions were voluntary, the extent to which a mental disorder or learning disability has an impact on the offender's ability to exercise self-control or to engage with medical services will be a relevant consideration.

    2. any effect of the mental disorder or learning disability on the impact of the sentence on the offender; a mental disorder or learning disability may make it more difficult for the offender to cope with custody or comply with a community order.

- Determination and/or demonstration of steps having been taken to address addiction or offending behaviour

 SG2-1 – SG2-12

Appendix 8

2020 Supplement to Handbook of YOUTHS in the Criminal Courts

E1 Introduction

The Court of Appeal has emphasized the importance of detailed consideration of the Guideline *Sentencing Children and Young People Overreaching Principles* (R v JT 2018 EWCA Crim1942) and the significance of considering maturity and development as well as chronological age. The Guideline applies if the offence was committed when under 18, whatever the age on sentence (R v Hobbs 2019 EWCA Crim 1003; R v Rexha 2018 EWCA Crim 1205).

H2.2 Amendment

The following offences are not 'grave crimes' and, if not offences of homicide, only summary trial would be possible:
- Causing death by driving disqualified RTA 1988 s 3ZC (maximum penalty ten years imprisonment)
- Causing death by careless or inconsiderate driving RTA 1988 s 2B (maximum penalty five years imprisonment)
- Causing death by driving unlicensed or uninsured RTA 1988 s 3ZB(maximum penalty two years imprisonment)

H3.13 *Amendment*

The final paragraph to read

The BA 1976 s 6(7) provides that a person who is convicted summarily of an offence under s6(1) or s6(2) shall be liable to imprisonment for a term not exceeding three months or to a fine not exceeding level 5 on the standard scale or to both and a person who is dealt with for contempt in the Crown Court shall be liable to imprisonment for a term not exceeding twelve months or to a fine or to both. A detention and training order may be imposed in the Crown Court (R v Mason Cooper 2018 EWCA 2628) but not in the youth court because the minimum term of a detention and training order is four months.

K4 Amendment

Neither a judge of the Crown Court nor of the Court of Appeal may sit as a district judge, under s66 Courts Act 2003, to impose a referral order. The case should be remitted to the youth court (R v Dillon 2017 EWCA Crim 2671).

L3

If the defendant first appeared at 17 but the proceedings were adjourned, with place of trial procedures being dealt with after he had attained 18 years of age, an indictable only offence must be sent to the crown court; a guilty plea could not be accepted and there could be no committal for sentence (R v Ford 2018 EWCA Crim 1751).

L6

Reaching the age of 18 is not to be treated as a 'cliff-edge'. Youth and maturity will be factors to inform a sentencing decision even if an offender is now eighteen (Attorney-General's Reference: R v Clarke; R v Anderson 2018 EWCA Crim 165. The Guideline *Sentencing Children and Young Offenders; Overreaching Principles (*Appendix Y1*)* continues to apply (R v Hobbs 2018 EWCA Crim 1003).

L6.2.2 ADD

Consecutive sentences / YOI detention

Where a defendant, now 18, committed an offence while under the supervision part of a DTO, a sentence of YOI detention for the new offence could not be made consecutive to a period of detention for breach of the DTO. Section 106 Powers of Criminal Courts (Sentencing) Act 2000 prevents this—in the same way that s 265 CJA 2003 prevents a prison sentence being made consecutive to time on recall from licence (*R v McGeechan (Jack)* [2019[EWCA Crim235).

L6.6. ADD

Allowing for time on remand

Only time remanded to youth detention accommodation counts automatically towards sentence. Time spent on a qualifying curfew will count as to one half of the relevant period but an order must be made by the court. [**D32**] Time spent in Local Authority accommodation does not count (R v Anderson 20187 EWCA Crim 2604). Whilst a court should consider making an appropriate reduction to a sentence, this will be rare and require very restrictive conditions (R v A 2019 EWCA Crim106).

N1 General

Jones v Birmingham City Council 2018 EWCA Civ 1189 confirms that these are not criminal proceedings so that the civil burden of proof applies and Article 6 of the ECHR is not engaged.

Index

Index